CompTIA Network+ N10-008 Certification Guide

The ultimate guide to passing the N10-008 exam

Glen D. Singh

BIRMINGHAM—MUMBAI

CompTIA Network+ N10-008 Certification Guide

Group Product Manager: Mohd Riyan Khan

Publishing Product Manager: Shrilekha Malpani

Senior Content Development Editor: Sayali Pingale

Technical Editor: Nithik Cheruvakodan

Copy Editor: Safis Editing

Book Project Manager: Neil Dmello

Proofreader: Safis Editing

Indexer: Sejal Dsilva

Production Designer: Joshua Misquitta

Marketing Coordinator: Nimisha Dua

First published: November 2018

Second edition: October 2022

Production reference: 1191022

Published by Packt Publishing Ltd.

Livery Place

35 Livery Street

Birmingham

B3 2PB, UK.

978-1-80323-606-3

www.packt.com

I would like to dedicate this book to the people in our society who have always worked hard in their field of expertise and who have not been recognized for their hard work, commitment, sacrifices, and ideas, but who, most importantly, believed in themselves when no one else did. This book is for you. Always have faith in yourself. With commitment, hard work, and focus, anything can be possible. Never give up, because great things take time.

– Glen D. Singh

Contributors

About the author

Glen D. Singh is an information security author and cybersecurity instructor. His areas of expertise are cybersecurity operations, offensive security tactics, and enterprise networking. He is a holder of many certifications, including CEH, CHFI, PAWSP, and 3xCCNA (in CyberOps, Security, and Routing and Switching).

Glen loves teaching and mentoring others and sharing his wealth of knowledge and experience as an author. He has written many books that focus on vulnerability discovery and exploitation, threat detection, intrusion analysis, incident response, network security, and enterprise networking. As an aspiring game-changer, Glen is passionate about increasing cybersecurity awareness in his homeland, Trinidad and Tobago.

I would like to thank God, the preserver of the universe, for all His divine grace and guidance. I would also like to thank Shrilekha Malpani, Sayali Pingale, Neil D'mello, and the wonderful team at Packt Publishing, who have provided amazing support throughout this journey. To the technical reviewer, Greg Gardner, thank you for your outstanding contribution to making this an amazing book.

About the reviewer

Greg Gardner is a former U.S. Navy Officer, government consultant, and technology expert. He has worked in the aerospace industry, at several dot-coms, at several data centers, at the Pentagon, and with most federal and many state agencies. He received his Master of Information Technology from Virginia Tech. Greg teaches and writes courseware for A+, Network+, Security+, CND, and CEH. Greg has taught at the high school and undergraduate levels as well as in private industry. He speaks at national technology conferences and has written two cyber-espionage novels.

As a long-time member of the IT community, it is my honor to be in the "give back" portion of my career. As a teacher, technology evangelist, and author, I strive to ensure that individuals who are making career changes or simply want to understand the fast-moving IT industry are prepared. Throughout my career, my family and spouse have been my greatest supporters – thank you.

Table of Contents

3

Ethernet Technology and Virtualization   89

4

Understanding IPv4 and IPv6 Addressing   143

5

Applied IPv4 Subnetting   195

6

Exploring Network Protocols and Services   223

7

Data Center Architecture and Cloud Computing   285

Part 2: Network Implementation

8

Networking Devices   315

9

Routing and Switching Concepts   351

10

Exploring Wireless Standards and Technologies   405

Part 3: Network Operations

11

12

13

Part 4: Network Security and Troubleshooting

14

Network Security Concepts   487

15

Exploring Cyberattacks and Threats   519

16

Implementing Network Security

17

Network Troubleshooting

18

Practice Exam   603

Assessments   629

Index   637

Other Books You May Enjoy   668

Preface

When breaking into the networking industry, you often hear people ask which certification is the best one to start pursuing. The CompTIA Network+ N10-008 certification is a vendor-neutral networking certification designed to help learners and certification holders to obtain the technical skills and hands-on experience needed to design, build, maintain, and troubleshoot modern-day network infrastructure to support the ever-growing demands of the network services, technologies, and resources that organizations heavily rely upon to support their business processes and users. Furthermore, this certification helps learners to validate their skills that are needed to support various types of network infrastructure and architectures on any platform while providing the learner with the specific skills that are needed by network professionals within the industry.

As a cybersecurity and networking lecturer with years of industry and academic experience, my goal is to help aspiring network and security professionals break into the industry. As technologies advance quickly, certification vendors such as CompTIA update their certification objectives to ensure learners acquire the latest knowledge and skills needed in the industry. Likewise, this new edition contains all-new updated content relevant to the CompTIA Network+ N10-008 exam objectives with practice questions, exercises, and labs to help reinforce learning and development. During the writing process of this book, I've used a student-centric and learner-friendly approach, helping you to easily understand the most complex topics, terminologies, and how to design, implement, and troubleshoot networks.

In this new edition, learners will become more aware of the various network architectures that are used within data centers and cloud service providers' environments, such as **Software-Defined Network** (**SDN**), and understand how SDN can be integrated into existing network infrastructures. Additionally, learners will encounter in-depth emphasis on new and emerging wireless standards and how businesses can leverage the flexibility of wireless technologies to support their business needs. Furthermore, we offer a dedicated focus on the network security principles, cyberattacks, threats, and network hardening techniques that are used to secure organizations from threat actors and data breaches.

This book begins by introducing you to networking models such as the **Open Systems Interconnection** (**OSI**) and **Transmission Control Protocol/Internet Protocol** (**TCP/IP**), which are responsible for helping systems exchange data over a wired or wireless network using a set of protocols that describes how data is encoded and formatted before it's sent to its destination. Then, you will explore common network topologies and network types used within many organizations around the world. Next, you will discover common Ethernet standards and how they are implemented in various network components and cable types within the modern network infrastructure. Additionally, you will gain a solid understanding of how to implement both IPv4 and IPv6 addressing within a network.

Furthermore, you will learn how to break down an IPv4 network block using a step-by-step approach for performing subnetting and **Variable Length Subnet Mask (VLSM)** for a multi-branch network. You will also explore common network protocols, services, and protocol types that are found on most modern networks. Then, you will discover data center architectures and the need for virtualization and cloud computing.

The second part of this book describes aspects of network implementation such as the role and function of common networking devices and security appliances required by organizations around the world. Then, you will explore routing and switching mechanisms that are used by routers and switches to efficiently forward messages to their destinations over a network. Additionally, you will learn about wireless networking, technologies, and security standards that are needed to design and implement a resilient and secure wireless network infrastructure.

The third part of this book covers network operations, examining best practices for measuring, monitoring, and improving the performance of a network, and detecting and resolving interface issues on devices. Furthermore, you will explore common plans, policies, and procedures that are developed and maintained within organizations to improve the security posture of their network infrastructure, and common agreements for employees. Additionally, you will discover how organizations implement **High Availability (HA)** within their networks to ensure critical services and resources are available for users, along with a look at disaster recovery best practices.

The final part of this book focuses on network security and troubleshooting concepts, covering the fundamentals of network security and risk management strategies for companies. Furthermore, you will learn about various types of cyber-attacks and threats on wired and wireless networks, and how threat actors perform human-based attacks. Furthermore, you will learn network security hardening techniques, wireless security best practices, common remote access technologies, and physical security. Lastly, you will discover how to use network troubleshooting methodology to efficiently discover and resolve common wired and wireless network issues using both hardware- and software-based tools.

By completing this book, you will be taken through an amazing journey from beginner to professional in terms of learning, understanding, and developing the skills and confidence needed to pass the official CompTIA Network+ N10-008 certification exam, while becoming well versed in a variety of network administration and security solutions as an aspiring network professional within the industry.

Who this book is for

This book is designed for beginners who are interested in starting a career in the field of networking and students who are pursuing the official CompTIA Network+ N10-008 certification. This certification guide is targeted at anyone, whether you're a beginner or seasoned professional who is looking to boost your career in network administration and operations. This book helps learners prepare to support various types of network infrastructure and platforms, while providing specific skills that are needed by the next generation of network professionals for the industry.

What this book covers

Chapter 1, Exploring the OSI Model and TCP/IP, introduces you to common networking models used to define how systems exchange messages over a network.

Chapter 2, Network Topologies and Connections, explores popular networking designs, types, and service provider links.

Chapter 3, Ethernet Technology and Virtualization, introduces you to Ethernet standards and technologies, cable types, and virtual networking concepts.

Chapter 4, Understanding IPv4 and IPv6 Addressing, introduces you to both IPv4 and IPv6 addressing structures and the types of IP addresses found on a network.

Chapter 5, Applied IPv4 Subnetting, introduces you to IPv4 subnetting and applying **Variable Length Subnet Masking** (**VLSM**) on a network.

Chapter 6, Exploring Network Protocols and Services, explores the roles and functions of common networking protocols and services.

Chapter 7, Data Center Architecture and Cloud Computing, introduces you to popular network architectures that are used within data center environments and cloud computing technologies.

Chapter 8, Networking Devices, introduces you to the roles and functions of common networking devices and security appliances.

Chapter 9, Routing and Switching Concepts, explores dynamic routing protocols, static routing concepts, and switching concepts to improve the performance and scalability of a network.

Chapter 10, Exploring Wireless Standards and Technologies, introduces you to wireless networking technologies and security standards.

Chapter 11, Assuring Network Availability, introduces you to best practices to ensure the availability and monitoring of network resources and assets.

Chapter 12, Organizational Documents and Policies, focuses on exploring common organizational plans, procedures, and security policies to prevent network and security incidents.

Chapter 13, High Availability and Disaster Recovery, explores high availability concepts to ensure critical network resources are always accessible, and describes disaster recovery concepts.

Chapter 14, Network Security Concepts, explores the need for information security, authentication systems, and risk management within organizations.

Chapter 15, Exploring Cyberattacks and Threats, focuses on various types of wired, wireless, and human-based cyberattacks and threats.

Chapter 16, Implementing Network Security, explores best practices for implementing countermeasures and mitigation techniques to prevent cyberattacks and threats.

Chapter 17, Network Troubleshooting, provides troubleshooting methodologies for detecting and resolving issues on wired and wireless networks using both hardware- and software-based tools.

Chapter 18, Practice Exam, provides a series of practice exercises to help reinforce your learning while preparing for the official certification exam.

To get the most out of this book

All exercises were completed on a system running Windows 10 as the host operating system with virtualization enabled on the processor.

Software/Hardware covered in the book	OS Requirements
Wireshark	Windows 10
Oracle VM VirtualBox	Ubuntu 20.04 Desktop
Oracle VM VirtualBox Extension Pack	
7-Zip	
Cisco IOS router (optional)	

All labs and exercises that were performed in this book used a free version of the required application to ensure you will be able to easily complete the exercises without the need for acquiring paid applications. However, you are free to use commercial tools and applications as needed.

After completing this book, using your imagination and wisdom acquired, attempt to create additional lab scenarios such as building a personal home lab environment using virtualization technologies and setting up virtual networks with virtual machines. This will help you to continue learning and exploring new technologies while further developing your skills as an aspiring network professional.

Download the color images

We also provide a PDF file that has color images of the screenshots/diagrams used in this book. You can download it here: `https://packt.link/a27qd`.

Conventions used

There are a number of text conventions used throughout this book.

`Code in text`: Indicates code words in text, database table names, folder names, filenames, file extensions, pathnames, dummy URLs, user input, and Twitter handles. Here is an example: "The wireless router is connected to the wired LAN via the network switch that's on the `172.16.1.0/24` network."

A block of code is set as follows:

```
*Apr 28, 15:53:58.5353: %LINEPROTO-5-UPDOWN: Line protocol on
Interface GigabitEthernet0/1, changed state to up
```

Bold: Indicates a new term, an important word, or words that you see onscreen. For example, words in menus or dialog boxes appear in the text like this. Here is an example: "To configure the duplex mode on a Windows operating system, open **Device Manager**, right-click on the interface, and select **Properties | Advanced tab**."

> **Tips or important notes**
> Appear like this.

Get in touch

Feedback from our readers is always welcome.

General feedback: If you have questions about any aspect of this book, mention the book title in the subject of your message and email us at `customercare@packtpub.com`.

Errata: Although we have taken every care to ensure the accuracy of our content, mistakes do happen. If you have found a mistake in this book, we would be grateful if you would report this to us. Please visit `www.packtpub.com/support/errata`, selecting your book, clicking on the Errata Submission Form link, and entering the details.

Piracy: If you come across any illegal copies of our works in any form on the Internet, we would be grateful if you would provide us with the location address or website name. Please contact us at `copyright@packt.com` with a link to the material.

If you are interested in becoming an author: If there is a topic that you have expertise in and you are interested in either writing or contributing to a book, please visit `authors.packtpub.com`.

Share your thoughts

Once you've read *CompTIA Network+ N10-008 Certification Guide - Second Edition*, we'd love to hear your thoughts! Scan the QR code below to go straight to the Amazon review page for this book and share your feedback.

https://packt.link/r/180323606X

Your review is important to us and the tech community and will help us make sure we're delivering excellent quality content.

Download a free PDF copy of this book

Thanks for purchasing this book!

Do you like to read on the go but are unable to carry your print books everywhere?

Is your eBook purchase not compatible with the device of your choice?

Don't worry, now with every Packt book you get a DRM-free PDF version of that book at no cost.

Read anywhere, any place, on any device. Search, copy, and paste code from your favorite technical books directly into your application.

The perks don't stop there, you can get exclusive access to discounts, newsletters, and great free content in your inbox daily

Follow these simple steps to get the benefits:

1. Scan the QR code or visit the link below

https://packt.link/free-ebook/978-1-80323-606-3

2. Submit your proof of purchase
3. That's it! We'll send your free PDF and other benefits to your email directly

Part 1:
Networking Concepts

In this part, you will be able to understand both the OSI reference model and TCP/IP stack, the purpose of network port numbers, protocols, and network design (topologies). Furthermore, you will be able to understand IP addressing and subnetting, fundamentals of virtualization, and cloud computing technologies.

This part of the book comprises the following chapters:

- *Chapter 1, Exploring the OSI Model and TCP/IP*
- *Chapter 2, Network Topologies and Connections*
- *Chapter 3, Ethernet Technology and Virtualization*
- *Chapter 4, Understanding IPv4 and IPv6 Addressing*
- *Chapter 5, Applied IPv4 Subnetting*
- *Chapter 6, Exploring Network Protocols and Services*
- *Chapter 7, Data Center Architecture and Cloud Computing*

1

Exploring the OSI Model and TCP/IP

As you embark on the journey of acquiring new knowledge and developing your skills as an aspiring network professional, you will be exploring the latest networking technologies and concepts needed by professionals within the networking and **Information Technology** (IT) industry. The CompTIA Network+ certification is filled with the latest technologies and content for the next generation of network professionals. It ensures learners gain the knowledge and in-demand skills needed to support the network infrastructure that organizations rely upon each day.

As an aspiring network professional, I'm sure you are very eager to dive into the technologies and start looking at network traffic, and even learn about cyber-attacks and network security solutions to help defend organizations from threat actors. However, all great journeys of becoming an expert within a field of study, such as networking, begin with developing a solid foundation and gaining a strong understanding of the fundamentals of network communication.

During this chapter, you will learn about the importance of and the need for using a protocol suite on a network to communicate with devices and share resources. You'll be exploring each layer of both the **Open Systems Interconnection** (OSI) and **Transmission Control Protocol/Internet Protocol** (TCP/IP) networking models, and how all the layers work together to ensure systems can exchange messages over a network. Additionally, you'll gain fundamental knowledge of how datagrams are encapsulated and de-encapsulated when devices send and receive messages. Lastly, you'll gain the hands-on skills of exploring the headers and fields found within packets using industry-recognized tools.

In this chapter, we will cover the following topics:

- The need for networking models

- Exploring the OSI model

- Understanding TCP/IP

- Data encapsulation concepts

- Analyzing network packets

Let's dive in!

Technical requirements

To follow along with the exercises in this chapter, please ensure that you have met the following requirement:

- Wireshark: `https://www.wireshark.org/`

The need for networking models

One of the most frequently asked questions from many learners who are starting their journey in the field of networking is, *what is a network*? A network is defined as having two or more computing devices interconnected, using a set of communication protocols (rules) that allow them to share a resource between themselves. A resource can be anything, such as a file on a centralized server, a multiplayer game on an online server, and even a network-connected printer. Networks are all around us and we use them every day to communicate with each other, share information, and even deliver an online service. The largest network in the world is the internet and every day it is continuously growing as more devices are connecting to it and organizations are joining their networks to the internet.

> **Important note**
>
> In the 1960s, the age before the internet, the US **Department of Defense (DoD)** provided financial funding to the **Defense Advanced Research Projects Agency (DARPA)**, which allowed computer scientists to start developing a prototype to allow academic institutions such as universities and government-funded research centers to establish a computer network over existing telephone lines. This early generation prototype was known as the **Advanced Research Projects Agency Network (ARPANET)**. However, the ARPANET was unable to support communication as expected and crashed when a user attempted to send an input such as a string of text across the ARPANET. Therefore, the project was dismissed.

While the internet is the largest network in the world, it is not owned by a single person, organization, or government, but various organizations globally have the responsibility of ensuring its sustainability, availability, security, and scalability. The following are important organizations that play key roles on the internet:

- **Internet Society (ISOC)**: The Internet Society is a non-profit organization whose mission is to encourage the open development, usage, and evolution of the internet in a way that is beneficial to everyone in the world. You can learn more about the Internet Society on their website at `https://www.internetsociety.org`.

- **Internet Engineering Task Force (IETF)**: The IETF is an organization with the responsibility of both developing and promoting internet technical standards such as protocol suites. Simply put, the IETF is responsible for ensuring the internet is a better place for all. You can learn more about the IETF on their website at `https://www.ietf.org`.

- **Internet Architecture Board (IAB)**: The IAB is a committee within the IETF that serves as an advisory board for overseeing the internet standards processes and the IETF architectural designs. You can learn more about the IAB on their website at `https://www.iab.org`.

- **Internet Assigned Numbers Authority (IANA)**: IANA is responsible for coordinating, distributing, and managing domain names, number resources, and protocol assignments on the internet and networks. Additionally, IANA oversees the **Autonomous System Number** (**ASN**) allocation and **Domain Name System** (**DNS**) root zone management. You can learn more about IANA on their official website at `https://www.iana.org`.

- **Internet Corporation for Assigned Names and Numbers (ICANN)**: ICANN is a non-profit organization that is responsible for the coordination, procedures, and maintenance of both namespaces and numerical spaces on the internet to ensure its stability and security. You can learn more about ICANN on their website at `https://www.icann.org`.

Imagine a world without computer networks; there would be so many challenges that both organizations and individuals would face each day. Imagine an employee of a company who wants to send a document to an employee of another organization. The traditional method would be to securely package the document with its contents within an envelope and use a courier service for delivery. However, using the internet and email services, the sender can attach the document file within an email message and forward it to the intended destination (recipient); the time it takes the message to be delivered between the sender and the recipient via the internet is highly reduced with the help of networking protocols compared to using traditional courier services.

Within the educational industry, there are many amazing certifications, qualifications, and study programs from various academic institutions around the world. Using the internet, educational institutions can deliver their learning content to students around the globe compared to the traditional on-campus learning method. Companies are also using networking technologies and the internet to extend their products and services beyond traditional borders. To ensure communication between networked devices such as computers works as expected, it's vital to understand the need for vendor-neutral networking models for intercommunication.

In today's world, many types of devices connect to our networks compared to traditional computers and servers. Some of these new devices include smart technologies and **Internet of Things** (**IoT**) devices such as smartphones and tablets, gaming consoles, and smart electronics and appliances. Connecting computers and IoT devices to a network is a seamless process and everything works as expected. However, back in the 1970s, early computer vendors started developing their proprietary networking models to allow their computers to intercommunicate and share resources over a network. For many organizations, this concept may have worked well if the company had bought computers from a specific computer vendor only. If, in the future, the company decided to purchase computers from another computer vendor, the company would not be able to create a unified network with all the computers from different vendors. This was one of the biggest issues with communication in the early days as each computer vendor developed its own proprietary networking model. As a result, companies would need to create separate networks for each vendor's device; this concept does not support network scalability for a growing company. This intercommunication issue led to the development of a common networking model that allows different devices to communicate over a network.

In the 1970s, the **International Organization for Standardization** (**ISO**) took the initiative on developing the OSI networking model for computer networks. The OSI model was designed to be a common standard for using networking protocols (rules) to allow intercommunication between devices that are connected over a network. However, the OSI model didn't have the traction needed to be implemented as a networking protocol suite within systems. At the same time during the 1970s, the US DoD also started working on developing a vendor-neutral protocol suite for intercommunication across computer networks; this protocol suite included the research and efforts of many organizations, such as universities and government agencies, to develop the networking protocols that made up the protocol suite we all know today as TCP/IP.

> **Important note**
>
> A network protocol is simply the rules and guidelines that are used by a device to allow communication or the exchange of messages from one device to another. There are many network protocols, each of which has a different purpose and characteristic. During this book, you will discover and learn about their functionalities and use cases.

In the 1980s and 1990s, organizations began implementing computer systems that supported various networking models such as those that were proprietary to specific computer vendors and even TCP/IP within their companies. As mentioned previously, companies experienced the challenge of interconnecting computers that used different networking models from computer vendors. Eventually, by the early 2000s, vendors had started to fully adopt and implement TCP/IP as the preferred network protocol suite to allow intercommunication between devices from different vendors. Hence, TCP/IP is considered to be the universal language of communication within the networking industry.

> **Important note**
>
> **AppleTalk** was a short-lived proprietary networking model created by Apple in 1985 and was used on Apple devices until 1995, when the TCP/IP protocol suite was adopted. Another short-lived networking model was **Novell NetWare**, a proprietary model created by Novell back in 1983 using the **Internetwork Packet Exchange** (**IPX**) networking protocol until 1995, when TCP/IP was adopted.

Having completed this section, you have gained an understanding of the importance of using a networking model to ensure devices can successfully communicate with one another over a network. In the next section, we will explore the roles and responsibilities of each layer of the OSI model.

Exploring the OSI model

The OSI model was originally developed to be an open networking model for computer networks to allow different devices to use a set of mutual protocols (rules) to allow communication between each other over a network. While the OSI model is commonly described as a reference model because it's not technically implemented on any networked devices such as computers, servers, or networking devices, networking professionals still use its terminology during their discussions and when writing documentation and publications. Therefore, as aspiring networking professionals within the industry, it's vital to gain a solid understanding of the characteristics and functionality of each layer within the OSI model.

The OSI model contains a total of seven layers that describe how communication occurs between one device and another over a network. Each layer of the OSI model has a unique role and responsibility to ensure a message from a sender contains all the necessary details to be successfully delivered to the intended destination. Imagine the challenges that would exist if networking models did not exist. Imagine writing a letter to a friend and posting it via the postal service with the hope it will be successfully delivered to the destination. However, if the address information is incorrect on the envelope, the postal service may have difficulties locating the destination. If the contents of the message are not correctly formatted or structured, the recipient of the message will not be able to clearly understand the contents. Similarly, on a network without a networking model or protocols, computers will have challenges ensuring their messages are delivered to their destination and that the contents of the messages are properly formatted and structured. Hence, the OSI model is a seven-layered networking model that contains the protocols (rules) and guidelines on how systems can communicate over a network.

The following diagram shows the seven layers of the OSI model:

Layer	Name	Protocol Data Unit (PDU)
7	Application	Data
6	Presentation	
5	Session	
4	Transport	Segment
3	Network	Packet
2	Data Link	Frame
1	Physical	Bits

Figure 1.1 – OSI model

As shown in the preceding diagram, the seven layers of the OSI model are in the following order:

- **Application**
- **Presentation**
- **Session**
- **Transport**
- **Network**
- **Data Link**
- **Physical**

At each layer of the OSI model, when a message exists at a specific layer, the message is commonly referred to as a **Protocol Data Unit** (**PDU**). A PDU is simply described as a single unit of data/information that can be transmitted from one host to another over a network. As the PDU is created at the Application layer of the OSI model of the host, it is referred to as data, which is the raw message. As the PDU travels down the OSI model, each of the lower layers is responsible for attaching additional information within a header onto the PDU to ensure proper addressing details are inserted to deliver the message. This process is commonly referred to as **encapsulation**. When a host on the network receives the message, the PDU travels upward on the OSI model, where each layer **de-encapsulates** the message, removing the header information until the raw message is delivered to the Application layer on the recipient device.

The following diagram shows an overview of the process of sending and receiving a message between two devices using the OSI model:

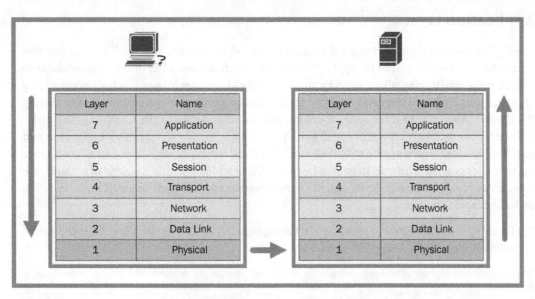

Figure 1.2 – Sending and receiving messages

As shown in the preceding diagram, when the computer sends a message, the message is created at the Application layer of the OSI model and works its way down the stack to the Physical layer. When the server receives the message through the network, the message is sent across the Physical layer and enters the Data Link layer before moving upward to the Application layer of the server.

Furthermore, the upper layers of the OSI model, such as the Application, Presentation, and Session layers, are designed to provide support for the application's functionality; in other words, they are designed to ensure the datagram (raw message) that's created by the sender can be transmitted across the network between the sender and receiver. The lower layers of the OSI model, such as the Transport, Network, Data Link, and Physical layers, focus on inserting the addressing information needed to deliver the datagram to the destination. Simply put, you can think of the lower layers as having the responsibility of ensuring end-to-end connectivity between hosts over a network.

Over the next few subsections, you will gain an in-depth understanding of the roles and responsibilities of each layer of the OSI model and how they help devices, such as computers, exchange messages between themselves and another host.

Application layer

The Application layer is the layer that is the closest to the end user, such as yourself. This layer provides an interface so that you can run the applications of a host such as a computer or even a smartphone to communicate with the underlying network protocols of the OSI model. To gain a better understanding of the responsibility and importance of the Application layer, imagine you're interested in visiting the CompTIA website to learn more about the examination details of the CompTIA Network+ N10-008 certification. A typical user will simply open their favorite web browser application and use their preferred search engine to find CompTIA's official website at www.comptia.org. Once the user clicks on the **Uniform Resource Locator** (**URL**) address, within a couple of seconds, the website downloads onto your device and the web browser renders the web language into something understandable to humans.

The following screenshot shows a standard web browser using HTTPS as the Application layer protocol to communicate with the CompTIA web server:

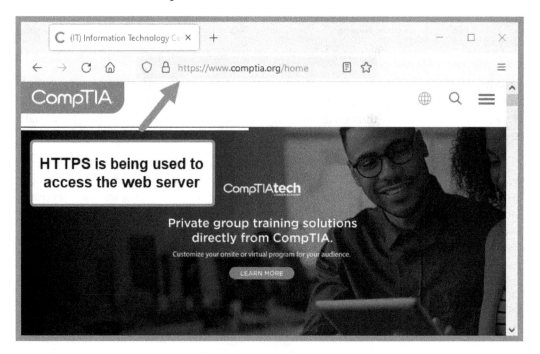

Figure 1.3 – Observing an Application layer protocol

While this process seems very simple and works well, there are a lot of underlying network protocols that work together to ensure your computer can access the internet and view the website. The end device, such as your computer or even smartphone, has an operating system that allows you to interact with the hardware components of your device to perform tasks. As a user, we generally install additional applications onto our operating system to add new functionality compared to the core functions and features that are present on the bare version of the operating system. Installing a web browser on your computer allows your operating system to interact with the **Hypertext Transfer Protocol** (HTTP) and **Hypertext Transfer Protocol Secure** (**HTTPS**) protocols. These are two examples of Application Layer protocols that allow you to interact/interface with web services on a network. Another example is using an email application such as Microsoft Outlook or Thunderbird running on your local computer to interact/interface with the **Simple Mail Transfer Protocol** (**SMTP**), an application layer protocol that is responsible for sending email messages over a network.

Each application layer protocol creates a datagram (raw message) or PDU that can only be interpreted by the same application layer protocol that created it. Simply put, a PDU created by HTTPS can only be interpreted by HTTPS and not another application protocol such as SMTP. As you may recall, a protocol is a rule that allows communication between devices over a network. Therefore, each protocol uses its own set of rules and structure for creating a PDU. At the Application layer, the PDU contains only the raw data created by the application layer protocol and does not have any addressing information needed to be delivered to the intended recipient. At the Application layer, the PDU is known as **Data**. Once the application layer protocol finishes its task of creating the PDU, it passes it down to the next layer, which is the **Presentation** layer.

Presentation layer

While the application layer protocols of the Application layer create system-dependent data (for example, ASCII or JPEG), the Presentation layer transforms it into an independent format. The PDU is then sent to lower layers to address the receiving system. This allows the Presentation layer on the receiving system to transform the data back into the system-dependent format (ASCII or JPEG) that the Application layer requires.

To gain a better understanding of the Presentation layer, imagine writing a letter to your friend. If you don't use the proper format of putting the destination delivery address and your sender's address on the external envelope, the postal service may experience some challenges when attempting to deliver the letter to the correct postal address. Overall, the Presentation layer ensures the PDU is formatted in a way that it will be supported by the lower layers of the OSI model and work on the actual network. Hence, it's important to ensure the PDU from the Application layer is formatted properly. At this layer of the OSI model, the PDU is still known as Data.

The following are the main responsibilities of the Presentation layer:

- Data formatting (encoding)
- Data compression
- Data encryption
- Data decryption

Once the Presentation layer finishes its task of formatting, encoding, and/or encrypting the PDU, it is sent down the OSI model stack to the next layer, known as the Session layer.

Session layer

Before a host can send a message to another host over a network, the sender needs to establish a logical session between itself and the destination device. The Session layer is responsible for ensuring that the devices across a network can create or establish a session between the sender and receiver. The Session layer is also responsible for maintaining the logical session (connection) between the hosts over the network. This allows each device to transmit their messages between themselves for the duration of the session. Lastly, the Session layer is responsible for terminating the logical session (connection) when both the sender and receiver are no longer communicating with each other. If the session is terminated during data transmission between the two hosts over the network, all data transmission will cease (stop) as well.

The following are the core functions of the Session layer:

- Create/establish a session
- Maintain the session
- Terminate a session

While the PDU exists within the Session layer, it is commonly referred to as Data. Once the Session layer completes its task, the PDU is sent down to the next layer within the networking model, known as the Transport Layer.

Transport layer

Networked devices such as computers, servers, and smart devices send and receive messages between each other very frequently and everything works well. Imagine if a client device such as a computer is requesting the web page from a web server on the internet. What occurs within the OSI model? At the Application layer of the client device, the HTTP application layer protocol of the OSI model creates an HTTP GET message to request the web page from the web server. Keep in mind that the Application layer is not responsible or concerned about how the data is delivered over the network. The data from the application layer protocol such as HTTP is sent down to the Transport layer.

> **Important note**
> In the TCP/IP protocol suite, the Transport layer is responsible for delivering the message between the Application layer and the network.

The Transport layer assigns a service port number to the PDU so that the receiving system will know how the Presentation layer should interpret and format the data. Then, the receiving system can read the data in the Application layer.

The following diagram shows a high-level visual representation of the client using HTTP to communicate with the same application layer protocol on the web server:

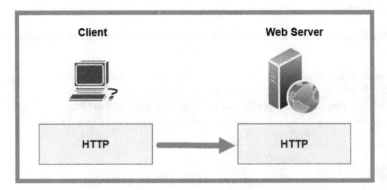

Figure 1.4 – Application layer protocol communication

The Transport layer ensures datagrams are delivered to the correct application layer protocol by assigning service port numbers to the PDU. Within an operating system that supports TCP/IP, there are 65,535 service port numbers.

The following diagram shows how these ports are categorized:

Port Range	Category
0 - 1,023	Well-known ports
1,024 - 49,151	Registered ports
49,152 - 65,535	Private/Dynamic ports

Figure 1.5 – Service port ranges

The service ports that exist within the range of well-known ports belong to the application layer protocols, which are very common on a network. Some of these common application layer protocols are HTTP, HTTPS, and SMTP. The registered port range belongs to users and organizations who have officially registered a service port number to operate on a custom build application or software. The private/dynamic range belongs to service ports that are temporarily used during communication, such as using a randomly generated service port on the sender's device as the source port.

While many people will think these ports are physical ports or interfaces on a device, these service ports are logical ports within an operating system. The service ports are the logical entry, while the exit ports on a system are used as doorways for sending and receiving datagrams on a network. You can think of a service port as a traditional airport that is used as a port of entry and exit of a country via air travel. Each service port number is logically mapped to an application layer protocol, so the Transport layer assigns the source and destination service port numbers to the PDU when it's received from the Application layer.

The following is a brief list of common application layer protocols and their corresponding service ports numbers:

Application Layer Protocol	Service Port Number
File Transfer Protocol (FTP)	20 & 21
Secure Shell (SSH)	22
Secure Copy (SCP)	22
SSH File Transfer Protocol (SFTP)	22
Telnet	23
Simple Mail Transfer Protocol (SMTP)	25
Domain Name System (DNS)	53
Hypertext Transfer Protocol (HTTP)	80
Hypertext Transfer Protocol Secure (HTTPS)	443

Figure 1.6 – Common application layer protocols

Using the same analogy from earlier, the Application layer on the client device sends the datagram to the Transport layer; the Transport layer encapsulates (inserts) a layer 4 header onto the datagram that contains both the source and destination service port numbers. Once the layer 4 header is added to the datagram from the Application layer, the PDU is referred to as a **segment**.

The following diagram shows a segment at the Transport layer containing a source and destination service port number with the data received from the application layer protocol:

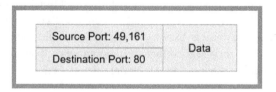

Figure 1.7 – Segment

As shown in the preceding diagram, the layer 4 header contains the source and destination service port numbers. The Data field contains the data received from the upper layer, such as the Application layer. The source service port number is a randomly generated number between 49,152 and 65,535. Since the source service port number is randomly generated by the operating system of the sender device, it is also referred to as an *ephemeral* port number. The source port number is important on the datagram as it informs the recipient about the sender's return address, similar to putting the return address information on a traditional letter. The destination service port number is inserted into the datagram, which informs the destination device about which application layer protocol to deliver the message to. For example, if the client is sending an HTTP message from itself to a web server on the internet, the Transport layer of the client device will insert a randomly generated source port number such as 49,161 and set the destination service port as 80. It uses port 80 since the application layer protocol on the destination device (web server) is running a web service that uses HTTP and HTTP uses service port 80 by default.

The following diagram shows a visual representation of the client sending a message to the web server that is running HTTP as the application layer protocol on service port 80:

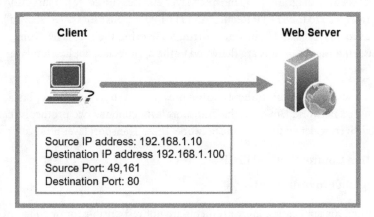

Figure 1.8 – HTTP Request message

The following diagram shows the addressing information used by the web server to respond to the client on the network:

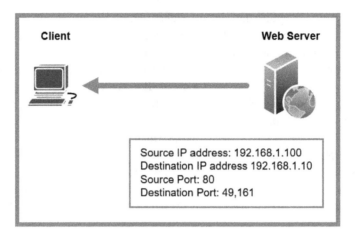

Figure 1.9 – HTTP Response message

As shown in the preceding diagram, the Transport layer ensures the correct source and destination services ports are assigned to the HTTP Request and HTTP Response messages. As you have learned thus far, the Transport layer is all about transporting/delivering the messages from one device to another while ensuring the datagrams are delivered to the appropriate application layer protocol on the destination device.

Thus far, we have focused a lot on understanding how service port numbers play a vital role in communication over a network. However, the Transport layer contains two protocols that assist with transporting and delivering datagrams over the network. These Transport layer protocols are as follows:

- **Transmission Control Protocol (TCP)**
- **User Datagram Protocol (UDP)**

As mentioned earlier, the application layer protocols are not responsible for or concerned about the delivery of messages from a sender to a receiver over the network. Hence, the Transport layer uses either TCP or UDP to ensure the messages from the Application layer of the OSI model are delivered to the destination host. The service ports on a system can use either TCP or UDP for communication over a network. Over the next couple of subsections, you will learn about the similarities and differences between TCP and UDP.

Transmission Control Protocol

The **Transmission Control Protocol** (**TCP**) is a connection-oriented protocol that establishes a logical connection between the source and destination devices before exchanging messages over a network. This connection is commonly referred to as the **TCP three-way handshake**.

The following diagram shows a high-level overview of the TCP three-way handshake between two devices:

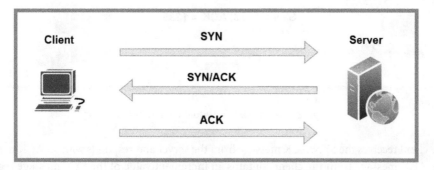

Figure 1.10 – TCP three-way handshake

The following is a breakdown of this process:

1. The client device wants to communicate with the server, so the client device sends a **synchronization (SYN)** message to the server. The SYN message is used to initiate a connection with the server. Within the SYN message, a randomly generated sequence number is created. This is used to indicate the beginning or starting sequence number for the data that will be transmitted from the client, as shown in the following diagram:

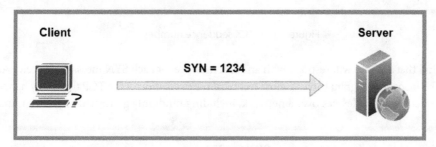

Figure 1.11 – SYN sequence number

2. The server receives the SYN message from the client and the server responds with an **acknowledgment (ACK)** message. Within the ACK message is an ACK sequence number; this number is the client's sequence number + 1. The server also includes a SYN message within its response, containing a randomly generated sequence number to inform the client it also wants to initiate a connection; this message is known as a **SYN/ACK**, as shown in the following diagram:

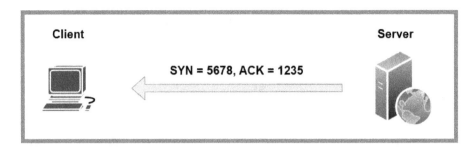

Figure 1.12 – SYN/ACK sequence number

3. The client receives the SYN/ACK message from the server and responds with an ACK message. The ACK message from the client contains an increment value of the SYN message received from the server, as shown in the following diagram:

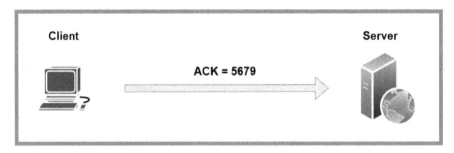

Figure 1.13 – ACK sequence number

Keep in mind that a device will respond with an ACK message for each SYN message it receives over a network. The following diagram shows a more technical representation of the TCP three-way handshake as it occurs between two devices over a network, including randomly generated sequence numbers:

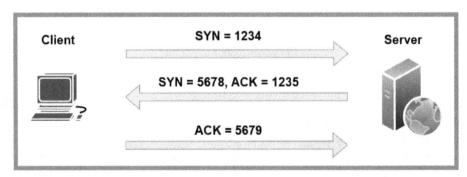

Figure 1.14 – TCP three-way handshake with sequence numbers

Using a network protocol analyzer tool such as Wireshark, network professionals can perform packet analysis on their network infrastructure and analyze the network traffic. The following screenshot shows the TCP three-way handshake captured using Wireshark on a real network:

No.	Source	Destination	Protocol	Info	
1	192.168.0.2	192.168.0.1	TCP	3m-image-lm(1550) → telnet(23)	[SYN] Seq=0 Win=32120
2	192.168.0.1	192.168.0.2	TCP	telnet(23) → 3m-image-lm(1550)	[SYN, ACK] Seq=0 Ack=1
3	192.168.0.2	192.168.0.1	TCP	3m-image-lm(1550) → telnet(23)	[ACK] Seq=1 Ack=1

Figure 1.15 – Wireshark capture

As shown in the preceding screenshot, packet #1 shows a sender, 192.168.0.2, sending a TCP SYN message that has a SYN sequence number of 0 to a destination device with an IP address of 192.168.0.1. Next, packet #2 indicates the device with the IP address of 192.168.0.1 responds with a SYN/ACK message that contains a SYN sequence number of 0 and an ACK sequence number of 1. Lastly, packet #3 indicates that the device with an IP address of 192.168.0.2 responds with an ACK message that contains an ACK sequence number of 1.

> **Important note**
>
> The sequence numbers used by TCP allow a destination device to easily reassemble incoming messages if they are received out-of-order compared to the order they were sent onto the network.

Once a TCP three-way handshake has been established, both hosts will begin sending messages to each other. When a client sends a message to another device using TCP as the Transport layer, the receiver of the message responds with an ACK packet to the sender. The ACK packet confirms the message was delivered successfully. If the sender does not receive an ACK packet from the intended destination host, after a while, the sender will attempt to retransmit the same message, repeating the process to ensure the message is delivered successfully. This is another benefit of using TCP when communicating over a network as it provides guaranteed delivery of messages and retransmits messages when needed.

When both hosts are no longer transmitting data between themselves over the network, TCP will attempt to gracefully tear down/terminate the connection using a four-step process, as shown here:

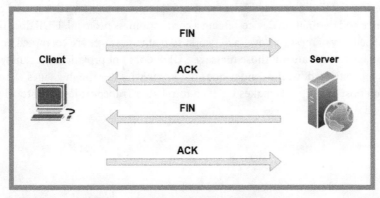

Figure 1.16 – TCP terminating a connection

As we can see, the client sends a **FINISH (FIN)** message to the server, indicating it no longer wants to maintain the session. The server responds with an ACK message to the client, indicating it is acknowledging that the client wants to terminate the connection. The server also sends a FIN message to the client to indicate it no longer wants to send any data. The final message is sent from the client – an ACK message – to confirm the termination.

The following are the benefits of using TCP as a transport layer protocol:

- Establishes a session such as the TCP three-way handshake before exchanging data.

- Provides reliability in delivering data over a network.

- Delivers data using the same order of delivery from the sender to the receiver.

- Uses flow control by creating a window size that has been mutually agreed upon between the source and destination hosts. The flow control window size determines the amount of data that can be sent at a time between the hosts.

While there are many benefits to using TCP as the preferred transport layer protocol, there are many disadvantages, such as the following:

- There is more overhead on a network when using TCP as the Transport layer protocol. For each message delivered to a destination device, the receiver responds with an ACK message.

- When a host is sending multiple messages to another host over a network, the messages are not sent all at once. TCP creates a logical window size between the source device and destination device that determines how much data can be sent at a time. TCP will send several messages within the TCP window and wait for acknowledgment messages from the receiver before sending more data. This creates a delay in the delivery of the messages.

In the next section, we will learn about the characteristics of another Transport layer protocol, the **User Datagram Protocol (UDP)**.

User Datagram Protocol

UDP is another Transport layer protocol that assists with delivering messages between devices over a network. Unlike TCP, UDP is a connectionless protocol that does not establish a logical connection between the source and destination devices. Being a connectionless protocol, UDP does not provide any guarantee of delivery of messages over a network, so if any messages are corrupted or discarded, UDP does not attempt to retransmit those messages. UDP does not provide any acknowledgments when messages are delivered, so the sender does not know whether the messages were delivered to the destination host or not. This makes UDP an unreliable Transport layer protocol within the networking model.

When using UDP as the preferred Transport layer protocol, the sender device does not use sequence numbers. As quickly as the datagrams from the Application layers are being sent down to the Transport layer, the Transport layer uses UDP and quickly places the datagrams on the actual network without adding any sequencing information. Therefore, when a destination host receives incoming messages over the network, there is no way to determine how to properly reassemble the messages in their correct order.

While TCP may seem to always be the preferred Transport layer protocol, UDP has some advantages, such as the following:

- Since UDP does not wait for any acknowledgment from the destination host, clients can send messages faster across the network to the destination devices. It is beneficial for application layer protocols that are time-sensitive such as **Voice over IP (VoIP)** and **Video over IP** solutions that are used in real time.

- Low overhead on the network since no acknowledgment messages are returning to the sender.

- UDP is commonly used with application layer protocols, which are not dependent on delivery or require acknowledgment.

- UDP is commonly used when applications have more efficient means of guaranteeing delivery of data and do not want the additional overhead TCP requires.

Once the Transport layer inserts its layer 4 header onto the datagram using TCP or UDP, it sends the segment down to the next layer on the OSI model. In the next section, we will learn about the role and functionality of the Network layer within the OSI model.

Network layer

The Network layer of the OSI model is responsible for ensuring the logical addressing information is inserted into the datagram. On a network, each device requires a unique **Internet Protocol version 4 (IPv4)** or **Internet Protocol version 6 (IPv6)** address that allows them to communicate with devices on their local and remote networks. The Network layer encapsulates a layer 3 header onto the datagram by inserting the source and destination IP addresses of the sender and destination host. Without inserting the source IP address onto the datagram, the recipient of the message will not be able to return any messages. Without including a destination IP address in the message, networking devices such as routers will not know how to forward the message to its intended destination. Once the PDU from the Transport layer is encapsulated with the layer 3 header, it is referred to as a **Packet**.

The following diagram shows a high-level overview of a client sending a message to a server:

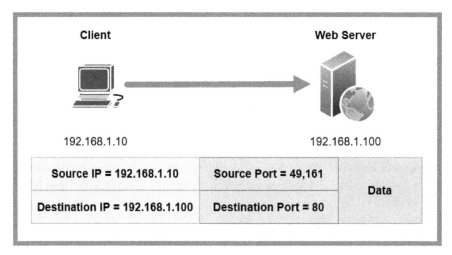

Figure 1.17 – Packet header

As shown in the preceding diagram, the packet contains a source IP address of 192.168.1.10, which belongs to the client device, and a destination IP address of 192.168.1.100, which belongs to the web server.

Additionally, the Network layer is responsible for the routing services that occur on the network. Devices such as routers are considered to be layer 3 devices that can interconnect different networks and forward packets between networking using the information within the layer 3 header of the packet, such as the destination IP address. Between a sender and receiver, there may be multiple routers and paths, and each time a router on the network receives a packet, it checks the destination IP address within the layer 3 header of the packet and the routing table on the router to determine whether a valid route to the destination exists. Therefore, a sender must insert the accurate layer 3 addressing (IP addresses) onto the layer 3 header of the packet to ensure networking devices such as routers can forward the packet to the intended destination.

> **Important note**
> The source IPv4 address on a packet may change due to the **Network Address Translation (NAT)** operating on a router. We will discuss the processes and needs of using NAT later in this book.

Internet Protocol (IP) is a connectionless layer 3 protocol that does not establish any logical connection or session between the sender and receiver of the message. Being connectionless simply means the IP will not create a dedicated, logical end-to-end session/connection before sending any data between the source and destination hosts over a network. Therefore, if packets are lost or corrupted during the transmission process, the messages are not retransmitted. Additionally, being connectionless does not notify the intended recipient about any incoming data/messages from a sender.

As the IP is a connectionless layer 3 protocol, it uses its best effort when transmitting data between sender and receiver devices over a network. Since it does not establish any end-to-end connections, it is unreliable and does not provide any guarantee that the data will be delivered to the destination host. However, it provides low overhead on the network as a connectionless protocol. Lastly, the IP indicates to the Transport layer whether or not to use the TCP, UDP, or other protocols in its header information. For example, if the data requires connection-oriented delivery, the IP will indicate TCP.

> **Important note**
>
> The operation of the IP is independent of the type of medium being used to transmit the data, such as wired, wireless, or even fiber optics. The lower layers, such as the Data Link layer of the OSI model, are responsible for ensuring the packets are prepared for the type of medium before they're placed on the actual network. The **Maximum Transmission Unit (MTU)** describes the maximum size of a message that can be supported by network media. The default MTU size is 1,500 bytes.

Once the Network layer encapsulates the datagram with a layer 3 header, it passes it down to the next layer of the OSI model, known as the Data Link layer.

Data Link layer

The Data Link layer of the OSI model is responsible for moving the datagrams from the upper layers onto the actual network. This layer handles the flow control regarding how much data is placed (outgoing) on the media, such as a wired, wireless, or fiber optics network medium. It also manages the flow control of incoming messages from the physical network that is going to the upper layers of the OSI model on a host device.

The Data Link layer ensures datagrams from the upper lowers of the OSI model can access the network media. This is because the upper layers are not concerned about the media type that is used to transport the data over the actual network. Whether the Network layer creates an IPv4 or IPv6 packet, the Data Link layer encapsulates a layer 2 header and trailer onto the packet, creating a **frame**. This frame is crafted by the Data Link layer to meet the requirements needed for it to be sent over the physical network media. Furthermore, the Data Link layer handles error detection to identify whether any incoming frames from the physical network are corrupted and discard them.

Within the Data Link layer, two sublayers assist with ensuring frames are encapsulated, de-encapsulated, and placed on the network:

- **Logical Link Control (LLC)**
- **Media Access Control (MAC)**

Over the next few subsections, you will learn about the functionality and roles of each of these sublayers within the Data Link layer of the OSI model.

Logical Link Control

Logical Link Control (**LLC**) is a sublayer within the Data Link layer of the OSI model and is responsible for ensuring there is communication between the networking applications, software, and protocols of the upper layers of the OSI model and the local host's device hardware such as the **Network Interface Card** (**NIC**). The NIC is a physical hardware-based component that allows a device such as a computer or a smartphone to interact with a wired or wireless network. The LLC inserts information within the frame, which indicates the network layer protocol that is being used within the frame. Additionally, the LLC allows many layer 3 protocols such as IPv4 and IPv6 to use the same network media and device.

Media Access Control

The **Media Access Control** (**MAC**) sublayer of the Data Link layer is responsible for performing the data encapsulation process and controlling access to the network device such as the NIC and network media (wired, wireless, or fiber optic). The MAC sublayer is also responsible for inserting the layer 2 physical addressing information onto the layer 2 header of the frame before placing it on the actual network media. The physical layer 2 address information is used to transmit and deliver frames being exchanged on a shared network medium. This layer 2 physical address is commonly referred to as a **MAC address** or a **Burned-In Address** (**BIA**).

A MAC address is a **48-bit** address that is embedded onto a NIC by the vendor of the device. The MAC address on a NIC is considered to be unchangeable as the vendor of the device hardcodes it into the firmware of the component, hence the name *burned-in address*. However, within the cybersecurity industry, the MAC address of a device can easily be changed by a threat actor or cybersecurity professional based on the use case.

The 48-bit (6-byte) binary MAC address is usually written in hexadecimal (ranges 0 – 9, A – F) to easily identify an address apart from another. The first 24 bits (3 bytes) of a MAC address is known as the **Organizationally Unique Identifier** (**OUI**) as it is assigned by the vendor of the device/NIC. The OUI portion of a MAC address can help both network and cybersecurity professionals determine the type/vendor of a device that is connected to a network. The last 24 bits (3 bytes) of the MAC address are uniquely addressed.

The following diagram shows an example of the OUI portion of a MAC address:

Organizationally Unique Identifier (OUI)	Assigned by the Vendor
3 Bytes	3 Bytes
24 Bits	24 Bits
00-60-5C	3d-d9-01
Cisco Systems	Device-Specific

Figure 1.18 – The OUI portion of a MAC address

MAC addresses are usually presented a bit differently based on the vendor of the device or operating system. The following are examples of the same MAC address in different formats:

- `0060.5c3d.d901`: This format is usually used by Cisco systems
- `00-60-5c-3d-d9-01`: This format is commonly used on Microsoft Windows operating systems
- `00:60:5c:3d:d9:01`: This format is found on Linux-based systems

> **Important note**
>
> MAC addresses are not case-sensitive. However, you may notice they are commonly presented in a lowercase format, while some devices may display them in uppercase.

As an aspiring network professional, you can perform a MAC address vendor lookup by using any of the following websites and pasting the MAC address into the necessary field:

- `https://macvendors.com`
- `https://macaddress.io`
- `https://www.wireshark.org/tools/oui-lookup.html`

The following screenshot shows an example of the OUI lookup while using the Wireshark OUI Lookup Tool:

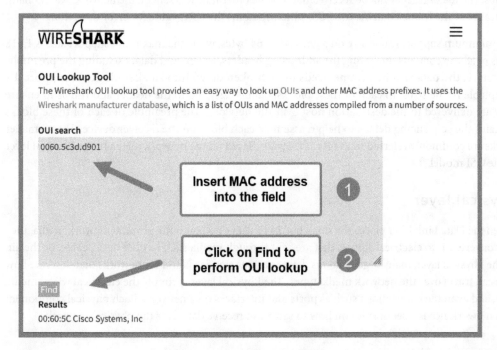

Figure 1.19 – OUI Lookup Tool

As shown in the preceding screenshot, the 00:60:5c code of the MAC address identifies the manufacturer of the device as Cisco Systems, Inc. This indicates that the device is most likely a networking device on the organization's network.

Furthermore, the MAC sublayer handles error detection by inserting a trailer into the frame. The trailer of the frame contains the **Frame Check Sequence (FCS)**, which includes the **Cyclic Redundancy Check (CRC)** value. The CRC is a one-way cryptographic, mathematical representation of the frame and its contents, which is calculated by using a process known as *hashing*. This helps systems validate the integrity of a message.

The following diagram shows a high-level overview of the layer 2 header and trailer of a frame:

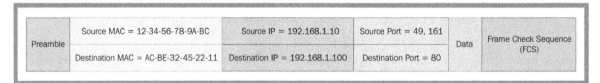

Figure 1.20 – Frame

As shown in the preceding diagram, the frame is encapsulated with a layer 2 header that contains the source and destination MAC addresses, as well as the preamble, which is used to identify the start of the frame with sequencing and synchronization. The preamble helps the receiver of the message determine where the frame begins and how to reassemble the message in the correct order. This is because the messages may not be received in the same order they was sent on the network. Additionally, the trailer of the frame contains the FCS, which contains the CRC value for error detection.

The minimum support frame size on a network is 64 bytes, while the maximum support size is 1,518 bytes of all the contents, including the addressing headers, trailer, and data, excluding the preamble. Therefore, the data within a frame needs to be broken down into smaller blocks to support the acceptable frame sizes. In each of these blocks, data is assigned to the header and trailer to ensure they are delivered to the destination host over the network. The preamble of each of these blocks contains the sequencing details to help reassemble each block on the receiver device. These smaller blocks are commonly referred to as **bits** as they are placed on the network media in the Physical layer of the OSI model.

Physical layer

When the Data Link layer places the small blocks of data (bits) onto the physical network media, they are converted into electrical signals that are sent through media such as fiber optic, cable, or the air. At the Physical layer, many organizations define various standards and frameworks that describe how data can travel over the network media types. The Physical layer is simply the electrical wires, media type, and even the connections such as ports and interfaces on a network. Each physical component on a network needs a set of rules on how to send and receive data over the physical network.

The following is a list of important organizations that govern how data can be sent over the physical network, how data can be encoded, and the signaling methods:

- **International Organization for Standardization (ISO)**
- **Telecommunications Industry Association/Electronic Industries Association (TIA/EIA)**
- **International Telecommunication Union (ITU)**
- **American National Standards Institute (ANSI)**
- **Institute of Electrical and Electronics Engineers (IEEE)**
- **Federal Communication Commission (FCC)**
- **European Telecommunications Standards Institute (ETSI)**

The Physical layer of the OSI model addresses the following elements to ensure data can be sent over a network:

- Physical components
- Encoding
- Signaling

The physical components are the hardware elements that you see on a network, such as the networking devices, the physical interfaces/ports on a device, the networking cables that are used to interconnect devices, and so on. Each hardware device, whether it's the NIC on a computer or a switch, uses a set of standards to ensure devices can transmit messages over the network.

The encoding process is handled by the Data Link layer before the bits are placed onto the Physical layer on the network. The encoding process describes the processes or methods used by a device to convert a stream of messages, such as bits, into code. This code is used to represent patterns that are recognizable by both the sender and receiver devices over the network. Think of an encoding process such as creating a mutual language that can be understood by two users or devices.

The signaling element of the Physical layer describes how the signals are created and placed on the physical network media by a sender device. The signals that are generated by the sender are electrical, wireless, or even optical (light), depending on the network media that is connected to a device. For example, a laptop connected to a wireless router will be converting the messages into a wireless signal before they are sent to the wireless router. A network device such as a switch may convert the messages into an electrical signal to place on a copper cable or into an optical signal (light) to place onto a fiber optic cable for transmission. These signals are usually represented using a 1 or 0 in the digital world; 1 may represent a high voltage on the wire while 0 may represent a low voltage on the wire.

With that, you have understood the fundamentals of the OSI model and how each layer plays a vital role in ensuring messages can be transmitted between a sender and receiver over a network. In the next section, we will learn about the TCP/IP protocol suite and how it compares to the OSI model.

Understanding TCP/IP

As mentioned previously, the US DoD developed a neutral networking model known as TCP/IP. This has been adopted by many computer and networking vendors. At the time of writing, TCP/IP is the dominating networking protocol suite and ensures devices can send and receive data over networks. Whether it's a private network within your home, office, or the internet, TCP/IP is implemented within all devices connected to a network.

While TCP/IP seems to specify only two networking protocols – TCP from the Transport layer and IP from the Network layer of the OSI model – they are the most commonly used on networks. The TCP/IP protocol suite is a group of networking protocols that all work together to ensure messages can be exchanged over any type of network between sender and receiver devices.

The original version of the TCP/IP protocol is made is up of four layers compared to the seven-layered OSI model. Modern versions of the TCP/IP protocol suite have five layers, splitting the bottom layer into Physical and Data Link layers.

The following diagram shows a comparison of the original TCP/IP protocol suite and the OSI model:

Layer	OSI Model	TCP/IP	Layer
7	Application	Application	4
6	Presentation		
5	Session		
4	Transport	Transport	3
3	Network	Internet	2
2	Data Link	Network Access	1
1	Physical		

Figure 1.21 – TCP/IP protocol suite

As shown in the preceding diagram, the following are the four layers of the TCP/IP protocol suite:

- **Application**
- **Transport**
- **Internet**
- **Network Access**

The Application layer of TCP/IP absorbs all the functionality and responsibilities of the Application, Presentation, and Sessions layers of the OSI model. The Transport layer of both the OSI model and TCP/IP has the same functionalities and responsibilities. The Internet layer of TCP/IP is equivalent to the Network layer of the OSI model. Lastly, the Network Access layer of TCP/IP is equivalent to both the Data Link and Physical layers of the OSI model.

> **Important note**
> The **Network Access** layer of TCP/IP is sometimes referred to as the **Link** layer or the **Network Interface** layer.

The following diagram provides a high-level overview of a computer sending a message that contains data to a server using the TCP/IP protocol suite:

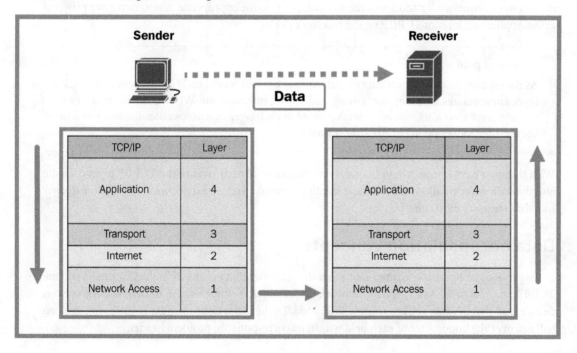

Figure 1.22 – TCP/IP protocol suite

As shown in the preceding diagram, the sender creates a message at the Application layer known as Data that is passed down to the lower layers and encapsulates a new header before it is placed on the physical network media. On the sender's device, the Transport layer encapsulates a header that contains the source and destination service port numbers and the Transport layer protocol such as TCP or UDP. The Internet layer encapsulates an IP header that contains the source and destination IP address and the IP version (IPv4 or IPv6). The Network Access layer encapsulates a header that contains the source and destination MAC addresses (physical addresses) and performs encodes, signals, and places the message onto the physical network media for transmission to the receiver.

On the receiver's end, the bits are accepted on the Network Access layer, which checks the integrity of the incoming message by checking the FCS within the frame's trailer. The Network Access layer also checks the destination MAC address found within the frame header to verify whether the message is intended for the actual receiver. Once everything is fine with the frame, the Network Access layer de-encapsulates the frame by removing the frame's header and trailer before sending it up to the Internet layer of the TCP/IP. At the Internet layer, the destination IP address found within the IP header of the packet is verified to determine whether it matches the IP address of the receiver. Once everything is fine with the packet, the Internet layer de-encapsulates the packet's header details and passes the message up to the Transport layer. At the Transport layer, the destination service port number is observed within the segment's header. The destination service port number is used by the Transport layer to determine which application layer protocol to deliver the message to. Once the Transport layer has identified the service port number to the corresponding application layer protocol, it de-encapsulates the Transport layer header and sends the raw datagram to the appropriate application layer protocol at the Application layer of TCP/IP on the receiver's device.

> **Important note**
>
> As data moves down a networking model, such as the OSI model or TCP protocol suite, each layer encapsulates a header containing addressing information. When a device receives a message over a network, the process is reversed as each layer de-encapsulates the headers and the message moves up to the Application layer.

With that, you have learned about the roles and functions of each layer of the TCP/IP protocol suite and the data encapsulation and de-encapsulation process. In the next section, we will dive deeper into data encapsulation concepts.

Data encapsulation concepts

In the previous sections, you learned a lot about the processes that occur within the OSI model and the TCP/IP protocol suite. As an aspiring network professional, it's important to understand the various fields found within Ethernet, IPv4, IPv6, TCP, and UDP headers. Over the next few subsections, you will discover the importance of each field within its corresponding protocol header.

Ethernet header

At the Data Link layer, when a packet is received from the Network layer, it is encapsulated with a layer 2 header and trailer. The following diagram shows each field within an Ethernet header:

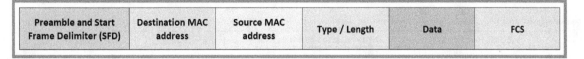

Figure 1.23 – Ethernet header

The following are the roles and functions of each field found within an Ethernet header:

- **Preamble** and **SFD**: The preamble is made up of 7 bytes and the **Start Frame Delimiter** (SFD) is 1 byte in size, so the entire field is a total of 8 bytes in size. This field within an Ethernet frame is used to synchronize messages being transmitted between a sender and receiver over a network. This field is also used to indicate the start of the frame to the receiver.

- **Destination MAC address**: This field is 48 bits (6 bytes) in length and contains the layer 2 physical address (MAC address) of the next device to receive the message.

- **Source MAC address**: This field is 48 bits (6 bytes) in length and contains the layer 2 physical address of the sender of a frame.

- **Type / Length**: This field is 2 bytes in length and contains details that are used to identify the upper layer protocol (IPv4, IPv6) that is encapsulated within a frame.

- **Data**: The data field ranges between 46 to 1,500 bytes and contains the raw data from the Application layer of the networking model. All Ethernet frames are required to be at least 64 bytes in length. If the frame is less than 64 bytes, additional bits, known as a *pad*, are inserted to increase the size of the frame to the minimum length.

- **FCS**: The **Frame Check Sequence** (FCS) field is made up of 4 bytes in length and it's used to verify the integrity of a frame and detect errors.

> **Important note**
>
> Frames that are less than 64 bytes are known as **runts**, while frames that are greater than 1,500 bytes are known as **jumbo frames** or **giants**.

Combining all the fields of an Ethernet header except for the preamble and SFD fields provides a frame length between 64 to 1,518 bytes. Next, you will learn about the fields within the IPv4 and IPv6 headers.

IP headers

At the Network layer of the OSI model and Internet layer of the TCP/IP protocol suite, when a segment is received from the Transport layer, it is encapsulated with a layer 3 header that is commonly referred to as an IP header. The following diagram shows the field within an IPv4 header:

Version	Internet Header Length	Differentiated Services (DS)		Total Length	
		DSCP	ECN		
Identification				Flag	Fragment Offset
Time-to-Live (TTL)		Protocol		Header Checksum	
Source IP Address					
Destination IP Address					
Options					

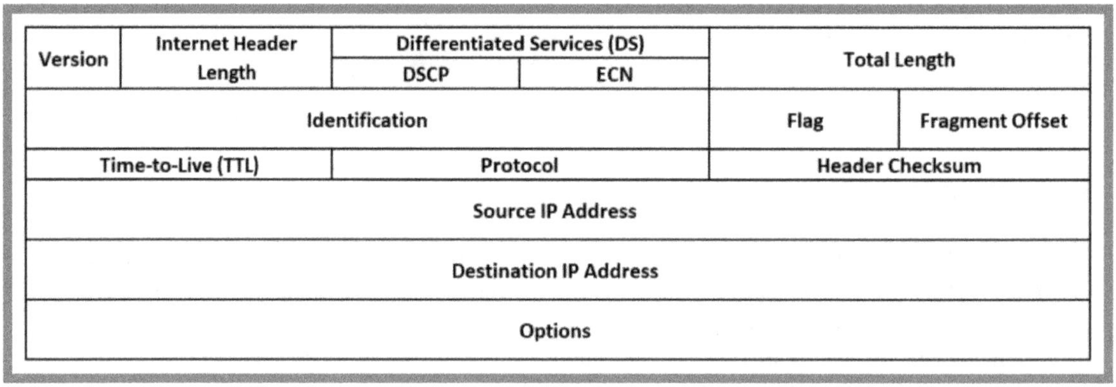

Figure 1.24 – IPv4 header

The following is a description of each field within an IPv4 header:

- **Version**: This field is made up of 4 bits and is used to identify the message as an IPv4 packet.

- **Internet Header Length**: This field is made up of 4 bits and is used to indicate where the header section ends and the data section starts.

- **Differentiated Services** or **DiffServ (DS)**: This field is made up of 1 byte (8 bits) and is used to determine the priority of the packet on the network. Within the DS field, the 6 most significant bits (from the left to right in a binary number) are used to present the **Differentiated Service Code Point (DSCP)**, while the 2 least significant bits (from right to left in a binary number) are used to represent the **Explicit Congestion Notification (ECN)** details.

- **Total length**: This field is made up of 16 bits (2 bytes) and is used to indicate the total size of the IPv4 packet.

- **Identification**: This field is made up of 16 bits (2 bytes) and is used to provide identification numbering to each fragmented packet that belongs to an original message.

- **Flags**: This field is made up of 3 bits and is used to indicate whether the packet is to be fragmented or not.

- **Fragment offset**: This field is made up of 13 bits and is used to indicate the sequencing position of a fragmented packet.

- **Time To Live (TTL)**: The TTL field is made up of 1 byte (8 bits) and is used to determine the life of the packet as it is transmitted between a sender and receiver over the network. Each time a layer 3 device such as a router receives a packet, it decreases the TTL value by 1 before forwarding it to the next device toward the destination. If the TTL value of a packet reaches 0, it is discarded on the network.

- **Protocol**: This field is made up of 1 byte (8 bits) and is used to indicate the payload type that is enclosed within the packet.

- **Header checksum**: This field is made up of 2 bytes (16 bits) and is used to determine whether there's any corruption within the IPv4 header.

- **Source IP address**: This field contains the source IPv4 address of the sender, which is 32 bits (4 bytes) in length.

- **Destination IP address**: This field contains the destination IPv4 address of the intended recipient, which is 32 bits (4 bytes) in length.

- **Options**: This field is optional as it's not always used.

The Network and Internet layers can also be encapsulated within an IPv6 header on the segment to create a packet. The following are the fields within an IPv6 header:

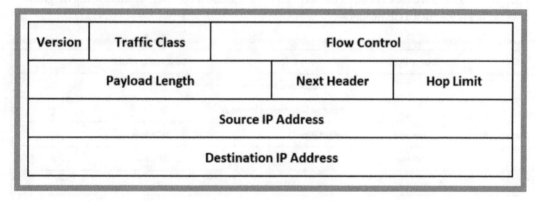

Figure 1.25 – IPv6 header

As shown in the preceding diagram, there are fewer fields within an IPv6 header compared to those found within an IPv4 header. The following is a description of each field found within an IPv6 header:

- **Version**: This field is 4 bits in length and is used to identify this packet as an IPv6 packet on the network.

- **Traffic class**: This field is 8 bits (1 byte) in length. It has the same functionality as the DS field found within an IPv4 packet.

- **Flow control**: This field is 20 bits in length and is sometimes referred to as the **Flow Label**. This field is used to inform the routers on the network to use the same type of handling for IPv6 packets that has the same flow control/flow label information.

- **Payload length**: This field is 16 bits (2 bytes) in length. It is used to represent the length of the enclosed data or payload in the IPv6 packet.

- **Next header**: This field is 8 bits (1 byte) in length. It is used to indicate the payload type that is enclosed within the IPv6 packet.

- **Hop limit**: This field is 8 bits (1 byte) in length and it has the same role and functions as the TTL field found within an IPv4 packet.

- **Source IP address**: This field contains the 128-bit IPv6 address of the sender.

- **Destination IP address**: This field contains the 128-bit IPv6 address of the receiver.

Next, we will learn about the fields found within a TCP header of a segment.

TCP header

Some application layer protocols use **Transmission Control Protocol** (**TCP**) as the preferred Transport layer protocol to ensure data is delivered between a sender and a receiver. The following diagram shows the fields within a TCP header:

Source Port			Destination Port	
Sequence Number				
Acknowledgement Number				
Header Length	Reserved	Control Bits	Window	
Checksum			Urgent	
Options				
Application Layer Data				

Figure 1.26 – TCP header

The following is a description of each field within a TCP header:

- **Source port**: This is a 16-bit (2-byte) field that contains the source service port number of the source application layer protocol.

- **Destination port**: This is a 16-bit (2-byte) field that contains the destination service port number for the destination application layer protocol.

- **Sequence number**: This is a 32-bit (4-byte) field that is used during the reassembly process on the receiver device.

- **Acknowledgment number**: This is a 32-bit (4-byte) field that is used to indicate that the message (data) has been received. This value will be the sequence number + 1.

- **Header length**: This is a 4-bit field that is sometimes referred to as the **data offset** field. It indicates the length of the TCP header.

- **Reserved**: This is a 6-bit field reserved for future usage.

- **Control bits**: This is a 6-bit field that is used to specify various TCP flags such as URG, ACK, PSH, RST, SYN, and FIN. These are sometimes referred to as the **Flag** field.

- **Window**: This is a 16-bit (2-byte) field that indicates the number of bits or bytes that can be accepted during data transmission between a sender and receiver.

- **Checksum**: This is a 16-bit (2-byte) field that is used to detect any errors within the TCP header.

- **Urgent**: This is a 16-bit (2-byte) field that is used to indicate urgency on the TCP header.

- **Options**: This is an optional field within the TCP header that can range between 0 and 320 bits in length.

- **Application layer data**: This field contains the data that's been received from the application layer protocol.

The following six TCP flags are found within the control bit field within a TCP header:

- **URG**: Indicates urgency on the TCP segment

- **ACK**: Indicates acknowledgment of a message

- **PSH**: Performs the push function

- **RST**: Used to reset a connection

- **SYN**: Indicates a synchronization message with a synchronization sequence number

- **FIN**: Indicates to gracefully terminate (finish) a session

Next, let's learn about the fields found within the UDP header of a segment.

UDP headers

Not all application layer protocols use TCP – many use the **User Datagram Protocol** (**UDP**) to ensure low overhead and faster transmission. The following diagram shows the fields within a UDP header:

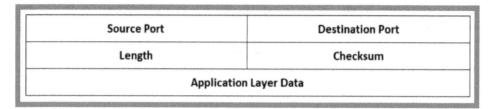

Figure 1.27 – UDP header

As shown in the preceding diagram, there are fewer headers within a UDP header compared to TCP. As a result, UDP provides less overhead on the network. The following is a description of each field within a UDP header:

- **Source port**: This is a 16-bit (2-byte) field that contains the source service port number of the source application layer protocol

- **Destination port**: This is a 16-bit (2-byte) field that contains the destination service port number for the destination application layer protocol

- **Length**: This is a 16-bit (2-byte) field that indicates the length of the UDP header

- **Checksum**: This is a 16-bit (2-byte) field that is used for detecting any errors within the TCP header

- **Application layer data**: This field contains the data that's been received from the application layer protocol

With that, you have explored the various fields found within various protocol headers such as Ethernet, IP, TCP, and UDP. In the next section, we will learn how to start analyzing network packets using Wireshark.

Analyzing network packets

Packet analysis is a technique that's used by both networking and cybersecurity professionals to see what's happening within their networks. Many protocol analyzer applications allow professionals to capture network traffic and analyze the state of the network. Network professionals use protocol analyzers to identify the type of traffic, whether any issues are occurring, and to assist with troubleshooting.

In this section, you will gain hands-on experience with Wireshark, a popular network protocol analyzer for identifying the fields within network packets. To get started with this exercise, follow these steps:

1. First, go to https://www.wireshark.org/download.html to download the latest version of Wireshark on your computer. Once the download is complete, start the installation process and use the default options when installing the application onto your computer. Ensure you install the PCAP driver when prompted.

2. We'll be using a sample capture file within this exercise. To download the sample file for this exercise, go to `https://wiki.wireshark.org/SampleCaptures` and download the `http_with_jpegs.cap.gz` file, as shown in the following screenshot:

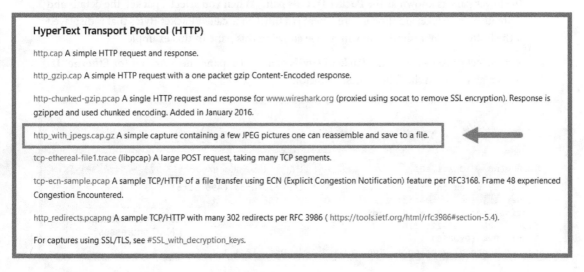

HyperText Transport Protocol (HTTP)

http.cap A simple HTTP request and response.

http_gzip.cap A simple HTTP request with a one packet gzip Content-Encoded response.

http-chunked-gzip.pcap A single HTTP request and response for www.wireshark.org (proxied using socat to remove SSL encryption). Response is gzipped and used chunked encoding. Added in January 2016.

http_with_jpegs.cap.gz A simple capture containing a few JPEG pictures one can reassemble and save to a file.

tcp-ethereal-file1.trace (libpcap) A large POST request, taking many TCP segments.

tcp-ecn-sample.pcap A sample TCP/HTTP of a file transfer using ECN (Explicit Congestion Notification) feature per RFC3168. Frame 48 experienced Congestion Encountered.

http_redirects.pcapng A sample TCP/HTTP with many 302 redirects per RFC 3986 (https://tools.ietf.org/html/rfc3986#section-5.4).

For captures using SSL/TLS, see #SSL_with_decryption_keys.

Figure 1.28 – Sample capture file

3. Next, open the **Wireshark** application on your computer, click on **File | Open**, and select the `http_with_jpegs.cap.gz` file that you downloaded in the previous step. Once the file has opened within Wireshark, you'll see all the packets and their contents, as shown in the following screenshot:

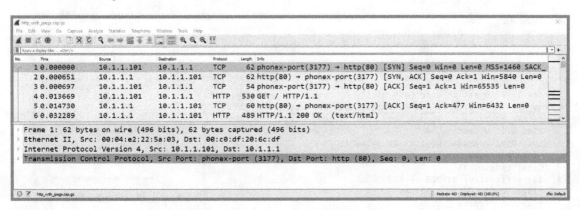

Figure 1.29 – Wireshark user interface

As shown in the preceding screenshot, the upper pane is known as the **Packet List** pane, which shows all the packets, the packet number, the absolute time from the point the capture started, the source and destination IP addresses, protocols, packet lengths, and summary information. The lower pane is known as the **Packet Details** pane. When you select a packet, the details and contents of the packet are shown here. There is a third pane called **Packet Bytes** that is displayed at the bottom of Wireshark. We will not be showing this pane in this example.

4.   Next, select packet #1 from the **Packet Details** pane and expand the **Ethernet** (or **Ethernet II**) header, as shown in the following screenshot:

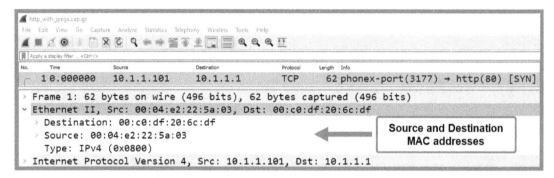

Figure 1.30 – Packet #1 Ethernet header

As we can see, the Ethernet header contains the source and destination MAC addresses, as well as the protocol type of the upper layer (Network/Internet layer).

5.   Next, expand the **Internet Protocol** header of packet #1 to view the IP header and its contents, as shown in the following screenshot:

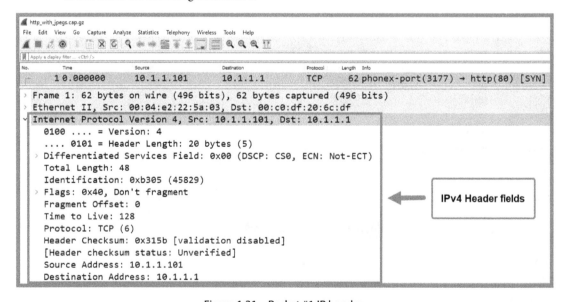

Figure 1.31 – Packet #1 IP header

As we can see, the IP header shows the version, **Differentiated Services** fields, total length, source and destination IP addresses, and all their fields.

6.   Next, expand the **Transmission Control Protocol** header of packet #1 to display its fields, as shown in the following screenshot:

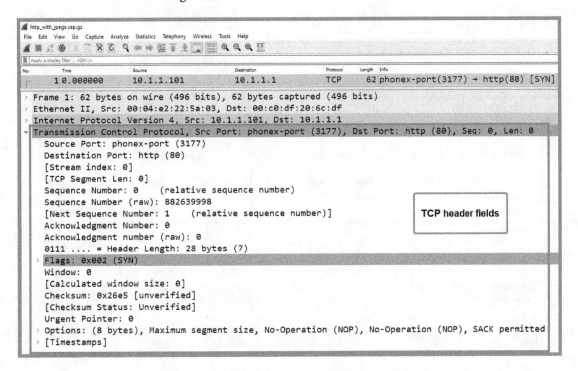

Figure 1.32 – Packet #1 TCP header

As we can see, the TCP header contains the source and destination service port numbers, TCP flag (SYN), sequence numbers, and so on. Notice that Wireshark automatically resolves the application layer protocol based on the service port number.

Important note

If Wireshark does not automatically resolve public IP addresses to hostnames or service port numbers to application layer protocols, simply enable the resolution features by selecting **Edit | Preferences | Name Resolution** to enable **Resolve MAC addresses**, **Resolve transport names**, and **Resolve network (IP) addresses**.

---

7.   Next, select packet #2 from the **Packet Details** pane and expand the **Ethernet** header, as shown in the following screenshot:

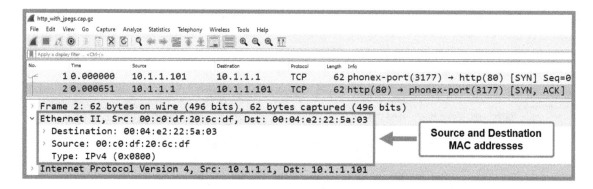

Figure 1.33 – Packet #2 Ethernet header

As we can see, the source and destination MAC addresses are now in reverse order.

8.   Next, expand the **Internet Protocol** header of packet #2 to view the IP header and its contents, as shown in the following screenshot:

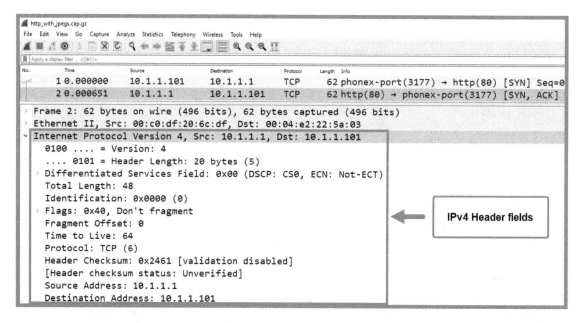

Figure 1.34 – Packet #1 IP header

As we can see, the source and destination IPv4 addresses are in reverse order as the web server is responding to the client.

9. Next, expand the **Transmission Control Protocol** header of packet #2 to display its fields, as shown in the following screenshot:

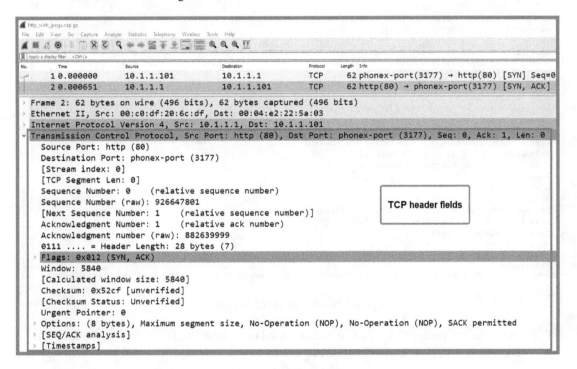

Figure 1.35 – Packet #2 TCP header

As we can see, the source and destination service ports are reversed compared to packet #1. The TCP flag indicates that packet #2 is a SYN/ACK response.

10. Next, select packet #3 and expand the **Transmission Control Protocol** header, as shown in the following screenshot:

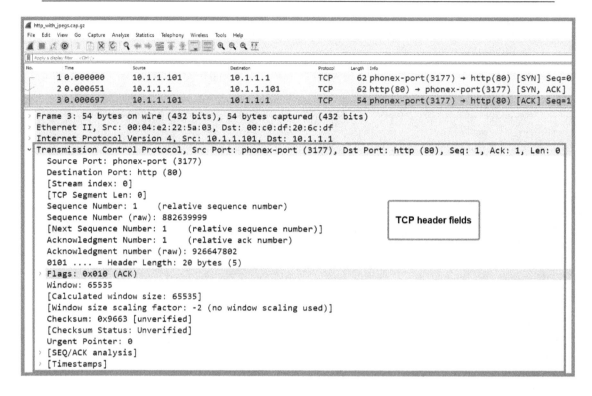

Figure 1.36 – Packet #3 TCP header

As we can see, packet #3 is a TCP ACK that is used to establish the TCP three-way handshake between 10.1.1.101 and 10.1.1.1.

11. Next, select packet #4 and expand the **Hypertext Transfer Protocol** header, as shown in the following screenshot:

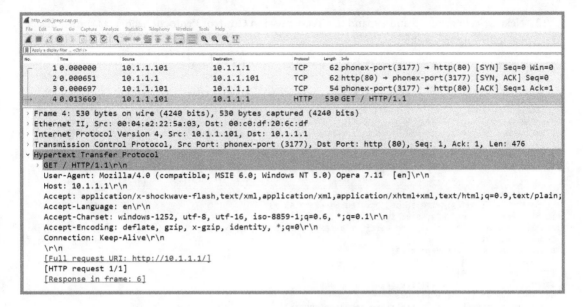

Figure 1.37 – Packet #4 HTTP header

As shown in the preceding snippet, packet #4 is sent from the client device (10.1.1.101) to the web server (10.1.1.1) and Wireshark shows the contents of the application layer protocol (HTTP).

> **Important note**
>
> HTTP is an unsecure protocol that does not provide any security such as data encryption. This means that anyone can view its contents using a protocol analyzer application.

12. Next, select packet #5 and expand the **Transmission Control Protocol** header, as shown in the following screenshot:

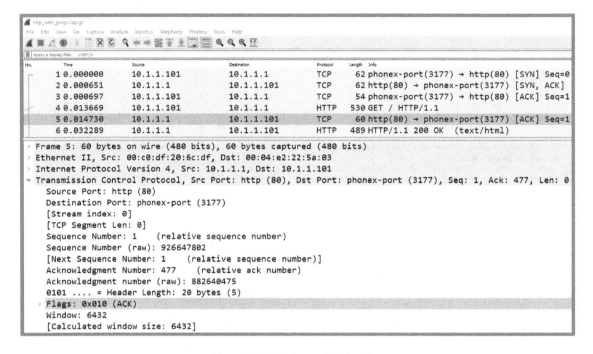

Figure 1.38 – Packet #5 TCP header

As we can see, packet #5 is a TCP ACK packet that is sent from the web server to the client, indicating that the HTTP message was received.

13. Next, select packet #6 and expand the **Hypertext Transfer Protocol** header, as shown in the following screenshot:

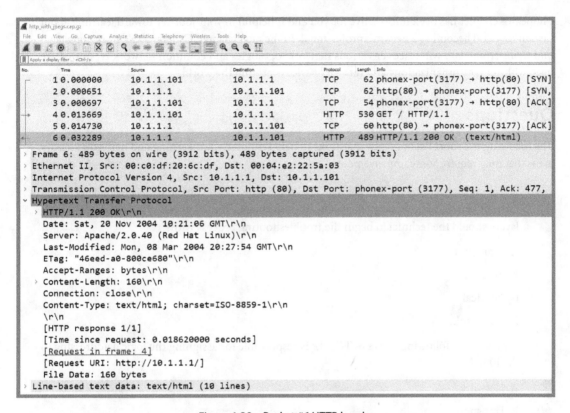

Figure 1.39 – Packet #6 HTTP header

As we can see, the response from the web server is visible using Wireshark.

Having completed this section, you have gained hands-on skills with Wireshark to identify the fields and their values within network packets.

Summary

In this chapter, you explored each layer of both the OSI reference model and the TCP/IP protocol suite. You discovered the roles and responsibilities of each layer and saw their purpose in ensuring messages are delivered successfully between source and destination hosts over a network. Additionally, you can describe, compare, and even contrast the layers between the OSI reference model and the TCP/IP protocol suite. As an aspiring network professional, you have also acquired the fundamental skills of understanding how the encapsulation and de-encapsulation process works between each layer, and even explored the headers of packets using a protocol analyzer application.

I hope this chapter has been informative for you and is helpful in your journey toward learning about networking and becoming a network professional. In the next chapter, *Chapter 2, Network Topologies and Connections*, you will discover various network topologies and common network types that are used within many organizations and service providers around the world.

Questions

The following is a short list of review questions to help reinforce your learning and help you identify areas that may require some improvement:

1. A technician has received a ticket that describes some CRC errors that have been detected on the network that are causing poor network performance for the users. Which of the following layers should the technician begin the troubleshooting process with?

    A. Transport

    B. Internet

    C. Physical

    D. Data Link

2. Which of the following layers of TCP/IP is responsible for assigning the logical addressing to the PDU?

    A. Network

    B. Transport

    C. Internet

    D. Network Access

3. Which of the following is a connectionless protocol?

    A. HTTP

    B. TCP

    C. LLC

    D. IP

4. Which of the following layers is not part of the OSI model?

    A. Application

    B. Internet

    C. Network

    D. Transport

5. Service port 25 is associated with which of the following protocols?

    A. SMTP

    B. DNS

    C. HTTP

    D. SSH

6. Which of the following layers of the OSI model is responsible for data encryption?

    A. Network Access

    B. Application

    C. Session

    D. Presentation

7. How many bits are there within a MAC address?

    A. 49

    B. 32

    C. 48

    D. 128

8. How many bits are there in an IPv4 address?

    A. 32

    B. 49

    C. 128

    D. 16

9. Which of the following layers is responsible for placing the data in the actual network media?

    A. Internet

    B. MAC

    C. LLC

    D. Network

10. Which of the following is not a valid MAC address?

    A. `0c:2d:c4:41:8b:66`

    B. `3d:f2:51:bf:40:b9`

    C. `4f:95:I5:b2:68:ca`

    D. `c5:fe:00:4f:73:e6`

Further reading

To learn more about network port numbers and protocols, check out `https://hub.packtpub.com/understanding-network-port-numbers-tcp-udp-and-icmp-on-an-operating-system/`.

Network Topologies and Connections

2

Designing a network to provide scalability, security, and redundancy with fault tolerance is essential to any network design and model. As an aspiring network professional, it's important to learn the building blocks of designing an optimal and resilient network infrastructure for the growing demand of organizations to support their business services and users. Understanding how network topologies can affect traffic flow within an organization is important to gain a solid understanding of designing a suitable network for any organization.

During this chapter, you will explore various network layouts and how they affect traffic flow within an organization. Next, you will explore various network types and devices that are interconnected to expand and share network resources over large geographic distances. Furthermore, you will understand how organizations and residential customers can connect to the service provider's network.

In this chapter, we will cover the following topics:

- Understanding network topologies
- Discovering network types
- Identifying service-related entry points
- Comparing provider links

Let's dive in!

Understanding network topologies

Network professionals design, implement, maintain, and troubleshoot networking technologies to ensure organizations can share resources between their users and devices within their company. Some networks are small, such as those within homes. These small networks usually have a few networked devices such as computers, smart appliances, **Internet of Things** (**IoT**) devices, and a couple of networking devices, such as a wireless router to create a wireless network and an **Internet Service Provider** (**ISP**) modem to provide internet service.

While small networks are very common to many users, within an organization, there are lots of devices based on the number of users, networks, and networking services within the company. Within an organization, there are many computers, laptops, servers, and smart/IoT devices. To interconnect all the devices within an organization, the company invests in purchasing many networking switches, routers, access points, and security appliances.

> **Important note**
>
> A network switch allows end devices such as computers, printers, and servers to connect to the actual organization's network. A router is a network device that interconnects two or more different networks together.

Interconnecting networking devices such as switches and routers seems simple as you can use a networking patch cable to make a physical connection between each device. However, if you interconnect networking devices without using a proper network design with industry best practices, you'll just be setting yourself up for a lot of future networking issues. As an aspiring network professional, it's very important to understand the various layouts of networking devices that are used to build a network. This idea of creating a layout of a network is commonly referred to as a **topology** or **network topology**.

Network topologies are used to help IT professionals understand how systems and devices are interconnected and to identify areas of improvement or where an issue may exist. Networking topologies can be described as **physical** or **logical**. A physical network topology contains a high-level overview showing the actual arrangement and placement of devices within an organization, such as the geographic location, such as city, as well as building names and floor and closet names. The physical network topology also shows the types of network connections and connectors since they are used to represent the type of network cables and how they are connected between devices within the organization.

The following diagram shows a simple example of a physical network topology:

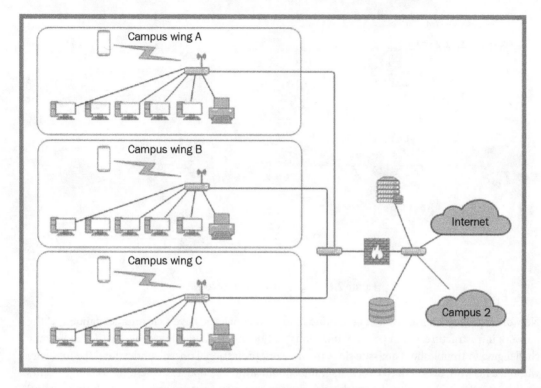

Figure 2.1 – Physical network topology

The logical network topology is a low-level diagram that focuses on the technical details of the network, such as the IP addresses and schemes, which demonstrate how data flows across the organization. The logical network topology diagram provides details about the different devices, such as switches, routers, and firewalls.

The following diagram shows an example of a logical network topology:

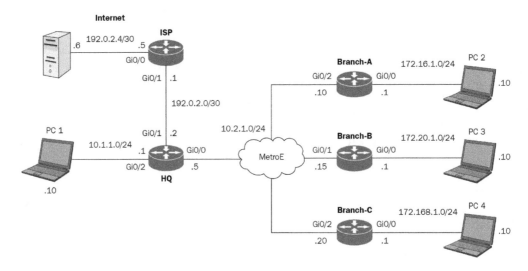

Figure 2.2 – Logical network topology

Network topology diagrams are not too difficult to create once you have a clear understanding of the network infrastructure within your organization. Without network topology diagrams, it can become challenging to troubleshoot an issue since the network professional doesn't understand the topology without a network diagram. Network diagrams should always be updated whenever a change occurs on the network. A change can be anything such as an upgrade, implementing new technologies and devices, and replacing or even decommissioning a device.

The following are some resources you can use to draw network topology diagrams:

- **Diagrams.net**: https://www.diagrams.net/ (free)

- **LibreOffice Draw**: https://www.libreoffice.org/discover/draw/ (free)

- **Microsoft Visio**: https://www.microsoft.com/en-us/microsoft-365/visio/ flowchart-software (commercial)

Many diagram and flowchart applications are used by many professionals within various industries. I recommend evaluating different diagram applications to determine which works best for you and meets your requirements. Some people may prefer a free application, while others may prefer a commercial product; each has its advantages and disadvantages. Keep in mind that your network diagrams should always be clear and easy to understand by anyone who is viewing them. In the past, I've seen diagrams created by networking professionals who have a lot of knowledge and skills, but due to less focus on soft skills such as communication and presentation, their diagrams were a bit challenging to understand. As an aspiring networking professional, it's important to have the essential soft skills and a creative imagination.

In the next section, you will discover the key characteristics of various types of network topologies.

Types of network topologies

A network topology defines the layout of how devices such as computers and networking devices are interconnected to allow traffic to flow within an organization. There are various types of network topologies, and each has its advantages and disadvantages. In this section, you'll discover various physical topologies.

Bus

The **bus** topology is a very old and legacy network topology that is no longer being used on modern networks. This type of network topology was designed to use a single networking cable as the main backbone of the entire network. This single backbone allowed nodes such as computers to connect to and access any resource on the network.

The following diagram shows an example of a traditional bus topology:

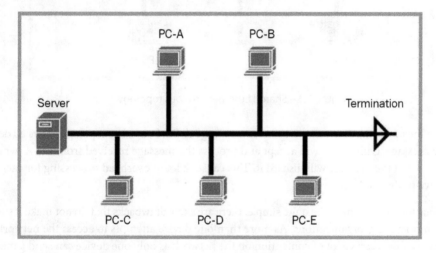

Figure 2.3 – Bus topology

As shown in the preceding diagram, all nodes are connected to the same networking cable (backbone), which allows each node to access the resources on the server or those that are shared from one node to another. On each end of the backbone networking cable, some terminators are installed to terminate or ground the cable if there are any unwanted electrical signals on the wire. Remember, computers and networking devices produce electrical signals that travel along a wire, such as a networking cable between nodes and devices. If there are additional or unwanted electrical signals on the wire and there's no place to discharge those signals, it can affect the devices connected to the networking cable.

In **Shared Ethernet**, the message is sent to a specific destination **Media Access Control** (**MAC**) address. Each node on the physical segment receives the message but only the **Network Interface Card** (**NIC**) whose MAC address matches the destination MAC address in the destination section of the Ethernet frame will accept the message (packet). All other NICs will discard this message (packet). This is true if the NICs are in non-promiscuous mode, which is the default mode.

The following diagram shows an example of a host sending a Shared Ethernet message:

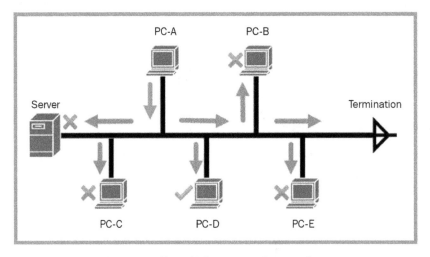

Figure 2.4 – Shared Ethernet on a bus topology

As shown in the preceding diagram, *PC-A* sends a message to *PC-D*, in a bus topology where all devices receive the message. Only *PC-D* will accept and process the message received from *PC-A*, while all other recipients of the message will discard it. This causes a lot of overhead processing for each host and excessive traffic on the network.

While the bus topology seems to be quite simple, there are a few drawbacks that do not make it suitable to support modern-day organizations. As more than one device attempts to access the network and send messages, this creates a lot of contention on the network as only one device can send a message at a time. Imagine if an organization is using a bus topology as their preferred network topology and many devices are attempting to communicate with each other at the same time – there will be a lot of contention to access the physical network. If multiple devices broadcast their message, network collisions can occur, where the packets become corrupted on the network, which causes a device to retransmit the message over the network.

The following diagram shows an example of a possible network collision when two nodes transmit:

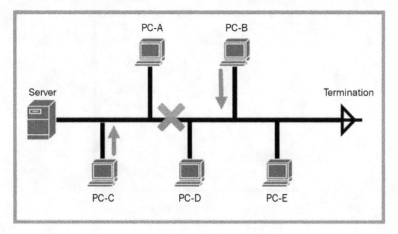

Figure 2.5 – Network collision

Another drawback of using the bus topology is its usage of a single backbone cable; there is no redundancy if a network failure was to occur. If there's a break at any point along the backbone network cable, this will result in an entire network outage where devices will not be able to communicate. Furthermore, this type of network topology has a lot of limitations for organizations that are growing. The bus topology does not support scalability or the ability to grow.

Now that you have learned about the key characteristics of the bus topology, let's explore the fundamentals of the ring network topology.

Ring

The **ring** topology is another older, legacy network topology that is no longer used within modern organizations. This type of network topology is designed to interconnect end devices such as computers in a ring format, where one host is connected to another host, and so on to create an actual ring.

The following diagram shows an example of a traditional ring topology:

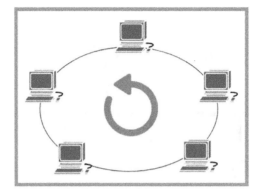

Figure 2.6 – Ring topology

As shown in the preceding diagram, each host (device) is interconnected to another host to create the ring topology. Within this type of topology, communication only occurs in a single direction. Therefore, if *PC-A* wants to communicate with another device, the message is sent in a single direction only and this method is applied to all devices on the network.

There's a dual ring topology that has two logical ring connections on each node on the network. The dual ring allows communication to occur in opposite directions on each ring. Here, one ring will allow traffic to flow clockwise only, and counterclockwise in the other ring.

The following diagram shows an example of a dual ring topology:

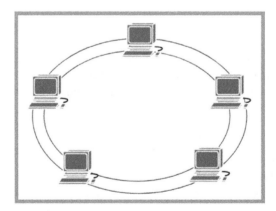

Figure 2.7 – Dual ring topology

While the ring topology seems simple, there are a few drawbacks to using this type of topology. Since communication occurs in a single direction, the message from the sender is passed along the way to each host on the network until it arrives at the intended destination host. Since the message of a sender passes to each host toward the destination, only one host can send a message at a time on the network. Since all nodes are interconnected, if a node within the ring topology is not available on the physical network, the entire network goes down, and the devices will not be able to communicate.

Now that you're familiar with the ring topology, let's learn about the star topology.

Star

The **star** topology is a common network topology used on many networks within organizations. The star topology allows the hosts to connect to a single networking device such as a switch. This topology ensures that if any host on the network wants to send a message to another host, the sender will forward the message to the network switch, which forwards the message to the intended destination host.

The following diagram shows a star topology:

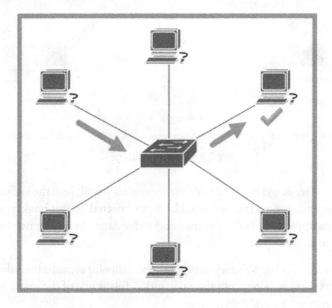

Figure 2.8 – Star topology

As shown in the preceding diagram, the switch functions as the network intermediary device to forward messages between a sender and receiver on the network. If one host on the network is offline or unavailable, the entire network is not affected except the bus and ring topologies, so the hosts can continue to send and receive messages simultaneously. In the star topology, if the central networking device such as the switch goes down or becomes unavailable, the entire network or all the connected hosts to the switch will be affected and won't be able to communicate.

The following diagram shows a visual representation of a network outage in a star topology:

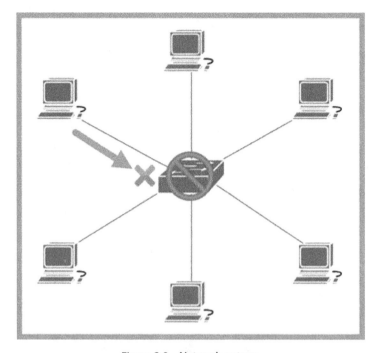

Figure 2.9 – Network outage

As shown in the preceding diagram, there isn't any redundancy built into the simple star topology. Since the switch is not available, all the connected hosts are affected. In this book, you will learn how network professionals implement fault tolerance and redundancy to ensure network services and resources are always available to users.

When working with a star topology, it's easy to support scalability for organizations that are increasing the number of devices that can connect to their networks. This is one of the major benefits of using a star topology – its support for scalability.

The following diagram shows how a star topology supports scalability:

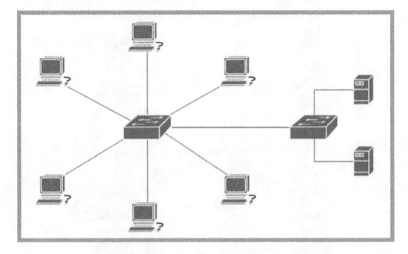

Figure 2.10 – Scalability in a star topology

As shown in the preceding diagram, if the organization wants to connect more hosts to the network, the network professional can connect another switch that will be able to support more hosts. When designing a network for an organization, scalability is one of the many factors that that networking professionals need to consider. Imagine if a network professional designed and built a network without the support to grow; if the organization needs to connect new devices to the network, there won't be any support. Thus, the network professional will need to redo the network design to support a growing organization. Furthermore, scalability does not only apply to the increase of connected devices – it needs to support the increase of network traffic and traffic types too.

Now that you have gained the fundamental knowledge of star network topologies, let's explore mesh topologies.

Mesh

Mesh topologies are currently used within various organizations or parts of their networks. In a mesh topology, each device within the network is connected to all other devices, creating a physical and logical mesh design. A mesh network topology provides full redundancy for traffic flow between any source and any destination as all devices are interconnected.

The following diagram shows an example of a mesh topology:

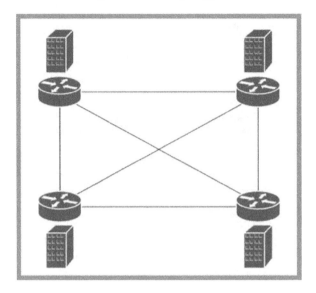

Figure 2.11 – Mesh topology

As shown in the preceding diagram, each router is connected to all other routers, thus creating multiple and redundant paths within the network. If one path goes down or becomes unavailable, there are multiple other paths available to forward network traffic between a source and a destination. Redundancy is another key factor network professionals need to consider when designing a network for an organization. Without redundancy, a network failure can result in the unavailability of network resources to users and the organization.

While having multiple redundant connections from one node to all other nodes in a mesh topology, this type of network topology can be complex to troubleshoot if an issue should occur due to the number of available paths. Additionally, if a new node joins the topology, the number of connections increases, which means there's also an increase in the cost to maintain the network. The formula to determine the number of links is N(N-1)/2. For example, if there are five devices, the total number of links is 5(4)/2 = 20/2 = 10. Adding just one additional device means there are 15 total links: 6(5)/2 = 30/2 = 15.

The following diagram shows an example of the number of connections needed as the network grows:

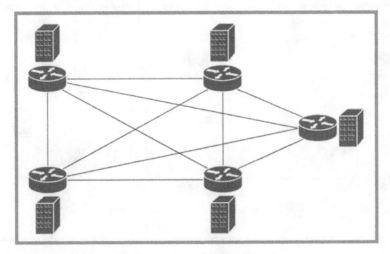

Figure 2.12 – Mesh network

As shown in the preceding diagram, as more nodes join the mesh topology, the number of required connections increases between each device. As a result, if an organization is implementing a mesh network design to interconnect all their branch offices, similar to what's shown in the preceding diagram, the organization needs to pay the ISP for each **Wide Area Network (WAN)** circuit (connection) between the branch routers. As you can imagine, the more connections/links there are in a mesh topology increases the expenditure of the organization and the complexity of configuring the nodes, such as routers, within the network. While the mesh topology provides the most redundancy, it becomes quite costly and complex as the network increases in size.

While the mesh topology has its advantages and disadvantages, organizations need to weigh the difference to determine whether it is the best design to fit their needs. Next, you will learn about the characteristics of the hybrid network topology.

Hybrid

Within many organizations, you will commonly find a mixture of many different network topologies implemented within the company. As an organization grows, so does the network to support the additional number of connected devices and new services. The **hybrid** topology is a combination of two or more different topologies that are interconnected to create a unified network.

The following diagram shows an example of a hybrid topology:

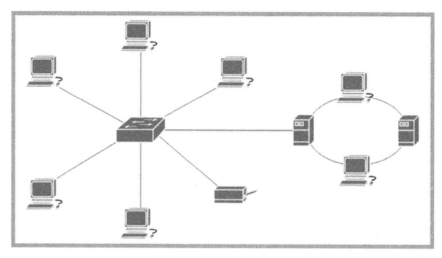

Figure 2.13 – Hybrid topology

As shown in the preceding diagram, the network consists of both star and ring topologies. Often, network professionals use different combinations of network topologies within their organizations to interconnect end devices such as computers and servers, as well as interconnect their branch offices together to share resources.

Now that you're aware of the characteristics of the hybrid topology, next, you will learn about the hub and spoke topology.

Hub and spoke

The **hub and spoke** topology is designed to provide a centralized node that acts as the main hub for all other nodes to interconnect. The hub on this topology acts as the central referencing point for all traffic between other nodes on the network. Each node is connected to the hub and these connections are referred to as spokes. This network topology does not allow nodes to directly connect; rather, all network traffic is sent through the hub within this topology, which is responsible for forwarding traffic to another node on the network.

The following diagram shows an example of a hub and spoke topology interconnecting different locations:

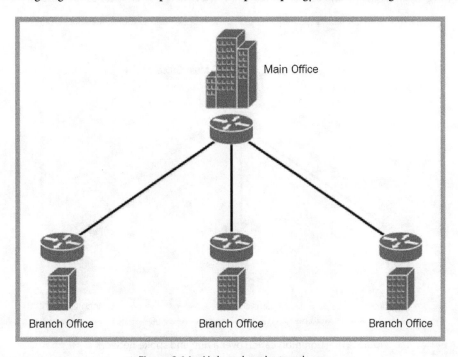

Figure 2.14 – Hub and spoke topology

As shown in the preceding diagram, the organization has one main office that will function as the headquarters that contains all the servers, while three remote branch offices will be used to provide services to customers are various geographic locations. Whenever a user or device needs to access a resource at another branch location, the traffic is sent to the main officer router (hub), which then forwards the traffic to the destination network.

The following diagram shows one branch office sending a message to another branch office:

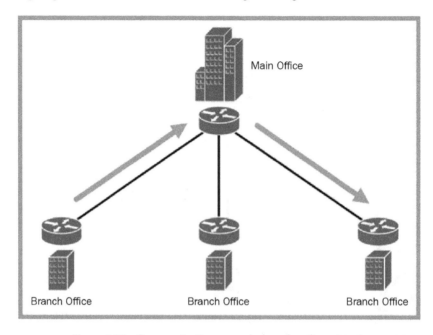

Figure 2.15 – Communication over a hub and spoke network

As shown in the preceding diagram, there are no direct connections between each spoke on the network. All spokes (branch offices) have to forward their traffic through the hub (main office), which is responsible for inspecting and routing network traffic to their destination.

The hub and spoke topology is commonly used by medium-sized and large organizations to interconnect their remote branch offices to their main office location. This topology is a cost-efficient design that allows organizations to save on internet subscription fees and improve their security monitoring.

Having completed this section, you have learned how to identify each type of network topology within the networking industry. In the next section, you will discover various network types and their characteristics.

Discovering network types

While there are many network topologies within the networking industry, there are also many network types, and each has characteristics. Network types are used to define the geographic boundary or limitation of a network and help network professionals understand the relationship between the connected devices within the network.

In this section, you will discover the key characteristics of various network types and gain a strong understanding of how each network type may differ from the others.

Peer-to-peer

In a **peer-to-peer** model, each client is logically connected and shares their resources with other clients on the network without the need for a centralized, dedicated server to provide the resources. If a client within the peer-to-peer network has a printer, that client can be configured to share the printer as a resource with other clients on the network. The client that is sharing the printer or resource becomes a server, while the others hosts (computers) on the network are clients that are accessing or requesting the resource.

The following diagram shows a logical overview of a peer-to-peer network model:

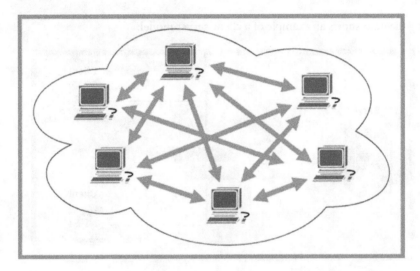

Figure 2.16 – Peer-to-peer model

As shown in the preceding diagram, there is no centralized management of any network resource or service. As a result, peer-to-peer networking does not support scalability well and may change to ensure all the clients on the network have access to the resources. Peer-to-peer networks are typically implemented as workgroups in many small organizations.

A real-world example of a peer-to-peer network is sharing files using a *torrent*. A torrent, or torrenting, allows a user to share files on their computer across a network such as the internet. A user who has a file to share with others uses a torrent manager application to create a torrent file and shares the torrent file with other users on the internet. The torrent file contains information about the file, file type, size, and so on, so when a user adds the torrent file to their torrent manager, the manager seeks the location of the file over the internet and establishes a peer-to-peer logical connection to all nodes that have the torrent file active on their computers/devices. In the world of torrenting, *seeds* or *seeders* are the computers that have the complete file on their device and share it with others to download. On the other hand, *leeches* or *leechers* are devices that download the file from each peer, preferably the seeds, until it reaches 100% download completion.

However, on a peer-to-peer network, there's no centralized management of resources, and security is a huge concern as each node is responsible for managing its security posture. Next, you will learn about the client-server model.

Client-server

The **client-server** network model contains dedicated devices that provide a resource or service to hosts on a network. These devices are referred to as servers. A server can be any device running an application that allows other hosts on the network to access the resources stored or being provided by the server.

The following diagram shows an example of a client-server model:

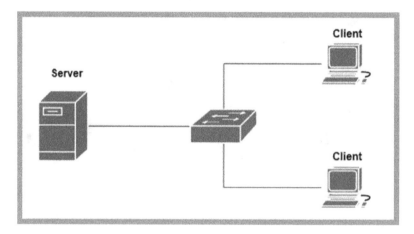

Figure 2.17 – Client-server model

As shown in the preceding diagram, the server can be configured as a file server to centrally store files and data for other devices and users on the network. The clients on the network are the devices that are requesting a service or resource. In a client-server model, scalability allows the network to grow while ensuring the resources are centrally accessible by all clients on the network. This is a major advantage of using a client-server model compared to a peer-to-peer networking model.

Next, you will learn about the fundamentals of a **personal area network** (**PAN**).

Personal area network

A PAN is a small network that is usually created by a user to interconnect their devices, such as a laptop, smartphone, wireless headphones, or a wireless printer. A user can set up a wired or wireless network to ensure their devices are connected to the same network. However, keep in mind that this type of network is not designed to connect to a larger network with other devices.

The following diagram shows an example of a PAN network:

Figure 2.18 – Personal area network

As shown in the preceding diagram, the user creates a small network to allow their devices to share resources within a very short distance. A real-world example of a PAN is connecting a laptop and smartphone to a wireless printer at home to print pictures. Another example is establishing a Bluetooth connection between a smartphone and another Bluetooth-enabled device to share files.

Within a PAN network, each device is responsible for managing its security. Next, you will learn about the characteristics of a **local area network (LAN)**.

Local area network

A LAN is a small network that exists within a single geographic location, such as within a building. A LAN allows all devices within an office location or building to be interconnected and share resources. Imagine starting an organization where you've acquired a building to provide office spaces for your employees, computers, and servers. Interconnecting all the devices, such as the computers, servers, and network printers, into a single physical network creates a LAN that allows everyone and all devices on the same network to easily share resources.

The following diagram shows an example of a LAN network type:

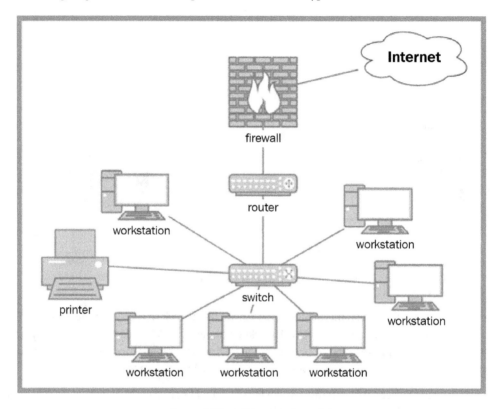

Figure 2.19 – LAN network model

As shown in the preceding diagram, the network contains a few workstations that are used by the employees within a small office, and each end device, such as a computer and printer, is connected to the network switch. The switch connects to the router, which functions as the **default gateway** to forward traffic from the internal network to a remote/foreign network such as the internet.

> **Important note**
>
> Without a default gateway device such as a router at the edge of a logical IP network, clients will not be able to communicate with remote networks or devices.

The router connects to the firewall to filter inbound and outbound traffic between the internal network and the internet. All the devices shown within the preceding diagram represent a LAN as they are all interconnected and within a single, small geographic location.

While LANs are created for organizations that only reside in a single location, some organizations will grow and open new branch offices in different geographic locations and will need to extend their network. Next, you will learn about extending a LAN over a large geographic distance.

Wide area network

A **wide area network (WAN)** allows organizations to extend their LAN and its resources over a large geographic distance. Why do we need a WAN? Business owners will usually create an organization with a single office location; as the company grows the demand for their products and services, so does the company. When a company starts with a single office location, a LAN is created within the building or office space to interconnect all devices and share resources such as files, and even the network printer. As the demand for the organization's products and services increases, the business owner(s) will hire more employees to ensure the demand is met while improving the business processes and so on.

As time goes by, the organization will grow and create new remote office locations within other cities or countries to support its customers. The organization may have all its servers located at its main office and want to share access with employees who are working at a remote office. Using a WAN allows the organizations to extend their LAN from their main office over a large geographic distance to each of the remote offices as needed.

The following diagram shows a WAN interconnecting two office locations:

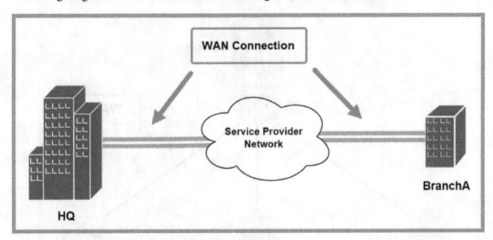

Figure 2.20 – WAN

As shown in the preceding diagram, the WAN connection is established by a **Managed Service Provider (MSP)** or an **Internet Service Provider (ISP)**. The service provided will implement the networking infrastructure throughout a city or country to support the demand for managed networking services and solutions. Usually, an organization that wants to interconnect its branch offices will contact various service providers for a consultation and the cost of the WAN services. The organization chooses the service provider that meets its business needs. The MSP or ISP is responsible for establishing and maintaining the WAN network for the organization. All traffic sent into a WAN connection by an organization remains private as the traffic passes through the service provider's network infrastructure. WAN solutions are managed services from service providers as they are responsible for the configuration, deployment, maintenance, and troubleshooting of the service on behalf of their customers.

What if an organization has multiple branch offices? How can internet services be established for all locations of the company? One solution is to implement a WAN solution and an internet service at each office location. The WAN solution will be used to share the network resources between branches, while the internet services provide access to the online services and resources that are outside the company's network.

The following diagram shows a WAN connection being used to create a hub and spoke topology to connect each remote office to the main office location; each office location has a dedicated internet connection:

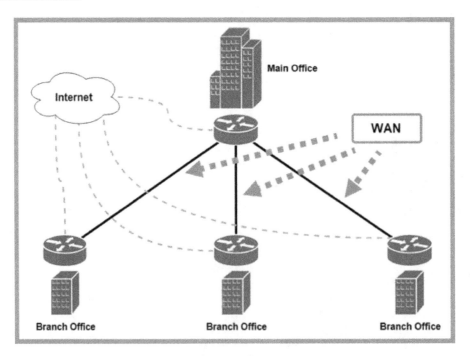

Figure 2.21 – Hub and spoke WAN connection

As shown in the preceding diagram, the organization has a hub and spoke topology for the WAN solution, while each office location has a dedicated internet service. While this setup may seem appropriate if the branch offices were located within different countries, where each country has its own ISP to supply internet services, if each branch office is located within the same country, it's not cost-efficient as the organization is charged for the internet service at each branch location, including the main office.

A better solution for an organization that has multiple branch offices within the same country is to create a hub and spoke topology for the WAN solution and implement a single internet connection at the main office. The internet service can be redistributed within the WAN connected to each branch router.

The following diagram shows an example of using a hub and spoke topology for a WAN solution while redistributing the internet to each branch office within the same country:

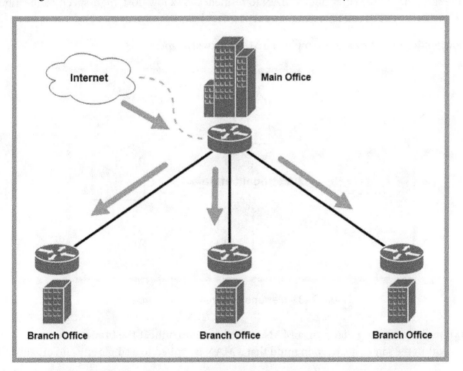

Figure 2.22 – Hub and spoke WAN topology with internet connectivity

As shown in the preceding diagram, the WAN connections are established between the main office and each branch office; the internet service is implemented at the main office only. Network professionals can configure the networking devices at the main office to redistribute the internet service through the WAN connection to each branch office. This design allows an organization to save a lot of money on their internet services when the branch offices are usually in the same country.

> **Important note**
>
> It is possible to redistribute internet services through a WAN connection to a branch office in another country, but the latency (response time) and network performance will not be optimal.

Next, you will learn about a network type that covers a city.

Metropolitan area network

Around the world, there are very large cities with many people, businesses, and fun things to do all day. In large cities, some organizations have multiple branch offices within the same city and need interconnectivity between their offices to share resources with employees. Using a **metropolitan area network (MAN)**, a service provider can interconnect all the branch offices of a single company within the same city. Some cities offer a MAN to residences as a low-cost, high-speed connection to the internet. These MANs can be used to incentivize residents to move to that city.

The following diagram shows an example of a MAN network type:

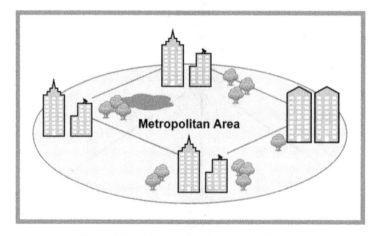

Figure 2.23 – Metropolitan area network type

As shown in the preceding diagram, a MAN is used to interconnect the branch offices of a single company within the same city. Keep in mind that a MAN is limited to a single city and organization.

Next, you will learn about a wireless network type that bridges a wired and wireless network topology.

Wireless local area network

Years ago, networks within organizations consisted of computers, servers, and networked devices that were connected using a wired connection. In the era of mobile computing, each person can have a mobile, portable device such as a laptop computer that contains all the essential components of a desktop computer but in a smaller and compact form factor. People no longer need to sit stationary at a single location to do work on their computers – they can work or learn using their laptops at any location that's comfortable and convenient to them.

As the mobile and IoT industry started, the demand for mobile computing and smart devices increased. This led to organizations implementing wireless networking infrastructure to support the need to connect wireless-capable devices onto their corporate network to share the same resources as the wired devices.

Within a wireless network, there's at least one wireless router, which is a multilayer (switch, access point, and router) device that performs routing between the wired network and wireless network. The wireless router generates a wireless signal using radio frequencies on the 2.4 GHz, 5 GHz, and 6 GHz bands based on the **Institute of Electrical and Electronics Engineers (IEEE)** 802.11 standard. The wireless network generated by the wireless router is on a unique **Internet Protocol (IP)** network, while the wireless router is connected to a wired network on a different IP network. Hence, a wireless router performs routing between the two different IP networks, from wireless to wired, and between the different IP networks.

> **Important note**
>
> Wireless routers are commonly used on small networks such as within homes and small businesses. An **Access Point (AP)** is a layer 2 device that provides a wireless network to allow wireless clients to establish a connection and access the resources on the wired network.

The **Wireless Local Area Network (WLAN)** is a wireless local area network that has one or more APs or wireless routers to allow wireless capable clients to connect and share resources. APs are connected to a network switch that provides wireless connectivity to wireless clients, as shown in the following diagram:

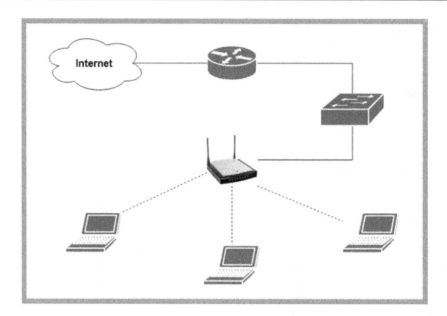

Figure 2.24 – WLAN network type

As shown in the preceding diagram, the laptop establishes a wireless connection to the wireless router. For the clients to access the resources on the wired network and the internet, the wireless router is connected to a network switch using a network cable. If wireless clients such as laptops are placed further away from the wireless router, the reception of the wireless signal by the client device will become weaker and the bandwidth will be affected.

Next, you will discover another network type that is commonly used within large educational institutions, such as universities.

Campus area network

In the world of academia, there are many universities around the world. Some universities have a single, large campus with many buildings containing classrooms, lecture halls, administrative offices, and so on, while other universities have multiple campuses at different geographic locations. For larger universities with many campuses, the network engineers within those academic institutions need to interconnect each campus to each other to ensure the users on each campus network can access and share resources. This type of network is commonly referred to as a **campus area network** (**CAN**).

The following diagram shows an example of a university with two campuses that are interconnected using a CAN:

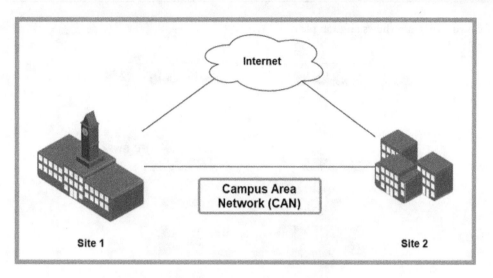

Figure 2.25 – Campus area network

As shown in the preceding diagram, *Site 1* and *Site 2* are interconnected using a CAN network connection that is maintained by the university.

Next, you will learn about a special network type that is designed to support large storage servers.

Storage area network

Within large organizations and data centers, there are dedicated networks that are designed to support a large number of dedicated services that store data. Within each storage or file server, there are a lot of hardware-based redundancy technologies implemented such as a dual **Network Interface Card (NIC)** to support **NIC Teaming**, a technology that allows more than one NIC to be used to redundant network connections on a server. Another common technology within the file or storage servers is using **Redundant Array of Independent Disks (RAID)** to support data redundancy between multiple drives on a single server.

A **storage area network (SAN)** is a dedicated area within an organization's network or data center that is used to physically implement multiple storages or file servers. The SAN is designed with both fault tolerance and redundancy in mind to ensure the network is always available. Additionally, the SAN needs networking devices such as switches and devices optimized for fiber channels, a technology that allows Ethernet over fiber optic cables. Using fiber optic cables ensures high bandwidth is supported within the SAN.

The following diagram shows an example of a SAN:

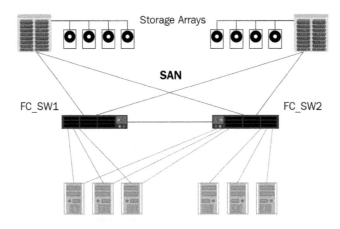

Figure 2.26 – Storage area network

As shown in the preceding diagram, each server has dual-homed connections to each fiber switch to support network redundancy. Redundancy is needed on the network so that if one networking device fails or a path is unavailable, the networking devices can automatically detect the failure on the network and re-route the network traffic using a backup or alternative path.

Software-defined wide area network

Within a **software-defined network (SDN)**, a controller is implemented that acts as the brain of the network. In a traditional network, each networking device, such as a router or switch, has a brain that tells the device how to forward traffic. Therefore, each device has to make its own, independent decision whenever it has to forward a packet to a destination. Implementing SDN allows a centralized controller to be implemented on a network. Here, the controller becomes the central brain of all the network devices, removing the decision-making function of each networking device on the network.

A **software-defined wide area network (SD-WAN)** allows networking professionals to define their intent for a network such as a WAN and allow the software to configure the network to operate. Organizations commonly use traditional WAN technologies to interconnect their branch and remote offices to share resources. With SD-WAN, organizations can allow the software to automatically configure the WAN solution while continuously optimizing the connection between branches for improved performance.

The following diagram shows an example of an SDN controller and networking devices:

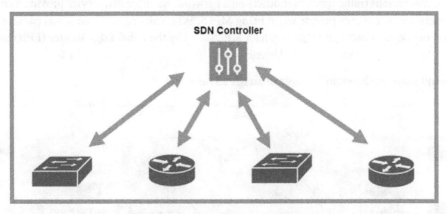

Figure 2.27 – SDN networking concepts

The idea of SDN allows networking professionals to easily manage the entire network as it grows by using the controller on the network. The controller can proactively monitor the network for any potential issues that may occur and take proactive actions to mitigate the issue. When working with SD-WAN or SDN, new networking devices can be configured to establish a connection to the SDN controller. Once a connection has been established, the SDN controller can automatically push configurations to each newly connected networking device.

Next, you will learn about a service provider technology for interconnecting multiple branch offices of an organization.

Multiprotocol label switching

Multiprotocol label switching (**MPLS**) is a service provider technology that allows organizations to interconnect their branch offices over a large geographic distance. Within the service provider's network, a private and dedicated MPLS connection is established to interconnect an organization's offices (remote sites). When working with MPLS, the organization (customer) can use various types of interfaces or connection methods to forward traffic to the service provider's network. Simply put, the connection to the service provider's network is interface-independent, allowing the organization (customer) to use a **Metro Ethernet** (**MetroE**), fiber optic, or even a **Digital Subscriber Line** (**DSL**) connection. Within the MPLS network, the ISP can logically create a bridge to interconnect all the branch offices of an organization (customer) quite easily without depending on a specific interface type or connection type.

Within an MPLS network, service providers can enhance the **Quality of Service (QoS)** that applies prioritization of various traffic types over others on a network. Additionally, service providers ensure the customers' traffic remains private when using MPLS. When an organization sends packets into an MPLS network, each packet is tagged with an MPLS label by the **Label Edge Router (LER)** on the **Provider Edge (PE)** of the service provider's network.

The following diagram shows an example of an MPLS network:

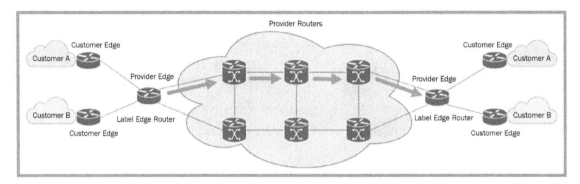

Figure 2.28 – MPLS network

As shown in the preceding diagram, two customers are using MPLS to interconnect their branch offices. When *Customer A* sends traffic into the MPLS network, it arrives at the *LER*, which is located at the PE of the service provider's network. The *LER* inserts an MPLS label into each packet received from *Customer A* with a unique label before forwarding the packet to the *Provider Routers*. When a *Provider Router* receives a packet, it inspects the *MPLS* label to determine how to forward the packet to its destination without needing to open the contents of the packet to view the header information.

Next, you will learn about routing encapsulation technologies that are used to establish a secure connection between remote offices and the main office of an organization.

Multipoint generic routing encapsulation

The **generic routing encapsulation (GRE)** is a tunneling technology that allows an organization to establish a tunnel between one site (office) to another over the internet. When working with GRE tunnels, it allows network professionals to establish a point-to-point tunnel between two offices only. GRE works well when there's a small number of branch offices for a single organization as each GRE tunnel per remote site (office) is only a unique IP network.

The following diagram shows an example of a GRE tunnel for a single organization:

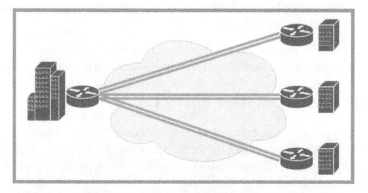

Figure 2.29 – Traditional GRE tunnels

As shown in the preceding diagram, each branch office has a GRE tunnel to the main office router over the internet. Each GRE tunnel is responsible for encapsulating packets between each branch office to the main office. However, traditional GRE tunnels do not support scalability well as each tunnel is on its own IP network. Furthermore, if one of the branch offices wants to send a message to another branch office, the traffic is sent to the hub (main office router), which is then forwarded to the destination network, like in a traditional hub and spoke topology.

In **multipoint generic routing encapsulation** (**mGRE**), both the hub router and each branch office router can be configured to support dynamic mGRE. This method allows a branch router to automatically establish a GRE tunnel to another branch router if needed. Unlike the traditional GRE method of using a *hub and spoke* model, mGRE allows the routers within the mGRE network to automatically establish, maintain, and terminate mGRE tunnels between any routers within the network.

The following diagram shows an example of an mGRE network:

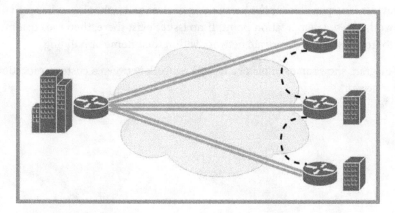

Figure 2.30 – mGRE tunnels

As shown in the following diagram, each branch router can establish an mGRE tunnel with another branch router, allowing branch offices to directly communicate and share resources without the need to use the traditional hub and spoke network topology.

Having completed this section, you have learned about the various network types and their characteristics. In the next section, you will explore the different service-related entry points to a customer network.

Identifying service-related entry points

A service-related entry point is simply the point where both a service provider and their customer's network interconnect. Imagine contacting an ISP for residential internet service for your home. Usually, the customer, such as yourself, will already have a LAN with various types of networked devices such as computers, printers, and so on.

The **demarcation point** or **demarc** is the location where the service provider and the customer's networks meet. If the ISP provides the customer with a modem, then the modem is the demarcation point on the network. The demarcation point also identifies the boundary that the ISP can provide support, such as troubleshooting issues, to ensure the internet service is working as expected.

The ISP will dispatch a crew to visit your location to implement their network infrastructure between the service provider network and your building or home. For customers opting for a fiber connection, the ISP crew will establish a connection between the **Fiber Access Terminal** (**FAT**) on the service provider network to the customer premise by using an optical drop cable. The FAT is simply an **Optical Termination Box** (**OTB**) that allows the ISP crew to easily manage multiple fiber connections to customers' locations and to function as a termination point for the optical drop cable from the customer premises. The FAT allows the ISP to supply its customers with **fiber-to-the-home** (**FTTH**) services. Next, a fiber patch cable is used to connect the panel box installed on the customer's premises to the fiber modem installed by the technology within their home. At this point, the customer can connect their LAN to the fiber modem to access the internet.

The service provider is responsible for the networking devices and technologies between the service provider's network and the demarcation point. If no issues exist there, then the customer has the responsibility to troubleshoot their private network within their home or building.

The following diagram shows an example of a typical network between a customer location and the service provider network:

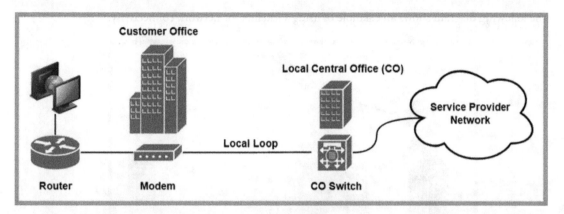

Figure 2.31 – Service provider network

As shown in the preceding diagram, the demarcation point can be identified as the modem that is installed within the customer's location, such as their building or home. The service provider is responsible for everything that's between the modem and the service provider's network.

Another component that is commonly installed by the service provider on the customer's building is a device known as a **SmartJack**. This is a special hardware-based component that functions as a **Network Interface Unit** (**NIU**) that provides feedback to a service provider such as an ISP. The SmartJack helps ISPs to determine whether there's an issue that exists between the service provider's network and the demarcation point at the customer's end by providing a remote loopback.

Having completed this section, you have learned about service-related entry points on a network. Next, you will explore various types of provider connectivity methods.

Comparing provider links

Service providers such as ISPs provide their customers with various services such as WAN and internet solutions. Additionally, ISPs provide various methods to allow their customers to connect to the internet and WAN solutions. In this section, we will be covering a wide range of provider connectivity methods and their characteristics.

Satellite

Sometimes, an organization or residential customer may be geographically located within an area where there isn't any fiber optic or copper lines installed in the community. Service providers can use satellite technologies to allow their customers to access the internet or interconnect remote branch offices to a WAN service.

The following diagram shows an example of using a satellite for network connectivity:

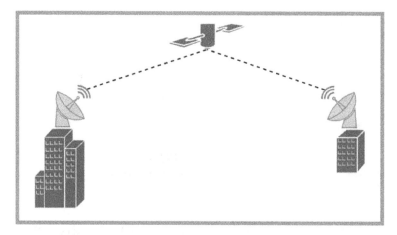

Figure 2.32 – A satellite link

As shown in the preceding diagram, there's a satellite dish installed at the customer's location that provides a connection to a satellite in orbit. The orbital satellite relays data between the **customer Premise Equipment (CPE)** to the service provider equipment, then through the service provider's network to the internet.

Satellite technology is commonly implemented in areas that do not allow service providers to implement physical cabling to the customer location. When working with satellite technologies, the satellite dish needs a line of sight for communication. Therefore, if an object blocks the line of sight or there are bad weather conditions, the connection (signal) will be affected. Furthermore, this type of technology can provide high latency (response time), which may not be suitable for time-sensitive applications such as **Voice over IP (VoIP)** or **Video over IP** solutions.

Next, you will learn about another type of provider link that uses copper lines.

Digital Subscriber Line

The **Digital Subscriber Line (DSL)** is a service provider technology that is commonly used to provide internet services to residential/home users. This technology allows the ISP to install a modem in the subscriber's (customer's) building or home.

There are two types of DSL within the service provider industry, as follows:

- **Symmetric DSL (SDSL):** In SDSL, both the upload and download bandwidths are the same values. This solution is generally a very expensive option.

- **Asymmetric DSL (ADSL):** In ADSL, the upload and download are not the same. The download speed is generally much higher than the upload speed.

The DSL model is used to connect to the traditional telephone lines within the service provider network. These telephone lines are commonly referred to as the **Public Switched Telephone Network (PSTN)** lines and sometimes as the **Plain Old Telephone Service (POTS)** lines. The PSTN lines connect to a **Digital Subscriber Line Access Multiplexer (DSLAM)**, which forwards the customer traffic from a region to the ISP network, then to the internet.

The following diagram shows a DSL network:

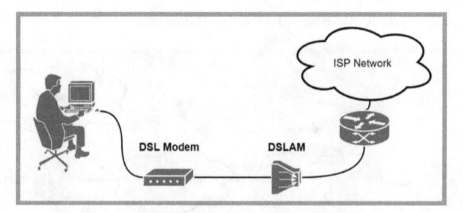

Figure 2.33 – DSL network

As shown in the preceding diagram, the user has a DSL model that splits the analog telephone signal and the digital signal to ensure the user can connect to the internet and use the telephone system without issues. Generally, DSL uses digital signals and requires a splitter, a hardware-based component to separate the telephone signal from the internet signal. One of the disadvantages of using a DSL is it works up to an average of 5.5 km in distance. Therefore, the further away a subscriber (customer) is from the DSLAM, the service quality will be impacted. This is commonly referred to as **attenuation** – that is, the loss of signal over distance within these lines.

> **Important note**
>
> A modem is used to convert an analog signal into a digital signal and vice versa. The terminology used to describe this conversion is **modulation** and **demodulation**.

Next, you will discover how service providers distribute internet services through their cable network to customers.

Cable

Many cable TV companies provide internet service to their customers over their existing cable networks. Cable TV and internet services are commonly distributed to home/residential customers compared to business customers using fiber optic. Service providers install a cable modem in their customers' locations, such as in their homes, which allows the cable modem to connect to the service provider's **Cable Model Termination System (CMTS)** via coaxial cables.

The following diagram shows a simple overview of the CMTS network:

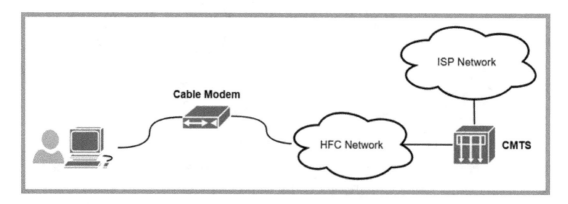

Figure 2.34 – CMTS model

As shown in the preceding diagram, the ISP's backbone network is connected to the CMTS network infrastructure. The **Hybrid Fiber-Coaxial (HFC)** infrastructure is a telecommunication provider's hybrid network that supports both fiber and coaxial infrastructure. The HFC network is used to connect all the cable modems from the customer location to the CMTS, then to the internet via the service provider's network.

When using a cable, it uses **Data over Cable Service Interface Specification (DOCSIS)**, which is an international telecommunication standard that supports 10 Gbps download speeds and 1 Gbps upload speeds. Unfortunately, the total bandwidth is shared as more customers use the cable network. As a result, as more customers use the internet at the same time, each customer will notice their internet speed is reduced.

Next, you will learn how businesses used dedicated lines to ensure their network bandwidth was guaranteed.

Leased line

A leased line allows a service provider to interconnect an organization's branch offices together. When using leased lines, the network bandwidth on the leased line is dedicated to the organization (customer) and always available, regardless of whether the customer uses it. Leased lines are expensive since they are dedicated to allocating network bandwidth to the paying customer to interconnect their remote offices.

The following diagram shows an example of an organization using leased lines to interconnect their main office with their branch offices over a service provider's network:

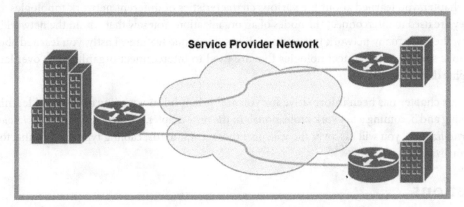

Figure 2.35 – Leased lines

The following are the major benefits of using leased lines for connectivity:

- Provides a connection with dedicated bandwidth
- This dedicated connection is provided between the customer and the service provider network

However, since leased lines provide a dedicated and not shared connection, this type of connection is usually more costly as the bandwidth is statically allocated to the customer.

Next, you will learn about the characteristics of metro optical links.

Metro optical

Metro optical is a type of provider link that allows an organization to access the service provider's network for internet access and even WAN solutions. The metro optical network consists of fiber optic cables that are used to provide very high-speed network connectivity between the customer and the service provider's network.

This type of network usually costs less than typical **Synchronous Optical Networking (SONET)** and **Synchronous Digital Hierarchy (SDH)** and works with Ethernet technologies. SONET is used on fiber optic networks, which allows a large quantity of data to be transported over great distances. On the other hand, SDH is simply described as a multiplex technology and a variant of SONET.

Having completed this section, you have discovered and learned about various provider links that allow organizations to access service providers' networks.

Summary

In this chapter, you learned about the various characteristics of different network topologies and how they are used to interconnect the nodes of an organization. You saw that within the networking industry, there are many network types and each has its unique features. Lastly, you learned about the various service provider technologies that are used to interconnect organizations over large geographic distances.

I hope this chapter has been informative for you and is helpful in your journey toward learning networking and becoming a network professional. In the next chapter, *Chapter 3, Ethernet Technology and Virtualization*, you will discover the various Ethernet standards, cabling types and connectors, and virtualization.

Questions

The following is a short list of review questions to help reinforce your learning and help you identify areas that may require some improvement:

1. Which network type is commonly used to extend a LAN over a great distance?

    A. Hub and spoke

    B. WAN

    C. Hybrid

    D. DSL

2. Which of the following network technologies has very high latency when interconnecting remote offices?

    A. Satellite

    B. Cable

    C. WAN

    D. CAN

3. Which of the following service provider technologies provides high-speed internet access over traditional telephone lines?

    A. Metro optical

    B. Cable

    C. DSL

    D. MPLS

4. Which of the following service provider technologies labels the incoming packets from a customer's network while improving faster forwarding of the packets through the service provider's network?

    A. ADSL

    B. Cable

    C. mGRE

    D. MPLS

5. If two mobile devices establish a Bluetooth connection, which type of network is created?

    A. CAN

    B. Peer-to-peer

    C. PAN

    D. MAN

6. Which of the following network types allows network professionals to automate the configuration of WAN solutions?

    A. mGRE

    B. SD-WAN

    C. MPLS

    D. SDSL

7. Which of the following network topologies allows only one end device to communicate at a time?

    A. Star

    B. Ring

    C. Peer-to-peer

    D. MAN

8. Which of the following is an operating frequency for wireless networks?

    A. 5.6 GHz

    B. 5.4 GHz

    C. 2.5 GHz

    D. 2.4 GHz

9. The routers on the edge of the service provider MPLS network are known as what?

    A. Provider routers

    B. CPE

    C. LER

    D. None of the above

10. Which of the following provider links uses coaxial to distribute internet and TV service to customers?

    A. Leased line

    B. DSL

    C. Cable

    D. Satellite

Further reading

To learn more about the topics that were covered in this chapter, check out the following links:

- *Networking Basics*: `https://www.cisco.com/c/en/us/solutions/small-business/resource-center/networking/networking-basics.html`

- *What is Computer Networking?*: `https://www.cisco.com/c/en/us/solutions/enterprise-networks/what-is-computer-networking.html`

- *What is Network Topology?*: `https://www.cisco.com/c/en/us/solutions/automation/network-topology.html`

3

Ethernet Technology and Virtualization

In the world of networking, Ethernet is the predominant technology found within the **local area networks (LANs)** of organizations. While Ethernet is very common, network professionals need to be aware and have a strong understanding of various Ethernet technologies and standards that are used within the networking industry, as well as how these standards and technologies help professionals to improve their network design and performance.

In this chapter, you will learn about various types of network connections and media types used for wired communication within an organization. You will explore various wiring standards and the various characteristics of copper and fiber cabling, as well as their advantages and use cases. Furthermore, you will gain a solid understanding of cable management and termination points that are used by service providers and organizations to interconnect their networks. Lastly, you will learn about Ethernet and virtualization technologies.

In this chapter, we will cover the following topics:

- Types of connections
- Ethernet standards
- Virtual networking concepts

Let's dive in!

Technical requirements

To follow along with the exercises in this chapter, please ensure that you have met the following hardware and software requirements:

- Windows 10 Enterprise: `https://www.microsoft.com/en-us/evalcenter/evaluate-windows-10-enterprise`
- Oracle VM VirtualBox: `https://www.virtualbox.org/wiki/Downloads`
- Oracle VM VirtualBox Extension Pack: `https://www.virtualbox.org/wiki/Downloads`

Types of connections

While working within the networking industry, you will commonly discover many organizations' networks uses wired and wireless connections to interconnect their users' devices to the network. Within environments with a lot of desktop computers and servers, wired connections are mostly implemented since the desktop computers are stationary and less likely to move from one location to another. On the other hand, servers are usually implemented within the server room and mounted onto a server rack and won't be moved to a new location unless needed by the organization. Hence, there are a lot of wired connections, which allows network professionals to connect end devices to the network.

There are two main types of wired connections that are commonly used within organizations on their networks, as follows:

- Copper
- Fiber optic

Over the next few sub-sections, you will learn about the characteristics, advantages and disadvantages, and use cases of each type of network medium.

Copper cables

One of the most common types of network media you will find in many organizations and networks is copper cables. These are inexpensive network cables that are very easy to implement within buildings, office spaces, and homes. As an aspiring network professional, it's important to understand the fundamentals of each type of cable used within the industry.

There are two types of copper cables that are used within networks:

- **Unshielded Twisted Pair (UTP)**
- **Shielded Twisted Pair (STP)**

UTP cables are very common and you will find them in almost any network within an organization and even **Small Office/Home Office (SOHO)** networks. These allow network professionals to connect users' devices, such as computers and IP phones, to the network to access and share resources. The UTP cables are referred to as *unshielded* because the physical cable does not contain a protective coating to prevent the actual conductors from absorbing **electromagnetic interference (EMI)** from machinery and other components. When a device such as a computer wants to send a message to another device over a network, the **Network Access** layer of the **Transmission Control Protocol/Internet Protocol (TCP/IP)** networking model converts the message into an appropriate signal for the network media before placing the message onto the actual network.

Copper cables transmit electrical signals over the wire in short distances and networking devices can decode the signals into packets and data. As these electrical signals are transmitted along a copper wire, the conductors, which are the actual copper wires, can absorb EMI from nearby devices and other electrical wires. When this occurs, the bits that are being transmitted in the form of electrical signals along a copper wire (medium) between devices will become corrupted and the sender will need to retransmit any messages that are damaged or corrupted.

Additionally, copper networking cables as referred to as *twisted pair* cabling. Within each UTP cable, there's a total of 8 individual wires that have a unique color coating. These wires are twisted in a total of 4 pairs to improve the resiliency against EMI from nearby devices and adjacent electrical wires.

The following figure shows a UTP cable:

Figure 3.1 – UTP cable

While UTP cables are very susceptible to EMI, the twisting of the conductors (copper wires) reduces the likelihood of messages being corrupted. Keep in mind that while the cables are twisted within the outer jacket, it still does not stop EMI from being absorbed by the copper conductors. Therefore, it's not recommended to implement UTP cables in areas or zones that contain a lot of machinery that emits EMI.

Another type of copper cable used within the networking industry is an STP cable. This is another type of twisted cable with the addition of protective shielding around the twisted conductors within the outer jacket.

The following figure shows an STP cable:

Figure 3.2 – STP cable

As shown in the preceding figure, the STP cable has shielding (a foil coating) around the twisted pair of wires. This protective shielding is used to prevent EMI from entering the copper conductors within the cable. Unlike UTP cables, which are inexpensive, STP cables are usually a bit more expensive because of the additional layer of protection within the cable's design. Hence, network professionals commonly implement STP cables within environments that have a lot of EMI.

As you have learned, networking professionals always need to understand the need for implementing the appropriate type of cable within various types of environments. The outer jacket of both the UTP and STP cables are made using **Polyvinyl Chloride (PVC)**, a material that releases toxic/harmful fumes to humans when burnt. These are known as non-plenum-rated cables. Sometimes, network professionals need to run network cabling within the plenum spaces of a building or office space. The plenum areas within an organization are the spaces that allow airflow to support heating and ventilation. Imagine if non-plenum-rated cables such as those that are made using PVC are installed within the ventilation air spaces, and these cables were to burn during a fire emergency within a building – the toxic fumes would be harmful to all employees and people within the organization.

Hence, it's highly recommended to implement plenum-rated cables within the plenum spaces within buildings when needed. Depending on your country, it may be required by the building codes and regulations to support the safety of people within a building.

The following diagram shows an example of a plenum-rated cable:

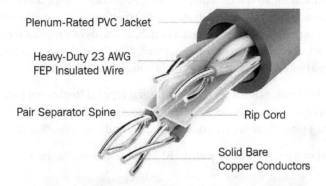

Figure 3.3 – Plenum-rated cable

As shown in the preceding diagram, plenum-rated cables contain a plenum-grade outer jacket to prevent fire from burning the conductors; there's also a pair of separator spines to keep each pair of twisted cables separate from other pairs. As you can imagine, plenum-rated cables are more expensive compared to non-plenum-rated cables. Keep in mind that plenum-rated cables are less toxic when they are burnt during a fire and it's important to properly plan which type of cables to use and how many are needed before starting a project.

Various types of copper cables are used to interconnect end devices to the network. The **Telecommunication Industry Association** (**TIA**) created a cabling standard that's used by networking professionals within the industry. The TIA standard defines various categories for networking cables. These cables are described as a **category** (**Cat**) cable followed by a number. Each category defines how the cable can be applied to a network, its support speed, such as bandwidth, and the maximum length for data transmission.

The following is a list of various types of category cables that are commonly found within organizations:

- **Cat 3**: Supports speeds up to 10 Mbps with a maximum distance of 100 meters

- **Cat 5**: Supports speeds up to 100 Mbps with a maximum distance of 100 meters

- **Cat 5e**: Supports speeds up to 1 Gbps with a maximum distance of 100 meters

- **Cat 6**: Supports speeds up to 1 Gbps with a maximum distance of 100 meters

- **Cat 6a**: Supports speeds up to 1 Gbps and 10 Gbps with a maximum distance of 100 meters

- **Cat 7**: Supports speeds up to 1 Gbps and 10 Gbps with a maximum distance of 100 meters

- **Cat 8**: Supports speeds up to 40 Gbps with a maximum distance of 30 meters

While a network cable may specify a maximum distance, in reality, these copper cables experience attenuation as the electrical signal travels along the wire. Attenuation is the loss of signal as it travels along a medium from a source to a destination. Therefore, if you use a single 100-meter cable to interconnect two devices such as a computer and a switch, as one device sends a message to the other in the form of an electrical signal on the media (network cable), the electrical signal will experience attenuation as the signal get weaker as it travels further away from the sender.

The ends of the twisted pair cables are terminated by various types of **Registered Jack (RJ)** connectors. To terminate the ends of a CAT 3 cable, an RJ-11 connector is used on both ends of the cable. The RJ 11 connector contains 4 pins; these are commonly used on traditional landline telephone systems.

The following figure shows a CAT 3 cable with an RJ 11 connector on its end:

Figure 3.4 – Cat 3 with an RJ 11 connector

Additionally, the RJ 45 connector is an 8-pin connector that is used on most modern Ethernet cables, such as CAT 5 and above. The following figure shows an Ethernet cable with an RJ 45 connector:

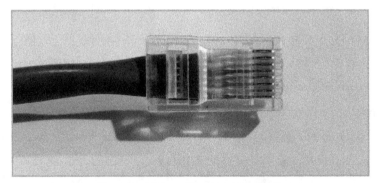

Figure 3.5 – Ethernet cable with an RJ 45 connector

The **TIA-568** standard helps networking professionals and organizations maintain consistency within their networks. The TIA has created two cabling termination standards that indicate how each conductor within a cable is terminated to a corresponding pin within an RJ 45 connector. The following are the two cabling standards that are used within organizations:

- **TIA-568A**

- **TIA-568B**

The following diagram shows the TIA-568A termination standard for an RJ 45 connector:

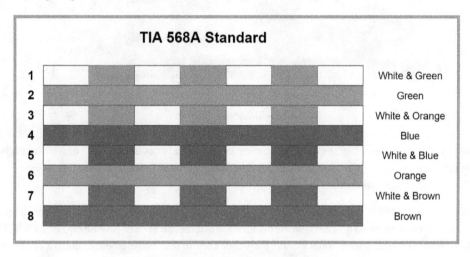

Figure 3.6 – TIA-568A standard

As shown in the preceding diagram, each conductor has a unique color code that is matched to a unique pin within the RJ 45 connector.

The following diagram shows the TIA-568B termination standard for an RJ 45 connector:

TIA 568B Standard

Pin	Color
1	White & Orange
2	Orange
3	White & Green
4	Blue
5	White & Blue
6	Green
7	White & Brown
8	Brown

Figure 3.7 – TIA-568B standard

As shown in the preceding diagram, the termination of the pin layouts in the TIA-568B standard is a bit different from the TIA-568A standard. Here, the cables in pins 1, 2, 3, and 6 switch positions from TIA-568A to TIA-568B standards.

A straight-through cable is formed by terminating a twisted-pair cable run with the same pin-to-pair assignments on both ends. As an example, if the TIA-568B standard is used on one end of a cable, the same TIA-568B standard is used to terminate the other end. In this manner, each pin in a connector on one end of the cable corresponds to the same pin on the other end of the cable. A crossover cable, on the other hand, is formed by swapping the pair going to pins 1 and 2 with the pair to pins 3 and 6. This is equivalent to terminating one end according to the TIA-568A standard, and the other end according to the TIA-568B standard. This mixture of standards is significant because it swaps the pins used for transmission and reception on equipment, allowing two similar devices to communicate.

The following diagram shows a comparison of the TIA-568A and TIA-568B standards:

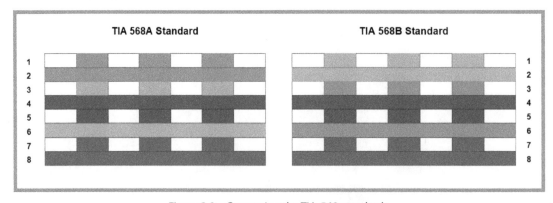

Figure 3.8 – Comparing the TIA-568 standards

Straight-through cables are commonly used to interconnect different types of devices together, while crossover cables are used to interconnect the same type of devices together. Therefore, straight-through cables (also called patch cables) are used to connect computers to switches or switches to routers, whereas crossover cables are used to connect switches to other switches, routers to other routers, computers to routers, and computers to computers. However, modern equipment often possesses a feature called **Automatic Medium Dependent Interface Crossover** (**Auto MDI-X**), which automatically detects that a crossover cable is required on a link and logically swaps the pins used for transmission or reception accordingly, allowing a straight-through cable to be used instead.

Another type of copper cable is coaxial. This type of cable usually has a foil coating around the copper core to protect it from EMI. Coaxial cables contain multiple layers of protection to prevent harm to the copper conductor at the core. This type of cable transmits its electrical signals through an inner core of either solid or stranded copper, or copper-clad steel. This inner conductor is surrounded by a layer of insulating material (usually plastic), which is itself surrounded by braided copper cable. This outer braided copper cable (which is usually grounded) serves to protect the inner core from EMI (keeping noise in the radio frequency domain out of the core) and signal leakage (keeping signals through the core inside of the coaxial cable). The inner insulating material (sometimes called a dielectric material) serves to separate the two conductors in the cable, while the outermost insulating sheath serves to cover and protect the outer braided jacket, and the entire cable by extension.

The following figure shows a coaxial cable:

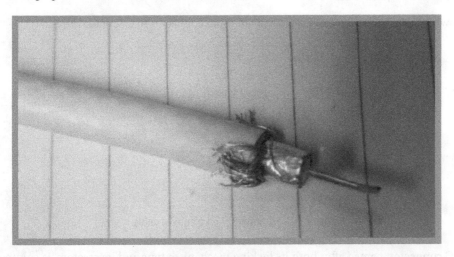

Figure 3.9 – Coaxial cable

Coaxial cables use the **Radio Guide/Grade** (**RG**) standard for their specification. In particular, the **RG-59** legacy standard is used on older TVs and cable modems with a termination point of 75 Ohms. However, the newer **RG-6** standard that is used on cable TV and broadband internet services has a termination point of 75 Ohms.

The following are the various layers of a coaxial cable, from the outer to inner layers:

- **Protective coating**: Made using PVC and protects the internal media from external elements and environmental factors

- **Braided shielding**: Prevents EMI from reaching the copper conductor

- **Foil shielding**: Prevents **Radio Frequency Interference** (**RFI**) from reaching the copper conductor

- **Dielectric Insulator**: An insulator to separate the copper conductor and the braided shielding, and to keep the copper conductor at the center of the coaxial cable

- **Copper conductor**: Used to transmit the electrical signals along the cable

The following three types of connectors are used on coaxial cables:

- **F-pin connector**

- **Bayonet Neill-Concelman** (**BNC**) connector

- **T type connector**, which is used to interconnect three coaxial cables together

One of the most common types of connectors used to terminate the end of a coaxial cable is the F-pin connector. The F-pin connector is used on coaxial cables, which are commonly attached to cable modems, televisions, and VCRs.

The following figure shows a coaxial cable with an F-pin connector to terminate the end:

Figure 3.10 – F-connector on a coaxial cable

The BNC connector, named after both its locking mechanism type and its creators, is commonly used at the end of coaxial cables to transmit **Radio Frequency** (**RF**) signals for equipment such as televisions and radios. The BNC connectors are primarily made in 75 Ohms and 50 Ohms variants so that they can be used in cables with similar impedance. Mismatches between the connector and the cable results in attenuation of the RF signals across the link. BNC connectors are attached to coaxial cables with the aid of a crimper, while male and female connectors are attached by joining and turning them in a quarter rotation.

The following diagram shows a T-connector:

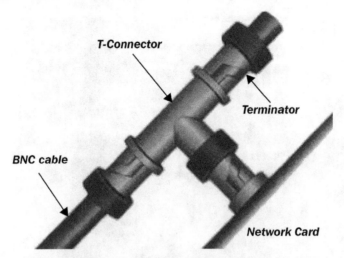

Figure 3.11 – T-connector

The following figure shows a BNC connector for a coaxial cable:

Figure 3.12 – BNC connector

Sometimes, you may need to connect a copper cable to a switch that supports only fiber optic connectors or vice versa. Using a media converter such as a copper-to-fiber converter will convert the electrical signals on the copper cable to light signals for a fiber optic cable, whereas a fiber-to-copper media converter is used to convert the light signals from a fiber optic cable to an electrical signal for a copper cable.

The following figure shows a coaxial to fiber media converter:

Figure 3.13 – Coaxial to fiber media converter

The preceding figure shows a Transition Network DS3/E3 COAX to Fiber Media Converter from Diversity-IT; credit goes to Diversity-IT for this figure.

Now that you are familiar with copper cables and components, next, you will learn about fiber optic cabling and its technologies.

Fiber optic cables

Although copper cables are still used in the vast majority of networks, fiber optic cables continue to replace copper cables in many sections of modern networks. These cables transmit data using pulses of light that are sent down a thin core of plastic or glass, which is surrounded by a material called cladding. This combination of core and cladding allows for the light to be transmitted through the process of either total internal reflection or continuous refraction of the light.

The following figure shows a fiber optic cable:

Figure 3.14 – Fiber optic cable

Compared to copper cables, fiber optic cables provide a lot of advantages, such as the following:

- Fiber optic cables allow faster throughput of data over the cable since fiber optic cables use **Light Emitting Diodes** (**LED**) or lasers to transmit data in the form of light rather than electrical signals. Also, photons travel at a higher speed than electrons, meaning that bits of data are delivered across the ends of fiber cables faster than in copper cables.
- Cables can be run for longer lengths since attenuation over fiber optic cables is lower than that of copper cables. Copper cables are typically rated for a maximum length of 100 meters, while fiber optic cables can run for many kilometers before needing a repeater.
- Fiber optic cables are immune to EMI.

However, there are a few drawbacks to using fiber optic cables within an organization:

- Fiber optic cables are more expensive compared to copper cables
- Fiber optic cables are very fragile and easy to break as the core is either glass or plastic

The following diagram shows the structure of a fiber optic cable:

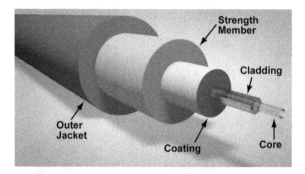

Figure 3.15 – Fiber optic cable structure

As shown in the preceding diagram, the fiber optic cable contains multiple layers of protection to prevent damage to the core. Each layer, such as the outer jacket, strength member, coating, and cladding, shields the core (glass or plastic) from external and environmental factors.

There are two major categories of fiber cables: single-mode and multimode. In the following subsections, you will explore the difference between these categories.

Single-mode fiber

In the context of fiber optic cables, a mode defines the method in which a wave travels through space. A **single-mode fiber** (**SMF**) optic cable is constructed to transmit only one mode of light through the fiber (in a direction parallel to the fiber). Thus, these cables consist of a core with a diameter that is quite small concerning the diameter of the cladding, since it only needs to accommodate a single mode of light. For example, one type of SMF cable is called 9/125 fiber, which means that the core is 9 **micrometers** or **microns** (**μm**) in diameter, while the cladding is 125 μm. Light through SMF can consist of multiple frequencies, but all of these frequencies follow a single path through the fiber.

SMF is usually used for fibers that need to span several kilometers in distance. Since all light waves follow a single mode, concepts such as modal dispersion (the spreading of light due to different modes) are not applicable, meaning that the attenuation of the light through the fiber is low and allows these links to span several kilometers without the need for an optical repeater. The light sources for SMF are usually lasers. Due to this requirement for laser light that can align well with the small diameter of SMF, transceivers (transmitters and receivers at either end of the fibers) are often more expensive than their **multimode fiber** (**MMF**) counterparts. SMF often operates using wavelengths of 1,310 nm or 1,550 nm, and the cable coating is often colored yellow.

Multimode fiber

MMF cables are constructed with much larger diameters than their SMF counterparts. For example, one common type of MMF is 62.5/125, meaning that the cable has a diameter of 62.5 μm, compared to the 9 μm of some SMF cables. This wider core allows multiple modes of light to propagate through the fiber, giving rise to additional losses due to phenomena such as modal dispersion, and limiting the maximum link length to much lower distances than SMF.

However, because of the wider core diameter, less precise transceivers can be used, allowing the cost of MMF systems to be generally lower than equivalent SMF systems. As an example, MMF transceivers may be constructed using less expensive LEDs instead of lasers as light sources. Therefore, network professionals need to weigh the cost of their fiber systems with their expected link distances appropriately, and determine whether the extra cost of SMF systems is necessary for the links that they require, or whether MMF would suffice for their situation.

Fiber connectors

The **Lucent Connector** (**LC**) is a type of fiber connector that was created by the Lucent Corporation. The connectors consist of a small plastic latch, similar to an RJ 45 jack, which helps secure the fiber connector to the port, and a 1.25 mm ferrule, which is used to align the fiber optic cable with the connector. Because of this small ferrule size, the LC connector is a small form factor connector, making it suitable for high-density fiber deployments such as in data centers.

The **Straight Tip** (**ST**) or bayonet connectors are a type of fiber connector that was created by AT&T. These types of connectors were popular in the late 1980s and 1990s, and consist of a larger ferrule (2.5 mm) and a twist-type, spring-loaded, cylindrical, nickel-plated, or stainless steel bayonet connector for locking. Its uses have declined in the last few years because other connectors (such as LC connectors) are less expensive and easier to connect and disconnect.

Subscriber Connectors (**SCs**), also known as Square Connectors or Standard Connectors, are connectors that were developed by **Nippon Telegraph and Telephone** (**NTT**). They are push-pull square-shaped connectors with 2.5 mm, spring-loaded, ceramic ferrule, and snap-in connector latches. They are easy to disconnect/reconnect and can be found in many network installations.

Mechanical Transfer Registered Jack (**MT-RJ**), also known as **Media Termination Recommended Jack**, are small, duplex fiber connectors, with both fibers terminating on a single 2.45 x 4.4 mm ferrule. They are roughly half the size of SCs and are easy to connect/disconnect from their ports using plastic latches, similar to RJ 45 connectors. Two pins, located on transceivers, allow easy alignment of the connector.

The following diagram shows various fiber connectors:

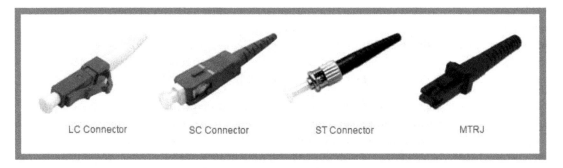

Figure 3.16 – Fiber connectors

As shown in the preceding diagram, each fiber connector has a unique form factor. Credit goes to AD-net Technology CO., LTD for their image.

Fiber transceivers

A transceiver is a component that is required to be inserted into a cage or slot on certain pieces of networking equipment, such as a switch, to provide an interface for certain types of copper or fiber cable to connect.

The following are common fiber transceivers:

- **Gigabit interface converter (GBIC)**
- **Small form-factor pluggable (SFP)**
- **Enhanced small form-factor pluggable (SFP+)**
- **Quad small form-factor pluggable (QSFP)**
- **Enhanced quad small form-factor pluggable (QSFP+)**

GBIC is a hot-swappable (can be removed and reinserted while equipment is powered on) transceiver that introduced the concept of removable transceivers, as opposed to fixed physical ports on networking devices, allowing for more flexibility in network links. Due to the appeal of GBICs, modern networking equipment requires transceivers (combined transmitter/receiver devices) on many ports to provide interfaces for different types of copper and fiber optic connectors, and cables to connect to the equipment.

The following figure shows a GBIC module from FiberStore:

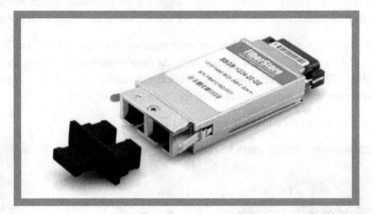

Figure 3.17 – GBIC module

SFP devices are compact, hot-swappable devices that are extremely common in modern networks, facilitating data rates of 1-2.5 Gbps through LC connectors (using both MMF and SMF) and data rates of 1 Gbps for twisted pair copper cables (using RJ 45 connectors). SFPs have largely replaced GBICs because of their smaller size. For fiber SFPs, transceivers exist to facilitate link lengths from several hundred meters to several kilometers, while copper SFPs are usually rated for a maximum of 100 m.

The following figure shows an SFP module from FiberStore:

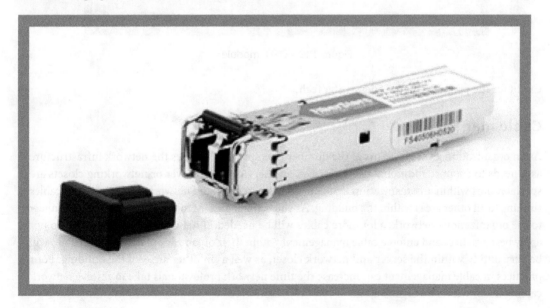

Figure 3.18 – SFP module

SFP+ supports higher data rates, and some equipment supports SFP+ transceivers, which are commonly used for 10 Gbps links using SMF or MMF cables. Copper SFP+ modules, which provide 10 Gbps speeds over twisted pair cables, also exist, but they are less common and more expensive.

QSFP and QSFP+ support even higher data rates; some equipment supports QSFP or QSFP+, which provide capacities of 4 Gbps and 40 Gbps, respectively. As their names suggest, they are constructed from four individual SFP or SFP+ channels, which are aggregated to provide four times the speed with significant space savings on devices, allowing for more dense deployments.

The following figure shows a QSFP module for a Brocade device:

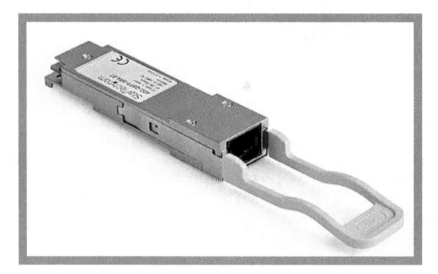

Figure 3.19 – QSFP module

Credit for the preceding figure goes to StarTech.

Cable management

As an organization grows in terms of the number of employees, so does the network infrastructure as it needs to support additional users, devices, and services. The server or networking closets are special rooms within an organization that contain many servers and networking devices with cables running to all other areas within the building. As you can imagine, as more users and devices connect to the organization's network, a lot more cables will be needed. If networking professionals do not apply best practices and enforce cable management within their organization, networking cables will be very untidy within the server and network closet, as well as in other areas of the building. Poor practices in cable management can increase the time network professionals take to resolve network cabling issues within an organization.

Implementing best practices with cable management allows networking professionals and organizations to use a systematic approach to organizing and managing all the networking cables within an organization. Additionally, it helps networking professionals quickly and easily identify individual networking cables when troubleshooting issues on the network. Furthermore, maintaining a tidy workspace and environment also reduces the likelihood of networking cables being damaged.

Cable termination points

There's a wide range of termination points in the context of networking. Cables from different telecommunication and internet service providers often terminate at a particular location in a network, while cables on downlinks to a customer's network may terminate at a different location. There are two common network termination blocks within many organizations, as follows:

- **66 block**
- **110 block**

66 and 110 blocks are two types of punch-down blocks that are commonly used to connect copper wires in networking systems. In a punch-down block, individual copper wires are pressed down into open-ended slots using a *punch-down tool*, causing two sharp metal blades in the slot to cut into the insulation of the wire, thus achieving electrical connectivity.

The following figure shows a 66 block from Major Custom Cable, Inc.:

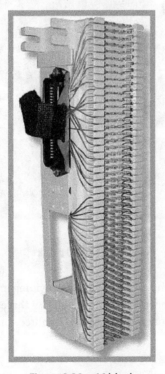

Figure 3.20 – 66 block

> **Important note**
>
> **Krone** is a European alternative to the traditional 110 block, while **Bix** is an alternative to the 66 block.

The 66 block is so named because of its model number, but it provides slots to accommodate 25 pairs or 50 split pairs of Cat 3 copper wire. The 66 blocks are often used for voice/telephone cabling within an organization.

The following figure shows a 110 block:

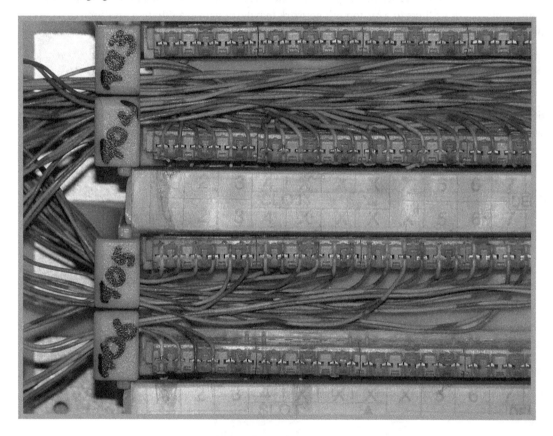

Figure 3.21 – 110 block

The 110 blocks are an upgraded version of the 66 blocks, providing increased slot density and meeting newer standards of twisted-pair copper cables, thus allowing these blocks to accommodate higher bandwidth links. The 110 blocks can often accommodate hundreds of Cat 5 and beyond copper cables.

Patch panels

In the context of networking, patch panels are pieces of equipment that facilitate the Physical Layer connections between links. Different patch panel types allow connections to be made between different types of cables. For example, fiber optic patch panels (or fiber distribution panels) provide ports for different types of fiber connectors (LC, SC, and so on), allowing connectivity to and between different strands of fiber cables. These panels are frequently used at locations where trunk cables (cables containing many individual copper or fiber cables) enter premises, allowing these individual cables to be terminated in a manner that is easy to manage on the premises. Patch (or jumper) cables are usually used to connect equipment to the ports of these patch panels or to connect between ports on the panels.

The patch panel allows networking professionals to connect wall jacks within the office space with a drop cable to the patch panel within the network closet. The patch panel then connects to a switch because the device, such as a computer, is not directly connected to the switch. This simplifies the configuration that's done on the switch.

> **Important note**
> The fiber distribution panel uses the same concept as the copper patch panel. A fiber distribution panel has extra space to allow the fiber cables to be wrapped in a circular/loop format to prevent the fiber core from bending.

Having completed this section, you have covered the fundamentals of various cabling connections and standards that are commonly found within the network industry. In the next section, you will discover various types of Ethernet standards that every networking professional needs to know.

Ethernet standards

Ethernet is the de facto technology that is used on all modern LANs within organizations. Ethernet helps both end devices and networking devices to communicate over both a wired and wireless network infrastructure using various networking protocols and standards. As you may recall, protocols are simply the rules, procedures, and methodologies that are used to govern how information and data are sent across a network between systems.

As with all technologies in the world, various Ethernet standards are maintained by the **Institute of Electrical and Electronics Engineers (IEEE)** that define how communication occurs across a wired network, whether the network media is copper or fiber optic cables. The **IEEE 802.3** standard is used on LANs for communication and there are many variants of this standard. Each variant specifies the type of media used for communication between devices and the support speed/bandwidth of the interface of a device.

Since the IEEE 802.3 standard was developed many years ago, the standard has had many new revisions over time to support newer features and capabilities. These various IEEE 802.3 standards are implemented within both copper and fiber optic network cabling, which follows the BASE standard.

The BASE standard helps networking professionals identify the specific characteristics of a cable, such as the following:

- **Transmission speed**: Defines the support bandwidth of the media such as 10 Mbps, 100 Mbps, 1,000 Mbps (1 Gbps), and 40 Gbps or greater

- **Signaling method**: BASE band signaling is the default signaling method that allows devices on a LAN to use the entire supported bandwidth of a media to transmit data between a source and destination while using a single data channel

- **Media type**: The media type of the networking cable, such as copper or fiber cable

The following is a list of common Ethernet standards for copper media:

- **10BASE-T**: Known as IEEE 802.3i, it supports Ethernet speeds of 10 Mbps with a signaling method of BASE that uses Twisted Pair (T) media (Cat 3) with a maximum distance of 100 meters.

- **100BASE-TX**: Known as IEEE 802.3u, it supports Fast Ethernet speeds of 100 Mbps with a signaling method of BASE that uses a Pairs of Twisted Pairs (TX) media (Cat 5) with a maximum distance of 100 meters.

- **1000BASE-T**: Known as IEEE 802.3ab, it supports a Gigabit Ethernet speed of 1,000 Mbps or 1 Gbps with a signaling method of BASE that uses Twisted Pair (T) media (Cat 6) with a maximum distance of 100 meters.

- **10GBASE-T**: Known as IEEE 802.3an, its supports 10 Gbps with a signaling method of BASE that uses Twisted Pair (T) media (Cat 6, Cat 6a, and Cat 7). The Cat 6 cables have a reduced distance of 55 meters when working with the 10GBASE-T standard with supported distances of 55 meters for Cat 6, 100 meters for Cat 6a, and 100 meters for Cat 7.

- **40GBASE-T**: Known as IEEE 802.3bq, this supports 40 Gbps with a signaling method of BASE which that Twisted Pair (T) media (Cat 8) with a maximum distance of 30 meters.

The following table shows a summary of Ethernet standards for copper cables:

Signaling Method	Ethernet Standard	Media Type
10BASE-T	IEEE 802.3i	Twisted Pair (Cat 3)
100BASE-TX	IEEE802.3u	Twisted Pair (Cat 5)
1000BASE-T	IEEE 802.3ab	Twisted Pair (Cat 6)
10GBASE-T	IEEE 802.an	Twisted Pair (Cat 6, 6a & 7)
40GBASE-T	IEEE 802.11bq	Twisted Par (Cat 8)

Figure 3.22 – Ethernet standards for copper cables

The Ethernet standard (IEEE 802.3) supports two environments: **shared** or **switched** mediums. The shared medium describes an environment in which all devices contend with one another for a spot of the network to communicate without being disrupted by other devices. This contention between devices can be solved, but on Ethernet networks that use copper cables, whenever a device such as a computer wants to send a message, it will attempt to access the network via the media and transmit the message across the network. In reality, there are usually multiple devices on the same network that also want to transmit their message at the same time. However, only one device can transmit at a time. This creates a content-based network where multiple devices are trying to access the network simultaneously to send their messages over the wire.

To solve this problem on a content-based network, the **Carrier Sense Multiple Access/Collision Detection (CSMA/CD)** methodology can be used. It allows only one device to transmit at a time on a wired Ethernet network. Before a sender transmits a message, it will check the media to determine if there is an existing electrical signal. If a signal is detected on the media, the sender will not transmit the message and re-check after some time to determine whether a signal still exists on the media. If no signal is detected on the media, the sender will transmit its message over the network to the destination host. However, without CSMA/CD, if two devices transmit at the same time on a content-based network, a collision occurs, causing the signals from the two senders to collide and become corrupted.

The following diagram shows a flow of actions that occur in CSMA/CD on a wired network:

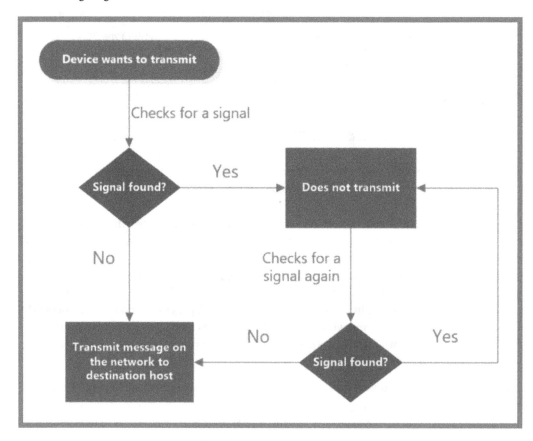

Figure 3.23 – CSMA/CD flowchart

The following is a list of common Ethernet standards for fiber optic media:

- **100BASE-FX**: Known as IEEE 802.3u, this supports Fast Ethernet speeds of 100 Mbps on long-range **Multimode Fiber (MMF)**

- **100BASE-SX**: Known as IEEE 802.3u, this supports Fast Ethernet speeds of 100 Mbps on short-range MMF

- **1000BASE-SX**: Known as IEEE 802.3z, this supports Gigabit Ethernet speeds of 1,000 Mbps or 1 Gbps on short-range MMF

- **1000BASE-LX**: Known as IEEE 802.3z, this supports Gigabit Ethernet speeds of 1,000 Mbps or 1 Gbps on long-range **Single-Mode Fiber (SMF)**

- **10GBASE-SR**: Known as IEEE 802.3ae, this supports 10 Gigabit Ethernet speeds on short-range MMF

- **10GBASE-LR**: Known as IEEE 802.3ae, this supports 10 Gigabit Ethernet speeds on long-range SMF

The following table shows a summary of Ethernet standards for fiber optic cables:

Signaling Method	Ethernet Standard	Media Type
100BASE-FX	IEEE 802.3u	Long-range MMF
100BASE-SX	IEEE 802.3u	Short-range MMF
1000BASE-SX	IEEE 802.3z	Short-range MMF
1000BASE-LX	IEEE 802.3z	Long-range SMF
10GBASE-SR	IEEE 802.3ae	Short-range MMF
10GBASE-LR	IEEE 802.3ae	Long-range SMF

Figure 3.24 – Ethernet standards for fiber optic cables

Having completed this section, you have explored various types of Ethernet standards that are common within the industry and are found on networking cables and interfaces on devices. In the next section, you will explore virtualization technologies.

Virtual network concepts

Long ago, whenever IT professionals set up a server within their organization, the server operating system was installed directly on the storage device, such as the **Hard Disk Drive (HDD)**. If you wanted to install another operating system on the same HDD, you would need to create a logical partition on the HDD and install the second operating system on the new partition. However, when powering on the physical server, only one operating system can be booted in the memory of the server. While running a single operating system at a time on a computer or server, the operating system has full access to all the hardware-based components, such as the processor, memory modules, storage drives, and so on. This allows the operating system to operate to its fullest potential and leverage all the available computing power to perform tasks and calculations.

However, an operating system does not always utilize hardware-based components all the time. There are many times when an operating system on a device such as a laptop, server, or even a smartphone will idle and use the least resources when there are no tasks or operations to perform. Imagine installing Windows Server 2022 on a very powerful server with a lot of memory, a high-end processor, and a lot of storage capacity but the operating system is using an average of 5-10% of the processor or less than 25% of the memory daily. As a result, there are a lot of unutilized computing resources on the server but the operating system is not leveraging it due to fewer resource-intensive applications and services that are running on the device. This is known as **server sprawl**.

The following screenshot shows the Task Manager on a Windows device that is under-utilized:

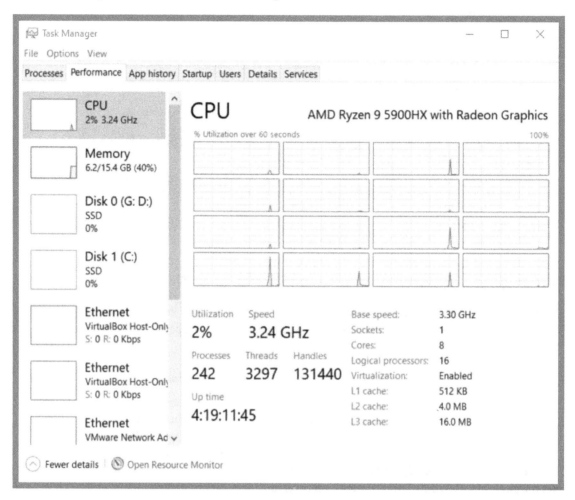

Figure 3.25 – Task Manager

What if you can install and run multiple operating systems at the same time on the same device? The legacy method would create a partition for each bootable operating system, but this method would allow only one operating system to run at a time. However, using a hypervisor application allows IT professionals to virtualize all the hardware-based components of a physical computer or server to allow virtual machines to be created.

Hypervisors

A hypervisor is an application that allows IT professionals to virtualize all the hardware-based components on a computer, such as its processor, memory, storage drives, network adapters, sound and video cards, optical drives, and even USB controllers. The hypervisor allows us to create a virtual environment to install guest operating systems on create a virtual machine. The hypervisor ensures the virtual environment is created to support the guest operating system, so a guest operating system will think it's running on physically supported hardware components. As an example, imagine running the Android mobile operating system as a virtual machine within a virtual environment on top of a Windows operating system. The hypervisor ensures the virtual hardware components meet the specification to support the guest operating system, which is the Android mobile operating system.

When creating a virtual machine, the user, such as yourself, can customize each virtual machine environment and assign the number of processor cores, memory, and even storage allocation to each virtual machine. This technique allows IT professionals to run multiple virtual machines at the same time on a single physical computer or server so long as the hardware-based resources are fairly allocated to each running virtual machine.

Using virtualization technologies within organizations allows companies to reduce the number of physical servers within their buildings. As a result, fewer servers will reduce the expenditure cost of maintaining the components within each physical server. Furthermore, it will reduce the amount of space needed to store physical servers in the organization as one physical server can be running multiple virtual servers at the same time. Additionally, virtualization can help reduce the power consumption within the server room since there are fewer physical servers needed. This is because virtualization allows legacy operating systems to run on hypervisors.

> **Important note**
>
> The operating system that is installed within a virtual machine is referred to as the **guest operating system**, whereas the operating system that is installed on the storage device of a server, such as the hard drive, and booted into memory is referred to as the **host operating system**.

There are two types of hypervisors within the industry and each has a separate deployment model:

- Type 1 hypervisor
- Type 2 hypervisor

The Type 1 hypervisor is sometimes called a bare-metal hypervisor because it is installed directly on the hardware, such as the storage device, and boots into the memory of the server. This type of hypervisor has direct access to all hardware-based components on the server. As a result, each virtual machine has direct access to the hardware, so each virtual machine can operate more efficiently.

The following diagram shows the Type 1 hypervisor deployment model:

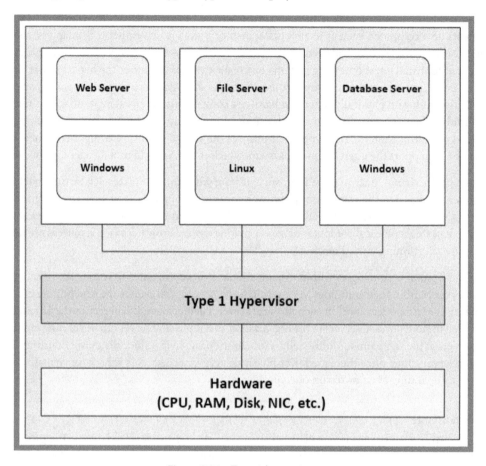

Figure 3.26 – Type 1 hypervisor

As shown in the preceding diagram, there's no host operating system installed on the storage that will run on top of the hardware-based components. When the server is powered on, the Type 1 hypervisor application will load from the storage drive into memory and control all the hardware-based components, allowing the user to create and manage virtual machines.

Type 1 hypervisors are good for physical servers that are stationary. When installing a Type 1 hypervisor onto a physical server, a static IP address is assigned to ensure IT professionals can manage the hypervisor and all its features over a network.

> **Important note**
>
> Type 1 hypervisors are good in a data center setting. They can replace numerous physical servers by virtualizing several high-end server operating systems onto one physical server. All networking can be abstracted so that static IP addresses can be assigned to each VM. Furthermore, the hypervisor allows for centralized management of multiple VMs.

The following screenshot shows the user interface of VMware ESXi, a Type 1 hypervisor:

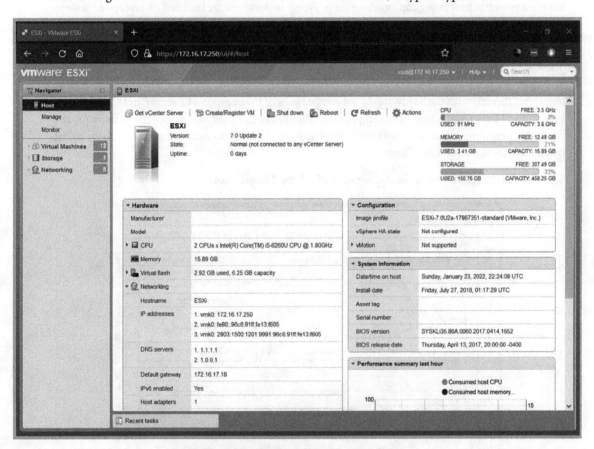

Figure 3.27 – VMware ESXi user interface

As shown in the preceding screenshot, VMware ESXi has a web-based user interface that allows you to easily manage a network. There are many Type 1 hypervisors available from trusted providers on the internet; some are commercial and others are free.

The following is a list of well-known free Type 1 hypervisors:

- **VMware ESXi**: `https://www.vmware.com/products/esxi-and-esx.html`
- **Proxmox**: `https://www.proxmox.com`
- **XCP-ng**: `https://xcp-ng.org`

While Type 1 hypervisors are amazing, there are not suitable for laptops since they are portable and have less powerful processing capabilities. Often, Type 2 hypervisors are installed on laptops or desktop computers. Installing a Type 1 hypervisor on a laptop is possible but accessing the user management interface will not be feasible.

The Type 2 hypervisor is an application that runs on top of an existing host operating system such as Microsoft Windows, Apple macOS, or Linux. This deployment does not allow the hypervisor application to interact directly with the hardware-based components of the computer or server, unlike the Type 1 hypervisor. However, the host operating system still utilizes the hardware resources to function and perform operations as needed; any remaining hardware-based resources are made available to the hypervisor for the virtual machines.

The following diagram shows the deployment of a Type 2 hypervisor:

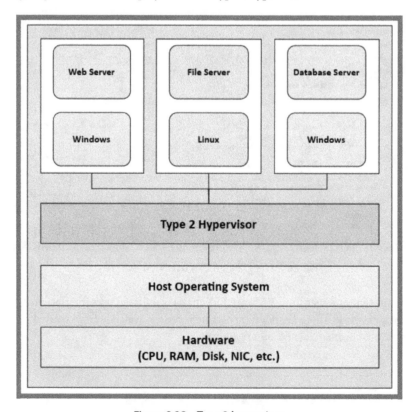

Figure 3.28 – Type 2 hypervisor

As shown in the preceding diagram, the host operating system runs on top of the hardware-based resources of the computer and uses any computing resources it needs to operate and perform tasks; the remaining resources are available to the virtual machines through the hypervisor application.

The following is a list of popular commercial and free Type 2 hypervisors:

- **VMware Workstation Pro**: `https://www.vmware.com/products/workstation-pro.html`
- **VMware Player**: `https://www.vmware.com/products/workstation-player.html`
- **Oracle VM VirtualBox**: `https://www.virtualbox.org/`
- **Parallels**: `https://www.parallels.com`

Using a Type 2 hypervisor on a computer or server allows you to run your host operating system and multiple virtual machines at the same time. Each virtual machine is an operating system in a virtual, isolated environment. Therefore, if one virtual machine is compromised by malware, the other virtual machines and the host operating system are not affected. However, if the virtual machines are networked to each other and the host operating system, the malware can spread through the virtual network within the hypervisor to other systems.

Virtual networking components

Creating a virtual machine can be very interesting and a bit exciting, especially if your duties are similar to those of a virtualization or cloud engineer. However, as aspiring network professionals, we must not forget that our network infrastructure also needs to be able to support a high amount of traffic, scalability, fault tolerance, and redundancy. As mentioned previously, one of the main benefits of virtualizing servers is being able to reduce the physical storage space for equipment such as servers and save on purchasing dedicated appliances. This concept also applies to networking devices such as switches and routers, and security appliances such as firewalls.

Network function virtualization

On a traditional network, you will commonly discover that there are many physical networking switches and routers that are used to interconnect end devices and other networks. Additionally, you'll see physical security devices such as firewalls on the perimeter networks of organizations to filter both inbound and outbound network traffic and prevent traffic.

Nowadays, networking professionals use a concept known as **Network Function Virtualization** (NFV), which allows organizations to implement virtual networking devices within a hypervisor that provides the same functionality, features, and services as traditional physical devices. Imagine an organization running its security appliances such as a firewall and networking devices such as routers and switches within a hypervisor on a physical server with other virtual machines.

NFV provides the same major benefits of using virtualization within an organization, such as the following:

- With networking devices running in a virtualization environment, there's no need to upgrade the hardware components of a physical device

- Multiple networking and security appliances can be running at the same time on a server, which reduces the need for physical space traditional physical device needs

- Reduces the overall power consumption as multiple virtual devices are operating on a single server

- There's no need for specific hardware components for a virtual networking device as the hypervisor ensures the virtual environment is suitable

A virtual switch has the same function and capabilities as a hardware-based physical network switch; the difference is the virtual switch operating system is installed on a hypervisor that is running on a physical server on the network. Networking professionals can configure a virtual switch to provide the same functionalities and services as a physical switch on the network. Similarly, virtual routers can perform routing and IP services to a network, as would a physical router on a traditional network. The Cisco **Cloud Services Router (CSR)** 1000V is a virtual router from Cisco that allows networking professionals to be implemented on a hypervisor. The Cisco ASAv is a virtual firewall that can be implemented by organizations on their private cloud infrastructure and the public cloud on various cloud providers' infrastructure.

Virtual network interface card

A hypervisor allows multiple virtual machines to run at the same time on a single physical computer or server device. Each virtual machine can be configured with unique networking configurations, such as allowing internet access to a virtual machine, placing a virtual machine within an isolated network, creating a network between the virtual machine and the host operating system only, and allowing a virtual machine to connect to the physical network or sharing the internet service through the host operating system.

Each virtual machine within a hypervisor has a **Virtual Network Interface Card (vNIC)**, which allows the virtual machine to access a network. The vNIC on a virtual machine has the same features and capabilities as a physical NIC installed on a regular computer or server. The only difference is that the vNIC can be used to set up network connections on and between virtual machines on a hypervisor application.

The following diagram shows virtual machines with vNICs:

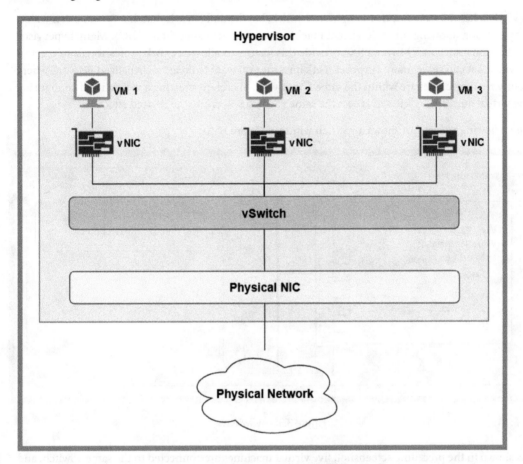

Figure 3.29 – vNICs on virtual machines

As shown in the preceding diagram, each virtual machine within the hypervisor has a vNIC, which allows them to access the host machine, other VMs on the host, other VMs on other hosts, other hosts on the network, or the internet, depending on the configuration with other virtual machines within the same hypervisor using a vSwitch. A virtual machine can have multiple vNICs installed to allow the virtual machine to access multiple networks at the same time.

vSwitch

A vSwitch has the same features as a physical switch, but the difference is that the vSwitch exists within a hypervisor, allowing multiple virtual machines to connect using their vNICs. Many hypervisor applications, such as VMware ESXi, provide this feature to allow network professionals to create a vSwitch that can serve many purposes. Let's imagine you want to create a virtualized network where your virtual machines are within the same IP network. Therefore, creating a vSwitch and configuring the virtual machines' vNICs to access the same vSwitch will create the desired effect.

The following screenshot shows a vSwitch within VMware ESXi:

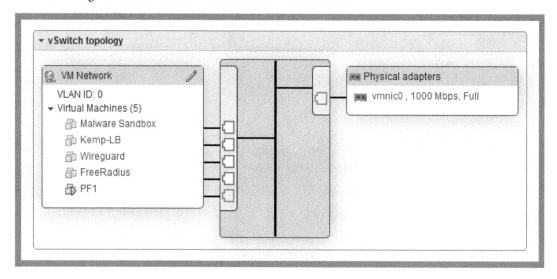

Figure 3.30 – vSwitch

As shown in the preceding screenshot, five virtual machines are connected to the same vSwitch, and the vSwitch is connected to the physical NIC on the server to provide access to the physical network within the organization.

Lab – creating a virtual machine

In this hands-on exercise, you will learn how to create a virtual machine on your computer using Oracle VM VirtualBox as the preferred hypervisor application. Before getting started with this exercise, the following are some important requirements:

- Ensure your processor on your computer supports **VT-x/AMD-V** virtualization features

- Ensure the virtualization features are enabled on your processor via the BIOS/UEFI

- You will need at least 2 GB of available memory and at least 20 GB of available space on your storage drive

Once you're all set, please use the following instructions to get started.

Part 1 – creating the virtual environment

Follow these steps:

1. First, you will need to download the Oracle VM VirtualBox hypervisor application by going to `https://www.virtualbox.org/wiki/Downloads` and choosing a software package based on the host operating system on your computer:

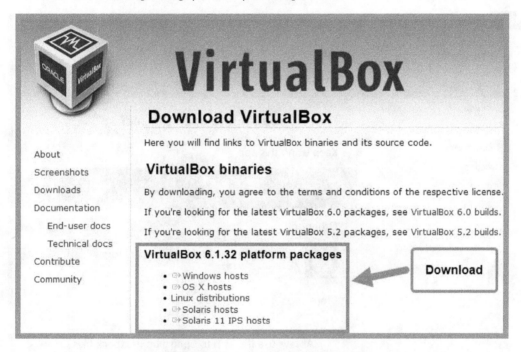

Figure 3.31 – Oracle VM VirtualBox download page

2. Next, on the same download page, download **VirtualBox 6.1.32 Oracle VM VirtualBox Extension Pack** onto your computer. This Extension Pack provides additional features to the hypervisor, which may be required later in this book:

> **VirtualBox 6.1.32 Oracle VM VirtualBox Extension Pack**
>
> - ⇨ All supported platforms
>
> Support for USB 2.0 and USB 3.0 devices, VirtualBox RDP, disk encryption, NVMe and PXE boot for Intel cards. See this chapter from the User Manual for an introduction to this Extension Pack. The Extension Pack binaries are released under the VirtualBox Personal Use and Evaluation License (PUEL). *Please install the same version extension pack as your installed version of VirtualBox.*

Figure 3.32 – Oracle VM VirtualBox Extension Pack

3. Next, you will need to install the Oracle VM VirtualBox platform package that you downloaded in *Step 1*. During the installation process, use the default configurations and settings provided by the installer.

4. Next, to install **Oracle VM VirtualBox Extension Pack**, right-click on the extension pack and choose **Open With | VirtualBox Manager** to begin the installation. Ensure you accept the user agreement to continue the installation process:

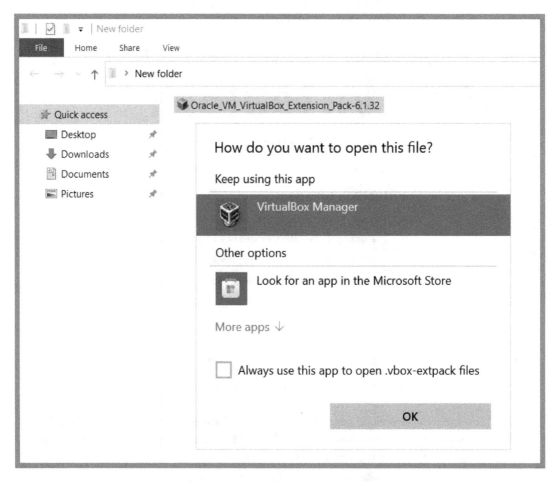

Figure 3.33 – VirtualBox extension pack

5. Next, you will need to download an evaluation copy of **Windows 10 Enterprise** from **Microsoft Evaluation Center** at https://www.microsoft.com/en-us/evalcenter/evaluate-windows-10-enterprise. Simply choose **ISO – Enterprise**, click **Continue**, and complete the form to receive a download link for the ISO file:

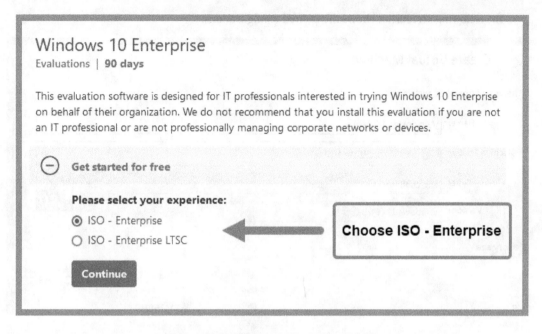

Figure 3.34 – Windows 10 Enterprise ISO file

You'll need to select the 32-bit or 64-bit edition to start the download of the ISO file onto your computer. Once the Windows 10 Enterprise ISO file has been downloaded onto your computer, proceed to the next step.

6. Open the **VirtualBox Manager** application and click on **New** to create a virtual machine within the hypervisor.

7. Next, on the **Create Virtual Machine** window, click on **Expert Mode** to use the expert mode options for creating the virtual machine.

8. The **Create Virtual Machine** user interface will switch to **Expert Mode**. Use the following parameters to create the virtual machine environment:

   - **Name**: Windows 10 VM

   - **Type**: Microsoft Windows

   - **Version**: Windows 10 (64-bit)

   - **Memory size**: 4,096 MB or greater

   - **Hard disk**: Create a virtual hard disk now

The following screenshot shows the desired configurations:

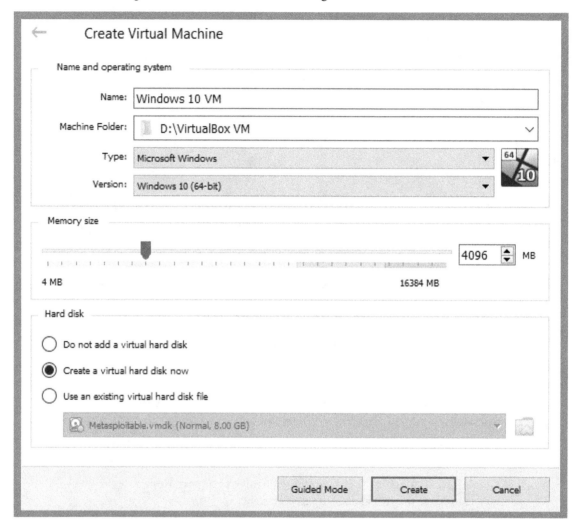

Figure 3.35 – Virtual machine configurations

Once you've set all the parameters, click on **Create** to proceed to the next step.

9. Next, **Create Virtual Hard Disk** will appear. Ensure you apply the following configurations and click **Create**:

- **File size**: 50 GB

- **Hard disk file type: Virtual Hard Disk (VHD)**

- **Storage on physical hard disk**: Dynamically allocated

The following screenshot shows the desired configurations:

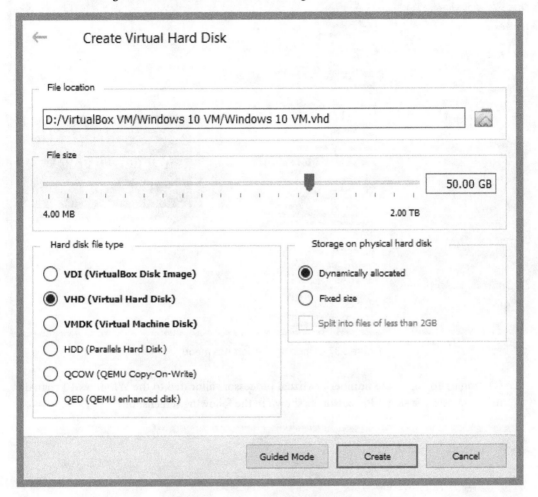

Figure 3.36 – Virtual hard disk configurations

10. Next, your virtual machine environment will be created and you'll return to **the VirtualBox Manager** main user interface. Select the **Windows 10 VM** virtual machine and click on **Settings**, as shown here:

Figure 3.37 – Opening the Settings menu

11. (Optional) To adjust the number of virtual processors allocated to the Windows 10 virtual machine, select **System | Processor**, as shown in the following screenshot:

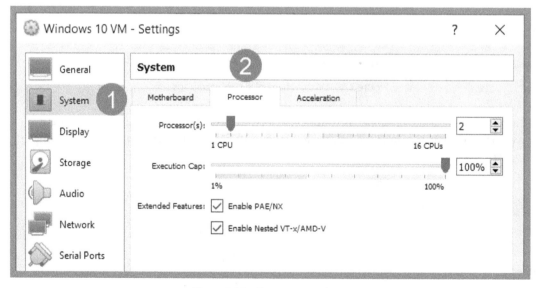

Figure 3.38 – Processor settings

12. Next, to adjust the vNICs on the Windows 10 virtual machine, select **Network | Adapter 1**. To share the internet access from your host operating system to the guest operating system within the virtual machine, ensure **Adapter 1** is enabled and set it to **NAT**, as shown here:

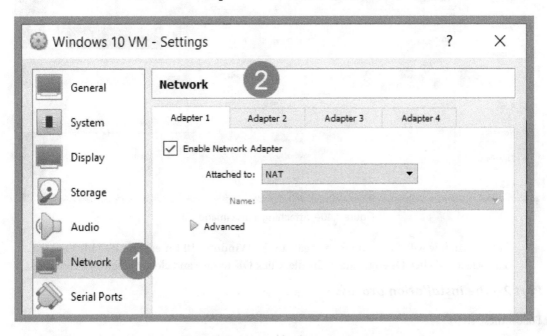

Figure 3.39 – Network adapter settings

13. Next, to attach the Windows 10 Enterprise ISO file to the virtual optical drive, select **Storage** and click on the **empty optical disk** icon. Then, in the **Attributes** section, select the **optical disk** icon to open the drop-down area. Select **Choose a disk File**, as shown here:

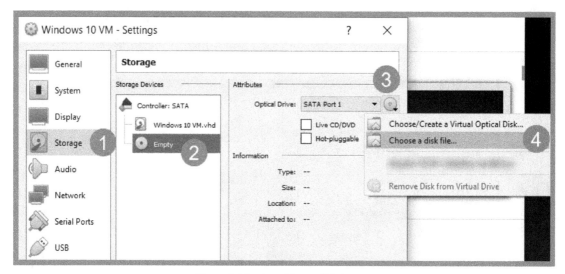

Figure 3.40 – Attaching a disk image

A new window will open. Simply navigate to the **Windows 10 Enterprise ISO file** location, and select and click **Open** to attach the file. Click **OK** to save and close the settings menu.

Part 2 – the installation process

Follow these steps:

1. Next, on the **VirtualBox Manager** main user interface, select **Windows 10 VM** and click on **Start** to power on the virtual machine.

2. The virtual machine will start and load the installation and boot files from the ISO file into the virtual memory on the virtual machine. On the **Windows Setup** window, click **Next**, as shown here:

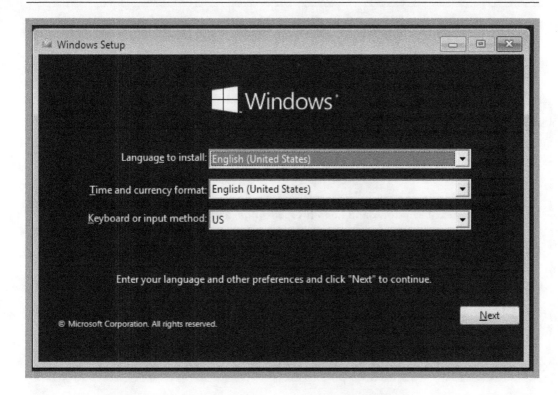

Figure 3.41 – The Windows Setup window

3. Next, click on **Install now** to set up and install Windows 10 Enterprise on the virtual environment:

Figure 3.42 – The installation confirmation window

4. Next, the **Applicable notices and license terms** window will appear. Simply accept the license terms and click **Next**.

5. Next, select **Custom: Install Windows only (advanced)**, as shown here:

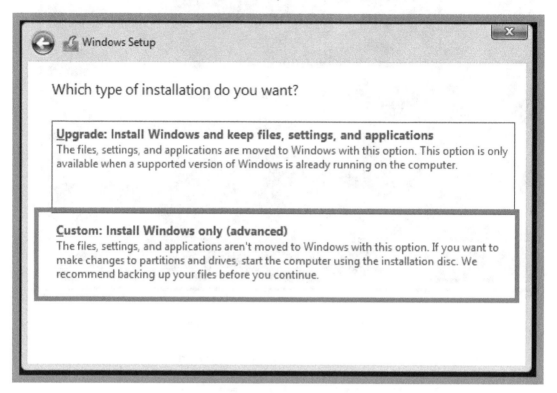

Figure 3.43 – Installation type

6. Next, you'll need to select the installation destination drive. Select the **Drive 0 Unallocated Space** option and select **Next**, as shown here:

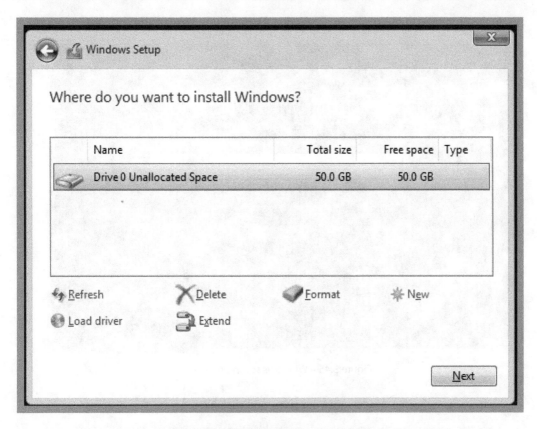

Figure 3.44 – Installation destination

The installation process will begin and will take a few minutes to complete. When the installation is completed, the operating system will automatically reboot on its own.

Part 3 – setting up Windows 10 Enterprise

Follow these steps:

1.   After the Windows 10 virtual machine reboots, select your region and keyboard layout and click **Yes** to proceed. The operating system will reboot again; this time, it can connect to the internet.

2. In the **Sign in with Microsoft** window, select **Domain join instead** and click **Next**:

Figure 3.45 – Windows setup process

3. Next, in the following window, set your name and click **Next**:

Figure 3.46 – Creating an identity

4. Next, set a password for your local user account and click **Next**:

Figure 3.47 – Setting a password

5. Next, you will need to confirm that the password has been configured correctly and set a few security questions.

6. Next, you will be prompted to adjust the privacy and Cortana settings. You can disable all the collection of data and disable Cortana to proceed. The setup process will complete on its own and the operating system will automatically reboot and present the desktop, as shown here:

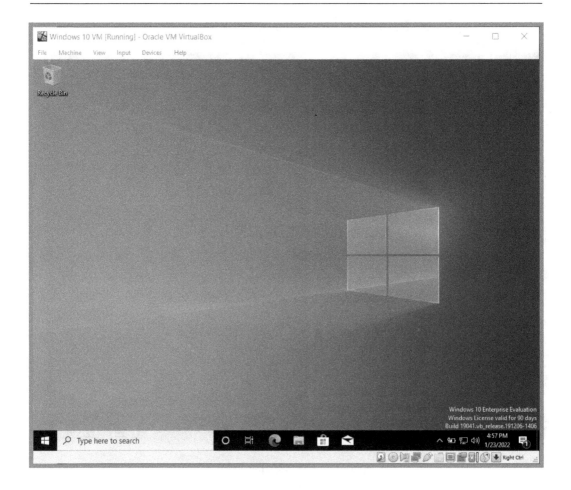

Figure 3.48 – Windows 10 user interface

Part 4 – installing guest additions

Follow these steps:

1. On the Windows 10 VM menu bar, select **Devices | Install Guest Additions CD image**, as shown here:

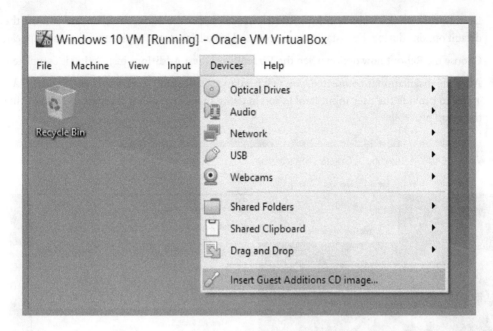

Figure 3.49 – Guest Additions

2. Within the Windows 10 Enterprise virtual machine, open **Windows Explorer** and go to **This PC**, where you will see that the **VirtualBox Guest Additions** virtual disk is present. Double-click to open it:

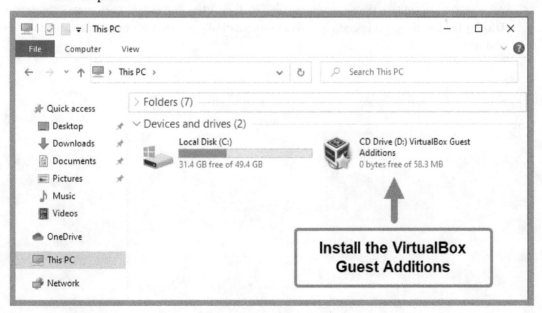

Figure 3.50 – Windows Explorer

3. Double-click on the **VboxWindowsAdditions** file to start the installation. Ensure you use the default options during the installation process and install any driver application that may appear.

4. Choose the **Reboot now** option when the **VirtualBox Guest Additions** installation is completed.

5. After the installation is completed, you will need to select **Input | Keyboard | Insert Ctrl + Alt + Del** to provide the user input field to log in using the user account that was created during the setup process:

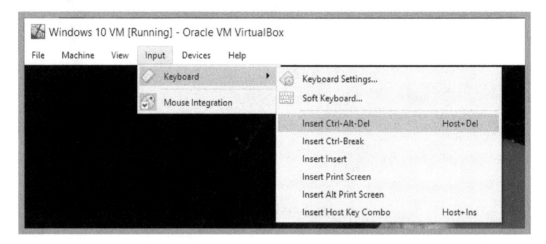

Figure 3.51 – Login window

6. After you've logged into the operating system, click on **View** and toggle **Auto-resize Guest Display** to allow the guest operating system to automatically scale to your monitor's resolution and size:

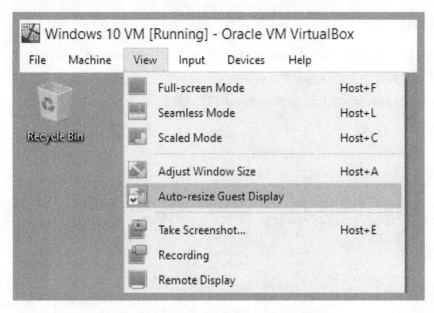

Figure 3.52 – Enabling Auto-resize Guest Display

Having completed this exercise, you have learned how to create a virtual machine and install Windows 10 Enterprise as a guest operating system on a hypervisor.

Summary

In this chapter, you learned about various Ethernet standards and their characteristics for copper and fiber cables, as well as their connection types. Furthermore, you learned about the importance of using cabling standards within organizations to maintain consistency and explored various virtualization technologies that are commonly used within the networking industry. Lastly, you gained skills in creating a virtual machine on a hypervisor.

I hope this chapter has been informative for you and is helpful in your journey toward learning networking and becoming a network professional. In the next chapter, *Chapter 4, Understanding IPv4 and IPv6 Addressing*, you will discover the various types and use cases of IPv4 and IPv6 addresses, and learn to perform subnetting.

Questions

The following is a short list of review questions to help reinforce your learning and help you identify areas that may require some improvement.

1. How many pairs of wires are there within an STP cable?

    A. 2

    B. 3

    C. 4

    D. 8

2. Which of the following cables is commonly used in telephone systems?

    A. Cat 5

    B. Cat 5e

    C. Cat 6

    D. Cat 3

3. Which of the following connectors is used in new coaxial cables?

    A. F-Type

    B. SFP

    C. RJ-48

    D. BNC

4. Which of the following fiber transceivers provides speeds of 40 Gbps?

    A. SFP

    B. QSFP+

    C. GBIC

    D. SFP+

5. Which of the following is true about fiber cables?

    A. Uses LEDs

    B. Cheaper than copper cables

    C. Less fragile than a coaxial cable

    D. All of the above

6. Which of the following is the standard for Ethernet?

    A. IEEE 802.15

    B. IEEE 802.11

    C. IEEE 802.3

    D. IEEE 802.16

7. Which type of hypervisor can run directly on top of the hardware components of a server?

    A. Type 2

    B. Type 0

    C. Type 1

    D. All of the above

8. Which of the following Ethernet standards supports 100 Mbps over a twisted pair cable?

    A. 10BASE-SX

    B. 100BASE-TX

    C. 100BASE-T

    D. 100BASE-LX

9. Which of the following Ethernet standards support 100 Mbps over long-range Multimode Fiber?

    A. 100BASE-FX

    B. 100BASE-SX

    C. 100BASE-LX

    D. 100BASE-LR

10. Which of the following Ethernet standards support 10 Gbps on short-range Single-Mode Fiber?

    A. 10GBASED-FX

    B. 10GBASED-LX

    C. 10GBASED-SR

    D. 10GBASED-LR

Further reading

To learn more about the topics that were covered in this chapter, check out the following links:

- *Basic Home Network Hardware Components*: `https://stevessmarthomeguide.com/networking-components/`

- *Network Cabling*: `https://fcit.usf.edu/network/chap4/chap4.htm`

- *What is Virtualization?*: `https://www.vmware.com/solutions/virtualization.html`

Understanding IPv4 and IPv6 Addressing

Each device connected to a network needs a logical address to be able to communicate with other devices and share resources. Without logical addressing, a sender will not be able to specify the delivery address or location for a message, and a recipient of a message will not know the sender's address if a response is needed. Within private networks within organizations and public networks on the internet, each device is assigned a logical address, which helps networking devices forward messages between a source and a destination.

In this chapter, you will understand the need for public and private IP address spaces and why it matters to networking professionals and organizations. You will gain a solid foundation in understanding the various types of IPv4 and IPv6 addresses, and why these address types are needed on networks. Lastly, you will explore IPv6 concepts and learn how to configure IP addresses on various devices.

In this chapter, we will cover the following topics:

- The need for IP addressing
- Exploring the structure of IPv4 and IPv6
- Types of IPv4 and IPv6 addresses
- Delving into IPv6 concepts
- Configuring IP addresses

Let's dive in!

Technical requirements

To follow along with the exercises in this chapter, please ensure that you have met the following hardware and software requirements:

- Windows 10: `https://www.microsoft.com/en-us/evalcenter/evaluate-windows-10-enterprise`

- Ubuntu 20.04 Desktop: `https://ubuntu.com/download/desktop`

- Cisco IOS router

The need for IP addressing

An **Internet Protocol** (**IP**) address is a Layer 3 logical address that is assigned to all devices on a network to allow communication between nodes on different IP networks. Imagine sending a letter to a friend or relative using traditional postal services. After writing the letter, you'll need to include the sender's address if the recipient wants to reply to your letter. Additionally, as the author of the letter, you'll need to include the destination mailing address to ensure the courier service has all the details needed to deliver the letter to the right address and person. What if you forgot to include the source/sender address on the letter? The recipient will not be able to send any replies to you. What if you haven't included the destination mailing address? The courier service will not be able to deliver the letter to the appropriate person.

Based on this analogy, the letter (message) is the electrical signal being generated by the sender's computer. Before the message is placed on the network, the sender's IP address is inserted as the source address and the recipient's IP address is included as the destination address. These addresses are required to ensure any networking devices along the way can forward the message to the intended recipient. Without proper addressing information (IP addressing) on the letter (message), the postal service (networking devices) will experience difficulties forwarding the letter correctly.

In the world of networking, the **Internet Assigned Numbers Authority** (**IANA**) is the governing body that is responsible for managing global **IP version 4** (**IPv4**) and **IP version 6** (**IPv6**) address assignments, **Autonomous System Number** (**ASN**) allocation to organizations that manage a large number of public networks, protocol assignment, and root **Domain Name System** (**DNS**) directories and services of the world.

On the internet, each device that is directly connected to the internet needs a unique IP address. If there are two or more devices with duplicate IP addresses that exist on the internet or within a private network, the networking devices that are responsible for forwarding packets will experience issues delivering a unique stream of packets from a sender to the correct destination host. To assist with distributing public IP addresses to **Internet Service Providers** (**ISPs**) around the world, IANA delegated the responsibility of IP distribution to five **Regional Internet Registries** (**RIRs**) around the world. Each RIR is responsible for distributing IPv4 and IPv6 address blocks to specific regions and geolocation.

The following are the five RIRs and their responsible geolocations:

- **African Network Information Center (AFRINIC):** Supports the continent of Africa

- **Asia-Pacific Network Information Centre (APNIC):** Supports regions of Asia and the Pacific

- **American Registry for Internet Numbers (ARIN):** Supports regions of Canada, the USA, and parts of the Caribbean

- **Latin America and Caribbean Network Information Centre (LACNIC):** Supports Latin America and parts of the Caribbean regions

- **Réseaux IP Européens Network Coordination Centre (RIPE NCC):** Supports Europe, the Middle East, and Central Asia

The following diagram provides a visual representation of how the public IP addresses are distributed to each RIR and the ISPs around the world:

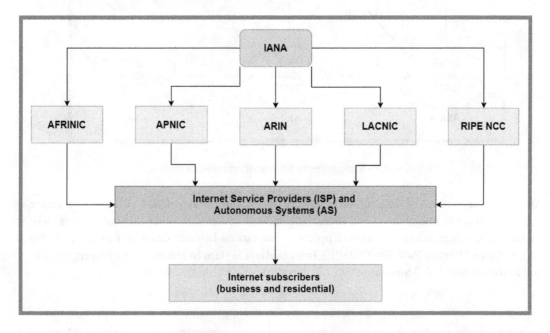

Figure 4.1 – IP network blocks delegation

As shown in the preceding diagram, each RIR is responsible for distributing IPv4 and IPv6 address blocks to ISPs and any **Autonomous System (AS)** within their responsible geolocation. An AS is simply any organization that is responsible for managing a large number of internet routing networks such as an ISP within a country or region. IANA assigns AS numbers to the various RIRs around the world. Then, the RIRs allocate these AS numbers to network operators such as ISPs. The ISPs use their AS numbers to share their network routing prefixes with other ISPs using the **Border Gateway Protocol (BGP)**.

> **Important note**
>
> BGP is an **Exterior Gateway Protocol (EGP)** that allows network operators such as ISPs to exchange their routing information with each other, allowing users on the internet to reach networks beyond their local ISP.

The following diagram shows a network representation of many interconnected network operators:

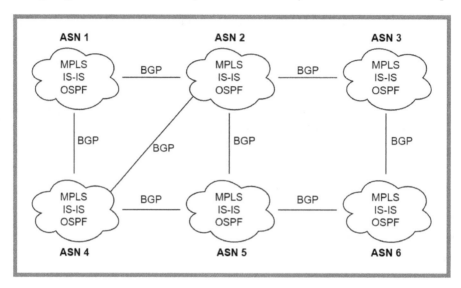

Figure 4.2 – Interconnected ISPs sharing network routes

As shown in the preceding diagram, each network operator or ISP is assigned a unique AS number that allows them to interconnect and share their network routes with other ISPs while using BGP to share their routes. Internally, network operators use various **Interior Gateway Protocols (IGPs)** such as **Open Shortest Path First (OSPF)**, **Intermediate System to Intermediate System (IS-IS)**, and **Multiprotocol Label Switching (MPLS)** to route traffic within their networks.

> **Tip**
>
> Many islands and continents are interconnected using submarine internet cables that are installed on the ocean's floor around the world. The following URL provides a visual map of the underwater submarine cables and the organizations that manage them: https://www.submarinecablemap.com/.

In the early days, back in January 1983, the world began seeing the deployment of IPv4 addresses – 32-bit logical addresses that are written in a dotted-decimal notation. While 1983 may seem to be a long time ago, the internet is still in its early phases and continuously growing as more devices and organizations' networks are connecting to it. As the internet began to grow quickly, IPv4 addresses for the internet were determined to one day be exhausted over time. As early as 1999, the world began to see a new generation of logical addresses being deployed, known as IPv6 addresses. These are 128-bit logical addresses that are written in hexadecimal notation.

IANA implemented the concept of creating two logical address spaces for IPv4 to help reduce the depletion of IPv4 addresses around the world. In the next section, you will learn about the importance of these two IPv4 address spaces and how they are used to reduce wastage while ensuring private networks can communicate on the internet.

Public versus private address spaces

IANA created two separate IPv4 address spaces to help reduce the depletion of IPv4 addresses around the world. These IPv4 address spaces are known as the **public address space** and the **private address space**. The public address space specified the IPv4 addresses that are routable on the internet and can be assigned to devices that are directly connected to the internet. The private address space specifies the classes and ranges of IPv4 addresses that are non-routable on the internet and can be assigned to devices on private networks only.

The following table shows the public classes of IPv4 addresses:

Class	Range	Default Subnet Mask
A	0.0.0.1 - 127.255.255.255	255.0.0.0
B	128.0.0.1 - 191.255.255.255	255.255.0.0
C	192.0.0.1 - 223.255.255.255	255.255.255.0
D	224.0.0.1 - 239.255.255.255	N/A
E	240.0.0.1 - 255.255.255.255	

Figure 4.3 – IPv4 public address space

As shown in the preceding table, classes A, B and C can be assigned to devices that are directly connected to the internet. The Class D address range is used for multicast communication between applications and services that operate on devices within a network, and the Class E address range is reserved for experimental uses.

> **Important note**
> The subnet mask is used to determine the network and host portion of an IP address, and the total number of IP addresses and usable IP addresses within a network.

In the early days of the internet, the IPv4 address space didn't have a proper structure as it does in today's world. Originally, the IPv4 address spaces used **classful** addresses, which describe how each IPv4 address class contains a specific number of networks. Here, each network contains a specific number of usable/assignable IPv4 addresses to host devices.

To get a better idea, the following table shows the IPv4 classful addressing information:

Class	Range	Default Subnet Mask	Number of Networks	Number of Usable IPv4 Addresses
A	0.0.0.1 - 127.255.255.255	255.0.0.0	126	16,777,214
B	128.0.0.1 - 191.255.255.255	255.255.0.0	16,384	65,534
C	192.0.0.1 - 223.255.255.255	255.255.255.0	2,097,152	254

Figure 4.4 – Classful IPv4 addresses

As shown in the preceding table, the classes of IPv4 addresses are the same as the public address space. However, within the Class A range, there's a total of 126 networks and each of those networks contains 16,777,214 usable IPv4 addresses that can be assigned to hosts on a network. The Class B range provides a total of 16,384 networks and each of those networks contains 65,534 usable IPv4 addresses that can be assigned to host devices on a network. Lastly, the Class C range contains a total of 2,097,152 networks and each of those networks contains 254 usable IPv4 addresses for hosts on a network.

One of the major issues with classful addressing is the wastage of unused IP addresses within an organization. Imagine that an organization with 2,000 devices requires a network block of addresses to assign to their company's network. A Class B address block would be most suitable in this situation. However, since any Class B network provides 65,534 usable IPv4 addresses, there will be a huge wastage of 65,534 – 2000 = 63,534 unused addresses that cannot be allocated to another organization. Simply put, organizations that were assigned very large IPv4 network blocks with too many addresses led to wastage. Keep in mind that during the era of classful addressing, all devices on the internet and those within private networks of the organization were all using classful addressing (public IPv4 addresses) that was routable on the internet.

Furthermore, let's say an organization has 400 devices and needs IPv4 addresses to assign to its network. The organization will need to lease a Class B address block that contains too many IPv4 addresses or multiple Class C address blocks to support the number of hosts. Therefore, classful addressing was not flexible enough to support organizations of various sizes.

Additionally, when the internet used classful addressing, the routers within service providers' networks contained very large routing tables, which affected the performance of a router on forwarding a packet to its destination. The routing table within a router contains routes (paths) that indicate how to reach a destination network. Therefore, for every packet that enters a router, the destination IP address is observed and the router checks the routing table for a route that matches the destination IP address. The router checks the routing table from top to bottom each time it has to perform a route lookup, stops with a suitable route it found, and forwards the packet using the route information. Imagine if routers on the internet have a very huge routing table, containing all the classful networks of the internet. Here, each router will take some time to go through its routing table to find a destination path to forward a packet. This is another issue with classful addressing on the internet.

When working with classful addresses, everyone needed to use the default subnet mask with the corresponding address block that was assigned to their organization. Companies were not able to logically segment their networks into multiple IP subnetworks from a single network block, which was not flexible for businesses of different sizes. A simple example is a business with 90 host devices that would be assigned a Class C network block that contains 254 usable IPv4 addresses. Any unused IPv4 addresses were not reallocated to another organization.

The idea of using classful addressing on the internet was not flexible to support the growth of the internet and organizations and did not minimize the wastage of IPv4 addresses. One solution was to implement **classless** addresses, which removed the need to use a default subnet mask for a specific range of IPv4 addresses. In this case, a Class A IPv4 address does not need to use the default subnet mask of 255.0.0.0 in classless addressing. When using classless addressing, the rules of using the default subnet mask are not applied, allowing networking professionals to use custom subnet masks with any IPv4 address.

To help reduce the wastage of public IPv4 addresses, IANA created the private IPv4 address space, which allows organizations to use a specific set of IPv4 addresses on private networks. These private IPv4 addresses are non-routable on the internet, which means if a computer is assigned a private IPv4 address, it will not be able to communicate with devices on the internet and vice versa. Imagine if all devices within the private networks of organizations were configured with a unique public IPv4 address – the public address space would be exhausted a lot quicker than expected. Therefore, the private address space allows organizations to assign a unique private IPv4 address on devices within their private networks without worrying about depleting the available number of public IPv4 addresses on the internet.

The following table shows the private IPv4 address space:

Class	Range	Default Subnet Mask
A	10.0.0.1 - 10.255.255.255	255.0.0.0
B	172.16.0.1 - 172.31.255.255	255.255.0.0
C	192.168.0.1 - 192.168.255.255	255.255.255.0

Figure 4.5 – Private IPv4 address space

As shown in the preceding table, the private IPv4 address spaces contain three classes of address ranges. Each class of address can be used within any organization's private network. This means two or more organizations can be using the same private IPv4 address classes within their private networks without causing any conflict.

> **Important note**
>
> The private IPv4 address is defined by **RFC 1918**: `https://www.rfc-editor.org/rfc/rfc1918.html`.

Simply put, if a device such as a computer was configured with a private IPv4 address and was directly connected to the internet, communication will not occur between the computer and devices on a public network such as the internet. **Internet Service Providers** (**ISPs**) usually implement security mechanisms such as an **Access Control List** (**ACL**) to filter traffic originating from their customers' networks that have source private IPv4 addresses, therefore separating the private and public address spaces from meeting each other. Before devices on a private IPv4 network can communicate with devices with public IPv4 addresses on the internet, the source private IPv4 address has to be translated into a public address.

Next, you will learn about a very common IP service that allows a private IPv4 network to communicate with a public network such as the internet.

Network Address Translation (NAT)

Network Address Translation (**NAT**) is an IP service that is commonly found on almost all private networks within organizations. NAT allows a private IPv4 source address to be translated into a public IPv4 address, allowing devices on a private network to communicate with devices on a public network. Without NAT, the private and public IPv4 address spaces will not be able to communicate and this would create a major issue. Imagine that organizations are implementing a private IPv4 addressing scheme on their private, internal networks and can't communicate with any servers or devices on the internet. To help ensure devices on a private IPv4 network can communicate with the internet, a NAT-enabled router is implemented between the networks.

The following diagram shows an example of a NAT-enabled router between a private and public network:

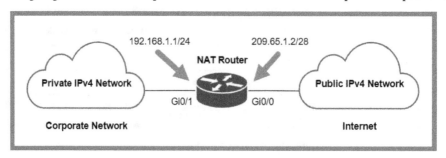

Figure 4.6 – NAT router

As shown in the preceding diagram, there's a private IPv4 network on the left that indicates an organization's private network while on the right there's the internet, where all devices are assigned a public IPv4 address. To interconnect these two different networks, a router is implemented to route traffic between the different networks. Additionally, to ensure devices on the private network can communicate with devices on the internet, NAT is configured on the router to translate any source IPv4 address that originates from the private network to the public IPv4 address that's configured on the router. Therefore, all outbound traffic from the corporate network to the internet will be assigned a new source IPv4 public address of 209.65.1.2. This allows devices on the internet to see the source traffic as originating from a device with a public IPv4 address of 209.65.1.2 and not from the private IPv4 network.

Usually, when a residential user subscribes to an internet service, the local ISP installs a modem on the customer's premises. The modem is a multi-functional device that allows the customer's private network to interconnect with the service provider's public network. Furthermore, the modem is preconfigured by the service provider to perform NAT, allowing the private IPv4 addresses of devices on the customer's network to be translated to the public IP address on the modem before the messages are sent out to the internet.

The following diagram is a visual representation of a NAT translation:

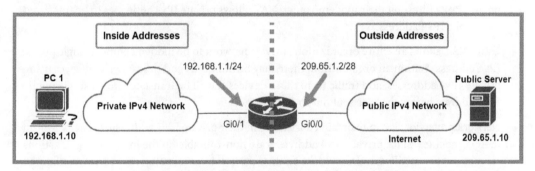

Figure 4.7 – NAT operations

As shown in the preceding diagram, all devices on the left are connected to the private IPv4 network, while all devices on the right are connected to the internet with a public IPv4 address. Additionally, the NAT-enabled router/modem identifies the addresses as **inside** and **outside**. The inside addresses are the private IPv4 addresses that are to be translated by the NAT-enabled router/modem. The outside addresses are those that are seen by all devices on the public address space – the internet. *PC 1* is connected to a private network within an organization and it's assigned a private IPv4 address of 192.168.1.10. This address is referred to as the Inside Local address. If *PC 1* attempts to send a message to the *Public Server* on the internet, the packets from *PC 1* will be restricted from entering the server provider's network and the internet.

The following steps explain how NAT works:

1. *PC 1* creates a packet with the source IPv4 address of 192.168.1.10 (*Inside Local*) and a destination address of 209.65.10 (*Outside Global*), and forwards the message to the default gateway (router) at 192.168.1.1.

2. The router inspects the source and destination IP addresses within the IP header of the packet to determine the destination and checks its routing table for a route (path).

3. Before the router forwards the packet to the internet, it translates the source private IPv4 address from 192.168.1.10 to the public IPv4 address on the router as 209.65.1.2 (*Inside Global*), then sends the packet to the destination server.

4. The *Public Server* will see the source IPv4 address of the packet as 209.65.1.2 (router) but not *PC 1* because NAT allows the private network to be hidden behind the public IPv4 address of the router.

The following are various advantages of using NAT on a network:

- The primary benefit of using NAT is to help conserve the public IPv4 address space by allowing organizations to use private IPv4 addresses on their internal networks and be assigned a single public IPv4 address on their modem/router. NAT allows private IPv4 addresses to be translated to a public IPv4 address.

- Using NAT allows an entire organization's private network to be hidden behind a single public IPv4 address. Within an organization, there may be hundreds and thousands of devices using private IPv4 addresses, and traffic from those devices can all be translated into a single public IPv4 address before they are sent out to the internet.

- Network professionals can maintain consistency in their private IPv4 addressing scheme within their companies. Since private IPv4 addresses are non-routable on the internet, organizations can use any private IPv4 address blocks on their private, internal networks. A NAT-configured router/modem handles all the translations of private IPv4 addresses to a public address.

While there are many benefits of using NAT on a network, there are some disadvantages that all network professionals need to know. The following are some disadvantages of NAT:

- Since the router or modem has to translate the private IPv4 address into a public one, network performance is affected. As traffic is sent to the router or modem to be translated before it is placed on the network, there is some delay as the router or modem has to perform the actual translation process.

- Since NAT modifies the IPv4 addresses on the packet, **Virtual Private Network** (**VPN**) solutions that use **IP security** (**IPsec**) to establish a secure logical tunnel over an unsecure network does not work well. When NAT changes the IPv4 addresses, it prevents the IPsec VPN tunnel from being successfully created.

- NAT modifies the IPv4 addresses within the packet, so end-to-end connectivity is lost between a sender and receiver. This makes it difficult for a receiver to determine the true source of a message, so the sender device can be hidden behind a public IP address on the internet.

Three types of NAT are commonly implemented within organizations by network professionals to allow devices on the private network to communicate with devices on the public network and vice versa. The following are the three common types of NAT:

- Static NAT

- Dynamic NAT

- **Port address translation (PAT)**

Static NAT allows network professionals to create a one-to-one mapping between an *Inside Local* address such as a private IPv4 address on an internal server to an *Inside Global* address such as the public IPv4 address on the router/modem internet-facing interface.

The following diagram shows an example of using Static NAT to access an internal web server:

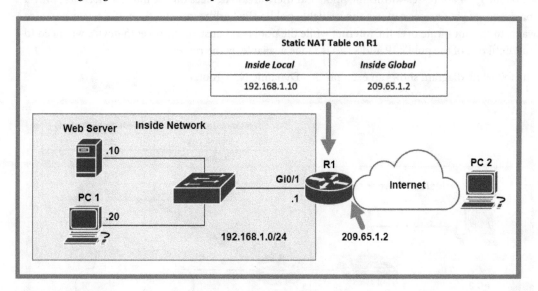

Figure 4.8 – Static NAT

As shown in the preceding diagram, there's an internal web server on a private IPv4 network that is inaccessible by any device on the internet. Network professionals can use Static NAT to create a one-to-one mapping between the private IPv4 address of the server (192.168.1.10) and the public IPv4 address on the router (209.65.1.2). Therefore, whenever a device on the internet such as *PC 2* connects to the public IPv4 address of 209.65.1.2, the router will forward all packets to 192.168.1.10, the internal web server. The user on the internet, *PC 2*, will not see the private IPv4 address on the internal network because it's being hidden behind the public IPv4 address on the router.

> **Important note**
>
> When using Static NAT, the one-to-one mapping remains as-is on the router or modem until it's modified by the network professional. Keep in mind that Static NAT mapping will forward all traffic types between a public IP address to a private IP address.

Whenever a company hosts an internal web server, they can either obtain a public IP address from their local ISP or assign a private IPv4 address and use static NAT to allow users from the internet to access the private internal server. Internet users would simply use the public IP address; when the organization's NAT-enabled router receives inbound traffic from the internet, the router checks for any valid NAT mappings for a valid entry. Once an entry is found, the traffic is sent to the private internal host. The internet user would think the server has a public address and not realize a NAT translation is taking place in the background.

Dynamic NAT allows network professionals to create a many-to-many mapping between multiple private IPv4 addresses and public IPv4 addresses address. In dynamic NAT, a pool of public IPv4 addresses are assigned to the private IPv4 addresses on a first come, first served basis. If there are six public IPv4 addresses within the pool, and there are 50 devices on the internal network, only a maximum of six devices can use the available public IPv4 addresses at a time. If a seventh device wants to communicate over the internet while the pool is exhausted, the seventh device will need to wait until one of the public IP addresses is made available by the router.

The following diagram shows an example of a Dynamic NAT router:

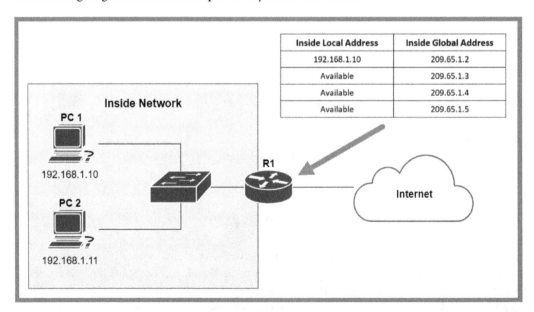

Inside Local Address	Inside Global Address
192.168.1.10	209.65.1.2
Available	209.65.1.3
Available	209.65.1.4
Available	209.65.1.5

Figure 4.9 – Dynamic NAT

As shown in the preceding diagram, when *PC 1* wants to communicate with a device on the internet, the router will check the NAT pool for an available public IPv4 address to translate the source private IPv4 address into a public address before forwarding the packet to the destination on the internet. While *PC 1* is using the 209.65.0.1 address, if another internal device such as *PC 2* wants to communicate with a server on the internet, the same process occurs on the NAT-enabled router and uses the next available public IPv4 address within the pool. However, if all addresses within the NAT pool are being used, additional devices on the internal network will need to wait until an address becomes available.

Port address translation (PAT), sometimes referred to as **NAT overload**, is one of the most common types of NAT that is found within many organizations and residential internet subscriber networks. PAT allows organizations and home users to perform a many-to-one translation. PAT allows multiple devices with private IPv4 addresses on the internal network to translate their source address to a single public IPv4 address using a NAT-enabled router or modem.

PAT is the most conservative type of NAT within the industry as it allows ISPs to assign a single public IPv4 address to each organization. The network professionals within companies can configure their routers to perform NAT overload, allowing multiple devices to translate their private addresses to the same public address for communication on the internet. Unlike Static and Dynamic NAT, NAT overload includes the source and destination service port numbers of each communication. Using the source and destination service port numbers allows the NAT-enabled router to uniquely identify and track each communication between the private (inside) and public (outside) networks.

The following diagram shows an example of NAT overload:

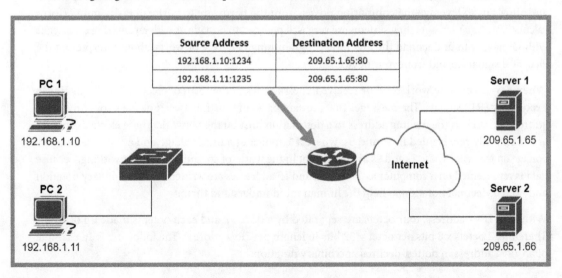

Source Address	Destination Address
192.168.1.10:1234	209.65.1.65:80
192.168.1.11:1235	209.65.1.65:80

PC 1
192.168.1.10

PC 2
192.168.1.11

Internet

Server 1
209.65.1.65

Server 2
209.65.1.66

Figure 4.10 – Port address translation

As shown in the preceding diagram, when *PC 1* wants to communicate with *Server 1* on the internet, *PC 1* creates a message to include the source and destination IPv4 addresses and service port numbers. When the message arrives at the NAT-enabled router or modem, the router records the source IPv4 address and service port number. Then, it translates the source private IPv4 address to the public IPv4 address while the source service port number remains unchanged. The NAT-enabled router keeps track of all translations, so any returning traffic from *Server 1* will be forwarded to *PC 1* only.

Having completed this section, you should now be able to describe the private and public IPv4 address spaces. You also discovered the various types of NAT and their use cases. In the next section, you will gain a deeper understanding of IPv4 and IPv6 address types.

Exploring the structure of IPv4 and IPv6

As an aspiring network professional, it's important to understand the structure of both IPv4 and IPv6 addresses and how they differ from each other. In this section, you will learn how to convert IPv4 addresses from binary into decimal and vice versa, and explore various address types and their use cases on a network.

Fundamentals of IPv4

Working with computers and servers is quite fascinating for many people as the age of technology is ever-growing and continuously evolving in so many ways. When working with computers or even an IoT device such as a smartphone, there's an operating system that controls the hardware components and allows us to leverage the computing power from the hardware to perform tasks and perform calculations. As a user, operating systems are very well polished to provide us with an amazing experience without having to understand the low-level programming language or worry about interpreting the electrical signals to and from your device.

When devices on a network send or receive a message, it's in the form of electrical, light, or **Radio Frequency** (**RF**) signals. The messages that are sent back and forth between devices contain logical addressing, such as the mailing address to a destination host on the network. These electrical signals are commonly represented in 1s and 0s, where a 1 indicates a high voltage and a 0 indicates a low voltage on the wire. These 1s and 0s are important in the world of computing and networking, because data is represented on a computer as 1s and 0s, and IP addresses are written in dotted-binary notation and dotted-decimal notation to help the human mind understand them.

Within an IPv4 address, four octets are separated by a dot (.), and each octet is made up of 8 bits. Therefore, 4 octets x 8 bits per octet = 32 bits in length per IPv4 address. The following is an example of an IPv4 address in dotted-decimal and binary notation:

	1st Octet	2nd Octet	3rd Octet	4th Octet
Dotted Decimal	192	168	10	20
Binary	1100 0000	1010 1000	0000 1010	0001 0100

Figure 4.11 – IPv4 address format

As shown in the preceding diagram, each octet has a total of 8 bits and each octet is separated with a dot (.), so the IPv4 address is 192.168.10.20 = 11000000.10101000.00001010.0 0010100. As an aspiring network professional, it's essential to learn how to convert IPv4 addresses between decimal and binary. This skill is needed to better understand how to perform subnetting and determine network ranges.

Converting binary into decimal

Let's take a further look into the format of an IPv4 address with its binary format. Since an IPv4 address is 32 bits in length with four octets, the following is an example of an IPv4 address in binary notation:

```
11000000.10101000.00000001.10000001
```

When presented with a binary number, the challenge is to convert the dotted-binary number into a dotted-decimal number. To better understand how the conversion process works, first, you need to understand the purpose of a base system or radix in mathematics. The radix (base) is a unique number that is used in a positioning system. In binary, the base is 2, so the radix is the number 2. Using the positioning system, the first position value (starting from right to left) is 0 to 7.

The following table shows base 2 (radix) when used in the positioning system with 8 bits (one octet):

Radix	2^7	2^6	2^5	2^4	2^3	2^2	2^1	2^0
Decimal	128	64	32	16	8	4	2	1

Figure 4.12 – Base 2 positioning system

Why did we use the range from 0 to 7 as our positioning values? We need to remember that the number zero (0) is the first of natural numbers and an integer on the numerical table, hence the reason we started with 2^0 as the first position. On the other hand, the last position is 2^7. This position represents the 8th position on the table. Since there are 8 bits in an octet, whenever you are converting an IPv4 address from binary into decimal notation, ensure you convert one octet at a time. This prevents any confusion or miscalculations during the conversion process.

> **Important note**
> In the world of mathematics, it's important to remember the rule that $A^0 = 1$.

To express the remaining positions with the radix of 2, the following is a further breakdown:

- $2^0 = 1$
- $2^1 = 2 \times 1 = 2$
- $2^2 = 2 \times 2 = 4$
- $2^3 = 2 \times 2 \times 2 = 8$
- $2^4 = 2 \times 2 \times 2 \times 2 = 16$
- $2^5 = 2 \times 2 \times 2 \times 2 \times 2 = 32$
- $2^6 = 2 \times 2 \times 2 \times 2 \times 2 \times 2 = 64$
- $2^7 = 2 \times 2 \times 2 \times 2 \times 2 \times 2 \times 2 = 128$

Additionally, the following list shows the full binary format to express each position value within an octet:

- $2^0 = 00000001 = 1$
- $2^1 = 00000010 = 2$
- $2^2 = 00000100 = 4$
- $2^3 = 00001000 = 8$
- $2^4 = 00010000 = 16$
- $2^5 = 00100000 = 32$
- $2^6 = 01000000 = 64$
- $2^7 = 10000000 = 128$

Now let's apply the theory to converting the IPv4 address of `11000000.10101000.00000001`
`.10000001` into a dotted-decimal notation. To perform this exercise, follow these steps:

1. Let's start with the first octet and place its values within the table, as shown here:

Radix	2^7	2^6	2^5	2^4	2^3	2^2	2^1	2^0
Decimal	128	64	32	16	8	4	2	1
Binary	1	1	0	0	0	0	0	0

Figure 4.13 – Converting the first octet

As shown in the preceding table, each bit value is aligned with the positioning system. Let's consider the columns with a binary number of 1. Here, the radix decimal value is ON. Therefore, within the table, both the 2^7 and 2^6 values are ON. This provides the following calculations:

$2^7 + 2^6 = 128 + 64 = 192$

2. Using the same principle from the previous step, let's assign the values of the second octet within the positioning system to determine its decimal value:

Radix	2^7	2^6	2^5	2^4	2^3	2^2	2^1	2^0
Decimal	128	64	32	16	8	4	2	1
Binary	1	0	1	0	1	0	0	0

Figure 4.14 – Converting the second octet

As shown in the preceding table, the bits that are 1 (ON) are 2^7, 2^5, and 2^3. This provides the following decimal value:

$2^7 + 2^5 + 2^3 = 128 + 32 + 8 = 168$

3. Next, let's convert the third octet by placing its bit values within the positioning systems, as shown in the following table:

Radix	2^7	2^6	2^5	2^4	2^3	2^2	2^1	2^0
Decimal	128	64	32	16	8	4	2	1
Binary	0	0	0	0	0	0	0	1

Figure 4.15 – Converting the third octet

As shown in the preceding table, the bit that's ON is $2^0 = 1$.

4. Next, let's convert the fourth octet by placing its bit values within the positioning system once more:

Radix	2^7	2^6	2^5	2^4	2^3	2^2	2^1	2^0
Decimal	128	64	32	16	8	4	2	1
Binary	1	0	0	0	0	0	0	1

Figure 4.16 – Converting the fourth octet

As shown in the preceding table, the following bit values are ON:

$$2^7 + 2^0 = 128 + 1 = 129$$

5. The final step is simply putting everything all together: `11000000.10101000.0000000` `1.10000001` = `192.168.1.129`.

> **Important note**
>
> If all bits are 1s within an octet, the total value will be `255`. This means each octet ranges from 0 to 255. This implies a valid IPv4 address will never have an octet greater than `255`.

Now that you have the skills to convert an IPv4 address from binary into decimal, let's take a look at converting an IPv4 address from decimal into binary.

Converting decimal into binary

In this exercise, you will learn how to use an eight-step method to convert an IPv4 address, `172.19.43.67`, from decimal into binary, one octet at a time. This eight-step method leverages the radix values in a slightly different approach while using basic subtraction to determine whether a bit is a 1 or 0.

The following are some guidelines to ensure the results are accurate:

- Always convert one octet at a time
- Always begin by subtracting the highest power of 2, which is 2^7 = `128`, while working downwards to the lowest power of 2, which is 2^0 = `1`
- If you can subtract the decimal number from the radix value, place a `1`
- If you are unable to subtract the decimal number from the radix value, place a `0`
- If you get a `0`, then subtract the decimal number from the next lower radix value

Let's start by converting the first octet, `172`, from decimal into binary with the following steps:

1. Is 172 – 128 (2^7) possible? Yes, with a remainder value of 44. Place a **1**.
2. Next, is 44 – 64 (2^6) possible? No, so carry the 44 forward to be subtracted from the next lower power of 2. Place a **0**.
3. Next, is 44 – 32 (2^5) possible? Yes, with a remainder value of 12. Place a **1**.
4. Next, is 12 - 16 (2^4) possible? No, so carry the 12 forward to be subtracted from the next lower power of 2. Place a **0**.
5. Next, is 12 – 8 (2^3) possible? Yes, with a remainder value of 4. Place a **1**.
6. Next, is 4 – 4 (2^2) possible? Yes, with a remainder value of 0. Place a **1**.

7. Next, is 0 – 2 (2¹) possible? No, so place a **0**.

8. Lastly, is 0 – 1 (2⁰) possible? No, so place a **0**.

Using the 1s and 0s from *Steps 1* to *8*, the binary value is `172 = 10101100`.

The following diagram shows a visual representation of each step during the calculation process of converting 172 into a binary number:

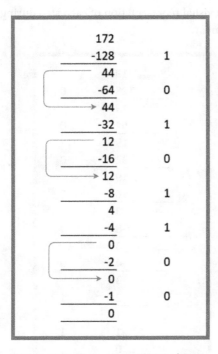

Figure 4.17 – Converting 172 into binary

Next, let's convert the second octet, `19`, from decimal into binary:

1. Is 19 – 128 (2^7) possible? No, so carry the 19 forward to be subtracted from the next lower power of 2. Place a **0**.

2. Next, is 19 – 64 (2^6) possible? No, so carry the 19 forward to be subtracted from the next lower power of 2. Place a **0**.

3. Next, is 19 – 32 (2^5) possible? No, so carry the 19 forward to be subtracted from the next lower power of 2. Place a **0**.

4. Next, is 19 - 16 (2^4) possible? Yes, with a remainder value of 3. Place a **1**.

5. Next, is 3 – 8 (2^3) possible? No, so carry the 3 forward to be subtracted from the next lower power of 2. Place a **0**.

6. Next, is 3 – 4 (2^2) possible? No, so carry the 3 forward to be subtracted from the next lower power of 2. Place a **0**.

7. Next, is 3 – 2 (2^1) possible? Yes, with a remainder value of 1. Place a **1**.

8. Lastly, is 1 – 1 (2^0) possible? Yes, with a remainder value of 0. Place a **1**.

Using the 1s and 0s from *Steps* 1 to 8, the binary value is 19 = 00010011.

The following diagram shows a visual representation of each step during the calculation process of converting 19 into a binary number:

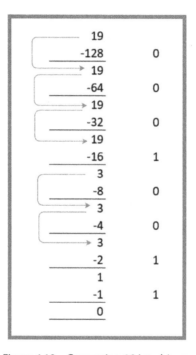

Figure 4.18 – Converting 19 into binary

Next, let's convert the third octet, 43, from decimal to binary:

1. Is 43 – 128 (2^7) possible? No, so carry the 43 forward to be subtracted from the next lower power of 2. Place a **0**.

2. Next, is 43 – 64 (2^6) possible? No, so carry the 43 forward to be subtracted from the next lower power of 2. Place a **0**.

3. Next, is 43 – 32 (2^5) possible? Yes, with a remainder value of 11. Place a **1**.

4. Next, is 11 - 16 (2^4) possible? No, so carry the 11 forward to be subtracted from the next lower power of 2. Place a **0**.

5.   Next, is 11 − 8 (2³) possible? Yes, with a remainder value of 3. Place a **1**.

6.   Next, is 3 − 4 (2²) possible? No, so carry the 3 forward to be subtracted from the next lower power of 2. Place a **0**.

7.   Next, is 3 − 2 (2¹) possible? Yes, with a remainder value of 1. Place a **1**.

8.   Lastly, is 1 − 1 (2⁰) possible? Yes, with a remainder value of 0. Place a **1**.

Using the 1s and 0s from *Steps* 1 to 8, the binary value is 43 = 00101011.

The following diagram shows a visual representation of each step during the calculation process of converting 43 into a binary number:

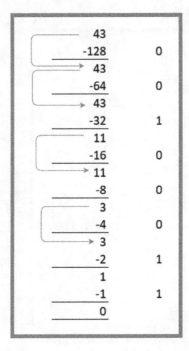

Figure 4.19 – Converting 43 into binary

Next, let's convert the third octet, 67, from decimal into binary:

1.   Is 67 − 128 (2⁷) possible? No, so carry the 67 forward to be subtracted from the next lower power of 2. Place a **0**.

2.   Next, is 67 − 64 (2⁶) possible? Yes, with a remainder value of 3. Place a **1**.

3.   Next, is 3 − 32 (2⁵) possible? No, so carry the 3 forward to be subtracted from the next lower power of 2. Place a **0**.

4.   Next, is 3 - 16 (2⁴) possible? No, so carry the 3 forward to be subtracted from the next lower power of 2. Place a **0**.

5. Next, is 3 – 8 (2³) possible? No, so carry the 3 forward to be subtracted from the next lower power of 2. Place a **0**.

6. Next, is 3 – 4 (2²) possible? No, so carry the 3 forward to be subtracted from the next lower power of 2. Place a **0**.

7. Next, is 3 – 2 (2¹) possible? Yes, with a remainder value of 1. Place a **1**.

8. Lastly, is 1 – 1 (2⁰) possible? Yes, with a remainder value of 0. Place a **1**.

Using the 1s and 0s from *Steps* 1 to 8, the binary value is 67 = 01000011.

The following diagram shows a visual representation of each step during the calculation process of converting 67 into a binary number:

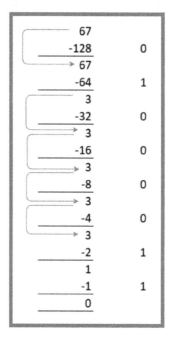

Figure 4.20 – Converting 67 into binary

Lastly, let's put everything all together and view the binary notation of 172.19.43.67:

	1st Octet	2nd Octet	3rd Octet	4th Octet
Decimal	172	19	43	67
Binary	10101100	00010011	00101011	01000011

Figure 4.21 – Binary and decimal notation

As shown in the preceding table, the IPv4 address is `172.19.43.67` = `10101100.0001001` `1.00101011.01000011`.

Understanding how to convert between binary and decimal is an essential skill within networking as you will need it to understand how to break down an IPv4 network block into smaller subnetworks.

In the next section, you will explore IPv6 concepts and discover the differences between IPv4 and IPv6 addresses.

Fundamentals of IPv6

Like IPv4, this new address has a format of its own. As you may recall, an IPv4 address consists of 32 bits in length and it's written in dotted-decimal notation for easier reading to the human mind. An IPv6 address consists of 128 bits in length and is written in hexadecimal notation. Hexadecimal contains both numbers and letters in the following range:

```
0 1 2 3 4 5 6 7 8 9 A B C D E F
```

This 128-bit address allows IPv6 to scale to 2^{128} IPv6 addresses, which allows 3.4×10^{38} IPv6 addresses that can be uniquely assigned to devices. Each IPv6 address is made up of 128 bits that are grouped into eight (8) hextets. Each hextet contains 16 bits, so `8 hextets x 16 bits per hextet = 128 bits` in length per IPv6 address.

The following is an example of an IPv6 address:

```
2001:0DB8:0000:1111:0000:0000:0000:0200
```

Notice each hextet contains hexadecimal values between `0` and `F` and each hextet is separated by a colon (`:`). In hexadecimal, the least value is `0` and the highest value is `F`, so each hextet ranges from `0000` to `FFFF`.

> **Important note**
> When writing or entering the values of an IPv6 address on a device, the letters are not case-sensitive, which means both lowercase and uppercase are accepted on both ends, as well as on networking devices.

Let's break down the following IPv6 address into a more simplified version:

```
2001:0DB8:0000:1111:0000:0000:0000:0200
```

First, all leading 0s in a hextet can be removed. When there are two or more hextets that are all zeros, a double colon (`::`) is used to replace the consecutive zeros within the IPv6 address. The following is a simplified version of the original IPv6 address:

```
2001:DB8:0:1111:0:0:0:200
```

Then, replace consecutive zero-only hextets with a double colon (: :). The following is a further simplified version:

```
2001:DB8:0:1111::200
```

> **Important note**
> The double colon (: :) can be used once in an IPv6 address.

Furthermore, when configuring an IPv6 address on a device such as a computer, server, or even a router, the host operating system of the device will accept both the full length of the address and the shortened versions. However, as an aspiring network professional, it's important to understand how to create the most simplified version of an IPv6 address.

As with all IPv4 addresses, there's usually a subnet mask to accompany it. The same also applies to IPv6. The default subnet mask or prefix length of an IPv6 address is /64. This means the first 64 bits of the IPv6 address represent the network portion of the address and the second portion represents the interface ID.

The following diagram shows the parts of an IPv6 address:

2001 :	0DB8 :	0000 :	1111 :	0000 :	0000 :	0000 :	0200
Global Routing Prefix			Subnet	Interface ID			

Figure 4.22 – IPv6 address structure

As shown in the preceding snippet, the first three hextets represent the **Global Routing Prefix** portion, which contains the first 48 bits of the address. This portion of the IPv6 address is assigned by the service provider such as the ISP. The fourth hextet (16 bits) represents the **Subnet** ID, which is used by the ISP to create subnetworks of the network block. The last 64 bits represent the **Interface ID** portion. Combining the Global Routing Prefix, Subnet ID, and Interface ID, a client is assigned a unique 128-bit IPv6 address on its network interface card.

Having completed this section, you have learned the fundamentals of both IPv4 and IPv6 addressing structures. In the next section, you will discover several addresses and their use cases on a network.

Types of IPv4 and IPv6 addresses

There are various types of IPv4 and IPv6 addresses and it's important to understand them as an aspiring network professional. In this section, you will gain a solid understanding of the key characteristics of each address type and discover their role in networks.

Automatic Private IP Addressing (APIPA)

When a client device such as a computer or even a smartphone is connected to a wired or wireless network, the device is automatically assigned an IPv4 or IPv6 address from a **Dynamic Host Configuration Protocol** (**DHCP**) server. In large organizations, companies usually implement one or more dedicated DHCP servers on the network to ensure redundancy and proper distribution of IP addresses to nodes on the network. However, within smaller environments such as **Small Office Home Offices** (**SOHOs**), you will likely not see a dedicated DHCP server. Rather, the modem or router you've been provided by the ISP provides the DHCP services for clients on the LAN.

What if a computer connects to a network and does not receive an IP address? What happens? There are many reasons a client device may not receive an IP address from the network, as follows:

- The client is unable to communicate with the DHCP server on the network
- The client is configured to use a static IP address that does not change
- The DHCP server is not present or offline on the network

By default, many client devices are configured to automatically communicate with a DHCP server and receive an IP address from it. However, if a client is unable to reach the DHCP server on the network, the client will automatically assign itself a special unique IPv4 address ranging from 169.254.0.1 to 169.254.255.254 with a default subnet mask of 255.255.0.0. This is a feature known as **Automatic Private IP Addressing** (**APIPA**), which is built into many operating systems such as Microsoft Windows.

> **Important note**
> On an IPv4 network, the APIPA address is sometimes referred to as an IPv4 **Link-Local** address. However, APIPA is a Microsoft-specific term for "Link-Local," which is preferred for Linux-based operating systems.

The following screenshot shows a Windows 10 client using an APIPA address on the network:

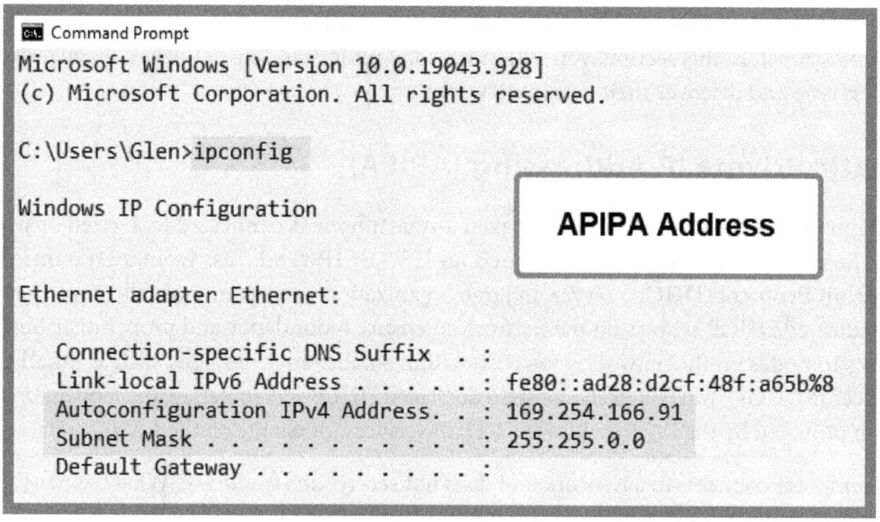

```
Command Prompt
Microsoft Windows [Version 10.0.19043.928]
(c) Microsoft Corporation. All rights reserved.

C:\Users\Glen>ipconfig

Windows IP Configuration                      APIPA Address


Ethernet adapter Ethernet:

   Connection-specific DNS Suffix  . :
   Link-local IPv6 Address . . . . . : fe80::ad28:d2cf:48f:a65b%8
   Autoconfiguration IPv4 Address. . : 169.254.166.91
   Subnet Mask . . . . . . . . . . . : 255.255.0.0
   Default Gateway . . . . . . . . . :
```

Figure 4.23 – APIPA address on a client

As shown in the preceding screenshot, the ipconfig command allows network professionals to view the local **Network Interface Card** (**NIC**) or network adapters on a Windows device and verify the IP addressing details on each network adapter. Furthermore, notice that the network adapter is using an IPv4 address that belongs to the APIPA range. Linux-based operating systems will use commands such as ifconfig, iwconfig, or ip instead of ipconfig.

Extended unique identifier (EUI-64)

On an IPv6 network, network professionals usually implement DHCPv6 servers to provide IPv6 addresses to clients. The DHCPv6 server keeps a record of each client that receives an IPv6 address and the lease time. However, on some IPv6 networks, network professionals implement a stateless IPv6 technology known as **Stateless Address Autoconfiguration** (**SLAAC**) that helps clients obtain global unicast IPv6 addresses on the network. One of the main differences between SLAAC and DHCPv6 is that SLAAC does not keep a record of each client's IPv6 address assignment or details.

When using SLAAC on an IPv6 network, SLAAC provides the network portion of the IPv6 address to the client – that is, the first 64 bits of the IPv6 address. The client uses a process known as **Extended Unique Identifier 64** (**EUI-64**) to convert its 48-bit **Media Access Control** (**MAC**) address into a 64-bit address, which will become the Interface ID portion of the IPv6 address. This allows the client to combine the 64-bit network prefix and the newly created EUI-64 address to create the 128-bit IPv6 address for the network adapter.

To get a better understanding of the EUI-64 process, let's imagine a computer is connected to an IPv6 network and is seeking a DHCPv6 server. However, SLAAC is enabled on the network and provides the client with `2001:DB8:0:1111::/64`, the network portion of the IPv6 address for its network adapter. The 48-bit MAC address is used on the computer's network adapter and the EUI-64 process is used to create the 64-bit interface ID portion of a 128-bit IPv6 address.

The following steps describe the EUI-64 process of converting a 48-bit MAC address of a network adapter to create a 64-bit address that will be used as the interface ID portion to create a unique IPv6 address:

1. First, split the 48-bit MAC address into half, separating the **Organizational Unique Identifier (OUI)** and the device portions, as shown in the following diagram:

FC	99	47		75	CE	E0
11111100	10011001	01000111		01110101	11001110	11100000

Figure 4.24 – EUI-64 process step 1

2. Next, insert the hexadecimal value, `FFFE`, in the middle of the 48-bit MAC address, as shown in the following diagram:

FC	99	47	FF	FE	75	CE	E0
11111100	10011001	01000111	**11111111**	**11111110**	01110101	11001110	11100000

Figure 4.25 – EUI-64 process step 2

> **Important note**
> FFFE is a value reserved by IEEE and can only appear in a EUI-64 generated from a EUI-48 MAC address.

3. Next, flip the seventh bit within the first byte so that a 0 will become a 1 or a 1 will become a 0. This bit indicates if the NIC is administered locally (0) or is globally unique (1), as shown in the following diagram:

11111110	10011001	01000111	**11111111**	**11111110**	01110101	11001110	11100000

Figure 4.26 – EUI-64 process step 3

4. Next, convert the binary into hexadecimal to view the EUI-64 portion of the address, as shown in the following diagram:

| FE | 99 | 47 | FF | FE | 75 | CE | E0 |

Figure 4.27 – EUI-64 process step 4

5. Lastly, putting it all together, the EUI-64 bit IPv6 address that will be assigned to the device's network adapter is 2001:DB8:0:1111:FE99:47FF:FE75:CEE0.

> **Tip**
>
> To easily identify a EUI-64 address, the hexadecimal value of FFFE is always in the middle of the Interface ID portion of the IPv6 address.

The following screenshot shows a Cisco router with a EUI-64 IPv6 address on its interface:

```
R1#show ipv6 interface gigabitEthernet 0/1
GigabitEthernet0/1 is up, line protocol is up
  IPv6 is enabled, link-local address is FE80::240:BFF:FE49:A302
  No Virtual link-local address(es):
  Global unicast address(es):
    2001:DB8:1:1::1, subnet is 2001:DB8:1:1::/64
```

Figure 4.28 – EUI-64 address on a router

As shown in the preceding screenshot, the IPv6 address can easily be identified as the result of the EUI-64 process since FFFE is within the middle section of the Interface ID portion of the address.

Unicast

Unicast addresses can be IPv4 and IPv6 addresses that are uniquely assigned to the network adapter of a device. Using a unicast address allows **one-to-one** communication between a sender and receiver device over a network.

The following diagram shows an example of a unicast network transmission between two devices:

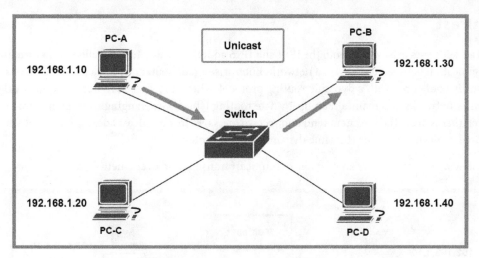

Figure 4.29 – Unicast communication

As shown in the preceding diagram, each device is assigned a unique IPv4 address on the network. Additionally, the IP address that's configured on each device is a unique unicast address, which allows any device to communicate with another device.

The following screenshot shows an interface on a Cisco IOS router that's been configured with a unicast address:

```
R1#show ipv6 interface gigabitEthernet 0/1
GigabitEthernet0/1 is up, line protocol is up
  IPv6 is enabled, link-local address is FE80::240:BFF:FE49:A302
  No Virtual link-local address(es):
  Global unicast address(es):
    2001:DB8:1:1::1, subnet is 2001:DB8:1:1::/64
```

Figure 4.30 – IPv6 unicast address

As shown in the preceding screenshot, the **Global Unicast Address** (**GUA**) is configured on the GigabitEthernet 0/1 interface on the router. This IPv6 address is similar to a public IPv4 address that is routable on the internet. The GUA IPv6 addresses are globally unique on the internet as they are routable on the internet. At the time of writing, GUA IPv6 addresses use the 2000::/3 network block of addresses.

Multicast

Multicast addresses exist within both the IPv4 and IPv6 address spaces. Multicast allows **one-to-many** communication between devices on a network. Enterprise-grade routers within a large organization are usually configured with a dynamic routing protocol, which allows each router to automatically learn new networks and maintain an up-to-date routing table by exchanging routing information between themselves. These routers send and receive messages to a multicast address group, which is only used by devices running the same dynamic routing protocol.

The following diagram shows an example of multicast transmission over a network:

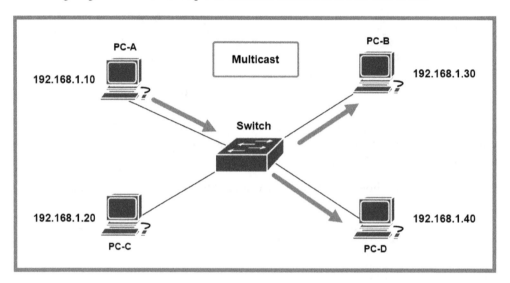

Figure 4.31 – Multicast communication

As shown in the preceding diagram, *PC-A* uses multicast to send messages to all devices that belong to the same multicast address group. Multicast IPv6 addresses have a network prefix of FF00::/8. The following is a list of IPv6 multicast addresses and their designated groups:

- FF02::1/12: All IPv6-enabled nodes on a network
- FF02::2/12: All IPv6-enabled routers on a network
- FF02::5/12: All routers that are running the **Open Shortest Path First** (**OSPF**) dynamic routing protocol
- FF02::A/12: All routers that are running the **Enhanced Interior Gateway Routing Protocol** (**EIGRP**) dynamic routing protocol

Next, you will learn about broadcast network transmission.

Broadcast

Broadcast allows **one-to-all** communication over an IPv4 network. Unlike IPv4 networks, IPv6 does not use broadcast addresses. Simply put, a computer that's connected to a network can send a single message to the network's broadcast address, which allows all devices within the same IP network to receive the message from the sender. Within a network that uses a Network ID of 192.168.1.0 and has a subnet mask of 255.255.255.0, the broadcast IP address will be 192.168.1.255.

The following diagram shows an example of broadcast transmission over a network:

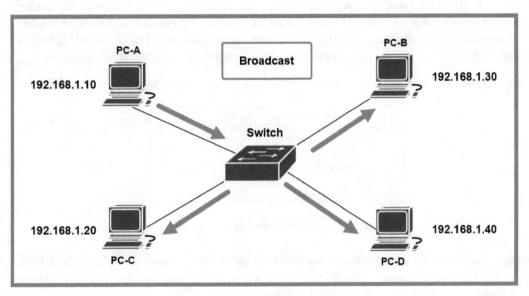

Figure 4.32 – Broadcast communication

As shown in the preceding diagram, *PC-A* sends a message to 192.168.1.255 and the message is delivered to all devices within the same IP network range. Keep in mind that having too many broadcast messages can affect the overall performance of the network, causing packet loss and high latency (slow response time) between devices.

Anycast

Anycast addresses exist on IPv6 networks and are used for **one-to-nearest** communication between devices over a network. Anycast allows the same unicast IPv6 address to be shared between multiple devices, such as servers on the internet. When a client such as a computer sends a message to an anycast IPv6 address, the message is delivered to the geographically nearest server that's configured with the anycast address.

Link-local

On an IPv6 network, each device is assigned two IPv6 addresses on its network adapter. One of the addresses is the IPv6 unicast address, which is used by the device when communicating with other hosts outside its local network. If the computer on an internal network within an organization wants to communicate with a server on the internet, the IPv6 unicast address will be used for this type of communication.

Additionally, an IPv6 **Link-Local** address is assigned to the same network adapter with the IPv6 unicast address. The IPv6 Link-Local address is used when devices are communicating with each other on the same IPv6 local area network. This address is unique in the same IPv6 network, which means another IPv6 network can be using the same range of IPv6 Link-Local addresses. IPv6 Link-Local addresses belong to the FE80::/10 network block. This address is similar to the IPv4 APIPA addresses.

The following screenshot shows the interfaces on a Cisco router assigned IPv6 Link-Local addresses:

```
R1#show ipv6 interface brief
GigabitEthernet0/0          [up/up]
    FE80::1
    2001:DB8:1:1::1
GigabitEthernet0/1          [up/up]
    FE80::1
    2001:DB8:1:2::1
```

Figure 4.33 – Link-local addresses on a router

As shown in the preceding screenshot, the interfaces on the Cisco router are assigned both IPv6 unicast and link-local addresses. The IPv6 link-local addresses can easily be identified as they begin with FE80 as the first hextet within the IPv6 address.

Loopback

On a device, whether it's a computer or even a networking device, there's an operating system that controls the hardware-based components and leverages the computing power to perform tasks and operations. On a system, there are running services that allow the operating system to perform tasks in the background and applications to provide additional functionality. However, the host operating system sometimes needs to communicate with these running services, the application, and itself. The loopback address allows a host device to send network traffic to itself, which allows network professionals to determine whether the **Transmission Control Protocol/Internet Protocol** (**TCP/IP**) network model is working properly on the local device.

The IPv4 loopback address ranges from 127.0.0.1 to 127.255.255.254 and has a default subnet mask of 255.0.0.0 (/8). However, it's quite common for network professionals to identify 127.0.0.1 as the loopback address as it's the first IPv4 address within the range, and it's mostly used when testing the loopback connectivity on a device.

The following screenshot shows how to test the loopback on a Windows operating system using the IPv4 loopback address:

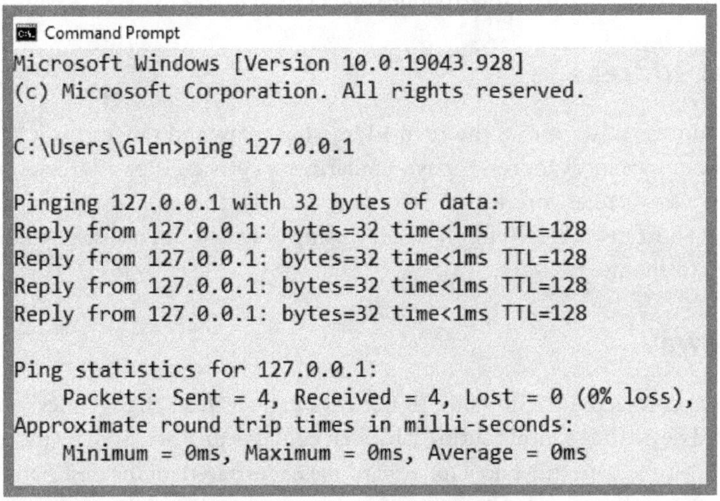

```
Command Prompt
Microsoft Windows [Version 10.0.19043.928]
(c) Microsoft Corporation. All rights reserved.

C:\Users\Glen>ping 127.0.0.1

Pinging 127.0.0.1 with 32 bytes of data:
Reply from 127.0.0.1: bytes=32 time<1ms TTL=128
Reply from 127.0.0.1: bytes=32 time<1ms TTL=128
Reply from 127.0.0.1: bytes=32 time<1ms TTL=128
Reply from 127.0.0.1: bytes=32 time<1ms TTL=128

Ping statistics for 127.0.0.1:
    Packets: Sent = 4, Received = 4, Lost = 0 (0% loss),
Approximate round trip times in milli-seconds:
    Minimum = 0ms, Maximum = 0ms, Average = 0ms
```

Figure 4.34 – IPv4 loopback address

As shown in the preceding screenshot, the ping tool was used to send four **Internet Control Message Protocol (ICMP) Echo Request** messages to the localhost using the IPv4 loopback address and the host responded to each message sent. This is an indication that TCP/IP is working fine for IPv4 connectivity.

In the IPv6 space, the loopback address is ::1/128, which allows network professionals to perform the same loopback testing on the TCP/IP network model on the local device. The following screenshot shows how to test the loopback on a Windows operating system using the IPv6 loopback address:

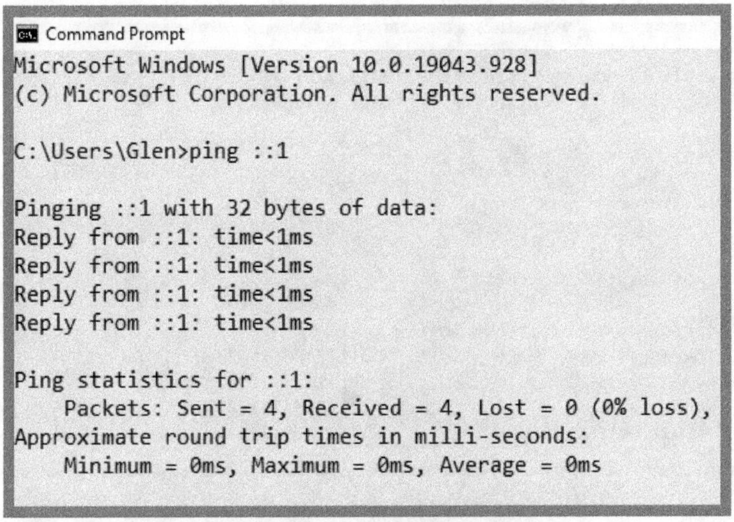

```
Command Prompt
Microsoft Windows [Version 10.0.19043.928]
(c) Microsoft Corporation. All rights reserved.

C:\Users\Glen>ping ::1

Pinging ::1 with 32 bytes of data:
Reply from ::1: time<1ms
Reply from ::1: time<1ms
Reply from ::1: time<1ms
Reply from ::1: time<1ms

Ping statistics for ::1:
    Packets: Sent = 4, Received = 4, Lost = 0 (0% loss),
Approximate round trip times in milli-seconds:
    Minimum = 0ms, Maximum = 0ms, Average = 0ms
```

Figure 4.35– IPv6 loopback address

As shown in the preceding screenshot, the `ping` tool was used to send four ICMP ECHO Request messages to the local host and four responses were returned. The loopback addresses exist on all devices that support TCP/IP, such as smartphones and even IoT devices.

Unique local address

A **unique Local** address exists within the IPv6 addressing space and ranges from `FC00::/7` to `FDFF::/7`. These unique local addresses have similarities to private IPv4 addresses on a network; they are unique to a private network within an organization and are non-routable on the internet. These unique local addresses are used for local addressing only and can be assigned to devices that do not need access to another network.

Default gateway

All devices that are connected to the same IP network can easily exchange messages and share resources. Each end device has a local routing table that contains the various network routes that are used by the local device to determine how to forward messages based on the destination IP address. The routing table of end devices is limited to the local area network and does not contain routes to public networks on the internet.

Therefore, if a device such as a computer attempts to forward a message to a host that does not exist within the same IP subnet as the sender, the computer will check its local routing table for a suitable route (path) to forward the packet. If a suitable route is not found, the sender will not be able to forward the message to the intended destination. Each device on a network requires a default gateway that allows them to forward messages when its local routing table does not contain a valid route for the destination of the message.

The following screenshot shows the default gateway address of a Windows 10 client on a private:

```
Command Prompt
Microsoft Windows [Version 10.0.19043.928]
(c) Microsoft Corporation. All rights reserved.

C:\Users\Glen>ipconfig

Windows IP Configuration


Ethernet adapter Ethernet:

   Connection-specific DNS Suffix  . :
   Link-local IPv6 Address . . . . . : fe80::ad28:d2cf:48f:a65b%8
   IPv4 Address. . . . . . . . . . . : 10.0.2.15
   Subnet Mask . . . . . . . . . . . : 255.255.255.0
   Default Gateway . . . . . . . . . : 10.0.2.2
```

Figure 4.36 – Default gateway

As shown in the preceding screenshot, the client has an IPv4 address of 10.0.2.15/24 with a default gateway of 10.0.2.2. Any time the client has to forward a message, it checks its local routing table for a valid route. If a valid route is not found for the destination IP address of the message, the client forwards the message to the default gateway. The default gateway is the default or primary doorway to communicate outside of a local network.

The following screenshot shows the routing table of a Windows 10 computer:

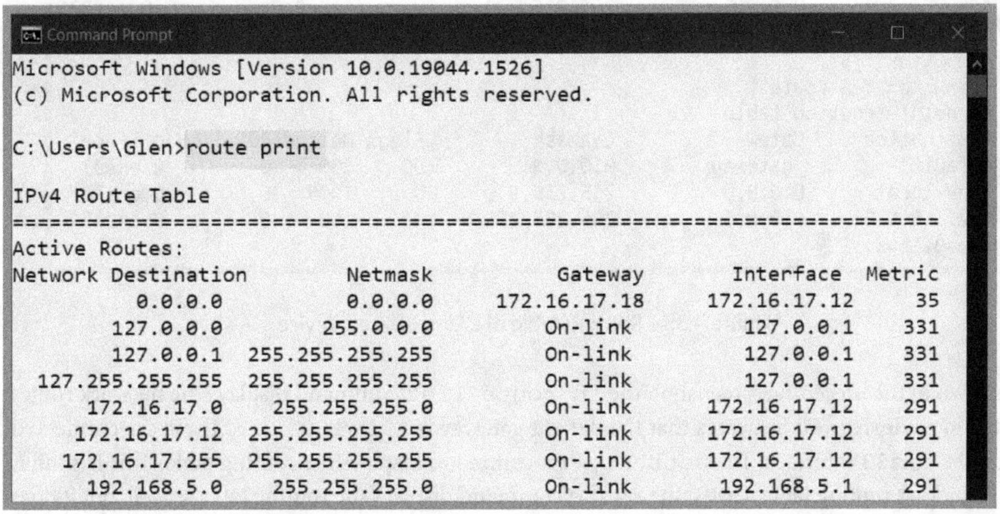

```
Command Prompt                                                  -    □    ×
Microsoft Windows [Version 10.0.19044.1526]
(c) Microsoft Corporation. All rights reserved.

C:\Users\Glen>route print

IPv4 Route Table
===========================================================================
Active Routes:
Network Destination        Netmask          Gateway       Interface  Metric
          0.0.0.0          0.0.0.0      172.16.17.18    172.16.17.12     35
        127.0.0.0        255.0.0.0         On-link         127.0.0.1    331
        127.0.0.1  255.255.255.255         On-link         127.0.0.1    331
  127.255.255.255  255.255.255.255         On-link         127.0.0.1    331
      172.16.17.0    255.255.255.0         On-link      172.16.17.12    291
     172.16.17.12  255.255.255.255         On-link      172.16.17.12    291
    172.16.17.255  255.255.255.255         On-link      172.16.17.12    291
      192.168.5.0    255.255.255.0         On-link       192.168.5.1    291
```

Figure 4.37 – Routing table of a Windows device

As shown in the preceding screenshot, the route print command is used to display the routing table of a Windows system. Looking closely, you'll see a list of destination networks, their network (subnet) masks, and their associated default gateways. A destination network of 0.0.0.0 with a subnet mask of 0.0.0.0 is a default route that points to the internet via a default gateway that has the 172.16.17.18 address.

The following screenshot shows the routing table of a Linux-based device running the Ubuntu Desktop operating system:

```
glen@linux:~$ ip route list
default via 192.168.5.2 dev ens33 proto dhcp metric 100
169.254.0.0/16 dev ens33 scope link metric 1000
192.168.5.0/24 dev ens33 proto kernel scope link src 192.168.5.129 metric 100
glen@linux:~$
glen@linux:~$ netstat -rn
Kernel IP routing table
Destination     Gateway          Genmask         Flags   MSS Window  irtt Iface
0.0.0.0         192.168.5.2      0.0.0.0         UG        0 0           0 ens33
169.254.0.0     0.0.0.0          255.255.0.0     U         0 0           0 ens33
192.168.5.0     0.0.0.0          255.255.255.0   U         0 0           0 ens33
glen@linux:~$
glen@linux:~$ route
Kernel IP routing table
Destination     Gateway          Genmask         Flags Metric Ref    Use Iface
default         _gateway         0.0.0.0         UG    100    0        0 ens33
link-local      0.0.0.0          255.255.0.0     U     1000   0        0 ens33
192.168.5.0     0.0.0.0          255.255.255.0   U     100    0        0 ens33
glen@linux:~$ █
```

Figure 4.38 – Routing table of a Linux-based device

As shown in the preceding screenshot, the `ip route list` command displays the network routes on the local device and indicates that the default gateway is `192.168.5.2`. These are connected using the `ens33` interface. The `netstat -rn` command displays the routing table. This is similar to a Windows routing table. Lastly, the `route` command displays the routing table as well, but it does not specify the IP address of the gateway.

Implementing a default gateway such as a router on the network allows end devices to forward their messages to the default gateway when their local routing table does not have a route for the destination of a packet. The default gateway is usually a Layer 3 device, such as a router, that connects the LAN of an organization to the internet.

The default gateway is configured with a default route that allows the router to inspect the destination IP address within each packet that is received from internal clients on the network. If the router receives a packet with a destination IP address that doesn't exist within the private networks of the organization, the router will forward it to the ISP's router on the internet.

In this section, you learned how to identify and describe the functionality of various types of addresses on a network. In the next section, you will learn how IPv4 and IPv6 can coexist on the internet.

Delving into IPv6 concepts

IPv4 and IPv6 addresses exist within different spaces and cannot natively communicate with each other. To help ensure devices that exist on both IPv4 and IPv6 networks can communicate with each other, various IPv6 technologies allow both versions of IP to coexist. Within this section, you will learn about each technique that allows the coexistence of IPv4 and IPv6 on networks.

Tunneling

While IPv4 is currently dominating most parts of the internet, there are many IPv6 public networks. However, not all organizations have adapted and implemented IPv6 networks within their company. One of the major concerns about having two different versions of IP on the internet or within an organization is that these two versions cannot communicate with each other natively. Simply put, if a device such as a computer is configured with an IPv6 address, it will not be able to communicate with devices on an IPv4 network. Furthermore, routers will not be able to transport an IPv6 packet over an IPv4 network without the help of tunneling.

Tunneling allows IPv6 packets to be transported over an IPv4 network. The forwarding router is responsible for encapsulating the IPv6 packet inside an IPv4 packet before sending it over the IPv4 network. This type of tunneling is referred to as 6to4 tunneling. 4to6 tunneling, on the other hand, allows an IPv4 packet to be encapsulated within an IPv6 packet so that it can be transported over an IPv6 network.

Dual stack

Another method for IPv4 and IPv6 to coexist within private and public networks is to implement dual stacking. Dual stacking both IPv4 and IPv6 addresses on the same NIC of an end device or interface of a networking device such as a router will allow the device to communicate efficiently on both IPv4 and IPv6 networks. If the device has sent a message to a host on an IPv4 network, it will use the IPv4 address that's configured on its local NIC or interface. If the device has to send a message to a host on an IPv6 network, the process is quite simple as it will use the IPv6 address that's configured on the local NIC or interface.

The following screenshot shows the wireless network adapter of a Windows 10 computer:

```
Wireless LAN adapter Wi-Fi 4:

   Connection-specific DNS Suffix  . :
   IPv6 Address. . . . . . . . . . . : 2803:1500:1201:
   Temporary IPv6 Address. . . . . . : 2803:1500:1201:
   Link-local IPv6 Address . . . . . : fe80::d5a1:7c64:407c:c8e3%28
   IPv4 Address. . . . . . . . . . . : 172.16.17.12
   Subnet Mask . . . . . . . . . . . : 255.255.255.0
   Default Gateway . . . . . . . . . : fe80::1%28
                                       172.16.17.18
```

Figure 4.39 – Dual stack NIC

As shown in the preceding screenshot, this is a wireless NIC of a Windows 10 computer that has been configured/assigned with both IPv4 and IPv6 addresses. The dual stack allows this network adapter on the device to communicate with both devices on IPv4 and IPv6 networks simultaneously.

Translation

As you learned earlier in this chapter, NAT allows a router to translate the source private IPv4 address into a public IPv4 address before forwarding the packet out on the internet. **Network Address Translation 64 (NAT64)** allows devices within an IPv6 network to communicate with hosts on an Iv4 network using an address translation that's similar to traditional NAT for IPv4 networks and devices. NAT64 is configured on routers to translate IPv6 addresses into IPv4 addresses, which allows IPv6-enabled devices to communicate with IPv4 hosts and vice versa.

Router advertisement

Devices on an IPv6 network automatically obtain a GUA IPv6 address using ICMPv6 messages. Whenever an IPv6-enabled device such as a computer is connected to an IPv6 network, it sends a **Router Solicitation (RS)** message to the network to discover any IPv6 routers. An IPv6-enabled router responds with a **Router Advertisement (RA)** message, which is used to inform the host on the network how to obtain a GUA IPv6 address.

Furthermore, the RA message provides the following network information to the client:

- The network prefix and the prefix length of the address
- The default gateway IPv6 address for the network
- The DNS server IP addresses and domain name

Additionally, the RA messages provide the following methods for configuring a GUA IPv6 address for a client on the network:

- **Stateless Address Autoconfiguration (SLAAC)**
- SLAAC with stateless DHCPv6
- Stateful DHCPv6

Next, you will learn about SLAAC and the methods used for configuring a GUA IPv6 address.

Stateless Address Autoconfiguration (SLAAC)

SLAAC allows devices on a network to be configured with a GUA IPv6 address without the need for a **Dynamic Host Configuration Protocol v6 (DHCPv6)** server. DHCP is a commonly used network protocol and allows a DHCP server to automatically distribute IP addresses to devices on a network. The DHCPv6 server distributes IPv6 addresses to the client.

However, in some IPv6 networks, there are no DHCPv6 servers available to provide IPv6 addresses to clients on the network. The following is the process of a client obtaining a GUA IPv6 address using SLAAC on an IPv6 network:

1. A client on the network sends an RS message to seek any IPv6-enabled routers.
2. The IPv6-enabled router responds with an ICMPv6 RA message and provides the network prefix and the prefix length.
3. The client uses the EUI-64 process to convert its 48-bit MAC address on the local NIC to create a 64-bit Interface ID. The 64-bit Interface ID is appended to the end of the 64-bit network prefix to create a 128-bit GUA IPv6 address for the client.

Additionally, the RA message from the router can indicate to the client to use both SLAAC and stateless DHCPv6 to obtain a GUA IPv6 address. In this situation, the RA messages inform the client device of the following instructions:

1. First, use SLAAC to create its own GUA IPv6 address.
2. Second, use the router's IPv6 Link-Local address as the default gateway for the network. The router's IPv6 Link-Local addresses are set as the source addresses within the RA message from the router to the client.
3. Lastly, use the stateless DHCPv6 server to obtain the DNS server addresses and domain names only. The stateless DHCPv6 server does not provide the IPv6 address, prefix length, or the default gateway.

Another method for a client to receive an IPv6 address from the network is using a stateful DHCPv6 server. A stateful DHCPv6 server has similar functionalities to a traditional DHCP server on an IPv4 network as it provides the following configurations to clients:

- GUA IPv6 address
- Prefix length
- DNS server addresses
- Domain name

While using a stateful DHCPv6 server on a network, the RA messages from the router provide the default gateway address to clients. The router's IPv6 Link-Local address is included within the RA message as the source address.

Having completed this section, you have explored the characteristics and use cases of various IPv4 and IPv6 address types on a network. In the next section, you will learn how to configure IP addresses on various types of devices.

Configuring IP addresses

In this section, you will gain the hands-on skills needed to configure and assign IPv4 and IPv6 addresses on various devices such as Windows and Linux operating systems, as well as a Cisco IOS router.

Windows operating system

In this hands-on exercise, you will learn how to configure an IP address on a Windows 10 operating system. To get started with this exercise, follow these steps:

1. First, on a Windows 10 device, click on the start icon that's located at the bottom-left corner of the desktop.

2. Next, within the **Windows Search** bar, enter Control Panel and click on the application.

3. Next, within the Windows **Control Panel**, click on **Network and Internet**, as shown in the following screenshot:

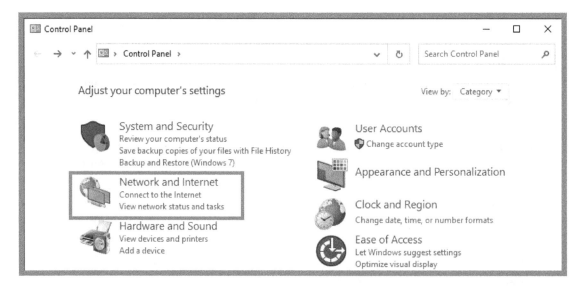

Figure 4.40 – Control Panel

4. Next, within the **Network and Internet** menu, click on **Network and Sharing Center**, as shown in the following screenshot:

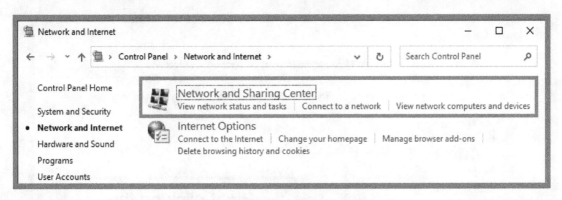

Figure 4.41 – The Network and Internet menu

5. Next, within the **Network and Sharing Center** area, click on **Change adapter settings**, as shown in the following screenshot:

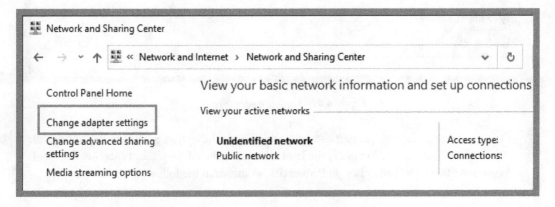

Figure 4.42 – Network and Sharing Center

6. Within the **Network Connections** menu, you will see a list of wired and wireless network adapters. Right-click on your network adapter and select **Properties**, as shown in the following screenshot:

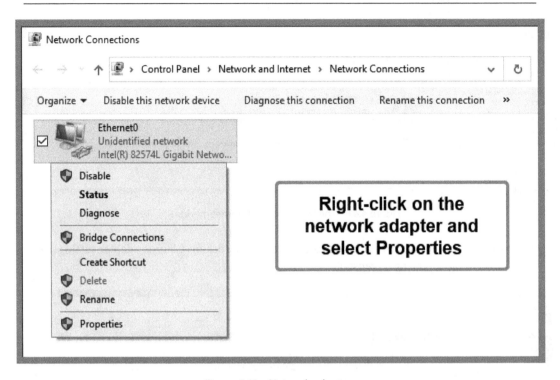

Figure 4.43 – Network adapters

7. On the network adapter's properties window, you have the option to change the settings of IPv4 and IPv6 addresses. To modify the IPv4 settings on the adapter, select **Internet Protocol Version 4 (TCP/IPv4)** and click on **Properties**, as shown in the following screenshot:

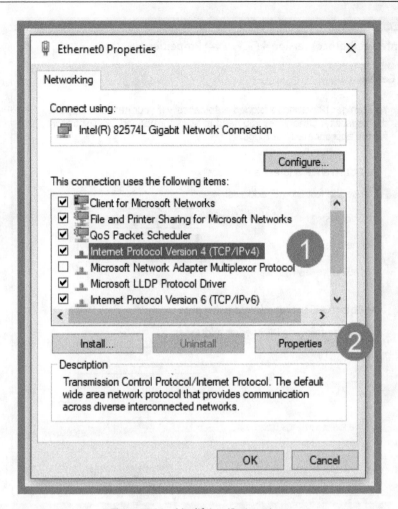

Figure 4.44 – Modifying IPv4 settings

8. Next, the IPv4 **Properties** window will appear. By default, the network adapter is configured to automatically obtain an IP address, subnet mask, default gateway, and DNS server addresses from a DHCP server on the network. To set a static IP address that does not change, you can modify the various options, as shown in the following screenshot:

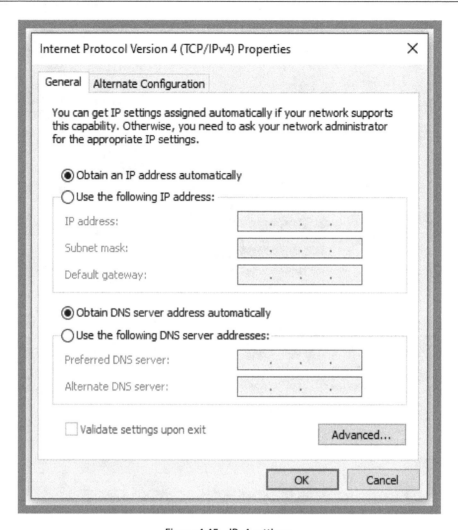

Figure 4.45 – IPv4 settings

If you modify the configurations on the network adapter, ensure you click on **OK** to save and apply the setting on the network adapter.

9. After changing the IPv4 and/or IPv6 settings on the network adapter, click on the Windows icon on the taskbar to open the *Start* menu and enter cmd or Command Prompt to quickly find and open the Windows **Command Prompt**.

10. Once the **Command Prompt** area is open, use the ipconfig and ipconfig /all commands to view the IP addressing information on the network adapter, as shown in the following screenshot:

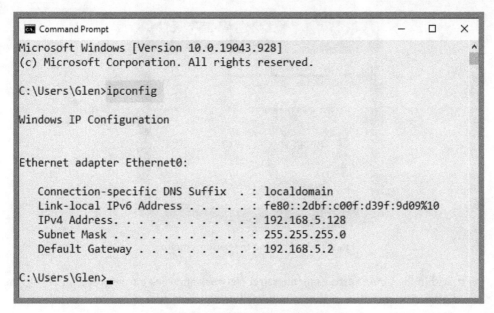

Figure 4.46 – Verifying IP configurations

As shown in the preceding screenshot, the `ipconfig` command helps network professionals quickly determine the IP address, subnet mask, and default gateway of a Windows device.

Tip

These steps can be achieved by using the `netsh interface ip set address name="Packt1" static 192.168.5.128 255.255.255.0 192.168.5.2` command in the Windows Command Prompt.

Having completed this exercise, you have gained the hands-on skills needed to configure and modify IP addresses on a Windows operating system. Next, you will learn how to modify the network adapter settings on a Linux-based device.

Linux operating system

In this hands-on exercise, you will learn how to configure and modify the IP address settings on a network adapter on a Linux-based operating system such as Ubuntu Desktop. To get started with this exercise, follow these steps:

1. On **Ubuntu Desktop**, click on the *power* icon at the top-right corner to expand the drop-down, then click on **Settings**, as shown in the following screenshot:

Figure 4.47 – Opening the Settings menu

2. Next, within the **Linux Settings** menu, select **Network** and click on the gear icon next to the wired network connection, as shown in the following screenshot:

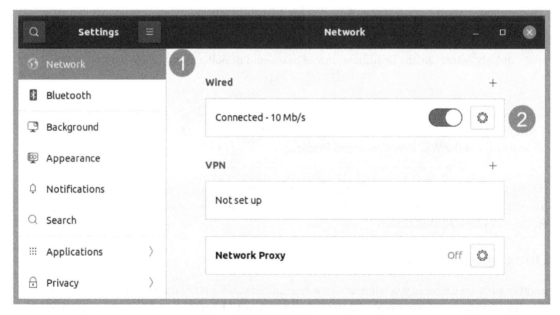

Figure 4.48 – The Settings menu

3. Next, within the adapter settings, select **IPv4** to change the IPv4 address, subnet mask, and DNS server addresses and create static routes, as shown in the following screenshot:

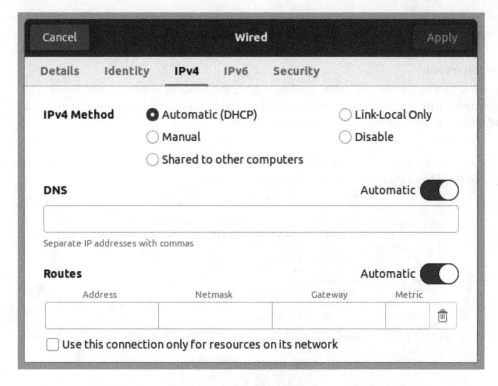

Figure 4.49 – IPv4 settings

If you modify any settings on the network adapter, ensure you click **Apply** to apply the configurations to the adapter of the Linux machine.

4. Next, you can open the **Terminal** area and use the `ip addr` command to determine the number of network adapters and the IP addresses that have been assigned to them, as shown in the following screenshot:

```
glen@linux:~$ ip addr
1: lo: <LOOPBACK,UP,LOWER_UP> mtu 65536 qdisc noqueue state UNKNOWN group default qlen 1000
    link/loopback 00:00:00:00:00:00 brd 00:00:00:00:00:00
    inet 127.0.0.1/8 scope host lo
       valid_lft forever preferred_lft forever
    inet6 ::1/128 scope host
       valid_lft forever preferred_lft forever
2: ens33: <BROADCAST,MULTICAST,UP,LOWER_UP> mtu 1500 qdisc fq_codel state UP group default qlen 1000
    link/ether 00:0c:29:bb:51:a5 brd ff:ff:ff:ff:ff:ff
    altname enp2s1
    inet 192.168.5.129/24 brd 192.168.5.255 scope global dynamic noprefixroute ens33
       valid_lft 1626sec preferred_lft 1626sec
    inet6 fe80::f05f:517f:c917:511b/64 scope link noprefixroute
       valid_lft forever preferred_lft forever
glen@linux:~$
```

Figure 4.50 – Verifying IP addresses

As shown in the preceding screenshot, the `ens33` network adapter on the Ubuntu machine has been assigned the `192.168.5.129/24` address.

> **Important note**
>
> Some networking tools may not be available within the Linux operating system. Simply use the `sudo apt update` and `sudo apt install net-tools` commands to install additional networking tools on the operating system.

5. Lastly, the `ifconfig` command provides a list of network adapters on the local machine and the IP addresses, as shown in the following screenshot:

```
glen@linux:~$ ifconfig
ens33: flags=4163<UP,BROADCAST,RUNNING,MULTICAST>  mtu 1500
        inet 192.168.5.129  netmask 255.255.255.0  broadcast 192.168.5.255
        inet6 fe80::f05f:517f:c917:511b  prefixlen 64  scopeid 0x20<link>
        ether 00:0c:29:bb:51:a5  txqueuelen 1000  (Ethernet)
        RX packets 337733  bytes 494266844 (494.2 MB)
        RX errors 114  dropped 134  overruns 0  frame 0
        TX packets 75584  bytes 4208843 (4.2 MB)
        TX errors 0  dropped 0 overruns 0  carrier 0  collisions 0
        device interrupt 19  base 0x2000

lo: flags=73<UP,LOOPBACK,RUNNING>  mtu 65536
        inet 127.0.0.1  netmask 255.0.0.0
        inet6 ::1  prefixlen 128  scopeid 0x10<host>
        loop  txqueuelen 1000  (Local Loopback)
        RX packets 782  bytes 68767 (68.7 KB)
        RX errors 0  dropped 0  overruns 0  frame 0
        TX packets 782  bytes 68767 (68.7 KB)
        TX errors 0  dropped 0 overruns 0  carrier 0  collisions 0
```

Figure 4.51 – Checking IP addresses and network adapters

As shown in the preceding screenshot, the `ifconfig` command provides meaningful information to network professionals to determine the current IP addresses on the available network adapters on the device.

Having completed this exercise, you have gained the hands-on skills to modify the IP address configurations on a Linux operating system. Next, you will learn how to configure IPv4 and IPv6 addresses on a Cisco IOS router.

Cisco IOS router

In this exercise, you will learn how to configure IP addresses on an interface on a Cisco IOS router. To get started with this exercise, follow these steps:

1. Connect to the Cisco IOS router using a **console cable** between the computer and the console port on the router, or connect to the router via remote access.

2. Next, use the following commands to configure an IPv4 address on a specific interface on the device:

```
Router> enable
Router# configure terminal
Router(config)# interface gigabitEthernet 0/1
Router(config-if)# ip address 192.168.1.1 255.255.255.0
Router(config-if)# no shutdown
Router(config-if)# exit
```

3. Next, to configure an IPv6 address on a Cisco IOS router, use the following commands:

```
Router> enable
Router# configure terminal
Router(config)# ipv6 unicast-routing
Router(config)# interface gigabitEthernet 0/1
Router(config-if)# ipv6 address 2001:1234:4567:89AB::1/64
Router(config-if)# no shutdown
Router(config-if)# exit
Router(config)# exit
```

4. Next, to view the IPv4 configurations on the GigabitEthernet 0/1 interface, use the `show ip interface` command, as shown in the following screenshot:

```
Router#show ip interface gigabitEthernet 0/1
GigabitEthernet0/1 is up, line protocol is up (connected)
  Internet address is 192.168.1.1/24
  Broadcast address is 255.255.255.255
  Address determined by setup command
  MTU is 1500 bytes
  Helper address is not set
  Directed broadcast forwarding is disabled
```

Figure 4.52 – Verifying the IPv4 address on an interface

5. Next, to view the IPv6 address on an interface, use the `show ipv6 interface` command, as shown in the following screenshot:

```
Router#show ipv6 interface gigabitEthernet 0/1
GigabitEthernet0/1 is up, line protocol is up
  IPv6 is enabled, link-local address is FE80::2D0:58FF:FE02:8002
  No Virtual link-local address(es):
  Global unicast address(es):
    2001:1234:4567:89AB::1, subnet is 2001:1234:4567:89AB::/64
  Joined group address(es):
    FF02::1
    FF02::2
    FF02::1:FF00:1
    FF02::1:FF02:8002
MTU is 1500 bytes
```

Figure 4.53 – Verifying the IPv6 address on an interface

Having completed this exercise, you have learned how to configure both IPv4 and IPv6 addresses on an interface on a Cisco IOS router.

Summary

In this chapter, you have gained a solid understanding of the need for logical addressing on a network and have discovered both the IPv4 and IPv6 address spaces. You learned about the importance of NAT to help preserve the IPv4 public address space while allowing devices on a private network to communicate with hosts on a public network. Furthermore, you have gained the hands-on skills to convert IP addresses between binary and decimal. Additionally, this chapter covered the characteristics of various IPv4 and IPv6 address types and their role on a network.

I hope this chapter has been informative for you and is helpful in your journey toward learning networking and becoming a network professional. In the next chapter, *Chapter 5, Applied IPv4 Subnetting*, you will gain hands-on skills as a network professional to break down network blocks into subnetworks using the technique of subnetting.

Questions

The following is a short list of review questions to help reinforce your learning and help you identify areas that may require some improvement:

1. Which of the following statements is true?

    A. There are 48 bits in a MAC address

    B. There are 48 bits within an IPv4 address

    C. There are 64 bits within an IPv6 address

    D. There are 32 bits within a MAC address

2. Which of the following is the default subnet mask for the 172.30.1.45 IP address?

    A. 255.0.0.0

    B. 255.25.2555.0

    C. 255.255.0.0

    D. 255.255.255.128

3. Which of the following classes does the 172.14.9.64 IP address belong to?

    A. Class A

    B. Class C

    C. Class E

    D. Class B

4. Which of the following IP addresses belongs to the RFC 1918 list of addresses?

    A. 172.29.0.45

    B. 172.32.4.67

    C. 172.15.76.69

    D. 172.14.100.45

5. Which type of address translation allows network professionals to map multiple private IP addresses to a single public address?

    A. Static NAT

    B. Dynamic NAT

    C. PAT

    D. All of the above

6. Which of the following addresses is not a valid IPv4 address?

    A. 129.34.67.25

    B. 185.56.32.87

    C. 118.454.45.23

    D. 23.78.23.99

7.   Which of the following is not a valid IPv6 address?

A. 2001:0DD8:0000:1111:0000:0000:0000:0200

B. 2001:0DE8:0000:1111:0000:0000:0000:0200

C. 2001:0DF8:0000:1111:0000:0000:0000:0200

D. 2001:0DG8:0000:1111:0000:0000:0000:0200

8.   Which of the following commands should you use to determine the current IP address configurations on a Windows operating system?

A. ipconfig

B. ifconfig

C. ip addr

D. route print

9.   Which of the following is a EUI-64 address?

A. 2001:DB8:0:1111:FE99:47FA:FE75:CEE0

B. 2001:DB8:0:1111:FE99:47FF:FE75:CEE0

C. 2001:DB8:0:1111:FE99:47FB:FE75:CEE0

D. 2001:DB8:0:1111:FE99:47FC:FE75:CEE0

10.   Which of the following techniques translates an IPv6 address into an IPv4 address?

A. NAT

B. PAT

C. NAT overload

D. NAT64

Further reading

To learn more about the topics that were covered in this chapter, check out the following links:

- *Number Resources*: https://www.iana.org/numbers

- *4 IP Configuration Commands Every SysAdmin Should Know*: https://www.comptia.org/blog/ip-configuration-commands

- *Talk Tech to Me: 9 Common Linux Network Commands*: https://www.comptia.org/blog/linux-network-commands

- *What is NAT?*: https://www.comptia.org/content/guides/what-is-network-address-translation

5

Applied IPv4 Subnetting

In this chapter, you will learn about the importance of the subnet mask and its role in helping network professionals determine the network and host portions of an address, and helping networking devices make forwarding decisions. Additionally, you will learn how to calculate the network prefix and network ID of IPv4 addresses and use subnetting techniques to create smaller network blocks to improve the efficiency of a network.

In this chapter, we will cover the following topics:

- Understanding the purpose of the subnet mask
- Delving into network prefixes and subnet masks
- Determining the network ID
- Understanding the purpose of subnetting
- IPv4 subnetting and VLSM

Let's dive in!

Understanding the purpose of the subnet mask

Both IPv4 and IPv6 addresses have an accompanying subnet mask. The subnet mask plays a very important role within the network and helps a sender device determine whether to forward a message to the default gateway or not. The following are the important key characteristics of the subnet mask and its responsibilities:

- An IPv4 subnet mask has the same length as an IPv4 address, which is 32 bits in length, while an IPv6 subnet mask is 128 bits in length.
- The subnet mask is used with an IPv4 or IPv6 address to help devices identify the network and host ports of the IP address.

- The subnet mask is used to help devices and network professionals determine the total number of IP addresses and usable (assignable) addresses within an IP network.

- The subnet mask helps a sender device determine whether the destination host is on the same IP network as the sender or on another network. If the destination host is on another IP subnet, the sender forwards the message to the sender's default gateway.

The following table shows the default subnet mask for each class of IPv4 addresses on both a private and public network:

Class	Default Subnet Mask
A	255.0.0.0
B	255.255.0.0
C	255.255.255.0

Figure 5.1 – Default subnet masks

As shown in the preceding table, the default subnet masks are assigned to their respective IPv4 address classes. When working with classful addresses, an IPv4 Class A address such as 10.10.10.1 will be assigned a default subnet mask of 255.0.0.0. On the other hand, an IPv4 Class B address of 172.16.4.3 will be assigned a default subnet mask of 255.255.0.0 and an IPv4 Class C address of 192.168.1.20 will be assigned a default subnet mask of 255.255.255.0.

Next, you will explore the principles of creating a network prefix when working with IPv4 addressing by using the information found within the subnet mask.

Delving into network prefixes and subnet masks

In this book, you may have seen various IPv4 and IPv6 addresses written in the format of 192.168.1.1/24 or 2001:DB8:0:1111:FE99:47FF:FE75:CEE0/64 and you're wondering what the /24 and /64 values are at the end of the IP addresses. The /x value that's appended to the end of the IP address is referred to as the **network prefix** and represents the subnet mask in a simplified format. Additionally, the x value is calculated based on the total number of bits, which are 1s within the subnet mask of the IPv4 or IPv6 address.

To gain a better understanding, let's consider an IPv4 address such as 10.1.2.3, which has a default subnet mask of 255.0.0.0. The following table shows the binary notation of the Class A subnet mask:

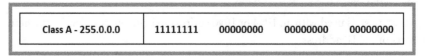

Class A - 255.0.0.0	11111111	00000000	00000000	00000000

Figure 5.2 – Class A subnet mask

As shown in the preceding table, there are a total of 8 bits, which are 1s within the subnet mask. Therefore, the network prefix is /8. Rather than writing the entire subnet mask with an IPv4 or IPv6 address, network professionals can simply append the network prefix at the end of an IP address.

The following table shows the binary notation of each default class of subnet mask:

Class A - 255.0.0.0	11111111	00000000	00000000	00000000
Class B - 255.255.0.0	11111111	11111111	00000000	00000000
Class C - 255.255.255.0	11111111	11111111	11111111	00000000

Figure 5.3 – Subnet masks

As shown in the preceding table, the following are the network prefixes for each default subnet mask:

- **Class A**: 255.0.0.0 - /8
- **Class B**: 255.255.0.0 - /16
- **Class C**: 255.255.255.0 - /24

Additionally, the subnet mask helps network professionals and devices determine the network and host portions of an IP address. The **network portion** of the IP address is the same for all devices within the same IP network, while the **host portion** of the IP address is unique to the interface of the end device only.

To determine the network and host portion of an IP address, you can simply convert both the IP address and subnet mask into binary notation, as shown in the following table:

10.0.0.0	00001010	00000000	00000000	00000000
255.0.0.0	11111111	00000000	00000000	00000000

Figure 5.4 – network ID of Class A

As shown in the preceding snippet, the 1s within the subnet mask that are aligned with the bits within the IP address are used to identify the network portion of the address, while the 0s within the subnet mask that are aligned to the remaining bits within the IP address indicate the host portion of the address. Placing a dotted line after the last 1 within the subnet mask will help you quickly identify the network and host portions of both IPv4 and IPv6 addresses.

Next, let's look at identifying the network and host portion of a Class B address that uses the default subnet mask:

172.16.0.0	10101100	00010000	00000000	00000000
255.255.0.0	11111111	11111111	00000000	00000000

Figure 5.5 – network ID for Class B

As shown in the preceding table, the first 16 bits within the subnet mask are all 1s, which indicates the first 16 bits within the IP address represent the network portion of the address. The bits that are 0s within the subnet mask indicate the host portion of the IP address.

Lastly, let's look at identifying the network and host portion of a Class C address that uses the default subnet mask:

192.168.0.0	11000000	10101000	00000000	00000000
255.255.255.0	11111111	11111111	11111111	00000000

Figure 5.6 – network ID for Class C

As shown in the preceding table, the subnet mask indicates the first 3 octets (24 bits) within the IP address representing the network portion and the last octet (8 bits) represents the host portion of the address.

During your journey in the field of network, you will commonly discover networks are using custom subnet masks such as 255.255.224.0. To calculate the network prefix, simply convert each octet from decimal into binary, as shown in the following steps:

1. Converting the first octet, 255, into binary will be 11111111.
2. Converting the second octet, 255, into binary will be 11111111.
3. Converting the third octet, 224, into binary will be 1110000.
4. Converting the fourth octet, 0, into binary will be 0000000.
5. Lastly, calculating the sum of all bits that are 1s from each octet will provide a network prefix of /19.

The following table shows a classless IPv4 address with a custom subnet mask:

192.168.1.54	11000000	10101000	00000001	0011	0110
255.255.255.240	11111111	11111111	11111111	1111	0000

Figure 5.7 – Custom subnet mask

As shown in the preceding table, the 1s within the subnet mask represent the network portion of the IP address, which is the first 28 bits. The 0s within the subnet mask represent the host portion of the address, which is the last 4 bits.

Now that you have the skills to both describe and understand the purpose of the network prefix, next, you will learn how to use a subnet mask to determine whether a destination host is on the same network as the sender.

Determining the network ID

During my experience within the networking industry, I have seen IT professionals mistakenly configure the incorrect IP address and/or subnet mask on devices within their network. As an aspiring network professional, it's important to understand how to identify whether devices are on the same IP network or not. Let's take a look at the following network topology, which contains a computer, a switch, and a router:

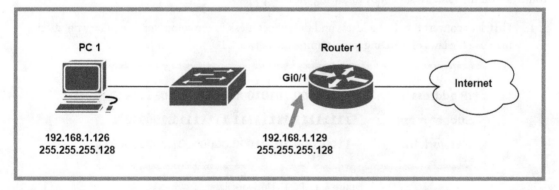

Figure 5.8 – Network topology

As shown in the preceding diagram, there's a small network that contains a computer with a label of **PC 1** that has an IPv4 address of 192.168.1.126 that uses a custom subnet mask of 255.255.255.128. On the same network, there's a router as the default gateway that provides access to the internet, which is configured using an IPv4 address of 192.168.1.129 with a custom subnet mask of 255.255.255.128.

In this scenario, the computer is connected to the same physical network as the router. If the computer has to send a message to a host on the internet, the computer forwards the traffic to its default gateway on the network. However, looking closely at the IPv4 addresses on both **PC 1** and **Router 1**, it seems like both devices are on the same IPv4 network, right? What if I told you that these two devices are not on the same IP network and won't be able to communicate with each other?

To determine why **PC 1** and **Router 1** will not be able to communicate with each other, you need to calculate the network IDs of each device. The **network ID** allows network professionals to identify which IP network a host belongs to. While devices within an organization are all interconnected to the same physical network, network professionals create unique IP subnetworks (subnets) where each subnet has a network ID, a range of usable IP addresses, and a broadcast address.

To determine the network ID of a host, devices and network professionals use a logical operation known as **ANDing**. The process of ANDing allows a system to accept two input values and provide a single output. The following are the laws of ANDing:

```
0 AND 0 = 0
0 AND 1 = 0
1 AND 0 = 0
1 AND 1 = 1
```

Using the laws of ANDing, devices and network professionals AND the IP address of a device against the subnet mask, the result of which is the network ID. Let's determine whether the computer and router are on the same IP subnet by following these steps:

1. First, let's convert the IPv4 address and the subnet mask of the computer into binary notation, then use the laws of ANDing to determine the network ID of the computer:

IP address	11000000.10101000.00000001.01111110
Subnet mask	11111111.11111111.11111111.10000000
Network ID	11000000.10101000.00000001.00000000

Figure 5.9 – PC 1's Network ID

As shown in the preceding diagram, the network ID for PC 1 in binary notation is `11000000.10101000.00000001.00000000`. Converting the binary notation into decimal will provide the network ID of the router as `192.168.1.0/25`.

2. Next, let's covert the IPv4 and subnet mask of the router into binary notation and use the laws of ANDing to determine the network ID, as follows:

IP address	11000000.10101000.00000001.10000001
Subnet mask	11111111.11111111.11111111.10000000
Network ID	11000000.10101000.00000001.10000000

Figure 5.10 – The router's network ID

As shown in the preceding diagram, the network ID for the router in binary notation is `1100 0000.10101000.00000001.10000000`. Converting the binary notation into decimal will provide the network ID of the router as `192.168.1.128/25`.

3. Lastly, let's compare the network IDs of both PC 1 and the router. PC 1 has a network ID of `192.168.1.0/25` and the router has a network ID of `192.168.1.128/25`. Since these network IDs are not the same, this means PC 1 and the router are not on the same IP subnet. Therefore, they will not be able to communicate with each other, even though they are connected to the same physical network.

Now that you've gained the skills to determine the network ID of a device by ANDing the IP address and subnet mask, next, you will learn about the importance of subnetting in the networking industry and how to calculate the total and usable IP addresses within a network.

Understanding the importance of subnetting

Imagine you're a network professional for an organization that has six branch offices within various cities of your country. Each branch office has no more than 50 end devices that need an IPv4 address. Your job is to assign an appropriate IPv4 addressing scheme within the entire organization to support all the remote offices and devices. At first, it will be very easy to assign a unique private IPv4 Class C address block to each of the six branches to meet the required number of IPv4 addresses per remote office, as shown:

- **Branch office 1**: `192.168.0.0/24`
- **Branch office 2**: `192.168.1.0/24`
- **Branch office 3**: `192.168.2.0/24`
- **Branch office 4**: `192.168.3.0/24`
- **Branch office 5**: `192.168.4.0/24`
- **Branch office 6**: `192.168.5.0/24`

While this IPv4 addressing scheme will work, it's not the most efficient scheme as there will be a lot of wastage of IPv4 addresses within each of the six branch offices. Let's take a closer look at why this is not the best solution:

1. First, let's use the following formula to calculate the total number of IPv4 addresses within a single IPv4 network block:

   ```
   Total IPv4 addresses = 2^H
   ```

   The total number of IPv4 addresses includes the network ID, the range, and the broadcast addresses within a network. The H value represents the number of host bits within the address.

2. Now, let's determine the number of host bits with any of the private Class C networks:

192.168.0.0	11000000	10101000	00000000	00000000
255.255.255.0	11111111	11111111	11111111	00000000

Figure 5.11 – Determining host bits

As shown in the preceding table, the bits that are 0s within the subnet mask represent the host portion of the IP address. Therefore, there are 8 host bits within the address.

3. Next, substituting the value of $H = 8$ in our formula provides the following results:

   $$
   \begin{aligned}
   \text{Total IPv4 addresses} &= 2^H \\
   &= 2^8 \\
   &= 256
   \end{aligned}
   $$

There are a total of 256 IPv4 addresses within a Class C network that uses the default subnet mask; this includes the network ID, the usable addresses, and the broadcast address.

> **Important note**
>
> When calculating the number of IP addresses that can be assigned to devices, we need to exclude the network ID and the broadcast addresses as these two addresses are not assignable to any device on an IPv4 network.

4. Next, to calculate the number of usable IP addresses within the network, use the following formula:

   ```
   Usable IPv4 addresses = 2^H - 2
   ```

Since there are 8 bits within any of the Class C address blocks that use the default subnet mask, the following calculations provide the results of usable IPv4 addresses:

```
Usable IPv4 address = 2^H - 2
                    = 2^8 - 2
                    = 256 - 2
                    = 254
```

To conclude, there are 254 usable IPv4 addresses per Class C network that uses a /24 network prefix.

If you were to implement a unique Class C network block within each of the six remote branches of the organization, there would be a huge amount of IP addresses being wasted. Therefore, using classful addressing with default subnet masks isn't the most suitable solution in some cases. Using a classless addressing scheme allows network professionals to create smaller networks with custom subnet masks with fewer usable IP addresses to avoid wastage by using a technique known as **subnetting**.

Subnetting provides the following benefits to organizations and network professionals:

- To efficiently distribute IP addresses with the least wastage
- To create more networks with smaller broadcast domains

So far, you have seen the importance of minimizing the wastage of IPv4 addresses within private and public networks. However, a large broadcast domain within an organization can affect the performance of the network. Imagine that there are 500 end devices such as computers, servers, and **Internet of Things** (**IoT**) devices, all interconnected to the same IP network. Each time a device sends a broadcast message, it's propagated throughout the entire network and all devices receive a copy of the message and process it. If more devices are generating broadcast messages on the network at the same time, these messages will eventually saturate the available bandwidth on the physical network, causing other traffic types such as voice and video to be discarded. Voice and video traffic types use **User Datagram Protocol** (**UDP**) as their preferred transport layer protocol as UDP is better for time-sensitive applications. However, since UDP does not provide reliability or guarantee of delivery, UDP traffic is most likely to be discarded when the network becomes saturated.

To reduce the size of a broadcast domain, subnetting allows network professionals to create smaller IP networks to support fewer devices. For example, while all devices are interconnected to the same physical network within an organization, a network professional can create a unique subnet for each department within the company such that the human resource team will be on a unique IP subnet, the accounting team will be on another IP subnet, and so on. If a device within the human resources team is generating broadcast messages, it's limited to the human resources IP subnet and will not propagate to another IP subnet within the organization. Therefore, other departments will not be affected and the broadcast messages are contained while improving the performance of the entire network.

Having completed this section, you have discovered the importance of subnetting and gained the hands-on skills to calculate the number of addresses within a network. Next, you will gain the hands-on experience that network professionals have to perform subnetting and VLSM.

IPv4 subnetting and VLSM

To further understand how subnetting helps network professionals, let's take a deeper dive into getting the hands-on skills on breaking down an IP address block to create subnets for an organization. In this exercise, let's imagine you're the network administrator or network engineer for a fictional organization that has a total of four offices that are interconnected using a **Wide Area Network (WAN)** solution, as shown in the following network topology:

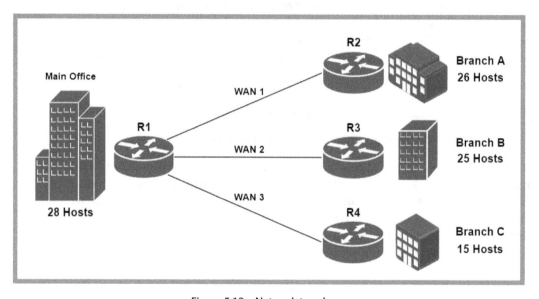

Figure 5.12 – Network topology

Your objective is to create an IPv4 addressing scheme for the entire organization, ensuring each office location has an IP subnet and that there's the least wastage of IP addresses per subnet. The following sub-sections will guide you through the process of subnetting.

Step 1 – determining the appropriate IPv4 block

To get started with subnetting as a network professional, you will need to determine the total number of networks within the organization and the size of the largest network. Three WAN networks are used to interconnect the remote branches to the main office and four **Local Area Networks (LANs)** within each office location, which is a total of seven networks.

Determining the number of networks and the size of the largest network within an organization helps you choose an appropriate address class for the organization. Each address class supports a unique amount of IPv4 networks and addresses based on their default subnet masks.

In this step, we'll be using the default subnet masks to help us determine the total number of IPv4 addresses within each IPv4 address class. The 1s within the subnet mask represent the network portion, while the 0s represent the host portion of the address, as shown in the following table:

	1st Octet	2nd Octet	3rd Octet	4th Octet
Class A - 255.0.0.0	11111111	00000000	00000000	00000000
Class B - 255.255.0.0	11111111	11111111	00000000	00000000
Class C - 255.255.255.0	11111111	11111111	11111111	00000000

Figure 5.13 – Subnet masks

Using the 2^H formula to calculate the total number of IPv4 addresses per class, the following results show the total size of each network per address class:

- Class A = 2^{24} = 16,777,216 total IP addresses
- Class B = 2^{16} = 65,536 total IP addresses
- Class C = 2^8 = 256 total IP addresses

To get a more realistic result, it's important to remember that the network ID and broadcast addresses can't be assigned to any device on an IPv4 network and need to be excluded to determine the usable number of IPv4 addresses that can be assigned to hosts on a network. Therefore, using the $2^H - 2$ formula, to calculate the number of usable IPv4 addresses, the following results show the available IPv4 addresses per address class:

- Class A = $2^{24} - 2$ = 16,777,214 usable IP addresses
- Class B = $2^{16} - 2$ = 65,534 usable IP addresses
- Class C = $2^8 - 2$ = 254 usable IP addresses

Since we have already determined the number of networks within the organization, the following is a further breakdown listing the size of each network:

- **Main Office LAN**: 28 hosts
- **Branch A LAN**: 26 hosts

- **Branch B LAN**: 25 hosts
- **Branch C LAN**: 15 hosts
- **WAN 1 (R1-R2)**: 2 IPs are needed
- **WAN 2 (R2-R3)**: 2 IPs are needed
- **WAN 3 (R3-R4)**: 2 IPs are needed

Implementing a Class A address block within the organization will result in over 16 million addresses being wasted since the largest network within the company has 28 host devices. Using a Class B address block with 65,534 usable IPv4 addresses will result in wastage of addresses too. However, using a Class C network block may seem to be the most appropriate as it's the small address Class with 254 usable IPv4 addresses.

> **Important note**
> When creating subnets, the size of each subnet should be able to fit the largest network within an organization.

Now that we've determined that a Class C address block will be appropriate for the organization, in the next step, you will learn how to further evaluate whether a single Class C address block can be broken down into seven subnets to fit each network in the company.

Step 2 – creating new subnets (subnetworks)

When creating subnets, it's important to convert the address block from dotted-decimal notation into binary notation as it helps easily identify the network and host portions of the address. Additionally, to create new subnets from an address block, you will need to convert some of the host bits into new network bits. This allows us to create more networks while reducing the number of IPv4 addresses that are available within each subnet.

Let's get started by using the first available Class C address block of 192.168.0.0/24 and converting both the address and default subnet mask into binary notation, as shown in the following table:

Network block	11000000 . 10101000 . 00000000 . **00000000**
Subnet mask	11111111 . 11111111 . 11111111 . **00000000**

Figure 5.14 – Network block and default subnet mask

As shown in the preceding table, the 1s within the subnet mask represent the network portion of the IP address and the 0s represent the host portion of the address. Simply put, the first 24 bits represent the network portion and the last 8 bits represent the host portion of the number. This means that all hosts within the 192.168.0.0/24 network will have the same network portion of the IPv4 address, while the host portion will be unique to the individual host device on the network.

To create subnetworks from a network block, you will need to convert host bits into network bits. These host bits are taken from the point where the 1s stop within the subnet mask. When converting host bits into network bits, the following formula is used to determine the number of new networks:

Number of networks = 2^N

The Nth value represents the number of host bits that are converted into network bits.

As mentioned previously, the host bits are taken from the point where the 1s stop in the subnet mask (from left to right). Let's start by converting one host bit into a network bit and determine the number of new networks that can be created:

Network block	11000000 . 10101000 . 00000000 . 0**0000000**
Subnet mask	11111111 . 11111111 . 11111111 . **1**0000000

Figure 5.15 – Converting one host bit

When we convert bits on the host portion of an address, the bit value is also changed within the subnet mask to represent the new network portion of the address. Using the aforementioned formula to determine the total number of networks, the following are the results:

Number of networks = 2^N

$$= 2^1$$

$$= 2$$

Therefore, converting one host bit isn't enough to create enough networks for the organization. Let's convert another host bit, as shown in the following table:

Network block	11000000 . 10101000 . 00000000 . 00**000000**
Subnet mask	11111111 . 11111111 . 11111111 . **11**000000

Figure 5.16 – Converting two host bits

Let's use our formula to determine the number of new networks when using 2 host bits:

```
Number of networks = 2ᴺ

                   = 2²

                   = 2 x 2

                   = 4
```

If we convert two host bits into new network bits, it will not be sufficient as these new bits will only provide us with four networks. Since our goal is to create seven new networks from the original address block with each new subnet able to support 28 hosts, let's convert an additional host bit into a network bit, as shown in the following table:

Network block	11000000 . 10101000 . 00000000 . 000**00000**
Subnet mask	11111111 . 11111111 . 11111111 . 111**00000**

Figure 5.17 – Converting three host bits

Let's use the aforementioned formula to determine the number of new networks when using three host bits:

```
Number of networks = 2ᴺ

                   = 2³

                   = 2 x 2 x 2

                   = 8
```

Converting three host bits into network bits will provide eight new subnetworks. As you have seen within our calculations, if fewer host bits are converted into network bits, the total number of new networks will not be sufficient for the organization. Therefore, converting an additional host bit into a network bit allows us to achieve the goal of seven networks with one extra network.

Having converted three bits from the host portion of the IPv4 address to be used as network bits to support the creation of new subnets, there are five remaining host bits within the host portion of the address, as shown in the following table:

Network block	11000000 . 10101000 . 00000000 . 000**00000**
Subnet mask	11111111 . 11111111 . 11111111 . 111**00000**

Figure 5.18 – Remaining host bits

To determine whether each of the eight new subnets will be able to support the largest network within the organization of 28 hosts, we need to calculate the total number of IPv4 addresses per network using the following formula:

```
Total IPv4 addresses = 2ᴴ
                     = 2⁵
                     = 2 x 2 x 2 x 2 x 2
                     = 32
```

Using five host bits within any of the eight new networks will provide a total of 32 IPv4 addresses, inclusive of the network ID and broadcast addresses for each network. However, since the network ID and broadcast addresses can't be assigned to devices within an IPv4 network, we need to exclude them. The following formula is used to calculate the number of usable (assignable) IPv4 addresses per network:

```
Usable IPv4 address = 2ᴴ - 2
                    = 2⁵ - 2
                    = (2 x 2 x 2 x 2 x 2) - 2
                    = 30
```

Based on the results, each of the eight new subnets will contain 30 usable IPv4 addresses that can be assigned to devices. As a result, we have found a workable solution of using a Class C address block and using mathematical calculations to determine whether it's suitable for the organization. Since this solution is workable, we are converting three host bits into network bits, and a new subnet mask is created for each of the new subnets, so they will be using 255.255.255.224 with a network prefix of /27.

> **Important note**
>
> When performing subnetting, the original address block is broken down into smaller networks called subnetworks (subnets), and the subnet mask changes to support each new subnet.

The following are important guidelines when creating new subnetworks:

- Ensure you do not modify/change the bits within the network portion of the IP address
- Ensure you do not modify/change the new host portion of the IP address
- Ensure you only modify the new network bits as these are used to create the new subnetworks

By changing the new network bits from 0s to 1s within the IP address, we can create all the possibilities for new network IDs. The following are the calculations for creating the eight new subnets:

Subnet 1	11000000 . 10101000 . 00000000 . 00**000000**	**192.168.0.0/27**
Subnet 2	11000000 . 10101000 . 00000000 . 001**00000**	**192.168.0.32/27**
Subnet 3	11000000 . 10101000 . 00000000 . 010**00000**	**192.168.0.64/27**
Subnet 4	11000000 . 10101000 . 00000000 . 011**00000**	**192.168.0.96/27**
Subnet 5	11000000 . 10101000 . 00000000 . 100**00000**	**192.168.0.128/27**
Subnet 6	11000000 . 10101000 . 00000000 . 101**00000**	**192.168.0.160/27**
Subnet 7	11000000 . 10101000 . 00000000 . 110**00000**	**192.168.0.192/27**
Subnet 8	11000000 . 10101000 . 00000000 . 111**00000**	**192.168.0.224/27**

Figure 5.19 – New subnets

As we can see, the first three bits within the 4th octet are the new network bits, and changing each bit value from 0 to 1 creates a new subnetwork. These are the network IDs for the new eight subnetworks with their new network prefix. Therefore, the last five bits within the 4th octet are the new host bits for each new subnet.

> **Tip**
>
> Since each subnet is equal in terms of total IP addresses, using the 2^H formula will help you quickly determine the incremental value between the subnet and determine the network IDs.

Now that you've calculated the network IDs for each of the eight new subnets, next, you will discover how to calculate the IP address ranges for each subnet.

Step 3 – assigning subnets to each network

In this step, you'll learn how to calculate the IP address ranges for each new subnet by determining the network ID, the first and last usable addresses, and the broadcast address per subnet.

To ensure your calculations are done efficiently, use the following guidelines:

- To determine the first usable IP address within a subnet, use the network ID + 1 formula. In binary notation, the first bit from the left is set to 1.

- To calculate the broadcast address within a subnet, use the Next network ID - 1 formula. In binary notation, it's when all the host bits are 1s within the address.

- To calculate the last usable IP address within a subnet, use the Broadcast Address - 1 formula. In binary notation, it's where all the host bits are 1s except the bit to the farthest right.

Using these guidelines, let's calculate the network range of the first subnet and assign it to the main office LAN network:

Subnet 1	11000000 . 10101000 . 00000000 . 00000000	192.168.0.0/27
First usable IP	11000000 . 10101000 . 00000000 . 00000001	192.168.0.1/27
Last usable IP	11000000 . 10101000 . 00000000 . 00011110	192.168.0.30/27
Broadcast	11000000 . 10101000 . 00000000 . 00011111	192.168.0.31/27

Figure 5.20 – Subnet 1 network range

As shown in the preceding table, the network ID is determined when all the host bits are 0s within the address. While the first usable IPv4 address is when the first bit from the right is only 1, the last usable address is when all the host bits are 1s except the bit to the farthest right of the address, and the broadcast address is when all the hosts are 1s.

Next, applying the same mathematical technique, let's determine the network range of the next subnet that will be assigned to the Branch A LAN network:

Subnet 2	11000000 . 10101000 . 00000000 . 00100000	192.168.0.32/27
First usable IP	11000000 . 10101000 . 00000000 . 00100001	192.168.0.33/27
Last usable IP	11000000 . 10101000 . 00000000 . 00111110	192.168.0.62/27
Broadcast	11000000 . 10101000 . 00000000 . 00111111	192.168.0.63/27

Figure 5.21 – Subnet 2 network range

Next, repeating our technique, let's calculate the network range of the third subnet that will be assigned to the Branch B LAN network:

Subnet 3	11000000 . 10101000 . 00000000 . 01000000	192.168.0.64/27
First usable IP	11000000 . 10101000 . 00000000 . 01000001	192.168.0.65/27
Last usable IP	11000000 . 10101000 . 00000000 . 01011110	192.168.0.94/27
Broadcast	11000000 . 10101000 . 00000000 . 01011111	192.168.0.95/27

Figure 5.22 – Subnet 3 network range

Next, let's determine the network range of the fourth subnet that will be assigned to the Branch C LAN network:

Subnet 4	11000000 . 10101000 . 00000000 . 01100000	192.168.0.96/27
First usable IP	11000000 . 10101000 . 00000000 . 01100001	192.168.0.97/27
Last usable IP	11000000 . 10101000 . 00000000 . 01111110	192.168.0.126/27
Broadcast	11000000 . 10101000 . 00000000 . 01111111	192.168.0.127/27

Figure 5.23 – Subnet 4 network range

So far, we can successfully assign the first four subnets to each LAN for each office location of the organization. However, three WAN networks are used to interconnect each branch router to the main office router. These WAN links are point-to-point connections that require only two IP addresses per WAN connection:

- **WAN 1**: Main office router to Branch A router – only two IP addresses are needed

- **WAN 2**: Main office router to Branch B router – only two IP addresses are needed

- **WAN 3**: Main office router to Branch C router – only two IP addresses are needed

If we were to assign the remaining subnets to any of the WAN networks, there will be a lot of wastage of IPv4 addresses. Since each subnet has 30 usable IPv4 addresses and each WAN link requires only two IP addresses, there will be a wastage of 28 IPv4 addresses per WAN link.

To further avoid wastage of IPv4 addresses within our new subnets while being able to assign IPv4 addresses to our WAN networks, we can use a technique known as **Variable Length Subnet Masking** (**VLSM**), which allows us to further break down a subnet into smaller subnetworks. Think of it as subnetting a subnet even further to reduce IPv4 address wastage on a network. We can use any of the remaining following subnets for VLSM:

Subnet 5	11000000 . 10101000 . 00000000 . 10000000	192.168.0.128/27
Subnet 6	11000000 . 10101000 . 00000000 . 10100000	192.168.0.160/27
Subnet 7	11000000 . 10101000 . 00000000 . 11000000	192.168.0.192/27
Subnet 8	11000000 . 10101000 . 00000000 . 11100000	192.168.0.224/27

Figure 5.24 – Unallocated networks

The preceding table shows the unallocated subnets that haven't been assigned to any networks within the organization of our scenario. Since these unallocated subnets are equal in size, we can use any one of these remaining subnets to perform our VLSM technique. To keep everything simple and easy to understand, the following subnets will be documented and reserved for future office locations:

Subnet 5	11000000 . 10101000 . 00000000 . 10000000	**192.168.0.128/27**
Subnet 6	11000000 . 10101000 . 00000000 . 10100000	**192.168.0.160/27**
Subnet 7	11000000 . 10101000 . 00000000 . 11000000	**192.168.0.192/27**

Figure 5.25 – Subnet reservations

The following subnet will be broken down using VLSM to create smaller subnetworks:

Subnet 8	11000000 . 10101000 . 00000000 . 11100000	**192.168.0.224/27**

Figure 5.26 – Eighth subnet

In the next step, you will learn how to perform VLSM on the eighth subnet to create small subnets to support the WAN links between the remote offices and the main office.

Step 4 – performing Variable-Length Subnet Masking (VLSM)

In this step, you will learn how to further break down a subnet to create smaller IP networks with smaller broadcast domains while efficiently distributing IP addresses with the least wastage. Since each of the three WAN links are point-to-point networks that require only two IP addresses, we can determine the number of host bits needed within an IP address to provide two usable IP addresses.

To calculate the number of usable IP addresses within a network, use the following formula:

`Number of usable IPv4 addresses = ` $2^H - 2$

As you may recall, H represents the number of host bits within an IP address.

To get started, let's convert the `192.168.0.224/27` subnet into binary notation to visualize the network and host portions of the address:

Network ID	11000000 . 10101000 . 00000000 . 11100000	192.168.0.224
Subnet mask	11111111 . 11111111 . 11111111 . 11100000	255.255.255.224

Figure 5.27 – Binary notation

As shown in the preceding table, there are five hosts within the network. If we use one host bit (the 32nd bit) from the 192.168.0.224/27 network ID within our formula, the following will be the result of usable IPv4 addresses:

```
Number of usable IPv4 addresses = 2ᴴ - 2

                                = 2¹ - 2

                                = 2 - 2

                                = 0
```

Using one host bit will result in 0 usable IP addresses. Let's use two host bits (the 31st and 32nd bits) from the same network ID, 192.168.0.224/27, within our formula to determine the number of usable IP addresses:

```
Number of usable IPv4 addresses = 2ᴴ - 2

                                = 2² - 2

                                = (2 x 2) - 2

                                = 4 - 2

                                = 2
```

Using two host bits provides two usable addresses. At this point, we have a solution for creating new subnets from the 192.168.0.224/27 network block, which has two usable IP addresses per new subnet. To ensure this solution is workable, the two host bits that we are going to use will remain as host bits – that is, 00 within the address. This leaves us with three remaining bits within the host portion of the 192.168.0.224/27 network block. These remaining bits will be converted into network bits for creating the new subnets.

The following formula provides the number of new subnets when converting three host bits into network bits:

```
Number of networks = 2ᴺ

                   = 2³

                   = 2 x 2 x 2

                   = 8
```

Converting three host bits into network bits will provide us with a total of eight new subnets from the 192.168.0.224/27 network block; each subnet will contain a total of four IPv4 addresses inclusive of two usable addresses. By creating eight new with two usable addresses, we can assign three of the eight new subnets to the existing WAN links; the remaining subnet can be documented as a reservation for the future growth of the organization.

The following table shows the effects of converting three host bits within the subnet mask into network bits to create eight new subnets from the 192.168.0.224/27 network block:

Network ID	11000000 . 10101000 . 00000000 . 11100000	192.168.0.224
Subnet mask	11111111 . 11111111 . 11111111 . 11111100	255.255.255.252

Figure 5.28 – Creating new network bits

As we can see, converting three host bits into network bits creates a new subnet mask of 255.255.255.252 or a network prefix of /30 for the eight new subnets from the 192.168.0.224 network block. Additionally, notice that two host bits are remaining within the host portion of the addresses. These host bits will ensure there are two usable addresses within each of the new subnets.

Before getting started with VLSM, please use the following guidelines to prevent any miscalculations of new subnets:

- Do not change or modify the original network bits within the network portion of the address
- Do not change or modify the new host bits within the host portion of the address
- Only change or modify the new network bits within the address

The following table shows all the possibilities of modifying the new network bits from the address by changing the 0s to 1s, creating eight new subnets from the 192.168.0.224 network block:

VLSM Subnet 1	11000000 . 10101000 . 00000000 . 11100000	192.168.0.224/30
VLSM Subnet 2	11000000 . 10101000 . 00000000 . 11100100	192.168.0.228/30
VLSM Subnet 3	11000000 . 10101000 . 00000000 . 11101000	192.168.0.232/30
VLSM Subnet 4	11000000 . 10101000 . 00000000 . 11101100	192.168.0.236/30
VLSM Subnet 5	11000000 . 10101000 . 00000000 . 11110000	192.168.0.240/30
VLSM Subnet 6	11000000 . 10101000 . 00000000 . 11110100	192.168.0.244/30
VLSM Subnet 7	11000000 . 10101000 . 00000000 . 11111000	192.168.0.248/30
VLSM Subnet 8	11000000 . 10101000 . 00000000 . 11111100	192.168.0.252/30

Figure 5.29 – VLSM networks

The preceding table shows the eight new networks that were created from the 192.168.0.224 network block. Each new subnet has a network prefix of /30 to support a total of four IPv4 addresses, inclusive of two usable addresses for the WAN point-to-point links within the organization.

The following are the calculations used to determine the network range of the first subnet that will be assigned between the main office router and Branch A router:

Subnet 1	11000000 . 10101000 . 00000000 . 11100000	192.168.0.224/30
First usable IP	11000000 . 10101000 . 00000000 . 11100001	192.168.0.225/30
Last usable IP	11000000 . 10101000 . 00000000 . 11100010	192.168.0.226/30
Broadcast	11000000 . 10101000 . 00000000 . 11100011	192.168.0.227/30

Figure 5.30 – WAN 1 allocation

The following are the calculations used to determine the network range of the second subnet that will be assigned between the main office router and Branch B router:

Subnet 2	11000000 . 10101000 . 00000000 . 11100100	192.168.0.228/30
First usable IP	11000000 . 10101000 . 00000000 . 11100101	192.168.0.229/30
Last usable IP	11000000 . 10101000 . 00000000 . 11100110	192.168.0.230/30
Broadcast	11000000 . 10101000 . 00000000 . 11100111	192.168.0.231/30

Figure 5.31 – WAN 2 allocation

The following are the calculations used to determine the network range of the third subnet that will be assigned between the main office router and Branch C router:

Subnet 3	11000000 . 10101000 . 00000000 . 11101000	192.168.0.232/30
First usable IP	11000000 . 10101000 . 00000000 . 11101001	192.168.0.233/30
Last usable IP	11000000 . 10101000 . 00000000 . 11101010	192.168.0.234/30
Broadcast	11000000 . 10101000 . 00000000 . 11101011	192.168.0.235/30

Figure 5.32 – WAN 3 allocation

Now that we've allocated the first three subnets to the WAN links within the organization, the following five subnets will be documented and reserved within the company to support future growth:

VLSM Subnet 4	11000000 . 10101000 . 00000000 . 11101100	192.168.0.236/30
VLSM Subnet 5	11000000 . 10101000 . 00000000 . 11110000	192.168.0.240/30
VLSM Subnet 6	11000000 . 10101000 . 00000000 . 11110100	192.168.0.244/30
VLSM Subnet 7	11000000 . 10101000 . 00000000 . 11111000	192.168.0.248/30
VLSM Subnet 8	11000000 . 10101000 . 00000000 . 11111100	192.168.0.252/30

Figure 5.33 – Reserved WAN subnets

These remaining WAN subnets will be needed in the future when the organization is growing and creating new remote offices. Planning for the future growth of an organization is important when designing an IP address scheme. Network professionals should consider the growth of each department within an organization, the growth of branch offices, and the entire organization as well. Using statistical data from human resources can assist in how the organization has grown within the past 5-10 years. Using this information can help network professionals determine an appropriate address class and how to create their subnetworks to support their company.

Lastly, the following table shows the allocation for networks with a /27 network prefix:

Subnet 1	Main Office LAN	192.168.0.0/27
Subnet 2	Branch A LAN	192.168.0.32/27
Subnet 3	Branch B LAN	192.168.0.64/27
Subnet 4	Branch C LAN	192.168.0.96/27
Subnet 5	Reserved	192.168.0.128/27
Subnet 6	Reserved	192.168.0.160/27
Subnet 7	Reserved	192.168.0.192/27
Subnet 8	No longer available	192.168.0.224/27

Figure 5.34 – Subnets for LANs

The following table shows the allocation for networks that use the /30 network prefix:

VLSM Subnet 1	WAN 1	192.168.0.224/30
VLSM Subnet 2	WAN 2	192.168.0.228/30
VLSM Subnet 3	WAN 3	192.168.0.232/30
VLSM Subnet 4	Reserved	192.168.0.236/30
VLSM Subnet 5	Reserved	192.168.0.240/30
VLSM Subnet 6	Reserved	192.168.0.244/30
VLSM Subnet 7	Reserved	192.168.0.248/30
VLSM Subnet 8	Reserved	192.168.0.252/30

Figure 5.35 – Subnets for WANs

Having completed this section, you have gained the hands-on skills to perform subnetting and VLSM as a network professional.

Summary

In this chapter, you learned about the importance of subnetting and the role it plays within the networking industry and the internet. You have acquired the skills to identify the network and host portions of addresses and determine the network prefix of an address. Furthermore, you have gained the hands-on skills needed to perform subnetting on a network address block to create subnetworks.

I hope this chapter has been informative for you and is helpful in your journey toward learning networking and becoming a network professional. In the next chapter, *Chapter 6, Exploring Network Protocols and Services*, you will explore various network protocols and traffic types.

Questions

The following is a short list of review questions to help reinforce your learning and help you identify areas that may require some improvement.

1. Which of the following is a valid host of the `172.16.150.0/23` network?

    A. `172.16.160.56`

    B. `172.16.150.256`

    C. `172.16.150.56`

    D. `172.17.150.1`

2. Which of the following is the first usable address of a network that has an end device with the `192.168.46.234/26` address?

    A. `192.168.46.192`

    B. `192.168.46.191`

    C. `192.168.46.187`

    D. `192.168.46.197`

3. Which of the following subnets does the host `10.45.67.32/19` address belong to?

    A. `10.45.97.0`

    B. `10.45.64.0`

    C. `10.45.63.0`

    D. `10.45.67.128`

4.   Which of the following is the broadcast address for the `172.30.56.48/28` network?

   A. `172.30.56.61`

   B. `172.30.56.62`

   C. `172.30.56.63`

   D. `172.30.56.64`

5.   Which of the following is a valid host of the `192.16.10.0/20` network?

   A. `192.16.15.100`

   B. `192.16.16.100`

   C. `192.15.15.100`

   D. `192.16.16.2`

6.   Which of the following is the first usable address of a network that has an end device with the `172.10.146.24/18` address?

   A. `172.10.148.1`

   B. `172.10.146.1`

   C. `172.10.148.1`

   D. `172.10.128.1`

7.   Which of the following subnets does the host `100.5.67.36/29` address belong to?

   A. `100.5.66.32`

   B. `100.5.66.64`

   C. `100.5.67.32`

   D. `100.5.67.0`

8.   Which of the following is the broadcast address for the `12.39.6.68/28` network?

   A. `12.38.6.79`

   B. `12.39.7.79`

   C. `12.39.8.79`

   D. `12.39.6.78`

9.   Which of the following is a valid host of the `12.100.90.0/23` network?

   A. `12.100.91.24`

   B. `12.100.91.257`

   C. `12.10.91.24`

   D. `12.10.93.24`

10. Which of the following is the first usable address of a network that has an end device with the 10.168.46.234/9 address?

A. 10.12.0.1

B. 10.167.0.1

C. 10.128.0.1

D. 10.12.0.1

Further reading

To learn more about the topics that were covered in this chapter, check out the following links:

- *What Is Network Segmentation?*: https://www.comptia.org/blog/security-awareness-training-network-segmentation

- *IP Addressing and Subnetting*: https://www.cisco.com/c/en/us/support/docs/ip/routing-information-protocol-rip/13788-3.html

- *Host and Subnet Quantities*: https://www.cisco.com/c/en/us/support/docs/ip/routing-information-protocol-rip/13790-8.html

6

Exploring Network Protocols and Services

Connecting computers, servers, and **Internet of Things** (**IoT**) devices on a network is a simple process, such as enabling the wireless connectivity features on the host device and selecting a wireless network within the vicinity. Sometimes, it's as easy as connecting a network cable between the end devices such as a computer to the networking device to access the resources on a network. Once a connection is made, everything seems to just work seamlessly, and we can send and receive email messages and browse the internet. However, there are many application and **network layer protocols** (**NLPs**) that all work together to help client devices, servers, networking devices, security appliances, smart devices, and even IoT devices communicate with each other on a network.

As an aspiring network professional within the industry, it's important to build a solid understanding of the key features and characteristics of common network protocols that assist devices in exchanging various types of messages over a network. In this chapter, we will explore the roles and features of various network and application layer protocols that are commonly used within many networks. Additionally, you will be able to identify the purpose of each protocol and how they are used to allow hosts to communicate on a network and share resources. Furthermore, you will gain a solid understanding of secure versus unsecure protocols and why data confidentiality is important as devices are exchanging messages. Lastly, you will discover the fundamentals of various networking services, which help users connect and communicate with each other.

In this chapter, we will cover the following topics:

- Network protocols
- Network protocol types
- Network services

Let's dive in!

Technical requirements

To follow along with the exercises in this chapter, please ensure that you have met the following hardware and software requirements:

- Wireshark: `https://www.wireshark.org/`
- 7-Zip: `https://www.7-zip.org/`

Network protocols

To build a strong foundation of the concepts of network protocols and communication, you must understand the roles and responsibilities of end devices and servers. End devices are very common on a network, and these devices usually require access to a service or resource. For instance, if you look around within an organization or your home, you'll see many end devices. These devices are computers, laptops, and IoT devices, which are all connected to a network. Servers are any device that provides the services and resources that are needed by end devices. For a client such as a computer to access the resources on a server, these two devices use a mutually agreed-upon network protocol that is responsible for exchanging messages over the network.

Network protocols are simply the underlying technology, rules, and procedures that define how a sender can package and format a message to be sent across a network to a destination host. Without protocols or rules for communication on a network, devices will not format or address a message properly before placing the message onto the network for delivery. When the receiver accepts the incoming message, the receiver may misinterpret the message due to a lack of formatting or addressing. Hence, many unique network protocols have their roles and functionality for communication over a network.

Many common protocols on a network are application layer protocols that operate at the application layer of both the **Open Systems Interconnection (OSI)** and **Transmission Control Protocol/Internet Protocol (TCP/IP)** networking models. These application layer protocols allow a user such as yourself to interface with the network. Using an application on your device such as a web browser, you can interact with web applications and web servers using **Hypertext Transfer Protocol Secure (HTTPS)** or use the **Microsoft Outlook** application to send email messages using **Simple Mail Transfer Protocol (SMTP)**.

As mentioned in *Chapter 1, Exploring the OSI Model and TCP/IP*, the **Transport layer** of the OSI and TCP/IP networking model is responsible for assigning the source and destination service port number based on the application layer protocol. Each application layer protocol is associated with a unique service port number that helps devices deliver a message to the appropriate application layer protocol. Hence, the Transport layer has a very important role and is responsible for ensuring messages are delivered to their destinations. These service ports are simply the doorways used by the operating system of a device to send and receive messages on a network.

The following table shows the major categories of service numbers and their ranges according to the **Internet Assigned Numbers Authority (IANA)**:

Port Groups	Range	Description
Well-known Ports	0 - 1,023	Used by common and popular services and applications
Registered Ports	1,024 - 49,151	These ports are assigned to specific entities for use with specific processes and applications
Private/Dynamic Ports	49,152 - 65,535	These are ephemeral ports which are used when a client application is communicating with a server

Figure 6.1 – Service port numbers

As shown in the preceding table, there are **65,535** service ports on an operating system. These services can be used with the **Transmission Control Protocol** (**TCP**) and/or **User Datagram Protocol** (**UDP**) Transport layer protocols of an operating system. An operating system will temporarily open a dynamic/ephemeral service port for sending only messages. A server that's providing a service or resource to clients on a network will open a well-known service port number to allow inbound connections from clients. Without an open service port number on an operating system, a device will not be able to send and receive messages. As a result, the device will not be able to communicate with others on the network.

In the following sub-sections, you will discover various application and network protocols that help users share resources and communicate efficiently over a network.

File protocols

As a network professional, you will commonly discover many file-sharing applications that allow devices, clients, and servers within organizations to provide file-sharing services to users on the network. Within the networking industry, there are various application and network layer protocols that are designed with the functionality to allow file transfer between devices over a network.

File Transfer Protocol

The **File Transfer Protocol** (**FTP**) is a very common file sharing protocol that operates in a client-server model, allowing users to connect to a file server to upload and download files over a network. FTP operates on service port 20 to allow data transfer between an FTP client and the FTP server, while service port 21 is dedicated to controlling commands and functions from the FTP client and FTP server.

The following diagram shows the first phase of an FTP connection between a client and server on a network:

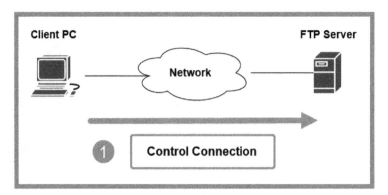

Figure 6.2 – Phase 1 of FTP

As shown in the preceding diagram, the computer with the FTP client application opens the connections to the FTP server on service port 21. Next, the client opens another connection to the server on service port 20 to transmit data traffic, as shown in the following diagram:

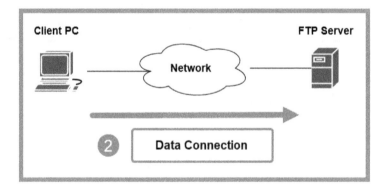

Figure 6.3 – Phase 2 of FTP

Lastly, the data is transferred from the FTP server on service port 20 to the client, as shown in the following diagram:

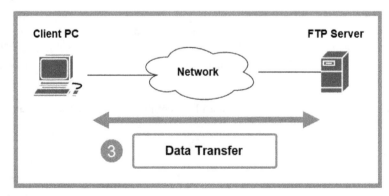

Figure 6.4 – Phase 3 of FTP

Imagine each employee within an organization only stores files on their local computers; if a user's computer were to experience a storage drive failure or get infected with malware, there would be a high risk that the data will be lost or corrupted. Storing files on a centralized file server on a network allows employees to upload, download, and share files with others, allowing multiple people to work together on the same files. The same principle applies to file sharing between networking devices and client systems on a network. So, whenever a network professional has to update the firmware of a router or a modem, these networking devices usually support FTP as a method to transfer the firmware from a computer to the modem over a network.

> **Important note**
> FTP uses service ports 20 (data) and 21 (control) by default.

As an aspiring network professional, it's important to consider the security of the network when implementing network services and protocols within an organization. While an FTP server is usually implemented within the internal network of a company, it's still important to use secure protocols whenever possible to reduce the likelihood of a cyberattack. FTP is one of the many protocols that does not provide any data encryption and sends the traffic in plaintext. Therefore, if a threat actor such as a hacker can intercept the traffic that's being exchanged between an FTP client and an FTP server, the hacker will be able to capture all the data and user credentials that were exchanged between devices. Hence, FTP is vulnerable to **Man-in-the-Middle (MiTM)** attacks.

SSH File Transfer Protocol

The **SSH File Transfer Protocol (SFTP)** allows a client to establish an encrypted tunnel using **Secure Shell (SSH)** to a file server that supports the SFTP protocol. Once the SSH connection is established between the client and server, both devices encapsulate the FTP packets within the SSH tunnel for file transfer over the network.

The following diagram shows a visual representation of SFTP over a network:

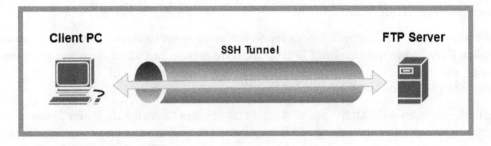

Figure 6.5 – SFTP

As shown in the preceding diagram, the computer establishes an SSH tunnel to the server on port 22 over the network and uses FTP to transfer files within the encrypted SSH tunnel. Using SFTP prevents a threat actor such as a hacker from identifying any confidential or sensitive data that's being exchanged over a network. The hacker will be able to intercept the traffic, but all the packets will be encrypted and the data will be unreadable.

> **Important note**
> SFTP uses service port 22 by default.

Network professionals should always use secure protocols such as SFTP whenever possible within their organization's networks and the internet. Without secure communication, hackers and other malicious users will be able to view our digital messages and capture confidential data. SFTP is one of the many secure protocols within the TCP/IP networking model.

File Transfer Protocol Secure

File Transfer Protocol Secure (**FTPS**), sometimes referred to as **FTP over SSL** (**FTP/S**), is another file transfer protocol that allows users to securely transfer files between a client and server over a network. SFTP uses **Secure Sockets Layer** (**SSL**) or **Transport Layer Security** (**TLS**) to encrypt the FTP messages that are being sent over the network between a client and server.

The client encrypts the FTP messages using SSL/TLS before placing the messages on the network to the destination FTP server. Compared to SFTP, as messages are sent across the network, there is no secure connection/tunnel; each FTPS packet is individually encrypted using SSL/TLS. Therefore, the FTP server will decrypt each FTPS message as they are received from the network and reassemble the messages into data.

However, FTPS operates on service port 990 and sometimes on service port 21. If a client on the network establishes a connection to the server on service port 990, it is considered to be **implicit FTPS**, which indicates the client intends to use SSL. As a result, the SSL handshakes will be exchanged between the client and server immediately.

On the other hand, if the client establishes a connection to the server on service port 21, it is known as **explicit FTPS**. When using explicit FTPS, the client connects to port 21 on the server and wants to use SSL with the server, additional steps are taken by sending either an AUTH SSL or AUTH TLS command from the client to the server.

Once the server receives the AUTH SSL or AUTH TLS command from the client over the network, the client and server will begin exchanging SSL handshakes and establish a secure connection. For this reason, when the client makes connections on service port 21 for FTPS, it's called explicit FTPS as the client has the option to enable better security mechanisms when needed to transfer sensitive files.

Trivial FTP

The **Trivial File Transfer Protocol** (**TFTP**) is a connectionless, lightweight version of FTP that allows network professionals to quickly upload and download files between a client and networking device over a network. In large organizations that have many networking devices such as routers and switches, network professionals update the operating systems and firmware of these devices to fix any bugs and security issues and improve the stability of the device. Enterprise-grade networking devices allow network professionals to configure switches and routers to load their operating systems from a remote TFTP server over a network at the boot time.

While networking devices have their operating systems stored locally, Cisco routers and switches can be configured to retrieve their operating system from a TFTP server at boot time. This method allows networking professionals to download and store the latest version of the operating system on a centralized TFTP server. When a networking device such as a Cisco router is powered on, it will check for a remote TFTP server and download the operating systems over the network and load it into the memory of the router. In the future, whenever a newer version of the operating system or firmware is available, network professionals can simply download the newer version and replace the older version on the TFTP server.

> **Important note**
> TFTP uses service port 69 by default.

The following diagram shows a visual representation of using TFTP on a network:

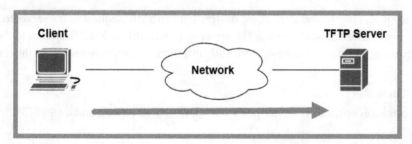

Figure 6.6 – TFTP service on a network

As shown in the preceding diagram, the client is connecting to the TFTP server on its default service port, 69, to upload or download files over the network. Being a connectionless protocol, TFTP uses UDP as the preferred Transport layer protocol, so it is lightweight and does not need acknowledgment messages when sending messages.

Server Message Block

The **Service Message Block** (**SMB**) is a common protocol that operates in a client-server model, allowing shared network resources such as printers, files, and directories to be shared in a Microsoft Windows environment.

The following are the three core functions of SMB:

- Starting, authenticating, and terminating sessions between a client and server
- Controlling access to files and printers
- Allowing applications to exchange information between devices on a network

The following diagram shows a visual representation of the client-server model of SMB:

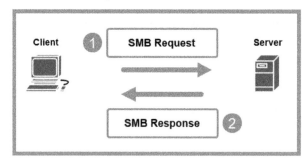

Figure 6.7 – Client-server model of SMB

As shown in the preceding diagram, the client devices send an **SMB Request** to the server to request the shared network resources on the server. The server responds with an **SMB Response** to the client, providing requesting additional information for authentication and providing access to the resources.

> **Important note**
> The SMB protocols operate on service ports 137 (UDP), 138 (UDP), and 445 (TCP).

While SMB is commonly used within a Microsoft Windows environment, Linux-based operating systems use a variation of SMB that is known as **SAMBA**. Lastly, Apple's macOS also uses SMB to share network resources between devices.

In this section, you learned about various networking protocols that help devices transfer files. Next, you will how network professionals can remotely access devices over a network.

Remote access protocols

Remote access protocols are special protocols that allow IT professionals to remotely access and manage devices over a network. Within an organization, there may be hundreds of servers and networking devices that are located at different remote offices. IT professionals usually configure remote management on these devices, which allows them to remotely connect and implement new configurations or perform troubleshooting to resolve any issues. Without remote access protocols, an IT professional will always need physical access to a device to perform any configuration changes or troubleshooting.

For instance, a few years ago, I was a network engineer for a regional **Internet Service Provider (ISP)** and my department was responsible for monitoring and resolving any networking issues that affected the performance of the service provider's network infrastructure and delivery of services. While working in the ISP, my team monitored networks within many different countries that had a lot of networking devices. If an issue occurs within any part of the network, whether it's within the same country as our offices or another country, a network engineer who is assigned to the service ticket will remotely connect to various networking devices within the service provider's network and perform troubleshooting to resolve the issues. Additionally, if any changes were to be made on the network, the same methodology applies – to remotely connect to the networking devices and administer the changes.

Using remote access protocols provides the convenience for IT professionals to centrally manage end devices, servers, and networking devices over a network. Additionally, it helps IT professionals save a lot of time from physically visiting the location of a server or network device. While remote access protocols provide a lot of conveniences, they also provide a security risk if an IT professional is using an unsecure remote access protocol to connect to a networking device. Unsecure protocols do not provide security features such as data encryption and sending messages in plaintext, allowing hackers to capture usernames and passwords.

Telnet

Telnet is an unsecure remote access protocol that allows IT professionals to remotely connect to devices such as computers, servers, networking devices, security appliances, and IoT devices. While Telnet is a legacy protocol and should not be used due to security concerns, many organizations still implement Telnet as a remote access protocol on their corporate networks.

The following screenshot shows the number of devices on the internet that have Telnet enabled for remote access:

Figure 6.8 – Shodan results

Shodan is an online service used by cybersecurity professionals to determine whether their organization's IT infrastructure is exposed to the internet. The preceding screenshot shows there are a lot of devices around the world that have Telnet enabled for remote access and management. If a hacker retrieves or guesses the correct user credentials for any device, the hacker will be able to access the target device over the internet.

> **Important note**
> Telnet uses service port 23 by default.

The following screenshot shows a reconstruction of packets that were exchanged between a client and a server using the Telnet protocol:

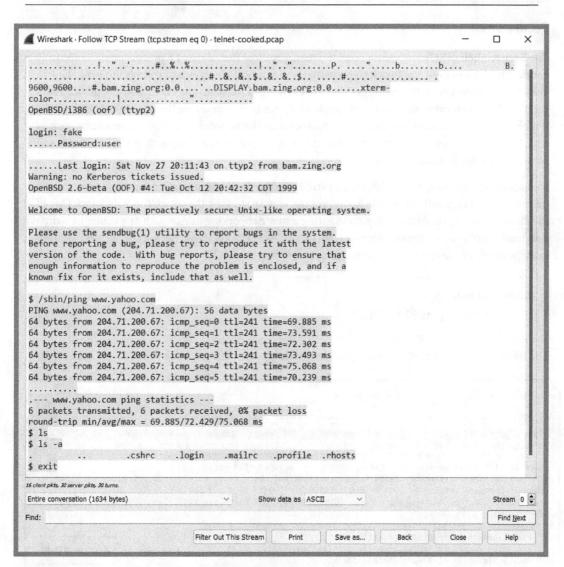

Figure 6.9 – Telnet messages

As shown in the preceding screenshot, the client and server exchanged messages and, using a packet analyzer such as **Wireshark**, reorganized all the Telnet messages and provided a simple overview of the communication that occurred between the client and server. The messages are displayed in plaintext because Telnet does not provide any data encryption, so it's an unsecure remote access protocol and is not recommended for use on a network.

Secure Shell

The **Secure Shell** (**SSH**) is a secure remote access protocol that allows IT professionals to securely connect to devices over a network to perform configuration changes and troubleshooting. Unlike Telnet, SSH encrypts all the messages that are exchanged between the client and the device that's running the SSH service, such as the networking device or the server on the network. Without SSH, it'll be risky to use unsecure remote access protocols on the network, whereby a threat actor such as a hacker can intercept the communication and capture confidential data such as the username and password needed to access a device.

SSH encrypts all messages, so a hacker can still intercept the communication between a source and destination, but they will not be able to decrypt the message to view the secret/concealed data. One of the most common procedures when configuring a new networking device such as a router or switch is to implement a secure remote access protocol such as SSH; this allows networking professionals to manage the device over a network using a secure protocol.

> **Important note**
> SSH uses service port 22 by default.

The following screenshot shows a sample Wireshark capture between a client and server using SSH:

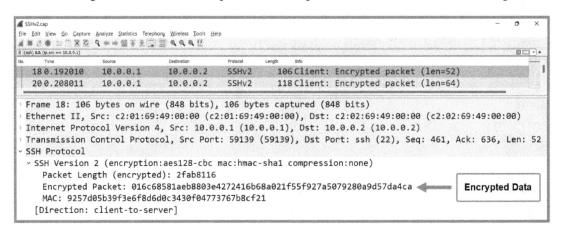

Figure 6.10 – SSH packet capture

As shown in the preceding screenshot, the client has an IP address of 10.0.0.1 and uses SSH to send encrypted messages to the server at 10.0.0.2. Wireshark helps determine the SSH version, encryption algorithm, and hashing algorithm for validating the integrity of the message, as well as the **Message Authentication Code** (**MAC**) value and the actual encrypted message/data. Therefore, the information displayed on the Wireshark interface is the same information that a hacker will be able to view and capture while the data is encrypted and safe.

Remote Desktop Protocol

Within a Microsoft Windows environment, IT professionals enable **Remote Desktop Protocol** (**RDP**), a native secure remote access protocol that is built into Microsoft Windows operating systems. Using RDP within an organization allows IT professionals to remotely manage Windows servers and desktop devices using a **Graphical User Interface** (**GUI**). This differs from SSH and Telnet, which provide a **Command-Line Interface** (**CLI**).

> **Important note**
>
> RDP operates on service port 3389.

The following screenshot shows a packet capture of RDP messages that were exchanged between two Microsoft Windows devices over a network:

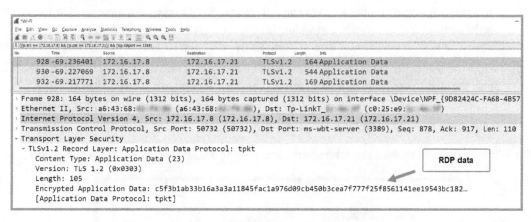

Figure 6.11 – RDP packet capture

As shown in the preceding screenshot, the client device has an IP address of 172.16.17.8 and it sends RDP messages to another host with an IP address of 172.16.17.21. The RDP message is encrypted using TLS, a security protocol that provides data security and privacy on a network. Furthermore, the packet capture reveals that the RDP messages are encrypted and prevent anyone from viewing the confidential data that's exchanged between the hosts on the network.

Email protocols

The way people communicate with each other has changed a lot over the years. Initially, a person would write a letter using the traditional method with a pen and paper or use a typewriter. Once the letter was written, it was enclosed within an envelope where the sender's information and destination addresses were inserted with a postal stamp. Then, it was given to the postal service organization for delivery to the intended recipient. Sending a traditional mail or package to someone can take some time before it arrives at the destination.

In today's world, sending a traditional letter to someone is almost replaced with electronic mail (email), which allows a sender to write a message using their computer or smartphone and send it over a network to the destination email address. Emails are typically delivered to their destination addresses within a few minutes compared to a traditional letter, where a courier service is used. Emails are commonly used to send letters, notices, memorandums, and share files as attachments between users. To ensure emails are transported and delivered over a network, various email protocols help devices format messages for transportation and delivery between a sender and destination address.

The SMTP is an email protocol that is used for sending emails from clients to email servers, and email servers to other email servers. The following process provides an overview of each phase of sending an email between a sender and destination:

1. When a user wants to send an email message to another person, the sender uses an email application such as **Microsoft Outlook** to compose and send the message.

2. The email application on the sender's computer uses SMTP to establish a connection to the sender's email server. When the connection is established, the email application uses SMTP to forward the email message to the sender's email server, which has service port 25 open by default.

3. When the sender's email server receives the email message, it also uses SMTP to forward the email message to the recipient's email server, which has service port 25 open by default.

4. When the email arrives on the recipient's email server, the server uses SMTP to send the message to the email application on the intended recipient's device.

The following diagram shows a visual representation of using SMTP to send emails over a network:

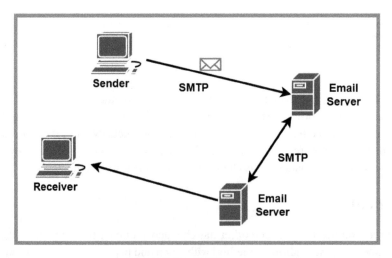

Figure 6.12 – SMTP process

The **Post Office Protocol** (**POP**) is a common email protocol that allows email clients such as Microsoft Outlook to download messages from email servers over a network. The email servers that use the POP service passively listen on TCP service port 110 for inbound requests from email client applications. Once a TCP connection is made between the client application and the email server on service port 110, the client downloads the email messages from the mailbox to the client. Once the emails have been downloaded, the email messages are deleted from the email server.

The following diagram shows a visual representation of the POP operations:

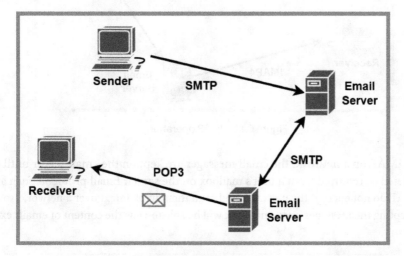

Figure 6.13 – POP operations

As POP deletes the email messages from the email server after downloading them onto the client device, there is no centralized location for storing the messages on a network. Hence, POP is not recommended for organizations that need a centralized backup solution for their resources.

The **Internet Message Access Protocol** (**IMAP**) is another common email protocol that allows email clients such as Microsoft Outlook to synchronize the email messages between the client application and email server via service port 143 by default over a network.

The following diagram shows a visual representation of IMAP on a network:

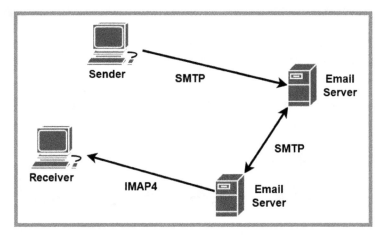

Figure 6.14 – IMAP operations

When using IMAP on a network, the email messages are kept on the email server until they are manually deleted or removed from a user's mailbox on the server. Email protocols such as SMTP, POP, and IMAP do not encrypt the messages and send them in plaintext over a network, so a hacker who is intercepting the messages over a network will be able to view the content of emails exchanged between users.

> **Important note**
> **POP version 3 (POP3)** and **IMAP version 4 (IMAP4)** are commonly used on networks.

The following screenshot shows a TCP stream of SMTP messages over a network within Wireshark:

No.	Time	Source	Destination	Protocol	Length	Info
5	0.383968	10.10.1.4	patriots.in	TCP	54	uaiact(1470) → smtp(25) [ACK] Seq=1 Ack=1 Win=65535 Len=0
7	0.732749	10.10.1.4	patriots.in	SMTP	63	C: EHLO GP
10	1.076669	10.10.1.4	patriots.in	SMTP	66	C: AUTH LOGIN
12	1.419595	10.10.1.4	patriots.in	SMTP	84	C: User: Z3VycGFydGFwQHBhdHJpb3RzLmlu
14	1.762058	10.10.1.4	patriots.in	SMTP	72	C: Pass: cHVuamFiQDEyMw==
16	2.122354	10.10.1.4	patriots.in	SMTP	90	C: MAIL FROM: <gurpartap@patriots.in>
18	2.465190	10.10.1.4	patriots.in	SMTP	93	C: RCPT TO: <raj_deol2002in@yahoo.co.in>
20	2.828143	10.10.1.4	patriots.in	SMTP	60	C: DATA
22	3.200683	10.10.1.4	patriots.in	SMTP	1514	C: DATA fragment, 1460 bytes
23	3.200726	10.10.1.4	patriots.in	SMTP	1514	C: DATA fragment, 1460 bytes
24	3.200744	10.10.1.4	patriots.in	SMTP	1514	C: DATA fragment, 1460 bytes

> Frame 11: 72 bytes on wire (576 bits), 72 bytes captured (576 bits)
> Ethernet II, Src: Netgear_d9:81:60 (00:1f:33:d9:81:60), Dst: Cradlepo_3c:17:c2 (00:e0:1c:3c:17:c2)
> Internet Protocol Version 4, Src: patriots.in (74.53.140.153), Dst: 10.10.1.4 (10.10.1.4)
> Transmission Control Protocol, Src Port: smtp (25), Dst Port: uaiact (1470), Seq: 319, Ack: 22, Len: 18
> Simple Mail Transfer Protocol

Figure 6.15 – Email message

As shown in the preceding screenshot, the **Info** column reveals sensitive information found within some SMTP packets, such as the username and password used by the client to access the email server on the network.

The following screenshot shows the TCP stream that was reassembled by Wireshark:

```
Wireshark · Follow TCP Stream (tcp.stream eq 0) · smtp.pcap                    —    □    ×

235 Authentication succeeded
MAIL FROM: <gurpartap@patriots.in>
250 OK
RCPT TO: <raj_deol2002in@yahoo.co.in>
250 Accepted
DATA
354 Enter message, ending with "." on a line by itself
From: "Gurpartap Singh" <gurpartap@patriots.in>
To: <raj_deol2002in@yahoo.co.in>
Subject: SMTP
Date: Mon, 5 Oct 2009 11:36:07 +0530
Message-ID: <000301ca4581$ef9e57f0$cedb07d0$@in>
MIME-Version: 1.0
Content-Type: multipart/mixed;
        boundary="----=_NextPart_000_0004_01CA45B0.095693F0"
X-Mailer: Microsoft Office Outlook 12.0
Thread-Index: AcpFgem9BvjjZEDeR1Kh8i+hUyVo0A==
Content-Language: en-us
x-cr-hashedpuzzle: SeA= AAR2 ADaH BpiO C4G1 D1gW FNB1 FPkR Fn+W HFCP HnYJ JO7s Kum6 KytW LFcI LjUt;
1;cgBhAGoAXWBkAGUAbwBsADIAMAAwADIAaQBuAEAAeQBhAGgAbwBvAC4AYwBvAC4AaQBuAA==;Sosha1_v1;7;{CAA37F59-1850-45C7-8540-
AA27696B5398};ZwB1AHIAcABhAHIAdABhAHAAAQABwAGEAdAByAGkAbwB0AHMALgBpBpAG4A;Mon, 05 Oct 2009 06:06:01 GMT;UwBNAFQAUAA=
x-cr-puzzleid: {CAA37F59-1850-45C7-8540-AA27696B5398}

This is a multipart message in MIME format.

------=_NextPart_000_0004_01CA45B0.095693F0
Content-Type: multipart/alternative;
        boundary="----=_NextPart_001_0005_01CA45B0.095693F0"


------=_NextPart_001_0005_01CA45B0.095693F0
Content-Type: text/plain;
        charset="us-ascii"
Content-Transfer-Encoding: 7bit

Hello


I send u smtp pcap file

Find the attachment
```

Figure 6.16 – Reassembled TCP stream

As shown in the preceding screenshot, Wireshark was able to reassemble all the data found within all SMTP packets exchanged between the client and the server to produce a TCP stream showing the plaintext messages that were exchanged in a dialog format. The messages displayed in red are sent from the client to the email server, while the messages in blue are messages from the email server to the client on the network.

Using unsecure protocols is not recommended due to a lack of security features such as data encryption to provide confidentiality and privacy. To solve the issue with security, **Simple Mail Transfer Protocol Secure (SMTPS)** is a secure email protocol that uses TLS to encrypt outbound emails over a network and uses service port number 587 by default. Additionally, the **Post Office Protocol Secure (POPS)** is a secure email protocol that uses SSL to encrypt the email messages that are being downloaded from an email server to an email application on the client and uses port 995 by default. Lastly, the **Internet Message Access Protocol Secure (IMAPS)** is a secure email protocol that operates on service port number 993 and uses SSL to encrypt the email messages between the client and server during the synchronization process.

HTTP and HTTPS

When communicating with a web server on a network or the internet, a user will typically open a web browser application on their device that uses HTTP to create a message that is recognizable to the web application running on the web server. HTTP is an unsecure protocol that does not provide confidentiality or data privacy and sends messages in plaintext over a network to a web server that uses service port number 80 by default.

The following screenshot shows an HTTP GET message that was sent from a client to a web server:

```
˅ Hypertext Transfer Protocol
  › GET /download.html HTTP/1.1\r\n
    Host: www.ethereal.com\r\n
    User-Agent: Mozilla/5.0 (Windows; U; Windows NT 5.1; en-US; rv:1.6) Gecko/20040113\r\n
    Accept: text/xml,application/xml,application/xhtml+xml,text/html;q=0.9,text/plain;q=0.8
    Accept-Language: en-us,en;q=0.5\r\n
    Accept-Encoding: gzip,deflate\r\n
    Accept-Charset: ISO-8859-1,utf-8;q=0.7,*;q=0.7\r\n
    Keep-Alive: 300\r\n
    Connection: keep-alive\r\n
    Referer: http://www.ethereal.com/development.html\r\n
    \r\n
    [Full request URI: http://www.ethereal.com/download.html]
    [HTTP request 1/1]
    [Response in frame: 38]
```

Figure 6.17 – HTTP message

As shown in the preceding screenshot, Wireshark can display the contents within the HTTP section of the packet between the client and web server on the network; HTTP does not encrypt the messages and sends them in plaintext. To resolve the security concerns of HTTP, it's recommended to use **HTTP over SSL (HTTPS)**, which is a secure version of HTTP that establishes a secure connection between the web browser and web server over the network while using service port number 443 by default.

> **Important note**
>
> HTTPS can use either SSL or TLS when connecting to a web server.

The following screenshot shows a client connecting to a web server using HTTP:

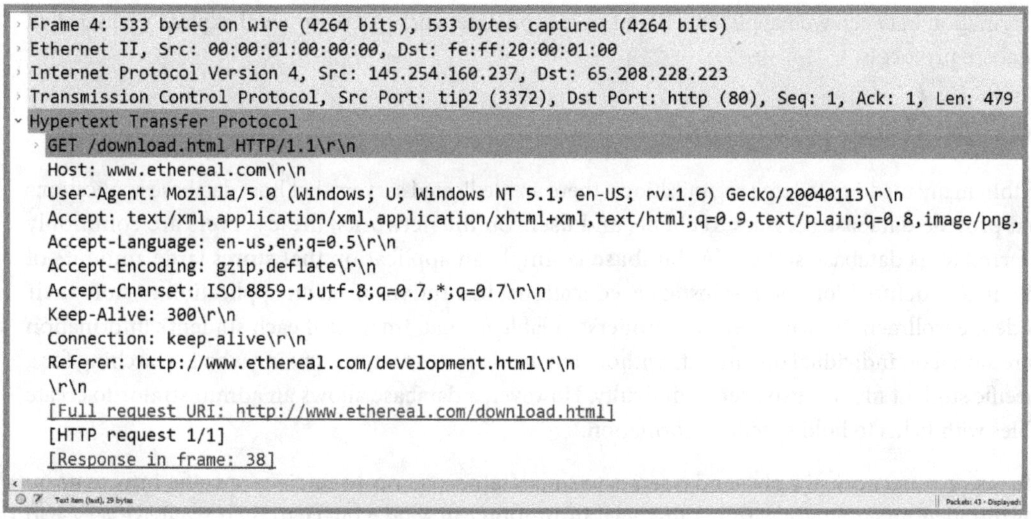

```
Frame 4: 533 bytes on wire (4264 bits), 533 bytes captured (4264 bits)
Ethernet II, Src: 00:00:01:00:00:00, Dst: fe:ff:20:00:01:00
Internet Protocol Version 4, Src: 145.254.160.237, Dst: 65.208.228.223
Transmission Control Protocol, Src Port: tip2 (3372), Dst Port: http (80), Seq: 1, Ack: 1, Len: 479
Hypertext Transfer Protocol
  GET /download.html HTTP/1.1\r\n
  Host: www.ethereal.com\r\n
  User-Agent: Mozilla/5.0 (Windows; U; Windows NT 5.1; en-US; rv:1.6) Gecko/20040113\r\n
  Accept: text/xml,application/xml,application/xhtml+xml,text/html;q=0.9,text/plain;q=0.8,image/png,
  Accept-Language: en-us,en;q=0.5\r\n
  Accept-Encoding: gzip,deflate\r\n
  Accept-Charset: ISO-8859-1,utf-8;q=0.7,*;q=0.7\r\n
  Keep-Alive: 300\r\n
  Connection: keep-alive\r\n
  Referer: http://www.ethereal.com/development.html\r\n
  \r\n
  [Full request URI: http://www.ethereal.com/download.html]
  [HTTP request 1/1]
  [Response in frame: 38]
```

Figure 6.18 – HTTP GET message

As shown in the preceding screenshot, the client device sends the HTTP GET message to service port 80 on the server and can see the contents of the message in plaintext. As network professionals and hackers will be able to determine the location of the resource that's being requested by the client device on the internet, it's not recommended to use unsecure protocols on a network due to data privacy concerns.

The following screenshot shows the contents of an HTTPS packet that was captured while it was sent from a client to a web server:

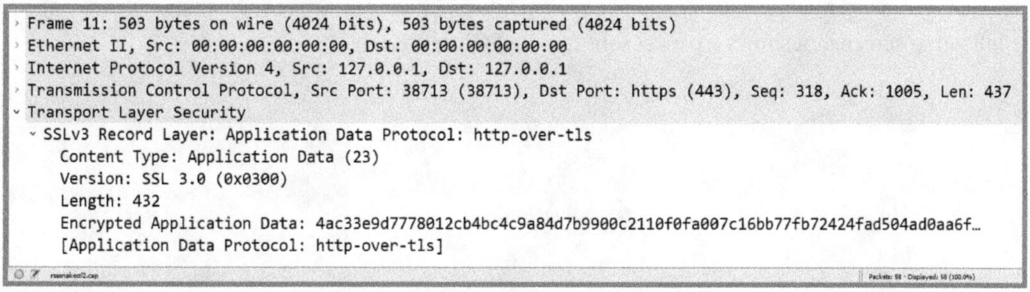

```
Frame 11: 503 bytes on wire (4024 bits), 503 bytes captured (4024 bits)
Ethernet II, Src: 00:00:00:00:00:00, Dst: 00:00:00:00:00:00
Internet Protocol Version 4, Src: 127.0.0.1, Dst: 127.0.0.1
Transmission Control Protocol, Src Port: 38713 (38713), Dst Port: https (443), Seq: 318, Ack: 1005, Len: 437
Transport Layer Security
  SSLv3 Record Layer: Application Data Protocol: http-over-tls
    Content Type: Application Data (23)
    Version: SSL 3.0 (0x0300)
    Length: 432
    Encrypted Application Data: 4ac33e9d7778012cb4bc4c9a84d7b9900c2110f0fa007c16bb77fb72424fad504ad0aa6f…
    [Application Data Protocol: http-over-tls]
```

Figure 6.19 – HTTPS message

As shown in the preceding screenshot, the contents of the HTTPS message are unreadable because it's encrypted, unlike HTTP. Using HTTPS allows users to securely connect to web servers and exchange messages between their web browser application and the web server over the network. Try to always use secure protocols such as HTTPS whenever possible to ensure data security and privacy.

With that, you've discovered common networking protocols that are used to send and retrieve information between web applications and clients on a network. Next, you will explore various data database protocols.

SQL database protocols

Within many medium to large organizations, there are dedicated servers that host database applications that provide database services to clients and users on the networks; these servers are commonly referred to as database servers. A **database** is simply an application that stores large amounts of data in a structured format. For instance, educational institutions need an application to store their student enrollment information in an understandable format. Imagine if each student's information were stored on individual documents without any fields and structure; anyone who is searching for a specific student file will experience difficulty. However, a database allows an administrator to create tables with fields to hold specific information.

Clients on a network simply send queries to the database server to retrieve specific information. For instance, an employee within a financial institution can send a query to their database server to retrieve the records of all people who opened an account within a specific period. Furthermore, the employee can be very granular with queries such as filtering age group, time range, gender, and so on. Database applications operate in a client-server model, whereby the user has the database client-side application installed on their computer, which connects to the database application that's running on the database server over the network.

The following are common database application protocols and their operating port numbers:

- **SQL Server** operates on service port 1433
- **SQLNet** operates on service port 1521
- **MySQL** operates on service port 3306

The following screenshot shows a packet sent to a MySQL server:

```
> Frame 6: 132 bytes on wire (1056 bits), 132 bytes captured (1056 bits)
> Ethernet II, Src: 00:00:00:00:00:00, Dst: 00:00:00:00:00:00
> Internet Protocol Version 4, Src: 192.168.0.254, Dst: 192.168.0.254
> Transmission Control Protocol, Src Port: 56162 (56162), Dst Port: mysql (3306), Seq: 1, Ack: 57, Len: 66
˅ MySQL Protocol
    Packet Length: 62
    Packet Number: 1
  ˅ Login Request
    > Client Capabilities: 0xa685
    > Extended Client Capabilities: 0x0003
      MAX Packet: 16777216
      Charset: utf8 COLLATE utf8_general_ci (33)
      Unused: 00000000000000000000000000000000000000000000000
      Username: tfoerste
      Password: eefd6d5562851bc5966a0b41236ae3f2315efcc4
```

Figure 6.20 – MySQL packet

As shown in the preceding screenshot, the client sends the username and password hash to the MySQL server on port 3306. Furthermore, notice that the user credentials are sent in plaintext as the MySQL database protocol does not encrypt messages by default.

Lightweight Directory Access Protocol

The **Lightweight Directory Access Protocol (LDAP)** is a common network protocol that is used to perform operations such as read, write, and query on a directory server over a network. A common directory service is the **Active Directory Domain Service (AD DS)** on a Microsoft Windows Server operating system. Active Directory allows IT professionals to centrally manage all users and connected devices on a Windows domain within an organization. Simply put, IT professionals join all computers on the Windows domain and create the users' accounts on Active Directory. Additionally, Active Directory allows policies to be applied to users, groups, and computer accounts on the Windows domain.

> **Important note**
>
> The Windows server that is running the AD DS role is commonly referred to as the **Domain Controller (DC)**.

To gain a better idea of how LDAP works, the following steps provide details of when a user is connecting to a Windows domain using Active Directory:

1. The user powers on their computer and is prompted to log in using their domain user account.

2. The user enters their username and password on the Windows client computer.

3. The Windows client computer converts the user's password into a **New Technology LAN Manager (NTLM)** hash value because the Microsoft Windows operating system does not store users' passwords in plaintext.

4.   The user's username and password hash is sent to the DC using LDAP.

5.   The DC checks the Active Directory service to determine the authenticity of the user's credentials and applies policies.

6.   The DC informs the Windows client device on whether to allow the user to log in and the policies to apply.

The communication that occurs between the Windows client device and the DC uses LDAP by default. However, LDAP is an unsecure network protocol that operates on service port 389 by default on directory servers.

The following screenshot shows the information captured from an LDAP message on a network:

```
[+] Listening for events ...

[SMB] NTLMv2-SSP Client    : 192.168.42.23
[SMB] NTLMv2-SSP Username  : REDTEAMLAB\bob
[SMB] NTLMv2-SSP Hash      : bob::REDTEAMLAB:dfcd20c1317287a1:57A3BBBE56FA9A3F9A67AEE
20B1BD124:010100000000000080F0706BB295D701EE6249EE418CC89300000000020008004A0055004E
004A0001001E00570049004E002D004F004D0042005700570053005000490045004500450037000040340057
0049004E002D004F004D0042005700570053005000490045004500450037002E004A0055004E004A002E004C
004F00430041004C00030014004A0055004E004A002E004C004F00430041004C00050014004A0055004E
004A002E004C004F00430041004C000700080080F0706BB295D70106000400020000000008003000300000
000000000001000000020000020D6265CA99359070E75C00205F6C3A43CDEC000C918DE7CA1E5DB82B3
6E70A50A00100000000000000000000000000000000000009002400630069006600730002F003100390032
002E003100360038002E00340032002E003200030030000000000000000000000
```

Figure 6.21 – LDAP message

As shown in the preceding screenshot, the contents of an LDAP message from a client to a DC were captured and the data was sent in plaintext. A hacker who is intercepting the packets on a network will be able to capture the client's source IP address, the domain name, and the username and password hash of the user.

> **Important note**
> LDAP uses the X.500 standard, which defines how information is stored and organized within a directory server.

Since LDAP is an unsecure protocol that does not provide confidentiality and data security, it's recommended to use **LDAP Secure** (**LDAPS**), which uses SSL/TLS for data encryption to ensure privacy on a network. LDAPS operates on service port 636 by default.

Syslog

Networking devices, servers, and even end devices generate log messages that contain information and critical details about events that occur. Network professionals use the information found within log messages to identify if a problem has occurred and what caused the problem. Since each networking device generates a log message, this means a network professional will need to manually log into a device to view the logs for that device only. This process can be very time-consuming and inefficient.

Many networking devices, servers, and end devices support a common network protocol that allows them to forward their log messages over a network to a centralized logging server. This protocol is known as **Syslog**. The Syslog protocol allows devices to generate logs for events that occur on a device. For example, if an interface on a router has been disabled or enabled, a Syslog message is created that contains all the necessary details about the event.

The following is the default format of a Syslog message that is generated by Cisco devices:

```
seq no: timestamp: %facility-severity-MNEMONIC: description
```

The following is a breakdown of each component of a Syslog message:

- `seq no`: Represents the sequence number that is assigned to the log message.
- `timestamp`: Includes the date and time the message was generated by the device. The date and timestamp are taken from the system clock on the host device.
- `facility`: Represents what the log message is referencing on the event that has occurred, such as the source of the problem or protocol.
- `severity`: Includes a severity code that helps network professionals determine the importance of the event.
- `MNEMONIC`: Inserts text that is uniquely used to describe the event.
- `description`: Contains a brief description of the event.

The following is an example of a Syslog message generated by a Cisco device:

```
*Apr 28, 15:53:58.5353: %LINEPROTO-5-UPDOWN: Line protocol on
Interface GigabitEthernet0/1, changed state to up
```

The following table contains the Syslog severity levels, their names, and descriptions:

Severity Name	Severity Level	Description
Emergency	0	System is unusable
Alert	1	Immediate action is needed
Critical	2	Critical condition
Error	3	Error condition
Warning	4	Warning condition
Notification	5	Normal but significant condition
Informational	6	Informational message
Debugging	7	Debugging message

Figure 6.22 – Syslog severity levels

The Syslog protocol uses UDP service port number 514 by default over a network. Keep in mind that Syslog is used to gather logging information that helps network professionals with monitoring and troubleshooting issues within an organization. Syslog allows network professionals to configure devices to send their log messages to a specific logging destination, such as a centralized logging server.

Session Initiation Protocol

Voice over IP (**VoIP**) is a very common technology that allows organizations to implement a telephone system on their existing TCP/IP network. The telephones have an IP address assigned on the network that converts a person's voice into a digital signal in the form of packets to be transmitted over a network. The IP phones communicate with a **Unified Communication Server** (**UCS**) that contains the call routing features, voicemail settings, hunt groups, and other calling functions that are needed by the organization.

One of the major benefits of using a VoIP system within an organization is the cost efficiency of the telephone charges. An employee can simply pick up their IP phone and dial the extension number of another employee within the same organization and won't be billed for the internal call as the communication is occurring within the organization's network. When an employee uses their IP phone to call another employee, the IP phone uses the **Session Initiation Protocol** (**SIP**), a common network protocol that provides real-time transmission of both voice and video traffic over a network.

> **Important note**
>
> SIP operates on service port 5060 by default and does not encrypt messages over the network. However, there's a secure version of SIP that operates on service port 5051.

Real-time protocols such as SIP use UDP as their preferred Transport layer protocol as it provides faster transmission and low overhead on the network compared to TCP. However, since UDP messages have a high priority to be discarded on a congested network, network professionals usually implement **Quality of Service (QoS)** technologies on the network to guarantee the allocation of network bandwidth to specific traffic types such as VoIP and **Video over IP**.

Next, you will discover common networking protocol types such as TCP, UDP, and ICMP.

Network protocol types

There are so many protocols and protocol types on a network and learning them can take a lifetime to master. However, as an aspiring network professional, it's important to understand the fundamentals of common network protocol types that are found within many organizations. Network protocol types are simply the set of rules that are used to describe how a device such as a computer communicates with another device over a network. If two devices are used, whether they are the same type of devices or different, both systems need to negotiate on a common set of rules. These common rules are referred to as the network protocol type.

Over the next few sub-sections, you will learn about the fundamentals of ICMP, TCP, and UDP.

Internet Control Message Protocol

Internet Control Message Protocol (ICMP), defined by RFC 792, is typically used to provide error reporting on a network. Common networking tools such as **Ping** and **Traceroute** are built into many operating systems and allow network professionals to invoke ICMP to check end-to-end connectivity between hosts on a network, identify the path a packet is traveling between a source and destination, and even measure the latency between hops on a network.

The following table provides a breakdown of each ICMP type by name, code, and description:

Type	Name	Code
0	Echo Reply	0
3	Destination Unreachable	0 - Nework Unreachable
		1 - Host Unreachable
		2 - Protocol Unreachable
		3 - Port Unreachable
		4 - Fragmentation needed and "Don't Fragment" was set
5	Redirect	0 - Redirect for the Network
		1 - Redirect for the Host
8	Echo Request	0
11	Time Exceeded	0 - Time to Live (TTL) exceeded
		1 - Fragment reassembly time exceeded

Figure 6.23 – ICMP codes and types

As shown in the preceding table, various ICMP codes and types are inserted within an ICMP packet. For instance, the following screenshot shows a connectivity test between my computer and Google's DNS server on the internet:

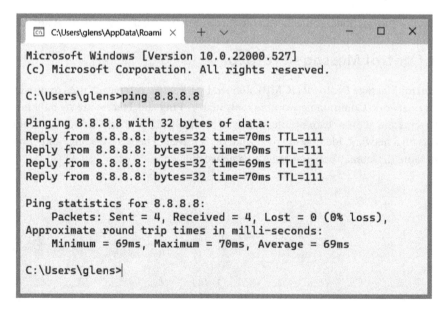

Figure 6.24 – Using ping to test connectivity

As shown in the preceding screenshot, the local host sent four **ICMP Echo Request** messages to Google's DNS server on the network and received four **ICMP Echo Reply** messages. The following screenshot shows the ICMP type and code value for the **ICMP Echo Request** message with the source and destination IP addresses and port numbers:

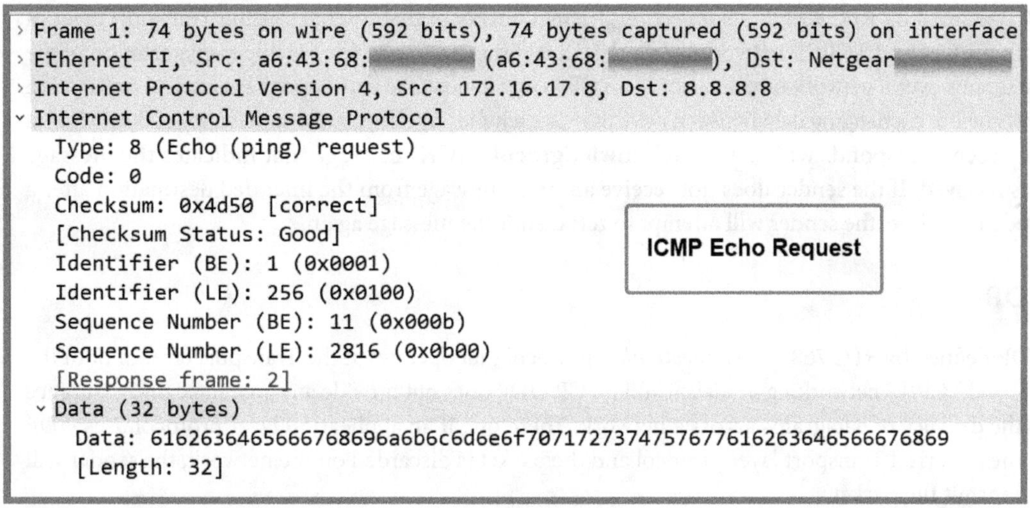

```
> Frame 1: 74 bytes on wire (592 bits), 74 bytes captured (592 bits) on interface
> Ethernet II, Src: a6:43:68:          (a6:43:68:          ), Dst: Netgear
> Internet Protocol Version 4, Src: 172.16.17.8, Dst: 8.8.8.8
v Internet Control Message Protocol
    Type: 8 (Echo (ping) request)
    Code: 0
    Checksum: 0x4d50 [correct]
    [Checksum Status: Good]
    Identifier (BE): 1 (0x0001)                ┌──────────────────────────┐
    Identifier (LE): 256 (0x0100)              │    ICMP Echo Request      │
    Sequence Number (BE): 11 (0x000b)          └──────────────────────────┘
    Sequence Number (LE): 2816 (0x0b00)
    [Response frame: 2]
  v Data (32 bytes)
      Data: 6162636465666768696a6b6c6d6e6f707172737475767761626364656667 6869
      [Length: 32]
```

Figure 6.25 – ICMP Echo Request message

For each **ICMP Echo Request** message that's received and processed by a host, an **ICMP Echo Reply** is returned. The following screenshot shows the ICMP type and code values within an **ICMP Echo Reply** message:

```
> Frame 2: 74 bytes on wire (592 bits), 74 bytes captured (592 bits) on interface
> Ethernet II, Src: Netgear          (9c:3d:cf:          , Dst: a6:43:68:
> Internet Protocol Version 4, Src: 8.8.8.8, Dst: 172.16.17.8
v Internet Control Message Protocol
    Type: 0 (Echo (ping) reply)
    Code: 0
    Checksum: 0x5550 [correct]
    [Checksum Status: Good]                     ┌──────────────────────────┐
    Identifier (BE): 1 (0x0001)                 │     ICMP Echo Reply       │
    Identifier (LE): 256 (0x0100)               └──────────────────────────┘
    Sequence Number (BE): 11 (0x000b)
    Sequence Number (LE): 2816 (0x0b00)
    [Request frame: 1]
    [Response time: 69.797 ms]
  v Data (32 bytes)
      Data: 6162636465666768696a6b6c6d6e6f707172737475767761626364656667 6869
      [Length: 32]
```

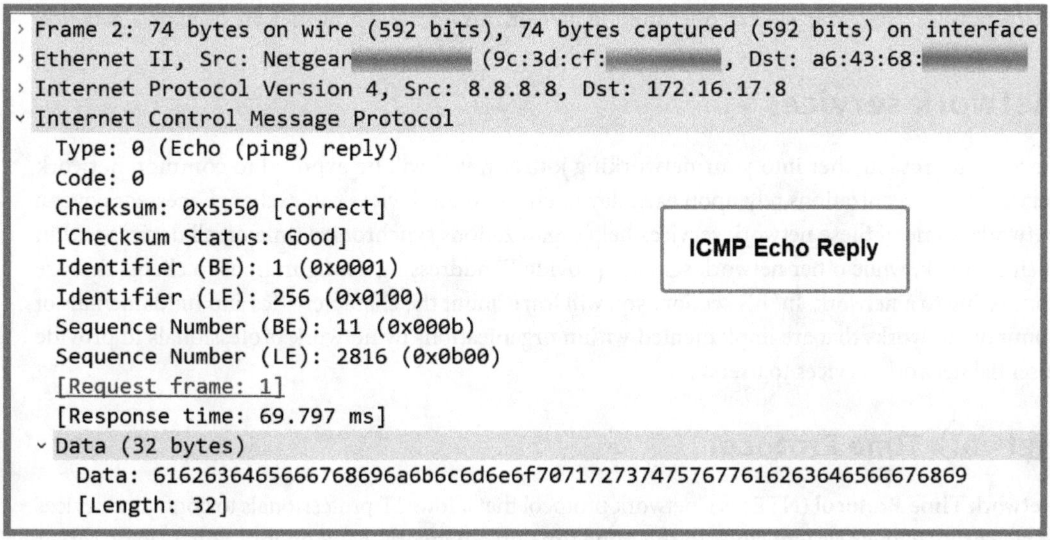

Figure 6.26 – ICMP Echo Reply message

Network professionals use various free and commercial software-based tools that use ICMP to assist with identifying any potential issues on a network and resolving them.

TCP

TCP, defined by RFC 793, is a *connection-oriented* protocol that operates at the Transport layer of both the OSI and TCP/IP networking models. It is designed to provide reliable transportation of the datagrams over a network by establishing a TCP 3-way handshake between the source and destination hosts before exchanging data between devices. For each message sent between devices on the network, the receiver responds with a TCP **acknowledgment** (**ACK**) message that indicates the message was received. If the sender does not receive an ACK message from the intended destination after a predefined time, the sender will attempt to retransmit the message again.

UDP

UDP, defined by RFC 768, is a *connectionless* protocol that operates at the Transport layer of both the OSI and TCP/IP networking models. Unlike TCP, UDP does not provide any guarantee or reassurance of the delivery of datagrams across a network. Therefore, if an application layer protocol uses UDP as the preferred Transport layer protocol and the packet is discarded on the network, the sender will retransmit the packet.

As quickly as the application layer is sending data down the TCP/IP networking model, UDP will be forwarding those messages quickly further down the model and then onto the network. UDP is not concerned about whether the messages are delivered to the intended destination. However, it provides faster data transmission and less overhead on the network compared to TCP.

Having completed this section, you have learned about common network protocol types and their characteristics. Next, you will explore common network services and how they are used on a network.

Network services

As you progress further into your networking journey, you will be exposed to common network services that organizations rely upon each day to ensure their devices can exchange messages over a network. Some of these network services help organizations synchronize time on all devices within their network, while other network services provide IP addressing configurations to clients that are connecting to a network. In this section, you will learn about the characteristics and fundamentals of common networks that are implemented within organizations by network professionals to provide essential network services to users.

Network Time Protocol

Network Time Protocol (**NTP**) is a network protocol that allows IT professionals to configure devices to synchronize their system clock to the same time on a network. NTP operates on a client-server model that uses UDP service port 123 by default. Without NTP on a network, IT professionals will need to manually configure the time on each device such as computers, servers, networking devices, and security appliances within the organization. This process can be very time consuming, which can lead to misconfigurations and mismatches in the time set on many devices.

When time is synchronized on the system clocks on all devices, it ensures all devices have the same time set. This is important for ensuring automated tasks are executed on time and in the proper sequence. Imagine if IT professionals configure various tasks on servers and systems to be undertaken automatically at a specific time of day for each day of the week. If the time on the devices is not accurate, the tasks will not be performed when needed. Furthermore, when a device is generating Syslog messages, it's important to include the time and date in each log message to help network professionals determine when an event or incident has occurred. Without time synchronization, the time inserted into Syslog messages will not correlate with the events on other networking devices. This will create a challenge for network professionals to determine the actual sequence of events that occurred on the network.

> **Important note**
>
> NTP is an unsecure protocol that allows hackers to exploit its security vulnerabilities. However, NTP allows authentication between an NTP server and NTP clients over a network.

The following diagram shows the NTP architecture and hierarchical structure:

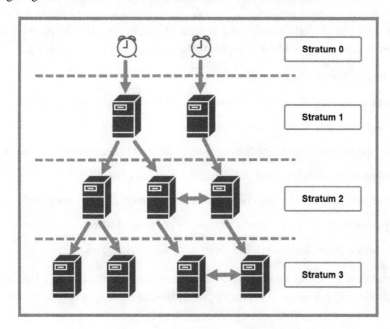

Figure 6.27 – NTP hierarchical structure

As shown in the preceding diagram, the NTP hierarchical structure is made up of clients, servers, and stratum levels. The NTP servers are devices that provide the time for NTP clients on a network.

> **Important note**
> The NTP stratum levels range from 0 to 15, where level 0 contains the authoritative sources.

Each stratum level 0 contains the primary time servers and are known as the authoritative sources on the network that have the most accurate time. Servers at stratum level 1 synchronize their time clocks with devices on stratum 0, while devices on stratum 2 synchronize their time with those devices on stratum 1 and so on.

Dynamic Host Configuration Protocol

The **Dynamic Host Configuration Protocol** (**DHCP**) is a common network protocol and service that allows network professionals to automatically distribute IP addresses to client devices on a network. When an end device such as a computer or smartphone is connected to a network, it requires an IP address, subnet mask, default gateway address, and **Domain Name System** (**DNS**) server address. These IP addresses allow the client to communicate with devices on the same network and remote networks.

Imagine if network professionals have to statically/manually assign IP addresses to each device that's connecting to their organization's network; the process will be time-consuming and lead to duplication of IP address assignment. To help simplify the process of distributing IP addresses on a network, network professionals implement a DHCP server, which allows them to configure the following:

- **Scope**: The range of IP addresses (pool)
- **Exclusion ranges**: The IP addresses that should not be distributed on the network
- **Reservation**: Reserves IP addresses from the pool
- **Dynamic assignment**: Dynamically assigns an IP address to a client on the network
- **Static assignment**: Statically configures an IP address on a client
- **Lease time**: Sets the time that the client can use the IP address given from the DHCP server
- **Scope options**: Additional operations that can be configured when creating the scope
- **Available leases**: Identifies the available lease time for an IP address

Whenever a client device such as a computer connects to a network, it will seek a DHCP server on the network to retrieve IP addresses to communicate with other hosts on the same network.

> **Important note**
>
> A DHCP client sends a DHCP message from a source service port of 68. The DHCP server operates on service port 67 by default.

To gain a better idea of the DHCP process, the following steps outline the DHCP 4-way handshake that occurs when a client connects to a network with an active DHCP server:

1. The client connects to the network and sends a DHCP **Discover** message, seeking a DHCP server on the network:

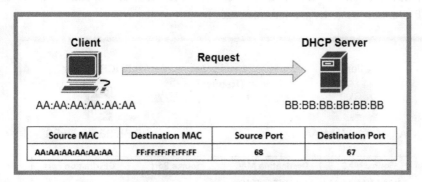

Figure 6.28 – DHCP Discover message

As shown in the preceding diagram, the client includes its source **Media Access Control** (**MAC**) address and source port number, which is 68. The client inserts the destination MAC address as FF:FF:FF:FF:FF:FF with the broadcast MAC address for a Layer 2 network and the destination port number, which is 67. The source IP address on the packet is left blank while the destination IP address is set to 255.255.255.255.

2. Next, the DHCP server responds with a DHCP **Offer** message, which contains the IP address needed by the client for communication on the network:

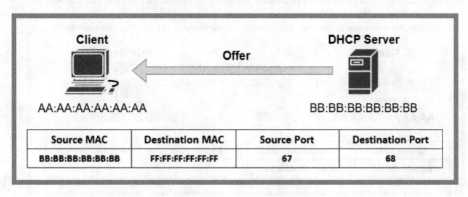

Figure 6.29 – DHCP Offer message

As shown in the preceding diagram, the DHCP **Offer** message is sent from the DHCP server to the client on the network. The DHCP **Offer** message contains the source MAC address and source port number 67 of the DHCP server. This message also contains the destination MAC and destination port number 68 of the client on the network.

> **Important note**
> The DHCP **Offer** message is sometimes sent as unicast or broadcast to the client on the network.

3. Next, the client sends a DHCP **Request** message to the DHCP server, indicating that it will use the IP addresses from the previous message:

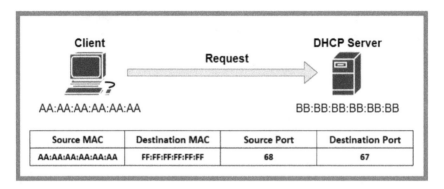

Figure 6.30 – DHCP Request message

As shown in the preceding diagram, the client sends a Layer 2 broadcast message to the DHCP server on the network, even though the client knows the MAC address of the DHCP server from the DHCP **Offer** packet.

4. Lastly, the DHCP server responds with a DHCP **Acknowledgment** unicast message to confirm the client can use the IP address provided from the addressing pool on the server:

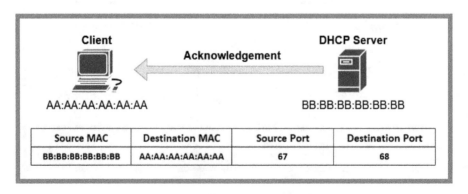

Figure 6.31 – DHCP Acknowledgement message

The client is allowed to use the IP addresses provided by the DHCP server for the duration of the lease. If the client wants to extend the lease of communication on the network, the client can send a DHCP **Request** (unicast) message to the DHCP server to request the renewal of the lease.

What if a client connects to the organization's network but the DHCP server is located on another IP subnet? How will the client be able to get the IP addresses from the server? Sometimes, network professionals will configure a DHCP server with multiple address pools and implement it in a centralized location. However, when a client connects to a network, it will send a DHCP Discover message, which is only broadcast to a Layer 2 network. This means that any Layer 2 broadcast messages will not be able to propagate beyond a router.

The following diagram shows a router blocking a **DHCP Discover** message from propagating to another network:

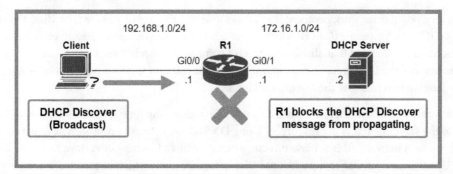

Figure 6.32 – Router blocks Layer 2 broadcast message

As shown in the preceding diagram, routers and other Layer 3 devices do not propagate Layer 2 broadcast messages beyond their source network. As a result, the **DHCP Discover** message from the client will not be able to reach the DHCP server on another network.

To solve this issue, configuring the router to be a **DHCP Relay** agent will allow the router to forward DHCP messages between clients and DHCP servers over a network, as shown here:

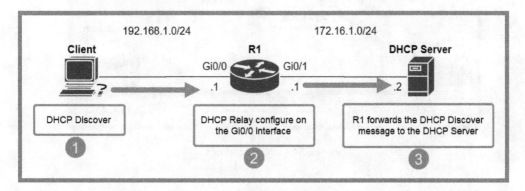

Figure 6.33 – DHCP Relay agent

The GigabitEthernet 0/0 interface on the router is configured with the following configurations to allow the router to relay the DHCP messages between the 192.168.1.0/24 network and the DHCP server:

```
R1(config)# interface GigabitEthernet 0/0
R1(config-if)# ip helper-address 172.16.1.2
R1(config-if)# exit
```

Keep in mind that the ip helper-address command is applied to the interface on the router that receives DHCP Discover messages from clients.

DNS

DNS is a very popular network protocol that allows a device to resolve a **Fully Qualified Domain Name (FQDN)** or a hostname to an IP address over a network. As you know already, each device on a network has an IP address that allows end-to-end communication between hosts. Imagine if you need to remember the IP address of each web server on the internet that you want to visit – it will be quite challenging to remember these logical addresses.

What if a server's IP address has changed and you don't know the new IP address? How will you connect to the server to access the resources? Using DNS allows network professionals to implement a DNS server on a network. This is like a directory that contains a listening of various hostnames that maps to IP addresses, similar to a traditional telephone directory, which contains a list of people's names and their telephone numbers.

The following diagram shows a typical DNS transaction between a client and DNS server:

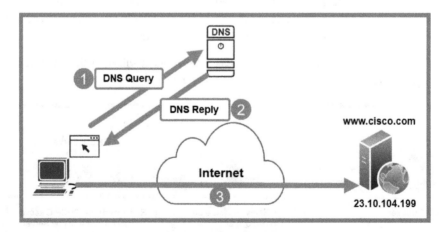

Figure 6.34 – DNS operations

The following is a breakdown of the DNS operations shown in the preceding diagram:

1. The client wants to establish a connection to www.cisco.com but does not know the IP address of the web server. Therefore, the client sends a **DNS Query** message to the DNS server on service port 53, requesting the IP address of www.cisco.com.

2. The DNS server receives this **DNS Query** and performs a lookup within its database and finds the record. The DNS server responds with a **DNS Reply** that contains the IP address of www.cisco.com.

3. The client receives the **DNS Reply** information and connects to the IP address found in the response from the DNS server.

> **Important note**
> DNS servers use port UDP port 53 by default. However, a DNS server can exchange zone records with another DNS server by using TCP port 53.

Within a DNS server, network professionals can create various types of records containing specific IP addressing information. The following are a list of record types and their purpose:

- **Address** (A versus AAAA): The A record maps a hostname to an IPv4 address, while the AAAA record maps a hostname to an IPv6 address

- **Canonical name** (CNAME): The CNAME record allows an alias to be mapped to a domain name

- **Mail Exchange** (MX): The MX records contain the addresses of mail exchangers on a domain

- **Start of Authority** (SOA): The SOA record specifies the authority of the domain

- **Pointer** (PTR): The PTR record maps an IP address to a hostname

- **Text** (TXT): The TXT record contains text information that helps a domain owner validate ownership of a domain

- **Service** (SRV): The SRV record contains the service records for the domain

- **Name Server** (NS): The NS record contains the name servers for a domain

The following screenshot shows an example of performing a DNS lookup using the native nslookup tool within a Microsoft Windows operating system:

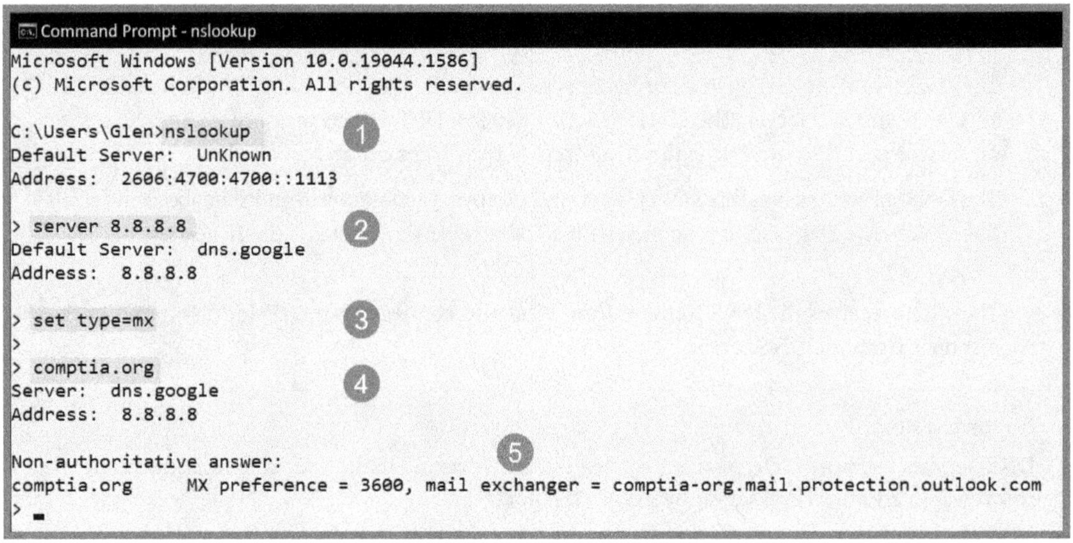

```
cmd Command Prompt - nslookup
Microsoft Windows [Version 10.0.19044.1586]
(c) Microsoft Corporation. All rights reserved.

C:\Users\Glen>nslookup                    1
Default Server:  UnKnown
Address:  2606:4700:4700::1113

> server 8.8.8.8                          2
Default Server:  dns.google
Address:  8.8.8.8

> set type=mx                             3
>
> comptia.org                             4
Server:  dns.google
Address:  8.8.8.8

Non-authoritative answer:                              5
comptia.org     MX preference = 3600, mail exchanger = comptia-org.mail.protection.outlook.com
> ▃
```

Figure 6.35 – DNS lookup

As shown in the preceding screenshot, the `nslookup` tool allows network professionals to troubleshoot DNS-related issues on a network. The following is a breakdown of each step shown in the preceding screenshot:

1. When the `nslookup` command is entered in the Windows **Command Prompt**, it provides the current DNS server that's configured for the host device. The address information that's returned is retrieved from the configurations of the host device.

2. Using the `server <ip address/hostname>` command allows the network professional to specify another DNS server to send queries while using nslookup.

3. Next, the `set type` command is used with a DNS record type to indicate which record type to query.

4. Lastly, entering a domain name such as `comptia.org` will send the query to `8.8.8.8` for the MX record type.

5. The results indicate the information was retrieved from a non-authoritative source/server and the hostname (or IP address) of CompTIA's email server(s) were found.

> **Important note**
>
> An **authoritative DNS server** is the final holder of an IP address for a domain name or hostname on a network. The authoritative DNS server for a domain contains the original DNS records that are associated with a domain. However, the **recursive DNS server** or **non-authoritative DNS server** does not hold the original DNS records for a domain but queries an authoritative server when needed.

Each domain name that's available on the internet contains the root (`.`) and a **Top-Level Domain (TLD)** such as `.com`, `.net`, or `.org` within the name, such as `cisco.com`. However, hostnames are usually assigned to servers such as `www.cisco.com`. This is commonly referred to as an FQDN since it contains a TLD, the hostname, and the domain. Using an FQDN allows network professionals and devices to specify the location of a device on a network.

The following diagram shows an example of a global hierarchy of root DNS servers, which contains the record for their corresponding TLDs:

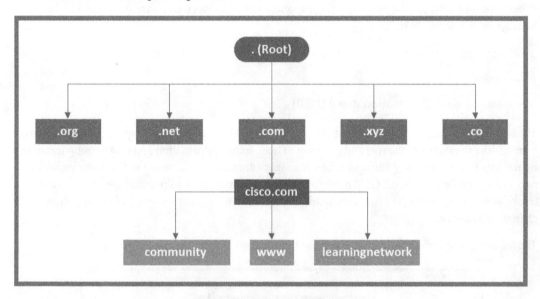

Figure 6.36 – Root DNS servers

As shown in the preceding diagram, the `.com` root DNS server contains all the DNS information about all the registered domain names that use the `.com` TLD. The `.com` root DNS server contains the DNS information for the `cisco.com` domain and its hostnames.

There are many trusted DNS servers on the internet that provide improved performance, speed, and security. The following are some examples of trusted DNS servers:

- **Cloudflare DNS**: `https://1.1.1.1/`
- **Quad9 DNS**: `https://www.quad9.net/`
- **OpenDNS**: `https://www.opendns.com/`
- **Google Public DNS**: `https://developers.google.com/speed/public-dns`

Keep in mind that you should always use trusted DNS servers whenever possible as they provide improved performance on hostname resolution and security features to filter malware and malicious websites.

Simple Network Management Protocol

The **Simple Network Management Protocol** (**SNMP**) is a common network protocol that allows network professionals to remotely manage and monitor networking devices, security appliances, and servers within their organization. SNMP helps network professionals collect information about the performance and status of a device to determine whether an issue exists, as well as how long the issue has been occurring based on historical data.

When working with SNMP, three main components need to work together to create a **Network Management System** (**NMS**):

- Manager

- Agent

- **Management Information Based** (**MIB**)

The Manager is an application that's installed on the network professional's computer or centrally on a server. The manager has the role and function to both collect information and make configurations on devices that are running the agent. The manager can retrieve information from agents on the network by sending an SNMP GET message that instructs the agent to respond with the requested information. Additionally, the manager sends SNMP SET messages to an agent when configuration changes are needed.

The following diagram shows a simple representation of SNMP messages on a network:

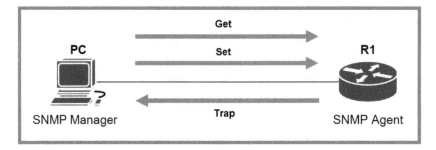

Figure 6.37 – SNMP messages

The SNMP agent is configured on the networking device, such as a switch or router. The SNMP agent is the actual component on the networking device that communicates with the SNMP manager application and vice versa. The MIB is a database that contains the information needed by the agent to find and retrieve data from a device. Simply put, the network professionals use the manager to retrieve information from a device that's running an SNMP agent. The SNMP agent uses MIB to locate the requested information within the networking device and responds to the agent with the collected data.

> **Important note**
> SNMP operates on UDP service port 161 by default. However, the SNMP manager uses UDP service port 162.

The following are the three current versions of SNMP:

- **SNMPv1**: Has bad security features such as no data encryption or authentication mechanisms
- **SNMPv2**: This version of SNMP also contains bad security features
- **SNMPv3**: Supports data encryption and authentication

Having completed this section, you have learned about various network services, along with their role and functions on a network. In the next section, you will learn how to analyze various traffic and protocol types on a network.

Lab – analyzing FTP packets

In this hands-on exercise, you will learn how to analyze FTP packets using Wireshark. To get started with this exercise, follow these steps:

1. Go to `https://wiki.wireshark.org/SampleCaptures` and download the `iseries.cap` file, as shown here:

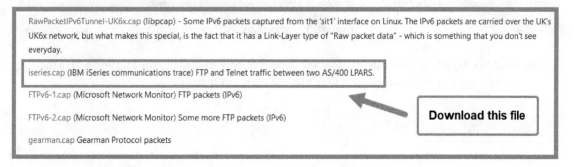

Figure 6.38 – FTP sample file

2. Next, launch the Wireshark application on your computer and click on **File | Open**, as shown here:

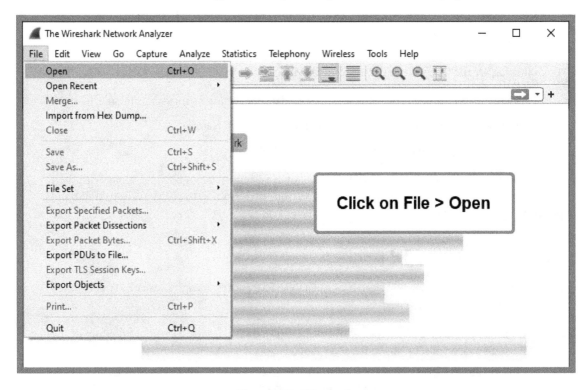

Figure 6.39 – Wireshark

3. Next, the **Open Capture File** window will appear. Simply navigate to the location where the iseries.cap file is stored, select the file, and click on **Open**:

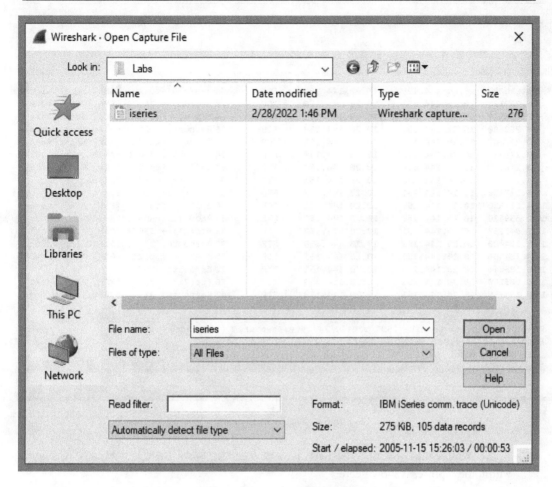

Figure 6.40 – Loading a .pcap file

4. Next, Wireshark loads all the information found within the captured packets and shows the source and destination IP addresses, source and destination service port numbers, protocols, and the data found in each packet:

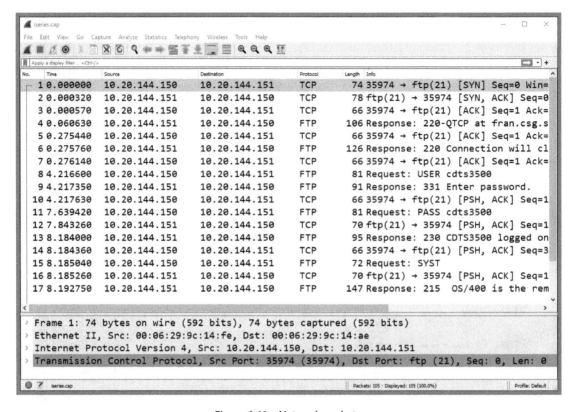

Figure 6.41 – Network packets

5. In the **Display Filter** bar on Wireshark, type `ftp` and hit *Enter* to filter all the FTP packets within the capture, as shown here:

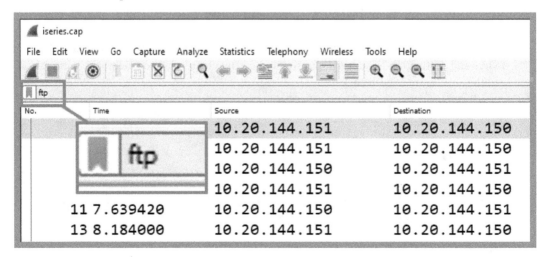

Figure 6.42 – Filtering FTP packets

6. Next, you will notice Wireshark displays the packets that are related to FTP only:

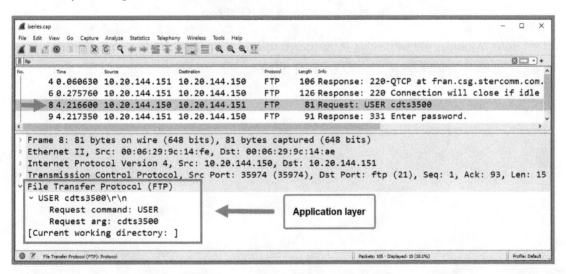

Figure 6.43 – FTP packets

As shown in the preceding screenshot, sensitive information is shown within the **Info** column of each FTP packet, such as the user credentials sent from the client to the FTP server on the network and the step-by-step actions performed between each device.

7. Next, select **packet #8** to display the packet details and the data found within the Application layer of the packet, as shown here:

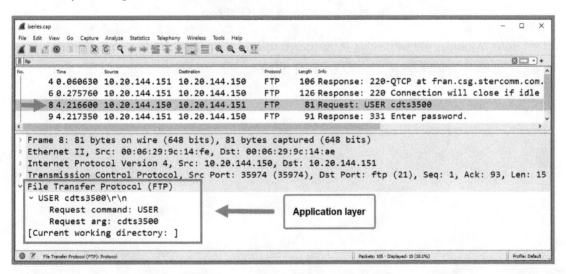

Figure 6.44 – Analyzing FTP packets

As shown in the preceding screenshot, the username was sent in plaintext to the server on the network. Additionally, you can see the source and destination IP addresses and service port numbers.

8. Next, to view the entire conversation between the FTP client and server, right-click on **packet #4** and select **Follow | TCP Stream**, as shown here:

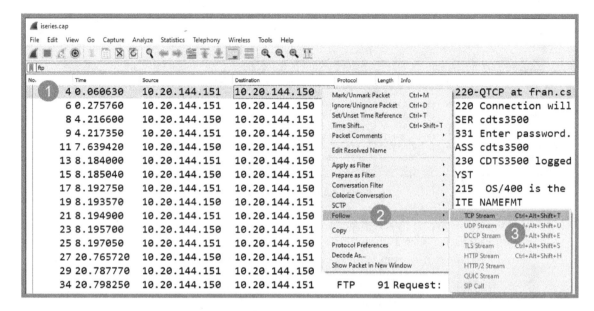

Figure 6.45 – Following the TCP stream

9. Next, Wireshark will reassemble all the packets that are part of the TCP stream and open a new window displaying the entire transaction of messages between the client and server:

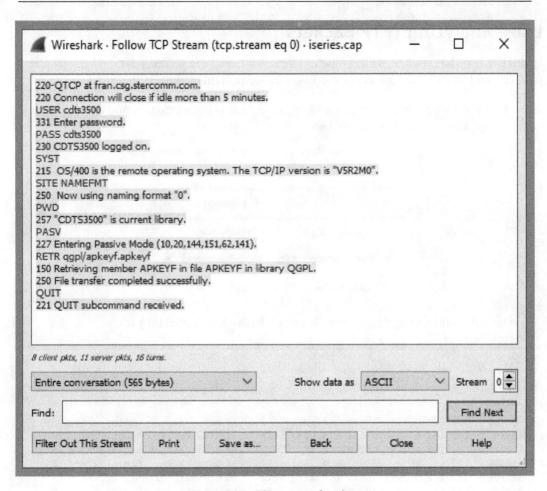

```
Wireshark · Follow TCP Stream (tcp.stream eq 0) · iseries.cap        —    □    ✕

220-QTCP at fran.csg.stercomm.com.
220 Connection will close if idle more than 5 minutes.
USER cdts3500
331 Enter password.
PASS cdts3500
230 CDTS3500 logged on.
SYST
215  OS/400 is the remote operating system. The TCP/IP version is "V5R2M0".
SITE NAMEFMT
250  Now using naming format "0".
PWD
257 "CDTS3500" is current library.
PASV
227 Entering Passive Mode (10,20,144,151,62,141).
RETR qgpl/apkeyf.apkeyf
150 Retrieving member APKEYF in file APKEYF in library QGPL.
250 File transfer completed successfully.
QUIT
221 QUIT subcommand received.

8 client pkts, 11 server pkts, 16 turns.

Entire conversation (565 bytes)  ⌄    Show data as  ASCII  ⌄  Stream 0 ⬍

Find:                                                                Find Next

Filter Out This Stream    Print    Save as...    Back    Close    Help
```

Figure 6.46 – TCP stream of packets

As shown in the preceding screenshot, the messages from the server to the client are displayed in blue, while the messages from the client to the server are displayed in red. You can see the username and password that were used to access the server and the commands entered by the user on the client device.

10. Lastly, close the **TCP Stream** window and Wireshark.

Having completed this lab, you have discovered the various fields and values that are found within FTP messages. In the next hands-on exercise, you will explore the difference between FTP and TFTP messages.

Lab – analyzing TFTP packets

In this hands-on lab, you will explore how TFTP packets learn to reconstruct data and extract files from captured TFTP packets on a network. To get started with this exercise, follow these steps:

1. Go to `https://wiki.wireshark.org/SampleCaptures` and download the `tftp_rrq.pcap` file, as shown here:

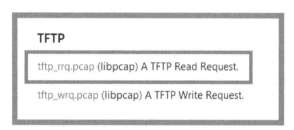

Figure 6.47 – TFTP packet capture file

2. Next, open the `tftp_rrq.pcap` file using Wireshark to view all the packets:

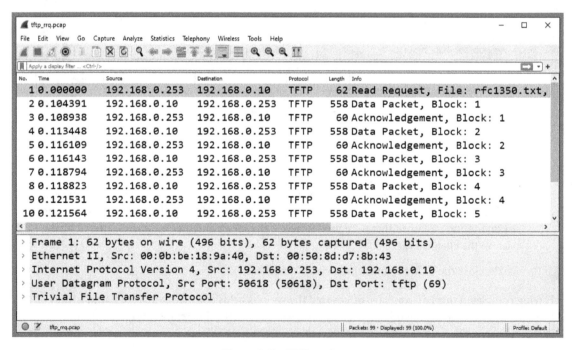

Figure 6.48 – TFTP packets

As shown in the preceding screenshot, **packet #1** is a **Read Request** message from the client to the TFTP server on the network and it's requesting the `rfc1350.txt` file. Next, the file is transferred in multiple data blocks from the server at `192.168.0.10` to the client at `192.168.0.253` over the network.

3. Within a total of 99 packets, the entire text file is transferred from the server to the client. To view the entire `rfc1350.txt` file, select **File | Export Objects | TFTP**, as shown here:

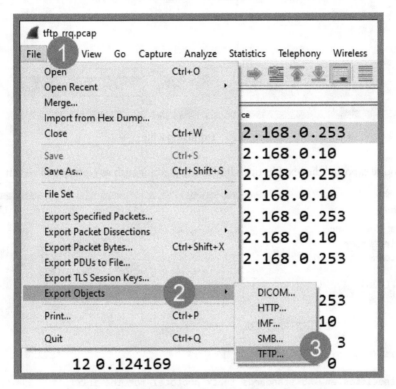

Figure 6.49 – Export menu

4. Next, the **Export Object** window will appear and display the files that were found within the entire capture file, as well as the packet number that's associated with finding the file. To extract the file from the packet capture, select the file and click on **Save**, as shown here:

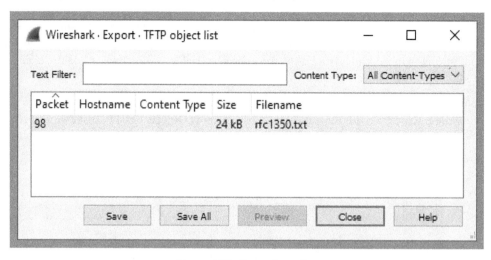

Figure 6.50 – Exporting a file

5.   Once you've exported the text file, open it with a text editor such as **Notepad** to view its contents:

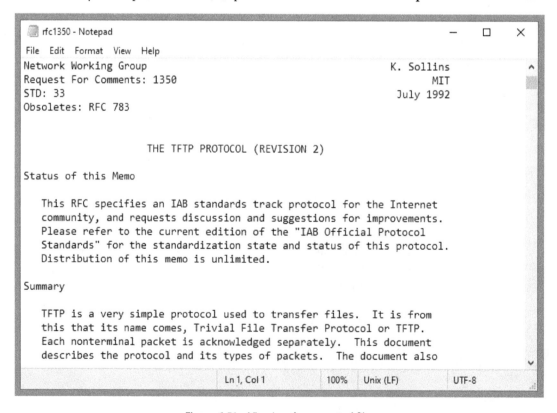

Figure 6.51 – Viewing the exported file

Having completed this exercise, you have learned how to analyze TFTP packets using Wireshark and extract the files that are transferred between a client and a server. In the next lab, you will explore captured SMB packets.

Lab – analyzing SMB packets

In this hands-on exercise, you will explore the security risks and discover how data is exchanged over a network between hosts that uses the SMB protocol. To get started with this exercise, follow these steps:

1. First, go to `https://www.7-zip.org/` to download the **7-Zip** application and install it on your computer, as shown here:

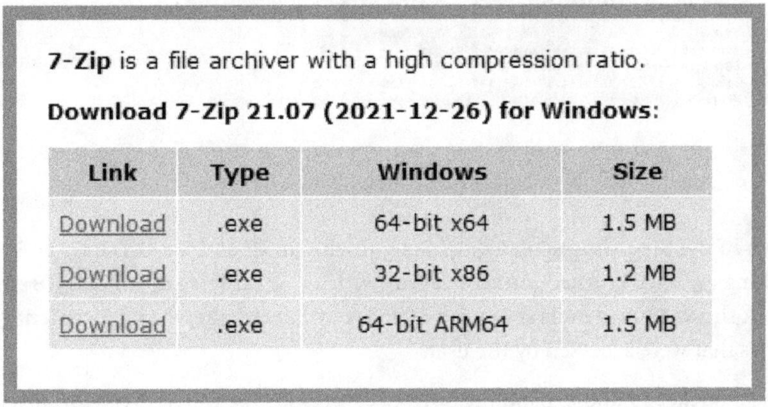

Link	Type	Windows	Size
Download	.exe	64-bit x64	1.5 MB
Download	.exe	32-bit x86	1.2 MB
Download	.exe	64-bit ARM64	1.5 MB

7-Zip is a file archiver with a high compression ratio.

Download 7-Zip 21.07 (2021-12-26) for Windows:

Figure 6.52 – 7-Zip application

2. Next, go to `https://wiki.wireshark.org/SampleCaptures` and download the `smbtorture.cap.gz` file onto your computer, as shown in the following screenshot:

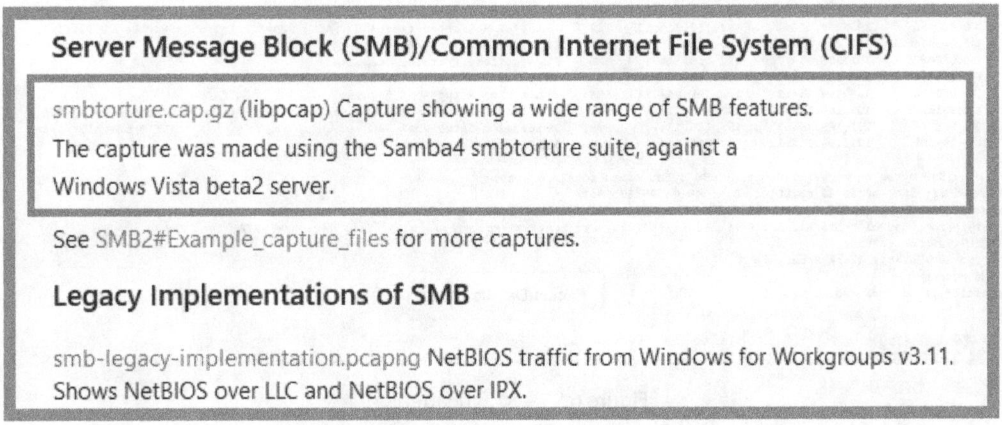

Server Message Block (SMB)/Common Internet File System (CIFS)

smbtorture.cap.gz (libpcap) Capture showing a wide range of SMB features. The capture was made using the Samba4 smbtorture suite, against a Windows Vista beta2 server.

See SMB2#Example_capture_files for more captures.

Legacy Implementations of SMB

smb-legacy-implementation.pcapng NetBIOS traffic from Windows for Workgroups v3.11. Shows NetBIOS over LLC and NetBIOS over IPX.

Figure 6.53 – SMB sample capture file

3. Next, use the 7-Zip application to unzip/extract the `smbtorture` Wireshark capture file.

4. Open the extracted `smbtorture` file using the Wireshark application, as shown here:

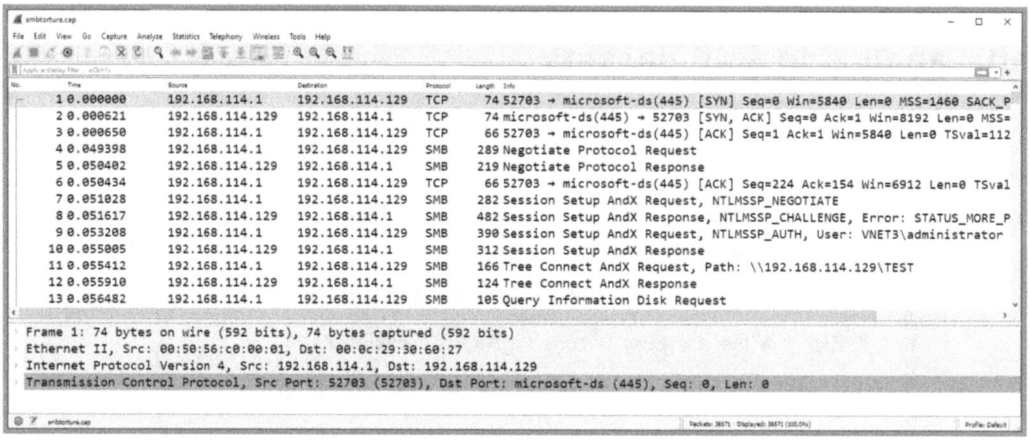

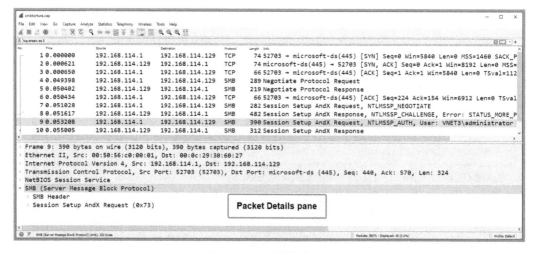

Figure 6.54 – SMB packets

As shown in the preceding screenshot, a client with an IP address of 192.168.114.1 is establishing an SMB connection to a server with an IP address of 192.168.114.129. Wireshark shows some details about the **TCP 3-way handshake**, the user credentials, and the directories that were accessed by the user.

5. Next, select **packet #9** and expand the **SMB (Server Message Block Protocol)** field within the **Packet Details** pane on Wireshark:

Figure 6.55 – SMB header

6. Next, expand **Session Setup AndX Request | Security Blob | GSS-API Generic Security Service Application Program Interface | Simple Protected Negotiation | negTokenTrag | NTLM Secure Service Provider**. Here, you will see the username, NTLM hash, hostname of the client, and domain name that was used to request access to the SMB server:

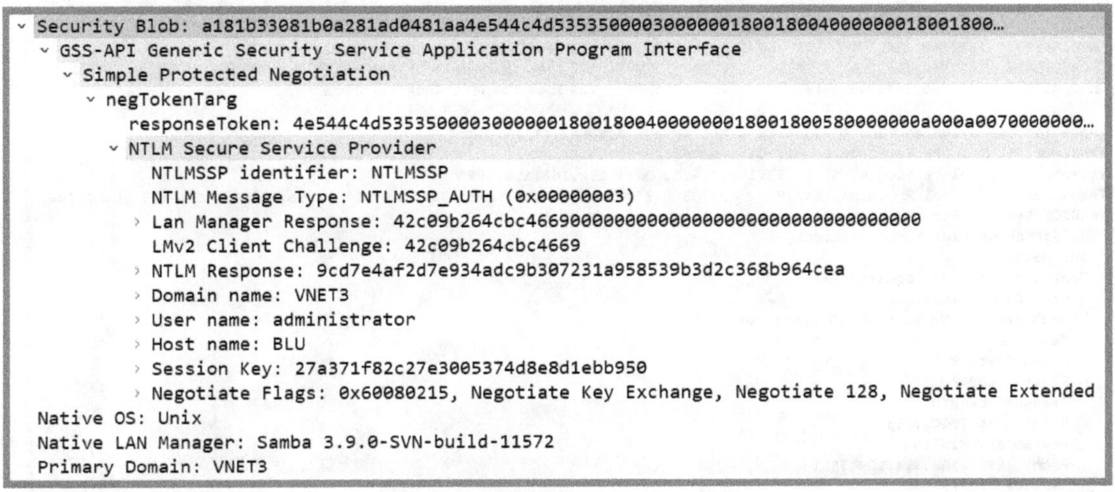

```
v Security Blob: a181b33081b0a281ad0481aa4e544c4d535350000300000018001800400000018001800...
  v GSS-API Generic Security Service Application Program Interface
    v Simple Protected Negotiation
      v negTokenTarg
          responseToken: 4e544c4d535350000300000018001800400000018001800580000000a000a0070000000...
        v NTLM Secure Service Provider
            NTLMSSP identifier: NTLMSSP
            NTLM Message Type: NTLMSSP_AUTH (0x00000003)
          > Lan Manager Response: 42c09b264cbc4669000000000000000000000000000000000000000000
            LMv2 Client Challenge: 42c09b264cbc4669
          > NTLM Response: 9cd7e4af2d7e934adc9b307231a958539b3d2c368b964cea
          > Domain name: VNET3
          > User name: administrator
          > Host name: BLU
          > Session Key: 27a371f82c27e3005374d8e8d1ebb950
          > Negotiate Flags: 0x60080215, Negotiate Key Exchange, Negotiate 128, Negotiate Extended
Native OS: Unix
Native LAN Manager: Samba 3.9.0-SVN-build-11572
Primary Domain: VNET3
```

Figure 6.56 – SMB Request message

As shown in the preceding screenshot, the client sent all the information the SMB server needs to validate the identity and authenticity of the client before providing access to the shared network resources on the server.

7. Next, select **packet #11** to view the path (directory) that's being requested by the client on the server:

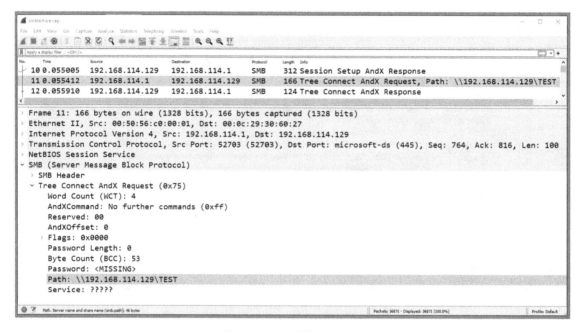

Figure 6.57 – SMB directory

As shown in the preceding screenshot, the client is requesting access to the \\192.168.114.129\TEST directory on the SMB server.

8. Next, scroll through the remaining packets within the capture file and try to identify what the user is doing on the SMB server on the network. Some packets' information will reveal the user is creating, modifying, and even deleting some of the files on the server.

9. Next, to view all the files that were transmitted between the client and server, on **Wireshark**, select **File | Export Objects | SMB**, as shown here:

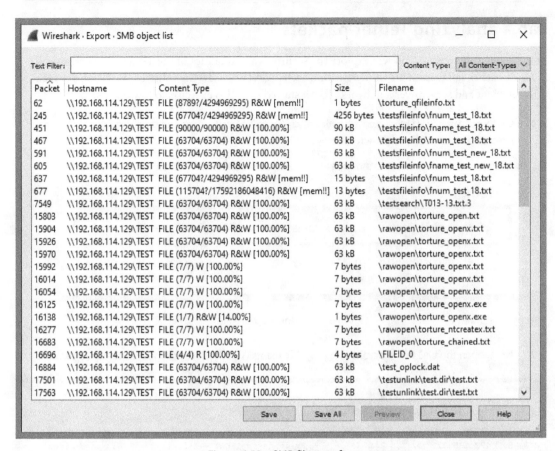

Figure 6.58 – SMB file transfers

As shown in the preceding screenshot, Wireshark was able to reassemble all the files that were exchanged using the SMB protocol between the client and server. You can choose to extract one or more files by using the **Save** and **Save All** buttons on the **Export** window.

10. Lastly, when you're finished working with Wireshark and analyzing the packets, you can close the application and document your findings as it will help you gain a better understanding of how communication occurs over a network.

Having completed this hands-on exercise, you have explored the SMB protocol using Wireshark, a protocol analyzer that provides you with the details found within each packet on a network.

Lab – analyzing Telnet packets

In this hands-on exercise, you will explore the security vulnerabilities of the Telnet protocol, as well as how a hacker can reassemble the data within each packet and view the entire conversation between a Telnet client and server over a network. To get started with this exercise, follow these steps:

1. Go to `https://wiki.wireshark.org/SampleCaptures` and download the `telnet-cooked.pcap` file, as shown here:

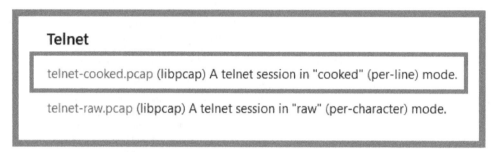

Figure 6.59 – Telnet capture file

2. Next, open the `telnet-cooked.pcap` file using Wireshark to view all the captured packets:

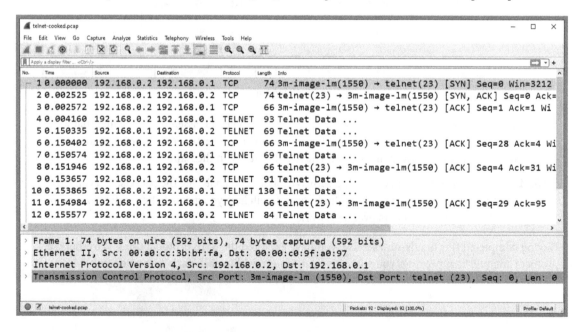

Figure 6.60 – Telnet packets

As shown in the preceding screenshot, there's a client with an IP address of `192.168.0.2` that is establishing a Telnet session to a server with an IP address of `192.168.0.1`.

3. Next, right-click on **packet #1** and select **Follow | TCP Stream** to view the entire conversation between the client and the Telnet server on the network:

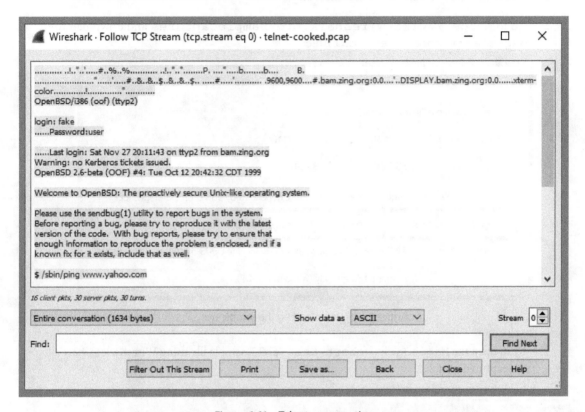

Figure 6.61 – Telnet conversation

As shown in the preceding screenshot, Wireshark was able to reconstruct the entire conversation that occurred between the client and server that were using the Telnet protocol. The message written in red is sent from the client to the server, while the messages written in blue are those from the server to the client. As mentioned previously, Telnet is an unsecure protocol that does not encrypt the messages between devices over a network. As a result, a threat actor such as a hacker can intercept the messages on a network and capture any sensitive and confidential information, as you have seen in this exercise.

Having completed this exercise, you have learned how a threat actor can view the information found within unsecure network protocols and have understood why it's important to always use secure protocol whenever possible. In the next lab, you will learn how to listen to a VoIP call using Wireshark.

Lab – reassembling a SIP telephone conversation

In this hands-on lab, you will discover the security flaws found within the SIP protocol and how to assemble all the SIP packets and listen to a VoIP conversation that occurred over a network. To get started with this hands-on exercise, follow these steps:

1. Go to `https://wiki.wireshark.org/SampleCaptures` and download the `MagicJack+ short test call` file:

SIP and RTP

aaa.pcap Sample SIP and RTP traffic.

SIP_CALL_RTP_G711 Sample SIP call with RTP in G711.

SIP_DTMF2.cap Sample SIP call with RFC 2833 DTMF

MagicJack+ Power On sequence SIP and RTP traffic generated by power on the MagicJack+

MagicJack+ short test call A complete telephone call example

sip-rtp-opus-hybrid.pcap SIP and OPUS hybrid payloads, include OPUS-multiple frames packets.

rtp-opus-only.pcap RTP Opus payloads only (without SIP/SDP).

Figure 6.62 – Downloading the sample file

2. Next, open the `MagicJack+ short test call` sample file using Wireshark to view all the captured packets:

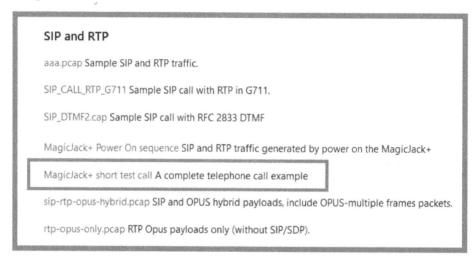

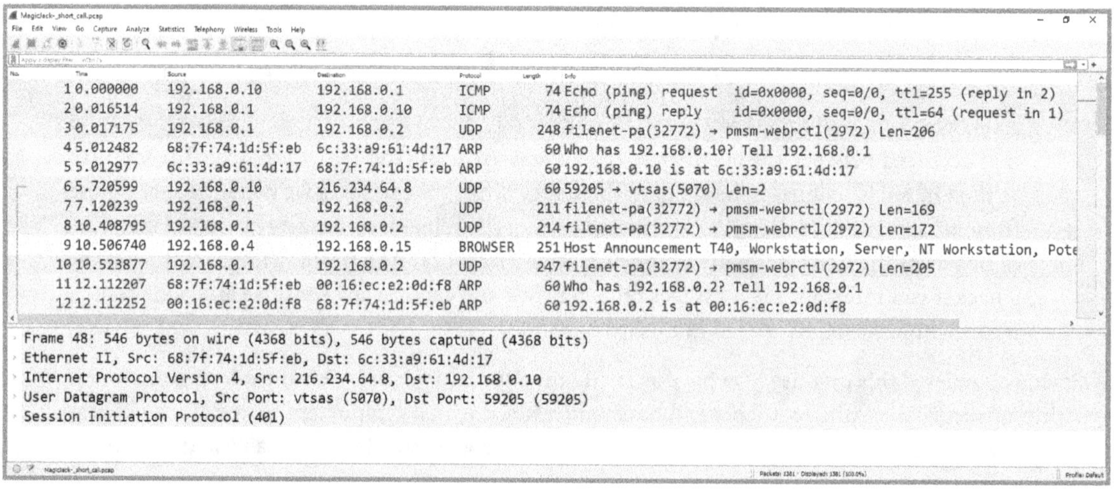

Figure 6.63 – SIP packet capture

3. Next, click on **Telephony | VoIP Calls** on the Wireshark menu bar:

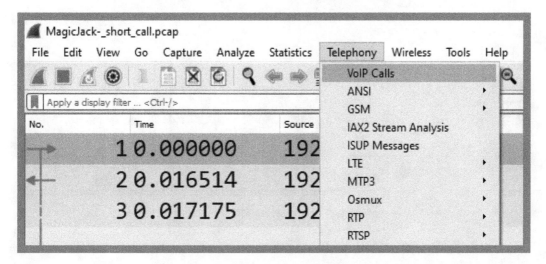

Figure 6.64 – Telephony menu

4. Next, the **VoIP Calls** window will appear and display all the VoIP conversations that were found within the packet capture. You may need to press **Prepare Filter** before clicking on **Play Streams** to listen to the SIP call:

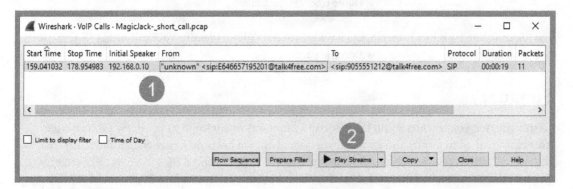

Figure 6.65 – VoIP calls

5. Next, Wireshark will reassemble all the data found in the SIP packets and create an audio playback. Simply click the **Play** icon to play the audio:

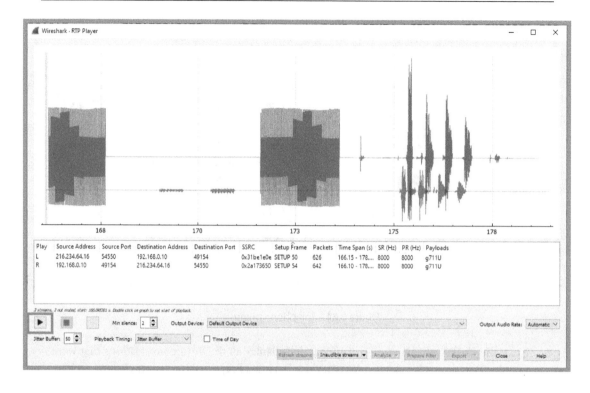

Figure 6.66 – Playing audio

Having completed this hands-on lab, you have gained the skills to identify VoIP calls using Wireshark and even listen to the audio found within the packets.

Summary

In this chapter, you learned about the roles and functions of common networking protocols and how they are used to format and exchange messages between hosts on a network. Additionally, you discovered various remote access protocols, such as Telnet, SSH, and RDP, as well as their security features. Furthermore, you discovered email protocols, database protocols, web protocols, directory protocols, and even VoIP protocols on networks.

As an aspiring network professional, you have gained the hands-on skills to perform packet analysis on various network protocols such as FTP, TFTP, Telnet, and SIP while observing how each protocol sends and receives data between devices. Lastly, you explored common network services that are needed within many organizations to ensure devices can communicate with other hosts on the network.

I hope this chapter has been informative for you and is helpful in your journey toward learning networking and becoming a network professional. In the next chapter, *Chapter 7, Data Center Architecture and Cloud Computing*, you will learn about the fundamentals of various data center architectures and cloud computing technologies and design models.

Questions

The following is a short list of review questions to help reinforce your learning and help you identify areas that may require some improvement:

1. Which of the following protocols is used to download emails from an email server on a network?

   A. SMTP

   B. POP

   C. IMAP

   D. All of the above

2. A network administrator is connected remotely to a router on the network. However, a hacker was able to capture the username and password used by the network administrator to log into the device. Which of the following protocols was most likely being used by the network administrator?

   A. RDP

   B. SSH

   C. HTTP

   D. Telnet

3. A network administrator wants to securely upload files to a device over a network. However, the network administrator was able to connect to port 22 on the destination host. Which of the following protocols is being used by the network administrator?

   A. FTPS

   B. SSH

   C. SFTP

   D. HTTPS

4. A network administrator is configuring an email server to securely send emails to their destinations. Which of the following protocols should be used?

   A. SMTPS

   B. DNS

   C. SMTP

   D. SSMTP

5. Which of the following transport protocols does not guarantee that messages are sent over a network?

    A. SIP

    B. TCP

    C. IP

    D. UDP

6. A network administrator wants to monitor the performance of all networking devices within their organization. Which of the following protocols will most likely allow the network administrator to retrieve the status information of a device?

    A. SNMP

    B. NTP

    C. DHCP

    D. RDP

7. A network administrator wants to secure the communication between a directory server and clients on the network. Which of the following protocols is most suitable for this task?

    A. LSDAP

    B. LDAPS

    C. SLDAP

    D. LDAP

8. Which of the following messages is sent to a DHCP server to confirm the use of an IP address?

    A. Discover

    B. Acknowledgment

    C. Offer

    D. Request

9. Which of the following tools allows a network administrator to test connectivity between hosts on a network?

    A. Traceroute

    B. ICMP

    C. Ping

    D. Telnet

10. A network administrator wants to forward log messages from all networking devices to a centralized logging server. Which of the following is the default service port for Syslog?

    A. 154

    B. 541

    C. 514

    D. 415

Further reading

To learn more about the topics that were covered in this chapter, check out the following links:

- *What Is a Network Protocol, and How Does It Work?*: https://www.comptia.org/content/guides/what-is-a-network-protocol

- *What is the difference between authoritative and recursive DNS nameservers?*: https://umbrella.cisco.com/blog/what-is-the-difference-between-authoritative-and-recursive-dns-nameservers

7

Data Center Architecture and Cloud Computing

As an aspiring network professional, you will soon realize how quickly technologies are evolving to support the demand of organizations around the world. Large organizations and service providers are allowing others to lease and rent the resources within their data centers around the world. This allows your organization to simply pay for the resources that are used within another organization's data center. At the time of writing, many organizations are going into and are already within the data center industry and are becoming cloud service providers.

In this chapter, you will discover how network professionals design enterprise networks to support scalability, fault tolerance and redundancy, security, and **Quality of Service (QoS)**. Furthermore, you will learn how administering and managing your network can be improved by using a controller-based solution that provides the instructions to networking devices within an organization. Additionally, you will explore various technologies that are used to build and maintain a **Storage Area Network (SAN)** and you will gain a solid foundation in cloud computing and its technologies.

In this chapter, we will cover the following topics:

- Understanding network architecture
- Discovering software-defined networking
- Exploring data center architectures
- Delving into storage area networks
- Fundamentals of cloud computing

Let's dive in!

Understanding network architecture

As an aspiring network professional, it's essential to understand the importance of designing an optimal network architecture to support both the current and future demands of an organization. Quite often, many organizations experience a lot of network congestion with too many broadcast messages propagating their network and users complaining about the high latency (slow response times) between their end devices and the servers on the network. Without a proper network design, network security and cybersecurity professionals experience challenges when implementing security solutions and countermeasures to mitigate cyberattacks and threats.

For instance, imagine an organization that's experiencing a lot of network congestion and security issues within its network. If the organization upgrades its network infrastructure with new networking devices and cabling, it doesn't necessarily mean its problems are resolved. It all begins with a great network architecture design to ensure various issues such as network congestion, slow response times, security concerns, and network outages are reduced.

When designing a network for an organization, whether it's a small, medium, or large network, it's important to consider the following factors:

- Fault tolerance and redundancy
- Scalability
- Security
- QoS

Fault tolerance simply defines the ability of a device to continue functioning and providing its services to a network when one or more components are affected. In other words, a device can continue operating after a component failure has occurred. Networks must be designed with fault tolerance to ensure if a networking device such as when a router or a switch has a failure, the network is built to quickly detect the failure and recover to forward traffic between its source and destination.

The following diagram shows a simple network that supports fault tolerance using redundancy:

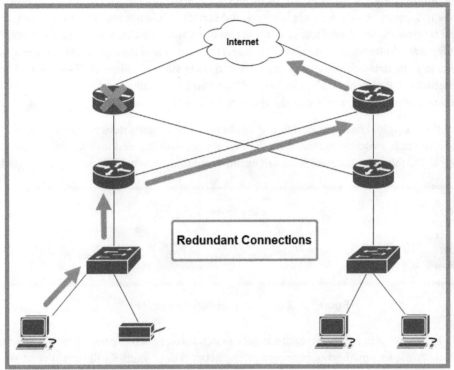

Figure 7.1 – Fault tolerance and redundancy

As shown in the preceding diagram, network professionals can implement fault tolerance on their network by creating **redundancy** of multiple paths between a source and a destination. Therefore, if a path is no longer available due to a faulty network cable or device, the existing networking devices can detect the failure and redirect network traffic through a different path while ensuring the availability of network services.

Many networks forward traffic using **packet switching**, which allows a sender to break down a single message into smaller packets to be transported over a shared network. This allows a message such as an email to be broken down into multiple smaller packets that are easier to transport over a network. Each packet contains the necessary source and destination addressing information needed to deliver to the destination host. When using a packet-switching network, each packet may use a different path based on the current network conditions such as available bandwidth, reliability, and load on the network. With a fault tolerance network that uses redundancy, packet switching is possible and provides better delivery of messages from the source to the destination.

Scalability is another important factor that needs to be considered by network professionals when designing or upgrading a network for an organization. Implementing scalability allows a network to easily grow to support new devices, applications, and services while not impacting the performance of existing services that are being accessed by current users within the organizations. Organizations grow as they hire additional staff members to support the demands of their products and services. As more users join the network, so does the number of devices such as computers, laptops, and smart devices. Network professionals will implement additional switches to allow new end devices to connect to the network, allowing users to access the resources and services.

However, if the original network design did not support scalability, network professionals may daisy-chain multiple switches together with the concept of providing a connection to all devices on the network. The following diagram shows an example of multiple switches daisy-chained together:

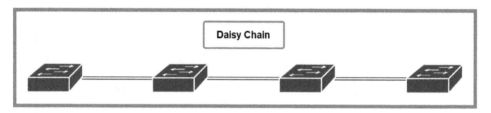

Figure 7.2 – Daisy chain network connections

As shown in the preceding diagram, each network switch is connected to another switch in a daisy-chain effect. While this method of interconnecting networking switches will provide end-to-end connectivity of devices on a network, it does not efficiently support scalability and redundancy. If any of the switches were to experience a failure, connectivity along the daisy chain would be affected, so interconnecting network switches using the daisy chain method is not recommended as it will lead to additional issues in the future.

Security is needed within all organizations in all industries around the world. With the increase in cyberattacks and newly emerging threats, organizations need to safeguard their assets from threat actors such as hackers. Designing a network to support network security and cybersecurity solutions is needed. Security solutions such as firewall appliances, **Intrusion Prevention Systems (IPSs)**, and endpoint security solutions are simply forms of security solutions needed for organizations to mitigate again cyberattacks.

Without network security solutions within an organization's network, the network professionals will not be aware of their network and assets being compromised by a hacker until it's too late. Organizations that invest in their network security and cybersecurity solutions are reducing the time to detect an intrusion and are continuously working on improving their security solutions and protecting their assets.

Quality of Service (QoS) is a common technology that allows network professionals to configure networking devices such as routers and switches to prioritize network bandwidth for specific traffic types. Many application layer protocols use **Transmission Control Protocol (TCP)** as it provides guaranteed delivery of messages between a source and destination. However, many other protocols use **User Datagram Protocol (UDP)** as their preferred transport layer protocol. UDP is connectionless and has no guarantee that datagrams will be delivered. Because of this, if a network becomes congested, messages sent using UDP have a higher probability of being discarded.

Many traffic types are time-sensitive and need to be delivered as soon as possible within an organization such as **Voice over IP (VoIP)** and **Video over IP**. Many organizations have been investing a lot of money into their collaboration solutions such as telepresence, allowing employees to use both VoIP and Video over IP solutions to communicate in real time with each other beyond borders. Imagine if the packets are not being delivered in real time and some are dropped off the network due to congestion; the employee on the receiving end of the call will not be receiving the message in real time and parts of the conversation will be lost on the network. To solve this issue, QoS is implemented on the network to ensure specific traffic types are guaranteed allocated network bandwidth for prioritization over other network traffic types.

Creating a network architecture for an organization seems to be a difficult process as you need to consider a model that supports scalability, fault tolerance and redundancy, security, and QoS. To save the day, Cisco has a wide range of validated design guides that help network professionals to use a **proof of concept (POC)** model with best practices and recommendations to implement a suitable network design within their organization.

Over the next few sub-sections, you will explore two common models from the Cisco-validated design guides that are used within enterprise organizations. These are the Cisco 3-tier and 2-tier architectures.

Cisco 3-tier architecture

A very common network architecture that is found within many large organizations is the 3-tier architecture, which contains three layers of network switches. Each layer has a specific role and function that adds simplification to the network design and helps network professionals easily add, expand, and manage the network.

The following diagram shows the 3-tier architecture module:

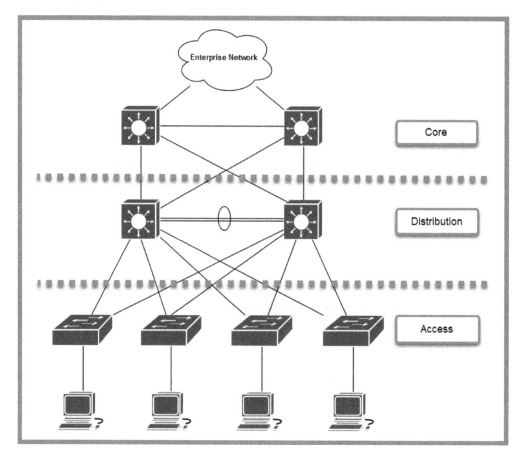

Figure 7.3 – 3-tier architecture

The **access layer**, also known as the **edge layer**, is responsible for providing network connectivity and access from end devices to the network and resources. Typically, network professionals implement access layer switches that operate at Layer 2 of the **Open Systems Interconnection** (**OSI**) and **Transmission Control Protocol/Internet Protocol** (**TCP/IP**) network models. At the access layer, there is no redundancy for end devices that are connected to the network as a typical computer has a single **Network Interface Card** (**NIC**) that uses a wired connection to the network switch.

The **distribution layer**, also known as the **aggregation layer**, is responsible for providing link aggregation and redundancy for the access layer switches on the network. There are usually two distribution layer switches within a branch office; each access layer switch will connect to each distribution layer switch to ensure redundancy between end devices. In the event a distribution layer switch is offline/unavailable, the access layer switch can automatically detect that a path is no longer available and forward the frames to another distribution layer switch on the network. Typically, traffic within a branch office/network flows between the access and distribution layers.

> **Important note**
>
> Layer 3 switches are implemented within the Distribution and Core layers of the network architecture as they provide both Layer 2 and Layer 3 functionality such as routing.

The **core layer** is notably the high-speed backbone of the network architecture. It provides interconnectivity and redundancy for the distribution layers within an organization with many branch offices. Therefore, network traffic is sent to the core layer when the destination is located in another branch office.

The following diagram provides a physical topology of the 3-tier architecture:

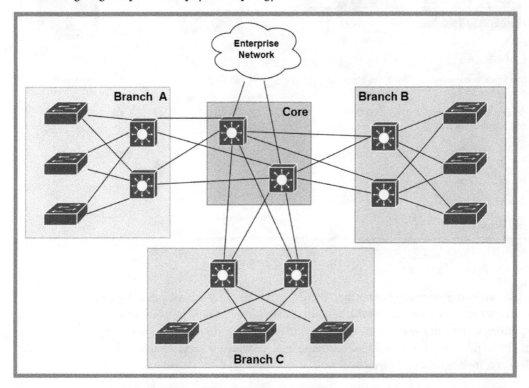

Figure 7.4 – Physical topology of the 3-tier architecture

As shown in the preceding diagram, each branch office has two distribution layer switches that interconnect each access layer switch. If the **Local Area Network** (**LAN**) within **Branch A** needs to expand as more users are joining the organization, the network professional can simply implement another access layer switch to support the additional users and devices at the location, hence it's easy to scale the network to support new devices. Furthermore, each distribution layer switch is connected to each core layer switch on the network to ensure there is redundancy within the organization. Lastly, the core layer is used to interconnect each branch office together and forward traffic to the routers and the internet.

The following screenshot shows the product page of various types of switches on Cisco's website:

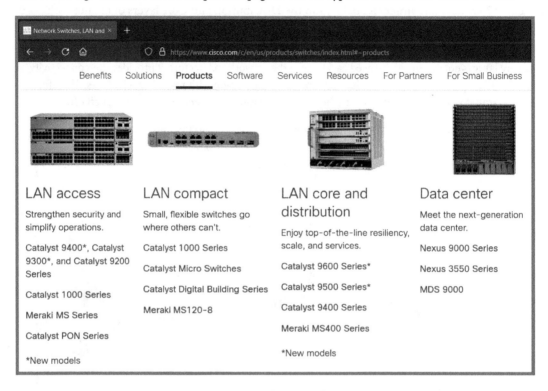

Figure 7.5 – Cisco switches

As shown in the preceding screenshot, there are various types of switches for specific segments of a network such as access layer switches and distribution and core layer switches. Therefore, when acquiring a network switch for an organization, it's important to determine which type of switch and model is suitable and meets all the requirements to provide the services and features to support the network, applications, and users.

> **Tip**
>
> Each series and models of switches have a data or product sheet that contains all the specifications of the device. As an aspiring network professional, ensure you visit the vendor website for the device details and become familiar with the datasheet of the device to determine if it's a suitable device needed by your organization or network solution.

The 3-tier architecture has a lot of benefits for large organizations, such as the following:

- Uses a multi-layered design to support scalability and redundancy while ensuring each layer is defined by its role and function

- Support modularity to help network professionals with their design elements, which can be replicated and applied within their entire organization while being consistent

- Eliminates the flat-network design, which does not support scalability and redundancy for large enterprise organizations

> **Tip**
> To learn more about the Cisco 3-tier architecture design, please go to `https://www.cisco.com/c/en/us/td/docs/solutions/CVD/Campus/cisco-campus-lan-wlan-design-guide.html`.

While the 3-tier architecture is recommended as it provides scalability, fault tolerance, and redundancy, it can be quite costly to implement within smaller organizations. Therefore, the 2-tier architecture is designed to provide the same characteristic as the 3-tier architecture for smaller organizations.

Cisco 2-tier architecture

The 2-tier architecture is designed for smaller organizations that have a smaller network and budget. The 2-tier architecture consists of two layers instead of three. The 2-tier architecture provides the same benefits as the 3-tier model such as support for scalability, fault tolerance and redundancy, security, and QoS but with a smaller design.

The following diagram shows the 2-tier architecture:

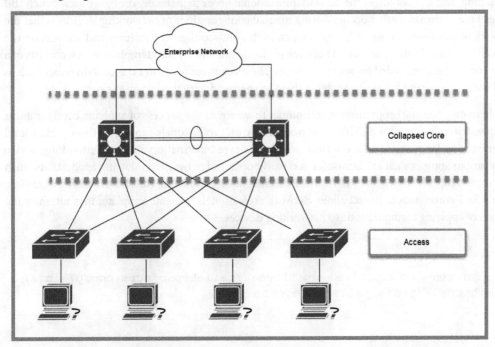

Figure 7.6 – 2-tier architecture

As shown in the preceding diagram, the 2-tier architecture contains a **collapsed core layer** and **access layer**. The collapsed core layer is simply a consolidation of the core and the distribution layers into a single layer. Typically, network professionals can implement either core or distribution layer switches within the collapsed core layer of the network. Furthermore, the access layer has the functionality to provide network connectivity of end devices to the actual network. Lastly, keep in mind that each access layer switch is connected to each switch within the collapsed core layer to provide fault tolerance and redundancy.

Having completed this section, you have gained an understanding of both the 3-tier and 2-tier network architectures, which are commonly used within small to large organizations. In the next section, you will take a deep dive into software-defined networking concepts and technologies.

Discovering software-defined networking

Software-defined networking (**SDN**) allows network professionals to automate the configurations and management of networking devices within an organization using a controller-based solution. Traditionally, a network professional will need to acquire networking devices such as routers and switches from the vendor, unbox each device, perform operating system and firmware upgrades, apply configurations on each networking device, and verify that the configurations are working as expected. This process seems quite normal as it's the traditional method that's been adapted for many years within the networking industry.

The downside of using the traditional method is that many tasks seem to be a bit repetitive and time-consuming, and let's not forget the network professional needs to manually configure each switch and router. One of the issues that occurs during manual configurations of networking devices is that the network professional can make human errors, such as misconfiguring features and services on the device. Additionally, many seasoned network professionals will create a template, which consists of a set of configurations needed for specific devices. However, these templates can contain issues such as outdated configurations and not applying them to specific device models on the network.

An alternative is using programming techniques to automate the process of applying configurations to networking devices over a TCP/IP network. Network professionals can use **Python**, a high-level programming language to create scripts, which retrieves information about a networking device from various sources such as Microsoft Excel workbooks and network monitoring applications. Such information includes hostnames, IP addresses, subnet masks, and so on. Additionally, using a template engine for Python such as **Jinga2** allows network professionals to create templates that automate the process of applying configurations to networking devices.

> **Tip**
> To learn more about Jinga, take a look at `https://palletsprojects.com/p/jinja/` and `https://jinja.palletsprojects.com/`.

Within a Cisco environment, **Zero Touch Provisioning** allows network professionals to configure a new networking device such as a Cisco switch or router to automatically retrieve configurations when it's connected to a network. This saves time and reduces the likelihood of misconfigurations on new networking devices.

While these methods seem a lot better than manually configuring networking devices, these still require a lot of manual work without you realizing it. The network engineering industry is adapting to controller-based solutions, which allow network professionals to centrally manage an entire network from a single pane of glass (dashboard). Therefore, network professionals no longer need to apply configurations manually to network devices – they can simply apply their intent to an SDN controller and the controller will apply the necessary configurations on the network. This is known as **intent-based networking (IBN)**. Next, you will explore the components that are used within an SDN environment.

Components of SDN

In a traditional network architecture, each networking device makes its own decisions on how to forward a message to a destination. Simply put, each networking device has a brain that makes the choices and decisions on forwarding messages and has its set of configurations. Since networking devices on a traditional network operate autonomously from each other, it's important to understand the role and functions of the three planes that exist within each networking device:

- Management plane
- Data plane
- Control plane

The **management plane** is responsible for allowing network professionals to manage network devices using various communication channels and protocols. Some management protocols include **Secure Shell (SSH)**, **Hypertext Transfer Protocol Secure (HTTPS)**, and **Simple Network Management Protocol (SNMP)**. Without the management plane on a networking device, it would be quite difficult to manage and monitor a device over a network.

The **data plane** on a networking device is responsible for receiving and forwarding messages between a source and a destination. When a message is received by a switch, the destination **Media Access Control (MAC)** address is inspected within the frame header. The switch will check the **Content Addressable Memory (CAM)** table or **MAC address table** to determine how to forward the frame to its destination. Additionally, a router will inspect the packet header for the destination IP address and check its local routing table for a suitable path to forward the packet to its destination.

The **control plane** on a networking device is responsible for controlling how the entire device operates. The control plane is the actual brain of the device and tells it how to make its forwarding decisions on the network. Various routing protocols help routers determine how to forward a packet to a destination, while switches use various Layer 2 forwarding algorithms for determining how to forward a frame to a destination host on the network. All the algorithms and mechanisms that are responsible for determining how a device handles messages exist within the control plane.

Within an SDN architecture, the SDN controller manages the control plane's role and functionality for all the networking devices. Simply put, the control plane (brain) function is no longer handled by each networking device – the function is now controlled and managed by the SDN controller, as shown in the following diagram:

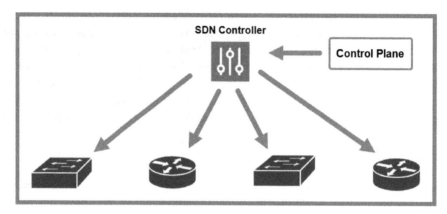

Figure 7.7 – SDN architecture

Using an SDN within a large network allows network professionals to log into the SDN controller, which provides full visibility of everything on their networks, such as the health and performance of the network and devices. The SDN controller can predict potential network issues and provide recommendations on how to resolve them and implement proactive solutions. Furthermore, using the SDN controller allows network professionals to centrally manage all networking devices within their entire organization from a single dashboard interface.

The SDN controller can manage all the networking devices by using the **Southbound Interface** (**SBI**) **application programming interface** (**API**). The SBI simply utilizes the following methods to manage a networking device:

- NETCONF
- OpenFlow
- **Command-line interface (CLI)**
- SNMP
- OpFlex

Additionally, the network professional can access the SDN controller via the **Northbound Interface** (**NBI**) API, which provides visibility of the entire network through a single pane of glass (dashboard). Practically speaking, network professionals access the user interface of the SDN controller by using a **Graphical User Interface** (**GUI**) or retrieving information using a **Representational State Transfer** (**REST**) API.

The following screenshot shows the user interface of the Cisco **Digital Network Architecture (DNA)** Center:

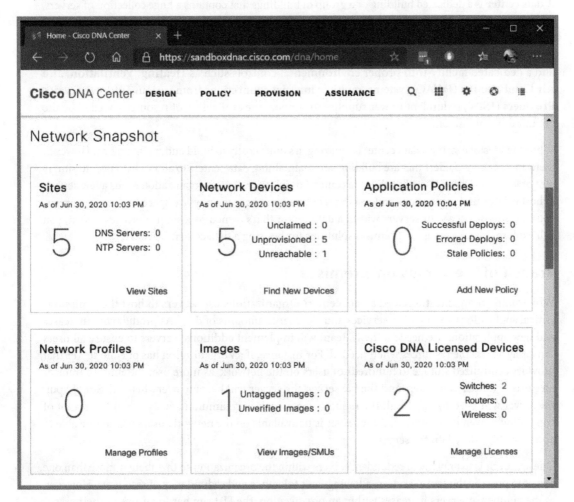

Figure 7.8 – Cisco DNA Center

Cisco DNA Center is an SDN controller that allows networking professionals to design and implement policies, perform device provisioning tasks, and continuously monitor their network for performance issues.

Having completed this section, you have learned about the importance and benefits of using SDN technologies within networks and how network professionals reduce the time of identifying and resolving issues while using a proactive approach. In the next section, you will discover various data center architectures.

Exploring data center architectures

A **data center** is a dedicated building or a group of buildings that contains a huge collection of servers, networking devices, and security appliances that are maintained by an organization. Medium and large organizations create a data center that allows IT professionals to house all their servers and critical applications within a dedicated space on their network. This concept allows centralized management and a dedicated facility with proper environmental controls such as **Heating, Ventilation, and Air Conditioning** (**HVAC**) systems, multiple internet connections from various **Internet Service Providers** (**ISPs**), redundant power supplies to support the availability of resources needed by the organization, and so on.

While the idea of owning a data center is amazing, it's quite costly to build and maintain one. However, there are service providers that are building and maintaining data centers to allow customers to simply rent or lease the resources within the data center. For instance, if your organization needs a few servers to host your critical applications and resources but does not have the physical space to store the servers, you can simply place your servers within a data center that's owned by a service provider. Next, you will explore branch versus on-premises solutions for housing a data center.

Branch office versus on-premises

Why would an organization need a data center? Organizations use servers to host their mission-critical applications and provide services and store large amounts of data. As productivity increases and new applications are needed, the IT team will implement additional servers to ensure all users can easily access the resources when needed. For instance, if an organization has one file server that provides centralized storage to hundreds of users on the network, as more users attempt to transfer files between their computers and the file server, the server will become overwhelmed. Simply put, the server will need to handle all the requests from each user simultaneously, which uses a lot of computing power. Furthermore, if the server is unavailable on the network, users will not be able to access the files stored on the server.

One approach is to implement redundant servers within the organization so that there is more than one server to provide the same services, allowing fault tolerance and redundancy of resources. However, as the number of servers increases within an organization, the IT team has to ensure all their assets, such as the servers, are always available to users on the network. This means that system administrators and IT technicians need to perform routine maintenance procedures to ensure everything is working fine while actively monitoring the health of each device on the network.

An on-premises solution simply means an organization has its servers within its company's building and they are maintained by in-house IT professionals. The advantage of using an on-premises model is the IT professionals have physical access to the servers and the organization has full ownership of the devices and equipment. However, if one of the servers has a faulty component or is unavailable, the in-house IT professionals are responsible for resolving the issues as quickly as possible and ensuring users have access to the resources.

As an organization increases and creates more branch offices, the IT team of the company needs to ensure their users, such as the employees, have access to all the network resources to efficiently perform their daily duties. Companies will typically contact their local telecommunication provider or ISP to **Wide Area Network (WAN)** solution to interconnect their branch offices, such that the users on a remote branch office will be able to access the resources at the main office and so on. Alternatively, the company can implement a **Virtual Private Network (VPN)** solution to internet their branch offices while removing the cost of paying an ISP for a managed service.

Sometimes, an organization sees the benefits of using a data center from a service provider to host their servers and applications since data centers are designed to provide uptime availability, ensuring resources are always available to users and customers. While hosting your servers and applications in a data center, it's important to consider the following factors:

- The connectivity methods between the data center and your location

- The security and data privacy concerns of using a data center from a service provider

- The expenses associated with paying a service provider versus an on-premises solution

Colocation is another type of solution that is commonly used by many organizations. A colocation solution is usually a type of data center that allows customers to rent physical server rack spaces, internet bandwidth, servers, and other equipment. Using a colocation allows companies to bring their own devices to the data center's location, where they will be hosted by the service provider.

Spine and leaf

A data center uses a special 2-tier architecture known as the **spine and leaf** architecture, which supports scalability and East-West traffic flow. The spine and leaf network architecture contains two layers of network switches that are designed specifically to operate in data center networks. The top row of switches is known as the **spine** switches or the backbone switches as they are used to create a full mesh by interconnecting each spine switch to all switches within the lower layer, as shown in the following diagram:

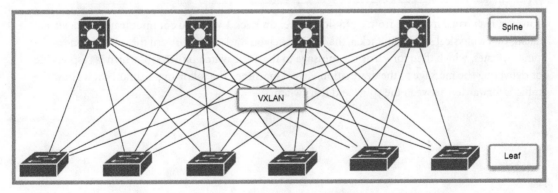

Figure 7.9 – Spine and leaf architecture

Furthermore, the switches on the lower layer are referred to as **leaf** switches. Each leaf switch is connected to each spine switch, creating a full mesh for redundancy. Additionally, the leaf switches are also known as **Top-of-Rack (TOR)** switches since they allow servers to connect to the network. The following diagram shows multiple physical servers within multiple racks and that each physical server is connected to a leaf switch:

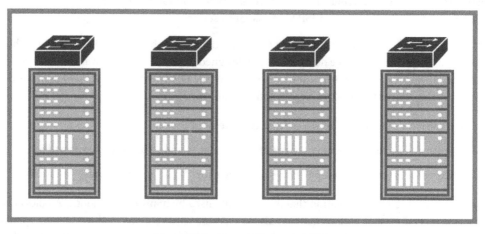

Figure 7.10 – Top-of-Rack switching

As shown in the preceding diagram, each server within a single rack is connected to the TOR switch on the same rack. Therefore, if a virtual machine from one of the servers within Rack 1 wants to communicate with a virtual machine within another server on Rack 1, the TOR switch on Rack 1 will handle forwarding the traffic between servers and virtual machines within Rack 1 only.

> **Important note**
> *North-South* traffic flow occurs between a server and outside the data center, while *East-West* traffic flow occurs between servers and virtual machines within the data center.

However, if a virtual machine from a physical server on Rack 1 wants to communicate with a virtual machine on a physical server on Rack 3, the TOR switch on Rack 1 will forward the traffic to one of the spine switches, which then forwards the message to the TOR switch on Rack 3, which is responsible for delivering the message to the destination virtual machine. The following diagram shows how the traffic is forwarded between the spine and leaf switches:

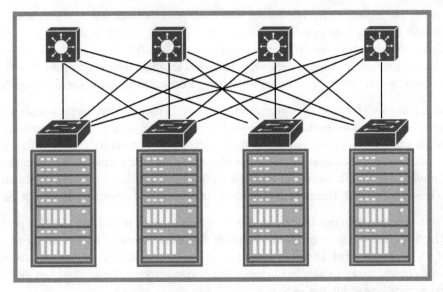

Figure 7.11 – Forwarding traffic between the spine and leaf switches

Each switch within the spine and leaf architecture is a layer 3 switch and uses dynamic routing protocols to forward traffic between servers and devices. This architecture uses a technology known as **Virtual Extensible LAN** (**VXLAN**), which allows data centers to easily scale to meet the demands of providing cloud computing services to users. As more server racks are implemented within the data center, the spine and leaf architecture allows data center engineers to easily scale the network to support more devices. Implementing an additional leaf switch allows more servers to join the data center network. Furthermore, it's easy to implement additional spine switches to support the increase of leaf switches.

Having completed this section, you have learned about the fundamentals of data center architecture and design. In the next section, you will learn about storage area networks.

Delving into storage area networks

Data is the most valuable asset to any organization and needs to be safeguarded at all times from threat actors such as hackers. While cybersecurity professionals work continuously to ensure their organization's assets are protected, it's important to consider hardware failures can occur on devices that are storing data such as **Hard Disk Drives** (**HDDs**) and **Solid State Drives** (**SSDs**) on a computer, server, or **Network Attached Storage** (**NAS**).

Imagine if an organization does not have any centralized file server on the network and everyone stored critical files on their local computers. Whenever a user wants to share a document with another person, they would attach the file to an email message. If a user's computer were to be infected with malware or experience hardware failure, there's a risk that data will be lost on the local device.

An organization can implement NAS devices on their **Local Area Network (LAN)**, which allows users to centrally store files on a dedicated device over a TCP/IP network. A NAS, as its name suggests, is a small enclosure that contains a few HDDs that operate in a cluster. This allows users on a network to access the storage unit over a computer network. NAS devices are efficient for small networks with a few users as it allows the company to save money while using a dedicated and centralized storage device.

If business is going well for an organization, more employees may be hired as the organization is expanding, which means more users and devices are joining the network. In a larger organization, NAS devices are not efficient to support hundreds or thousands of users who are regularly transferring files over a network. Having dedicated storage servers with lots of storage drives that have been configured using **Redundant Array of Independent Disks (RAID)** to provide redundancy between the storage drives of a server is essential. Therefore, if one storage fails within the server, the data is not lost.

However, some organizations that have the necessary resources invest in building a SAN to provide a dedicated high-speed network to interconnect all their data storage pools of servers and devices. The concept of a SAN is to ensure high-speed access between users and the dedicated storage servers, as well as provide maximum availability by implementing fault tolerance and redundancy on the storage devices and applications within the SAN.

The following diagram shows a typical SAN design:

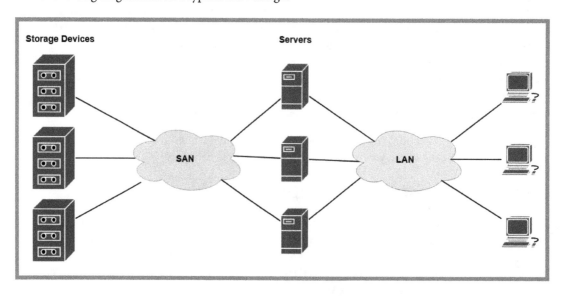

Figure 7.12 – SAN architecture

As shown in the preceding diagram, the SAN contains the dedicated storage servers and disk arrays and uses a fiber channel to ensure there is support for high data rates between the file servers and the users in the organization. Furthermore, there are SAN switches that are dedicated networking devices that interconnect with storage servers and have the responsibility of moving network data through the SAN. Next, you will explore common network connections that are implemented within an SDN environment.

Connection types

Since a SAN supports many storage devices such as servers with various storage arrays, it's important to ensure that SAN can support the huge bandwidth needed between the SAN and other parts of the organization's network from users.

The following are various components within an SDN environment:

- **Fiber Channel** (**FC**) is simply a very high-speed network that is designed to support very low latency (fast response times) and high throughput between devices. Using an FC within a SAN has many advantages compared to using traditional copper cables. Using an FC allows network professionals to run fiber cables beyond the limitation of 100 meters and transfer data at gigabit speeds compared to copper cables, which experience attenuation (loss of signal) over distance. When implementing FC within a network, an FC **Host Bus Adapter** (**HBA**) is installed on each storage server and networking device within the SAN. For each HBA on a device, multiple ports allow data to be exchanged.

- **Fiber Channel over Ethernet** (**FCoE**) allows FC frames to be encapsulated within an Ethernet message for transportation over a network. The objective of using Ethernet is to provide a mutual technology over a network that allows multiple traffic types such as FC and **Internet Protocol** (**IP**) to be delivered over a high-speed network that uses fiber optic cables. However, access to network resources is usually limited to a LAN.

- **Internet Small Computer Systems Interface** (**iSCSI**) allows fiber communication over a routable network compared to FCoE. Simply put, if there are users over different IP networks within the organization, iSCSI is a better solution because FCoE provides access to users on the same network (LAN).

Having completed this section, you have explored the fundamentals of SAN and its components. Next, you will take a deep dive into exploring cloud computing, models, and services.

Fundamentals of cloud computing

Cloud computing is one of the most demanding and trending topics within the IT industry as more organizations are migrating their services, applications, and servers to the cloud. As an aspiring network professional, it's essential to understand cloud computing, the types of cloud deployment models, and cloud services.

Cloud computing can be demystified as paying for the resources you use within a cloud service provider's data center. Imagine your organization wants to acquire additional servers to host new applications and services needed by the employees to perform their daily duties. Some of the concerns of acquiring new servers are the time it takes for the vendor to ship the servers to the customer's location, the time it takes the IT staff members to set up and deploy the applications on the servers, and any additional maintenance on the equipment if any issues should occur in the future.

What if your organization can simply pay for the resources used within someone else's data center such as Microsoft Azure, **Amazon Web Services (AWS)**, or **Google Cloud Platform (GCP)**? Simply put, your organization can create a user account on a cloud service provider's website, select the type of services needed, use the online calculator to get an estimate for the cost of hosting the services on the preferred cloud provider's data center, and deploy the servers and services within minutes compared to weeks. That's right – rather than waiting for a few weeks to receive physical servers from a vendor, using cloud computing allows professionals to deploy new servers and applications on the internet within a matter of minutes. Furthermore, if no one wants to use a service, application, or server within a cloud provider's data center, you can terminate it within seconds and stop paying for it.

Cloud computing providers allow their customers to use a **pay-as-you-go** model, which means you can *pay per minute* or *hour*, depending on the preferred cloud provider. This allows organizations to save a lot of money and time as they can start and stop servers as needed. Most importantly, the customer is not responsible for handling the physical maintenance of the servers within the cloud service provider's data center, which removes that responsibility from your IT staff. However, the customer is responsible for the security management of any services, applications, and servers that are deployed within any cloud provider's data center. Hence, cloud engineers need a solid understanding of security concepts and best practices for securing data and assets on the cloud.

The word *cloud* simply means the customer is using a service, application, or server within a data center that cannot be seen by the customer or is physically accessible. For instance, anyone on the internet with a credit card can create a user account on the Microsoft Azure, AWS, or GCP website and deploy a server within just a few minutes. As a customer, do you see the physical server within the data center? Simply put, in most cases, you do not see the actual servers, but you can communicate with the server using the internet; the internet is a collection of many public networks that are managed by many ISPs around the world.

There are many advantages to using cloud computing technologies, such as the resources within a cloud provider's data center being accessible from anywhere at any time. For instance, services such as Google Workspace and Microsoft 365 allow companies to outsource their email services to Google and Microsoft cloud solutions. With Google Workspace and Microsoft 365, this eliminates the need for a company to set up mail exchange servers within their networks. Using these email solutions allows a company to simply pay per user per month and if a user needs additional storage on their mailbox, the company can simply pay an additional fee for the specific user. Overall, all users will be able to access their mailbox (email inbox) from anywhere at any time using an internet connection as the services are hosted and maintained by the email solution provider.

Cloud computing helps companies reduce the need for physical appliances, equipment, and devices at their location. Simply put, it reduces the physical space needed to house physical servers. Cloud providers allow their customers to quickly *spin up* (create) a new virtual server on the cloud within a few minutes while allowing the customer to *scale up* or *scale down* the computing resources on the server. As more computing power is needed on a virtual server on the cloud, a customer is provided with features to increase the computing resource, such as increasing the number of virtual processors, memory such as virtual **Random Access Memory** (**RAM**), storage drives, and NICs. This is commonly referred to as *scaling up*. *Scaling down* is referred to as reducing the computing resources on a server as the demand is lower.

Organizations that use cloud computing technologies reduce the need for a dedicated IT team. However, there is a huge demand for cloud engineers with specialized skills needed to deploy, maintain, and secure solutions on Microsoft Azure, AWS, and GCP. Each of these top cloud providers has developed a learning path and certification tracks to help the new generation of IT professionals to learn cloud computing.

> **Important note**
>
> A **tenant** is a single customer on a cloud provider platform. **Multi-tenant** is when multiple customers use the same cloud provider platform. **Tenant isolation** allows multiple customers to use the same shared resources within the data center but each customer is isolated from accessing another customer's resources.

Cloud computing providers support elasticity and scalability. **Elasticity** simply allows a system to adapt to the workload and changes of the environment, such that a customer can quickly provision and de-provision servers and applications as needed within a cloud provider's data center. For instance, if your organization needs one web application to host a website, as more users connect and interact with your web server, there will be an increase in demand for computing power to process each web request. With elasticity, your organization can create additional web servers within a few minutes with the same web application and implement a load balancer to distribute the inbound web request between each web server.

Scalability within cloud computing allows organizations to increase and decrease the resources needed based on the demand. For instance, you may need one Linux server on the cloud to perform some tasks. As you increase the workload on the server, you will eventually notice that each task takes longer to be completed. Increasing the virtual number of processes and memory can allow more tasks to run at the same time while ensuring each process is allocated sufficient computing resources.

Furthermore, security is everyone's concern. Within a cloud computing environment, the customer is responsible for managing the security of the resources they place within a cloud service provider's data center. For instance, if you spin up a new virtual server that runs Windows Server 2022 or a Linux-based server, you are responsible for securing your virtual machine on the cloud. Therefore, if you do not apply device hardening techniques and best practices on the virtual server, there's a high risk a threat actor such as a hacker can compromise and take over your virtual server on the internet.

Over the next few sub-sections, you will discover various cloud deployment models, service models, and connectivity solutions.

Deployment models

When deploying a cloud computing solution for an organization, four models are commonly used by cloud engineers and service providers. The **private cloud** model is where any organization such as your company owns the data center, and the infrastructure is managed by your IT team. Within the private cloud model, the resources are only accessible to the employees of the organization and no one else.

The following diagram shows a representation of a private cloud model that can only be accessed by the organization and its employees:

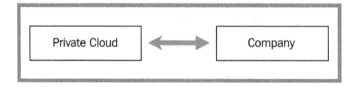

Figure 7.13 – Private cloud model

The **public cloud** model is available to anyone on the internet. These are public cloud service providers such as Microsoft Azure, AWS, GCP, and many more. The public cloud allows anyone to create virtual servers and deploy applications and services on a data center that shares its resources with others and uses a pay-as-you-go model. In a public cloud model, the cloud service provider is responsible for all physical hardware maintenance.

The following diagram shows a representation of the public cloud and your organization, which is sharing the resources with others:

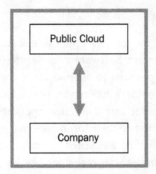

Figure 7.14 – Public cloud model

The **hybrid cloud** model is a mixture of the private and public cloud deployment models. It allows an organization's data, servers, and applications to be locally backed up on its private data center and replicated to an online public cloud solution provider. This solution is quite costly to maintain but provides an excellent solution for disaster recovery and business continuity practices.

The following diagram provides a representation of a hybrid cloud deployment model:

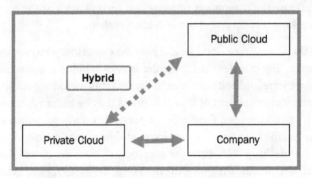

Figure 7.15 – Hybrid cloud model

Lastly, the **community cloud** model is where several organizations share the resources on a cloud platform. These can be groups of companies with similar interests or partnerships all accessing and sharing resources within a data center or cloud service provider.

Cloud service models

Various cloud service models define how services, applications, and resources are delivered to users from a cloud service provider's data center. **Software-as-a-Service (SaaS)** is a very common service model that allows the cloud solution provider to offer access to the user interface of the application that's being hosted within the cloud provider's data center. For instance, organizations that use Google Workspace or Microsoft 365 do not need to install the client application on each user's computer. Each user can simply access the web application on their corporate email and other collaboration tools using a standard web browser. The user is neither concerned nor has access to manage the host operating system or the hardware components of the servers that are hosting the application.

The **Platform-as-a-Service (PaaS)** service model is designed for developers who require a bit more control over their operating or working environments. When working with a PaaS solution, the cloud service provider allows the user or developer to make changes to the operating system and the programming frameworks that are running on the host operating system. However, the user does have access to the underlying hardware resources on the server.

The **Infrastructure-as-a-Service (IaaS)** service mode allows the user to manage physical hardware and software resources on the virtual server on the cloud provider's data center. This model allows the user to increase and decrease the computing resources on servers, such as the number of processes, memory, storage, networking interface, and the operating system.

Desktop-as-a-Service (DaaS) is where a cloud service provider can deliver a virtual desktop environment to a user over the internet. The cloud service provider is responsible for managing all the backend maintenance such as hardware and software requirements. This includes backups and storage and updates. However, security management of DaaS solutions may be a shared responsibility between the cloud service provider and the user. DaaS offers a **persistent desktop**, which keeps the data and changes made by a user. So, the next time the user logs onto the virtual desktop, everything is already there. In a **non-persistent desktop**, each time the user logs off from the virtual desktop, all data and settings are cleared from the system. Therefore, the next time the user logs on, a clean virtual desktop environment is presented.

Lastly, the **Infrastructure as Code (IaC)** model focuses on managing the resources within a cloud service provider's data center and the virtual machines on servers, load balancers, and networking using the same versioning method as DevOps engineers.

Cloud connectivity solutions

Hosting applications, servers, and other resources on a cloud service provider's data center is awesome but ensuring your organization and users have secure access is very important. Not having secure access to the resources on your data center or a cloud provider's data center is a huge security risk. This is because a threat actor can intercept the communication channel between your users and the resources on the cloud, capturing sensitive and confidential information.

Using a VPN allows a secure, encrypted connection to be established over an unsecure network such as the internet. Setting up a VPN between your organization's network and the resources on a cloud service provider's data center is a common solution used by many organizations. Using a VPN allows the company to save a lot of money while protecting data-in-motion over the internet. However, the company will be responsible for managing its VPN solutions and ensuring users can access the resources when needed.

Another method for connecting to a cloud service provider's data center is using a **private-direct connection to the cloud provider**. Many ISPs provide direct connectivity solutions between an organization (customer) and a data center. These connectivity solutions are usually secure within the ISP network to ensure no unauthorized parties can intercept the communication channel between the customer and the data center.

Having completed this section, you gained the skills and knowledge to identify various cloud computing technologies, service and deployment models, and connectivity methods.

Summary

In this chapter, you learned about the 3-tier and 2-tier network architectures, which are commonly implemented by network professionals within small to large organizations. You have discovered the benefits of using these network architectures to support scalability, fault tolerance and redundancy, security, and QoS. Furthermore, you have explored the fundamentals of SDN and how it helps network professionals to predict potential issues in their network and improves the management of all networking devices. Lastly, you can now describe SAN technologies and cloud computing since you explored various deployment models and their benefits to organizations.

I hope this chapter has been informative for you and is helpful in your journey toward learning networking and becoming a network professional. In the next chapter, *Chapter 8, Networking Devices*, you will learn about the roles and functions of various networking and networked devices that are commonly found within organizations.

Questions

The following is a short list of review questions to help reinforce your learning and help you identify areas that may require some improvement.

1. Which of the following layers allows a server to connect to the network?

    A. Core

    B. Access

    C. Distribution

    D. Data Link

2.   The collapsed core is a combination of which of the following?

A. Core, access, and distribution

B. Core and access

C. Access and distribution

D. Distribution and core

3.   Which of the following is a benefit of using the 3-tier architecture?

A. Single-layer network

B. QoS

C. Security

D. Scalability

4.   Which of the following components is responsible for determining how a device forwards traffic on a network?

A. Routing protocol

B. Management plane

C. Control plane

D. Data plane

5.   Which of the following network architectures is used within a data center?

A. 2-tier

B. Spine and leaf

C. 3-tier

D. All of the above

6.   Which of the following SAN technologies does not allow access beyond a local area network?

A. IP

B. TCP/IP

C. iSCSI

D. FCoE

7. Which of the following cloud models allows an organization to access shared resources with others?

   A. Public

   B. Hybrid

   C. Community

   D. Private

8. Which of the following service models provides a virtual desktop interface for a user?

   A. SaaS

   B. DaaS

   C. IaaS

   D. PaaS

9. Which of the following connectivity methods allows an organization to securely access the resources on a data center while saving cost?

   A. Leased line

   B. VPN

   C. Metro Ethernet

   D. MPLS

10. Which model provides access to the user interface of an application that's hosted on a cloud provider's data center?

    A. SaaS

    B. DaaS

    C. IaaS

    D. PaaS

Further reading

To learn more about the topics that were covered in this chapter, check out the following links:

- *Enterprise Campus 3.0 Architecture: Overview and Framework*: `https://www.cisco.com/c/en/us/td/docs/solutions/Enterprise/Campus/campover.html`

- *What is Software-Defined Networking (SDN)?*: `https://www.vmware.com/topics/glossary/content/software-defined-networking.html`

- *Cisco Data Center Spine-and-Leaf Architecture: Design Overview White Paper*: `https://www.cisco.com/c/en/us/products/collateral/switches/nexus-7000-series-switches/white-paper-c11-737022.html`

- *Why storage area networks are important*: `https://www.ibm.com/topics/storage-area-network`

- *Cloud Computing*: `https://www.ibm.com/cloud/learn/cloud-computing`

- *What is Desktop as a Service (DaaS)?*: `https://www.vmware.com/topics/glossary/content/desktop-as-a-service.html`

- *What is infrastructure as code (IaC)?*: `https://docs.microsoft.com/en-us/devops/deliver/what-is-infrastructure-as-code`

Part 2:
Network Implementation

This part describes common networking devices and their deployment models, security appliances and their functionality on a network, various routing and switching technologies, and wireless networking standards.

This part of the book comprises the following chapters:

- *Chapter 8, Networking Devices*
- *Chapter 9, Routing and Switching Concepts*
- *Chapter 10, Exploring Wireless Standards and Technologies*

Networking Devices

As an aspiring network professional, you will soon discover that there are many types of networking and networked devices within organizations and office spaces. Each networking device has unique characteristics, roles, and functions in forwarding messages from a source to a destination, such as from your computer to a server on the internet. Understanding the role and function of each networking device will provide you with better knowledge and wisdom on designing an efficient network using the appropriate devices where needed, to ensure users and client devices are able to access and share resources.

During the course of this chapter, you will explore the roles and functions of various networking devices that are commonly configured and implemented within organizations when building an enterprise network. Additionally, you will discover the purpose of security appliances and how they are used to detect and mitigate cyber-attacks and threats. Furthermore, you will understand the characteristics of common networked devices that are attached to a network.

In this chapter, we will cover the following topics:

- Understanding networking devices
- Exploring security appliances
- Types of networked devices

Let's dive in!

Understanding networking devices

Networking devices are intermediary devices that are used to build and extend a network to allow users to access and share resources. End devices such as computers and laptops are able to operate on their own and perform tasks as needed by the user. Computers are able to store data on their local storage devices, and users are able to physically transport data between devices using a USB storage device such as a USB flash drive or an external storage drive. This method of sharing data is suitable for a small organization with a few users, and not for larger organizations with hundreds and thousands of employees.

As an organization increases in size, network professionals are required to ensure each user is able to access and share resources over a network. Networks are built by professionals using various intermediary networking devices that accept a message from a sender device and determine the best suitable path to forward to its destination. There are various networking devices within the industry and it's very important to understand the role, function, and how each device forwards traffic along a network between a source and destination.

Hub

A network hub is a legacy networking device that operates at Layer 1 of the **Open System Interconnection (OSI)** networking model. The network hub was an early generation networking device that allowed end devices to be interconnected and share resources; however, this type of networking device became obsolete due to its limitation and lack of support for scalability and the inefficiency of forwarding messages between the source and destination.

Unlike many modern network devices that forward a message between a sender and receiver, a network hub operates like a repeater device, which simply accepts an incoming electrical signal on the wire and rebroadcasts it through all other interfaces on the hub. To put it simply, if four computers are connected to a hub, and PC 1 sends a message into the hub, the hub will rebroadcast the message to all other devices that are connected to the hub.

The following diagram shows how a hub forwards a message:

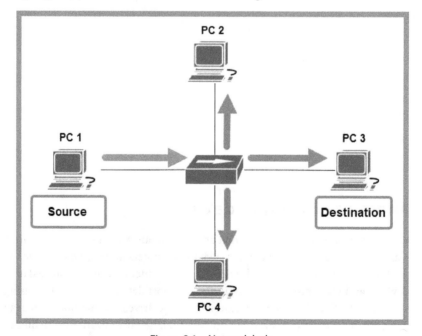

Figure 8.1 – Network hub

As shown in the preceding diagram, **PC 1** wants to send a message to **PC 3** on the network. **PC 1** creates a message in the form of an electrical signal and places the message onto the media (copper cable). When the hub receives the message (electrical signal) from **PC 1**, it simply rebroadcasts the message out of all other interfaces to all other devices on the network. To put it simply, devices such as **PC 2** and **PC 4** receive a copy of the message that was only intended for **PC 3**; this creates a security concern on the network.

Furthermore, imagine that an organization has many more devices and is using a network hub to interconnect all end devices and share resources. As you can imagine, a hub is a non-smart device that simply rebroadcasts incoming signals throughout the network. In a large network with many hubs, each device that sends a message will be rebroadcasted through the entire network, therefore creating excess or unnecessary traffic within various sections of a network, which can lead to network congestion.

A single collision domain is created for all devices that are connected to the hub. A **collision domain** is simply a segment of the network where a packet collision can occur due to more than one device transmitting a message at a time on a shared network segment. Once packet collision occurs, the message is discarded and the sender has to transmit the message again.

The following diagram shows the effects of using only hubs on a network:

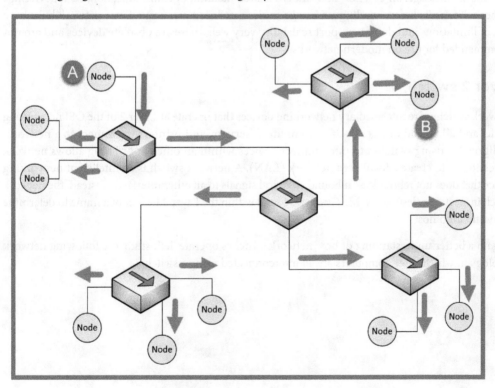

Figure 8.2 – Issues with hubs

As shown in the preceding diagram, **Node A** sends a message to **Node B** on the network. However, as the message is transported to the destination, each hub along the way is rebroadcasting and sending a copy of the message to other devices on the network. As a network grows with more hubs and devices, network congestion is bound to happen, which can cause packet loss and high latency. Furthermore, the collision domain increases, as more hosts are connecting to a network with hubs.

Since a network hub simply rebroadcasts messages without inspecting the destination **media access control (MAC)** address or the destination IP address of a message, what if two different devices send a message to the hub? A network collision will occur, causing the packets from both senders to be corrupted, therefore, only one device can transmit a message at a time while all others have to wait on a hub network. If a network collision occurs and/or the packets are corrupted, the sender of the message will resend the message.

To prevent issues on a hub network, end devices such as computers use **Carrier Sense Multiple Access with Collision Detection (CSMA/CD)**. Before an end device places a message (electrical signal) on the media, the device checks the media for the presence of a signal. If a signal is detected, it means another device is already using the media/network and is transmitting a message. Therefore, the device waits and checks the media again until no signals are detected, and then proceeds to transmit the message. Since a hub network is a shared medium of communication, each device has to check the media before sending a message or else a collision can occur. Since network hubs have a lot of limitations and do not support scalability very well, these are obsolete devices and are not recommended for use on modern networks.

Layer 2 switch

Network switches are intermediary networking devices that operate at Layer 2 of the OSI networking model and allow end devices such as computers, servers, and printers to connect to a network. Additionally, using switches to interconnect devices within an office or building allows network professionals to create a **local area network (LAN)**. A network switch is an intelligent networking device that does not rebroadcast inbound electrical signals to all other interfaces; instead, the network switch inspects the destination MAC address found within the Layer 2 header of a frame to determine the destination host.

To gain a better understanding of how network switches operate, let's study the following network topology in which three computers are all interconnected using a switch:

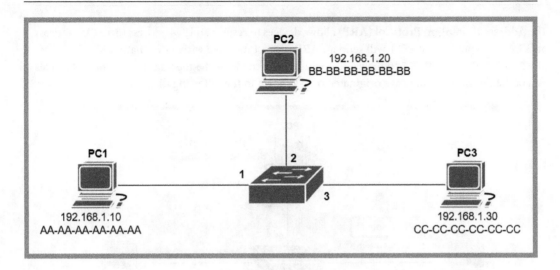

Figure 8.3 – Network topology with a switch

As shown in the preceding diagram, each computer is assigned an IPv4 address and has a unique MAC address on its **network interface card** (**NIC**). When a switch boots up, it does not know which computer is connected to any of the local interfaces on the switch. Only when a device such as a computer sends a message does the switch inspect the source and destination MAC addresses within Layer 2 of the frame, which is used to populate the **content-addressable memory** (**CAM**) table.

> **Important note**
>
> The CAM table is used by Cisco switches to store MAC addresses that are learned by an interface and helps the switch determine how to forward a message to a destination on the network. Each time a frame enters an interface, the switch will check the source MAC address and if the source MAC address was never seen before on the inbound interface, the switch will temporarily store it in the CAM table and map it to the interface. This is how switches populate entries within a CAM table. Keep in mind that the contents of the CAM table are stored in **random access memory** (**RAM**), and the contents are lost whenever the switch loses power or reboots.

Let's imagine that PC 1 wants to send a message to PC 3 but doesn't know the destination host's MAC address. What happens next? On a network, all senders will need to include source and destination MAC addresses within the Layer 2 header, and the source and destination IP addresses in the Layer 3 header. Since switches operate at Layer 2, they will not be able to view the Layer 3 header details but only MAC addresses in the Layer 2 header of the frame. Therefore, it's essential that the source and destination MAC addresses are inserted correctly on a frame before placing the message on the network for delivery.

The **Address Resolution Protocol (ARP)** allows devices to resolve an IPv4 address to a MAC address on a LAN. To put simply, PC 1 will send an ARP request message with a destination MAC address of FF:FF:FF:FF:FF:FF to the switch, which will broadcast the message to all other interfaces except the interface the message originated on, as shown in the following diagram:

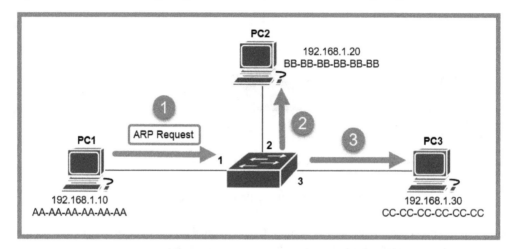

Figure 8.4 – ARP request message

As shown in the preceding diagram, the ARP request message is sent to the switch and is broadcasted to all other interfaces. Additionally, the source MAC address of the frame is stored on the CAM table and is mapped to interface 1, as shown in the following table:

Interface	MAC Address
1	AA-AA-AA-AA-AA-AA
2	
3	

Figure 8.5 – CAM table

Next, PC 2 and PC 3 will receive the ARP request message and inspect the requested target IP address of 192.168.1.30. Since PC 2 has an IP address of 192.168.1.20, it will discard the message and not respond. PC 3 has the target IP address and will respond directly to PC 1 with its MAC address using an ARP reply message.

The following diagram shows an ARP reply message:

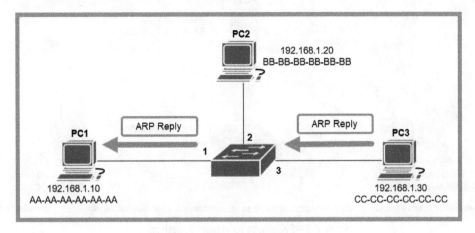

Figure 8.6 – ARP reply message

When the switch receives the ARP reply message from PC 3, it inspects the source and destination MAC. PC 3's source MAC address is stored within the CAM table and is mapped to interface 3, and the switch forwards the ARP reply directly to the destination host since the switch had previously recorded PC 1's MAC address on the CAM table.

The following table shows the entries of the CAM table after receiving the ARP reply from PC 3:

Interface	MAC Address
1	AA-AA-AA-AA-AA-AA
2	
3	CC-CC-CC-CC-CC-CC

Figure 8.7 – CAM table updated

At this point, the switch knows where PC 1 and PC 3 are located based on the entries within the CAM table and their MAC addresses. Additionally, PC 1 knows the MAC address of PC 3 and inserts it within the destination MAC address field of the frame, and sends the message on the network. The switch will inspect the destination MAC address within the Layer 2 header of the frame and check the CAM table to determine which interface knows about the destination MAC address, and forward the message out of interface 3, as shown in the following diagram:

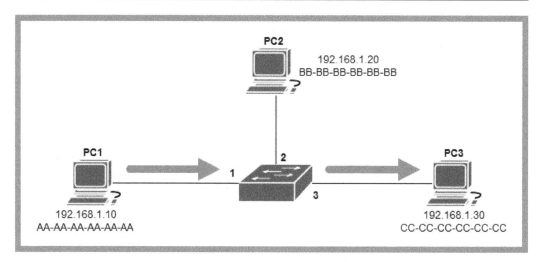

Figure 8.8 – Switching forwarding method

Once a switch already knows PC 3 is connected to interface 3, it sends the message directly to the destination host on the network.

However, there's another real-world scenario where the sender device (such as a computer) knows the destination host's MAC address but the switch doesn't. Whenever a switch receives a frame, it will inspect the destination MAC address and check the CAM table to determine how to forward the message to its destination, as you already know. In the event that a switch does not know the location of the destination host because the MAC address is not found within the CAM table, the switch will flood the message out of all interfaces except the interface the message originated on.

This means all devices that are connected to the switch will receive a copy of the message, except the sender. Each device, upon receiving the message from the switch, will inspect the destination MAC address to determine whether they are the intended recipient or not. If a device receives a message and the destination MAC address of the frame does not match the MAC address of the device, the message is discarded. However, if a device receives a message and the destination MAC address of the frame matches the MAC address of the device's NIC, the frame is processed and sent to the upper layers of the network model.

Switches help reduce the size of a collision domain as compared to hubs on a network. Since switches are intelligent devices and forward frames to their destination by inspecting the destination MAC addresses, switches are able to isolate a collision to a per-interface level. To put it simply, each interface on a switch represents one collision domain, hence it's recommended that only one device is connected to each switch interface. Hence, a 48-port switch will contain 48 collision domains.

> **Tip**
>
> Each interface/port on a switch represents one collision domain. Therefore, a switch with eight ports has eight collision domains.

The following diagram shows a representation of collision domains on a switch:

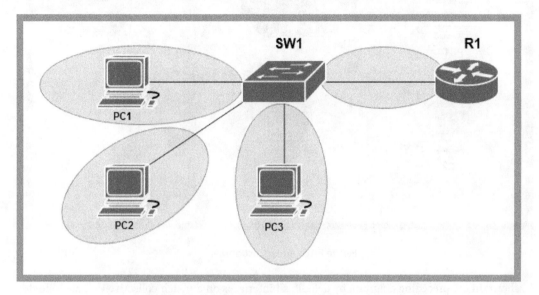

Figure 8.9 – Collision domains

As shown in the preceding diagram, there are four collision domains, and since one device (such as a computer) is attached to each interface on the switch, the possibility of a collision occurring between a computer and the switch is reduced. However, if a device sends a Layer 2 broadcast message with a destination MAC address of FF:FF:FF:FF:FF:FF, the switch will forward the message out of all interfaces, thus creating a single broadcast domain. A broadcast domain is simply described as a network segment that all devices can reach by using a Layer 2 broadcast message.

The following diagram shows a broadcast domain on a network switch:

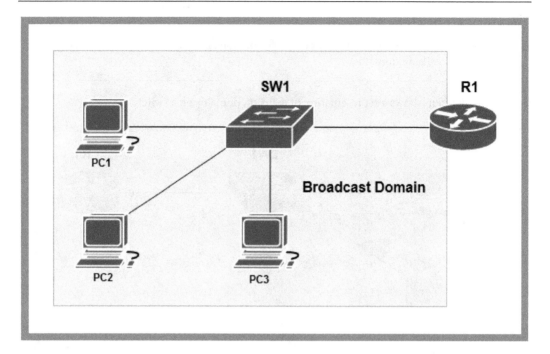

Figure 8.10 – Broadcast domain

As shown in the preceding diagram, by default, all interfaces on a switch collectively create a single broadcast domain that allows all devices to be reached by a Layer 2 broadcast message. As a network professional, creating smaller Layer 2 broadcast domains helps to improve network efficiency and overall performance.

Layer 3 capable switch

Network switches are commonly referred to as Layer 2 devices that operate at the data link layer of the OSI networking model and have the capabilities to forward frames based on the destination MAC addresses. Nowadays, there are Layer 3 network switches, which operate at the network layer of the OSI networking model. These Layer 3 switches allow network professionals to interconnect and perform routing between different **virtual local area networks** (**VLANs**) within an organization.

Large organizations implement VLANs within their physical network, which allows network professionals to logically segment a physical network into small broadcast domains, allowing each department (such as human resources, sales, IT, and so on) to be on their own logical network. Therefore, if a device within the sales VLANs generates a broadcast message, it's limited to devices within the same VLAN only. Since an organization may have multiple VLANs, hosts within a VLAN will not be able to communicate with devices on another VLAN. To ensure VLANs are able to exchange messages with each other, a Layer 3 device is needed to route traffic between one VLAN and another.

One of the most common Layer 3 devices is a router, which allows network professionals to interconnect two or more different networks together. However, network professionals can use a Layer 3 switch that provides routing functionalities as a router to allow communication between VLANs within an organization. Keep in mind that routers are dedicated Layer 3 devices for forwarding packets that have additional Layer 3 functionalities such as advanced data, security, and voice features. However, a Layer 3 switch can perform both Layer 2 functions and Layer 3 routing functions on a network. Using a Layer 3 switch allows the organization to reduce the cost of a dedicated router on the network to perform inter-VLAN routing.

Bridge

A network bridge is a special networking device that operates at Layer 2 of the OSI networking model and allows network professionals to divide the network into multiple collision domains. If you recall, older networks were built using a hub to interconnect end devices and extend a network within an office space or building. However, the downside of using a hub is it creates a single, large collision domain with all connected devices, which isn't good for performance and security. To put it simply, if a computer sends a message to a hub, it is rebroadcasted to all devices on the network. Additionally, if two more computers transmit a message at the same time, a packet collision will occur.

The following diagram shows a single, large collision domain that's created using hubs:

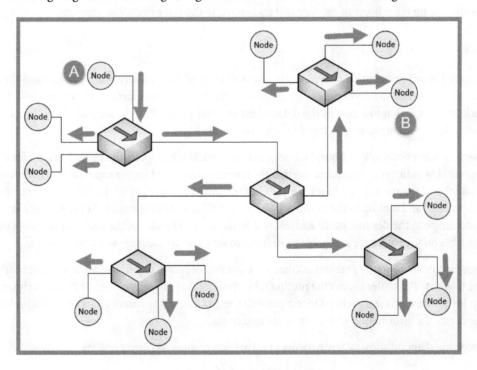

Figure 8.11 – Broadcast domain

Network professionals can implement a bridge into a large collision domain to create two smaller collision domains on a network. The following diagram shows a network topology with two collision domains that are separated by a bridge in the middle:

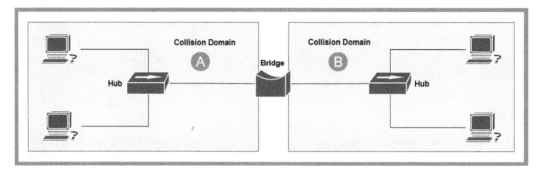

Figure 8.12 – Creating a smaller collision domain

As shown in the preceding diagram, **Collision Domain A** is separated from **Collision Domain B** by a bridge. Therefore, if PC 1 and PC 2 send a message at the same time, a packet collision will occur and affect the devices that are connected to **Collision Domain A** only, leaving **Collision Domain B** unaffected. However, if PC 1 sends a broadcast message, all devices (such as PC 2, PC 3, and PC 4) will receive the message because they are still connected to the same broadcast domain.

Router

Routers are Layer 3 devices that operate at the network layer of the OSI networking model and allow network professionals to interconnect two or more different networks together. These are dedicated networking devices that function as the default gateway and forwarding device that allows hosts on one network to communicate with hosts on another network.

Whenever a router accepts an inbound message such as a packet, it inspects the Layer 2 header for the destination MAC address to determine whether the message is intended for the router. If the destination MAC address of the message matches the MAC of the inbound interface of the router, the frame is de-encapsulated and sent up to the network layer of the OSI networking model. At the network layer, the router inspects the destination IP address within the Layer 3 header of the packet and checks the routing table on the router for a suitable route/path to forward the message to its destination.

Each router contains a routing table that contains a number of routes to various destination networks and the internet. The router checks the routing table from top to bottom each time it has to perform a lookup before forwarding a packet. Once a suitable route is found, the router stops the route lookup and processes the information within the matching route.

The following diagram shows a few networks that are interconnected using routers:

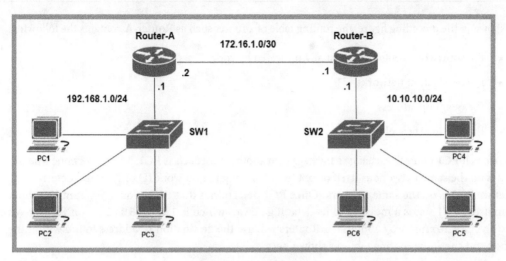

Figure 8.13 – Network diagram

As shown in the preceding diagram, there are three networks that are interconnected using two routers. Each router has a local routing table that tells the router how to forward an incoming packet to its destination. **Router-A** has two directly connected networks, 192.168.1.0/24 and 172.16.1.0/30. Networks that are directly connected to a router will automatically appear within the routing table when the router boots up. The 10.10.10.0/24 remote network will not automatically appear in the routing table of **Router-A** by default as it is a remote network and it's not directly connected. However, the 10.10.10.0/24 and 172.16.1.0/30 networks will automatically be inserted in the routing table of **Router-B** by default as they are directly connected.

The following snippet shows the routing table of **Router-A**:

```
Router-A#show ip route
Codes: L - local, C - connected, S - static, R - RIP, M - mobile, B - BGP
       D - EIGRP, EX - EIGRP external, O - OSPF, IA - OSPF inter area
       N1 - OSPF NSSA external type 1, N2 - OSPF NSSA external type 2
       E1 - OSPF external type 1, E2 - OSPF external type 2, E - EGP
       i - IS-IS, L1 - IS-IS level-1, L2 - IS-IS level-2, ia - IS-IS inter area
       * - candidate default, U - per-user static route, o - ODR
       P - periodic downloaded static route

Gateway of last resort is not set

     10.0.0.0/24 is subnetted, 1 subnets
O       10.10.10.0/24 [110/2] via 172.16.1.1, 00:01:05, GigabitEthernet0/1
     172.16.0.0/16 is variably subnetted, 2 subnets, 2 masks
C       172.16.1.0/30 is directly connected, GigabitEthernet0/1
L       172.16.1.2/32 is directly connected, GigabitEthernet0/1
     192.168.1.0/24 is variably subnetted, 2 subnets, 2 masks
C       192.168.1.0/24 is directly connected, GigabitEthernet0/0
L       192.168.1.1/32 is directly connected, GigabitEthernet0/0

Router-A#
```

Figure 8.14 – Routing table

As shown in the preceding figure, the routing table of a router such as **Router-A** contains the following:

- The source of a route that is usually indicated by code

- The destination network

- The next hop address

- The exit interface of the router

Therefore, if **PC1** wants to exchange a message with another host such as **PC2**, it will determine whether **PC2** is on the same network as itself or not by calculating the network ID of **PC1** and determining whether **PC2** is on the same network. Once **PC1** determines that **PC2** is on a different IP subnet from itself, **PC1** sends a message to its default gateway, which is 192.168.1.1 on **Router-A**'s GigabitEthernet 0/0 interface. Routers will use the destination IP address found within the packet and check the routing table, as shown here:

```
Router-A#show ip route
Codes: L - local, C - connected, S - static, R - RIP, M - mobile, B - BGP
       D - EIGRP, EX - EIGRP external, O - OSPF, IA - OSPF inter area
       N1 - OSPF NSSA external type 1, N2 - OSPF NSSA external type 2
       E1 - OSPF external type 1, E2 - OSPF external type 2, E - EGP
       i - IS-IS, L1 - IS-IS level-1, L2 - IS-IS level-2, ia - IS-IS inter area
       * - candidate default, U - per-user static route, o - ODR
       P - periodic downloaded static route

Gateway of last resort is not set

     10.0.0.0/24 is subnetted, 1 subnets
O       10.10.10.0/24 [110/2] via 172.16.1.1, 00:01:05, GigabitEthernet0/1
     172.16.0.0/16 is variably subnetted, 2 subnets, 2 masks
C       172.16.1.0/30 is directly connected, GigabitEthernet0/1
L       172.16.1.2/32 is directly connected, GigabitEthernet0/1
     192.168.1.0/24 is variably subnetted, 2 subnets, 2 masks
C       192.168.1.0/24 is directly connected, GigabitEthernet0/0
L       192.168.1.1/32 is directly connected, GigabitEthernet0/0

Router-A#
```

Figure 8.15 – Routing table

Router-A uses the network route that is highlighted in the preceding figure and forwards the packet out of its GigabitEthernet 0/1 interface to **Router-B**, which is assigned the 172.16.1.1 address. The process is repeated on each router for every incoming packet to determine how to forward the message to its destination, and eventually, the packet will be delivered to the destination. Routers are simply essential networking devices that help network professionals to interconnect different physical and IP networks together.

Each interface on a router represents a collision domain, hence it's recommended that only one device should be connected to an interface, which prevents packet collisions from occurring. Additionally, each interface on a router is also attached to a broadcast domain, hence routers stop a Layer 2 broadcast from propagating from one network to another.

Let's study the following network diagram and identify the number of collision domains and broadcast domains:

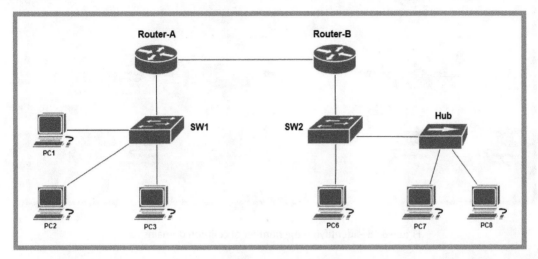

Figure 8.16 – Network diagram

There are three broadcast domains, as shown in the following diagram:

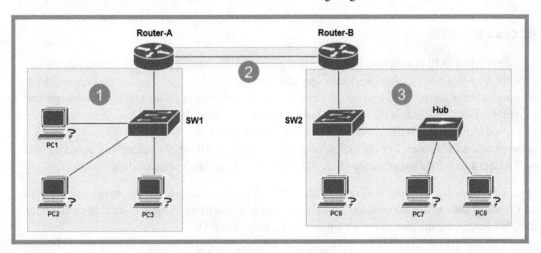

Figure 8.17 – Identifying the number of broadcast domains

There are eight collision domains, as shown in the following diagram:

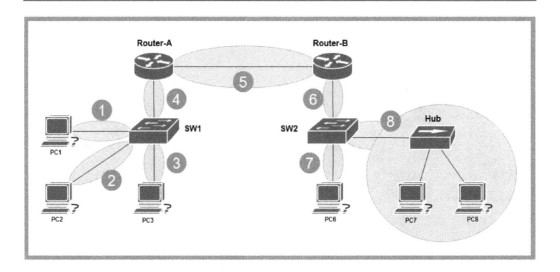

Figure 8.18 – Identifying the number of collision domains

As a network professional, it is important that you can identify the number of collision domains and broadcast domains. Routers do not forward a Layer 2 broadcast message from one broadcast domain to another.

Access point

An **access point** (**AP**) is a networking device that allows Wi-Fi-capable devices to connect to a wired network, allowing users to share resources and access services. While the core of many organizations' networks is wired connections between devices, wireless networking provides a lot of convenience and support for mobility. Wireless networking allows network professionals to easily extend the capabilities of a wired network to a wireless network by simply connecting an AP to a network switch. Since a network operates at Layer 2 of the OSI networking model, the AP simply generates wireless signals on 2.4 GHz and 5 GHz based on the IEEE *802.11* standards for wireless networking.

Once a client such as a laptop connects to an AP, the client has access to the resources and services on the wired network. Implementing a wireless network allows users to roam around the office with their Wi-Fi-capable devices and work within the vicinity of the AP.

The following diagram shows a small wireless network with an AP:

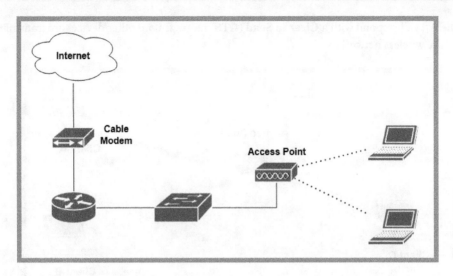

Figure 8.19 – Wireless network

There are various IEEE *802.11* wireless standards in the wireless networking industry, however, it's important to know that older APs that use the IEEE *802.11a/b/g/n/ac* standards create a contention-based wireless network for all connected clients.

The following steps are written in layman's terms to provide clarity on how a wireless client proceeds to send a message on a wireless network:

1. **Client-A** wants to send a message to another wireless client that is connected to the same AP.

2. Before **Client-A** transmits the message, it sends a **Request to Send** (**RTS**) message to the AP to determine whether the wireless network is clear to send the message.

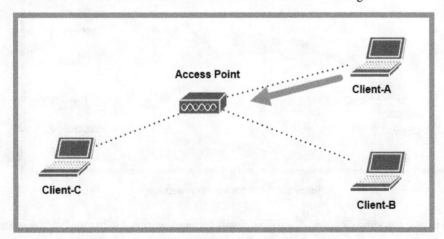

Figure 8.20 – Requesting status from the AP

3. The AP will respond with a **Clear to Send** (**CTS**) message if no other devices are transmitting on the wireless network.

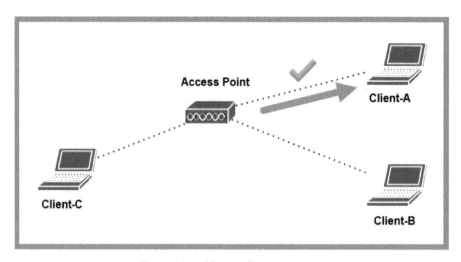

Figure 8.21 – AP providing a response

4. Then, **Client-A** will send the message to the AP that is responsible for forwarding it to the destination host on the wireless network.

5. The AP will simply rebroadcast the message to all other connected hosts similar to a hub on a wired network.

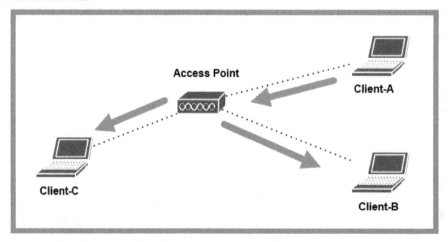

Figure 8.22 – AP forwarding message

As shown in the preceding diagram, all wireless clients that are associated with an AP that operates on IEEE *802.11a/b/g/n/ac* wireless standards are all on a single collision domain and broadcast domain.

Wireless networks that use IEEE *802.11a/b/g/n/ac* use **Carrier Sense Multiple Access with Collision Avoidance (CSMA/CA)** to avoid collision of frames on a wireless network. With CSMA/CA, a wireless client will first check with the AP to determine whether the network is clear to send or not. The AP will respond to the client with an all-clear or not. This method prevents collisions of more than one client wanting to transmit a message over the wireless network.

Important note

Newer wireless routers and APs that use the IEEE *802.11ax* (Wi-Fi 6) standard do not contain the limitations and shortcomings of previous generations of wireless networking standards. To put it simply, devices that are connected to a Wi-Fi 6 network do not need to use CSMA/CA, as IEEE *802.11ax* has improved on forwarding traffic more efficiently, but they can still use RTS/CTS to communicate with legacy APs.

Another type of wireless networking device that's commonly implemented within small office networks and homes is a wireless router. A wireless router is an all-in-one device that contains the function of an AP, switch, and router in a single device. The AP feature allows the wireless router to create a wireless network on 2.4 GHz and 5 GHz frequencies according to the IEEE *802.11* standard for wireless networking. Furthermore, on the back of a typical wireless router are a few interfaces that are known as switch ports or switch interfaces; these interfaces allow a user to establish a wired connection between their end device and the wireless router. These switch ports operate as a typical Layer 2 network switch, where all devices that are connected to the wireless router using a wired connection will all be able to communicate with each other.

Lastly, the wireless router performs routing functions such as routing traffic between the wireless and wired network. The wireless network is assigned an IP subnet that's uniquely different from the IP subnet that's used on the wired network. To put it simply, a smartphone that's connected to a wireless router will obtain an IP address that's different from the IP addresses that are being used on the wired LAN.

The following diagram shows a typical wireless network with a wireless router:

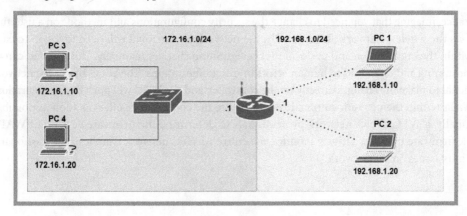

Figure 8.23 – Wireless router

As shown in the preceding diagram, **PC 1** is assigned an IP address from the `192.168.1.0/24` network, and it's connected to the wireless router. The wireless router is connected to the wired LAN via the network switch that's on the `172.16.1.0/24` network. Therefore, the wireless router performs routing between these two different types of networks (wired and wireless) and between the different IP networks.

Wireless LAN controller

A **wireless LAN controller** (**WLC**) is a special networking device that allows network professionals to efficiently manage all the **wireless access points** (**WAPs**) within an organization from a centralized controller on the network. If an organization has multiple WAPs, the network professionals can simply log in to each device and perform configuration changes, upgrade the firmware, and troubleshoot to resolve any issues.

A few WAPs are just good enough for a small to medium-sized organization with few wireless devices such as laptops and smart devices. However, as the organization provides more wireless devices to employees, network professionals need to ensure the wireless network infrastructure is able to support the increase in wireless devices that are connecting to the wireless network and provide sufficient bandwidth for each device to exchange messages. Therefore, network professionals will implement additional WAPs within the organization to ensure there is sufficient coverage of the wireless signals while eliminating any dead zones, ensuring wireless clients can connect to any WAP within the organization and have access to resources.

As more WAPs are implemented to support wireless clients, network professionals need to continuously monitor the performance of the wireless network to ensure the network is operating optimally. If a WAP is unavailable due to a faulty firmware update or hardware deficiency, wireless clients within the range of the faulty WAP will be affected, and users who rely on the wireless network will be affected as well. Using a WLC allows network professionals to configure each WAP on the network to establish a connection to the WLC. Network professionals can simply log in to the WLC with a web interface and centrally manage the entire wireless network.

For instance, imagine that you need to change the security configurations and methods on a user that can access the wireless network. Traditionally, the network professional will need to log in to each WAP within the organization and perform the configuration changes manually. This method can be time-consuming and often lead to human errors in misconfigurations. The WLC allows the network professional to make the changes directly on the controller, and the WLC will push the configurations to all WAPs within the network automatically to ensure the changes take effect as soon as possible. Additionally, a WLC allows network professionals to determine the firmware version of WAPs, schedule firmware updates, actively monitor the entire wireless network from a single dashboard, and identify issues on the network.

A WLC can be implemented as an on-premises solution or in the cloud. Overall, the WLC is simply a custom operating system or firmware that's running on a hardware-based device. Each deployment provides its own set of advantages and disadvantages, therefore it's important to evaluate which type of deployment is most suitable for the organization while providing the most benefits to achieve the objectives.

Load balancer

A **load balancer** is a special networking device that allows network professionals to distribute the inbound network and application traffic types across a cluster of servers that are providing services and/or resources to users. Imagine that an organization has created a web server and connects it to the internet to host an e-commerce web application to enable the company to sell its products and services to anyone online. For each user on the internet who connects and performs a transaction on the web server, some processing power is used per transaction. As more users connect and perform more transactions, the utilization of computing resources on the server will continue to increase, and eventually, the server will become overwhelmed and perform slowly. As a result, users will be affected due to the slow performance of the server and its incapability to handle a large number of users and their transactions.

One solution is to deploy multiple servers to host the same e-commerce web application, and implement a load balancer device on the network to accept incoming messages from users on the network and distribute the load evenly across the cluster of servers; therefore, one server will not be handling all the transactions. Furthermore, since each server will be able to perform optimally, the load balancer ensures any one server is not overwhelmed with the number of web request messages from the users on the internet.

The following diagram shows a load balancer deployed on a network:

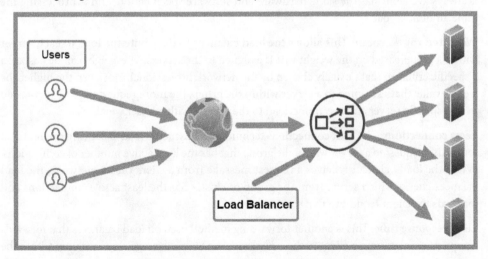

Figure 8.24 – A load balancer on a network

As shown in the preceding diagram, any incoming traffic from users on the internet is intercepted by the load balancer, which is responsible for distributing the network and application traffic types to the group of servers, ensuring each server is not overburdened with a lot of transactions or requests.

Load balancers can be implemented on a network as a hardware-based device or an application that runs on a hypervisor or cloud environment. Load balancers typically operate at either Layer 4 or Layer 7 of the OSI networking model. The Layer 4 load balancers can distribute network traffic based on common transport layer protocols, while Layer 7 load balancers can distribute the load based on common application layer protocols such as **Hypertext Transfer Protocol Secure (HTTPS)**.

Furthermore, load balancers are able to provide fault tolerance; in the event of a server within the cluster being unavailable or offline, the load balancer can simply distribute the incoming load of network traffic to the available servers within the cluster. However, load balancers can operate in an `Active/Active` state, which allows the distribution of network and application traffic between all active servers within a cluster. They can also operate in an `Active/Passive` state, which allows the distribution of the load to an active server only and performs a failover to a standby server if the active server is no longer available.

The following are the four most common algorithms that are used by load balancers that determine how the load is distributed to servers on a network:

- **Round robin**: This is the most common and simplest method that's used on load balancers to distribute the load to multiple servers. The round robin method simply forwards a request message from a user to each server within the group in turn, and when the load balancer reaches the last server within the group/cluster, it will start again from the first server to the second and third and so on. While this forwarding method is simple, it's not the most efficient for traffic distribution, as the load balancer assumes each server within the group or cluster is always available, has the same hardware and software specification, and is processing the same amount of load.

- **Weighted round robin**: This allows the load balancer to distribute the load to each server within a group based on the weight that is assigned to the servers. The weight can be based on a specific criterion that's usually chosen by the network professional. However, the higher the weight value that's assigned to a server within the group, the more requests will be forwarded to that specific server and less traffic/load to the servers with a lesser weight value.

- **Least connections**: The least connections technique is a dynamic load-balancing method that forwards a request to a server within the group that has the least active number of connections. When the load balancer receives a request message from a client on the network, the load balancer checks which server from the group or cluster has the least active connections and forwards the client request to that server.

- **Least response time**: This is another forwarding method used on load balancers that forwards a request message from a client to the server with the lowest average response time within the group of servers.

Proxy server

A **proxy server** is simply a server on the network that performs the function of a relay between clients and servers on a network. Proxy servers are commonly implemented by network professionals to prevent hackers from invading a corporate network within an organization, and it does this by intercepting all the messages between the clients and servers.

Within companies, proxy servers are commonly used to perform URL filtering by inspecting the destination URL that a user is trying to reach. If the URL is within the blacklist of web addresses, the proxy server does not forward the client request to the destination. However, if the destination URL exists within the whitelist of allowed web addresses, the proxy server forwards the message to the destination server.

The following diagram shows a proxy server on a network:

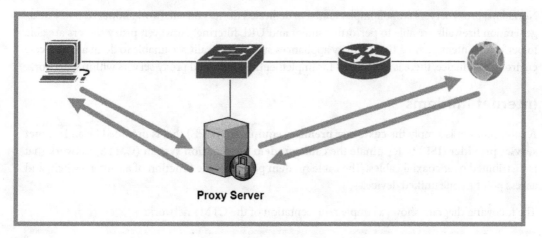

Figure 8.25 – Proxy server on a network

As shown in the preceding diagram, when PC 1 wants to send a message to the public server on the internet, PC 1 is configured to forward all web request messages to the proxy server on the network for inspection. Then, the proxy server will check the destination URL and determine whether it's allowed or denied. If the web request is permitted, the proxy server forwards the message to the web server. When the web server responds, the proxy server intercepts the response messages and caches the data before forwarding a copy to PC 1.

> **Important note**
> WAPs or wireless routers can also function as proxy servers on a network.

Proxy servers are common in performing the caching of content; therefore, when a client sends a web request to the proxy server, it checks its cache to determine whether the data already exists or not. If a cached version of a web page already exists within the memory of the proxy server, it is sent to the client on the network. Caching helps an organization reduce the amount of internet bandwidth consumption; however, the cache also means there's the likelihood that an outdated version of a web page is sent to a client.

The following are common types of proxy servers:

- **Forward proxy** – This is a common type of proxy that intercepts a client's request message and forwards it to the destination on the internet
- **Reverse proxy** – This type of proxy server intercepts and forwards the request message from devices that are on the internet to the servers on the internal network of the organization

Nowadays, proxy servers are still implemented as dedicated devices on a network, however, many next-generation firewalls are able to perform content and URL filtering. However, proxy servers are able to perform content caching that security appliances such as firewalls are unable to do in a large-scale environment, hence, there is still a need for implementing dedicated proxy servers within a network.

Internet modems

A cable modem is simply the **customer premises equipment** (**CPE**) that is provided by an **internet service provider** (**ISP**) to terminate the **cable modem termination system** (**CMTS**) network that is distributed over coaxial cables. The cable modem performs the function of a router, switch, and access point in one unified device.

The following diagram shows a simple representation of the CTMS network:

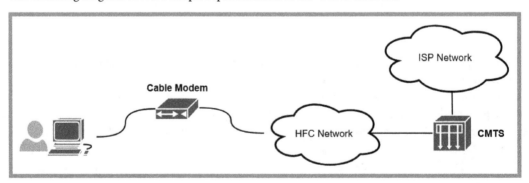

Figure 8.26 – CMTS network

As shown in the preceding diagram, the ISP implements the CMTS network infrastructure and distributes the cable TV and internet services over the **hybrid fiber-coaxial** (**HFC**) infrastructure to their customers. A cable modem is installed at the customer's location to interconnect the customer's private network to the HFC and CMTS infrastructure to access internet services.

As you may have realized, modems are all-in-one devices that perform multiple roles such as functioning as a router between the customer's and the ISP's networks, operating as a switch to allow the customer to physically connect a few devices, and providing a wireless signal as an AP to allow users to connect their wireless capable devices.

Digital subscriber line (DSL) modems are another type of modems provided by ISPs that distributes internet services over the **public switched telephone network** (**PSTN**) lines, sometimes called the **plain old telephone service** (**POTS**) lines.

The following diagram shows a representation of a typical PSTN network with a DSL modem:

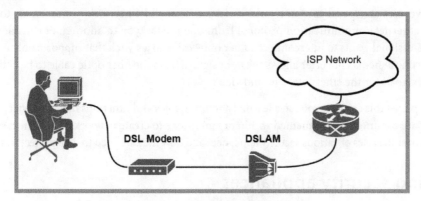

Figure 8.27 – DSL modem

As shown in the preceding diagram, the DSL modem is installed at the customer's location, and terminates and converts the signals from the ISP's network, allowing the devices within the customer's network to access the internet services.

Repeater

A repeater, sometimes referred to as a Wi-Fi extender/repeater, is a Layer 1 device that simply accepts a signal and regenerates the same signal at a higher power. These devices can be commonly found on wireless networks that are implemented by network professionals within a building or compound area. An AP contains one or more antennas that are used to emit a radio frequency signal, allowing wireless clients to connect to the AP and share resources. However, the antennas of an AP or wireless router can only emit a signal that is strong enough to travel over a certain distance before it starts getting weaker as the distance increases.

Physical obstacles such as concrete and steel walls absorb the wireless signals, therefore, preventing the signals from traveling further away from the AP. Hence, network professionals implement repeaters in strategic locations within their building or compound to capture the signals from the APs and regenerate the same signal. This technique helps reduce dead zones within the wireless network, ensuring there is maximum coverage of the wireless signals for all wireless clients within the organization.

Voice gateways and media converters

Voice gateways allow an organization to interconnect their enterprise **Voice over IP** (**VoIP**) network to the telecommunication service provider's network using various connectivity methods such as PSTN and **Session Initiation Protocol** (**SIP**) technologies. Within an organization, you will commonly find a VoIP network with IP phones, a **unified communication server** (**UCS**), and networking devices configured to perform the routing of calls between users within the organization. Using a voice gateway allows users to establish calls outside the organization's network using a telecommunication service provider.

Media converters are specialized networking devices that allow network professionals to easily convert an ethernet communication protocol from one media type to another. For instance, if a network professional wants to interconnect a fiber optic cable to a switch that supports only ethernet interfaces, using a media converter allows the light signals from the fiber optic cable to be converted to electrical signals for the ethernet cable, and vice versa.

Having completed this section, you have learned about the roles and functions of various networking devices that are commonly implemented within organizations to create networks. In the next section, you will discover the roles of various security appliances and how they are used to help protect a network.

Exploring security appliances

Cybersecurity is one of the most demanding fields within the IT industry, as threat actors such as hackers are always looking for new ways to compromise systems and networks within organizations and steal their data. Security appliances are specialized devices that are designed to protect a system or a network from cyber-attacks and threats. In this section, you will learn about the roles and features of firewalls, **intrusion detection systems** (**IDSs**), and **intrusion prevention systems** (**IPSs**) on systems and networks.

Firewall

A firewall is a network-based security appliance or host-based application that is designed to filter malicious traffic between networks. Network security professionals commonly implement network-based firewalls between the corporate network of their organization and the internet. The intention is to filter any potentially dangerous traffic originating from the internet that's attempting to enter the private network of the organization.

The internet is the most unsafe network in the entire world and organizations need to monitor and filter network traffic to and from their networks. While it's important to filter inbound traffic from the internet, it's equally important to filter outbound traffic from the corporate network to the internet. If an organization's network is compromised with malware, it usually attempts to infect other systems on the internet. By using a firewall to monitor and filter outbound traffic, network security professionals are able to detect and block any potentially malicious traffic that's also leaving the organization, preventing the threat from spreading to devices on the internet.

The following diagram shows a typical hardware-based firewall that's implemented within a company:

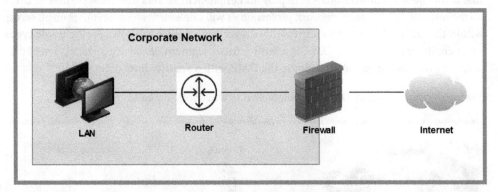

Figure 8.28 – Network-based firewall

As shown in the preceding diagram, a network-based firewall is implemented to filter traffic between the internet and the corporate network of an organization. The advantages of using a network-based firewall are it's a hardware-based device that sits between two or more networks and has the capabilities of filtering traffic between those networks. However, network-based firewalls have to be carefully configured by a security professional to efficiently filter traffic. If a firewall is misconfigured, malicious traffic can be allowed from the internet to the internal networks of the organization. Additionally, threat actors may be able to discover the security vulnerability within the misconfiguration of the security appliance and exploit it.

Next-generation firewalls are able to perform **deep packet inspection (DPI)** by decrypting any encrypted packets to inspect the Layer 7 protocol for any potential threat or malware that may be embedded within an application-layer protocol. Additionally, next-generation firewalls are able to perform **data loss prevention (DLP)** to prevent employees from sending confidential data and files outside the organization's network; however, these are just a few of the many features within firewalls that help network security professionals to protect their organization's assets.

When deploying network-based firewalls, it's important to identify the following security zones:

- **Outside zone**: The outside zone is identified as a network that does not belong to the organization such as the internet. Traffic that originates from the outside zone is considered to be unsafe and not trusted, therefore, any interface in the firewall that's assigned to the outside zone has a security level of 0 by default. The firewall will automatically not permit any traffic that is originating from any interfaces that have a security level of 0 by default.

- **Inside zone**: The inside zone is identified as a network that is managed by the organization, and is usually the internal corporate network within the company. The inside zone is usually assigned a security level of 100, which is fully trusted by the firewall. Therefore, any traffic that originates from the inside zone will automatically be permitted to access any other networks or zones that are attached to the firewall.

- **Demilitarized zone (DMZ)**: The DMZ is a semi-trusted zone within the organization's network that allows network professionals to deploy and implement servers that are accessible to users on the internet. For instance, network professionals will implement an on-premises email server within the DMZ and configure a firewall with very strict rules to allow specific traffic types to an email server. Since the DMZ is a semi-trusted segment of the organization's network, security professionals usually configure the DMZ with a security level of 50.

The following diagram shows all three zones attached to a network-based firewall:

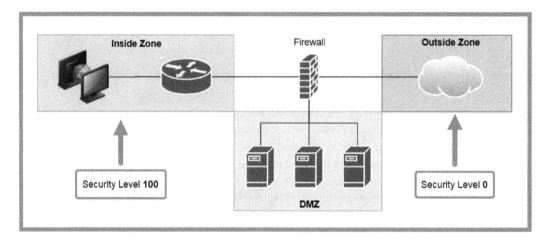

Figure 8.29 – Security zones on a firewall

The security levels assigned to each zone are very important as they determine whether the firewall will permit or deny traffic between a *zone*. By default, Cisco firewall appliances allow traffic that originates from a zone with a higher security level to a zone with a lower security level, while denying traffic originating from a zone with a lower security level to a zone with a higher security level. Put simply, the firewall does not trust traffic originating from zones with lower security levels.

By default, the following rules are applied to a network-based firewall:

- Traffic originating from the inside zone is permitted to the DMZ
- Traffic originating from the inside zone is permitted to the internet
- Traffic originating from the DMZ is not permitted to the inside zone
- Traffic originating from the DMZ is permitted to the outside zone
- Traffic originating from the outside zone is not permitted to the inside zone
- Traffic originating from the outside zone is selectively permitted based on the firewall rules to the DMZ

> **Important note**
>
> Packet filtering firewall rules are created using the five tuples: source IP address, destination IP address, source port number, destination port number, and protocol. The five tuples are used to identify a flow/stream of traffic between a source and a destination. Therefore, when creating a firewall rule to permit or deny traffic, it's important that the network security professional has a clear understanding of the source and destination of the traffic flow.

There are host-based firewalls that are simply security applications that are installed on a host device such as a computer with the capabilities of filtering network traffic entering and leaving the host device. Unlike network-based firewalls, which can filter traffic between networks, host-based firewalls are capable of filtering traffic on the host device only.

The following snippet shows the Windows Defender Firewall on a Windows 11 device:

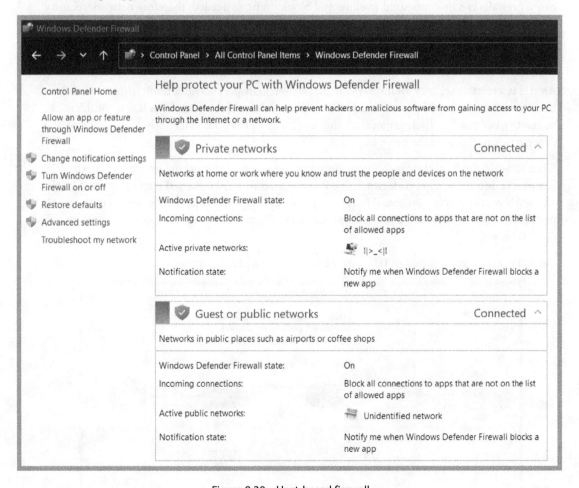

Figure 8.30 – Host-based firewall

Many operating systems, such as Microsoft Windows and various flavors of Linux, have a built-in native firewall that filters traffic on the host device. However, many antimalware applications provide a third-party host-based firewall to improve threat detection and prevention. Whether there's a network-based firewall implemented within an organization's network, it's recommended to ensure all host-based firewalls are enabled on all client and end devices.

Imagine that an organization has disabled all their host-based firewalls within the entire company and implemented a single network-based firewall between their corporate network and the internet. The network-based firewall is a single layer of protection and failure, and if it is misconfigured or unable to detect malware entering the corporate network, the malware can easily spread to all end devices within the company's network. If the host-based firewall is disabled on each end device, there is nothing really stopping the malware from attempting to compromise other hosts within the internal network. Hence, it's important to ensure host-based firewalls are enabled at all times. Both host- and network-based firewalls can be configured to allow and block traffic as needed, therefore network security professionals should configure firewall rules accordingly rather than disable a firewall completely.

IPS/IDS

An IDS is a reactive security solution system that is used to inspect network traffic, detect whether an intrusion is found within a packet, and send an alert if an intrusion is found. An IDS is considered to be reactive because it will trigger an alert after a security intrusion is detected but does not stop the cyber-attack or threat on the network.

Since IDSs do not have the capability of stopping an intrusion as it occurs on a network, the IDS sensor is connected to a network switch that is configured within a **switched port analyzer (SPAN)**. The SPAN port is simply a dedicated interface on the network switch that takes a copy of the network traffic that is flowing between a source and destination through the switch and out the SPAN port to the IDS sensor.

The following diagram shows an IDS sensor connected to a SPAN port on a switch:

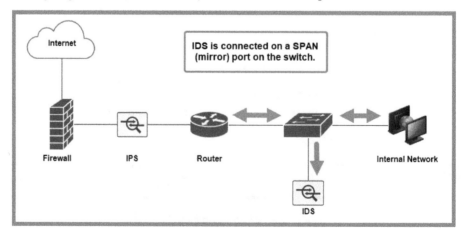

Figure 8.31 – IDS sensor on a network

As shown in the preceding diagram, the IDS sensor receives a copy of the network traffic passing through the switch for analysis. If an intrusion is detected, the IDS reacts and triggers an alert but does not stop the attack as it's happening on the network. IDSs are commonly used by security professionals to understand how attacks occur on a network and what the objectives of a threat actor are. Using intelligence collected from an IDS can provide a lot of information on how hackers are performing new and sophisticated cyber-attacks.

The IPS is a proactive security solution system that sits in line with network traffic, inspecting and detecting any intrusions. If an intrusion is detected, the IPS immediately blocks the intrusion and sends an alert. Unlike the IDS, the IPS has the capability of stopping an intrusion as it occurs on the network.

The following diagram shows an IPS on a network:

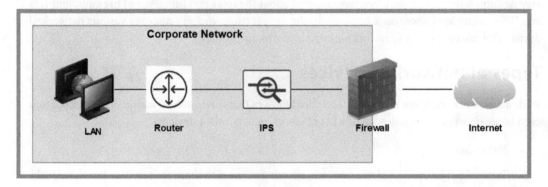

Figure 8.32 – IPS on a network

As shown in the preceding diagram, the IPS is placed between the network-based firewall and the internal network of the organization. Some firewalls are not able to detect intrusions within various traffic types, hence the need for a detected security solution that has the capabilities of detecting intrusions that are missed by the firewall on the network. Additionally, the IPS is placed behind the firewall and inspects traffic that is entering and leaving the corporate network only, hence the reason for its placement between the firewall and corporate network.

Years ago, **network-based intrusion detection systems** (**NIDSs**) and **network-based intrusion prevention systems** (**NIPSs**) were detected as hardware-based security appliances. Nowadays, these are built into next-generation firewalls and are activated with a software license from the firewall vendor.

There are **host-based intrusion detection systems** (**HIDSs**) and **host-based intrusion prevention systems** (**HIPSs**) that are security applications installed on host devices such as computers. HIDSs and HIPSs have the same function as the network-based deployment with the exception that HIDSs and HIPSs can only monitor the security events within a host. They can also monitor network traffic coming into the host. Additionally, they are often used as file integrity checkers.

The following are the four types of alerts that are generated by an IDS and IPS:

- **False positive**: An alarm is triggered, but no threats exist

- **False negative**: No alarm is triggered, but a threat does exist

- **True positive**: An alarm is triggered, and a threat does exist

- **True negative**: No alarm is triggered, and no threat exists

Network security professionals continuously improve the rules within an IDS and IPS to ensure there are fewer *false positives* and *false negatives*. Therefore, each alert has to be investigated by a security professional to determine whether it's a real security intrusion or not.

Having completed this section, you have learned about the roles and functions of firewalls, and IDS and IPS security appliances on a network. In the next section, you will discover various networked devices that are commonly found within organizations and homes.

Types of networked devices

Within a network, there are many host and client devices that can be found within organizations and even home networks. The following is a list of common networked devices:

- VoIP phone.

- Printers can be connected to a network, allowing all users to share the resource simultaneously.

- Physical access control devices.

- IP cameras can connect to a wired and/or wireless network, allowing a user to remotely access and manage the cameras.

- **Heating, ventilation, and air conditioning** (**HVAC**) sensors are implemented within a data center to detect changes in the temperature of the room. The sensors communicate with the HVAC system to ensure the temperate is properly controlled within the room to ensure all devices are cooled.

- **Internet of Things** (**IoT**) devices such as smart refrigerators, smart speakers, smart thermostats, and smart doorbells.

- **Industrial control systems (ICS)** such as **supervisory control and data acquisition (SCADA)** systems are systems that are implemented within an industrial plant that automate and control many processes for the day-to-day operations of the facility.

Having completed this section, you have discovered common networked devices that are commonly found within an organization and home network.

Summary

During the course of this chapter, you have explored the roles and functions of a wide range of networking devices and security appliances that are commonly implemented within organizations to forward traffic between a source and a destination. Additionally, you have explored the need for security appliances and solutions such as firewalls, IDSs, and IPSs within a network. Lastly, you have gained insights into the type of devices that are connected to a network, such as IoT devices.

I hope this chapter has been informative for you and is helpful in your journey toward learning about networking and becoming a network professional. In the next chapter, *Chapter 9, Routing and Switching Concepts*, you will explore various routing protocols and how they work to ensure routers are able to forward packets to their destinations, and various switch configurations that are used to segment a physical network to improve performance.

Questions

The following is a short list of review questions to help reinforce your learning and help you identify areas that require some improvement:

1. Which of the following devices operates at Layer 1?

    A. Router

    B. Hub

    C. Firewall

    D. Switch

2. Which of the following devices is used to interconnect different networks?

    A. Firewall

    B. Hub

    C. Switch

    D. Router

3. Which of the following devices is used to manage all the APs within an organization?

    A. WLC

    B. Bridge

    C. WAP

    D. Switch

4. Which of the following devices can be used to forward traffic between VLANs?

    A. Layer 2 switch

    B. Bridge

    C. Hub

    D. Layer 3 switch

5. Which of the following can a network professional use to distribute network traffic between multiple servers on a network?

    A. Router

    B. Layer 3 switch

    C. Load balancer

    D. Proxy server

6. Which of the following devices is provided by the ISP to interconnect a customer network to their CMTS network?

    A. Bridge

    B. Cable modem

    C. Router

    D. DSL modem

7. Which of the following wireless standards does not need to use CSMA/CA?

    A. IEEE 802.11ax

    B. IEEE 802.11a

    C. IEEE 802.11n

    D. IEEE 802.11ac

8. Which of the following blocks an intrusion on a network?

    A. HIPS

    B. NIDS

    C. HIDS

    D. NIPS

9. Which of the following alert types is best used to describe when no threat exists on a network and an alert is generated?

   A. False negative

   B. True negative

   C. False positive

   D. True positive

10. Which of the following methods is used to prevent collisions on a wired contention-based network?

    A. CSMB/CD

    B. CSMA/CD

    C. CSMD/CA

    D. CSMA/CA

Further reading

To learn more on the subject, check out the following links:

- *What is a next-generation firewall?* https://www.cisco.com/c/en/us/products/security/firewalls/what-is-a-next-generation-firewall.html

- *What is a Wireless LAN Controller?* https://www.cisco.com/c/en/us/products/wireless/wireless-lan-controller/what-is-wlan-controller.html

- *What is an IPS?* https://www.vmware.com/topics/glossary/content/intrusion-prevention-system.html

9

Routing and Switching Concepts

Routing and switching are core networking functionalities, and every aspiring network professional needs a solid understanding of how various types of devices forward traffic to their destinations. Many protocols are configured on routers to forward packets, and switches use various methods to forward frames to their destinations.

In this chapter, you will explore how routers make their forwarding decisions to ensure packets are delivered to their destinations. You will gain a solid understanding of the various dynamic routing protocols, their algorithms, and the metrics used to determine the best path to a destination network. Furthermore, you will discover various configurations that are commonly implemented on managed switches to help improve the performance of a network.

In this chapter, we will cover the following topics:

- Exploring routing concepts
- Understanding routing protocols
- Bandwidth management
- Delving into switching concepts
- Exploring VLAN
- Understanding switch port configurations

Let's dive in!

Exploring routing concepts

Routers are Layer 3 devices that operate at the Network layer of the **Open Systems Interconnection** (**OSI**) and the Internet layer of the **Transmission Control Protocol/Internet Protocol** (**TCP/IP**) networking models. Routers are one of the most essential networking devices found within private and public networks as they allow network professionals to interconnect two or more different networks together, and forward packets to their destinations. For instance, routers can interconnect different IP subnets, allowing devices on one IP network to communicate with hosts on another IP network and interconnect networks with different media types, such as an Ethernet network with a fiber optic.

Routers are built to perform many Layer 3 operations such as **Network Address Translation** (**NAT**) and filtering traffic using **Access Control Lists** (**ACLs**). Some routers even support **Virtual Private Network** (**VPN**) capabilities, allowing network professionals to set up *site-to-site* and *remote access* VPNs. However, all routers have a core function, which is to *route/forward* packets to their destinations efficiently using the most suitable path. For instance, have you ever wondered how your computer or smartphone can communicate with servers on the internet or how routers can forward your packets to the intended destination network or host? Routers are configured with routing protocols, which use an algorithm that helps them determine the best path or route to a destination. Between your device and a server on the internet, many paths are available that can be used to forward the packets from your device to the destination over the internet. However, not all paths are suitable due to various factors within each path.

For instance, imagine if the routers within an **Internet Service Provider** (**ISP**) network forward packets along paths that were heavily congested with a lot of network traffic (load). All the internet subscribers of that particular ISP will experience high latency, which causes slow response times when they are communicating with hosts on the internet. Using dynamic routing protocols helps routers calculate the best path from a source to a destination by assigning metric values to various factors about a patch, such as the following:

- Cumulative bandwidth
- Latency
- Reliability
- **Outgoing load (TX load)**
- **Receiving load (RX load)**
- Hop count
- Path

However, each algorithm within the dynamic routing protocol uses one or more factors to determine and install the best path to a destination within the routing table of a router. Each router has a local routing table that contains a list of destination routes/paths. This simply tells the router how to forward a packet to its destination.

The following diagram shows a computer that wants to send a message to a remote device:

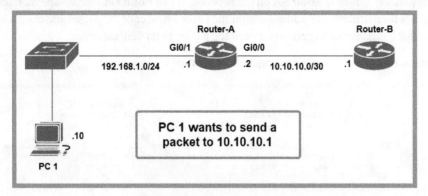

Figure 9.1 – Network diagram

As shown in the preceding diagram, **PC 1** wants to send a message to **Router-B**, which has been configured with an IP address of 10.10.10.1. Before **PC 1** places the message on the network media, it checks its local *routing table* to determine whether the destination exists within the same network as **PC 1** or on a remote network.

The following screenshot shows the routing table within **PC 1**:

```
Command Prompt

C:\Users\Glen>route print
===========================================================================
Interface List
 13...00 0c 29 f7 9e ab ......Intel(R) 82574L Gigabit Network Connection
  1...........................Software Loopback Interface 1
===========================================================================

IPv4 Route Table
===========================================================================
Active Routes:
Network Destination        Netmask          Gateway       Interface  Metric
          0.0.0.0          0.0.0.0      192.168.1.1     192.168.1.10    281
        127.0.0.0        255.0.0.0         On-link         127.0.0.1    331
        127.0.0.1  255.255.255.255         On-link         127.0.0.1    331
  127.255.255.255  255.255.255.255         On-link         127.0.0.1    331
      192.168.1.0    255.255.255.0         On-link      192.168.1.10    281
     192.168.1.10  255.255.255.255         On-link      192.168.1.10    281
    192.168.1.255  255.255.255.255         On-link      192.168.1.10    281
        224.0.0.0        240.0.0.0         On-link         127.0.0.1    331
        224.0.0.0        240.0.0.0         On-link      192.168.1.10    281
  255.255.255.255  255.255.255.255         On-link         127.0.0.1    331
  255.255.255.255  255.255.255.255         On-link      192.168.1.10    281
===========================================================================
Persistent Routes:
  Network Address          Netmask  Gateway Address  Metric
          0.0.0.0          0.0.0.0      192.168.1.1  Default
===========================================================================
```

Figure 9.2 – PC 1 routing table

Since 10.10.10.1 does not exist within the 192.168.1.0/24 network, **PC 1** sends the message to its **default gateway**, which is **Router-A** on the network. When **Router-A** receives the message from **PC 1**, it inspects the destination IP address within the Layer 3 header of the packet and checks its local routing table for a suitable route/path to forward the packet to its destination.

The following screenshot shows the routing table of **Router-A**:

```
Router-A#show ip route
Codes: L - local, C - connected, S - static, R - RIP, M - mobile, B - BGP
       D - EIGRP, EX - EIGRP external, O - OSPF, IA - OSPF inter area
       N1 - OSPF NSSA external type 1, N2 - OSPF NSSA external type 2
       E1 - OSPF external type 1, E2 - OSPF external type 2, E - EGP
       i - IS-IS, L1 - IS-IS level-1, L2 - IS-IS level-2, ia - IS-IS inter area
       * - candidate default, U - per-user static route, o - ODR
       P - periodic downloaded static route

Gateway of last resort is not set

     10.0.0.0/8 is variably subnetted, 2 subnets, 2 masks
C       10.10.10.0/30 is directly connected, GigabitEthernet0/0
L       10.10.10.2/32 is directly connected, GigabitEthernet0/0
     192.168.1.0/24 is variably subnetted, 2 subnets, 2 masks
C       192.168.1.0/24 is directly connected, GigabitEthernet0/1
L       192.168.1.1/32 is directly connected, GigabitEthernet0/1

Router-A#
```

Figure 9.3 – Routing table of a Cisco router

As shown in the preceding screenshot, the routing table contains a list of destination routes (paths) that are known to the router. The code listed in the upper portion of the snippet indicates how a route was learned by the router. For instance, in the lower portion of the snippet, there are various *parent routes* and *child routes*. The child routes can easily be identified as they are indented compared to the parent routes, which are not in the routing table. Each child route has a code that indicates how the router was learned; the C code indicates the route is directly connected to the router, while the L code indicates it's a local route that points to a specific IP address. Additionally, each route contains a destination network followed by the exit interface of the router or the next hop address.

> **Important note**
>
> A router will check its routing table using a top-down approach until it finds a suitable route. Once a suitable route is found, the router stops searching and forwards the packet to the destination based on the details specified within the route. A network route will specify the *exit interface* of the router and/or the *next hop* address. The *exit interface* simply indicates which port on the router should be used to forward the packet to its destination. The *next hop* address is the IP address of the next router to receive the packet along the way to the destination.

Therefore, **Router-A** uses the following network route to forward the packet to **Router-B**:

```
C       10.10.10.0/30 is directly connected, GigabitEthernet0/0
```

Simply put, **Router-A** will forward the packet out from its `GigabitEthernet 0/0` interface, to which **Router-B** is connected. However, if a default gateway or router does not have a valid route to a destination network, it will return a *Destination Unreachable* message to the sender.

Now that you have a better idea of the concept of routing, next, you will take a deep dive into understanding how various dynamic routing protocols help network professionals choose the best path to a destination.

Understanding routing protocols

Routers can populate their routing tables with directly connected routes or networks that are attached to the local interfaces of a router. However, a router is unable to determine the path/route to a destination network that is not directly connected, such as a remote network on the internet or a network that is attached to another router within an organization.

For instance, the following screenshot shows the *routing table* of **Router-A**, which has two directly connected routes/networks on the local router:

```
Router-A#show ip route
Codes: L - local, C - connected, S - static, R - RIP, M - mobile, B - BGP
       D - EIGRP, EX - EIGRP external, O - OSPF, IA - OSPF inter area
       N1 - OSPF NSSA external type 1, N2 - OSPF NSSA external type 2
       E1 - OSPF external type 1, E2 - OSPF external type 2, E - EGP
       i - IS-IS, L1 - IS-IS level-1, L2 - IS-IS level-2, ia - IS-IS inter area
       * - candidate default, U - per-user static route, o - ODR
       P - periodic downloaded static route

Gateway of last resort is not set

      10.0.0.0/8 is variably subnetted, 2 subnets, 2 masks
C        10.10.10.0/30 is directly connected, GigabitEthernet0/0
L        10.10.10.2/32 is directly connected, GigabitEthernet0/0
      192.168.1.0/24 is variably subnetted, 2 subnets, 2 masks
C        192.168.1.0/24 is directly connected, GigabitEthernet0/1
L        192.168.1.1/32 is directly connected, GigabitEthernet0/1

Router-A#
```

Figure 9.4 – Routing table

As shown in the preceding diagram, **Router-A** contains the `10.10.10.0/30` network, which is directly connected to its `GigabitEthernet 0/0` interface, and the `192.168.1.0/24` network, which is directly connected to the `GigabitEthernet 0/1` interface.

The following diagram provides a visual representation of the *routing table* within **Router-A**:

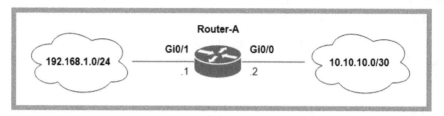

Figure 9.5 – Network topology

However, what if the network topology were to expand to include additional networks that are interconnected with multiple routers? This can be seen in the following diagram:

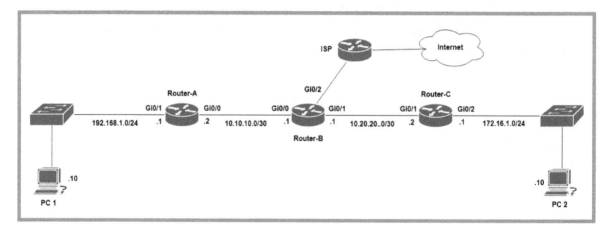

Figure 9.6 – Network diagram

As shown in the preceding diagram, **Router-A** is not directly connected to the 10.20.20.0/24 and 172.16.1.0/24 networks. Therefore, if **PC 1** wants to send a message to **PC 2** over the network, **Router-A** will not be able to forward the message until those networks are known to **Router-A**. As a result, if **PC 1** forwards a packet to **Router-A** with the destination IP address of 172.16.1.10, **Router-A** will return a *Destination Host Unreachable* message to **PC 1** because a route to the destination host or network does not exist within the routing table of **Router-A**.

The following screenshot shows the routing table of **Router-A** on the topology:

```
Router-A#show ip route
Codes: L - local, C - connected, S - static, R - RIP, M - mobile, B - BGP
       D - EIGRP, EX - EIGRP external, O - OSPF, IA - OSPF inter area
       N1 - OSPF NSSA external type 1, N2 - OSPF NSSA external type 2
       E1 - OSPF external type 1, E2 - OSPF external type 2, E - EGP
       i - IS-IS, L1 - IS-IS level-1, L2 - IS-IS level-2, ia - IS-IS inter area
       * - candidate default, U - per-user static route, o - ODR
       P - periodic downloaded static route

Gateway of last resort is not set

      10.0.0.0/8 is variably subnetted, 2 subnets, 2 masks
C        10.10.10.0/30 is directly connected, GigabitEthernet0/0
L        10.10.10.2/32 is directly connected, GigabitEthernet0/0
      192.168.1.0/24 is variably subnetted, 2 subnets, 2 masks
C        192.168.1.0/24 is directly connected, GigabitEthernet0/1
L        192.168.1.1/32 is directly connected, GigabitEthernet0/1

Router-A#
```

Figure 9.7 – Router-A routing table

As shown in the preceding screenshot, **Router-A** does not have a network route for the 172.16.1.0/24 network, so it will not be able to forward any packets to **PC 2** with an IP address of 172.16.1.10.

The following screenshot shows the response from **Router-A**, which indicates it does not have a valid route to the destination host:

```
C:\>ping 172.16.1.10

Pinging 172.16.1.10 with 32 bytes of data:

Reply from 192.168.1.1: Destination host unreachable.
Reply from 192.168.1.1: Destination host unreachable.
Reply from 192.168.1.1: Destination host unreachable.
Request timed out.

Ping statistics for 172.16.1.10:
    Packets: Sent = 4, Received = 0, Lost = 4 (100% loss),
```

Figure 9.8 – Destination unreachable message from the router

A network professional can resolve this issue by configuring **Router-A**, **Router-B**, and **Router-C** with a dynamic routing protocol that automatically shares network routes between routers, allowing them to update their routing tables of network topology changes while ensuring each router knows how to forward packets to its intended destination. Many dynamic routing protocols are commonly implemented within organizations by network protocols. Each protocol has unique characteristics that define how they choose the most suitable path to a destination.

In the next section, you will learn about the fundamentals of various dynamic routing protocols and how each of these protocols determines the best path to a destination.

Dynamic routing

Dynamic routing protocols are designed to help routers automatically learn about designation networks by sharing routing information with other routers. The routing information that's shared between routers within an organization is used to add the best suitable route to a destination network within the routing table of each router. Additionally, if a network or path is no longer available, the dynamic routing protocol automatically detects changes within the network topology, sharing updated routing information with all routers within the network to ensure their routing table is always up to date. Hence, if a router receives a packet with a destination IP address and the router no longer has an available route to the destination, the router informs the sender that the destination host or the network is unreachable.

> **Important note**
> Each dynamic routing protocol is designed with an algorithm that calculates the best suitable path to a destination by determining the **metric** (cost) of each available path and choosing the path with the least metric to install within the routing table.

Dynamic routing protocols provide the following benefits:

- Automatically discover remote networks by sharing routing information between routers on a network

- Maintain an up-to-date routing table on all routers within the network

- Choose the best suitable destination path to forward packets to their destinations

- Can find a new best path in the event the current path is no longer available

The following diagram shows a breakdown of each dynamic routing protocol within the industry:

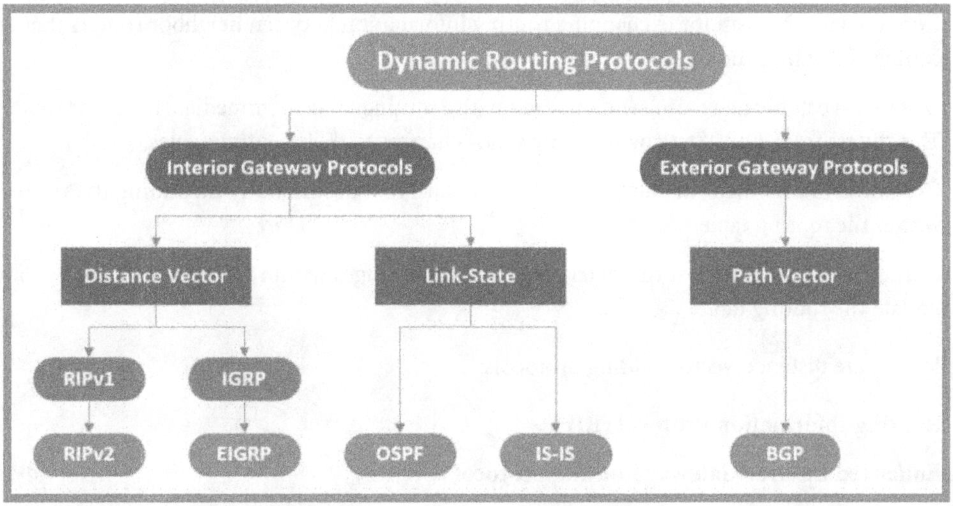

Figure 9.9 – Dynamic routing protocols

As shown in the preceding diagram, there are routing protocols that belong to **Interior Gateway Protocols** (**IGPs**) and **Exterior Gateway Protocols** (**EGPs**). IGPs are simply dynamic routing protocols that are implemented within an organization that does not share routing information on the internet. For instance, organizations with private networks implement IGPs on their routers to share routing information. When all routers know about all networks within an organization, it's commonly referred to as a converged network.

> **Important note**
>
> **Interior Gateway Routing Protocol** (**IGRP**) is a legacy Cisco proprietary routing protocol that is no longer implemented on networks and has been replaced with its successor, **Enhanced Interior Gateway Routing Protocol** (**EIGRP**).

Additionally, IGPs are further divided into two sub-categories: **Distance-Vector** protocols and **Link-State** protocols. The distance-vector protocols forward packets based on distance and direction. Each distance-vector routing protocol uses an algorithm to calculate the best path to the destination host or network and sends that information to the neighbor routers that are using the same routing protocol. The distance-vector routing protocols use factors that are relative to distance and direction, such as hop counts, bandwidth, reliability, outgoing and receiving load, and delays.

Additionally, the algorithms within distance-vector routing protocols consist of the following factors:

- Contain a mechanism for exchanging routing information between neighbor routers that are configured within the same routing protocol.

- Distance-Vector routers also send out their entire routing table to immediate neighbor routers. This differs from Link-State, which only sends changes to their routing tables.

- Contain a mechanism for calculating the best path to a destination and adding the route(s) within the routing table.

- Contain a mechanism that can detect and adapt to changes within the network topology and update the routing table.

The following are distance-vector routing protocols:

- **Routing Information Protocol (RIP)**
- **Enhanced Interior Gateway Routing Protocol (EIGRP)**

However, the link-state routing protocol uses the cumulative bandwidth to a destination network as the metric. Each router that is configured with a link-state routing protocol builds its topological map of the entire network, which helps the router determine the shortest path to the destination. Link-state routing protocols will only send an update to a neighbor router if there's a change within the network topology.

The following are link-state routing protocols:

- **Open Shortest Path First (OSPF)**
- **Intermediate System - Intermediate System (IS-IS)**

EGPs are dynamic routing protocols that are implemented between ISPs to share public networks. These networks are more aptly referred to as **Autonomous Systems (ASs)**. IGP routes internal to one AS, whereas EGP routes between AS(s). For instance, at the time of writing, the **Border Gateway Protocol (BGP)** is the only EGP that exists within the networking industry, and it's used between ISPs to share their public networks with other ISPs on the internet. Hence, BGP is the path-vector routing protocol that allows ISP routers to learn about other public networks and maintain an up-to-date routing table with BGP routes.

Administrative distance

A router can be configured with multiple dynamic routing protocols to operate simultaneously. Each routing protocol that's operating on the router will use its algorithm to determine the best path to a destination network. However, which route needs to be added to the routing table? A route to a destination network can only appear once within the routing table. Simply put, if a router is configured with EIGRP and OSPF routing protocols and each of these routing protocols determines the best path to a destination, the router has to make a decision on which route from these two protocols will be added to the routing table since duplicates are not supported.

Usually, network professionals only configure one routing protocol within their organization. However, there are situations where more than one routing protocol is operating on the same router within a company's network and each routing protocol determines the best path based on its algorithm.

Cisco IOS routers use **administrative distance** (**AD**) to determine the trustworthiness of a route to be added to the routing table. Each dynamic routing protocol is assigned a unique AD value, which helps the router determine which route source is most trustworthy compared to others.

The following table shows the AD values for each route source for Cisco IOS routers:

Route Source	Administrative Distance
Directly connected	0
Static route	1
EIGRP summary route	5
External BGP	20
Internal EIGRP	90
OSPF	110
IS-IS	115
RIP	120
External EIGRP	170
Internal BGP	200

Figure 9.10 – Administrative distance chart

As shown in the preceding table, each route source and protocol has a unique AD value assigned that helps the router choose a route source. The router chooses the route source to a destination network that has the lowest AD value. For instance, if a router is configured with both EIGRP and OSPF, and each of these routing protocols determines the best path to a destination, the EIGRP route will be added to the routing able of the router because EIGRP has a default AD value of 90 compared to OSPF, which has an AD value of 110. However, if a network professional configures a static route to the same destination network, the static route will be prioritized and added to the routing table as its AD value is 1.

Over the next few sub-sections, you will gain a solid foundation on various distance-vector, link-state, and path-vector routing protocols that are used on the internet and within private networks of organizations.

RIP

RIP is a legacy, distance-vector routing protocol that is no longer implemented by network professionals on large enterprise networks due to its many limitations. RIP uses the **Bellman-Ford** algorithm, which uses hop count as the metric to calculate the best path to a destination network. The hop count is simply calculated by the number of routers (hops) that exist in the destination. RIP uses a maximum hop count of 15, which decrements by 1 each time a router has to forward the packet to the next hop along the way to the destination. If the hop count value on the packet reaches 0, the last router to change it to 0 will discard the packet. The hop count value within RIP is like the **Time To Live (TTL)** value within an IP packet; if the TTL reaches 0, it's discarded on the network. Additionally, RIP uses UDP port 520 to exchange messages between RIP-enabled routers.

The following diagram shows a network topology that contains routers that have been configured with the RIP dynamic routing protocol:

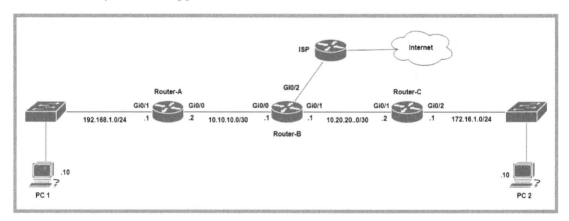

Figure 9.11 – Routers using the RIP dynamic routing protocol

Let's assume **Router-A, Router-B**, and **Router-C** are all managed by an organization and have been configured with RIP as the preferred dynamic routing protocol. The following screenshot shows the RIP routes that have been installed within the routing table of **Router-A**:

```
Router-A#show ip route
Codes: L - local, C - connected, S - static, R - RIP, M - mobile, B - BGP
       D - EIGRP, EX - EIGRP external, O - OSPF, IA - OSPF inter area
       N1 - OSPF NSSA external type 1, N2 - OSPF NSSA external type 2
       E1 - OSPF external type 1, E2 - OSPF external type 2, E - EGP
       i - IS-IS, L1 - IS-IS level-1, L2 - IS-IS level-2, ia - IS-IS inter area
       * - candidate default, U - per-user static route, o - ODR
       P - periodic downloaded static route

Gateway of last resort is 10.10.10.1 to network 0.0.0.0

     10.0.0.0/8 is variably subnetted, 3 subnets, 2 masks
C        10.10.10.0/30 is directly connected, GigabitEthernet0/0
L        10.10.10.2/32 is directly connected, GigabitEthernet0/0
R        10.20.20.0/30 [120/1] via 10.10.10.1, 00:00:15, GigabitEthernet0/0  ①
R     172.16.0.0/16 [120/2] via 10.10.10.1, 00:00:15, GigabitEthernet0/0  ②
     192.168.1.0/24 is variably subnetted, 2 subnets, 2 masks
C        192.168.1.0/24 is directly connected, GigabitEthernet0/1
L        192.168.1.1/32 is directly connected, GigabitEthernet0/1
R*  0.0.0.0/0 [120/1] via 10.10.10.1, 00:00:15, GigabitEthernet0/0  ③

Router-A#
```

Figure 9.12 – Routing table

As shown in the preceding screenshot, there are three network routes that were discovered and added to the routing table of **Router-A**. These routes are both highlighted and labeled with numbers 1, 2 and 3. The first remote network route is described as follows:

- R: The R code indicates the network route was learned and added to the routing table via RIP.

- 10.20.20.0/30: This portion of the network route indicates the destination network by its network prefix.

- [120/1]: The value of 120 indicates the AD for RIP. The AD of a dynamic routing protocol indicates the trustworthiness of a routing protocol. RIP has a default AD of 120 on Cisco routers. The value of 1 represents the metric of the route. Since RIP uses the hop count as the metric, we can determine that the destination network is one hop away.

- 10.10.10.1: This value within the route indicates the next hop address – that is, the next Layer 3 device (router) that will receive the packet from **Router-A**.

- **Timer**: The time value increases so long as the route is installed within the routing table of a router. This time helps network professionals determine how long the router has known about this route and whether any changes within the network topology have occurred.

- **Exit interface**: The exit interface indicates the interface that will be used to forward the packet to its destination.

While RIP seems to be a good dynamic routing protocol to automatically learn about networks and share routing information with other routers, many drawbacks make it unsuitable for many organizations. The following are the disadvantages of using RIP on a network:

- RIP broadcasts the entire routing of each router every 30 seconds, regardless of whether a network topology change occurred or not

- RIP does not support large networks with greater than 15 hops

- RIPv1 does not support networks that use custom subnet masks

- RIPv2 supports **Variable Length Subnet Mask (VLSM)** but doesn't allow you to manually specify the custom subnet mask during the configuration process

> **Important note**
>
> **RIPng** is the next generation of RIP and supports IPv6 routing. RIPv1 and RIPv2 support IPv4 routing on networks. RIPng uses UDP port 521 to exchange messages between routers.

Having understood the fundamentals of RIP in this section, next, you will gain a solid foundation on the OSPF routing protocol.

OSPF

Open Shortest Path First (OSPF) is a link-state dynamic routing protocol that's commonly used within many organizations' networks that are interoperable and with mixed vendor devices. OSPF uses its own datagrams and is tagged in the IP protocol as protocol number 89, so it does not use TCP or UDP. Additionally, OSPF uses the **Shortest Path First (SPF)** algorithm, which determines the *cumulative bandwidth* to a destination network and chooses the path with the lowest cost. This is the fast path compared to a path with a higher cost, which results in a slower link.

Being a link-state dynamic routing protocol, each OSPF-enabled router exchanges Hello packets with their neighbor routers to establish an adjacency, which is like a mutual handshake between routers. Once the handshake has been established, each router will exchange **Link-State Advertisements (LSAs)** of their directly connected networks to their neighbor routers, which contain information about the state and the cost of how to reach the links. Once all the OSPF-enabled routers collect the LSAs from each router on the network, they will build the **Link-State Database (LSDB)**, which is commonly referred to as the topology table. Hence, each OSPF-enabled router knows the entire network topology compared to routers that have been configured with distance-vector routing protocols. Once the LSBD is completed, the SFP algorithm is used to determine the best path or shortest path to all known destination networks and adds those paths within the routing table of each OSPF-enabled router.

Important note

OSPF-enabled routers send Hello packets to their neighbor routers every 10 seconds by default to indicate their presence on the network. However, a neighbor router is considered to be down or unavailable if a Hello packet is not received within 40 seconds. If a neighbor router is down, all the networks that have been learned from the neighbor router will be removed from the routing table.

The following network topology shows routers that have been configured with the OSPF dynamic routing protocol:

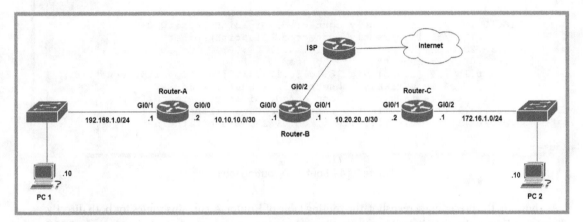

Figure 9.13 – OSPF network topology

As shown in the preceding network topology, **Router-A**, **Router-B**, and **Router-C** are all managed by the same organization, and they are configured to use the OSPF dynamic routing protocol to share routing information. Therefore, each router will share routing information about their directly connected networks with their neighbor routers.

The following screenshot shows the routing table of **Router-A**:

```
Router-A#show ip route
Codes: L - local, C - connected, S - static, R - RIP, M - mobile, B - BGP
       D - EIGRP, EX - EIGRP external, O - OSPF, IA - OSPF inter area
       N1 - OSPF NSSA external type 1, N2 - OSPF NSSA external type 2
       E1 - OSPF external type 1, E2 - OSPF external type 2, E - EGP
       i - IS-IS, L1 - IS-IS level-1, L2 - IS-IS level-2, ia - IS-IS inter area
       * - candidate default, U - per-user static route, o - ODR
       P - periodic downloaded static route

Gateway of last resort is 10.10.10.1 to network 0.0.0.0

      10.0.0.0/8 is variably subnetted, 3 subnets, 2 masks
C        10.10.10.0/30 is directly connected, GigabitEthernet0/0
L        10.10.10.2/32 is directly connected, GigabitEthernet0/0
O        10.20.20.0/30 [110/2] via 10.10.10.1, 00:00:13, GigabitEthernet0/0   ①
      172.16.0.0/24 is subnetted, 1 subnets
O        172.16.1.0/24 [110/3] via 10.10.10.1, 00:00:03, GigabitEthernet0/0   ②
      192.168.1.0/24 is variably subnetted, 2 subnets, 2 masks
C        192.168.1.0/24 is directly connected, GigabitEthernet0/1
L        192.168.1.1/32 is directly connected, GigabitEthernet0/1
O*E2 0.0.0.0/0 [110/1] via 10.10.10.1, 00:01:28, GigabitEthernet0/0   ③

Router-A#
```

Figure 9.14 – Router-A's routing table

As shown in the preceding screenshot, the routing table of **Router-A** contains routes for both directly connected networks, as indicated by the C code, and remote networks that were learned via the OSPF routing protocol, as indicated by the O code. Furthermore, notice that all the OSPF routes have the same AD value of 110 on the router as it's the default AD for OSPF routes. However, the third OSPF route, whose code is O*E2, indicates it's an external route that was redistributed using the OSPF routing protocol. Its purpose is to act as a default route to the internet.

> **Important note**
> OSPFv2 is used on IPv4 networks, while OSPFv3 is used on IPv6 networks.

Having completed this section, you have learned about the fundamentals of OSPF. Next, you will learn about a hybrid routing protocol that's mostly used in Cisco environments.

EIGRP

EIGRP is a hybrid, dynamic routing protocol that's implemented within organizations. EIGRP was a Cisco proprietary routing protocol until 2013, but organizations were long using OSPF as their preferred routing protocol as it is interoperable with mixed vendor equipment. EIGRP uses protocol number 88, which is encapsulated directly into IP datagrams, rather than TCP or UDP. However, unlike other routing protocols, EIGRP uses **Diffusing Update Algorithm** (**DUAL**) to calculate the best path to a destination and a backup path to the same destination. Simply put, EIGRP calculates a backup route for each primary route that is stored within the routing table of a router while ensuring the backup path is loop-free, and that it is ready to be placed within the routing table whenever the primary route is no longer available.

DUAL uses the following factors as metrics to calculate the best path and a backup path:

- Bandwidth
- Delay
- Reliability
- **Outgoing load (TX load)**
- **Receiving load (RX load)**

By default, DUAL uses bandwidth and delay to calculate the metric for the best path and backup path to a destination network, while the other remaining metrics are disabled by default. However, network professionals have the option to enable all five metrics on Cisco IOS routers if they wish.

The following network topology shows routers that have been configured with the EIGRP dynamic routing protocol:

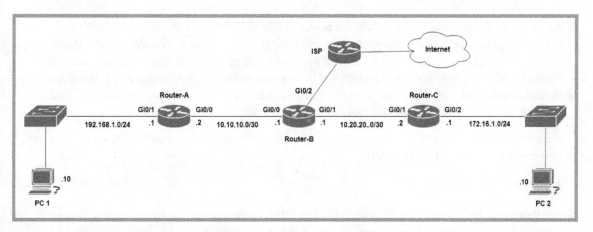

Figure 9.15 – EIGRP-enabled routers

As shown in the preceding network topology, let's assume **Router-A**, **Router-B**, and **Router-C** have all been configured with EIGRP as the preferred routing protocol. DUAL will calculate the metric (cost) to reach each network and install the paths within the routing tables of each router.

The following screenshot shows the EIGRP network routes within routing table of **Router-A**:

```
Router-A#show ip route
Codes: L - local, C - connected, S - static, R - RIP, M - mobile, B - BGP
       D - EIGRP, EX - EIGRP external, O - OSPF, IA - OSPF inter area
       N1 - OSPF NSSA external type 1, N2 - OSPF NSSA external type 2
       E1 - OSPF external type 1, E2 - OSPF external type 2, E - EGP
       i - IS-IS, L1 - IS-IS level-1, L2 - IS-IS level-2, ia - IS-IS inter area
       * - candidate default, U - per-user static route, o - ODR
       P - periodic downloaded static route

Gateway of last resort is 10.10.10.1 to network 0.0.0.0

     10.0.0.0/8 is variably subnetted, 3 subnets, 2 masks
C       10.10.10.0/30 is directly connected, GigabitEthernet0/0
L       10.10.10.2/32 is directly connected, GigabitEthernet0/0
D       10.20.20.0/30 [90/3072] via 10.10.10.1, 00:04:04, GigabitEthernet0/0 ①
     172.16.0.0/24 is subnetted, 1 subnets
D       172.16.1.0/24 [90/3328] via 10.10.10.1, 00:00:15, GigabitEthernet0/0 ②
     192.168.1.0/24 is variably subnetted, 2 subnets, 2 masks
C       192.168.1.0/24 is directly connected, GigabitEthernet0/1
L       192.168.1.1/32 is directly connected, GigabitEthernet0/1
D*EX 0.0.0.0/0 [170/5376] via 10.10.10.1, 00:03:45, GigabitEthernet0/0       ③

Router-A#
```

Figure 9.16 – Routing table

As shown in the preceding screenshot, the routing table of **Router-A** contains paths for remote networks that are not directly connected to the local router, these remote network routes are labeled with numbers 1, 2 and 3. Notice that the D code was used to indicate network routes that were learned via the EIGRP routing protocol and that each of these routes has a default AD value of 90. However, the default route that was redistributed via EIGRP has a code of D*EX and a default AD value of 170 since it's used to send packets outside the company's network.

Next, you will learn about the fundamentals of the routing protocol, which is used by ISPs to exchange routing information over the internet.

BGP

BGP is a path-vector routing protocol that's used by ISPs to exchange routing information with each other. BGP operates on TCP port number 179. Unlike the IGPs that are used within organizations' networks, BGP is a very slow converging routing protocol that does not send updates as soon as a change occurs on the network topology. Hence, BGP was designed to operate between ASs such as ISPs on the network. Therefore, if a public network goes down an ISP, BGP will not immediately tell the other neighbor ISPs but wait a while to determine if the network will be restored.

The following diagram shows the different ASs, such as ISPs, interconnected using BGP to share their routing information:

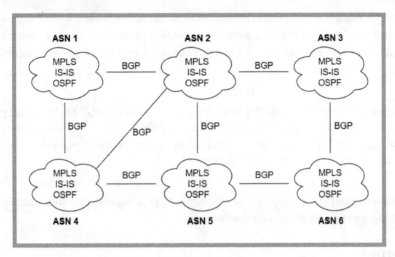

Figure 9.17 – ASs

As shown in the preceding diagram, each ISP is assigned a unique **Autonomous System Number (ASN)** that allows one ISP to establish an adjacency with another ISP using BGP to share routing information of their public networks. An AS is simply a large collection of public networks that are all managed by a single organization such as an ISP. Within each ISP's administrative domain, they use IGPs and other service provider technologies to forward traffic within their service provider network. However, BGP allows an AS to advertise their public networks to other ISPs around the world, ensuring each ISP knows how to forward packets to any public network on the internet.

> **Important note**
>
> When discussing the topic of BGP, it's common to think this version of BGP is strictly designed for the internet. However, there are two versions of BGP: **External BGP (eBGP)** and **Internal BGP (iBGP)**. eBGP is used between different ASs, while iBGP is used within an AS.

The following screenshot shows the BGP routing table of a router:

```
ACME1#show ip bgp
BGP table version is 6, local router ID is 192.168.0.1
Status codes: s suppressed, d damped, h history, * valid, > best, i - internal,
              r RIB-failure, S Stale
Origin codes: i - IGP, e - EGP, ? - incomplete

   Network          Next Hop            Metric LocPrf Weight Path
*  1.1.1.0/30       1.1.1.1                  0      0      0 65003 ?
*> 1.1.1.4/30       1.1.1.1                  0      0      0 65003 i
*> 1.1.1.8/30       1.1.1.1                  0      0      0 65003 i
*> 172.16.10.0/24   1.1.1.1                  0      0      0 65003 ?
*> 192.168.0.0/24   0.0.0.0                  0         32768 i

ACME1#
```

Figure 9.18 – BGP routing table

As shown in the preceding screenshot, the destination networks are on the left, while the paths to those networks are on the right. Since BGP is a path-vector routing protocol, each path shown within the BGP routing table presents an AS and not the number of hops away to reach the destination network.

> **Tip**
>
> If you're interested in seeing more BGP routing tables, check out the *BGP Looking Glass* project that was created and is maintained by many ISPs around the world; this is because they allow limited access to their BGP routers on the internet to anyone. Simply type the Google search term `bgp looking glass` in your web browser.

Next, you will learn about static routing and why network professionals use this technique within their networks to forward packets to their destinations.

Static routing

Static routing allows network professionals to manually configure destination network routes within the routing table of a router. Static routes always take precedence over any network route that was learned using a dynamic routing protocol. Since static routes have a default AD of 1, it's lower than the AD of any dynamic routing protocol, and if you recall, the AD defines the trustworthiness of a route. Hence, if a network professional creates a static route to a destination network, the router will automatically trust this route over others.

Network professionals can configure static routes on all routers within a small network. However, if the network topology changes, the static routes within the routers will not automatically update the changes within the topology compared to dynamic routing protocols. Simply put, static routes do not adapt to the changes of the network – they require a network professional to always update the configurations of static routes within all the routers of an organization. Hence, static routing is workable for small networks that change frequently and where there are fewer IP networks.

However, if a network professional misconfigures a static route on a router, the router will not forward packets correctly to the intended destination network. As a result, these misconfigurations can affect the performance of a network and routing packets between a source and a destination. Another common issue when using static routing is that a router will still forward packets to a network that is no longer reachable, simply because the static route that's configured within the route tells the device how to forward packets and does not update the routing table if the network topology changes. Removing or modifying a static route requires the skills of a network professional.

As an organization's network grows over time, since routers do not automatically learn remote networks by default, network professionals will need to implement a static route for each destination network on each router. Additionally, the complexity of troubleshooting issues increases as the network topology gets larger as more static routes are installed within the routing table of each router.

The following are various types of static routes:

- **Standard static route**: This type of static route specifies how to reach a destination network.

- **Default static route**: A default static route is used when no other routes within the routing table of a router match the destination IP address of a packet. This type of route is usually configured to forward packets to the internet.

- **Floating static route**: This type of static route functions as a backup route to a primary route on a router. For instance, if a primary route is no longer available, a floating static route is usually configured with an AD that is higher than the primary route.

- **Summary static route**: A summary static route is used to represent multiple destination IP networks in the form of a single, consolidated static route. Summary static routes are used to reduce the size of a routing table that has too many routes that are forwarding traffic to the same destination.

The following diagram shows a simple network topology where each router has been configured with static routing to forward traffic to remote networks:

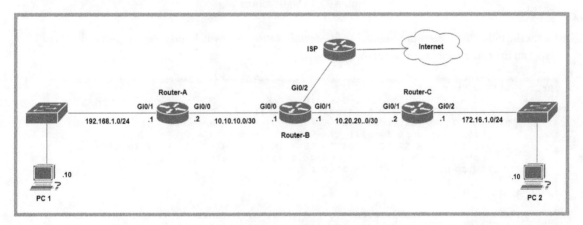

Figure 9.19 – Network topology

As shown in the preceding diagram, **Router-A** has to be configured with static routes to forward traffic to 10.20.20.0/30, 172.16.1.0/24, and the internet, as these networks are not directly connected to the router.

The following screenshot shows the static routes within the routing table of **Router-A** that are used to forward packets to the 10.20.20.0/30 and 172.16.1.0/24 networks:

```
Router-A#show ip route
Codes: L - local, C - connected, S - static, R - RIP, M - mobile, B - BGP
       D - EIGRP, EX - EIGRP external, O - OSPF, IA - OSPF inter area
       N1 - OSPF NSSA external type 1, N2 - OSPF NSSA external type 2
       E1 - OSPF external type 1, E2 - OSPF external type 2, E - EGP
       i - IS-IS, L1 - IS-IS level-1, L2 - IS-IS level-2, ia - IS-IS inter area
       * - candidate default, U - per-user static route, o - ODR
       P - periodic downloaded static route

Gateway of last resort is 10.10.10.1 to network 0.0.0.0

      10.0.0.0/8 is variably subnetted, 3 subnets, 2 masks
C        10.10.10.0/30 is directly connected, GigabitEthernet0/0
L        10.10.10.2/32 is directly connected, GigabitEthernet0/0
S        10.20.20.0/30 [1/0] via 10.10.10.1
      172.16.0.0/24 is subnetted, 1 subnets
S        172.16.1.0/24 [1/0] via 10.10.10.1
      192.168.1.0/24 is variably subnetted, 2 subnets, 2 masks
C        192.168.1.0/24 is directly connected, GigabitEthernet0/1
L        192.168.1.1/32 is directly connected, GigabitEthernet0/1
S*    0.0.0.0/0 [1/0] via 10.10.10.1

Router-A#
```

Figure 9.20 – Static routes

Lastly, the following screenshot highlights the *default static route*, which indicates the *gateway of last resort* on the routing table of **Router-A**:

```
Router-A#show ip route
Codes: L - local, C - connected, S - static, R - RIP, M - mobile, B - BGP
       D - EIGRP, EX - EIGRP external, O - OSPF, IA - OSPF inter area
       N1 - OSPF NSSA external type 1, N2 - OSPF NSSA external type 2
       E1 - OSPF external type 1, E2 - OSPF external type 2, E - EGP
       i - IS-IS, L1 - IS-IS level-1, L2 - IS-IS level-2, ia - IS-IS inter area
       * - candidate default, U - per-user static route, o - ODR
       P - periodic downloaded static route

Gateway of last resort is 10.10.10.1 to network 0.0.0.0

      10.0.0.0/8 is variably subnetted, 3 subnets, 2 masks
C        10.10.10.0/30 is directly connected, GigabitEthernet0/0
L        10.10.10.2/32 is directly connected, GigabitEthernet0/0
S        10.20.20.0/30 [1/0] via 10.10.10.1
      172.16.0.0/24 is subnetted, 1 subnets
S        172.16.1.0/24 [1/0] via 10.10.10.1
      192.168.1.0/24 is variably subnetted, 2 subnets, 2 masks
C        192.168.1.0/24 is directly connected, GigabitEthernet0/1
L        192.168.1.1/32 is directly connected, GigabitEthernet0/1
S*    0.0.0.0/0 [1/0] via 10.10.10.1

Router-A#
```

Figure 9.21 – Default static route

As shown in the preceding screenshot, the default static route is used when no other routes within the routing table of a router have a match for the destination IP address within a packet. Additionally, the next hop address of a default static route is used as the gateway of last resort on the router.

Having completed this section, you have learned about the fundamentals of static routing and dynamic routing. Next, you will explore bandwidth management tools to ensure specific data types are prioritized over a network.

Bandwidth management

Within an organization's network, many devices and users are sending and receiving messages to/from each other. Some users are uploading and downloading files from the internet, while others are having a teleconference meeting using a **Voice over IP** (**VoIP**) or **Video over IP** solution. Overall, many different traffic types are traveling along a network. Some of these traffic types are using a connection-oriented protocol such as **Transport Control Protocol** (**TCP**), while others are using a connectionless protocol such as **User Datagram Protocol** (**UDP**).

One of the major differences between TCP and UDP is that TCP provides guaranteed delivery for packets over a network. If a packet is not delivered to its intended destination, the sender will retransmit the message until the destination host provides an acknowledgment. Packets that use TCP as their preferred transport layer protocol have a higher priority on the network because TCP provides guaranteed delivery. Therefore, if a network becomes saturated or congested with too many packets, each device that wants to send a message tries to access the available bandwidth on the network to transmit its packets, which becomes an issue.

Furthermore, each networking device has two buffers for temporarily storing messages that are awaiting to be processed and forwarded to their destinations. These are known as **port-based memory** and **shared memory**. The port buffer exists on each interface of a networking device and is used to temporarily store inbound messages that have to be processed by the device. Additionally, the port buffer is used to temporarily store outbound messages that have already been processed by the device and are waiting to be placed on the physical network.

The shared memory of a networking device is simply used to temporarily store all the messages in a common buffer that is shared by all the interfaces and memory of the networking device. If a networking device buffer is filled, any additional messages will be dropped from the network. If TCP messages are dropped, the sender will retransmit them to the destination. However, if UDP messages are dropped from the network, the sender will not retransmit because UDP does not have any mechanism to determine whether a packet arrived at a destination or not.

For instance, voice and video traffic types use UDP as their preferred transport layer protocol because UDP provides better capabilities for delivering messages that are time-sensitive over a network compared to TCP. Imagine speaking to a colleague using a VoIP telephone within your office and the dialog is not smooth as some packets are being sent and received more slowly than others, while some packets are being dropped because another employee is transferring a huge file and saturating the network.

Network professionals use two types of solutions to ensure specific traffic types have a high priority of accessing the bandwidth over others on a network, as follows:

- **Traffic shaping**
- **Quality of Service (QoS)**

Traffic shaping allows network professionals to create delays of some traffic types using a traffic profile. This technique is commonly used to improve the latency and optimize the performance of a network while increasing the allocation of bandwidth for specific traffic types. Simply put, if a sender is transmitting too many packets that are congesting the network, networking devices such as switches can create a delay or slow down the amount of traffic between the host and destination over the network, thus allowing other traffic types to access the bandwidth. This allows higher priority traffic to flow with optimal speed over the network while lower priority traffic is delayed.

QoS is another solution that is commonly implemented within many organizations' networks that helps control traffic on a network while ensuring the improved performance of mission-critical applications over limited network capacity.

The following metrics are used within QoS to measure types of traffic over a network:

- **Bandwidth**: Bandwidth is the number of bits that can be transmitted in a second between a source and a destination.
- **Congestion**: In a network, congestion results in packets being delayed while they're arriving at their destinations. Congestion occurs when there is a lot more traffic on the network, which saturates all the available bandwidth.
- **Delay**: Delay is used to measure the time a packet takes to travel between a source and a destination. This is commonly referred to as **latency**. Users on a congested network usually experience high latency (slow response time).
- **Jitter**: Jitter measures the variation in the delay times of incoming packets on a network. For instance, on an optimal network, all packets that are received from the same sender should have the same latency. However, jitter increases on the network as users are sending and receiving messages and saturating the network.
- **Packet loss**: Packet loss measures how many packets are discarded or dropped between a source and destination over a given time. Any discarded TCP messages are retransmitted while UDP messages are not resent. Having too many packet losses can affect the performance of a network as some devices will retransmit dropped messages while others may not, depending on the transport layer protocol.

The following steps show how QoS prioritizes traffic on a network:

1. **Classification**: Inbound traffic on a networking device is inspected and placed within a waiting queue based on the **Differentiated Services (DS)** field of an IPv4 packet and the **Traffic Class** field of an IPv6 packet.

2. **Marking**: This is the process where the QoS tools on the networking device modify one or more fields within the packet header to insert a value.

3. **Queuing**: This phase is responsible for managing all the queues for outgoing messages on a networking device. Traffic is sent out of a networking device based on its priority.

4. **Policing and shaping**: The policing feature is responsible for discarding or dropping packets, while the shaping feature is responsible for keeping or holding the packets within a queue.

5. **Congestion avoidance**: This feature is used to reduce the amount of congestion that exists within a network to reduce packet loss.

The following diagram shows the classification process when using QoS:

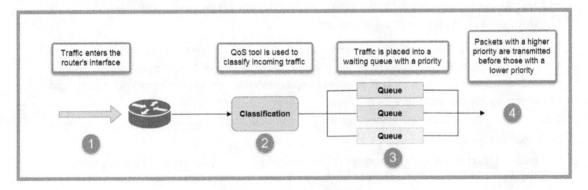

Figure 9.22 – Classification process

As shown in the preceding diagram, traffic enters the router's inbound interface and it's classified by the QoS tool within the device. After the classification process, the traffic is placed within a waiting queue with a priority value assigned to the message. The messages with a higher priority within a queue are forwarded to the network compared to messages with a lower priority.

Having completed this section, you have gained an understanding of bandwidth management techniques such as traffic shaping and QoS. In the next section, you will discover various switching concepts.

Delving into switching concepts

As you have learned so far, network switches are designed and configured to forward frames to their destinations over a network. However, network switches have a lot of additional cool features that allow network professionals to enable special services and functions on a network. In this section, you will learn how network professionals can distribute power over network cables to wireless access points and VoIP phones, prevent a Layer 2 loop on a switching network, aggregate multiple physical links into a single logical link between switches, and discover connected devices on a network.

PoE

Power over Ethernet (PoE) is the technology that allows **Direct Current (DC)** power over a copper Ethernet cable to devices to reduce the need for a dedicated power supply and **Alternating Current (AC)** power outlets. For instance, imagine you're a network professional who has been assigned to install an access point in the center of a ceiling within a large office space. Before installing the access point, you notice that the closest AC power outlet is located in the furthest corner of the room. Additionally, attaching a power extension cord to the access point while running the power cord above the ceiling is perhaps not a good idea due to safety concerns.

Enabling the PoE feature on a PoE-supported switch will allow DC power to be distributed along the Ethernet cable to the access point, hence reducing the need for a dedicated power supply and AC power outlet. The same concepts are commonly implemented to provide power to VoIP phones and IP cameras within organizations.

> **Important note**
> Since an Ethernet cable is used to support both PoE and data, PoE does not add any additional Ethernet capabilities to the data that's transported along the same cable.

PoE is defined by **IEEE 802.3af**, which was created in 2003. It specifies how electrical power can be delivered to another device by using the spare pairs within a copper Twisted Pair cable. These spare pairs are pins 4 and 5 or pins 7 and 8. However, PoE can use the data pairs of an Ethernet cable; these pairs are pins 1 and 2 or pins 3 and 6. The concept of using PoE within networks allows organizations to save a lot of money by reducing the need for AC outlets and dedicated power supplies for devices. PoE provides up to 15.4 watts of DC power with a maximum of 350 **milliamps (mA)** of electrical current. **PoE+**, an improved variation of PoE, was defined by **IEEE 802.3at** in 2009, which provides an increased power rating of up to 25.5 watts with a maximum of 600 mA of electrical current to devices.

> **Important note**
> There are two modes of PoE: A and B. Mode A delivers power on the data pairs (1, 2, 3, and 6), while mode B delivers power on the spare pairs (4, 5, 7, and 8).

Therefore, before a network professional purchases PoE switches for their organization, it's important to check the power rating of their PoE-supported devices such as access points, IP cameras, and VoIP phones to determine which version of PoE is more efficient to distribute power to these devices – that is, PoE or PoE+.

Spanning-Tree

When designing a network topology for any organization, it's essential to implement redundancy and fault tolerance to ensure multiple paths are available between a source and a destination. While redundancy seems to be good, it's also very bad for network professionals. When multiple switches are interconnected to create redundancy, the design also creates a Layer 2 loop. Simply put, a Layer 2 loop exists whenever there are two or more available paths between a sender and the destination hosts on a switch network.

The following diagram shows the 3-tier architecture that's commonly implemented within large organizations:

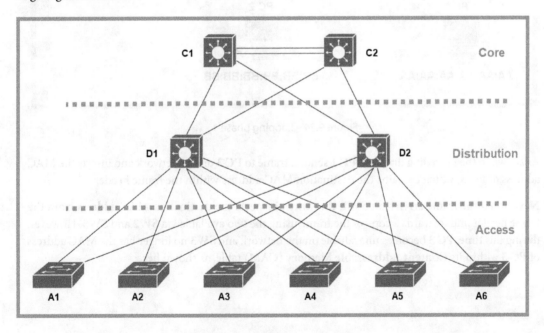

Figure 9.23 – 3-tier architecture model

As shown in the preceding diagram, the model allows scalability and provides lots of redundancy between each layer. The access layer allows end devices to connect and access the resources on the network, the distribution layer provides link aggregation, **Quality of Service (QoS)**, and inter-VLAN routing, and the core layer is the high-speed backbone of the network that interconnects the distribution layer between remote branch offices.

Let's take a look at how a Layer 2 loop is formed when there are redundancy paths within a switch network. The following diagram shows a small network with a redundant path between **PC 1** and **PC 3**:

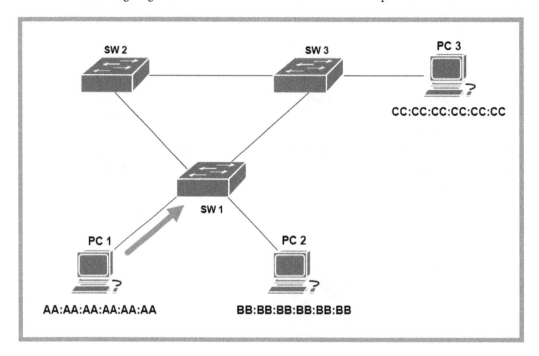

Figure 9.24 – Looping phase 1

As shown in the preceding diagram, **PC 1** sends a frame to **PC 3** on the network and inserts the MAC address of **PC 3**, which contains the destination MAC address within the frame header.

Next, when the frame arrives on **SW1**, the switch inspects the destination MAC address from the frame header and forwards a copy of the frame using the two available via **SW2** and **SW3**. However, during this time, **PC 3** becomes unavailable on the network and **SW3** no longer has the MAC address of **PC 3** within its **Content Addressable Memory** (**CAM**) table, as shown here:

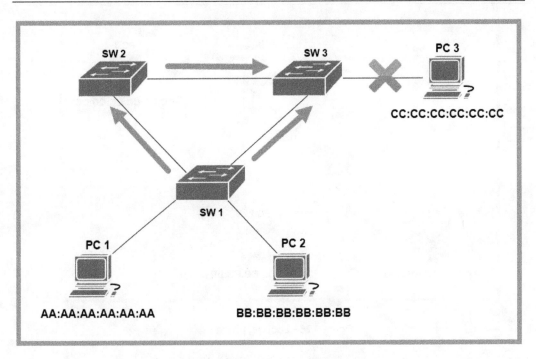

Figure 9.25 – Looping phase 2

Since **SW3** no longer has the MAC address of **PC 3** within its CAM table, when **SW3** receives the inbound message from **SW1**, it will flood the frame out of all other ports except the interface the message arrived on. The same will occur when **SW3** receives the frame from **SW2** as it's the default behavior of switches whenever the destination MAC address is not found within their CAM table, as shown here:

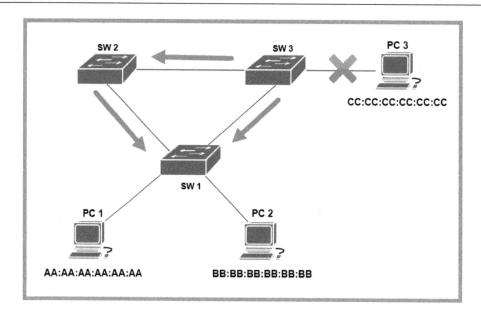

Figure 9.26 – Looping phase 3

This loop will occur on all switches within the topology, so long as each switch does not know how to find the destination host on the network. For this reason, each switch will simply regenerate the frame and rebroadcast it over and over, as shown in the following diagram:

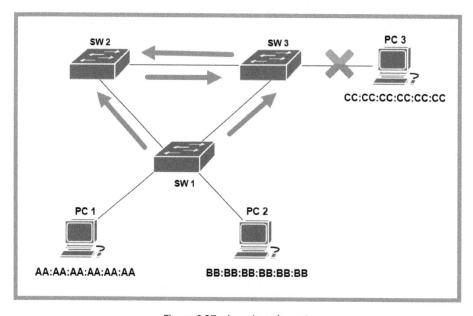

Figure 9.27 – Looping phase 4

The frames will be looping in a never-ending cycle because frames do not contain TTL fields like packets. Packets contain TTL fields that are assigned a value (number) before leaving a sender's device. Each hop (router) along the way to the destination will decrease the TTL value by 1. This ensures packets do not live forever on a network if a routing loop should occur. Additionally, if the TTL value of a packet reaches 0 before it arrives at its intended destination, the router that decreases the TTL to 0 will simply discard the packet on the network. Since frames do not have a TTL assigned to them, frames will not be automatically discarded and create a broadcast storm that can congest an entire network.

Another issue with redundant paths on a switch network is creating duplicate messages between a source and a destination host. To better understand how duplication can occur on a network with redundancy, let's take a look at the following diagram, where **PC 1** is sending a message to **PC 3**:

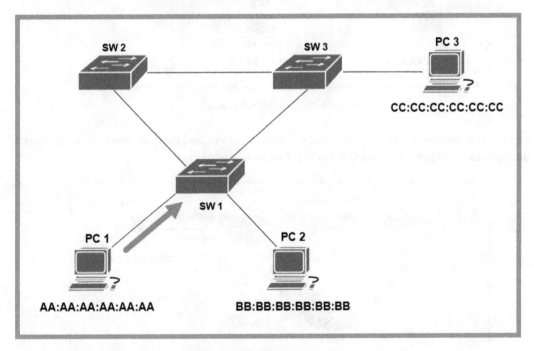

Figure 9.28 – Duplication phase 1

Without any loop prevention mechanisms on the network, when **SW1** receives the frame of **PC 1**, it will forward it to **PC 3** using the two available paths via **SW 2** and **SW 3**. Then, **SW 3** will forward both messages from **SW 1** and **SW 2** to **PC 3**, as shown in the following diagram:

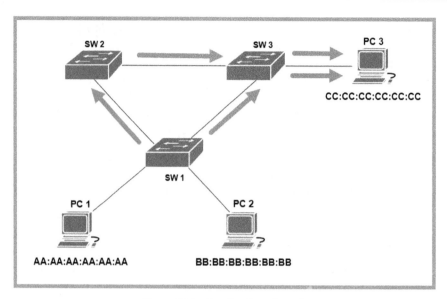

Figure 9.29 – Duplication phase 2

Since **PC 3** receives two copies of the message, it will respond twice, and the duplication of the responses will duplicate as it's being sent to **PC 1**, as shown in the following diagram:

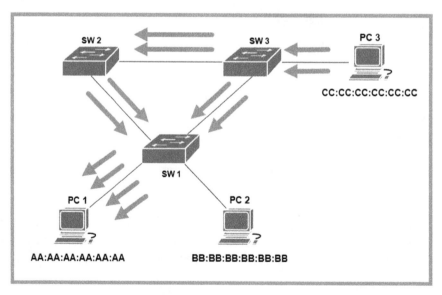

Figure 9.30 – Duplication phase 3

To resolve the issues that are created by redundancy on a switch network, the **Spanning-Tree Protocol (STP)** was designed as a Layer 2 loop prevention protocol that can detect any physical Layer 2 loops on a network and logically block the redundant path. This ensures only one active logical path between a source and destination is available.

> **Important note**
> STP is defined by the **IEEE 802.1D** standard for Layer 2 loop prevention on networks.

The following diagram shows a network topology with STP enabled on all switches that have already blocked a redundant path:

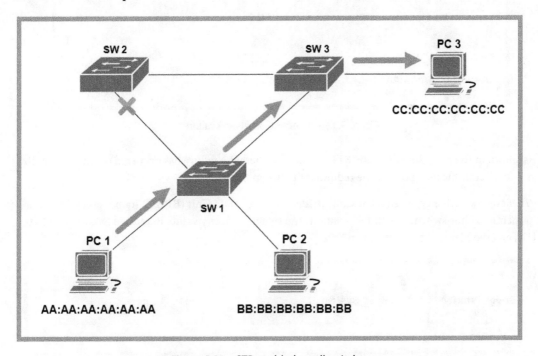

Figure 9.31 – STP enabled on all switches

As shown in the preceding diagram, whenever **PC 1** wants to send a message to **PC 3**, there is one active logical path between both devices that prevents a Layer 2 loop on the network. However, if the primary path is unavailable, STP can detect whether a path is unavailable and automatically redirect the flow of traffic using a backup path, as shown in the following diagram:

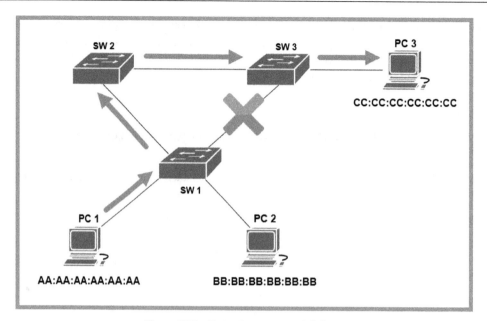

Figure 9.32 – Detecting a network failure

As shown in the preceding diagram, STP can detect whether a failure has occurred on an active path and redirect traffic using one of the redundant paths on the network.

Whenever a switch is powered on, it sends **Bridge Protocol Data Unit (BPDU)** frames every 2 seconds to their neighbor switches. A BPDU contains the switch's priority value, **Extended System ID (Ext-ID)**, and the MAC address, as shown here:

Bridge Priority	Extended System ID	MAC Address
4 Bits	12 Bits	48 Bits

Figure 9.33 – BPDU frame

The information within the BPDUs from each switch is used to elect a special switch as the **Root Bridge**. The Root Bridge informs all other switches to create one logical, loop-free path between any devices on the network. Therefore, if multiple switches are interconnected to create physical redundancy, the Root Bridge will ensure all physical redundant paths are logically blocked and only one active, loop-free path is available. The switch with the lowest bridge priority gets elected as the Root Bridge on the network.

However, since all Cisco switches have a default bridge priority of 32768, network professionals commonly configure their core or distribution layer switches to become the Root Bridge on the network by lowering the bridge priority by decrements of 4096. Hence, the switch with the lowest bridge priority becomes the Root Bridge. If all the switches have the same default bridge priority of 32768, then the switch with the lowest MAC address value will be elected are the Root Bridge on the network.

Once the Root Bridge has been elected, all the other switches on the network will create a logical path that points to the Root Bridge as it becomes the *central reference point* for all traffic within the network.

To get a better understanding of how STP identifies redundant paths and ensures only a loop-free path is active on the network, let's take a look at the following network topology:

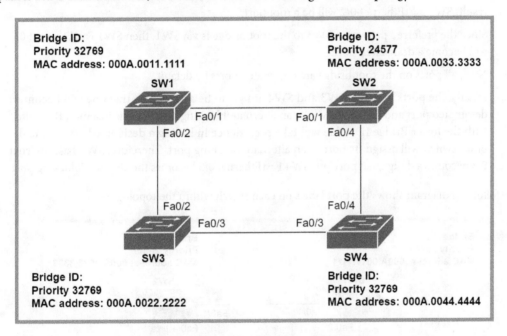

Figure 9.34 – Spanning-Tree network topology

As shown in the preceding diagram, each switch has a priority value (priority + Ext-ID value) and a unique MAC address. The following is my strategy for identifying the root bridge and port states on a network:

1. **Identify the root bridge**: The root bridge is the central reference port for all traffic within the **Virtual Local Area Network (VLAN)**.

2. **Identify root ports**: These are ports closest to the root bridge but not on the root bridge.

3. **Identify designated ports**: These are non-root ports that are in a forwarding state.

4. **Identify alternate/blocking ports**: These are ports that are logically blocked by STP to prevent a Layer 2 loop on a redundant path.

You must follow these steps to identify the root bridge and port status on the topology:

1. SW2 has the lowest priority value and therefore becomes a Root Bridge.

2. Next, the root ports are those that are closest to the root bridge, therefore SW1 FastEthernet 0/1 and SW4 FastEthernet 0/4 are root ports.

3. Next, we need to determine the port roles on SW3. There are two paths from SW3 to the root bridge – that is, SW3 to SW1 and SW3 to SW4 – and both of these paths have the same interface bandwidth. Then, we need to observe the Bridge ID values on both SW1 and SW4 such that the switch with a lower Bridge ID value will be the preferred path to the root bridge. Therefore, SW1 has a lower Bridge ID value because its MAC address is lower compared to SW4. As a result, SW3 FastEthernet 0/2 will be a root port.

4. Since the preferred path from SW3 to the root bridge is via SW1, then SW1 FastEthernet 0/2 will become a designated port.

5. Next, all ports on the root bridge are designated ports by default.

6. Finally, the ports between SW3 and SW4 are yet to be assigned so that one will become a designated port and the other will be an alternate/blocking port. In this instance, the switch with the lower Bridge ID value will take precedence in having a designated port while the other switch will assign its port to an alternate/blocking port. Therefore, SW3 FastEthernet 0/3 becomes a designated port and SW4 FastEthernet 0/3 becomes the alternate/blocking port.

The following diagram shows the port labels on each switch within the topology:

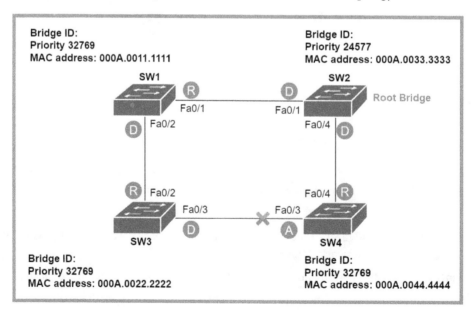

Figure 9.35 – STP port labels

Next, you will learn about a common networking technology that allows network professionals to perform port aggregation by combining multiple physical links into a single logical link.

Port aggregation

EtherChannel or **port aggregation** allows network professionals to combine multiple physical links into a single logical connection between switches to aggregate the bandwidth between devices. However, if a network professional connects two network cables to each of the Gigabit Ethernet interfaces of two switches, only one link will be active for transmitting messages; the other will be logically blocked by STP to prevent a Layer 2 loop, as shown in the following diagram:

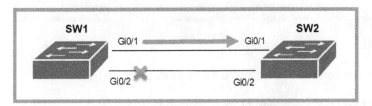

Figure 9.36 – STP blocking a redundant path

As shown in the preceding diagram, the objective was to combine or aggregate the bandwidth of both Gigabit Ethernet interfaces to create a sum of 2 **Gigabits per second (Gbps)** between **SW1** and **SW2**. However, since there are redundant links between both switches, STP will block one of the two links to prevent a Layer 2 loop from forming on the network.

To solve this issue, you can use Etherchannel, which allows a network professional to successfully aggregate the bandwidth of two or more physical connections to create a single logical link between switches to support greater bandwidth between devices. When using EtherChannel, the existing switch interfaces are used to create the actual EtherChannel link, so network professionals do not need to upgrade the hardware components of a switch that already supports the technology. Furthermore, EtherChannels create load balancing of network traffic between switches on a network, which helps with traffic aggregation while providing redundancy.

The **Link Aggregation Control Protocol (LACP)** is an open source protocol defined by **IEEE 802.3ad** that allows any vendor of switches to form EtherChannels between switches on a network. An LACP Etherchannel is formed when two switches use the Active LACP mode on their interfaces. The following table shows the results of the different LACP modes on **SW1** and **SW2**:

LACP		
SW1	**SW2**	**Status**
On	On	Yes
Active/Passive	Active	Yes
On/Active/Passive	No Configuration	No
On	Active	No
On/Passive	Passive	No

Figure 9.37 – LACP modes

The following are the requirements for establishing an EtherChannel between switches on a network:

- The same type of interface must be used between switches

- The same number of interfaces must be used between switches

- The speed and duplex need to be the same on all interfaces that are forming the EtherChannel

- The same configurations must be applied to all interfaces that are forming the EtherChannel

The following diagram shows an example of an EtherChannel that's unable to be formed because there's a duplex mismatch on **SW1**:

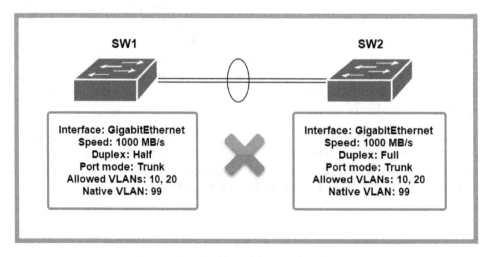

Figure 9.38 – Unable to form an EtherChannel

When the configurations are the same on the interfaces that are being used to create the EtherChannel between **SW1** and **SW2**, the EtherChannel is established between switches, as shown here:

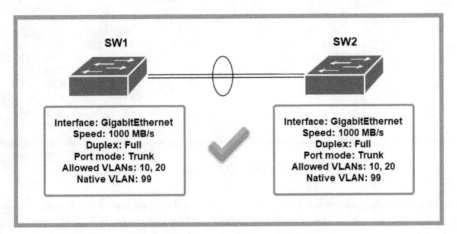

Figure 9.39 – Establishing an EtherChannel

If one of the physical interfaces of an EtherChannel is unavailable or has any misconfigurations, the entire EtherChannel is broken and all the physical interfaces will function independently from each other.

Next, you will learn about various network discovery protocols that are commonly used on networks to help devices and network professionals map a network topology.

Neighbor discovery protocol

As an aspiring network professional, it's nice to have an always up-to-date network topology diagram to help determine the type of networking devices, their capabilities, and interfaces used to connect to another device, their model numbers, and even IP addresses.

The **Cisco Discovery Protocol (CDP)** is a Cisco proprietary protocol that operates between Layers 2 and 3 of the OSI networking model. CDP is used to assist Cisco switches to learn about their directly connected neighbors, such as other switches and routers. On Cisco devices, CDP is enabled by default to exchange advertisement messages using a multicast address of 01:00:0C:CC:CC:CC.

A CDP message contains the following details about the sender device:

- Cisco IOS version of the switch or router
- Device model and type
- Connected interfaces for both local and remote devices
- The hostname of the device

The following screenshot shows the devices that are connected to a Cisco switch that uses CDP:

```
SW3#show cdp neighbors
Capability Codes: R - Router, T - Trans Bridge, B - Source Route Bridge
                  S - Switch, H - Host, I - IGMP, r - Repeater, P - Phone
Device ID     Local Intrfce   Holdtme    Capability    Platform    Port ID
R1            Gig 0/1         157            R          C2900       Gig 0/1
SW1           Fas 0/24        157            S          2960        Fas 0/24
SW2           Fas 0/23        157            S          2960        Fas 0/23
R1            Gig 0/1         157            R          C2900       Gig 0/1.10
R1            Gig 0/1         157            R          C2900       Gig 0/1.20
R1            Gig 0/1         157            R          C2900       Gig 0/1.30
SW3#
```

Figure 9.40 – CDP details

As shown in the preceding screenshot, Device ID indicates the hostname of the directly connected device, Local Interface identifies the interface used by the connected device, Holdtime indicates how long the information will remain in the table, Capability indicates the type of device, Platform indicates the model of the device, and Port ID indicates the local interface that's used to establish the connection.

Since CDP is a Cisco proprietary protocol, it's not interoperable with non-Cisco devices on a network. However, the **Link-Layer Discovery Protocol (LLDP)** is another discovery protocol that operates over Layer 2 of the OSI network model and is supported on both Cisco and non-Cisco devices. LLDP is defined by **IEEE 802.1AB**, which makes it interoperable on other vendor devices and provides similar details as the CDP on a network.

The following screenshot shows the LLDP details on a Cisco switch:

```
SW3#show lldp neighbors
Capability codes:
    (R) Router, (B) Bridge, (T) Telephone, (C) DOCSIS Cable Device
    (W) WLAN Access Point, (P) Repeater, (S) Station, (O) Other
Device ID          Local Intf    Hold-time   Capability       Port ID
SW1                Fa0/24        120         B                Fa0/24
R1                 Gig0/1        120         R                Gig

Total entries displayed: 2
```

Figure 9.41 – LLDP details

Hence, in many organizations with mixed vendor equipment, LLDP is the preferred neighbor discovery protocol to help both network professionals and networking devices identify the types of device on their network.

Having completed this section, you have learned about various switching concepts and technologies. In the next section, you will explore how network professionals can segment a physical network into smaller logical networks.

Exploring VLAN

In most networks, there are a lot of different traffic types, such as voice traffic generated from VoIP phones, video traffic from surveillance systems and telepresence equipment, and data traffic from end devices such as computers, servers, and printers. Imagine that an organization wants to segment these traffic types by implementing separate and dedicated network equipment for each type of traffic. This would mean creating three physically isolated networks to keep each traffic type apart from the other. The disadvantage of performing physical segmentation is the high cost of purchasing dedicated network equipment to build these networks.

With the evolution of the networking industry, we can create a fully converged network to allow all traffic types to use the same physical network while implementing logical segmentation of traffic using network switches. This allows for the creation of a single, well-designed physical network for voice, video, and data traffic while segmenting traffic types within an organization. As an aspiring network professional, you're probably wondering whether there will be any sort of interference between these traffic types over the same physical network.

Network professionals implement a **Virtual Local Area Network** (**VLAN**) within their switches to segment physically connected components on switches. This allows them to be logically organized. There are many benefits to implementing VLANs, such as the following:

- Improving network performance and management
- Reducing the size of a broadcast domain
- Improving network security
- Reducing cost

VLANs are used to improve the performance of a network by reducing the size of a broadcast domain. For instance, all devices that are assigned to a VLAN will be able to receive a broadcast message from a device within the same VLAN. Think of a VLAN as a logical network; devices within the same logical network can reach each other by using a broadcast. Since a broadcast is contained within a VLAN, devices that are assigned to another VLAN will not be affected.

Simply put, if all the devices within the **Human Resources** (**HR**) department were assigned to VLAN 10 and a computer within the HR department was generating a lot of broadcast messages, only devices within the HR department would be affected.

The following diagram provides a visual representation of VLANs within a company:

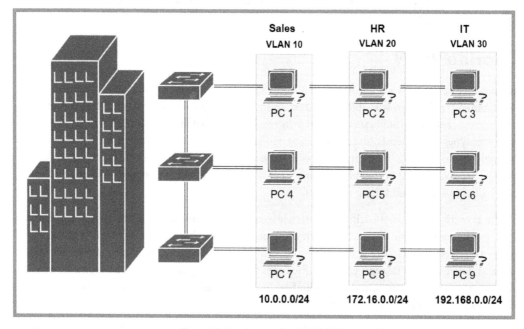

Figure 9.42 – Network with VLANs

As shown in the preceding diagram, if **PC 2** generates a lot of broadcast messages, only **PC 5** and **PC 8** will be affected as they belong to the same VLAN as **PC 2**.

VLANs are created on network switches and network professionals can assign a VLAN to an interface. Therefore, any device that sends a frame to a switch interface will be assigned an **IEEE 802.1Q** tag, which contains the VLAN ID of the interface. This technique ensures all frames are tagged with a VLAN ID, which helps the switch logically separate one piece of VLAN traffic from another.

To understand how VLAN tagging is used within a switch, let's take a look at the following diagram, which represents a switch:

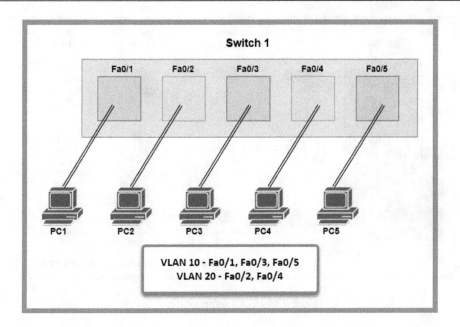

Figure 9.43 – VLAN assignment to each interface

As shown in the preceding diagram, each computer is connected to each interface of the switch, and a VLAN ID is assigned to each port. Therefore, if **PC 1** sends a broadcast to the switch, all inbound traffic on the Fa0/1 interface will be automatically tagged with VLAN 10. Since the message from **PC 1** is a broadcast, the switch will forward the message to all other ports that are assigned to the VLAN. Therefore, the broadcast message will be sent from both the Fa0/3 and Fa0/5 interfaces, and **PC 3** and **PC 5** will receive the message from **PC 1**. Overall, devices that are located on another VLAN, such as VLAN 20, are not affected by the broadcast from **PC 2**, so each VLAN is logically isolated from the other VLANs within the switch.

Since each VLAN is logically isolated from the other, each VLAN must be assigned a unique IP subnet, as shown in the following diagram:

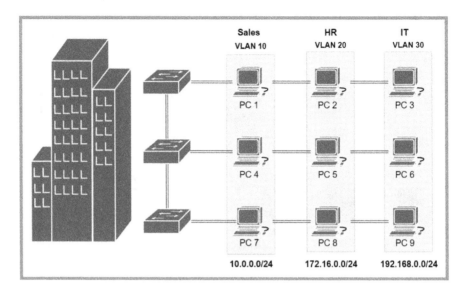

Figure 9.44 – VLAN segmentation

However, to ensure intercommunication between VLANs, network professionals will need to implement a Layer 3 or a dedicated router that has been configured to perform inter-VLAN routing, a technique that allows devices from one VLAN to communicate with devices on another VLAN.

Trunk links are point-to-point connections from switch-to-switch or switch-to-router. Trunks allow multiple VLANs to carry their traffic between switches and routers. Unlike access ports, which allow only one statically assigned VLAN on the interface, a trunk link allows many VLANs at the same time.

Types of VLANs

Various types of VLANs are created on a network. The following are the common types of VLANs within organizations:

- **Default VLAN**: The default VLAN is simply the VLAN that is created by the vendor. The default VLAN is VLAN 1 and all the interfaces of the switch are assigned to VLAN 1 by default, so a new enterprise-grade switch will work out of the box. However, since all interfaces are assigned to VLAN 1 by default, it's not recommended to use the default VLAN for security reasons. Unfortunately, network professionals are unable to rename or delete the default VLAN on a switch.

- **Data VLAN**: The data VLAN is usually configured to transport traffic generated by end devices such as computers, servers, printers, and access points.

- **Native VLAN**: The native VLAN is used to transport *untagged* traffic on an IEEE 802.1Q trunk link. Whenever an end device such as a computer sends traffic to a switch, the receiving switch port inserts an IEEE 802.1Q tag VLAN ID into the frame; this is known as *tagged* traffic. Untagged traffic does not originate from a VLAN; it is self-generated traffic from the switch itself, such as CDP and LLDP messages.

- **Management VLAN**: The management VLAN is used to remotely access the switch over a network for management purposes. Simply put, the management VLAN is also referred to as a **Switch Virtual Interface (SVI)** and is configured with an IP address and subnet mask.

- **Voice VLAN**: Voice traffic uses UDP, which does not provide any reliability for the delivery of each packet. Since a converged network is the recommended type of network infrastructure, having a dedicated network for all voice traffic is preferable. Using a dedicated VLAN to transport voice traffic will ensure that all the voice traffic is kept separate from the other traffic types on the physical network.

> **Important note**
>
> Only one data VLAN can be assigned to a switch port; this type of assignment will create an **access port** on the switch. Two VLANs can be assigned to an access port, but only if the other is a voice VLAN; therefore, only one data and one voice VLAN are allowed on a single access port.

The following diagram shows that VLAN 10 and 20 have been configured on the network, but the connection between the two switches is an access port that's only been statically assigned VLAN 10:

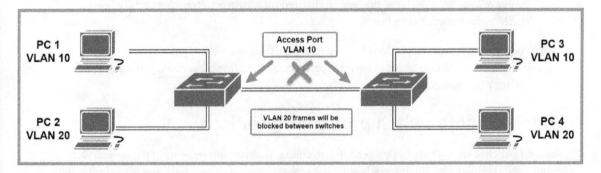

Figure 9.45 – Issues with access ports

As shown in the preceding diagram, **PC 1** and **PC 3** will be able to exchange messages between the two switches but **PC 2** and **PC 4** will not be able to communicate with each other. To solve this issue, a trunk is needed between the two switches to allow both VLAN 10 and 20 traffic, as shown here:

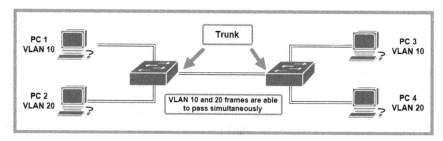

Figure 9.46 – Trunk links

The following are some key points about port tagging and IEEE 802.1Q:

- When a source device such as a computer sends a frame into a switch port, the switch will insert an IEEE 802.1Q tag into the frame.

- Access ports allow network professionals to configure one data VLAN on an interface.

- The IEEE 802.1Q tag contains the VLAN ID that is assigned to the switch's interface. This tag helps the switch isolate one piece of VLAN traffic from another VLAN, so each VLAN is logically separated from the others.

- The IEEE 802.1Q tag is kept on the frame, so long as it is passing between switches.

- The IEEE 802.1Q tag is only removed when the switch is sending outbound traffic from an access port.

- Trunks are special interfaces that are configured on a switch to transport multiple pieces of VLAN traffic between switches.

Having completed this section, you have learned about the fundamentals of port tagging using VLANs and how they are used to help improve network performance. In the next section, you will learn about various switch port configurations.

Understanding switch port configurations

Managed switches allow a network professional to configure many components of the device, such as enabling and disabling each interface, adjusting the support bandwidth on a port, and even configuring the speed and duplex settings on each interface. These are just a few of the many changes network professionals can apply to any port on a switch. Unlike unmanaged switches, network professionals can't log into the device or make any modifications to how the switch operates. An unmanaged switch simply operates like a basic switch and forward frames to its destination – that's about it.

A managed switch provides the additional capabilities and features that are needed by network professionals within the industry to ensure messages are delivered efficiently and quickly to their destinations. In this section, you will explore the importance of various switch port/interface configurations and their effects on a network.

Duplex and speed

Duplex simply defines how communication can occur between two devices on a point-to-point connection. Within networking devices, security appliances, and end devices, each of these devices has a network adapter that supports the following duplex modes:

- Half

- Full

- Auto

Half duplex allows only one device to communicate at a time on a point-to-point connection, such as two switches that are connected or a computer that is connected to a switch. Simply put, if two switches are connected and their connected interfaces are operating in half duplexes, one switch can send frames while the other receives. If the sender stops transmitting, then the other device can transmit its messages. For instance, devices that are connected to a hub such as computers operating on half duplex can prevent packet collisions by using **Carrier Sense Multiple Access/Collision Detection (CSMA/CD)**.

A full duplex allows two devices to simultaneously exchange messages at any time over a point-to-point network connection. For instance, the following diagram shows two switches that are connected that can both exchange messages with each other at the same time, unlike half duplex:

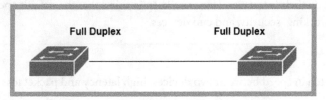

Figure 9.47 – Full duplex

However, the default duplex mode on many devices such as switches, routers, and computers is auto duplex. This enables the automatic negotiation sensing feature, which allows one device to sense the operating mode of another device and media, allowing the device to match the duplex mode.

The following diagram shows two switches that have their interfaces configured in auto mode:

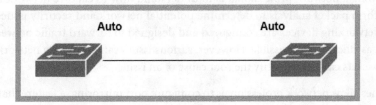

Figure 9.48 – Auto mode

As shown in the preceding diagram, the interfaces on both switches are operating in auto duplex mode. Ideally, after a few seconds, both switches will automatically negotiate and operate in either a full or half duplex. By default, they should negotiate to operate in full duplex but if there are any issues with a cable (media), network adapter, or even the drivers on either device, the duplex mode can result in a half duplex. However, it's recommended to statically configure the operating state of switch interfaces to ensure the best performances and reduce the time to troubleshoot an issue.

> **Important note**
> If there's a mismatch in the duplex between two devices, high latency and packet loss can occur.

Speed defines the maximum throughput or transmission speeds that are supported on an interface of a device. The following are various supported speed configurations on networking devices:

- **10**: Operates at 10 Mbps
- **100**: Operates at 100 Mbps
- **1,000**: Operates at 1,000 Mbps
- **Auto**: Uses an auto-negotiation sensing feature to detect and match the speed of another device

It's recommended to ensure devices that are connected on a point-to-point connection have the same speed configurations on their interfaces. However, keep in mind that the default operating mode for speed is auto on networking, security, and end devices.

> **Important note**
> If there's a mismatch in speed between two devices, high latency and packet loss can occur.

Having completed this section, you learned about the importance of ensuring both speed and duplex settings match on all devices within a network to prevent any issues. Next, you will learn about how network professionals can capture a copy of network traffic that passes through a switch.

Port mirroring

A part of becoming a network professional is to understand how to capture network traffic from a switch to perform packet analysis to determine potential network and security issues within an organization. Networking devices are configured and designed to forward traffic between a source and destination as efficiently as possible. However, various issues can occur on a network over time, and analyzing packets can help identify the root cause of an issue.

Managed switches allow network professionals to configure port mirroring, a feature that's built into many switches within the networking industry. When port mirroring is configured and enabled on a switch, the switch has to create a copy of all the traffic and remote both Layer 1 and Layer 2 pieces of data from each message before sending it out to a network security monitoring device.

> **Important note**
>
> **Cisco** commonly refers to port mirroring as **Switch Port Analyzer (SPAN)**, while **3Com** uses the term **Roving Analysis Port (RAP)**.

The following diagram shows a switch with port mirroring configured to mirror network traffic:

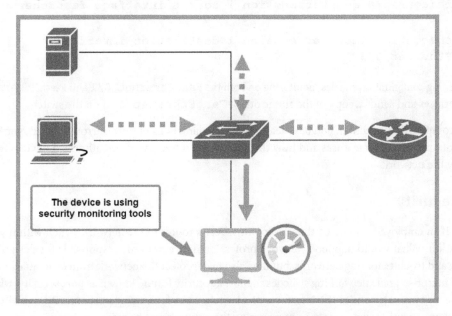

The device is using security monitoring tools

Figure 9.49 – SPAN on a network switch

As shown in the preceding diagram, the switch is configured with port mirroring to create a copy of all network traffic that is passing through the switch. A copy is forwarded to the device with a network security monitoring tool such as **Intrusion Detection System (IDS)** or even a protocol analyzer such as **Wireshark**.

The following are some key points of using the built-in port mirroring feature within supported switches:

- The port mirroring feature is already built into enterprise-grade networking switches.
- Port mirroring removed both Layer 1 and Layer 2 pieces of data from each message before sending it to the destination device.
- Network professionals need to apply the necessary configurations to create the mirror interfaces.
- **Remote SPAN (RSPAN)** can be configured on a larger network to capture traffic between switches that share a VLAN. This is the Cisco terminology for remote port mirroring.

The following is an example of SPAN configurations for a Cisco 2960 switch:

```
Switch(config)# no monitor session 1
Switch(config)# monitor session 1 source interface fastEthernet
0/1
Switch(config)# monitor session 1 source interface fastEthernet
0/2
Switch(config)# monitor session 1 destination interface
fastEthernet 0/3
```

The preceding configuration enables monitoring on both the FastEthernet 0/1 and FastEthernet 0/2 interfaces and sends a copy of the traffic out of FastEthernet 0/3 on the switch.

Having completed this section, you have learned the fundamentals of port mirroring. Next, you will learn about port security features and how they can be used to prevent unauthorized devices from accessing the network.

Port security

Imagine if an employee connected their laptop or wireless router to the network switch within your organization. What would happen? Network professionals are not only responsible for designing, building, and troubleshooting networks, but they also help protect the network from cyberattacks and threats. Enterprise-grade networking switches support a security feature known as **port security**, which applies security restrictions to the interfaces of a switch. Therefore, using port security on switches helps prevent unauthorized devices from accessing the network and its resources.

The following are the capabilities of port security when applied to an interface on a switch:

- Filters inbound traffic based on the source **Media Access Control** (**MAC**) address of the sender device

- Various security violation modes are used to either disable the interface automatically or restrict traffic from entering the interface

- Allows a network professional to statically assign a permitted MAC address on an interface

- Allows network professionals to automatically learn about and store trusted MAC addresses within the configurations of the switch

Keep in mind that port security is applied to an interface and that if an attacker is connected to an active interface that's not configured with port security, the attacker will be able to access the network. Furthermore, port security filters inbound traffic based on the source MAC address of a trusted device. A seasoned hacker can easily spoof the MAC address of their device to an address that's trusted by the switch and connect to the network while pretending to be a trusted device.

Auto MDI-X

The **Auto-Medium-Dependent Interface Crossover** (**Auto MDI-X**) feature is simply an auto-sensing mechanism that's built into the firmware or operating systems of switches, which allows the device to detect the type of cable being used to connect the switch to another device. For instance, before Auto MDI-X, network professionals needed to use a crossover cable to interconnect the same type of device together, such as a switch to another switch or a router to another router, while a straight-through cable was used to interconnect different types of devices.

Nowadays, network professionals can use either a straight-through or crossover cable to interconnect two switches without worrying if it's the right type of cable. The Auto MDI-X feature will simply detect the cable type and devices, then make the adjustments within the firmware or operating system to transmit and receive messages on specific pins within the interface on the switch.

Having completed this section, you have learned about various switch port configurations and how network professionals can use these features to help improve how a switch handles incoming traffic. Now, let's summarize this chapter.

Summary

In this chapter, you learned how to identify the characteristics of various dynamic routing protocols and determine how a router makes its forwarding decisions. Additionally, you explored the concepts of using static routing to forward packets on a router. Then, you discovered how network professionals can improve bandwidth management within a network with limited capacity to support all applications.

Furthermore, you explored various switching technologies such as delivering power over Ethernet, Layer 2 loop prevention mechanisms, link aggregation, and neighbor discover protocols. Lastly, you learned about various switch port configurations and how they are applied to help improve the performance of a network.

I hope this chapter has been informative for you and is helpful in your journey toward learning networking and becoming a network professional. In the next chapter, *Chapter 10, Exploring Wireless Standards and Technologies*, you will explore various wireless networking technologies and standards that are commonly implemented within organizations.

Questions

The following is a short list of review questions to help reinforce your learning and help you identify areas that may require some improvement:

1. Which of the following routing protocols has an administrative distance of 110?

   A. BGP

   B. EIGRP

   C. OSPF

   D. RIP

2. Which of the following routing protocols uses hop count as its metric?

   A. OSPF

   B. RIP

   C. EIGRP

   D. BGP

3. Which of the following routing protocols builds an entire topology table within each router before forwarding packets to their destination?

   A. RIP

   B. EIGRP

   C. BGP

   D. OSFP

4. Which of the following routing protocols is used between ISPs?

   A. EIGRP

   B. BGP

   C. IGRP

   D. EGP

5. Which of the following best describes the variation of delay times of incoming packets on a network?

   A. Jitter

   B. Delay

   C. Latency

   D. Ping

6. Which of the following is the newer standard for PoE+ on network switches?

    A. IEEE 802.1D

    B. IEEE 802.1Q

    C. IEEE 802.3at

    D. IEEE 802.3af

7. Which of the following standards is used to prevent Layer 2 loops on a network?

    A. IEEE 802.1D

    B. IEEE 802.1Q

    C. IEEE 802.3at

    D. IEEE 802.3af

8. Which of the following is a discovery protocol?

    A. Auto MDI-X

    B. OSPF

    C. LACP

    D. LLDP

9. Which of the following standards defines how a switch inserts the VLAN ID within a frame?

    A. IEEE 802.1D

    B. IEEE 802.1Q

    C. IEEE 802.3at

    D. IEEE 802.3af

10. Which of the following is used to filter traffic based on the source MAC address of a device?

    A. Auto MDI-X

    B. SPAN

    C. Port security

    D. All of the above

Further reading

To learn more about the topics that were covered in this chapter, check out the following links:

- *What Is Administrative Distance?*: https://www.cisco.com/c/en/us/support/docs/ip/border-gateway-protocol-bgp/15986-admin-distance.html

- *What is Power over Ethernet (PoE)?*: https://www.cisco.com/c/en/us/solutions/enterprise-networks/what-is-power-over-ethernet.html

- *Understand and Configure STP on Catalyst Switches*: https://www.cisco.com/c/en/us/support/docs/lan-switching/spanning-tree-protocol/5234-5.html

- *Configuring VLANs*: https://www.cisco.com/c/en/us/td/docs/switches/datacenter/sw/5_x/nx-os/layer2/configuration/guide/Cisco_Nexus_7000_Series_NX-OS_Layer_2_Switching_Configuration_Guide_Release_5-x_chapter4.html

10

Exploring Wireless Standards and Technologies

Wireless networking has been around for many years, and it's continuously being improved to support new technologies and capabilities for efficiently delivering messages over a non-wired network. It provides the convenience of mobility, allowing employees to use laptops, smartphones, and tablets within the vicinity of their company's wireless network. Moreover, wireless networking allows network professionals to create a metaphorical bridge between wired networks and wireless devices by using access points. It also allows wireless routers to allow these wireless clients to access the resources on a wired network. Therefore, users with a wireless network adapter can roam around the office or building while staying connected to the corporate network.

During the course of this chapter, you will be exploring various wireless communication standards that are commonly used within the industry and how each standard differs from the other. You will gain a solid understanding of various wireless networking concepts, such as discovering various wireless frequencies, how wireless devices communicate, and the types of antennas that are used to transmit messages. Lastly, you will dive into understanding various wireless security standards that are used to provide privacy using data encryption algorithms between clients and access points on a wireless network.

In this chapter, we will cover the following topics:

- Exploring wireless networking
- Delving into wireless security
- Exploring cellular technologies

Let's dive in!

Exploring wireless networking

When designing a wireless network for an organization, it's important to consider the components needed, the number of wireless clients that need access to the wireless network, and the location of these clients within an organization. The components needed are access points or wireless routers based on the size of the organization and the number of users on the wireless network.

For instance, wireless routers are common wireless networking devices that are commonly found within **Small Office Home Office (SOHO)** networks. This type of wireless networking device is simply a router, switch, and access point within a single unified device. A wireless router is suitable for small wireless networks such as those within homes and small office environments.

The following snippet shows the back of a Cisco Linksys 160N wireless router:

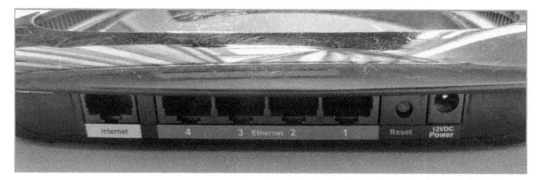

Figure 10.1 – Wireless router

As shown in the preceding snippet, there are five interfaces that allow wired ethernet connections. The **Internet** port, sometimes referred to as the **Wide Area Network (WAN)** port, allows a network professional to establish a wired connection from the internet modem to the wireless router for the purpose of providing internet access to devices that are connected to the wireless router. Without internet access on the wireless router, wireless clients will be able to communicate with each other but won't be able to access any resources on the internet.

The following diagram shows the connection between an internet modem and a wireless router:

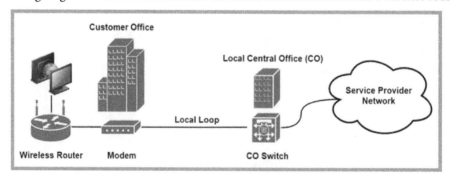

Figure 10.2 – Providing internet to a wireless router

Additionally, the wireless router has one or more ethernet ports that operate like a typical network switch, allowing network professionals to interconnect clients with each other using a wired connection. The built-in switch within the wireless routers functions like a typical network switch that forwards frames between devices on the wired and wireless networks. Therefore, all devices that are connected to the wireless router, whether on the wireless or wired network, will be able to communicate and exchange messages with each other.

Furthermore, the wireless router leverages the built-in access point feature to generate radio frequencies within the 2.4 GHz and/or 5 GHz band to create a wireless network, allowing wireless clients to connect to the device. The router functionality allows devices that are connected to the wired and wireless network types to intercommunicate with each other. Additionally, the router feature allows network professionals to create a **Dynamic Host Configuration Protocol (DHCP)** server within the wireless router to provide IP addresses, subnet mask, default gateway, and **Domain Name System (DNS)** server addresses to all connected clients.

The following diagram shows different networks that exist when using a wireless router:

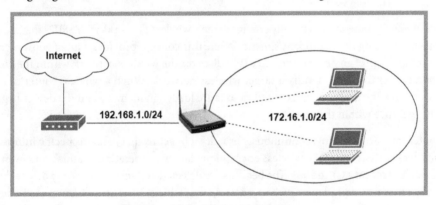

Figure 10.3 – Wireless networking

As shown in the preceding diagram, clients that are connected to the wireless network that's generated by the wireless router use IP addresses on the `172.16.1.0/24` network, whereas the network that exists between the modem and the internet port of the wireless router is in the `192.168.1.0/24` network range. Hence, the router function is used to forward packets between these different IP subnets and to the internet.

In medium-sized to large organizations, access points are commonly implemented to provide wireless coverage to all areas within a building. Access points simply generate a radio frequency that is supported by wireless devices, allowing wireless clients, such as mobile devices, to establish a connection to the access point and access the resources on the wired network. Unlike wireless routers, access points do not have any routing or switching functionality; they are simply used to create a wireless network and forward frames to the wired network and vice versa. This is a thin-client access point, one that has no configuration capability. They are connected to a wireless controller. Fat-client access points, on the other hand, can be individually configured and don't require a controller.

Clients that are connected to access points receive an IP address that is provided to the clients on the wired network. Hence, access points are simply used to allow wireless clients to access resources on the organization's network seamlessly as if they were connected to the wired network.

Up next, you'll learn how a wireless router and access points advertise themselves to nearby wireless clients within the vicinity while wireless clients search for previously associated wireless networks.

Beacons, probes, stations, and SSIDs

The **Service Set Identifier** (**SSID**) is simply the name of the wireless network that allows wireless clients to identify one wireless network from another. Imagine if setting an SSID was not an option on the wireless router or access point, it'll be quite challenging for users to identify their wireless network from another network. Home users and organizations usually change the default SSID that's configured by the vendor of the device to a name that's recognizable. However, as a good security practice, organizations should not set an SSID that can easily identify the organization's network or lure a hacker.

For instance, many IT professionals usually configure their wireless networks with SSIDs that are easily identifiable such as using their company's name. While this concept provides a lot of convenience in allowing the employees of an organization to easily discover the wireless network within the vicinity, it also helps a hacker to easily identify a target wireless network. When a wireless router or access point is powered on, the firmware and configurations are loaded in memory and the device begins to broadcast its presence within the vicinity.

Wireless routers and access points continuously broadcast **beacons** that contain specific information about themselves such as the SSID, wireless encryption standard, operating channel, and even their **Media Access Control** (**MAC**) address. The beacons are detected and inspected by any device that has a supported wireless network adapter such as smartphones, tablets, **Internet of Things** (**IoT**) devices, and laptops, therefore allowing a user to identify wireless networks within the vicinity.

The following diagram shows a wireless router broadcasting beacons:

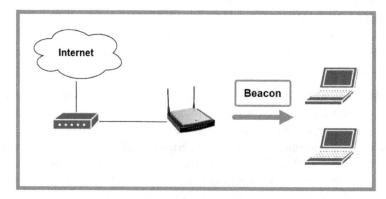

Figure 10.4 – Wireless beacons

As shown in the preceding diagram, as wireless clients move into the range of the wireless signal that's generated by the wireless router or access points, they will be able to capture the beacons and inspect them to determine the wireless network that's close by.

Wireless routers and access points provide the capability of disabling the SSID broadcast as a technique of hiding your wireless network from wireless clients. However, this technique does not add any layer of security as a seasoned hacker or cybersecurity professional can discover a hidden wireless network within a few seconds using very specialized skills, such as performing wireless reconnaissance by capturing beacons and probes. By analyzing the data within the captured beacons and probes, a seasoned hacker will be able to determine the type of clients and wireless routers within the area, hidden wireless networks, type of security configurations applied to the networks, and even the approximate distance between the attacker's machine and the target wireless router and clients.

If an IT professional chose to disable the SSID broadcast feature, the wireless router will not insert the SSID but still include all other information within each beacon that will be broadcasted.

The following snippet shows the basic configuration page of a wireless router:

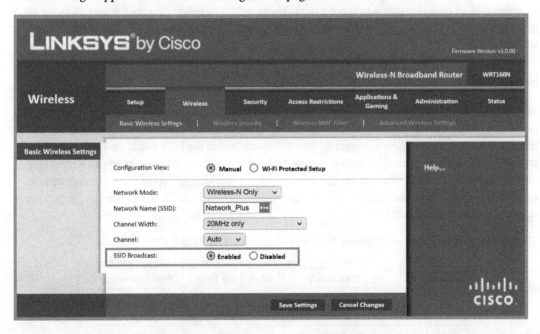

Figure 10.5 – Wireless router basic configuration page

As shown in the preceding snippet, the basic wireless configuration page allows a user to configure the wireless operating standard, SSID, channel width, channel number, and whether to enable or disable the SSID broadcast on the device.

When a wireless client (station) establishes a connection to a wireless router or access point, it's referred to as an **association**. When a client joins a wireless network, the client saves both the SSID and password into a **Preferred Network List (PNL)** that allows the user to easily re-join the same wireless network in the future. This enables the wireless network adapter on a client to begin sending probes for each entry within the PNL on the device. The **probes** allow the client to seek any of the wireless networks via their SSIDs that are stored within the PNL. Once a wireless network is found within the signal range, the client will attempt to create an association with the wireless network.

> **Important note**
>
> Wireless clients, such as laptops, smart TVs, and IoT devices, are examples of stations on a wireless network. The terms *wireless clients* and *stations* are used interchangeably during discussions and literature.

A seasoned hacker or cybersecurity professional can capture the probes to determine the wireless networks that are stored on a client and attempt to perform an *AP-less attack* to retrieve the password/passphrase of an organization's wireless network. However, many newer devices are now allowing IT professionals to prevent the client from automatically connecting to a saved wireless network that's within range.

Frequencies, ranges, and channels

The **Institute of Electrical and Electronics Engineers (IEEE)** is the governing body that created and currently maintains the standards and frameworks for both electrical and electronics specifications that include computers and wireless networking. The 802 committee of the IEEE holds the responsibility of creating and maintaining many common standards that are used by both computing and networking devices, such as Ethernet, Bluetooth, and Wi-Fi. The .11 working group of the 802 committee is specifically responsible for the wireless networking standard such as the IEEE 802.11 wireless networking standard within the industry.

The following tables show the different IEEE 802.11 wireless standards:

Standard	Frequency	Max. Data Rate	Year Introduced
IEEE 802.11	2.4 GHz	2 Mbps	1997
IEEE 802.11b	2.4 GHz	11 Mbps	1999
IEEE 802.11a	5 GHz	54 Mbps	1999
IEEE 802.11g	2.4 GHz	54 Mbps	2003
IEEE 802.11n	2.4 GHz & 5 GHz	300 Mbps	2009
IEEE 802.11ac	5 GHz	1 Gbps	2013
IEEE 802.11ax	2.4 GHz & 5 GHz	9.6 Gbps	2019

Figure 10.6 – Wireless standards

As shown in the preceding table, there are many generations of IEEE 802.11 within the wireless networking industry. The original IEEE 802.11 standard was designed to operate on a 2.4 GHz frequency and supported a maximum data transfer rate of 2 **Megabits per second (Mbps)**, however, this original standard was not implemented on any device. IEEE 802.11b became the first official wireless standard that was implemented on devices that operated on 2.4 GHz and provided a maximum data transfer rate of 11 Mbps.

IEEE 802.11a operates on the 5 GHz frequency and provides a maximum data transfer rate of 54 Mbps. The IEEE 802.11g standard operates at 2.4 GHz and supports maximum transfer rates of 54 Mbps. However, IEEE 802.11n (Wi-Fi 4), also known as Wi-Fi 4, operates on both the 2.4 GHz and 5 GHz frequencies and supports **Multiple In Multiple Out (MIMO)**, which improves the maximum data transfer rate up to 300 Mbps. Later wireless standards, such as IEEE 802.11ac (Wi-Fi 5), operate on the 5 GHz frequency and provide a maximum data transfer rate of 1 **Gigabit per second (Gbps)**.

The latest version of the wireless standard, IEEE 802.11ax (Wi-Fi 6), uses both 2.4 GHz and 5 GHz frequencies and provides a maximum data transfer rate of 9.6 Gbps. Overall, the speed and bandwidth that are supported on wireless networks are aligning with the speeds on wired networks, allowing users to exchange messages very quickly.

The IEEE 802.11 standards use the 2.4 GHz range, which has a total of 14 channels that range from 2.400 GHz to 2.490 GHz, with each individual channel having a width size between 20 MHz to 22 MHz for transporting messages between devices on the wireless network. Since these individual channels are very close to each other, it's recommended to configure the wireless routers and access points with non-overlapping channels, such as channels 1, 6, and 11.

The following diagram shows a representation of the non-overlapping channels:

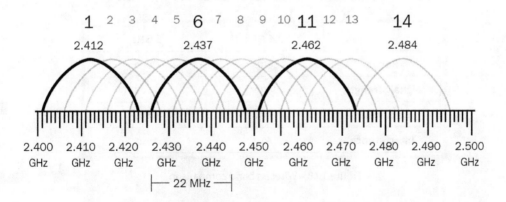

Figure 10.7 – Non-overlapping channels

As shown in the preceding diagram, channels 1, 6, and 11 are the only channels within the 2.4 GHz range that do not overlap with each other. However, channel 14 on the 2.4 GHz is restricted for usage in many countries, hence you will commonly discover wireless networks are using channels 1 to 13.

It's important to ensure your organization's access points aren't using any channels that are overlapping with other access points within the vicinity as it will create interference and affect the performance of the wireless network.

However, the earlier generations of IEEE 802.11 use the 2.4 GHz range and as a result, many organizations and home users who already have an existing wireless network are using the 2.4 GHz range. Therefore, if you were to implement a new wireless router or access point within your network, there's a high possibility that another access point within the same vicinity is using an overlapping channel as your wireless network. This issue is due to the limited number of available channels in the 2.4 GHz range for the IEEE 802.11 wireless network.

> **Tip**
>
> Using a Wi-Fi analyzer tool, such as **inSSIDer** from Metageek or the **Wi-Fi Analyzer** app from Microsoft Store, allows network professionals to view all nearby wireless networks, their operating frequencies and channels, SSIDs, vendors, and much more. Additionally, Wi-Fi analyzers help determine whether your wireless network is using an overlapping channel with another nearby Access Point.

The 5 GHz range supports a lot more channels compared to the 2.4 GHz band that ranges from channels 36 to 165. Unlike the 2.4 GHz band, the 5 GHz band allows devices to use channels 20 MHz, 40 MHz, 80 MHz, and 160 MHz using a technology known as **channel bonding**. Using channel bonding in the 5 GHz band allows wireless devices to transport more data over the wireless network, hence the 5 GHz band supports more bandwidth compared to the 2.4 GHz band.

The following table shows a comparison between the 2.4 GHz and 5 GHz bands:

	2.4 GHz	5 GHz
Range	Better	Good
Signal strength	Better	Good
Bandwidth	Good	Better
Interference	Most	Less

Figure 10.8 – Wireless band comparison

As shown in the preceding table, the 2.4 GHz band provides better signal strength, allowing the radio frequency signal to travel further away from the wireless router or access point, overall providing better range. The 5 GHz band, on the other hand, operates on a higher frequency and does not provide the same signal strength or range. However, the 5 GHz band supports more channels and channel bonding to provide greater bandwidth and less interference compared to the 2.4 GHz band.

SSID

The SSID allows network professionals to create a network name that's 32-bits in length, which helps users easily identify their preferred wireless network. When implementing a wireless network infrastructure within a building, office space, or home, it's important to understand the characteristics of various types of wireless network infrastructure deployment.

The topology of a wireless network can be infrastructure, ad hoc, or mesh modes. In infrastructure mode, a wireless Access Point is used as the network intermediary device to allow wireless clients to connect and share resources. While the ad hoc mode does not use any wireless intermediary devices, a wireless device such as a laptop can directly connect to another laptop to share resources. Lastly, in mesh mode, all wireless devices establish a connection with each other, hence creating a mesh topology.

A **Basic Service Set** (**BSS**) is the most common type of wireless infrastructure that contains a single wireless router or access point, allowing wireless clients within the vicinity to connect to it. The wireless router or access point is simply the intermediary wireless networking device that's used to forward WLAN frames between wireless clients and onto the wired network known as a **Distributed System Service** (**DSS**).

The following diagram shows a typical wireless network that's configured as a BSS:

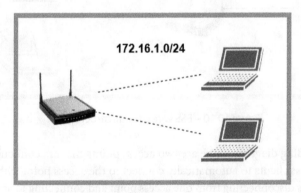

Figure 10.9 – BSS wireless infrastructure

> **Important note**
> Any wireless network that uses a wireless router or access point as the wireless network intermediary device is commonly referred to as **infrastructure mode**.

The **Extended Service Set** (**ESS**) is commonly found within medium-sized to large organizations with multiple access points connected to the same DSS (wired network). This wireless network exists when network professionals implement two or more access points that are connected to the same wired network. Each access point is configured with the same SSID, allowing a user with a laptop to roam between different access points within the office space or building of the organization. Roaming allows a user to automatically connect to another access point with the same SSID when moving out of range from one access point that has a weaker signal and closer to another that is broadcasting a stronger signal with the same SSID.

The following diagram shows a typical ESS wireless infrastructure:

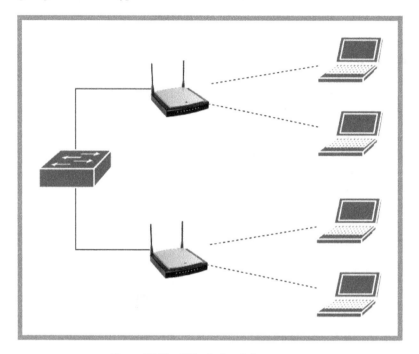

Figure 10.10 – ESS wireless infrastructure

As shown in the preceding diagram, there are two access points that are configured with the same SSID that allows wireless clients to automatically connect to the access point with the better signal. When a wireless client is disconnecting from one access point and connecting to another, the user will experience a temporary drop in wireless network connectivity until the wireless client re-establishes an association with the new access point.

An **Independent Basic Service Set** (**IBSS**) is a wireless network that does not use a wireless router or access point. In an IBSS, each wireless client is connected to every other wireless client within the vicinity, creating a wireless mesh network. This type of wireless network allows clients to share their resources directly with another client and it's commonly referred to as **ad hoc mode**.

The following diagram shows a typical IBSS wireless network:

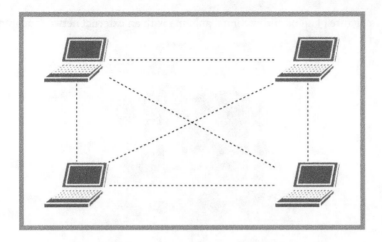

Figure 10.11 – IBSS wireless network

As shown in the preceding diagram, each wireless client, such as a laptop, can be configured to operate as an access point, allowing other wireless clients to connect and share resources with each other without the need for a dedicated wireless router.

Antenna types

When implementing a wireless infrastructure within an organization, the placement of wireless routers and access points is important to ensure there is proper coverage of the wireless signal for all wireless clients within a building or office space. If a wireless client is unable to receive an acceptable quality of signal from a wireless router, the transmission speeds for exchanging data between the wireless router and the wireless client is affected. Hence, it's important for network professionals to perform a **wireless LAN (WLAN)** survey to determine the number of access points needed and the placement of each access point to ensure there's full coverage of the organization.

There are various types of antennas that are installed on wireless routers and access points; each type of antenna determines how the signal is focused in a direction. For example, omnidirectional antennas do not focus the signal in a specific direction but emit the signal all around the antenna in any direction. Dipole antennas are an example of omnidirectional antennas; these are commonly within wireless radio devices and mobile cellular towers to send and receive signals in all directions.

The following is a picture of an omnidirectional antenna with an external network adapter:

Figure 10.12 – Omnidirectional antenna

While omnidirectional antennas work great to provide signal coverage within a home, office space, or building, it's not efficient in focusing a wireless signal in a specific direction. Directional antennas are better at radiating their signal more efficiently in a single direction. The following are examples of common directional antennas:

- Yagi antenna
- Dish antenna
- Parabolic antenna

Some of the wireless signals may radiate the signal to the sides of a focal point of a directional antenna while still focusing most of the signal in a specific direction.

MIMO concepts

Older wireless routers, access points, and wireless network adapters on clients were designed with a single antenna, which allowed the device to send and receive WLAN frames on the same antenna. This concept was referred to as **Single In Single Out (SISO)**.

The following diagram shows an example of SISO communication between an access point and a client:

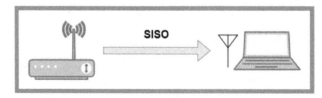

Figure 10.13 – Observing SISO

As shown in the preceding diagram, both the wireless client and wireless router are using the same antenna on their devices to send and receive messages. While this SISO allowed devices to communicate with each other, it was not efficient for sending more traffic on the wireless network.

Wireless device manufacturers began implementing multiple antennas on wireless routers, access points, and clients, allowing multiple antennas to send and receive messages simultaneously with the intention of increasing the throughput of the wireless network. This concept is referred to as **Multiple In Multiple Out (MIMO)**.

The following diagram shows an access point and client using MIMO to exchange messages:

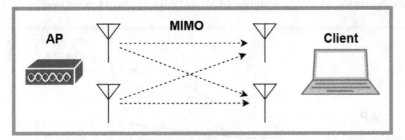

Figure 10.14 – Observing MIMO

On a wireless network with multiple wireless clients connected to the same wireless router, the wireless router can only transmit a stream of messages to one wireless client at a time, then to another client, and so on. Therefore, all wireless clients that are associated with the same wireless router or access point do not receive messages at the same time. This is referred to as **Single User Multiple In Multiple Out (SU-MIMO)**.

The following diagram shows a representation of SU-MIMO on a wireless network:

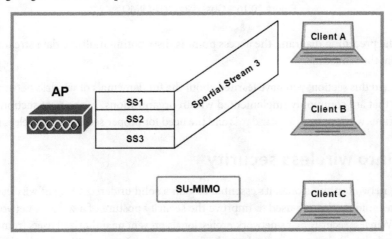

Figure 10.15 – Observing SU-MIMO

As shown in the preceding diagram, the access point has multiple streams for each wireless client but is unable to send the streams to each client at the same. Therefore, the access point will forward the stream for each client one at a time, ensuring messages are delivered to their destinations as quickly as possible.

However, wireless networks that use SU-MIMO have the limitation of forwarding a data stream to one wireless client at a time. The implementation of **Multi-User Multiple Input Multiple Out (MU-MIMO)** allows a wireless router or access point to forward all data streams to all wireless clients at the same time.

The following diagram shows a representation of MU-MIMO on a wireless network:

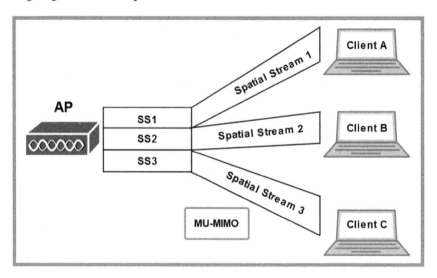

Figure 10.16 – Observing MU-MIMO

As shown in the preceding diagram, the access point is distributing multiple data streams to each wireless client at the same time.

Having completed this section, you have learned about the fundamentals of wireless networking and infrastructure that are commonly implemented within organizations. In the next section, you will learn about various wireless security standards and the need for proper security on wireless networks.

Delving into wireless security

As an aspiring network professional, it's essential to gain a solid understanding of wireless security concepts and techniques that are used to improve the security posture of a wireless network within organizations. Wireless security helps network professionals prevent unauthorized users from accessing the resources and prevent threat actors, such as a hacker, from capturing sensitive data that's exchanged between devices on the wireless network.

As more organizations implement wireless networks to support their mobile workforces, such as those who are using laptops and tablet computers, hackers are always looking for the *low-hanging fruit* such as the weakest points that can be easily compromised within an organization; wireless networks can be compromised as long as the hacker is within the vicinity of the wireless signal emitting from the access point. Hence, network professionals need to implement proper security solutions and best practices to reduce the risk of a potential cyber-attack on their systems and network.

Wireless encryption standards

Wired Equivalent Privacy (WEP) was one of the first generations of wireless security standards that were implemented on IEEE 802.11b wireless networks. The WEP security standard used the **Rivest Cipher 4 (RC4)** encryption algorithm to ensure confidentiality between the access point and wireless clients. However, many unresolved security vulnerabilities were found within the RC4 encryption algorithm that allow threat actors to easily compromise IEEE 802.11 wireless networks that used the WEP wireless security standard.

The following are key points about WEP:

- Uses a weak encryption algorithm
- Uses a small **Initialization Vector (IV)**, which is static and does not change, therefore increasing the likelihood of a threat actor determining the IV value that's exchanged between devices
- Uses 64-bit and 128-bit key sizes during the data encryption process
- Uses the RC4 stream cipher for data encryption
- Provides a 24-bit **Cyclic Redundancy Checksum (CRC)** for integrity checking

The **Wi-Fi Protected Access (WPA)** wireless security standard became the successor and replacement for the WEP security standard for wireless networks. WPA used a 128-bit key to perform data encryption on each WLAN frame by using the RC4 encryption algorithm with **Temporal Key Integrity Protocol (TKIP)**. TKIP ensures each WLAN frame was encrypted with a unique key before transmitting the frame over the wireless network. This technique simply inserted a sequence counter within each WLAN frame that prevented a threat actor, such as a hacker, from performing a replay attack on the wireless network. While WPA is using RC4 with TKIP, there are security vulnerabilities within both algorithms that allow hackers to easily compromise WPA wireless networks. Additionally, WPA provides a 48-bit CRC with a **Message Integrity Check (MIC)** for integrity checking for each WLAN frame that's transmitting over the network.

The following are key points of WPA:

- Uses a weak encryption algorithm
- Uses TKIP to encrypt each WLAN frame with a unique key
- Uses 128-bit keys during the data encryption process

- Uses the RC4 data encryption algorithm
- Provides a 48-bit CRC for data integrity

Wi-Fi Protected Access 2 (WPA2) is the successor and replacement for the WPA wireless security standard. WPA2 uses the **Counter Mode with Cipher Block Chaining Message Authentication Code Protocol (CCMP)** that is implemented within the **Advanced Encryption Standard (AES)** data encryption algorithm. CCMP allows AES to encrypt data within 128-bit blocks with a 128-bit key size. AES with CCMP prevented hackers from decrypting any messages that were exchanged over wireless networks that use WPA2 as the preferred wireless security standard.

Wi-Fi Protected Access 3 (WPA3) is currently the strongest and latest wireless security standard that uses **Simultaneous Authentication of Equals (SAE)** for data encryption. When WPA3 is implemented on personal networks, it uses a 128-bit key for data encryption and a 192-bit key on enterprise networks. Many new wireless routers and access points are supporting WPA3, however, there are many wireless clients supporting up to WPA2 standards. WPA3 supports backward compatibility for wireless clients that support WPA2, however, the wireless router or access point will scale down its wireless security standard from WPA3 to WPA2 to support older wireless clients. As a result, once the wireless router or access point uses WPA2, it inherits all of the security vulnerabilities of the older wireless security standard, such as brute force attacks, to retrieve the password/passphrase for the wireless network.

Authentication methods

After configuring the wireless security standard on a wireless router or access point, it's important to configure the authentication method for the wireless network. The authentication method simply defines how the wireless router or access point is going to validate an authorized wireless client before allowing access to the resources on the wireless network.

The **Pre-Shared Key (PSK)** allows the network professional to configure a password or passphrase on the wireless router or access point and it's shared with authorized users. When using PSK, all authorized users will know and share the same key for the network. However, if the key was shared with someone who is no longer authorized, the user will be able to access the wireless network provided that the network professional has not changed the key on the wireless router or access point.

Enterprise is another authentication method that allows network professionals to implement **IEEE 802.1X** for **Network Access Control (NAC)** using an **Authentication, Authorization, and Accounting (AAA)** server. The AAA server allows network professionals to create a user account for each authorized user for the wireless network on the centralized AAA server. Additionally, the network professional can configure authorization security policies on each user account that defines the user's privilege on the network. Furthermore, a AAA server has the capabilities of creating a log message for each activity performed by an authenticated user on the network for accountability purposes.

The following diagram shows an enterprise network topology including an AAA server:

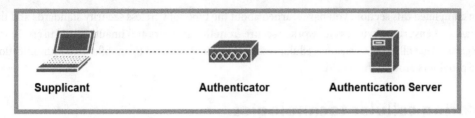

Figure 10.17 – AAA on an enterprise network

As shown in the preceding diagram, the **Supplicant** is simply the wireless client that wants to join the wireless network, the **Authenticator** is the wireless router or Access Point, and the **Authentication Server** is the centralized AAA server on the network. In this wireless infrastructure, each authorized user is assigned unique user credentials on the AAA server, therefore allowing better user management on the entire wireless network.

> **Important note**
>
> The authentication server can use either the **Remote Authentication Dial-In User Service (RADIUS)** or **Terminal Access Controller Access Control System+ (TACACS+)** authentication protocol. RADIUS is an open authentication protocol that is interoperable with different vendor devices while TACACS+ is a Cisco proprietary protocol that works with Cisco devices only.

Open authentication is the default authentication method on many wireless routers and access points. This method does not provide any authentication and allows any wireless device to connect and access resources on the wireless network. Additionally, this method does not provide any data encryption between the wireless client and the wireless router or access point. Many public wireless networks use open authentication that allows anyone in public to access the internet, however, this authentication method is not recommended for organizations as anyone can connect to it.

Wi-Fi Protected Setup (WPS) is an unsecure authentication method that eliminated the need to manually configure a password or passphrase on the wireless network. WPS simply provides an easy method to allow a wireless client authentication to a wireless network without the need for entering any credentials. Wireless routers or access points that are configured with WPS allow the network professional to simply press the physical WPS button of the wireless router and enable the WPS feature on the wireless client when a user needs to join the wireless network. Both devices will exchange a mutual 8-digit key, allowing the client to be authenticated to the wireless network. While WPS seems to be a convenient authentication method, it's highly unsecure as the 8-digit pin that's generated by the wireless router can be easily retrieved by hackers. Hence, it's recommended to disable WPS whenever possible on wireless networks.

A **captive portal** is simply a web-based portal that prompts a user on a wireless client to provide their user credentials when connected to a wireless network. Captive portals are commonly implemented by network professionals within hotels and coffee shops.

Having completed this section, you have learned about the types of wireless security standards and the importance of ensuring a wireless network is secure from threat actors and unauthorized users. In the next section, you will explore various cellular technologies that are used by mobile telecommunication service providers around the world.

Exploring cellular technologies

Cellular technologies have been around for quite some time and telecommunication providers are continuously improving the quality of service provided to their customers. Cellular technologies simply allow us to intercommunicate with each other using a cellular phone by connecting to a mobile telecommunication provider's network. While a mobile telecommunication service provider allows registered devices to connect to their network, the service provider has the ability to both track the geo-location of a connected mobile device and monitor the traffic types on their cellular networks.

2nd Generation (**2G**) is one of the most common generation cellular technologies within many countries around the world as it introduced both voice and text communication between mobile devices. 2G uses the **Global System for Mobile Communications** (**GSM**) technology that allows supported cellular devices to connect to the service provider's network and exchange voice and text messages with other users. Additionally, mobile telecommunication service providers used both **Enhanced Data rates for GSM Evolution** (**EDGE**) and **General Packet Radio Service** (**GPRS**) to provide data services of a 2G cellular network to mobile devices.

On the 2G network, **Time-Division Multiple Access** (**TDMA**) was a very common access method that divides the available bandwidth into different or separate time slots, allowing each device to be allocated a specific amount of bandwidth at a time to exchange messages over the service provider's network. The **Code-Division Multiple Access** (**CDMA**) is another common access method that ensures both the sender and receiver are transmitting messages using a mutually unique code pattern. This technique ensures both the sender and receiver are able to interpret the messages that are being exchanged between those devices over the service provider's network.

The **3rd Generation** (**3G**) is the successor of 2G that provides faster data services using both **High Speed Packet Access** (**HSPA**) and HSPA+. 3G used two technologies that are created from CDMA as the access method: the **Universal Mobile Telecommunications Systems** (**UTMS**) that introduced the **High Speed Packet Access** (**HSPA**) and HSPA+ that supports better data services over the mobile network. Additionally, 3G used **CDMA2000** that introduced the **Evolution Data Optimized** (**EVDO**) technologies for better data rates.

The following are important key points about 3G data rates:

- Uses UMTS with **Wideband Code Division Multiple Access** (**WCMDA**) that supports up to 2 Mbps, HSPA with download speeds of 14.4 Mbps and upload speeds of 5.57 Mbps, and HSPA+ that provides 42 Mbps download speeds and 11.5 Mbps upload speeds.

- Uses CDMA2000 that supports both upload and download speeds of 153 Kbps and uses EVDO that has 14.7 Mbps download speeds and 5.4 Mbps upload speeds.

The **4th Generation** (**4G**) is the successor of 3G that provides very high data rates using two technologies: **Worldwide Interoperability for Microwave Access** (**WiMAX**) that's defined by IEEE 802.16 and **Long-Term Evolution** (**LTE**). These mobile technologies provide an upgrade migration path for systems and devices on both the UMTS and GSM networks.

The following are important key points about 4G data rates:

- WiMax operates at 70 Mbps while WiMax 2.1 operates at 1 Gbps

- LTE supports 300 Mbps, LTE-A support 1 Gbps, and LTE-Pro support 3 Gbps

Currently, the **5th Generation** (**5G**) is the latest cellular technology within the mobile telecommunication industry. 5G still uses some of the existing 4G technologies within the mobile service provider's network but provides huge gigabit speeds with very low latency between devices. However, 5G technologies use MIMO with beamforming to boost/concentrate the signal in a specific direction to ensure a mobile device has coverage to access the cellular network.

Having completed this section, you have learned about various types of cellular technologies such as 2G, 3G, 4G, and 5G.

Summary

Over the course of this chapter, you have learned the fundamentals of various wireless networking technologies, such as wireless infrastructure within organizations and the importance of understanding operating frequencies and channels. Additionally, you have learned about the difference between various wireless network topologies such as BSS, ESS, and IBSS. Furthermore, you have gained a solid understanding of the characteristics of various wireless security standards and the importance of using strong data encryption algorithms to improve the confidentiality of wireless networks. Lastly, you have explored various cellular networking technologies and how they are used within the mobile telecommunication industry.

We hope this chapter has been informative for you and is helpful in your journey towards learning networking and becoming a network professional. In the next chapter, *Chapter 11*, *Assuring Network Availability*, you will learn about the importance of network operations such as monitoring a network to ensure the availability of services and resources.

Questions

The following is a short list of review questions to help reinforce your learning and help you identify areas that require some improvement.

1. Which of the following contains the SSID from an Access Point?

    A. IBSS

    B. Beacon

    C. Probe

    D. ESS

2. Which of the following frequencies provides greater distance for Wi-Fi networks?

    A. 5 GHz

    B. 6 GHz

    C. 2.4 GHz

    D. All of the above

3. Which of the following wireless network topologies allows network professionals to configure two or more Access Points with the same SSID that's connected to the same wired network?

    A. ISS

    B. BSS

    C. DSS

    D. ESS

4. Which of the following wireless security standards uses static, weak initialization vectors?

    A. TKIP

    B. WPS

    C. WEP

    D. WPA

5. Which of the following wireless security standards uses TKIP to improve security?

    A. WPA

    B. WPS

    C. WPA3

    D. WEP

6. Which of the following wireless security standards is not susceptible to a brute-force attack?

    A. WPA

    B. WPS

    C. WPA3

    D. WEP

7. Which of the following authentication methods uses IEEE 802.1X?

    A. Open Authentication

    B. PSK

    C. Enterprise

    D. Captive portal

8. When using AAA on a wireless network, which of the following devices has the role of the authenticator?

    A. Laptop

    B. Access point

    C. RADIUS server

    D. None of the above

9. Which of the following cellular technologies uses EDGE for data services?

    A. 2G

    B. 4G

    C. 5G

    D. 3G

10. Which of the following frequencies on an IEEE 802.11 network has the most interference?

    A. 5 GHz

    B. 6 GHz

    C. 2.4 GHz

    D. All of the above

Further reading

To learn more on the subject, check out the following links:

- *What is a Wi-Fi or wireless network*: https://www.cisco.com/c/en/us/solutions/small-business/resource-center/networking/wireless-network.html

- *What is a Wi-Fi Router*: https://www.linksys.com/us/r/resource-center/wifi-router/

- *What is an Access Point*: https://www.linksys.com/us/r/resource-center/what-is-a-wifi-access-point/

- *Wireless Network Standard*: https://www.technology.pitt.edu/help-desk/how-to-documents/wireless-network-standard

Part 3:
Network Operations

This part describes business continuity and disaster recovery concepts from a networking perspective. It further discusses network monitoring best practices, and organizational policies and documentation.

This part of the book comprises the following chapters:

- *Chapter 11, Assuring Network Availability*
- *Chapter 12, Organizational Documents and Policies*
- *Chapter 13, High Availability and Disaster Recovery*

11
Assuring Network Availability

Network professionals continuously monitor the performance of their network infrastructure to detect any possible or potential issue that may cause an outage or affect the delivery of services to users within an organization. As an aspiring network professional, it's important to understand the various tools and techniques that are commonly used by seasoned professionals within the industry to determine whether a network is performing as expected; you must know how to determine the root cause of the issue.

In this chapter, you will learn about the importance of ensuring the availability of network services and applications within an organization. You will learn about various network performance metrics and how they are used by network professionals to determine whether a network is performing optimally. In addition, you will explore various types of interface issues and how they can be detected and resolved by a network professional.

In this chapter, we will cover the following topics:

- Network performance metrics
- Understanding interface issues
- Environmental factors and sensors

Let's dive in!

Network performance metrics

Performance metrics help network professionals within the industry to determine whether their network is operating as expected or the delivery of network resources is affected. Network professionals use various tools and processes to collect data about the network. This data is then used for analysis and to generate reports that indicate the actual performance of the network. These statistics are recorded and commonly used to compare the current performance with past results; this comparison helps a network professional determine whether the current performance of the network is within the expected operating state or abnormal.

The following are some common performance metrics that are used to determine whether a networking device is operating as expected or whether there's a potential issue:

- Temperature
- **Central processing unit (CPU)** utilization
- Memory utilization
- Bandwidth
- Latency
- Jitter

Networking devices are continuously operating, processing, and forwarding messages to their destinations as quickly as possible over the network. Each day, during peak hours within an organization, all employees are accessing the network and devices are handling a lot of network traffic every second. The more load that's being processed by a networking device, the more computing power that's being utilized to quickly process and forward the messages. This increases the temperature of each device within the organization.

Network professionals commonly implement internal and/or external sensors with devices to closely monitor temperature changes. If the temperature is too hot or above normal, it can be an early warning of excessive utilization or a possible hardware issue on the device. Sometimes, if the operating system of a device detects that the temperature is too hot, it will automatically turn off the device to prevent hardware failure. However, if the temperature is too low, condensation can appear on the electronic components of the device.

Another common performance metric is CPU utilization on networking devices, security appliances, and servers. The CPU is simply the brain of the device that performs computational tasks. When devices such as routers and switches perform a lot of transactions and make forwarding decisions for thousands of messages, CPU usage will gradually increase as more tasks are being performed on the device. As the CPU utilization increases closer to 100%, the device will not be able to handle newer processes or perform additional computation tasks. Hence, if a network professional notices a networking device is not forwarding traffic as quickly as expected, they should check the CPU utilization to determine whether the computing power of the device is being exhausted; this may be a factor that is causing lower performance of the device.

The more memory that's available on a device allows the user to execute and run more applications simultaneously on a host. Networking devices contain built-in memory modules that function as **random access memory (RAM)**, allowing a limited number of applications to utilize the available amount of memory. Whenever messages are received on a networking device, they are stored within a buffer as the operating system processes each message before forwarding them to their destinations. Additionally, the available memory on a networking device affects the performance of how quickly messages are processed and forwarded to their destination. If there isn't enough available memory on a networking device, it's usually an indication of a fatal event that has occurred and requires immediate attention.

The following screenshot shows the CPU and memory utilization of a switch on a network:

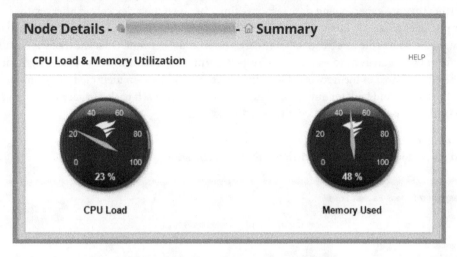

Figure 11.1 – CPU and memory utilization

As shown in the preceding screenshot, this network monitoring tool visualizes the CPU and memory utilization of a network switch within an organization.

The network bandwidth is simply the total amount of packets that can be transferred from a source device to a destination device within a given time. There are many factors involved when determining the network bandwidth, such as the Ethernet standards of networking cables, interfaces on networking devices, and the ports on end devices. Observing the bandwidth utilization and the types of traffic on a network helps network professionals collect and analyze the overall performance of the actual network and discover any problems such as congestion, latency, and physical issues, or even whether a security threat exists.

Various techniques are commonly used to collect and analyze network traffic, such as the following:

- **Simple Network Management Protocol (SNMP)**
- NetFlow
- **IP Flow Information Export (IPFIX)**

Using these methods to collect network traffic, network professionals can perform protocol analysis to determine whether there are any issues on the network, as well as the source of the issue.

Latency is simply the measurement of time between a request and response over a network. If users are reporting they are experiencing slow response times between their device and a server, there can be many possible causes. However, network professionals commonly capture network traffic between the source of the issues (the user's end) and the destination on the network. Once the traffic is captured, they perform packet analysis to examine the response times between various network segments to isolate the affected area of the network. Once the affected area has been identified, they can further examine the latency and look for any indication of changes within each packet, such as faulty packets or packets that are being retransmitted on the network.

The following screenshot shows a chart from a network monitoring tool indicating the average response time and packet loss on a network switch within an organization:

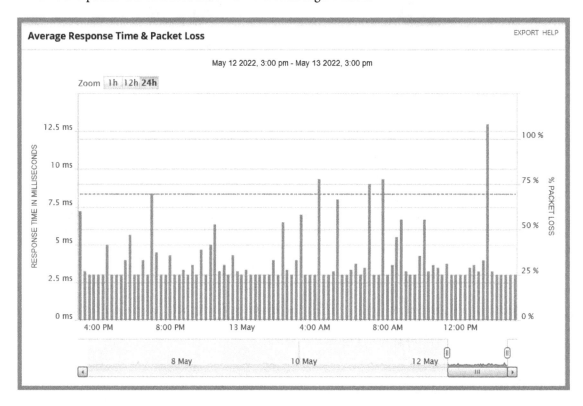

Figure 11.2 – Observing the response time and packet loss

As shown in the preceding screenshot, network monitoring tools help network professionals easily identify whether their devices are experiencing abnormal response times and packet loss. Furthermore, network monitoring tools can collect and archive data, which allows network professionals to reference historical data for any current issues or measure the performance of the network.

Furthermore, jitter is another common performance metric that's closely monitored by network professionals. Jitter measures the variation of delay times of incoming packets on a network. For instance, on an optimal network, all packets that are received from the same sender should have the same latency. However, jitter increases on the network as users are sending and receiving messages and saturating the network. **Voice over IP (VoIP)** and **Video over IP** solutions transport real-time media traffic over the network. Inconsistency between a source and destination can create a bad experience for the end user who is using a VoIP phone or video-conferencing application.

The following screenshot was taken from a network monitoring tool that's reporting the response time and packet loss on a switch:

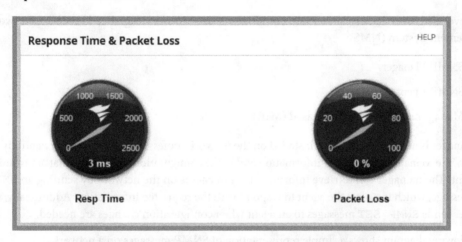

Figure 11.3 – Networking monitoring of latency and packet loss

As shown in the preceding screenshot, network monitoring tools provide easy-to-understand visualizations for network professionals to quickly determine whether the device is overwhelmed or not.

Next, you will learn about the importance of SNMP in monitoring network performance.

SNMP

SNMP is a common network protocol that allows network professionals to easily monitor devices within their organization. Network professionals usually configure their networking devices so that they can communicate with an SNMP Manager application that's either installed on their computer or a centralized server on the network. The SNMP Manager allows the network professional to easily collect statistical data from devices on the network, retrieve device statuses, and push configuration changes to network devices.

There are different versions of SNMP, as follows:

- **SNMPv1**: Does not support any security such as data encryption or authentication, hence it's not recommended for use.

- **SNMPv2**: This version of SNMP is an improvement on how SNMP handles communication between the SNMP Manager and SNMP Agent, but this version does not support data encryption or authentication. Hence, it's not recommended for use.

- **SNMPv3**: This version of SNMP is an improvement on prior versions and supports data encryption, integrity checking, and authentication.

When working with SNMP, three main components need to work together to create a **Network Management System (NMS)**:

- SNMP Manager

- SNMP Agent

- **Management Information Based (MIB)**

The Manager is an application that's installed on the network professional's computer or centrally on a server. The Manager must collect information and make configurations on devices that are running the agent. The manager can retrieve information from agents on the network by sending an SNMP GET message, which instructs the agent to respond with the requested information. Additionally, the manager sends SNMP SET messages to an agent when configuration changes are needed.

The following diagram shows a simple representation of SNMP messages on a network:

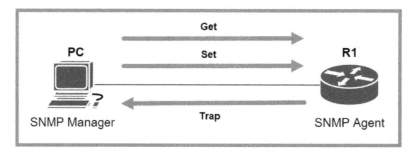

Figure 11.4 – SNMP messages

The Trap data units are sent from the Agent to the Manager as they contain data about changes or events that occurred on the device and only send information when a threshold has been met. Using traps greatly decreases network management bandwidth. The SNMP agent is configured on a networking device such as a switch or router. The SNMP agent is the actual component on the networking device that communicates with the SNMP manager application and vice versa. The MID is a database that contains the information needed by the agent to find and retrieve data from a device. Simply put, network professionals use the manager to retrieve information from a device that's running an SNMP agent. The SNMP agent uses MIB to locate the requested information within the networking device and responds to the agent with the collected data.

Network device logs

Networking devices, security appliances, servers, and end devices commonly generate logs, which are records of every event that has occurred on the device. Network professionals depend on the logs created by a device to determine the reason for an event. For instance, imagine if an organization experienced a network outage for a few minutes during the night. The networking devices will generate log messages for each event that occurred, including the timestamps and a description of the event. Network professionals can observe the logs before, during, and after the event from various devices within the affected area of the network to determine the reason for the outage and probable causes.

Logs are a great way to ensure proper accountability of events and actions on a network. Without network device logs, it's quite challenging to determine the reasons for events that occurred on a network.

The following screenshot shows various logs from networking devices within an organization:

TIME OF EVENT	MESSAGE
5/13/2022 3:27 PM ●	- GigabitEthernet3 · POLYCOM & DATA Down
5/13/2022 3:27 PM ●	- gigabitethernet17 · TO_CISCO_PHONE Up
5/13/2022 3:27 PM ⚠	Node has an average response time of 250 ms which falls above the 200ms threshold.
5/13/2022 3:27 PM ⚠	Node has dropped its average response time from above 200ms to 79 ms which falls below the 100ms threshold.
5/13/2022 3:27 PM ●	- gigabitethernet26 · Phone and Data Uplink Down
5/13/2022 3:27 PM ⚠	Gi2/7 Transmit Power Sensor on is Warning
5/13/2022 3:27 PM ⚠	Gi0/10 Receive Power Sensor on (Point Radix - Caribel) is Warning
5/13/2022 3:27 PM ⚠	Gi0/10 Receive Power Sensor on (Point Radix - Caribel) is Warning
5/13/2022 3:27 PM ⚠	Gi2/7 Transmit Power Sensor on is Warning
5/13/2022 3:27 PM ⚠	Hardware sensor Gi2/7 Transmit Power Sensor of hardware health monitoring on is warning
5/13/2022 3:27 PM ⚠	Node CFB has an average response time of 250 ms which falls above the 200ms threshold.
5/13/2022 3:27 PM ●	- gigabitethernet2 · Link to Cisco IP Phones Up

Figure 11.5 – Device logs

As shown in the preceding screenshot, various log messages contain timestamps, severity levels, and descriptions of the events displayed. As an aspiring network professional, it is important to monitor network changes and device logs closely to determine whether there are any issues or potential problems within your organization.

Traffic logs contain information and details about the traffic that flows between devices on a network. They allow network professionals to see a summary of all the traffic for a given time, contain specific details, and are commonly used for post-event analysis. For instance, network professionals can use network monitoring tools to view the past traffic pattern of a network, allowing you to compare past and present events.

The following screenshot shows a traffic log graph of a network switch over 24 hours:

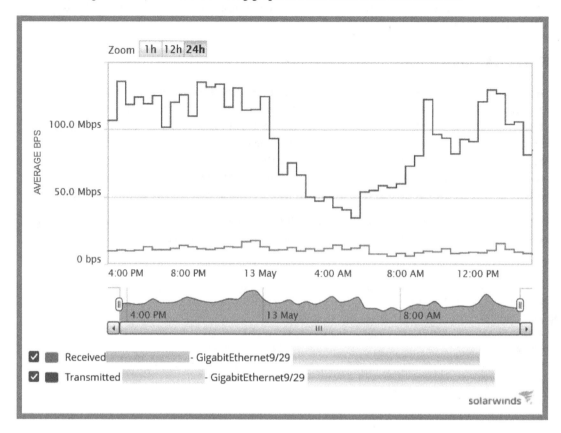

Figure 11.6 – Traffic log graph

As shown in the preceding screenshot, the graph shows the traffic patterns of a network switch over 24 hours, allowing a network professional to determine which time of day the network segment is mostly utilized and the average bandwidth that's being used on a daily, monthly, or annual basis.

Audit logs are common for determining specific information about who, what, and when an event occurred. For instance, audit logs help network professionals determine who and what resources were accessed on the network, the source and destination addresses, the timestamp of the event, and user information.

The following screenshot shows the security audit logs for a Windows 11 operating system:

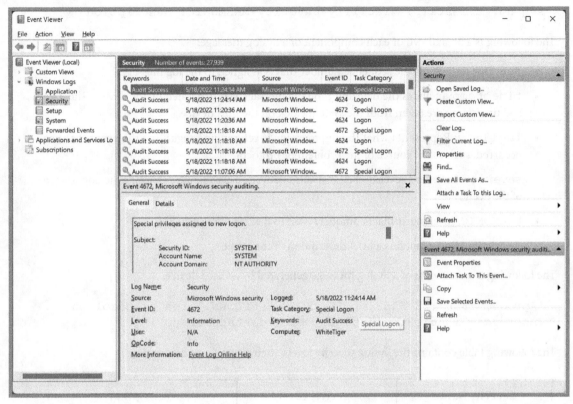

Figure 11.7 – Audit logs

As shown in the preceding screenshot, the audit logs are created on the device for every successful and unsuccessful logon attempt and special access event.

Networking devices, servers, and even end devices generate log messages that contain information and critical details about events that occur. Network professionals use the information found within log messages to identify whether a problem has occurred and what caused the problem. Since each networking device generates a log message, this means a network professional will need to manually log into a device to view the logs for that device only. This process can be very time-consuming and inefficient.

Many networking devices, servers, and end devices support a common network protocol that allows them to forward their log messages over a network to a centralized logging server. This protocol is known as **syslog**. The syslog protocol allows devices to generate logs for events that occur on a device. For instance, if an interface on a router has been disabled or enabled, a syslog message is created that contains all the necessary information about the event.

The following is the default format of a syslog message that is generated by Cisco devices:

```
seq no: timestamp: %facility-severity-MNEMONIC: description
```

The following is a breakdown of each component of a Syslog message:

- `seq no`: Represents the sequence number that is assigned to the log message.
- `timestamp`: Includes the date and time the message was generated by the device. The date and timestamp are taken from the system clock on the host device.
- `facility`: Represents what the log message is referencing regarding the event that has occurred, such as the source of the problem or protocol.
- `severity`: Includes a severity code that helps network professionals determine the importance of the event.
- `MNEMONIC`: Inserts text that is uniquely used to describe the event.
- `description`: Contains a brief description of the event.

The following is an example of a Syslog message generated by a Cisco device:

```
*Apr 28, 15:53:58.5353: %LINEPROTO-5-UPDOWN: Line protocol on
Interface GigabitEthernet0/1, changed state to up
```

The following table contains the Syslog severity levels, their names, and descriptions:

Severity Name	Severity Level	Description
Emergency	0	System is unusable
Alert	1	Immediate action is needed
Critical	2	Critical condition
Error	3	Error condition
Warning	4	Warning condition
Notification	5	Normal but significant condition
Informational	6	Informational message
Debugging	7	Debugging message

Figure 11.8 – Syslog severity levels

The Syslog protocol uses UDP service port number 514 by default over a network. Keep in mind that Syslog is used to gather logging information that helps network professionals with monitoring and troubleshooting issues within an organization. Syslog allows network professionals to configure devices so that they can send their log messages to a specific logging destination, such as a centralized logging server.

The following screenshot shows a collection of Syslog messages on a centralized logging server:

	TIME OF MESSAGE	HOSTNAME	SEVERITY	MESSAGE
☐	5/13/2022 3:24:50 PM	10.160.31.8	Error	135699: Gi0/6: Rx power high alarm, Operating value: -0.8 dBm, Threshold value: -3.0 dBm.
☐	5/13/2022 3:24:49 PM	10.10.2.12	Critical	8773971: * Security violation on port GigabitEthernet9/30 due to MAC address on VLAN 569
☐	5/13/2022 3:24:49 PM	10.10.2.12	Critical	8773970: * Security violation occurred, caused by MAC address on port GigabitEthernet9/30.
☐	5/13/2022 3:24:44 PM	10.10.2.12	Critical	8773968: * Security violation occurred, caused by MAC address on port GigabitEthernet9/30.
☐	5/13/2022 3:24:44 PM	10.10.2.12	Critical	8773969: * Security violation on port GigabitEthernet9/30 due to MAC address on VLAN 569
☐	5/13/2022 3:24:41 PM	10.160.20.243	Error	Junos: rpd[1832]: bgp_recv: peer (External AS received unexpected EOF
☐	5/13/2022 3:24:38 PM	10.10.2.12	Critical	8773967: * Security violation on port GigabitEthernet9/30 due to MAC address on VLAN 569
☐	5/13/2022 3:24:38 PM	10.10.2.12	Critical	8773966: * Security violation occurred, caused by MAC address on port GigabitEthernet9/30.

Figure 11.9 – Log messages

As shown in the preceding screenshot, the centralized logging server collects all the log messages from various devices on the network and performs both de-duplication and correlation, helping network professionals easily determine the sequence of events that occurred on the network.

Having completed this section, you have learned about the importance of monitoring a network and using various metrics to measure network performance. In the next section, you will understand how to identify interface issues on devices.

Understanding interface issues

Network professionals can log into a networking device, such as a switch or router, and check the status of each physical and logical interface on the device. By checking the interface's status, network professionals can quickly determine whether an interface has been misconfigured or is experiencing a physical issue that may result in connectivity issues between the sender and receiver devices on the network. In the following subsections, you will explore various status types that are used to identify a network-related issue on a device.

Checking the link state (up/down)

If the link state is up, it's an indication that the interface of a device is active and can both send and receive messages. The show interfaces command on Cisco IOS switches and routers allows network professionals to determine the status of an interface, as shown here:

```
SW1#show interfaces
FastEthernet0/1 is up, line protocol is up (connected)
  Hardware is Lance, address is 00d0.bc37.3901 (bia 00d0.bc37.3901)
 BW 100000 Kbit, DLY 1000 usec,
     reliability 255/255, txload 1/255, rxload 1/255
  Encapsulation ARPA, loopback not set
  Keepalive set (10 sec)
  Full-duplex, 100Mb/s
  input flow-control is off, output flow-control is off
  ARP type: ARPA, ARP Timeout 04:00:00
  Last input 00:00:08, output 00:00:05, output hang never
```

Figure 11.10 – Verifying the link's status

As shown in the preceding screenshot, FastEthernet0/1 has an up/up status, which indicates the interface can send and receive messages, and a network cable is physically connected. Additionally, the show ip interface brief command allows network professionals to obtain a summary of all interfaces on Cisco IOS switches and routers.

The following screenshot shows the output of the show ip interface brief command on a Cisco router:

```
R1.TT#show ip interface brief
Interface           IP-Address      OK? Method Status                Protocol
GigabitEthernet0/0  unassigned      YES unset  administratively down down
GigabitEthernet0/1  172.16.1.1      YES manual up                    up
GigabitEthernet0/2  192.168.1.1     YES manual up                    up
Vlan1               unassigned      YES unset  administratively down down
R1.TT#
```

Figure 11.11 – Checking all the interfaces on a Cisco router

As shown in the preceding screenshot, a network professional can determine whether an interface is assigned an IP address and the physical and logical status of the interface on the Cisco router. Furthermore, on a Windows operating system, the netsh interface ipv4 show interface and netsh interface ipv6 show interface commands allow you to see the status of all the interfaces on the device.

The following screenshot shows the IPv4 interface statuses on a Windows 11 computer:

```
C:\Users\glens>netsh interface ipv4 show interface

Idx     Met         MTU          State           Name
---  ----------  ----------  -------------  ---------------------------
  1         75  4294967295  connected      Loopback Pseudo-Interface 1
  7         25        1500  disconnected   Local Area Connection
 16         50        1500  connected      Wi-Fi
  8          5       65535  disconnected   OpenVPN Wintun
  3         25        1500  disconnected   Local Area Connection* 1
  9         25        1500  disconnected   Local Area Connection* 2
 14          5        1500  disconnected   Ethernet 2
 10         35        1500  connected      VMware Network Adapter VMnet1
 11         35        1500  connected      VMware Network Adapter VMnet8
```

Figure 11.12 – Checking IPv4 interface statuses

The following screenshot shows the IPv6 interface statuses on a Windows 11 computer:

```
C:\Users\glens>netsh interface ipv6 show interface

Idx     Met         MTU          State           Name
---  ----------  ----------  -------------  ---------------------------
  1         75  4294967295  connected      Loopback Pseudo-Interface 1
  7         25        1500  disconnected   Local Area Connection
 16         50        1472  connected      Wi-Fi
  8          5       65535  disconnected   OpenVPN Wintun
  3         25        1500  disconnected   Local Area Connection* 1
  9         25        1500  disconnected   Local Area Connection* 2
 14          5        1500  disconnected   Ethernet 2
 10         35        1500  connected      VMware Network Adapter VMnet1
 11         35        1500  connected      VMware Network Adapter VMnet8
```

Figure 11.13 – Checking IPv6 interface statuses

On the Linux operating system, the ip link show command allows you to see the statuses of all interfaces on the device, as shown here:

```
kali@kali:~$ ip link show
1: lo: <LOOPBACK,UP,LOWER_UP> mtu 65536 qdisc noqueue state UNKNOWN mode DEFAULT group default qlen 1000
    link/loopback 00:00:00:00:00:00 brd 00:00:00:00:00:00
2: eth0: <BROADCAST,MULTICAST,UP,LOWER_UP> mtu 1500 qdisc pfifo_fast state UP mode DEFAULT group default qlen 1000
    link/ether 08:00:27:0e:34:8d brd ff:ff:ff:ff:ff:ff
3: eth1: <NO-CARRIER,BROADCAST,MULTICAST,UP> mtu 1500 qdisc pfifo_fast state DOWN mode DEFAULT group default qlen 1000
    link/ether 08:00:27:9c:f5:48 brd ff:ff:ff:ff:ff:ff
4: eth2: <NO-CARRIER,BROADCAST,MULTICAST,UP> mtu 1500 qdisc pfifo_fast state DOWN mode DEFAULT group default qlen 1000
    link/ether 08:00:27:2d:52:3c brd ff:ff:ff:ff:ff:ff
5: docker0: <NO-CARRIER,BROADCAST,MULTICAST,UP> mtu 1500 qdisc noqueue state DOWN mode DEFAULT group default
    link/ether 02:42:1c:a5:df:c4 brd ff:ff:ff:ff:ff:ff
```

Figure 11.14 – Checking interface statuses on Linux

The following screenshot shows the output of the ip addr command:

```
kali@kali:~$ ip addr
1: lo: <LOOPBACK,UP,LOWER_UP> mtu 65536 qdisc noqueue state UNKNOWN group default qlen 1000
    link/loopback 00:00:00:00:00:00 brd 00:00:00:00:00:00
    inet 127.0.0.1/8 scope host lo
       valid_lft forever preferred_lft forever
    inet6 ::1/128 scope host
       valid_lft forever preferred_lft forever
2: eth0: <BROADCAST,MULTICAST,UP,LOWER_UP> mtu 1500 qdisc pfifo_fast state UP group default qlen 1000
    link/ether 08:00:27:0e:34:8d brd ff:ff:ff:ff:ff:ff
    inet 172.16.17.15/24 brd 172.16.17.255 scope global dynamic noprefixroute eth0
       valid_lft 86350sec preferred_lft 86350sec
    inet6 2803:1500:            /64 scope global dynamic noprefixroute
       valid_lft 259150sec preferred_lft 172750sec
    inet6 fe80::cc9c           /64 scope link noprefixroute
       valid_lft forever preferred_lft forever
3: eth1: <NO-CARRIER,BROADCAST,MULTICAST,UP> mtu 1500 qdisc pfifo_fast state DOWN group default qlen 1000
    link/ether 08:00:27:9c:f5:48 brd ff:ff:ff:ff:ff:ff
4: eth2: <NO-CARRIER,BROADCAST,MULTICAST,UP> mtu 1500 qdisc pfifo_fast state DOWN group default qlen 1000
    link/ether 08:00:27:2d:52:3c brd ff:ff:ff:ff:ff:ff
5: docker0: <NO-CARRIER,BROADCAST,MULTICAST,UP> mtu 1500 qdisc noqueue state DOWN group default
    link/ether 02:42:1c:a5:df:c4 brd ff:ff:ff:ff:ff:ff
    inet 172.17.0.1/16 brd 172.17.255.255 scope global docker0
       valid_lft forever preferred_lft forever
```

Figure 11.15 – Checking IP addresses

As shown in the preceding screenshot, a network professional can determine the status of all the interfaces on systems running Linux-based operating systems.

Checking the speed

The speed of an interface indicates how quickly a device can send and receive messages on that same interface. There are various types of interfaces on a networking device, such as Ethernet, which operates up to 10 Mbps, FastEthernet, which operates up to 100 Mbps, and GigabitEthernet, which operates up to 1,000 Mbps. It's important to ensure the speed configurations match on devices that are connected.

The following screenshot shows the current operating speed on the interface of a Cisco switch:

```
SW1#show interfaces fastEthernet 0/1
FastEthernet0/1 is up, line protocol is up (connected)
  Hardware is Lance, address is 00d0.bc37.3901 (bia 00d0.bc37.3901)
 BW 100000 Kbit, DLY 1000 usec,
     reliability 255/255, txload 1/255, rxload 1/255
  Encapsulation ARPA, loopback not set
  Keepalive set (10 sec)
  Full-duplex, 100Mb/s                    Speed
  input flow-control is off, output flow-control is off
  ARP type: ARPA, ARP Timeout 04:00:00
```

Figure 11.16 – Verifying the speed of an interface

However, on a Windows operating system, to verify the speed of the local interfaces, you must open **Device Manager**, right-click on the interface, and select **Properties | Advanced tab**, as shown here:

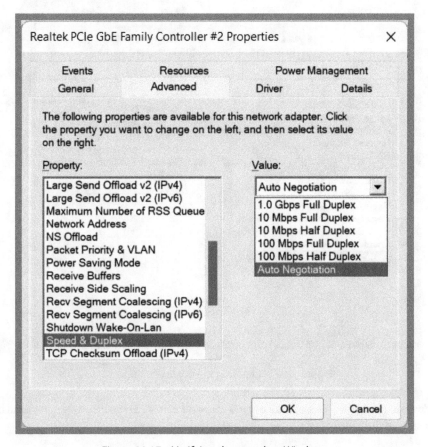

Figure 11.17 – Verifying the speed on Windows

As shown in the preceding screenshot, a network professional can manually configure the speed and duplex settings on the interface of the device.

Checking the duplex

Duplex is referred to as the common method where two devices are about to exchange messages. The duplex of an interface is usually set as **Auto** by default, but a network professional can manually configure the interface to operate in full or half duplex. To configure the duplex mode on a Windows operating system, open **Device Manager**, right-click on the interface, and select **Properties** | **Advanced tab**, as shown here:

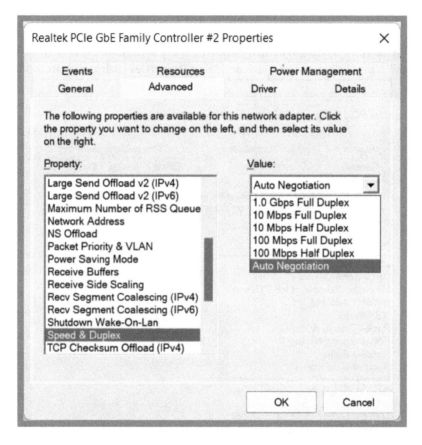

Figure 11.18 – Checking the duplex settings

On Cisco devices, the show interface status and show interfaces commands verify the current state of the speed on the interface, as shown here:

```
SW1#show interfaces fastEthernet 0/1
FastEthernet0/1 is up, line protocol is up (connected)
  Hardware is Lance, address is 00d0.bc37.3901 (bia 00d0.bc37.3901)
 BW 100000 Kbit, DLY 1000 usec,
     reliability 255/255, txload 1/255, rxload 1/255
  Encapsulation ARPA, loopback not set
  Keepalive set (10 sec)
  Full-duplex, 100Mb/s  ←──────  [ Duplex ]
  input flow-control is off, output flow-control is off
  ARP type: ARPA, ARP Timeout 04:00:00
```

Figure 11.19 – Verifying the duplex status on a Cisco switch

As shown in the preceding screenshot, network professionals can easily verify the current duplex status of an interface on Cisco switches on a network.

Checking the uptime/downtime

Checking the device's uptime can help networking professionals determine whether the device loses power at a certain time. If a device loses power unexpectedly, this should raise concerns for the network professionals.

On Cisco devices, the show version command provides the device's uptime, as shown here:

```
SW1#show version
Cisco IOS Software, C2960 Software (C2960-LANBASEK9-M), Version 15.0(2)SE4, RELEASE SOFTWARE
Technical Support: http://www.cisco.com/techsupport
Copyright (c) 1986-2013 by Cisco Systems, Inc.
Compiled Wed 26-Jun-13 02:49 by mnguyen

ROM: Bootstrap program is C2960 boot loader
BOOTLDR: C2960 Boot Loader (C2960-HBOOT-M) Version 12.2(25r)FX, RELEASE SOFTWARE (fc4)

Switch uptime is 39 minutes
System returned to ROM by power-on
System image file is "flash:c2960-lanbasek9-mz.150-2.SE4.bin"
```

Figure 11.20 – Checking the uptime

As shown in the preceding screenshot, the uptime reveals that the network switch has been running/powered on for the past 39 minutes. If a power outage occurs or the device loses power, the uptime will be reset. Therefore, network professionals can use the uptime on a networking device to determine whether a network outage was due to power loss within their organization.

Interface errors or alerts

What if network professionals configure the networking devices with the proper configurations but still experience packet loss and high latency? What could be the cause of this? Faulty network cables and interfaces are the most common causes of physical issues on a network. However, before changing the network cable or reassigning an interface, it's important to understand the types of errors and alerts that are created by a networking device.

The following screenshot shows the interface statistics of a Cisco switch:

```
Switch#show interfaces fastEthernet 0/1
FastEthernet0/1 is up, line protocol is up (connected)
  Hardware is Lance, address is 00d0.97c1.5801 (bia 00d0.97c1.5801)
 BW 100000 Kbit, DLY 1000 usec,
     reliability 255/255, txload 1/255, rxload 1/255
 Encapsulation ARPA, loopback not set
 Keepalive set (10 sec)
 Full-duplex, 100Mb/s
 5 minute input rate 0 bits/sec, 0 packets/sec
 5 minute output rate 0 bits/sec, 0 packets/sec
    956 packets input, 193351 bytes, 0 no buffer
    Received 956 broadcasts, 0 runts, 0 giants, 0 throttles
    0 input errors, 0 CRC, 0 frame, 0 overrun, 0 ignored, 0 abort
    0 watchdog, 0 multicast, 0 pause input
    0 input packets with dribble condition detected
    2357 packets output, 263570 bytes, 0 underruns
    0 output errors, 0 collisions, 10 interface resets
    0 babbles, 0 late collision, 0 deferred
    0 lost carrier, 0 no carrier
    0 output buffer failures, 0 output buffers swapped out
```

Figure 11.21 – Interface statistics

As shown in the preceding screenshot, there's a lot of statistical information within the lower section of the output, such as the number of packets that have entered the interface and the number of broadcast messages, along with a lot of details that are important to network professionals.

The following list describes each interface error type:

- **Input errors**: The input errors field indicates the total number of errors that were identified on the interface. These errors include the sum of the frame, giants, no buffer, runts, **Cyclic Redundancy Check (CRC)**, overrun, and any ignored counts.

- **Runts**: Runts are simply any packets that are discarded by the device because they are less than 64 bytes in size. These are sometimes caused due to a network collision between two devices.

- **Giants**: Giants are any packets that are discarded because they are greater than 1,518 bytes in size. Giants are usually caused by communication issues on the network.

- **CRC**: CRC errors are created when the checksum value within the trailer of a frame does not match the checksum generated by the receiver. If a mismatch in the checksum occurs, the integrity of the message is compromised. Additionally, CRC errors are caused due to a faulty network cable or interface.

- **Output errors**: Output errors are simply the total amount of all errors that prevent the transmission of any datagram from leaving the interface of the device.

- **Collisions**: Collisions are the total number of messages that were retransmitted because an Ethernet collision had occurred.

- **Late collisions**: Late collisions are any collisions that were detected after the first 512 bytes of the frame were transmitted.

Additionally, there are **encapsulation errors**, which are caused due to inconsistent configurations between switches such as a trunking encapsulation protocol such as **IEEE 802.1Q** and **Inter-Switch Link (ISL)**. ISL is a legacy Cisco proprietary trunking encapsulation protocol that allows Cisco switches to create a logical trunk link between themselves. However, ISL is not commonly implemented in Cisco environments, and IEEE 802.1Q is currently being used as the preferred encapsulation protocol for trunk links between switches.

Hence, it's important to ensure that if two switches are interconnected, the encapsulation protocol is the same between both devices.

Having completed this section, you have learned about various types of interface errors, their possible causes, and how to resolve them. In the next section, you will discover how environmental factors can affect the performance of network devices.

Environmental factors and sensors

Environmental factors can affect the performance of network devices and servers within an organization. Network professionals commonly configure and implement both software- and hardware-based sensors to detect temperature, humidity, and electrical power change on devices. If the temperature of a device is too hot, the operating system will automatically shut down to prevent physical damage to the hardware components of the device. Hence, networking devices and security appliances need proper cooling to ensure they continue to operate as expected.

Additionally, the humidity of the server room or network closet needs to be closely monitored. If the humidity is too low, static discharges can occur, which can damage hardware components. However, if the humidity is too high, there will be a lot of water vapor in the air. This creates condensation, which is bad for electrical and electronic components. Overall, a **heating, ventilation, and air conditioning (HVAC)** system is usually implemented to maintain and control the airflow and temperature within data centers, server rooms, and network closets to ensure devices are properly cooled.

The following are additional sensors that are commonly implemented:

- **Electrical sensors**: Monitors a device's circuit load (power).

- **Flood monitor**: Monitors whether there's water in the room.

- **NetFlow data**: This is a standard for collecting network statistics to determine the performance of the network. NetFlow uses a probe and a collector, where the probe watches network communication and the summary is sent to the collector.

Having completed this section, you have learned about the importance of monitoring environmental factors within a network to ensure its optimal performance within an organization.

Summary

In this chapter, you learned about the importance of ensuring the maximum availability of a network, its resources, and the services it provides to organizations. You also discovered various monitoring solutions and techniques that network professionals use to identify the performance and issues of network devices. Furthermore, you have explored various types of interface issues, their causes, and solutions.

I hope this chapter has been informative for you and is helpful in your journey toward learning about networking and becoming a network professional. In the next chapter, *Chapter 12, Organizational Documents and Policies,* you will learn about various organization plans and procedures that are needed during a disaster, as well as security hardening techniques.

Questions

The following is a short list of review questions to help reinforce your learning and help you identify areas that may require some improvement:

1. Which of the following is a common network performance metric?

   A. Memory

   B. Latency

   C. Bandwidth

   D. All of the above

2. Which of the following protocols would be preferred for time-sensitive traffic?

   A. HTTPS

   B. VoIP

   C. UDP

   D. SMTP

3. Which of the following network protocols can be used to monitor network devices?

    A. DHCP

    B. TFTP

    C. SMTP

    D. SNMP

4. Which of the following types contains information when a user logs into a device?

    A. Audit log

    B. Traffic log

    C. Device log

    D. All of the above

5. Which of the following helps network professionals determine how long a device has been powered on?

    A. Link state

    B. Uptime

    C. Duplex

    D. Interface status

6. Which of the following interface errors is best described as a packet that is less than 64 bytes?

    A. ISL

    B. CRC

    C. Runts

    D. FCS

7. Which of the following is a proprietary trunking encapsulation protocol?

    A. ISL

    B. DSL

    C. 802.1Q

    D. PPP

8. Which of the following systems can be used to control the temperature and humidity within a data center?

    A. UPS

    B. HVAC

    C. Generator

    D. All of the above

9. Which of the following can be used to collect network statistics?

    A. ISL

    B. DNS

    C. NetFlow

    D. Syslog

10. Which of the following severity names is assigned a severity level of 2 in Syslog?

    A. Warning

    B. Alert

    C. Critical

    D. Emergency

Further reading

To learn more about what was covered in this chapter, check out `https://www.dnsstuff.com/free-network-monitoring-software`, which specifies the top free network monitoring tools.

12

Organizational Documents and Policies

As an aspiring network professional, it's essential to understand the business processes and operations of an organization, as it will help you to align the IT objectives with the business goals better. Sometimes, non-technical procedures require the resources of the technical staff to complete, such as implementing a change within the IT services and resources to enhance the productivity of employees. Additionally, there are many non-technical plans and procedures that all technical staff need to know, such as security policies, recovery from disasters and incidents, and how to create and maintain proper documentation for systems and networks within the organization.

During this chapter, you will understand the importance of various types of plans and procedures that are commonly implemented and enforced within many organizations to ensure there are fewer risks to the business processes, and how to recover from a cyber-attack. Furthermore, you will explore various security policies that are used by security professionals to improve the security posture of systems and networks, and common types of documentation that must be maintained within any organization by IT professionals.

In this chapter, we will cover the following topics:

- Plans and procedures
- Hardening and security policies
- Common documentation
- Common agreements

Let's dive in!

Plans and procedures

Each organization usually has its own plans and procedures, which are commonly well-documented to ensure each employee has access to the most up-to-date form of documentation whenever needed. Plans and procedures are created to ensure each employee follows a standard set of rules or guidelines that are used to achieve a common goal or meet an objective. If each employee used their own unique method of completing the same task, only some of the employees would be able to achieve the objective, while others may not. Additionally, there may be employees who can complete the same task faster than others, while some may take quite some time.

Therefore, creating a standard set of plans and procedures that are shared with employees helps ensure each person can follow the same set of guidelines to complete a task and achieve the same goals. These plans and procedures are usually tested to ensure the most efficient method to achieve a specific goal. However, it's important to understand that as an organization grows and the IT team implements new technologies within the company to support the demand of users, plans and procedures need to be updated to ensure employees are aware of the most efficient methods of meeting an objective.

During this section, you will be exposed to common plans and procedures such as change management, incident response, disaster recovery, business continuity, and the need for standard operating procedures.

Change management

Change management simply focuses on ensuring that a change is beneficial to the organization and that it's applied as efficiently and effectively as possible while ensuring users are affected as little as possible during and after the change being made. Before a technical or non-technical change is implemented within an organization, the change has to go through an entire life cycle to ensure all the procedures are thoroughly followed by the people who are implementing the change – such that, the change has to be approved by the *Change Management Board*. They read carefully and determine whether the procedures are efficient, that those who are going to perform the change have the right set of skills and qualifications, that the impact of the change is minimal, and there's a contingency plan to roll back the change if the implementation does not go as planned and standby staff to assist if the primary staff are unable to continue or roll back the change.

To put it simply, changes have to be carefully evaluated to determine what is being changed and how it is going to affect the users within the organization. For instance, imagine the IT staff members upgraded the version of the Microsoft Office suite of applications that are installed on everyone's computer over one weekend within a company. Tech-savvy users will be able to adapt to the new user interface quickly and continue working – however, users who are not tech-savvy may find difficulties in adapting to the newer user interface and performing tasks using the various applications without prior training. For the users who are affected, productivity decreases and some tasks will take longer to complete until everyone can adapt to the change.

What if the IT staff members created training videos and various step-by-step documentation that was user-friendly and distributed them to employees before making the change? This would help all the employees to gain a better experience in transitioning from the older user interface to the new interface while helping the users to understand what has changed. Additionally, the IT staff can roll out the change in phases, such as one organizational department at a time, to monitor and gather the user experience, which could be used to help improve how to implement the change in the future within additional organizational departments.

The following are the typical phases of change management:

1. **Request** – Requesting to implement a change in the organization
2. **Evaluate** – Determining whether the change is needed to improve the business process
3. **Authorize** – Gaining authorization from the change advisory board before making the change
4. **Implement** – Performing the change within the organization (on the part of the change owner, the person who is performing the change)
5. **Documentation** – Documenting everything about the change for future reference

During a change, things may not always go quite as planned. Having a *rollback* or *remediation* plan helps IT professionals to reverse the change in the case of some unforeseen problem with the change. For instance, imagine you're performing a change to upgrade the operating system on a core switch within your network. During the upgrade process, something didn't go quite as planned – the switch seems to be frozen and no longer responds to any commands you're sending to the switch. If a rollback or remediation plan was not created before starting the change, you will spend a lot of time troubleshooting and restoring the switch to a working state.

As an aspiring IT professional, it is important to always remember that not everyone sees what you see, and therefore cannot adapt as quickly to change. The change has to be evaluated to determine what is being changed and how it is going to affect the users within the organization. Change management helps reduce the downtime of the network and resources while reducing the risks within an organization. Additionally, the change that's going to be made must be beneficial to the organization while ensuring the change does not create additional issues for the company and its resources.

Incident response plans

The field of cybersecurity is quite an amazing and in-demand industry around the world. Each day, we discover new security vulnerabilities within systems, and cybersecurity professionals are working continuously to implement security controls and countermeasures to mitigate the risks of being compromised by a threat actor such as a hacker. While there are a vast number of job roles within the cybersecurity industry, incident responders are in high demand. Incident response professionals are responsible for containing a threat and recovering from a cyber-attack that affects an organization. Overall, the incident response team are the cybersecurity professionals who help an organization prevent and recover from a real-world cyber-attack.

However, all organizations need an incident response plan, which is a set of procedures and tools that are commonly used by the cybersecurity team to efficiently identify, contain, and recover from cyber-attacks and threats. The incident response plan is designed to help organizations quickly adapt to the ever-changing security landscape of new emerging threats and quickly respond using a uniform, systematic approach to any threat of a cyber-attack.

It's important to document and keep track of all the incidents that occur within an organization. Keeping proper documentation can help a professional to determine whether a similar incident has occurred in the past and if so, what actions were taken. When documenting an incident, it's important to include as many details as possible in the description, record the time and date, location, persons involved, actions taken to resolve the issue, and lessons learned. Keeping track of incidents can help security professionals to look for any patterns of similar incidents in past records.

When an incident occurs, the right people must be involved to help resolve the issues. The organization may have a dedicated incident response team that is trained in resolving security incidents. The IT security management team or IT technical staff may also be involved in remediating the security incident. If a person within the technical team is unable to resolve the issue, the incident should be escalated to someone senior with more expertise in security.

Some companies will have a **Cyber-Incident Response Team** (**CIRT**), which is responsible for monitoring and resolving all security incidents within the organization. The CIRT is made up of professionals who are trained and qualified in various security incident response techniques. Most importantly, the CIRT is focused on incident response, analysis, and reporting.

Designing an incident response plan is all well and good but the plan needs to be tested regularly. The plan should be tested a few times per year. The testing of the plan should be scheduled. The plan should be tested before an actual security incident occurs. It's important to document the outcome after testing the plan. Look for any areas that need improvement and test again. Continuous testing helps cybersecurity professionals be better prepared in the event of a real cyber-attack or threat – frequent testing also helps improve the incident response plan to be more effective at handling incidents within the organization.

According to the *NIST SP 800-61 Rev. 2* documentation in the *Computer Security Incident Handling Guide*, the following are the phases of incident handling:

1. Preparation
2. Detection and analysis
3. Containment, eradication, and recovery
4. Post-incident activity and analysis

The following diagram shows the NIST incident response and handling model:

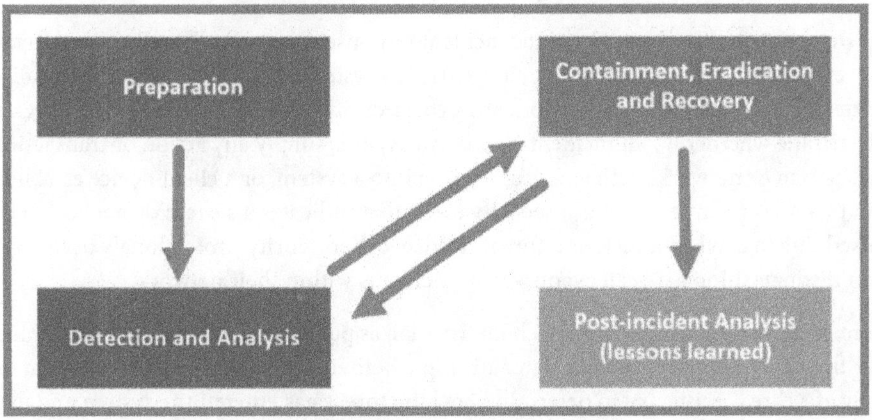

Figure 12.1 – The incident handling process

Over the next few subsections, you will gain better insights into the roles and responsibilities of each phase within the incident response phases.

> **Important note**
>
> The *NIST SP 800-61 Rev. 2* documentation in the *Computer Security Incident Handling Guide* can be found at `https://csrc.nist.gov/publications/detail/sp/800-61/rev-2/final`.

Preparation

The **preparation** phase focuses on gathering a list of all the assets within the organization. An asset is simply anything that has value to the company; assets can be tangible, intangible, or people. Tangible assets are any physical objects that are valuable such as networking devices and servers. Intangible assets are digital objects that do not have a physical form such as data, license keys for applications, organization policies and procedures, business processes, and intellectual property.

During the preparation phase, network and security professionals must create a baseline of their network and system's performance when everything is working under normal conditions. These baselines help cybersecurity and networking professionals to determine what is considered to be a *normal* traffic flow between the assets within the network. Furthermore, it is important to develop a communication plan that outlines who should be contacted if a security incident should occur within the organization and a plan of action for each possible security incident that can occur.

Detection and analysis

During the **detection and analysis** phase, the incident response team must be well-trained to identify a security event efficiently and quickly when it occurs on a system or the network of the organization. Events are generated all the time on a network and cybersecurity professionals need to investigate each event to determine whether it's an incident or not. An event is simply any action or transaction that occurs on a system or network, such as a user logging into a system, or a client device establishing a connection to a server. An incident is a security event that indicates a system or network has been compromised due to a cyber-attack or a threat. Hence, cybersecurity professionals need to keep a close eye on distinguishing between events versus incidents within their network.

Furthermore, it's important to collect as much information as possible on the security event or incident to improve the analysis phase, such as determining whether a threat exists in the system or not. Additionally, if a threat exists, try to determine how the threat has entered the system and network of the organization. Using security appliances to actively monitor systems and networks improves threat identification as they occur in real time.

Containment, eradication, and recovery

When a security incident occurs within an organization, the incident (or threat) must be contained as quickly as possible to prevent it from spreading and causing damage to other systems on the network. The goal of the **containment** phase is to simply stop a threat such as malware spreading to other systems on the network or a hacker from compromising additional machines.

Once the threat is contained, the eradication phase is initialized to remove the threat from any compromised or infected systems on the network. The **eradication** phase ensures systems are thoroughly disinfected to ensure there are no longer any infections present on any system within the organization. However, during the eradication phase, the incident response team will need to revisit the *detection and analysis* phase to verify that there are absolutely no more traces of the threat on any of the systems within the organization.

Once all traces of the threat are eliminated, then the **recovery** process begins, which focuses on restoring systems to an acceptable working state in terms of their operating systems, applications, and data. The recovery phase also includes performing data recovery from backups, replacing compromised systems, and re-installing the host operating systems and applications.

Post-incident analysis

After an incident is resolved, it's important to use the opportunity to learn from the experience of the cyber-attack or threat. The lessons learned will help improve the incident response plan and its effectiveness, and the efficiency and preparedness of the incident response team for future security events and incidents.

The business continuity plan

The **Business Continuity Plan** (**BCP**) is a set of guidelines that is used to help restore the organization's services and business functions whenever a disaster has occurred. A **Business Impact Analysis** (**BIA**) is used to help professionals to identify the most critical business processes, procedures, and resources that are needed to ensure the organization can continue to operate and function. The BIA contains a systematic method that also helps professionals to determine the potential effects of disruption on critical business processes and operations within a company. Additionally, it's essential to determine the availability that is needed by those business processes and resources that may be affected.

Many organizations use various metrics to measure the availability of their systems, such as assigning a percentage value to their uptime and downtime on an annual basis. For instance, many cloud service providers advertise their availability in terms of 99.999% annually. More 9s appended to the end of the percentage value simply indicates that more uptime is guaranteed by the service provider.

When developing a business continuity plan, it's important to consider the following factors:

- **Exercises (tabletop)** – When planning for business continuity, it's important to perform regular exercises to ensure everyone is prepared. These exercises can cost a lot of money and be very time-consuming. However, a *tabletop exercise* allows an organization to reduce costs and time by simply discussing a simulated disaster. In a tabletop exercise, people do not physically participate but rather discuss what happens at the reached stage of the plan.

- **After-action reports** – After completing a disaster recovery exercise, an after-action report is required. This report may contain the details of each step of the methodology and any explanations of the procedures. Make sure that you cover the details of everything that worked smoothly and anything that did not work as expected.

- **Failover** – Having a failover site is important; if a disaster occurs, you already have an alternative site and plans in place for migrating your systems. Ensure all data is fully replicated or synchronized between the organization and the failover site.

- **Alternative business practices** – During a disaster, things may not always go as planned. It's important to alternate between different methods of achieving the same task. This technique is useful in the case that the network or devices such as printers are not available to print a receipt for a customer. It's important to ensure proper documentation is kept for all the primary and alternative business processes before a disaster occurs.

Having explored the importance of business continuity planning, next, you will explore disaster recovery planning and how it plays a vital role within organizations.

Disaster recovery plans

Disaster recovery planning focuses on ensuring an organization is well prepared and equipped to recover from any possible disaster that may be a risk to the company, its resources, and assets. It's essential to create a dedicated team of professionals for performing and handling disaster recovery for the organization – additionally, proper documentation of the company's infrastructure should always be up-to-date to help professionals during times of need. When developing a disaster recovery plan, the organization should perform continuous training and testing of the plan to ensure everyone understands their roles and responsibilities during an actual disaster.

> **Important note**
>
> The *NIST SP 800-34 Rev. 1* documentation in the *Contingency Planning Guide for Federal Information Systems* can be found at `https://csrc.nist.gov/publications/detail/sp/800-34/rev-1/final`.

The following are key terms in disaster recovery planning:

- **Recovery Time Objective (RTO)** – The RTO is simply the maximum amount of time that a system or resource can be unavailable before there is an unacceptable impact on other systems' resources, business processes, and critical functions of an organization

- **Recovery Point Objective (RPO)** – The RPO is simply the point in time before the disruption or outage of a system to which the business processes or data can be recovered or restored after the outage has occurred

Additionally, when creating a disaster recovery plan, it's essential that you clearly identify both the internal and external teams that are responsible for assisting the organization in restoring services and critical business functions to an acceptable level, enabling the organization to resume its operations. Furthermore, having proper documentation of key assets of the organization helps disaster recovery professionals to reduce the time to restore business operations. Hence, professionals should ensure that network configurations, both hardware and software details, and vendors are properly documented, and all documentation should be up-to-date at all times.

Furthermore, it's important to identify the recovery and failover sites and the redundancy hardware components that will be needed in the event of a disaster. If this information is unknown before a disaster, the time to restore an organization's business operations will be lengthy due to inefficiency and the unavailability of important information. Keep in mind that the disaster recovery plan is designed to be proactive, allowing professionals to be prepared to handle and respond to various types of disasters that may affect the organization.

Lastly, continuous training and testing of the disaster recovery plans ensure each person understands their role and responsibilities during a real disaster. Additionally, continuous testing allows professionals to identify gaps or procedures that need to be updated and improved. Furthermore, IT professionals test their failover processes often to ensure the process is working as expected. Any issues discovered during the testing phase are documented and updated to improve the plan.

The system life cycle

The **system life cycle** is used to define the life span of a system or technology that is supported by a vendor before the device or product becomes obsolete. If an organization continues to use end-of-life systems on its networks, it increases the security risks to the organization. End of life simply means that the vendor of the product is no longer providing any support, updates, and patches to resolve any software bugs and security vulnerabilities. Without these updates and patches, any newly discovered security vulnerabilities on the system will not be rectified and the risk of the system being compromised due to a cyber-attack or threat increases.

> **Important note**
> The system life cycle affects both software and hardware components.

The following are the phases of a system life cycle:

1. **Procurement** – Focuses on planning, negotiating, and acquiring a product or system from a vendor.

2. **Deployment** – Focuses on the implementation (installation) and integration of systems into the organization.

3. **Management** – Focuses on supervision such as keeping track of the hardware or software products while monitoring them to ensure they're performing as expected. Additionally, supporting the product or system to ensure it continues to operate and perform as needed.

4. **Decommission and disposal** – Focuses on replacing devices that are no longer functioning or supported by the vendor, preserving systems to continue providing the resources and services needed, and retiring systems that are end-of-life.

Understanding the importance of the system life cycle of systems within an organization reduces the security risks associated with using outdated devices and applications. While many organizations do not update their internal technologies such as devices and applications, they are left vulnerable to cyber-attacks and the failure of systems as a result.

Standard operating procedures

Standard operating procedures are simply step-by-step guidelines or instructions for performing a common task within an organization. These guidelines are designed to improve the efficiency of performing a task or action by an employee and are sometimes required for compliance with various regulatory standards within an industry. Furthermore, using standard operating procedures within an organization helps reduces the likelihood of either failures or miscommunication, as the guidelines are standardized within the company for each person to follow to achieve a given task.

Overall, the standard operating procedures contain the details about the organization's daily business processes and operations, while outlining the methods, techniques, and sequences used to complete a given task or objective. Organizations should have procedures for everything within the business, therefore ensuring each employee understands how to achieve the task using the guidelines. It's important to ensure that the standard operating procedures are clearly defined and well documented so that they are easy to understand and follow by anyone who reads them.

If a standard operating procedure is not clearly defined or written, the reader may have difficulties understanding how to perform the task and will take longer to complete the action. As a result, this can lead to inefficiency within the organization and affect business operations.

Having completed this section, you have learned about various plans and procedures that are commonly implemented within many organizations around the world. Furthermore, you have learned about their roles and responsibilities, and how they help organizations to improve their performance and operations.

Next, let's take a deep dive into discovering various security policies that are used to improve the security posture of devices and systems on a network.

Hardening and security policies

Network professionals mostly focus on designing, configuring, maintaining, and troubleshooting network-related issues within an organization. However, it's important for the next generation of network professionals to understand the role of various security policies that are used to help prevent malicious activities on a system and network by employees of the company.

Over the next few subsections, you will explore various hardening techniques and security policies that are commonly used to help improve the security posture of companies.

Password policies

Password policies are created by system administrators and security professionals with the intent of ensuring that any user who wants to create or update a password on a system or device meets the requirements for creating a complex password. Many systems and devices are protected with a username and password combination that can easily be compromised by a skilled cybersecurity professional or seasoned hacker. For instance, imagine if users within the organization set a simple and easy-to-remember password for their user accounts within the company. If a threat actor were to gain access to the network, the hacker would be able to perform an online password attack with the intent to discover the valid user credentials of any user on the network with a weak password.

Password policies usually contain the following rules and guidelines:

- Do not use the same password on multiple systems, devices, or user accounts.
- Ensure the password contains uppercase, lowercase, special characters, symbols, and numbers to increase its complexity.
- Ensure the password has a minimum length of eight characters or more.
- Create a policy to ensure a user is unable to reuse an older password on a system.
- Create a policy to ensure passwords are frequently changed every 30 to 60 days.
- Create a lockout policy to prevent access to a user account if there are continuous failed login attempts within a specific duration of time. For instance, three failed attempts within 60 seconds is an indication of a possible attempt of an account takeover.
- Ensure users understand how to recover their user accounts if their passwords are forgotten.

The idea of creating complex passwords on systems reduces the likelihood of a hacker being able to compromise the user account and gain access to the system. However, creating a unique complex password for each system can make them quite challenging to remember. Using password manager applications helps people to generate unique, complex passwords and store them. If you're using a password manager application, ensure you set a complex password for it and use **Two-Factor Authentication (2FA)** to prevent a threat actor from gaining unauthorized access to your passwords within the password manager.

Acceptable use policy

The **Acceptable Use Policy (AUP)** is very common within many organizations and educational institutions, containing the guidelines, rules of conduct, and constraints that an employee or a user must agree to before they are granted access to a system or network. For instance, without an AUP within an organization, employees will be unrestricted in their actions on company-owned equipment such as computers and smartphones. If an employee is unaware of the *dos* and *don'ts* within an organization, the employee can use the company-owned systems to access websites and resources that are not safe for work and websites that create an unproductive workforce.

> Tip
> If you're interested in obtaining a template of an AUP and the additional common security policies, please see the following link: https://www.sans.org/information-security-policy/.

During the onboarding process of an employee, the human resource department usually ensures the new employee thoroughly reads and signs the AUP documentation as an indication of accepting the terms and conditions of using the systems and company resources. Additionally, the AUP ensures each policy uses the company's systems and resources to benefit and improve the organization's business processes.

Bring your own device policies

Bring Your Own Device (BYOD) is a policy that allows the employees within an organization to use their personally-owned devices such as smartphones, tablets, and laptops for work-related activities in the company. This allows the employee to use their personal devices for accessing their corporate email accounts, performing daily work-related tasks, and accessing the organization's network, services, and resources.

While it may be convenient for employees to use their personal devices, this concept imposes greater security risks to the organization. Since these devices are not company-owned, they are not managed by the IT team of the company – hence, the IT team is unable to monitor the security posture of these personal devices. For instance, if an employee has a smartphone with an outdated operating system, that smartphone will be vulnerable to many new cyber-attacks and threats. If the smartphone contains malware that's unknown to the device owner and it's connected to the organization's network, the malware can infect and compromise other systems within the corporate network.

Overall, organizations that implement BYOD policies ensure their network is closely monitored for any suspicious activities and there are cybersecurity solutions that are implemented to profile each connected device to ensure they meet the minimum security requirements before they are permitted access to the network resources.

Remote access policies

The remote access policy simply defines the methods and techniques that allow an employee to securely connect and access the resources on an organization's network. Many organizations implement remote access configurations on their networking devices and security appliance to allow their IT team to conveniently access systems and devices over a network. However, when implementing remote access services on a device, it's important to always secure methods and protocols to provide data security between the client and server.

The following are common network protocols and techniques that allow remote access:

- **Secure Shell (SSH)**
- **Remote Desktop Protocol (RDP)**
- **Virtual Network Computing (VNC)**
- A **Virtual Private Network (VPN)**

Whether you're using SSH or a remote access VPN to securely access the networking devices and security appliances within your organization, the remote access policy should define the authorized users, their privileges, the preferred remote access protocol, acceptable usages, the VPN concentrator, and client configurations. Without remote access policies within organizations, a user may attempt to take advantage of their privileges that access a networking or security device.

Onboarding and off-boarding policies

The onboarding process is usually conducted whenever an organization hires a new employee. This process is important to ensure the employee is well trained in the business processes and operations, tasks, and security policies that are involved within their new role and the organization. Furthermore, when an employee leaves an organization, the off-boarding process must be effective. The off-boarding process focuses on ensuring the user accounts for the resigned employee are disabled rather than deleted, passwords for systems are changed, and any company-owned devices and equipment are returned.

Imagine if an organization never disabled user accounts or changed the passwords on their systems – the ex-employee could share that confidential information with hackers who could use those secrets to gain physical access to the building and remote access to systems.

The onboarding and off-boarding policies are simply the guidelines and rules that are used by the human resources department to help a new employee join the organization and to separate the employee from the company when the employee leaves.

Security policies

Security policies are simply documentation that explains how an organization plans to protect and secure its assets from cyber-attacks and threats. These documents are frequently updated to ensure the organization is adapting to the changes in the security landscape, as new and emerging threats surface very often.

The head of information security within an organization is usually the responsible person who will be tasked with developing various security policies that are designed to protect the organization's assets. An information security professional must understand the need for data protection, privacy, and security of all assets (whether tangible, intangible, or people). Furthermore, it's essential to understand the various risks that are associated with each type of security vulnerability that exists within the organization. Lastly, an information security professional also needs to consider both internal and external threats, as many professionals focus more on securing their systems from external threats, while leaving their internal systems and network unprotected.

Data loss prevention

Data Loss Prevention (**DLP**) includes features within many cybersecurity solutions such as firewall appliances, email solutions, and **Endpoint Detection and Response** (**EDR**) applications. DLP focuses on preventing anyone within the organization from exfiltrating sensitive and confidential data. DLP solutions help organizations to monitor for any potential data breaches where, if an employee or a threat actor is attempting to remove data from the company's systems and network, the DLP solution can detect and prevent the security incident in real time.

Upon completing this section, you have now learned about the various types of hardening and security policies that are commonly used within organizations. In the next section, you will learn about the common but important types of documentation that are needed as a network professional.

Common documentation

Each organization usually has a set of common documentation that helps network professionals to better understand the network design when planning for future upgrades, maintenance, and troubleshooting issues.

The following are common types of documentation for network professionals:

- **Physical network diagrams** – The physical network diagram contains a flood plan of the building or office space and shows how each networking device is interconnected and its location. Additionally, you can find a rack diagram that includes a server rack and all its interconnected servers, and network racks, showing all the networking devices and security appliances. Furthermore, physical network diagrams show the **Intermediate Distribution Frame** (**IDF**) and the **Main Distribution Frame** (**MDF**), which indicate how and where the physical network connections are terminated within the company.

- **Logical network diagrams** – This type of diagram shows the packet flow throughout a network within an organization by illustrating how devices are interconnected and able to communicate with each other. The logical network diagram contains information such as IP schemes, networking devices and types, network protocols, and gateways to the internet.

- **Wiring diagrams** – A wiring diagram shows how the physical connections and layout of networking cables are made throughout the organization. They help network professionals to better understand the physical connections between devices and how they are interconnected.

- **Site survey reports** – Before implementing a wireless network solution for an organization, a site survey is required to determine the number of Access Points and their placements to ensure maximum coverage. To complete a site survey report, it's important to understand the needs and requirements of the organization in terms of wireless technology; obtaining a floor plan or facility diagram will be very useful when determining wireless signal coverage and the Access Point placements. Furthermore, inspect the physical and network infrastructure of the building and identify the coverage area by performing an actual site survey and measuring the signal. During this time, determine potential locations where the Access Points could be implemented and document all the findings of the survey.

- **Audit and assessment reports** – This type of report provides a complete and detailed analysis of the network performance or network security analysis of the organization. The audit and assessment report is used to determine any issues that exist on the network and whether these issues are being resolved.

- **Baseline configurations** – Without capturing a baseline of systems or the network when it's operating at an acceptable state, a network professional will not be able to tell whether the current state of their network is operating abnormally or not. Additionally, baseline configurations are a set of configurations that are applied to a system or device that is considered to be acceptable and should only be changed or modified using a change management process.

This is the common documentation that helps network professionals to ensure the healthy operation of their network infrastructure. In the next section, you will discover common organizational agreements that ensure various parties understand what is expected.

Common agreements

Organizations need to ensure the people who are using their systems, such as employees, contractors, and service providers, do not share sensitive information with external parties, and understand what is expected from them.

The following are common agreements that are used within the business world between two parties:

- **Non-Disclosure Agreements (NDAs)** – This type of agreement is usually given by an organization to employees, contractors, and service providers who will be working on the organization's systems and network. The NDA is simply a legal document used to prevent anyone from disclosing sensitive and confidential information that's discovered on the organization's systems.

- **Service-Level Agreements (SLAs)** – The SLA is a common agreement that's given by a service provider to the customer that indicates the responsibility of the service provider and its role in providing and ensuring the delivery of the service to the customer and that this service meets the acceptable level.

- A **Memorandum of Understanding (MOU)** – This type of agreement is sometimes written in the form of a letter that contains the intention between two parties. However, the MOU is a less formal type of agreement that's commonly used within an organization and does not always require either party to sign.

Having completed this section, you have learned about common organizational documentation and its characteristics.

Summary

During this chapter, you have learned about the importance of performing change management to reduce the risks that are involved in implementing a change in a system, network, or organization. Additionally, you have discovered the various phases of incident response and planning and the need for incident response professionals within the industry. Furthermore, you have explored the role and function of various plans and procedures, common types of documentation, and agreements.

I hope this chapter has been informative for you and is helpful in your journey toward learning about networking and becoming a network professional. In the next chapter, *Chapter 13, High Availability and Disaster Recovery*, you will learn about various techniques that help network professionals to ensure their network is always up and running.

Questions

The following is a short list of review questions to help reinforce your learning and help you identify areas that require some improvement:

1. Which of the following phases are responsible for removing a threat from a system?

    A. Post-incident analysis

    B. Detection

    C. Containment

    D. Eradication

2. When developing a business continuity plan, which of the following helps professionals to improve the plan?

    A. An after-action report

    B. Failover sites

    C. Alternative business practices

    D. All of the above

3. The maximum amount of time for which a system can be unavailable before there is an unacceptable impact on other systems within an organization is known as what?

    A. The recovery point objective

    B. Incident handling

    C. The recovery time objective

    D. Recovery

4. Which phase in the system life cycle is responsible for keeping track of hardware and software products?

    A. Deployment

    B. Maintaining

    C. Monitoring

    D. Management

5. Which of the following types of policies helps reduce account takeovers?

    A. An acceptable use policy

    B. A password policy

    C. A BYOD policy

    D. All of the above

6. Which of the following prevents threat actors from exfiltrating data from an organization?

    A. The AUP

    B. DLP

    C. URP

    D. RDP

7. Which of the following agreements prevents a contractor from disclosing sensitive information?

    A. Security policies

    B. An MOU

    C. An SLA

    D. An NDA

8. Which of the following agreements is used to assure a given service to a customer?

    A. An SLA

    B. An MOU

    C. An NDA

    D. All of the above

9. Which of the following policies allows employees to use their personal devices on the organization's network to perform work-related tasks?

A. An MOU

B. BYOD

C. The AUP

D. None of the above

10. Which of the following can be used to ensure each employee uses a set of guidelines to achieve the same objectives within an organization?

A. DLP

B. SOP

C. An MOU

D. The AUP

Further reading

To learn more on the subject, check out the following links:

- *What is change management?* – https://www.techtarget.com/searchcio/definition/change-management

- *Incident management* – https://www.sans.org/white-papers/1516/

- *Security policy templates* – https://www.sans.org/information-security-policy/

13

High Availability and Disaster Recovery

As an aspiring network professional, one of the core roles and responsibilities is to always ensure the network services and resources are always available and accessible to the users on the network. Within large organizations, many users depend on the availability of the network infrastructure to provide the availability of various network services and resources that are essential for ensuring the business is operating continuously.

In this chapter, you will explore various techniques that are commonly implemented by IT professionals to ensure their systems and networks are always up and running to provide the necessary services and resources for their users. You will dive into both high availability and various disaster recovery concepts and gain a solid understanding of how various technologies are used to ensure fault tolerance while providing maximum uptime for resources.

In this chapter, we will cover the following topics:

- High availability concepts
- Disaster recovery concepts

Let's dive in!

High availability concepts

High availability (**HA**) is simply the ability of a system or a network to continuously operate without failure. For instance, network professionals implement various techniques and technologies into their network infrastructure to ensure it can continue operating without failing over a very long time. For instance, imagine if a switch or a router were to fail within a company; what will be the impact and how many users will be affected? What if the router was connecting the organization's internal network to the **internet service provider** (**ISP**) network? All the users within the organization will be affected and if the company was depending on resources or services that are hosted on a cloud provider's data center, those cloud resources will be inaccessible.

A common strategy for setting up HA within an organization is to implement **fault tolerance** in the form of *redundancy* in hardware components on devices and network infrastructure. For instance, imagine if a critical server within the company has one network adapter that allows network connectivity between the server and the clients. If the network adapter on the server were to fail, none of the users on the network will be able to access the resources hosted on the server. However, implementing two or more network adapters and connecting each network adapter from the server to two different switches provides redundancy in network connectivity between the server and the physical network.

When implementing HA techniques within a network, IT professionals must be familiar with the following key terminology:

- **Mean Time To Repair** (**MTTR**): This is the time required/needed to resolve an issue. For instance, if an IT professional spends a total of 60 hours per year repairing a server during an unplanned maintenance window and the server was repaired 8 times during that same year, then MTTR = Total repair time/number of repair = 60/8 = 7.5 hours.

- **Mean Time Between Failure** (**MTBF**): This is the predicted time between the outages of a system. For instance, if a critical server operates for 8,745 hours per year and experienced 10 failures within the same year, then MTBF = Total uptime/number of failures = 8745/10 = 874.5 hours.

- **Recovery Time Objective** (**RTO**): This is the goal of getting the system up and running back to a specific service level after an outage has occurred.

- **Recovery Point Objective** (**RPO**): This is determined by how data loss is considered to be acceptable or how far back the data goes to bring the system back online.

To become a professional within the networking industry, it's essential to have a solid understanding of the importance that HA plays within organizations and the various techniques that are used to provide network availability to users. In the following sub-sections, you will explore common HA techniques and discover their benefits.

Diverse paths

In today's world, many organizations are using services from cloud computing providers to help reduce the cost of maintaining their own IT infrastructure. Whenever an organization such as your employer is considering a cloud provider or a data center, it's important to consider the type of connectivity between your organization and the data center, and the number of connections needed. While some organizations will choose to have a single ISP to provide connectivity between your company and the data center, it's important to consider the possibility of an outage that may occur within your ISP's network. If ISP services are unavailable, your organization will not be able to access your resources that are hosted within the remote data center.

The following diagram shows an organization with a single connectivity path to the data center facility:

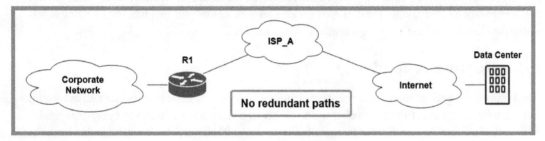

Figure 13.1 – No redundancy

As shown in the preceding diagram, if the router between the organization's corporate network and the internet goes down, users and client devices will not be able to access the resources on the internet.

Having multiple/diverse paths between your organization and the data center is an important factor to consider when implementing HA concepts. Multiple/diverse paths focus on ensuring an organization has more than one available path to and from a data center or the internet. Hence, if one ISP connection goes down, the redundant ISP connection will be enabled and allow the organization to continue accessing the resources within the data center.

The following diagram shows redundant ISPs providing connectivity:

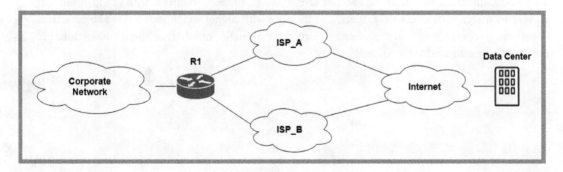

Figure 13.2 – Redundant ISP connections

Since data centers are hosting resources, servers, and devices for many customers, the data center also needs redundancy internet connections from various ISPs within the region. For instance, imagine if a data center had only one internet connection that is used to provide internet connectivity between the data center and the world. If this single connection were to be disrupted and becomes unavailable, the resources within the data center would be inaccessible to many users and organizations. Therefore, even data centers need redundancy connections from multiple ISPs to ensure their resources are available to users and organizations.

Since data centers use multiple ISPs for redundant internet connection, additional hardware such as networking and specialized devices are needed; network devices need to be configured with advanced routing protocols that can quickly route packets between a source and destination. Furthermore, the routing protocols that are used within the data center should be able to detect network changes and reconverge quickly. Using multiple ISPs for a data center provides greater redundancy, ensuring access to the data center resources is always available when needed.

Infrastructure redundancy

Any network designed around the concepts of stability and reliability must incorporate a large amount of fault tolerance. **Fault tolerance** refers to the ability of a system to continue to operate normally, despite the failure of one or more of its constituent parts. Fault tolerance is closely related to both the concept of HA, which is the ability of a system to operate properly and continuously for an extended period, and the concept of a single point of failure, which refers to any one component or entity in a system whose failure can affect the operation of the entire system.

Network professionals often purchase particular components and implement several types of configurations to design highly available fault-tolerant systems. One commonly implemented configuration is load balancing. **Load balancing** is a configuration technique that aims to disseminate workloads among all of the available resources. This technique is commonly implemented in servers. Incoming traffic from clients is initially directed at the load balancer, which then utilizes its preconfigured balancing algorithm to determine which of its backend servers will receive the traffic.

Common load balancing/scheduling algorithms include *round-robin* (a simple algorithm where requests are sequentially distributed to servers as they arrive), *weighted round-robin* (as with round-robin, but servers are assigned different weightings, and the ones with higher weightings receive larger shares of incoming requests), and *least connection* (servers with smaller numbers of client connections are preferred over saturated servers).

The following diagram shows the concept of a load balancer on the network:

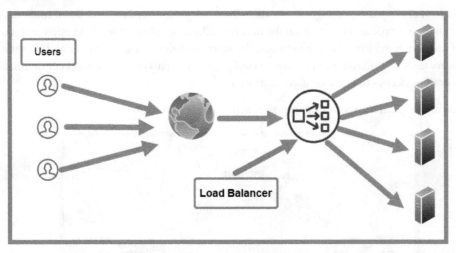

Figure 13.3 – Load balancer

As shown in the preceding diagram, this introduces the concept of clustering, which is another technique commonly used to provide high availability. **Clustering** refers to the aggregation of several nodes into a group, such that the group of nodes behaves as though it were a single node. For instance, the preceding diagram illustrates a server cluster, where each server delivers content to clients in the same manner as a single server would. Clustering adds a degree of fault tolerance to a system, so long as the cluster is configured correctly. For example, a cluster can be configured such that, even if a single node in the cluster fails, the other nodes continue to provide the overall function of the cluster, with the other nodes simply absorbing the increased workload.

Another technique commonly used to provide fault tolerance is **network interface card (NIC) teaming**. NIC teaming refers to a technique in which several NICs on a server are combined into a group to provide higher capacity or improved fault tolerance to the server. When configured to provide increased fault tolerance, NIC teaming balances traffic across all of the NICs and links in the group, allowing traffic to continue flowing if any of the individual NICs in the group fails.

This concept of combining several links into one highly available link can also be implemented on network equipment (such as switches) through the concept of **port aggregation**. Port aggregation allows several physical ports on devices to be combined into one logical port on the device. This process can be performed through particular protocols on devices such as the **link aggregation control protocol (LACP)**.

Active-active versus active-passive configurations

The concept of *active-passive* configurations allows network professionals to install and configure two devices of the same type and function on the network, allowing only one device to operate at a time. If one of the two devices fails on the network, the secondary device can take over and become the new primary device. Within the active-passive configuration, there's always constant communication between both devices as they are configured as a pair.

The following diagram shows an example of an active-passive scenario:

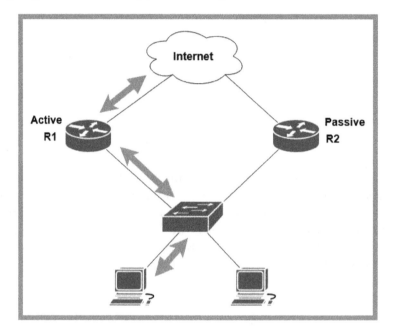

Figure 13.4 – Active-passive routers

As shown in the preceding diagram, two routers have been configured to operate in an active-passive mode, where **R1** is configured to operate as the primary router for forwarding packets between the internet and the internal network and **R2** becomes the standby router. While these two routers are online, they both exchange keep-alive messages with each other. If **R2** does not receive the keep-alive messages from **R1** after a specific time, **R2** will automatically assume the role of the primary router for forwarding packets to and from the internet for the internal clients.

Network professionals commonly configure various types of devices in an active-passive state. Some of these devices are switches, routers, firewalls, and even servers on a network. The configurations and real-time session information between devices in an active-passive state need to be constantly synchronized with each other as failover may happen at any time within an organization.

In an active-active state, two devices of the same type are configured and operating at the same time. This type of configuration is usually more complex to design and operate compared to the active-passive configuration. Since both devices are active and forwarding traffic at the same time, the packet can flow in many different directions.

The following diagram shows routers operating in an active-active state:

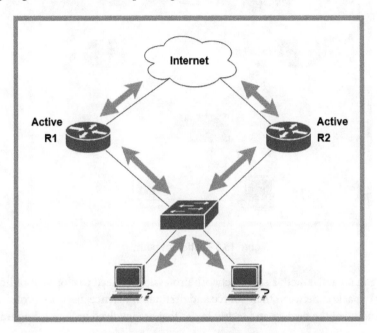

Figure 13.5 – Active-active routers

As shown in the preceding diagram, **R1** and **R2** are both operating in an active-active state. Therefore, traffic from one computer may take the outbound path through **R1** to access the internet, and returning traffic may not take the same path but use the path through **R2** and back to the computer.

The following diagram shows how data can flow in different directions:

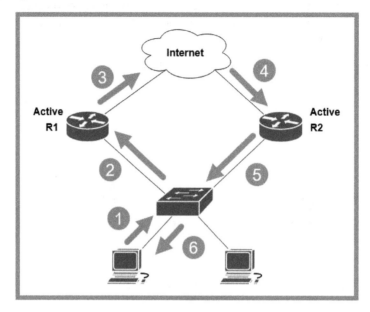

Figure 13.6 – Different paths

When operating in an active-active state, network professionals need to closely monitor and even control the flow of packets between their source and destination. Hence, network professionals need a solid understanding of the devices and technologies that are involved in forwarding traffic.

First hop redundancy

Typically, on a network, there will be a default gateway such as a router that is configured to forward packets to remote and foreign networks, such as public networks on the internet. Without a default gateway, clients and servers will not be able to exchange messages with devices that are beyond their subnet or local network. As a network professional, it's essential to ensure the default gateway is available and operating as expected.

The following diagram shows a network with a single default gateway:

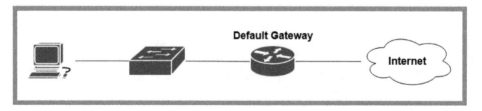

Figure 13.7 – Single default gateway

As shown in the preceding diagram, the computer has only one default gateway to the internet. If the default gateway becomes unavailable due to a failure or another cause, the clients on the internal network will lose connectivity to the internet. Around the world, many organizations depend on internet connectivity for various resources, such as accessing resources on a cloud provider's data center, communicating with external parties, research, and so on. Imagine if an organization has only one default gateway and it goes offline – what will be the impact on the users within the company?

Within the networking industry, there are various **first-hop redundancy protocols** (**FHRPs**) that allow network professionals to configure two routers of the same type to operate in an active-active or active-passive role, which helps provide redundancy for the default gateway. Routers that are using an FHRP share a virtual IP address and a virtual **media access control** (**MAC**) address. The virtual IP and virtual MAC address are assigned to the active router that is responsible for forwarding packets. In the event the active router is no longer available, the virtual IP and MAC address is reassigned to the standby router, which will now assume the role of the new active router on the network.

The following diagram shows two routers that are using FHRP:

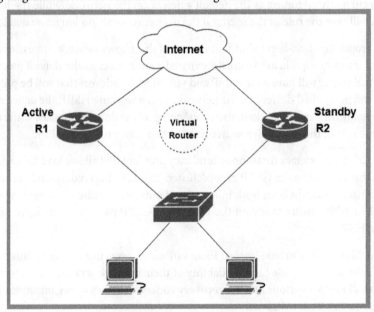

Figure 13.8 – First-hop redundancy

As shown in the preceding diagram, two routers have been configured with first-hop redundancy, which allows them to create a virtual router that has the role of the default gateway. The virtual router has a virtual IP address and a virtual MAC address that is shared with the clients on the networks. However, one of the physical routers such as **R1** will be an active router, while **R2** will be the standby router. If the active router, **R1**, goes offline, the failover will occur automatically and **R2** will become the new active router. Additionally, since the virtual IP and virtual MAC address are shared between both **R1** and **R2**, the clients will experience a minor interruption in network connectivity during the failover process.

Since clients, servers, and networked devices are provided the virtual IP and virtual MAC address of the virtual router, whenever the active router such as **R1** goes offline and the failover occurs, there is no need to inform the clients on the network as the virtual IP and virtual MAC address are assigned to the new active router, **R2**, on the network.

The following are FHRPs that are commonly used within the industry:

- **Virtual Router Redundancy Protocol (VRRP)**
- **Hot Standby Router Protocol (HSRP)**
- **Gateway Load Balancing Protocol (GLBP)**

VRRP is a common vendor-neutral first-hop redundancy protocol that allows network professionals to create a group of physical routers with the intent to create a virtual router on a network. Using VRRPv2 allows many routers to become part of the VRRP group, which enables them to share the virtual IP address as the default gateway address for the network. When using VRRP, the *master* is the router that is currently operating as the default gateway on the network, while the *backup* is the other router that will take the role of the *master* if the master router is no longer available.

HSRP is a Cisco-proprietary first-hop redundancy protocol that allows network professionals to group two Cisco routers into a group/cluster to create a virtual router to act as the default gateway for the network. The virtual router will have a virtual IP and virtual MAC address that will be provided to all clients, services, and networked devices on the network. When working HSRP, the *active* router is the router that is currently forwarding packets and is operating as the default gateway, while the *standby* router will take the role of the new active router if the actual active router is offline.

GLBP is another Cisco-proprietary first-hop redundancy protocol that allows load balancing between multiple routers that are within the GLBP group/cluster. This first-hop redundancy protocol allows network professionals to load-balance both inbound and outbound traffic while gaining the benefits of implementing first-hop redundancy on their network. GLBP uses the same *active* and *standby* router concept as HSRP.

Having completed this section, you have learned about various concepts that are commonly implemented by network professionals to provide high availability of their network services and resources. In the next section, you will explore various disaster recovery concepts that allow organizations to continue operating and recovering from a disaster.

Disaster recovery concepts

A disaster can occur at any time and without warning, and many organizations can be greatly impacted when a disaster happens. The impact of a disaster can affect the ability of an organization to continue operating, whether short-term or long-term. Hence, companies implement various disaster recovery plans and strategies to help recover whenever a real disaster occurs.

In the next few sub-sections, you will discover common practices that organizations use to help them recover when disasters do occur.

Recovery sites

In the event of a critical disaster at an organization's primary business location, it may be necessary for the company to move all of its staff to a backup location to ensure business continuity. These backup locations, also known as recovery sites, can be categorized into one of four groups, depending on how they are equipped, and the resources that are available at each site:

- **Hot site**: A hot site is a complete mirror image of an organization's primary location. It contains all of the equipment and data required for the staff to begin working again with little to no downtime. Hot sites contain the latest backups of data and configurations of equipment.

- **Warm site**: A warm site contains all of the physical infrastructures of the primary location, but requires staff to restore backups and configurations manually, meaning that recovery times are longer than with a hot site.

- **Cold site**: A cold site is a backup site that simply reserves space for the enterprise. Infrastructure must be transferred to this site and backups must be restored. Although cold sites require the longest time to restore business functions, they also have the lowest costs associated with them.

- **Cloud site**: A cloud site is simply a recovery site that is established within a cloud provider's data center and provides enough resources for the recovery process. Using a cloud site ensures there's no separate facility to manage as the physical maintenance is handled by the service provider. Although the cost can be a flat fee, it can vary based on the usage of resources within the cloud provider's data center. Keep in mind that the data and applications within a company's primary location still need to be moved to the cloud site.

In addition to choosing backup/recovery sites, network professionals must also choose which method of data backup they wish to employ. Three of the main methods are as follows:

- **Full backup**: All data in every file server for a backup is preserved every time a backup cycle is performed. This method allows data to be restored quickly since every backup contains all of the data required for restoration (requiring only one restoration to be performed). However, this method also requires the most time to perform and requires the most space on backup media.

- **Incremental backup**: A backup that records only the files that have been added or changed since the last backup. A full backup is performed first; then, incremental backups record the changes that occur after that initial full backup. Therefore, incremental backups require much less space and time to restore as they only record the changes that have occurred since the last backup (either incremental or full). However, they also require much more time to restore, requiring first the restoration of the last full backup, then the restoration of all subsequent incremental backups.

- **Differential backup**: This backup method provides a compromise between full and incremental backups. With this method, a full backup is performed initially. Then, on each subsequent backup cycle, a differential backup is run, recording the changes that have been made since the last full backup. In this way, restoration is quicker than with an incremental backup, requiring only the full backup and the last differential backup. This method also requires less space and time than continuous full backups.

It is also important to be familiar with **snapshots** when working with hypervisors and virtual machines. Snapshots record the state of a system at a particular instance in time. They do not back up (copy) the data within the system, but merely record how the data is organized within the system at the instant it is taken. Since they do not replicate data, snapshots are commonly used for recording different versions of a system. However, this lack of replication also means that they are not full backup solutions by themselves. Therefore, it is important to utilize other backup solutions in tandem with snapshots.

Facilities and infrastructure support

Organizations invest in various support systems to ensure their facilities and infrastructure are always up and running to provide the necessary resources to support their business, functions, and processes. Without electricity, electronic devices such as computers, servers, networking devices, security appliances, and physical security systems will not be operational.

An **uninterruptible power supply** (**UPS**) is an external unit that provides short-term backup power to a device. The UPS contains an internal, changeable battery that stores electrical current. A computer, server, or networking device receives power from the UPS while it is connected to the power outlet.

The following are common types of UPS:

- **Offline/standby**: This type of UPS is often seen within homes and small offices. They provide instant power to connected devices whenever a power outage occurs. Furthermore, when the UPS detects it's no longer receiving electrical power from the power outlet, it will automatically switch to the backup battery mode to supply short-term power to any connected devices.

- **Line-interactive**: This type of UPS provides additional protection against low and high voltage and power surges from the utility company.

- **Online/double conversion**: This type of UPS always provides electrical power from its inverter to any connected devices. This method allows no delays when an actual power outage occurs.

Some UPS devices support additional features such as auto shutdown, which sends a signal to a connected device such as a computer to automatically power off during a power outage. Additionally, many UPSs support phone line suppression to prevent any noise or irregularity in electrical signals on the phone lines.

On a server rack, IT professionals install a **power distribution unit** (**PDU**), which simply provides multiple power outlets to many servers on the same rack. The PDU is commonly used by IT professionals to both monitor and control the power capacity that's being provided and consumed by each server. IT professionals use common network protocols such as **Simple Network Management Protocol** (**SNMP**) to gather statistics and perform changes to the PDU over a TCP/IP network.

Medium-size to large organizations and data centers usually have one or more **generators** to provide long-term backup power to their facilities and infrastructure. The power can be unavailable for a very long time during a disaster and the organization may have critical servers and networking devices that need to be available to provide resources for the business. Using one or more generators can provide electrical power to an entire building for a long time. Unlike a UPS, which contains a backup battery to store power, a generator runs on fuel and may take a few minutes to get up and running to provide power to the building, so a UPS may be needed in the meantime.

A **heating, ventilation, and air conditioning** (**HVAC**) system is commonly implemented within data centers and organizations that provide temperature, humidity, and airflow control for a building. This type of system is usually integrated with the fire suppression system of the organization; if a fire occurs within a building, there will be a lot of toxic smoke that is harmful to humans. Therefore, the HVAC and fire suppression system needs to work together to control and extinguish the fire. Additionally, a computer system usually manages the equipment and components that are responsible for the cooling and heating decisions that are made for the workspaces and data centers.

Having a fire suppression system within a data center is mandatory for fire safety and compliance. Fire suppression systems within a data center do not use water as it's not good for large rooms with electronics such as servers. It's quite common to use a type of inert gas and chemical agents that are usually stored within large tanks that are dispersed during an actual fire. The gases and chemical agents remove/reduce the oxygen within the affected area, suppressing the fire.

Network device backup/restore

Network professionals spend a lot of time configuring network devices within their organizations to ensure these devices forward traffic to their destinations as expected. Configuring a new router or switch for your network may take a few minutes to administer the baseline configurations for initial device provisioning. However, a network professional will administer additional configuration to the device to ensure it is forwarding traffic efficiently to the destination as expected.

As an organization expands, so does its network infrastructure to support more users, devices, services, and applications. Hence, additional device configurations are needed for the network devices within the organization to support these changes and efficiently forward packets to their destinations.

As a result, network professionals need to understand the various states of network device configurations; the following are the different device states:

- **Actual**: This is the present state of a device and its current configurations on the network
- **Perceived**: This is the state that we think the device and its configurations should be in on the network
- **Desired**: This is the state that we want the device and its configurations to be in on the network

As a network professional, there are many times that changes may occur on the network, such as when implementing additional servers within the server rack with a new application. Here, we would think the networking devices are capable of handling the additional traffic on the network with their current configurations. This is known as the *perceived* state. However, after implementing the additional servers and applications, it was realized that the networking devices have the capabilities but lack the configurations to do so; this is the *actual* state. As network professionals, we would want all the networking devices within the company to be configured with additional device configurations to efficiently support the new servers and applications to ensure optimal performance of the network infrastructure; this is the *desired* state.

Furthermore, it's a very common practice within the IT industry to create multiple backups of each device configuration that's on the network. When creating backups, it's important to verify the backups are created properly and are not corrupted. Imagine if a network professional performs backups regularly and were to restore a backup configuration to a device, only to realize the backup file is corrupted. Hence, always check the integrity and verify the backup file(s) are not corrupted so that when they are needed to restore a system or device to a working state, the backups are good to go.

Having completed this section, you have learned about various disaster recovery concepts and how they can be used to help organizations restore their services and critical business functions during a disaster.

Summary

In this chapter, you learned about the importance of high availability and various techniques that network professionals use, such as creating multiple paths, implementing redundancy within the infrastructure, and using various first-hop redundancy protocols, to ensure users always have access to network resources and services when needed. Additionally, you have discovered various disaster recovery concepts, such as the need for recovery sites, support systems for both facilities and infrastructure, and creating backups of device configurations and systems.

I hope this chapter has been informative for you and is helpful in your journey toward learning networking and becoming a network professional. In the next chapter, *Chapter 14, Network Security Concepts*, you will learn about different types of cyber security threats and network attacks, and how to secure a wireless and wired network infrastructure using best practices and mitigation techniques.

Questions

The following is a short list of review questions to help reinforce your learning and help you identify areas that may require some improvement:

1. How can network professionals implement a fault-tolerant network infrastructure within their organization?

   A. Reduce the number of hubs on the network

   B. Increase the number of routers

   C. Implement redundancy

   D. All of the above

2. Which of the following best describes the goal of getting the system up and running back to a specific service level after an outage has occurred?

   A. Mean time between failures

   B. Recovery time objective

   C. Mean time to repair

   D. Recovery point objective

3. Which of the following is a non-proprietary protocol that's commonly used in a network that supports redundancy within the default gateway?

   A. GLBP

   B. HSRP

   C. FHRP

   D. VRRP

4. Which of the following sites costs the least to maintain?

   A. Warm site

   B. Cold site

   C. Cloud site

   D. Hot site

5. Which of the following best describes creating a backup of all the changes and new files that were created since the last full backup?

A. Differential backup

B. Full backup

C. Incremental back

D. None of the above

6. Which of the following devices provides short-term backup power to a server when a power outage occurs?

A. Generator

B. PDU

C. AVR

D. UPS

Further reading

To learn more about the topics that were covered in this chapter, check out the following links:

- *Disaster recovery site (DR site)*: `https://www.techtarget.com/searchdisasterrecovery/definition/disaster-recovery-site-DR-site`

- *What is fault tolerance*: `https://www.imperva.com/learn/availability/fault-tolerance/`

Part 4:
Network Security and Troubleshooting

This part focuses on securing both wired and wireless network infrastructures using various technologies and protocols, understanding various types of cyber attacks and threats on a network, and using network security best practices with countermeasures. Lastly, this section covers common network troubleshooting techniques and practice questions.

This part of the book comprises the following chapters:

- *Chapter 14, Network Security Concepts*
- *Chapter 15, Exploring Cyberattacks and Threats*
- *Chapter 16, Implementing Network Security*
- *Chapter 17, Network Troubleshooting*
- *Chapter 18, Practice Exercises*

14

Network Security Concepts

As an aspiring network professional, it's important to have a solid foundation in various network security concepts and principles. Designing, building, and maintaining networks is quite awesome within the industry, but hackers are always looking for new ways to compromise organizations and steal their data. Network professionals design a network with network security principles and technical controls to prevent and mitigate cyber-attacks and threats to help safeguard the assets of the company.

In this chapter, you will understand the need for network security principles and how they are used to help prevent various cyber-attacks and threats. Additionally, you will explore various techniques that are commonly implemented within large organizations to improve the authentication process between users and systems. Lastly, you will explore security and business risk management techniques that are used to help organizations identify and mitigate various types of risks.

In this chapter, we will cover the following topics:

- Understanding network security
- Exploring authentication methods
- Risk management

Let's dive in!

Understanding network security

Network security focuses on the techniques, policies, and security controls that are implemented within an organization's network infrastructure to prevent various types of malicious activities, threats, and cyber-attacks. Without network security solutions, anyone, whether it's an employee or a guest user, can intentionally or unintentionally perform malicious activities on the network that can cause damage to systems and data loss.

While threat actors are the typical people who will perform intentional cyber-attacks on a network, the trusted employees within the organization can perform unintentional actions, such as inserting a malware-infected USB drive into their work computer/systems without knowing the USB drive contains malware. Sometimes, an employee who is unaware of various threats may click a malicious link within a phishing email that's created by hackers. Hence, network security professionals need to consider the risks that are involved if the organization's assets are left unprotected.

Before implementing network security solutions and countermeasures to mitigate and prevent cyber-attacks and threats, it's important to identify the assets within the organization. Assets are simply anything that has value or is valuable to the organization. Without being able to identify the assets within a company, network security professionals will not be able to properly implement the best countermeasures and security controls to protect the asset from threats.

The following are the three categories of assets:

- **Tangible**: The tangible assets are simply any physical objects that have value such as networking devices, security appliances, servers, computers, and furniture.

- **Intangible**: These are the intellectual property and digital assets, which do not have a physical form. Intangible assets are data, software and application licenses, business processes and procedures, and intellectual property.

- **People**: The employees of an organization are of value as they are the ones who perform the day-to-day business processes to ensure the business continues to operate and provide services to customers. The employees need to be protected from human-based cyber-attacks and threats such as social engineering attacks.

In the field of network security, various types of security controls and countermeasures are commonly implemented to mitigate and prevent cyber-attacks and threats while protecting tangible and intangible assets, as well as people, within a company. To further understand the network security concepts, next, you will take a deep dive into exploring the pillars of information security and how they work together to protect data, systems, networks, and people.

Confidentiality, integrity, and availability

Information security focuses on protecting the most valuable asset of any organization: data. Data is created each day by users on computers, servers, networking devices, and even security appliances. Data is created in many ways such as a user creating a document on their computer to write a letter to another person, creating a spreadsheet that helps forecast future financial projections for the later months, and even creating an email message. Networking devices and security appliances generate logs, which contain important information about various transactions and causes of errors that occurred on the network that will be helpful to network and security professionals for troubleshooting issues.

Overall, data is created very often on systems, and we don't even realize it anymore as many organizations and people around the world have adapted to using digital technologies in their everyday lives. For instance, a computer with a word processing application was used to create and help develop the contents of this book while the author typed his thoughts using his keyboard. For each new document, file, or email created on a system such as a computer or a server, new data is created and written to the storage drives of the device.

Organizations store a lot of data that contains confidential information such as details that can be used to identify people; this type of data is commonly referred to as **personally identifiable information (PII)**. The following are examples of PII:

- A person's name
- Date of birth
- Credit card number
- Driver's permit/license number
- Any biological characteristics such as fingerprints, facial geometry, and more
- Mother's maiden name
- Social security number
- Bank account details
- Email address
- Telephone number
- Physical residential address

Additionally, healthcare providers store their patients' details on their systems, which can be used to profile a specific patient. This type of data is commonly referred to as **protected health information (PHI)**. The following are examples of PHI:

- The patient's name
- Telephone number
- Email address
- Residential address
- Any dates on medical records such as date of birth, date of deceased, date of administration, and discharge of the health facility
- Social security number
- Driver's permit/license number

- Biometric information about the patient

- Information about the patient's mental or physical health

- The health care provider's information for the patient

Nowadays, threat actors are developing more sophisticated malware such as **ransomware**, a type of crypto-malware that is designed to encrypt all the data on a system except for the operating system files and presents a payment window to the victim. By encrypting all the data on the system, the threat actor is holding your data hostage and requesting a ransom to be paid within a specific time frame; otherwise, the data will be wiped from the system. This technique is quite intelligent because threat actors can simply create ransomware and unleash it on the internet to compromise any connected systems that are vulnerable. Keep in mind that when ransomware infects a system, the threat actor can exfiltrate your data and sell it on the dark web.

To better understand how data can be vulnerable, the following are the various states of data you must know about:

- **Data in motion**: This is any data that is being sent from one device to another, either over a network or being transported using a portable storage device. Typically, devices are continuously exchanging messages with each other on the **Local Area Network** (**LAN**) within a building or over the internet. For instance, many network protocols that transport data over a network are unsecure by default, allowing hackers to intercept and capture sensitive information such as user credentials and confidential files. There are various techniques to protect data in motion, such as using secure protocols and **Virtual Private Network** (**VPN**) solutions.

- **Data at rest**: This is the data that is currently stored on a local or external storage drive that's not being used by an application or transmitted over a network. If a hacker compromises a server, the hacker will look for any confidential data that's on the local storage drives. Using disk and file encryption applications allows users to encrypt data and entire drives on a system to protect any data at rest.

- **Data in use**: This is any data is that currently being used or accessed by an application. This is the most vulnerable state of data. Simply put, imagine that you have created a password-protected document on your local disk drive to prevent unauthorized persons from reading the contents of the file. Whenever you need to access the file, it has to be decrypted and then viewed within the application. While an application is accessing data in its decrypted state, a hacker can compromise the system or application to access the data. To protect data in use, it's recommended to use trusted applications and ensure both the application and operating system are up to date.

The three pillars of information security are implemented in both administrative and technical security controls within organizations to help protect assets, including data from cyber-attacks and threats. The following are three elements are the pillars of information security:

- **Confidentiality**: Confidentiality ensures that only authorized users have access to resources such as systems or data on a network. Without confidentiality on a system or network, anyone, such as hackers and unauthorized people, will be able to access sensitive and confidential information. Using secure network protocols and VPN technologies protects data in motion and using file and disk encryption applications allows a user to encrypt data at rest on a storage drive. Threat actors will be able to access encrypted data – they just won't be able to use or consume it without the decryption key if the data is at rest.

- **Integrity**: Integrity ensures a message is not changed, modified, or altered in any way between the source and destination. Imagine sending a message such as an email to someone and, during the delivery process, a threat actor was able to intercept the message, read its contents, and modify the message before sending it off to the destination. The recipient, on reading the email, will not identify the message was altered during transmission. Using a trusted hashing algorithm allows users to validate whether a message was altered or not between a source and a destination. Another example is if you're downloading a file from a trusted website with a provided hash. After the download is completed, you can compare the provided hash with the hash you've generated for the file. If both hash values are the same, the integrity is verified, and the file's contents were not altered.

- **Availability**: Availability ensures the data and resources are available to authorized users. Various types of cyber-attacks focus on disrupting the availability of network services, applications, devices, and networks. For instance, threat actors commonly use a **Distributed Denial of Service (DDoS)** attack to disrupt public servers on the internet while preventing legitimate users from accessing the services. Network security professionals commonly implement cybersecurity solutions that are designed to mitigate and prevent cyber-attacks that are designed to affect the availability of systems and resources.

When implementing confidentiality, integrity, and availability within an organization, it's important to ensure there is a balance between each of the components to form the CIA triad, as shown in the following diagram:

Figure 14.1 – CIA triad

As shown in the preceding diagram, the CIA triad is usually drawn using a triangle, and at the end of each angle is one of the three elements – confidentiality, integrity, and availability. At the center of the CIA triad is a dot that represents an equal balance of each element. Some organizations may focus more on confidentiality and integrity, which reduces the availability (access) of resources to users on the network, including the employees. Hence, maintaining a good balance between the components will create great harmony.

Threats, vulnerabilities, and exploits

A **threat** is simply defined as anything that has the potential to cause harm or damage to a system. Additionally, a threat has the potential to violate any component of the CIA triad, such as retrieving confidential data, altering a message during transmission, and even disrupting network services and resources. A **vulnerability** is described as a security weakness or design flaw within a system. Hackers typically use an **exploit** that can take advantage of the security weakness of their target, allowing the hacker to compromise the system. You can think of an exploit as code that is designed to take advantage of a security weakness on an application, firmware, or operating system. As you dive further into the field of network security, cybersecurity, and information security, you will discover many types of internal and external threats that can compromise the confidentiality, integrity, or availability of a system.

Additionally, **zero-day** vulnerabilities are found and exploited by threat actors before they are known by the vendor of the product. For instance, operating systems and software vendors perform continuous and rigorous security testing on their products to discover and resolve any security flaws before making them available to their customers. However, there have been times when threat actors were able to discover and exploit a security weakness on an application before the software vendor was made aware of the vulnerability and had time to resolve it. Sometimes, a software vendor may take a few days or even months to roll out a security update or patches to resolve the zero-day vulnerability, leaving their customers' systems vulnerable and exploitable.

Whenever a new security vulnerability is discovered, it is commonly reported to the software vendor or directly to the **Common Vulnerabilities and Exposures (CVE)** and **National Institute of Standards and Technology (NIST) National Vulnerability Database (NVD)**, which is assigned a unique CVE reference number that provides details about the security vulnerability, affected systems, and how it can be mitigated.

The following screenshot shows an example of the CVE details of the EternalBlue security vulnerability on the Microsoft Windows operating system:

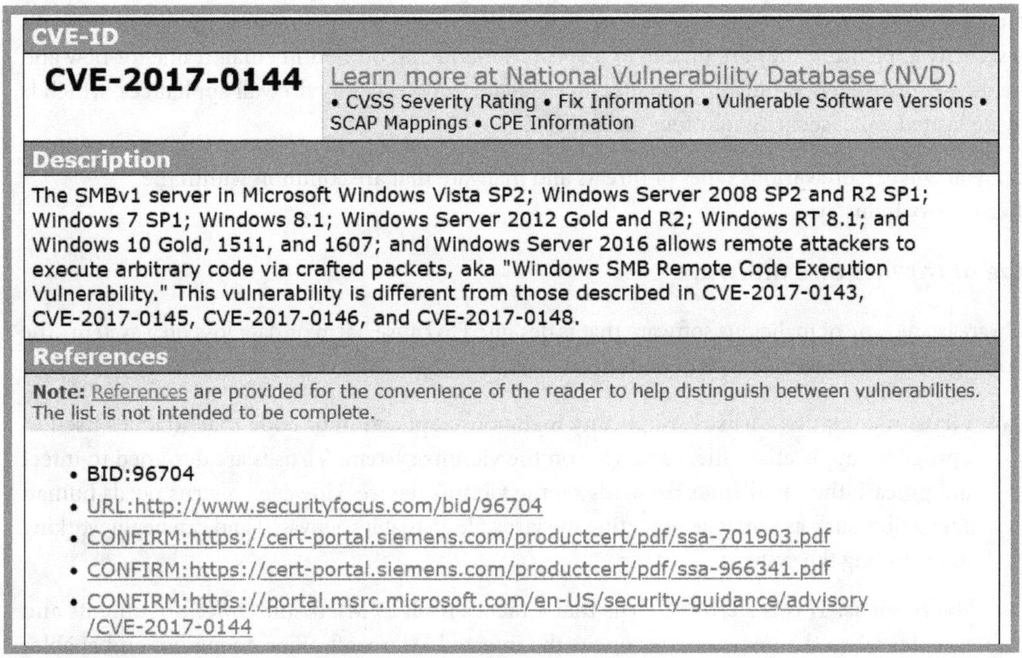

CVE-ID

CVE-2017-0144   Learn more at National Vulnerability Database (NVD)
• CVSS Severity Rating • Fix Information • Vulnerable Software Versions •
SCAP Mappings • CPE Information

Description

The SMBv1 server in Microsoft Windows Vista SP2; Windows Server 2008 SP2 and R2 SP1; Windows 7 SP1; Windows 8.1; Windows Server 2012 Gold and R2; Windows RT 8.1; and Windows 10 Gold, 1511, and 1607; and Windows Server 2016 allows remote attackers to execute arbitrary code via crafted packets, aka "Windows SMB Remote Code Execution Vulnerability." This vulnerability is different from those described in CVE-2017-0143, CVE-2017-0145, CVE-2017-0146, and CVE-2017-0148.

References

Note: References are provided for the convenience of the reader to help distinguish between vulnerabilities. The list is not intended to be complete.

- BID:96704
- URL:http://www.securityfocus.com/bid/96704
- CONFIRM:https://cert-portal.siemens.com/productcert/pdf/ssa-701903.pdf
- CONFIRM:https://cert-portal.siemens.com/productcert/pdf/ssa-966341.pdf
- CONFIRM:https://portal.msrc.microsoft.com/en-US/security-guidance/advisory/CVE-2017-0144

Figure 14.2 – CVE details of a known vulnerability

> **Tip**
>
> To learn more about the newly reported vulnerability and CVE details, be sure to check out `https://cve.mitre.org/`.

The NIST NVD website usually contains additional details about the security vulnerability, such as the vulnerability scoring, which is based on the **Common Vulnerability Scoring System** (**CVSS**) calculator for creating a community-recognized vulnerability score. This determines the severity level of a security weakness.

Internal threats can create a greater impact within an organization compared to external threats. While many organizations focus on implementing various security solutions to protect their corporate networks from external threats on the internet, many IT professionals do not always apply the same level of security to their internal networks. Threat actors such as hackers are aware that the internal security within many organizations is weak or does not even exist at all. Hence, it's easier to compromise an organization from the inside than to perform an external attack.

For instance, many organizations implement a next-generation firewall at their network perimeter to filter inbound and outbound traffic between their organization and the internet. Threat actors commonly craft phishing email messages, which are designed to trick a potential victim into clicking a malicious embedded link or execute the malicious attachment within the message. While firewalls are security appliances, they are unable to inspect inbound and outbound email traffic for new and emerging threats. Hence, phishing emails can easily go undetected by firewall appliances, which is why dedicated email security solutions are needed.

Next, you will explore various types of threats and malware that are common within the cybersecurity industry.

Type of threats and malware

Malware is any type of malicious software that is designed to cause harm or data loss on a system. The following are a list of various type of malware:

- **Virus**: A computer virus is simply any malicious application or code that attaches itself to a program, application, file, or service on the victim's system. Viruses are designed to infect and unleash their malicious payloads on the victim's device. However, a virus needs human interaction, such as someone executing the virus file so that it's activated and can begin working and infecting the system.

- **Macro virus**: This is a type of virus that attaches itself to Microsoft Office documents and executes when the unaware user opens the infected Microsoft office document and enables the macro feature. The macro feature within Microsoft Office allows a user to insert additional functionality into the document whenever a user opens the file. However, hackers have found methods to exploit this feature in Microsoft Office files.

- **Boot sector virus**: This type of virus infects the boot sector of a hard disk drive on a victim's computer. If the boot security has a virus, whenever the system boots and the operating system is running, the virus has the potential to compromise all aspects of the victim's computer.

- **Attachments**: Malicious attachments are commonly inserted and sent in phishing email messages to potential victims and organizations around the world. Email attachments may be malware-infected and are designed to compromise the unaware user's system.

- **Polymorphic virus**: This type of malware is designed to consistently change its coding to evade detection by antimalware solutions on systems and networks, but the role and function of the malware do not change.

- **Worm**: A computer worm is self-propagating malware that can spread to any connected system on its own without user interaction. Computer worms are designed to affect a system's usability by overwhelming or exhausting the available computing resources of the system.

- **Fileless virus**: This type of malware does not have a digital form compared to other traditional malware, which is usually attached to a file, service, or application. This type of malware simply does not exist as a file and does not have a virus signature, which allows it to evade threat detection systems. Additionally, fileless viruses are designed to run within the memory of the compromised system.

- **Rootkits**: This type of malware is designed to gain high-privilege access to the victim's system such as *root* on Linux-based systems and *administrator* or *system-level* privileges on Windows-based systems, allowing the malware to perform administrative tasks. Once a system is infected with a rootkit, it operates at the kernel level of the operating system, which is inaccessible by antimalware programs.

- **Keylogger**: A keylogger is an application that's commonly installed on a compromised system that captures all the keystrokes from the victim's keyboard. Keyloggers are both software and hardware based. The hardware-based keylogger is inserted between the user's keyboard and the computer to intercept all user input from their keyboard.

- **Trojan**: This type of malware is disguised to trick the potential victim into thinking it's a legitimate file or program. A hacker usually creates a Trojan to trick their victim into installing a computer game or a trusted program. Once the victim executes the trojan on their system, the payload is unleashed in the background while the victim thinks the application is legitimate.

- **Backdoor**: A backdoor is usually created on a compromised system by a Trojan. Backdoors allow hackers to gain access to the compromised system, unbeknownst to the victim.

- **Logic bomb**: This type of malware is installed on a system and remains dormant until a predefined action is triggered, activating the logic bomb to unleash its payload on the system. Logic bombs can be triggered based on the time, date, and even the user's actions.

- **Ransomware**: This is crypto-malware that encrypts all the data on a compromised system except the operating system. The operating system is left unharmed as the ransomware displays the payment window to the victim, requesting a ransom to recover the encrypted data. Since hackers are untrustworthy, it's not recommended to pay the ransom as there is no reassurance the hacker will provide the correct decryption keys to access your data.

- **Bot and botnet**: Hackers install a bot (robot) on each compromised system, which allows them to remotely control the compromised system over a network, hence creating zombies. A group of infected systems with bots are commonly referred to as a botnet (robot network). A single hacker can set up a **Command and Control (C2)** server on the network, which allows the hacker to send instructions to the C2 server. These are then relayed to all active bots within the botnet to launch a cyber-attack on a target on the internet.

- **Remote Access Trojan (RAT)**: Sometimes called a **Remote Administration Tool (RAT)**, this allows a hacker to remotely control a compromised system over a network.

- **Spyware**: This type of malware collects data about the user's activity on an infected system. It monitors and reports the victim's activities and behavior back to the hacker. The hacker collects the data, which is usually sold on the dark web.

- **Potentially Unwanted Program** (**PUP**): This is usually any unwanted application or software that is installed on your system. Sometimes, when a user is installing an application, there are additional third-party applications that may be bundled and installed on the user's device.

There are so many types of malware in the industry and being able to identify each type is beneficial in understanding whether a system is compromised by a specific malware or another type of threat.

Types of threat actors

While there are many types of threats and cyber-attacks, threat actors are the people responsible for performing the cyber-attacks and creating the threats within the industry. The following is a list of various categories of threats actors and their motives:

- **Advanced Persistent Threat** (**APT**): APTs are special hacking groups that design very sophisticated cyber-attacks and threats that are advanced and undetected by security solutions, persistent to remain on a compromised system and network while being a threat to the victim. APTs are created to remain on a compromised network while further exploiting additional systems on the network and exfiltrating data.

- **Insider**: Insider threats are described as the attacker already being within the organization's network, behind the company's security controls, and being able to attack any vulnerable systems. A disgruntled employee can be an insider threat as these are people whose intention is to disrupt the operations of the company by launching a cyber-attack.

- **State actors**: These are hackers who are hired by a nation's government to focus on national security and perform reconnaissance on other nations around the world. State actors, sometimes referred to as nation-state hackers, are always well funded to acquire the best technologies, tools, and training needed to develop advanced persistent threats to compromise their targets.

- **Hacktivist**: This threat actor is a person who uses their hacking skills to support a political or social agenda as an activist. Their actions include website defacement, launching massive DDoS attacks, and disclosing confidential records on the internet.

- **Script kiddie**: This is a novice type of hacker, sometimes a beginner who is not necessarily a kid or child, but someone who does not truly understand the technical details of performing a cyber-attack and creating a threat on their own. This is someone who follows the instructions or tutorials of real hackers to perform a cyber-attack on a target without understanding what is happening in the background and the impact. However, the actions of a script kiddie can cause equal or more damage to a system compared to a seasoned hacker.

- **Criminal syndicates**: These are well-funded groups of hackers who focus on financial gain. Each person within the group has a specialist role during the cyber-attack, such as someone who focuses strictly on the reconnaissance of the target, while another develops an APT and another on exploitation, and so on.

- **White hat hacker**: These are the cybersecurity professionals within the industry who uses their hacking skills to help companies secure their systems and networks.

- **Black hat hacker**: This type of hacker uses their skills for malicious purposes.

- **Gray hat hacker**: This type of hacker uses their skills for both good and bad intentions. This person can be a cybersecurity professional during their day job and uses their hacking skills for bad intentions at night.

- **Competitors**: Competitors are always seeking new methods to ensure their products, services, and solutions are always the best in the industry, above their opponents in the business sector. However, competitors may look for ways to damage the reputation of their opponents to create a competitive advantage of gaining new customers and more revenue. Some competitors may even hire a hacker to compromise and exfiltrate confidential documents and leak financial records on the internet.

Now that you're familiar with various types of threats and threat actors, next, you will learn about the importance of implementing least privilege for users on a network and how **role-based access control (RBAC)** can provide an additional layer of security.

Least privilege and RBAC

Imagine if, one day, all the employees within your organization had the same user privileges as each other. This would imply the customer service representatives have the same user privileges on their systems as the IT manager and senior members of staff, without any security restrictions to prevent unauthorized changes on their computers. To reduce these security risks, the *principle of least privilege* is applied to everyone to ensure a user has only enough user privileges on their systems to perform their daily duties while meeting the organization's goals and objectives.

Additionally, *rotation of duties* helps detect and reduce any fraudulent activities within an organization. This technique ensures each employee is rotated between different job functions every few months. Therefore, if a specific employee is performing unethical or fraudulent tasks within their current job over a certain period, it may be unnoticeable. However, when the new employee assumes the role of the previous one, the unethical practices will be noticeable, and management can determine the source of the issue.

Another common strategy within large organizations is using *separation of duties* to ensure no single employee has all the privileges to make a major technical change to a system. Separation of duties requires two different people who can use their combined knowledge to complete a major technical change on a system. For instance, the person who is responsible for modifying the configurations on the firewall should not be the same person who is authorizing those changes; there should be two people for this. This concept prevents a single person from taking over the system or network within an organization.

Sometimes, the human resource and management team suspects an employee is performing unethical or malicious activities on the network. By enforcing *mandatory vacation*, the employee will need to a take leave of absence from the workplace, where they will be unable to access the systems and networks while away. This allows the organizations to determine whether the employee is responsible for unethical or malicious activities on the network.

Lastly, RBAC is a type of access control method that is based on a user's job role and duties within the company. This access control ensures the user has the necessary privileges to perform their job efficiently and nothing more. IT professionals can implement this technical security control within their organization by leveraging the **Group Policy Object (GPO)** role within **Active Directory Domain Service (AD DS)** on Microsoft Windows Server. GPOs allow IT professionals to create security policies by indicating the permissions a user has on a company-owned system. For instance, if you want to prevent all users within the organization from accessing the **Control Panel** area or the **Settings** menu within the Microsoft Windows operating system, using a GPO allows you to configure this restriction and roll out the policy to all domain user accounts on the network. Within the *enterprise* versions of Microsoft Windows, IT professionals can create local GPOs on individual systems that will be applied to any user who logs into the computer.

Defense in Depth and zero trust

While cyber-attacks and threats are increasing each day and the need for cybersecurity professionals and solutions are increasing, organizations are starting to realize there are no prior warnings or indications their company is the next target until it's too late and their systems are compromised. While many organizations are already investing in acquiring cybersecurity solutions such as threat detection and prevention application and security appliances such as firewalls, they also need to understand the importance of implementing a multi-layered approach to improve their defenses against new and emerging threats.

While many organizations think they don't need cybersecurity solutions, hackers target anyone and any organization, despite the size of the company. For instance, if a small, private medical practitioner has a few computers within the office to perform daily business transactions and tasks, consider the network infrastructure that's used to interconnect these systems to share resources. The business may be using a small wired or wireless network; however, does the network have any security features and solutions implemented to prevent external and internal threats?

It's important to understand not all cyber-attacks and threats originate from the internet or externally. However, many organizations think a network-based firewall is enough to protect their assets and safeguard their systems and users from hackers and other threats. The downside is the network-based firewall is simply a single layer of security that can only filter traffic that passes through the device.

The following diagram shows a network-based firewall that's filtering inbound and outbound traffic:

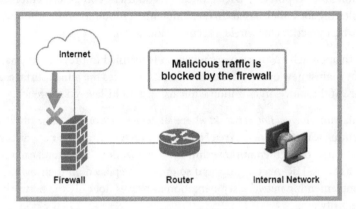

Figure 14.3 – Network-based firewall

While having a network-based firewall implemented between the internet and the internal network, it's important to understand that there are other types of threats and attacks that cannot be prevented or mitigated by a security appliance such as a firewall. What if the organization has a wireless network? Does the wireless router or Access Point use the latest wireless standard and is configured with a complexity password? Are there any unauthorized users who are connected to the wireless network? These are just some of the many questions we need to think about when considering the security of a wireless network.

While some organizations or small businesses think their network or systems do not contain any valuable data, all data is valuable to threat actors. For instance, a small medical practitioner may be using a laptop, computer, or tablet to store patients' information. If a threat actor were to compromise the laptop and steal the patients' data, they may be able to identify many patients and disclose their medical history to the public. As a result, the patients will be the victim because their PHI was stolen due to a lack of security controls, meeting compliance, or a lack of diligence of security of the patients' data by the medical provider. However, the medical provider is also the victim as their systems and networks were compromised by a threat actor.

As you may realize already, a single layer of security is not sufficient. A **Defense in Depth** approach is the concept of implementing multiple layers of security, which is designed to reduce the attack surface that the threat actor can exploit using a vulnerability while improving the security posture of an organization. For instance, rather than implementing only a network-based firewall to protect all the internal assets of an organization, using a Defense in Depth approach, you should implement **Endpoint Detection and Response** (**EDR**) applications on users' computers, enforce inbound and outbound email filtering for email-based threats, implement inbound and outbound web filter for web-based attacks, best practices for wireless security, and so on.

A Defense in Depth approach ensures an organization is fortified to prevent internal and external threats, it's resilient against new cyber-attacks and threats, reduces the attack surface, and improves the security posture of the entire organization while using a multi-layered approach.

While some organizations have a *flat network*, where all devices are on the same physical and logical network, implementing a **Virtual Local Area Network** (**VLAN**) within the network can help create and enforce logical network segmentation within the organization. Therefore, each organizational department, such as Sales, HR, Accounting, and so on, can be placed on their own, unique VLAN on the network. Implementing network segmentation improves not only the network performance but the network security too.

The following diagram shows the concept of VLANs on a network:

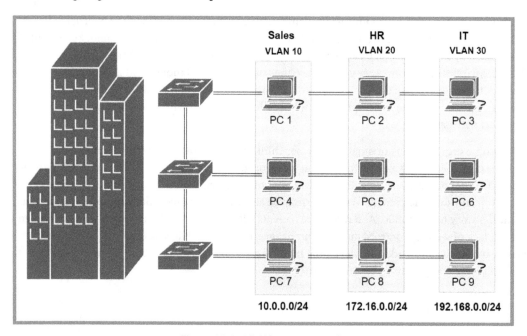

Figure 14.4 – VLANs on a network

As shown in the preceding diagram, there are many devices connected to the same physical network but the devices within their own organizational departments, such as Sales, HR, and IT, are on their own VLAN and IP subnet.

Additionally, many organizations have network-based firewalls that are filtering inbound and outbound traffic between their internal corporate network and the internet. However, the organizations may have a few servers that need to be accessible from users on the internet. Placing the servers on the internal network creates a major security risk as users from the internet will be able to access the internal network, which isn't good. However, creating a **screened subnet**, previously known as a **Demilitarized Zone (DMZ)**, allows security professionals to create a semi-trusted area on their network with strict rules to allow specific users and traffic types into the screened subnet.

The following diagram shows the concept of a screened subnet or DMZ:

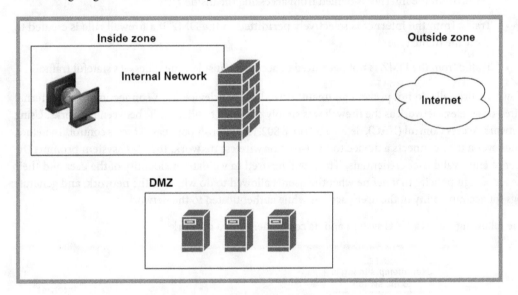

Figure 14.5 – Screened subnet

As shown in the preceding diagram, the screened subnet (or **DMZ**) contains all the publicly accessible servers within the organization, allowing users from the internet to access these systems. When implementing a network-based firewall, it's important to understand the importance of security zones:

- **Inside zone**: The inside zone is a fully trusted zone that has a security level of 100. This security zone is typical of an internal, corporate network, so the firewall will automatically trust all traffic that's originating from the inside zone.

- **Outside zone**: The outside zone is a no-trusted zone with a security level of 0. This security zone is typically a foreign network that is not owned or managed by the organization – it's commonly the internet. Therefore, the firewall will not trust any traffic that originates from the outside zone and simply drop or block the traffic.

- **DMZ**: This is the semi-trusted zone, also known as the *screened subnet*, which typically has a security level of 50.

The security zones and security levels play an important role within the firewall as it determines how traffic is filtered by default between each of the security zones based on the security levels:

- Traffic that originates from a security zone with a higher security level will be allowed to access a security zone with a lower security level

- Traffic that originates from a security zone with a lower security level will be denied from accessing a security zone with a higher security level

- Traffic from the inside zone is allowed to the DMZ and the outside zone

- Traffic from the internet is denied from accessing the inside zone

- Traffic from the internet is selectively permitted to the DMZ if a firewall rule is created to allow the traffic type

- Traffic from the DMZ is not permitted to access the inside zone unless it's stateful traffic

However, firewalls do not prevent an unauthorized user or device from connecting to the internal wired or wireless network as the firewall was simply designed to filter traffic between networks. Using **Network Access Control (NAC)**, defined by **IEEE 802.1X**, enforces port-based access control. Therefore, whenever a user connects a device to the wired or wireless network, the NAC system prompts the user to enter valid user credentials, which will be used to validate the identity of the user and their device, assign policies that define what the user is allowed to do while on the network, and generate logs for accountability of the user's actions while authenticated to the network.

The following shows a NAC system and its components on a network:

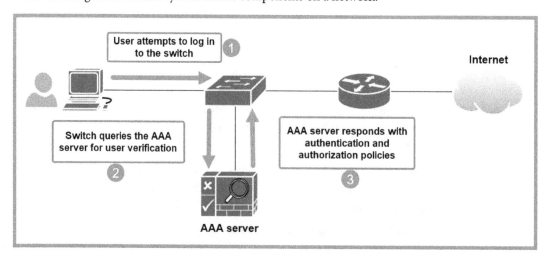

Figure 14.6 – NAC system

As shown in the preceding diagram, three essential components are part of a NAC solution. The supplicant is the client device that is connected to the wired or wireless network. Once the supplicant (computer) is connected to the network, the user will be prompted to enter their user credentials. The authenticator is the network switch, wireless router, or Access Point on the network, which is the intermediary device that allows the supplicant to access the network. The authentication server is the server and performs **Authentication, Authorization, and Accounting (AAA)** on the network. The user credentials, policies, and logs are created on the authentication server.

AAA is a framework that improves network security within an organization. AAA uses the following authentication protocols:

- **Remote Access Dial-In User Service (RADIUS)** is a common, open source AAA server that allows IT professionals to implement AAA within an environment with multi-vendor equipment. RADIUS operates on **UDP port 1812** for authentication and **UDP port 1813** for accounting. Keep in mind that RADIUS does not encrypt the entire packet on the network but only encrypts the password.

- **Terminal Access Controller Access-Control System Plus (TACACS+)** is a Cisco-proprietary authentication server that only operates with Cisco devices. TACACS+ operates on **TCP port 49** and encrypts the entire packet, protecting the data it contains.

Wireless networks that use IEEE 802.1X NAC commonly use **Extensible Authentication Protocol (EAP)**, a network authentication framework that is designed to securely handle the authentication messages between systems over a wireless network. EAP is commonly seen on wireless networks that use **Enterprise** mode with a RADIUS server compared to **Personal** mode with a **Pre-Shared Key (PSK)**.

The following are variations of EAP:

- **EAP Flexible Authentication via Secure Tunneling (EAP-FAST)**: This version of EAP was developed by Cisco as a replacement for the **Lightweight EAP (LEAP)** version, which was implemented in wireless networks that used the **Wired Equivalent Privacy (WEP)** security standard. EAP-FAST uses a **Protected Access Credential (PAC)** to handle the authentication process. PAC is similar to using a secure cookie between a web server and web browser; it's stored locally on the client that's being authenticated to the network and is used by the client to validate their authenticity to the system.

- **EAP Transport Layer Security (EAP-TLS)**: This uses TLS to provide stronger security on a network. EAP-TLS supports *mutual authentication*, such that both a client and server authenticate to each other, whereby both the client and server exchange digital certificates to validate their identities to each other.

- **EAP Tunnel Transport Layer Security (EAP-TTLS)**: This is a version of EAP that supports TLS tunneling for transporting messages between systems over a network. In EAP-TTLS, only the server needs a digital certificate, unlike in EAP-TLS, where both the client and server use certificates.

- **Protected EAP (PEAP)**: This version of EAP encapsulates EAP messages inside a TLS tunnel.

While NAC solutions are designed to enforce port-based access control to wired and wireless networks, companies add the following types of controls within their network to improve the network security while creating a Defense in Depth approach:

- **Technical controls**: These are the electronic and digital systems that are implemented to prevent unauthorized activities.

- **Administrative controls**: These are the security policies that are created and implemented within a company that is designed to manage how employees interact with the organization's systems. These administrative controls are usually in the form of security policies and procedures, human resource policies, and standard operating procedures.

- **Physical controls**: These are the physical objectives and controls such as doors, locks, fences, security guards, and so on that are used to secure a physical location such as a building or data center.

Furthermore, some organizations implement a **honeypot**, which is a type of computer system that is configured and implemented on a network to catch or trick threat actors into thinking it's a real system. A honeypot intends to lure attackers using a decoy such as mimicking a real production system on the network. When the attacker attempts to compromise and exploit the honeypot, cybersecurity professionals capture the data that's generated from specialized security monitoring tools on the honeypot, which indicates the attacker's action – that is, what the person is trying to do.

The data collected from a honeypot provides insights into the following:

- The source of the attacker

- The severity of the threat and cyber-attack

- What type of tools the attacker is using

- If your security solutions are capable of preventing the threat or cyber-attack

By implementing Defense in Depth within organizations, they can move closer to creating a **zero-trust** network. Zero trust simply focuses on not trusting anything or anyone until it's properly authenticated on the network. Can you imagine the security risks that are involved when a user connects their mobile device to a company's network? If the company's network does not support AAA or does not have any threat detection and prevention systems, malware on the user's device can spread onto the network and compromise the critical servers.

Having completed this section, you have learned about various network security concepts, such as the importance of the CIA triad, various types of threats and threat actors, and the importance of Defense in Depth. Next, you will explore various authentication methods that can be implemented on a network.

Exploring authentication methods

As humans, we can simply look at someone and recognize whether a person is a relative, friend, colleague, stranger, or foe. The human mind allows us to retain memories that contain details about what we see each day, such as recognizing a co-worker entering the office building each morning and greeting you. Likewise, security guards, who are present at various entry points on a compound or building, validate whether a person is an employee or a customer. Eventually, the security guards will become familiar with the employees of an organization and recognize their faces quickly.

Computer systems and their technologies are continuously advancing to help improve the lives of many people around the world while helping organizations improve their business operations and automation. Since many organizations rely strongly on computers to help perform many business processes and procedures, IT professionals need to ensure authorized people are using company-owned systems. For instance, what if an unauthorized user within the organization gained access to a computer system that is responsible for the **Heating, Ventilation, and Air Conditioning** (HVAC) system for the data center? What will the impact be if the user shuts down the cooling system?

Computer systems are different from the human mind and need processes to determine and validate the identity of a user before allowing them to access the resources of the system. By implementing authentication, IT professionals can configure various key elements that are used to identify a valid user on the system, such as a username and password combination. Whenever a user attempts to access the system, they are prompted to enter something that is known only to the valid user onto the system, such as a valid username and password. If the user credentials are correct, the system allows the user to access the resources. However, if the user credentials are inaccurate, the system restricts access and does not trust the user. You can think of authentication as a set of processes that are used by a system to validate the identity of a user.

Authentication plays an important role in computer systems in today's world, especially with the continuous increase in cybercrime that's happening each day. It has become an industry norm to ensure authentication is enabled on all systems within organizations, simply to reduce the risk of an unauthorized user gaining access to a system.

The following are various authentication factors:

- **Something you are**: A user can prove their identity to a system by using biometrics such as their fingerprint, facial recognition, voice, and iris and retina scanning.

- **Something you have**: A user can provide a security token such as a smart card or a USB token such as a *Yubikey*. Additionally, the system that the user is attempting to access can send an SMS message that contains a unique authentication code that can be used once by the user.

- **Something you know**: This can be a password, passphrase, **Personal Identification Number** (**PIN**), or even a series of patterns such as those on the locked screen of a smartphone.

- **Somewhere you are**: Systems allow a user to validate their identity via their geo-location. So, when a user is attempting to log into a system, the source IP address and/or **Global Positioning System (GPS)** location is used as an additional attribute.

- **Something you do**: This is an attribute that's personal to the user, such as their typing and handwriting patterns.

Typically, when a person acquires a new computer, laptop, or smartphone, they will enable authentication to ensure an unauthorized user is unable to access the contents and resources on the device. Similarly, network professionals will configure a local user account with a password to restrict unauthorized users from accessing their networking devices. Since the user account is created locally on the computer or networking device, whenever a user wants to access the system, they will need to enter their user credentials, which are checked against the local database. This database determines whether the account is valid. This method is commonly referred to as **local authentication** as the user credentials are created on the local system only.

If the same user attempts to log into another computer or a networking device, a valid user account needs to be created on the other systems too. The benefit of using local authentication is the computer system can quickly query its local database to determine whether the username and password combination exists or not. However, the downside is that the user account needs to exist on each system that the user needs access to. Therefore, if the user credential is changed on one device, it must be changed on all devices. Using AAA with NAC allows network professionals to implement a centralized authentication server that's running RADIUS, allowing networking devices to query the authentication server whenever a user attempts to log into a system.

Next, you will learn about the importance of implementing **multi-factor authentication (MFA)** on systems to prevent unauthorized users from gaining access to systems and accounts.

Multi-factor authentication

Creating a user account on a computer or an online website is quite simple; fill in some identification details and create a username (identity) and password. Whenever you're attempting to log into your online account, you'll be prompted to enter your username and password. Once the user credentials match on the system, you're authenticated. It's that simple. However, configuring only a password, passphrase, or pin is one factor that's used to validate your identity to the system. Simply put, if a hacker wants to compromise your email account, they can easily determine your username by looking at your email address. Then, the hacker will simply need to determine your password for the account. Once the password is retrieved, the hacker can access your account.

MFA is the concept of enabling additional layers of security on a user account to prevent hackers from performing account takeovers. With MFA implemented, a user will need to provide two or more authentication factors during the authentication process before the system allows the user access. For instance, when logging into your online email account, the website prompts you to enter your email address or username, as shown in the following screenshot:

Figure 14.7 – Google sign-in page

Next, the system prompts you to enter your password/passphrase to validate whether you're the authorized user for the account, as shown in the following screenshot:

Figure 14.8 – Password page

If you've configured MFA, the system will prompt you to use the additional factor next. In this example, I'm using a physical security token and received the following prompt to insert the USB device:

Figure 14.9 – Additional security

With MFA enabled on a system, a user must enter more than one factor to prove their identity. This means that if a username and password of a victim are known to a hacker, the hacker is less likely to compromise the user account if MFA is turned on. Many people are also using authenticator apps on their mobile devices where the authentication code is changed every 20 to 30 seconds. Therefore, if a hacker wants to access an online account with MFA enabled that uses an authenticator code, the hacker will need to use a unique code from the app.

Kerberos, single sign-on, and LDAP

Kerberos is a network authentication that is commonly implemented on Microsoft Windows operating systems and allows client devices such as computers to authenticate to a Domain Controller on a network. Microsoft Windows Server supports the **Active Directory Domain Service (AD DS)** role, which allows an IT professional to create a logical security domain. This allows IT professionals to centrally manage the security privileges of all users, groups, and devices that belong to the domain.

Important note

Active Directory allows IT professionals to create users, groups, and computer accounts on Windows Server. This allows IT professionals to centrally manage the security of devices and assign policies to users on the domain.

Kerberos allows users on a Microsoft environment to authenticate once on the domain and access all the resources without the need to re-enter their user credentials whenever they need access to a new resource. This concept is commonly referred to as **single sign-on (SSO)**. Additionally, SSO is commonly implemented on various online platforms. For instance, when a user logs into their Google account on the internet, the user can access all of Google's products and services without having to register or re-authenticate when accessing other services from Google.

To get a better idea of how Kerberos works, let's look at the three main components that all need to work together to ensure Kerberos provides SSO to users and systems on the network:

- **Client**: This is the user who logs into their client computer using their domain user credentials.

- **Key Distribution Center (KDC)**: The KDC is the Microsoft Windows server that is running the Active Directory role and services. It's the Domain Controller.

- **Application server**: The application server is simply a server that is providing a resource or service to users on the domain/network.

When a person enters their user credentials on a client computer that's connected to a domain, the client computer converts the password into a **New Technology LAN Manager (NTLM)** version 2 hash. Then, it sends both the username and the NTLMv2 hash of the password within a **Lightweight Directory Access Protocol (LDAP)** packet to the Domain Controller. As you may recall, LDAP is a common network protocol that is used to perform operations such as read, write, and query, on a directory server for records. A common directory server is a Windows Server that is running the Active Directory role.

The following steps outline the Kerberos process:

1. The user enters their credentials on their client's computer. The username and NTLMv2 hash of the password are sent across the network in an LDAP packet to the KDC:

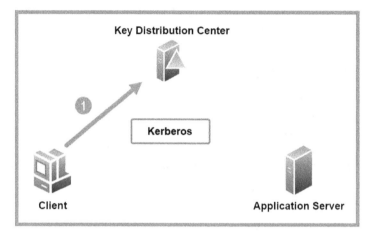

Figure 14.10 – Kerberos phase 1

2. Next, the **krbtgt** account is a local account that's automatically created on the KDC. It is responsible for creating and sending an encrypted and signed **Ticket Granting Ticket** (**TGT**) to the client:

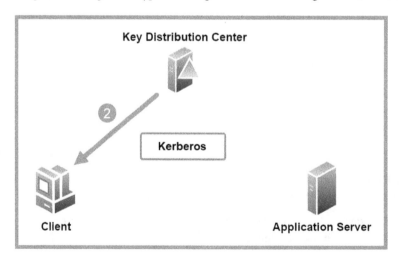

Figure 14.11 – Kerberos phase 2

3. The client keeps the TGT until the user is ready to access a resource such as the application server on the domain. The client sends the TGT to the KDC to request a **Ticket Granting Service** (**TGS**) ticket:

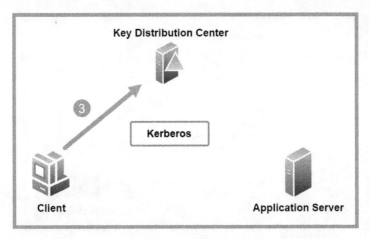

Figure 14.12 – Kerberos phase 3

4.   Next, the KDC uses the service's NTLM hash to encrypt the TGS and sends the TGS to the client:

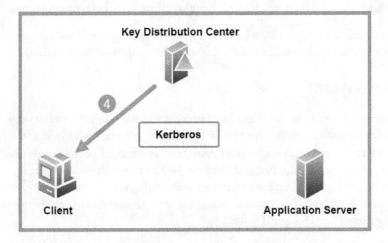

Figure 14.13 – Kerberos phase 4

5.   When the client computer connects to the application server on the domain, it provides the TGS ticket to access the services and resources on the server:

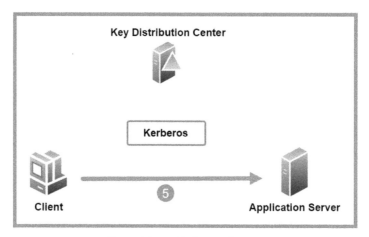

Figure 14.14 – Kerberos phase 5

As you have seen in the preceding phases, the user authenticates only once to the Windows domain using Kerberos with SSO and does not need to re-authenticate to access resources on the domain.

Having completed this section, you have learned about authentication methods on networks. Next, you will discover risk management techniques that are commonly used by organizations.

Risk management

Each day, people make decisions to mitigate and prevent various types of risks in their daily lives, workplaces, and organizations. In this context of network security, risk is defined as the likelihood/possibility that a threat actor can cause harm or damage to a system. IT professionals must be able to identify the assets that could be attacked and compromised by cyber-attacks and threats. As you may recall, assets are simply anything that has value to an organization and are usually tangible, intangible, and people (employees). By identifying the assets, security professionals will get a better idea of what needs to be safeguarded from potential threats.

Furthermore, IT professionals need to identify the various types of threats and threat actors and how they can potentially compromise the assets of the organization. A hacker will commonly perform reconnaissance to collect a lot of information about their target before launching an attack. The information that's collected is used to create a profile about the target and determine the technical infrastructure of the target. Sometimes, during the reconnaissance phase, the threat actor may discover exposed security vulnerabilities that can be exploited. However, the hacker usually proceeds to perform various types of scanning to determine if additional security vulnerabilities exist on devices that belong to the target. A large number of vulnerabilities found during the reconnaissance and scanning phases is an indication of a large attack surface.

From a cybersecurity perspective, each vulnerability found on a system has a severity score/rating that is determined by vulnerability assessment tools using the **CVSS calculator**. The CVSS calculator allows cybersecurity professionals to determine the vulnerability score for any security weaknesses or flaws found on a system, helping cybersecurity professionals prioritize their focus on high-risk vulnerabilities that can have a huge impact if exploited compared to low-risk vulnerabilities. The vulnerability score provided by the CVSS calculator is acceptable within the cybersecurity industry among professionals and organizations.

Overall, the main objective of risk management is to implement processes, procedures, and controls to reduce the security risks that can impact or compromise the assets of a company.

> **Important note**
> The CVSS 3.1 calculator can be found at `https://www.first.org/cvss/calculator/3.1` and `https://nvd.nist.gov/vuln-metrics/cvss/v3-calculator`.

The following are common risk response techniques:

- **Avoidance**: This technique focuses on stopping all activities that are creating risk within the organization.
- **Transference**: This technique involves contacting a third-party vendor such as a **Managed Security Service Provider** (**MSSP**) to both handle and manage the security risk on behalf of the organization.
- **Acceptance**: The organization understands its mission-critical processes and procedures that create risk. Without them, the organization cannot operate and accepts the risks.
- **Mitigation**: The organization implements various security controls to prevent the occurrence of risks.

Next, you will explore the importance of regular security risk assessments within organizations.

Security risk assessments

A **security risk assessment** helps organizations identify, assess, and even implement various security controls that are designed to prevent and resolve security vulnerabilities on their systems and networks. Can you imagine if organizations never performed security risk assessments on their infrastructure? There would be a lot of hidden security flaws in their applications, systems, and networks that can be exploited by hackers. For instance, many organizations around the world don't realize their systems have been compromised until a few months have passed. This is why there's a need for regular security risk assessments – to determine the current security posture with a gap analysis to indicate whether the number of security risks is reducing after each assessment and implementation of security controls.

Threat assessments allow cybersecurity professionals to research new, existing, and emerging threats in the industry to determine the future of cyber-attacks and the intention of threat actors. Since each type of threat actor has a unique motive for their attacks, it is important to understand their mindset and the type of tools being used to perform those attacks on targets. For instance, data is the most valuable asset to any organization, and it's found everywhere. Understanding the strategies and tools that are used by hackers allows cybersecurity professionals to use the same tools and techniques with the intent to discover security vulnerabilities on their company's systems, and then implement security controls to prevent a real cyber-attack from occurring. This involves taking a proactive approach to improving the security posture of the organization from threats.

The following are additional types of threats that can affect organizations:

- **Environmental**: These types of threats are natural and sometimes occur without any prior warning. Environmental threats include natural disasters such as flooding, hurricanes or cyclones, earthquakes, and so on.

- **Man-made**: These types of threats are created by people such as a disgruntled employee who wants to cause harm to the organization by destroying the data stored on the company's servers or disrupting the availability of network services and resources.

- **External**: These are threats that can originate from outside of the organization, such as a hacker or group of hackers launching a DDoS attack on the organization's web server on the internet.

A **vulnerability assessment** helps organizations identify the security vulnerabilities that exist on a system and determine their risk level. Since a security vulnerability is defined as the security weakness or flaw in a system that can be exploited by a threat actor such as a hacker, IT professionals must quickly discover these flaws and resolve them before a real hacker compromises their company. Additionally, vulnerability assessment tools help cybersecurity professionals test for specific vulnerabilities and help ensure systems are compliant with various industry security frameworks and standards. For instance, systems that are used to process payment cards must be **Payment Card Industry Data Security Standard (PCI DSS)**-compliant to ensure these systems meet the minimum level of security for data protection. Vulnerability assessments and tools assist in checking for compliance.

The following are common vulnerabilities in systems:

- **Default settings**: These are systems and devices that are deployed on a network using the same configurations as they had when they left the manufacturer.

- **Weak encryption**: These are systems that use insecure encryption technologies that allow a threat actor to gain unauthorized access to the system and data.

- **Unsecure protocols**: Unsecure protocols are network and application protocols that do not provide security features such as encryption to ensure privacy between the client and the server.

- **Open permission**: These are the full permissions of files and folders that are given to everyone, which can lead to security risks from users on the network.

- **Unsecure root accounts**: These are root accounts on Linux-based systems that do not contain complex passwords that are easy to compromise. Since root accounts are created on Linux-based systems, they're often used to discover *unsecure administrator accounts* on Windows-based systems that are vulnerable to account takeovers due to weak passwords.

- **Open ports and services**: Many unnecessary services run on a system. Some services may open a service port to allow inbound connections from a remote system. Then, a threat actor can launch a remote exploit across the network to take advantage of the vulnerable service on a target system.

Penetration testing is the technique used by authorized cybersecurity professionals with legal permission to simulate a real-world cyber-attack on the systems and networks that belong to an organization, using the same techniques and tools used by real hackers with the intent to discover hidden security vulnerabilities. At the end of a penetration test, the cybersecurity professional submits both an executive and technical report to the organization with details of any security vulnerabilities that were found during the time of the security assessment, from most critical to least. This will include details on how a real hacker will be able to compromise the vulnerabilities, and recommendations on how to prevent and mitigate the security risk.

Organizations use a penetration testing report to improve the security posture of their systems and networks that were tested by applying patches and updates, closing unused service ports, disabling unnecessary services, improving device configurations, and using secure network protocols for communication. It's important to perform continuous testing on systems and networks within companies to ensure all backdoors and security flaws are fixed before a real hacker compromises them.

Posture assessment helps organizations determine the security risks on mobile devices that are connecting to the corporate network. For instance, an organization with a **Bring Your Own Device (BYOD)** policy may be allowing their employees to connect their devices, such as smartphones, tablets, and laptops, to the company's wireless network. Since these personal devices are not managed by the organization's IT team, there's no way IT professionals can regularly implement operating systems and security updates on these devices.

Therefore, network and security professionals commonly implement security solutions such as the Cisco **Identity Services Engine** (**ISE**) to help determine the security posture of any connected device. The posture assessment checks each device to determine if it is trusted, whether the operating system is up to date, whether the device has an antimalware application, and the type of operating system. If the device has not been through the posture assessment, it is assigned to an isolated logical network, preventing the user and device from accessing the resources on the network.

> **Important note**
> **Process assessment** focuses on examining the existing business processes and procedures within the organization. This helps determine whether these processes are performing optimally with the expenses associated with each process to achieve the expected quality and goals.

Vendor assessment focuses on understanding and reducing the risks that are involved in working with a third-party vendor such as a service provider. There are many security concerns, such as whether the vendor has certified professionals to work on your equipment such as networking devices, security appliances, and servers within your organization. Additionally, it checks whether the vendor has a privacy policy for protecting their customer's data and whether the vendor is meeting various industry compliance and standards. For instance, an engineer may be required to be certified in a specific information security certification before working on systems that are designed to protect data. Important organizations screen each vendor and ensure they meet all the requirements before conducting any business.

In this section, you learned about various security risk assessment types and how they can be used to help organizations to identify and reduce security vulnerabilities.

Summary

In this chapter, you learned about the CIA triad and how network professionals can use it to improve data security within their organizations. Additionally, you learned about various types of security risks and threats that can cause harm to systems and networks in many companies. Furthermore, you discovered various types of authentication methods and how they can be used to reduce account takeovers while preventing unauthorized access to systems.

I hope this chapter has been informative for you and is helpful in your journey toward learning networking and becoming a network professional. In the next chapter, *Chapter 15, Exploring Cyberattacks and Threats*, you will learn about various types of attacks and threats, as well as how to identify them.

Questions

The following is a short list of review questions to help reinforce your learning and help you identify areas that may require some improvement:

1. Which of the following is responsible for ensuring authorized users have access to data?

    A. Availability

    B. Integrity

    C. Confidentiality

    D. All of the above

2. Which of the following prevents users from accessing a web server on the internet?

    A. Ransomware

    B. Black hat

    C. Trojan

    D. DDoS

3. Which of the following allows a hacker to exploit and compromise a system before the vendor can resolve the issue?

    A. Zero-day

    B. Day one attack

    C. Exploit

    D. Ransomware

4. Which of the following malware does not have a signature and runs in memory?

    A. Rootkit

    B. Fileless virus

    C. Boot sector virus

    D. Polymorphic virus

5. Which of the following best describes an employee who uses hacking skills to cause damage to the organization's systems?

    A. APT

    B. Hacktivist

    C. Black hat

    D. Insider

6. Which of the following allows network professionals to create logically isolated networks using their existing physical network infrastructure?

    A. Implementing routers

    B. Implementing switches

    C. Implementing VLANs

    D. Implementing bridges

7. Which of the following frameworks is associated with port-based access control?

    A. IEEE 802.1Q

    B. IEEE 802.1D

    C. IEEE 802.1w

    D. IEEE 802.1X

8. Which of the following is an open network authentication protocol that works with mixed-vendor equipment?

    A. RADIUS

    B. SSO

    C. TACACS+

    D. Kerberos

9. Which of the authentication methods grants a ticket to a user, allowing to user to provide the ticket to any server on the network to access its resource?

    A. RADIUS

    B. SSO

    C. TACACS+

    D. Kerberos

10. Which of the following checks whether a device has met all the security requirements before it's allowed access to the network resources and services?

    A. Vulnerability assessment

    B. Posture assessment

    C. Process assessment

    D. Threat assessment

Further reading

To learn more about the topics that were covered in this chapter, check out the following links:

- *What is the CIA Triad?*: https://www.fortinet.com/resources/cyberglossary/cia-triad

- *Cyber Security Threats*: https://www.imperva.com/learn/application-security/cyber-security-threats/

- *Zero Trust Security Explained: Principles of the Zero Trust Model*: https://www.crowdstrike.com/cybersecurity-101/zero-trust-security/

- *Use these 6 user authentication types to secure networks*: https://www.techtarget.com/searchsecurity/tip/Use-these-6-user-authentication-types-to-secure-networks

- *What is risk management and why is it important?* https://www.techtarget.com/searchsecurity/definition/What-is-risk-management-and-why-is-it-important

15

Exploring Cyberattacks and Threats

As an aspiring network professional, it's essential to understand the fundamentals of various types of cyberattacks, how they are performed by hackers, and the goal of the attack on a target. Security has become everyone's concern, whether you're beginning a career in the field of IT or already a seasoned professional. Each day, hackers are exploiting systems within organizations around the world and cybersecurity professionals are working continuously to create a proactive approach to prevent these attacks and stop hackers. Hence, network professionals, who are the architects of designing, implementing, and maintaining network infrastructure, also need to have a foundation in security threats and attacks.

In this chapter, you will learn how various types of network-based attacks are performed by threat actors and their impact on the confidentiality, integrity, and availability of systems and resources. Additionally, you will learn how hackers can perform wireless-based attacks to compromise both personal and enterprise wireless networks. Lastly, you will learn how threat actors can hack the human minds of their victims to trick them into revealing sensitive information.

In this chapter, we will cover the following topics:

- Exploring network-based attacks
- Understanding wireless attacks
- Delving into human and environmental attacks

Let's dive in!

Exploring network-based attacks

Threat actors such as hackers always look for security vulnerabilities in the systems and networks of their targets. A seasoned hacker will attempt to compromise the *low-hanging fruits*, as these are the security flaws that are easy to exploit on a system and do not require too much complexity in setting up the attack. Quite often, many people think security vulnerabilities are found only on applications and operating systems, but not on the network and its protocols. In the early days of the internet, many networking protocols were not designed with security features since it was not a concern as it is in today's world. Many of these unsecure network protocols make up the **Transmission Control Protocol/Internet Protocol** (**TCP/IP**) networking model, which is implemented on every device that's connected to a network. Therefore, the TCP/IP networking model contains a lot of vulnerabilities that can easily be exploited by hackers on a network, allowing them to perform various types of network-based attacks.

In this section, you will explore various types of network-based attacks that are common within the cybersecurity and networking industry.

Denial of service

A **Denial-of-Service** (**DoS**) attack is a common network-based attack that exploits the vulnerabilities within TCP/IP. This allows an attacker to compromise the availability of a network service or resource, thus preventing access to the resource from legitimate users on the network. For instance, imagine an organization has a web server on the internet that's hosting an e-commerce application that allows the company to sell its products to anyone online. Each potential customer uses the web browser on their computer to send an HTTP request message to the e-commerce web server, instructing the server to send its home page to the client. For each HTTP request message that is received on the server, computing resources such as CPU, memory, storage, and network bandwidth are allocated to process and respond to the user.

As more users send HTTP request messages to the server, the server allocates available computing resources to quickly process and respond to each message. If a hacker sends thousands of unsolicited HTTP request messages to the server, the server will continue to allocate any available computing resources to process each message. Simply put, the CPU and memory utilization will increase quickly, causing the server to be occupied with processing the bogus requests from the hacker and not responding to legitimate requests from the potential customers on the network. Overall, as this malicious activity continues, the server will eventually stop responding to any request message because it's too busy processing a huge amount of unsolicited messages, therefore denying legitimate users access to the services provided by the server.

The following diagram displays a hacker performing a DoS attack on a single server:

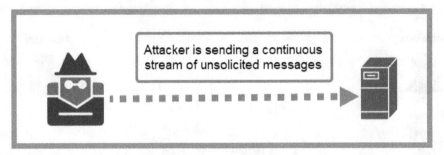

Figure 15.1 – DoS attack

As shown in the preceding diagram, the source of the attack is originating from a single geographic location – this is typically a single source IP address. Therefore, cybersecurity professionals can easily identify the source of the traffic by inspecting the source IP address within the IP header of the packet, then implementing an **Access Control List** (**ACL**) to restrict traffic. This ACL can be implemented on the edge router or firewall on the organization's perimeter network.

Launching a single DoS attack against a target can easily be mitigated. Additionally, the goal of performing a DoS attack is to ensure the target resources or services are unavailable to legit users. Sometimes, an organization may implement various technologies to ensure its critical servers are resilient against failures and cyberattacks. Therefore, a network and server may continue to provide services and resources to legitimate users while being under a DoS attack. In this situation, the threat actor will soon realize their attack is not creating a major impact, as expected, and that the target is still up and running.

However, if a group of hackers from different geographic locations all coordinate and launch a DoS attack on the same target, this is commonly referred to as a **Distributed Denial-of-Service** (**DDoS**) attack. A DDoS is an amplified version of a DoS attack as it originates from multiple, different geographic locations at the same time, and it is quite difficult to stop. While a cybersecurity professional will be able to determine the security incident that's happening, blocking all the source IP addresses can be quite challenging as there can be hundreds or even thousands of source IP addresses.

The following diagram shows a DDoS attack being performed against a single target:

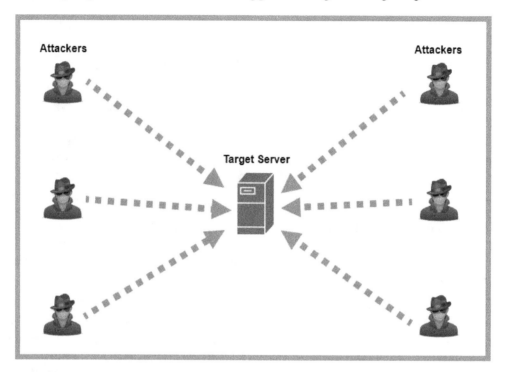

Figure 15.2 – DDoS attack

Sometimes, organizations are unable to stop or mitigate a massive DDoS attack and have to resort to disconnecting the affected server. This means disconnecting the affected server from the internet for a while before re-connecting it again. Hence, it is important to implement next-generation firewalls and internet security solutions with the capabilities of detecting and mitigating these attacks.

However, keep in mind that many seasoned hackers will attempt to fake their identity by changing their real source IP address to a fake IP address; this is known as **IP spoofing**. This technique is commonly used by hackers to prevent their real location or IP address from being known by cybersecurity professionals and law enforcement.

The following diagram shows an attacker who is spoofing their IP address:

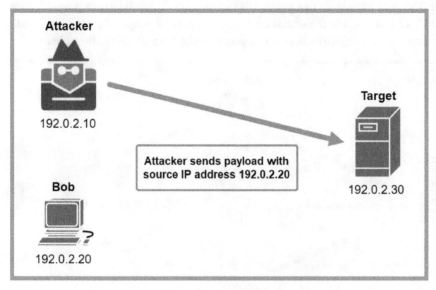

Figure 15.3 – IP spoofing

Hackers commonly use IP spoofing to perform a **Reflected DDoS** attack on their target. In a Reflected DDoS attack, the hackers spoof the target's IP address and set it as their own, then use the spoofed IP address to flood unsolicited packets to a public server such as a **Domain Name System (DNS)** server, which commonly responds to DNS query messages. When the public server receives unsolicited packets from the hackers, it will respond to the spoofed IP address that belongs to the actual target.

The following diagram shows a Reflected DDoS attack:

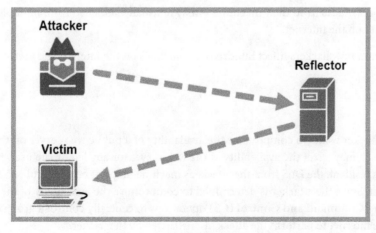

Figure 15.4 – Reflected DDoS attack

As shown in the preceding diagram, a threat actor has spoofed the IP address of the target server, then sent lots of DNS query messages to a public DNS server that responds to each query. The responses from the DNS server are sent to the actual target machine, thus creating a reflected attack. Additionally, hackers can use multiple reflectors to create an **Amplified DDoS** attack, as shown here:

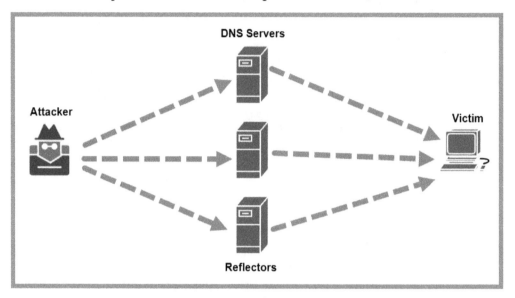

Figure 15.5 – Amplified DDoS attack

As shown in the preceding diagram, an infected machine is sending multiple request messages to multiple public servers on the internet. Each public server will respond to the spoofed IP address, so all the responses are sent to the target machine. Hackers do not necessarily choose one specific attack; they can use a combination or chain of attacks to compromise their targets. Most commonly, hackers do not launch DoS attacks from their machines – they're usually launched from multiple malware-infected machines on the internet.

Next, you will learn how hackers infect hundreds of machines on the internet and create an army of infected systems.

Botnets

Let's imagine a hacker wants to compromise the availability of a public web server on the internet. Using a DoS attack may affect the availability of the web server for any legitimate user. However, if the web server is resilient, the DoS from the attacker's machine may not be powerful enough to have a massive impact. Since the attacker is determined to compromise the availability of the target, the hacker can set up **Command and Control (C2)** operations to centrally control a group of infected machines on the internet to perform the attack, as instructed by the hacker.

When setting up C2 operations, the hacker will need to infect as many systems as possible on the internet with a bot. A **bot** is simply a type of malware that infects a system such as a computer or a server, allowing the hacker to take control and instruct the compromised system to perform malicious actions on other systems, making it a *zombie*. Typically, a hacker can compromise and install malware on trusted and popular web servers on the internet. Whenever an unaware user visits any of these malware-infected servers with their device, the bot is downloaded and installed on the user's machine. As more systems become infected with bots, it creates a huge network of infected systems known as a **botnet**, which is centrally managed by the hacker using a C2 server.

The following diagram shows a botnet that is being managed by a single hacker on the internet:

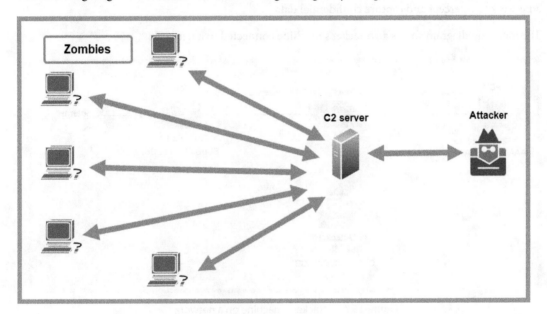

Figure 15.6 – Botnet

As shown in the preceding diagram, the botnet is metaphorically a robot army that awaits the instructions from the C2 server that is managed by the hacker. Whenever the hacker wants to launch a DDoS attack against a public server, the hacker connects to the C2 server and sends the instructions (commands). The C2 server will forward these instructions to any bot that lives on the internet, and they will execute the instructions and perform the attack on the target.

Next, you will learn about a Layer 2 attack that is commonly used by hackers, mostly on internal networks, to intercept data on unsecure communication channels.

On-path attack

An **on-path attack** or **Man-in-the-Middle (MiTM)** attack is a common network-based attack that occurs on an internal network within an organization. A hacker uses an on-path attack to intercept traffic over a communication channel, such as a wired or wireless network, to capture sensitive or confidential information that's transmitted over the network. As you have learned thus far, many networking protocols are responsible for communication between systems over a network. However, many common unsecure network protocols are used on modern networks. Unsecure network protocols do not provide data security features such as data encryption when transmitting a message over a network. This creates an opportunity for a threat actor who has gained unauthorized access to a network to intercept and capture confidential data.

The following diagram shows an attacker's machine connected to a network:

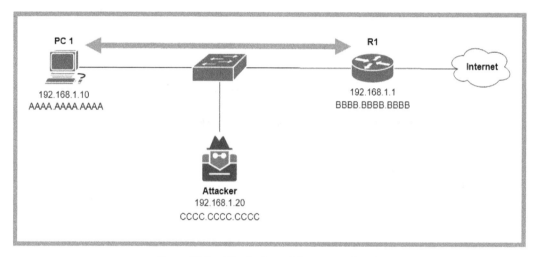

Figure 15.7 – Attacker's machine on a network

As shown in the preceding diagram, the attacker's machine is connected to the same network switch as PC 1 and the router. If PC 1 has to forward traffic to the internet, the traffic is sent to the switch and then to the router. The switch inspects the destination **Media Access Control** (**MAC**) address within the frame header, then forwards the message directly to the router. For the attacker's machine to intercept the traffic between PC 1 and the router, the attacker will need to exploit the security vulnerabilities within the **Address Resolution Protocol** (**ARP**).

> **Important note**
>
> ARP is a common network protocol that allows systems to resolve IP addresses to MAC addresses.

The attacker needs to perform ARP poisoning on the ARP caches on PC 1 and the router by sending gratuitous ARP messages to both devices. For instance, the attacker machines send gratuitous ARP messages to PC 1, which contain the IP address of the router and the MAC address of the attacker's machine. This technique poisons the ARP cache of PC 1 into thinking the router is now associated with the MAC address of the attacker's machine. Therefore, if PC 1 has to send any packets to the router, it will insert the attacker's MAC address as the destination's MAC address within the packet. Once the packet leaves PC 1 and is received by the switch on the network, the switch will then forward the packet to the attacker's machine.

Additionally, the attacker sends gratuitous ARP messages to the router to poison its ARP cache. The attacker machine creates gratuitous ARP messages that contain the IP address of PC 1 and the MAC address of the attacker's machine. Once the router receives and processes these messages, the router's ARP cache will automatically update to associate the attacker's MAC address with the IP address of PC 1. Therefore, many packets from the router to PC 1 will be sent to the attacker's machine on the network, hence allowing the attacker's machine to intercept bi-directional communication between PC 1 and the router.

The following are the technical phases during an on-path attack in a network:

1. The attacker machine is connected to the network but does not intercept the packets between PC 1 and the router, as shown here:

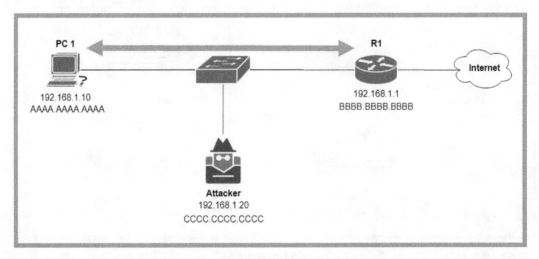

Figure 15.8 – Phase 1

2. The attacker machine sends a gratuitous ARP message to both PC 1 and the router that contains false IP-to-MAC address information. The attacker machine sends a gratuitous ARP message to PC 1 with `192.168.1.1 -> CC-CC-CC-CC-CC-CC` and to the router with `192.168.1.10 -> CC-CC-CC-CC-CC-CC`, as shown here:

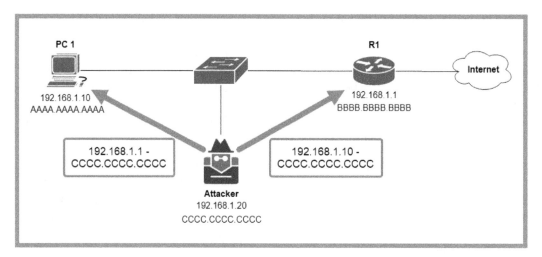

Figure 15.9 – Phase 2

3. Once the ARP caches on both PC 1 and the router have been poisoned with false information, whenever they forward messages to each other, the messages are sent to the attacker's machine, as shown here:

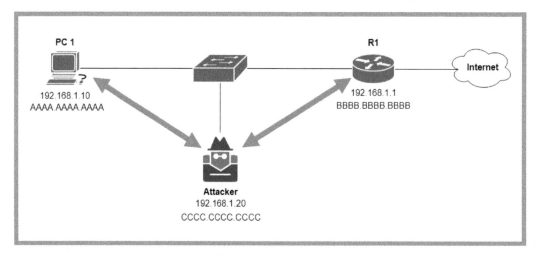

Figure 15.10 – Phase 3

4. Lastly, the attacker machine is also configured to forward messages between PC 1 and the router to reduce the likelihood of the messages being intercepted by a hacker on the network.

Network professionals can configure the **Dynamic ARP Inspection** (**DAI**) security feature on supported network switches to prevent on-path attacks and prevent devices from sending fake ARP messages on the network. DAI is a Layer 2 security mechanism on network switches that prevents hackers from spoofing their MAC address and performing on-path attacks. With DAI enabled on a Layer 2 network, only legitimate ARP requests and responses are permitted on the network.

DNS-based attack

DNS is a common network protocol that allows devices to resolve a **Fully Qualified Domain Name (FQDN)** or hostname to an IP address. As you already know, each device on a network has an IP address that allows end-to-end communication between hosts. For instance, if you want to visit www. cisco.com using your computer, a DNS query is sent to your preferred DNS server to request the IP address of the domain name. If the DNS server has the record, it responds to your computer with the IP address of www.cisco.com. Once your computer has the IP address of Cisco's web server, it will insert the IP address as the destination address of the packet.

The following diagram shows the sequence of events during a DNS query:

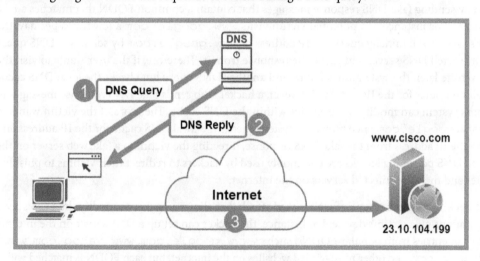

Figure 15.11 – DNS query

Imagine if you needed to remember the IP addresses of each web server on the internet that you wanted to visit; it would be quite challenging to remember these logical addresses. However, DNS servers are like online directory servers that contain a list of well-known domain names and their associated IP addresses. Therefore, your computer does not need a long list of hostname-to-IP address entries stored in a file on the local drive, which requires frequent updates for any changes to be made on the internet. Rather, you can configure your computer to send all its DNS query messages to a trusted, online DNS server on the internet.

The following are some examples of trusted DNS servers on the internet:

- **Cloudflare DNS**: https://1.1.1.1/
- **Quad9 DNS**: https://www.quad9.net/

- **Cisco's OpenDNS**: `https://www.opendns.com/`
- **Google Public DNS**: `https://developers.google.com/speed/public-dns`

Imagine that a DNS server has been misconfigured with default configurations, a weak password, or maybe the underlying operating system contains known security vulnerabilities and a hacker can exploit those security flaws and gain control of the DNS server. The hacker can perform various types of DNS-based attacks, such as the following:

- DNS poisoning
- DNS hijacking
- Domain hijacking

DNS poisoning is a type of attack that allows the hacker to modify the DNS cache on their victims' system by sending fake DNS response messages that contain a common FQDN that matches a fake IP address. For instance, if a potential victim visits `www.google.com` a few times per day, the victim's system will initially query the IP address of `www.google.com` by sending a DNS query to their trusted DNS server and cache the response from it. Therefore, if the user wants to visit the same website later, the system does not resend another DNS query but checks the local DNS cache on their computer for the IP address. However, a hacker who sends fake DNS response messages to a victim's system can modify these entries within the DNS cache. Therefore, if the victim wants to visit `www.google.com` once more, the system checks the local DNS cache for the IP address and will use the IP address from the fake DNS response, directing the victim to a fake web server on the internet. DNS poisoning attacks are commonly used by hackers to redirect their victims to phishing websites and malware-infected servers on the internet.

DNS hijacking is another type of DNS-based attack that allows a hacker to modify the DNS server configurations on a victim's device. For instance, the hacker can set up a DNS server on the internet with lots of entries from popular FQDNs, such as `www.google.com`, `www.yahoo.com`, `www.microsoft.com`, and other most-visited websites on the internet, but each FQDN is matched with a fake IP address that is assigned to a phishing website or a malware-infected web server on the internet. In this type of attack, the hacker manages their DNS server and its entries. Since the hacker changes the DNS server settings on the victim's system, all DNS queries will be sent to the hacker's DNS server.

Lastly, in a **domain hijacking** attack, the hacker can take control and ownership of a legitimate domain name and modify the DNS records that are associated with the domain. For instance, if a user purchases a domain name from a trusted domain registrar but does not secure their user account properly, a hacker can attempt to take over the user's account and their domain name. Once a hacker takes control of a legitimate domain name, they can create, delete, and modify DNS records and ensure users are redirected to untrusted websites on the internet. Additionally, the hacker can transfer the domain name to another domain registrar that's preferred by the hacker.

VLAN hopping

As you learned in *Chapter 9, Routing and Switching Concepts*, a **Virtual Local Area Network (VLAN)** provides a lot of benefits to organizations, such as improving network performance and security, reducing the cost of network infrastructure, and creating smaller broadcast domains without the need for separate dedicated networking devices. As an aspiring network professional, it's important to understand the security risks that are involved if switch interfaces/ports have been misconfigured with VLAN IDs.

VLAN hopping is a common Layer 2-based attack that allows a hacker to exploit a misconfigured switch port, allowing the hacker to access multiple VLANs simultaneously on the network. For instance, switch ports that are connected to end devices such as computers, servers, and printers are statically configured as access ports. Access ports are used to assign and transport only one piece of data, known as VLAN traffic, except for voice and data VLANs, which are assigned to the same access port on a switch.

The following diagram shows access ports on a switch and their associated VLANs:

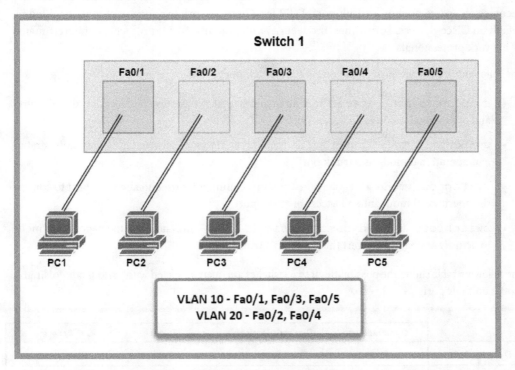

Figure 15.12 – Access ports

When two switches are interconnected, network professionals configure the interface of both switches as a trunk, which allows multiple VLANs to send their traffic between switches, as shown here:

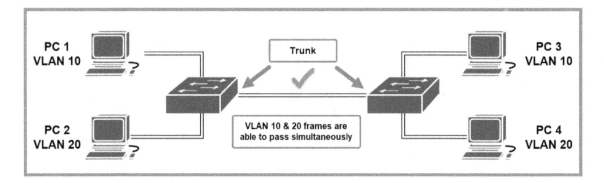

Figure 15.13 – Trunk interfaces

Sometimes, IT and network professionals do not always utilize best practices when configuring switch interfaces. For instance, Cisco switches use the **Dynamic Trunking Protocol (DTP)** to automatically negotiate the interface mode when another device is connected, regardless of whether the interface becomes an access port or a trunk port. DTP is a Cisco-proprietary protocol that's enabled by default on Cisco devices. Sometimes, the security vulnerability of this protocol is underestimated by network professionals.

The following are the various modes on a Cisco switch port:

- `switchport mode access`: This command is used to statically configure the administrative and operational mode as an access port
- `switchport mode trunk`: This command is used to statically configure the administrative and operational mode as a trunk port
- `switchport mode dynamic auto`: This command is used to allow the port to convert the operational mode into an access or trunk port
- `switchport mode dynamic desirable`: This command sets the negotiation mode to *actively attempt* to convert the port into a trunk port

The following table shows the possibilities if two switches are interconnected with various administrative modes on their ports:

	Dynamic Auto	Dynamic Desirable	Trunk	Access
Dynamic Auto	Access	Trunk	Trunk	Access
Dynamic Desirable	Trunk	Trunk	Trunk	Access
Trunk	Trunk	Trunk	Trunk	Limited Connectivity
Access	Access	Access	Limited Connectivity	Access

Figure 15.14 – DTP negotiation chart

By default, Cisco switches use `switchport mode dynamic auto` on all their interfaces. If a hacker connects their attacker machine to a misconfigured switch port, the hacker can inject fake DTP messages into the switch port, causing the interface to flip into a trunk state. This allows the hacker to access all the VLANs on the network.

The following diagram shows an attacker's machine connected to a misconfigured port on a switch, which means it can convert the port into an unauthorized trunk port:

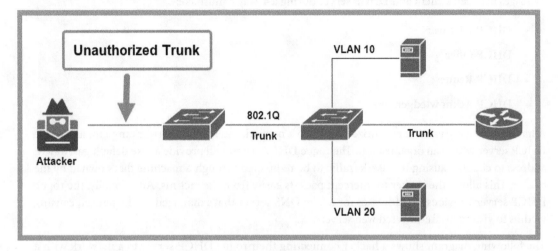

Figure 15.15 – Unauthorized trunk port

To mitigate this type of security vulnerability on switches, you can statically configure an interface as an access or trunk port. Statically configuring the interfaces will prevent the administrative mode from unexpectedly changing. Additionally, network professionals should disable any port negotiation features such as DTP when possible on the entire switch or the port of the device as applicable. On Cisco switches, the `switchport nonegotiate` command is used to prevent DTP frames from being generated on an interface.

Rogue DHCP

Dynamic Host Configuration Protocol (DHCP) is a common network protocol and IP service that allows network professionals to automatically distribute IP addresses to clients on a network. For instance, when a client connects to a network, they will need an IP address, subnet mask, default gateway, and DNS server configuration that allows them to communicate with other systems. Network professionals can manually assign and configure IP addresses on each device that connects to a network. However, this task can become complex and overwhelming since they need to manually keep track of the IP addresses that are assigned to each device to prevent duplication and human error. Additionally, if the IP addressing scheme within the organization needs to be modified, the network professional will need to manually change the IP addresses on each system accordingly.

Implementing a DHCP server on the network mitigates all these challenges, allowing the DHCP server to automatically distribute available IP addresses from a pool to each client device that connects to the network. Additionally, the DHCP server maintains records of the IP addresses that have been assigned to each client and their lease time. This prevents any IP addresses that have been assigned to devices on the network from being duplicated.

As you may recall from *Chapter 6, Exploring Network Protocols and Services*, DHCP uses the following messages between a client and DHCP server during a 4-way handshake:

- **DHCP Discover**

- **DHCP Offer**

- **DHCP Request**

- **DHCP Acknowledgement**

A hacker who has gained unauthorized access to a network can install a network implant as a rogue DHCP server within an organization. The rogue DHCP server will provide a fake default gateway IP address to clients, causing the user's traffic to be redirected through a machine that's owned by the hacker. This allows the hacker to intercept packets easily from the victims. Additionally, the rogue DHCP server provides IP addresses for a fake DNS server that's managed by the hacker, causing victims to visit malware-infected web servers.

The following diagram shows a hacker connecting their rogue DHCP server to a network with a legitimate DHCP server:

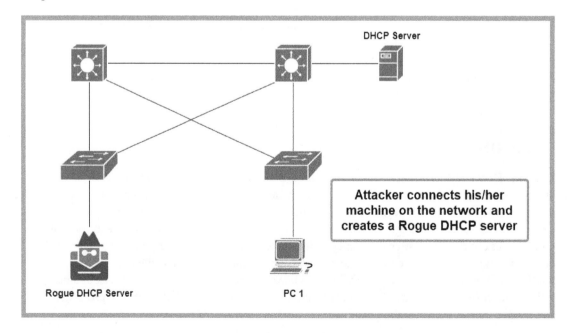

Figure 15.16 – Rogue DHCP server

Typically, the hacker will attempt to compromise the availability of the legitimate DHCP server to prevent it from sending **DHCP Offer** and **DHCP Acknowledgment** messages to clients that are requesting IP addresses or attempting to renew their leases. Once the legitimate DHCP server is offline or unavailable, whenever a client sends a **DHCP Discover** message on the network, the rogue DHCP server will respond with a DHCP Offer, thus providing the unaware client with fake IP addresses for the default gateway and DNS servers.

To mitigate rogue DHCP servers on a network, network professionals commonly implement the **DHCP Snooping** security feature within Cisco switches. DHCP Snooping sets all the ports on a Cisco switch as *untrusted ports* to prevent any inbound DHCP Offer and DHCP Acknowledgement messages from entering the network from untrusted sources. Therefore, the network professional configures the interface that is connected to the legitimate DHCP server as a *trusted port*, allowing the DHCP server to respond to clients on the network.

Password attacks

Whether you're creating an account on your local computer or an online account on your favorite website, setting a password reduces the likelihood of an unauthorized person gaining access to your account. However, various techniques are used by hackers to retrieve their victim's user credentials – that is, their username and password. Long ago, passwords were enough to prevent hackers and other malicious users from performing account takeovers and gaining unauthorized access to systems. However, nowadays, hackers can easily retrieve someone's user credentials using various techniques, such as social engineering the victim into revealing their username and password for their online email account, social media profile, or banking platform.

Typically, when a user is creating a password for their account, their username is commonly stored in plaintext while their password is sent through a hashing algorithm to create a one-way digest (hash) of the password before it's stored in a database. Therefore, the plaintext password is not stored in the database but the digest (hash) of the password is. Since the digest (hash) is a one-way function, it's considered to be irreversible, so the owners of the system that store the digest (hash) do not know the actual plaintext password. For instance, the newer versions of the Windows operating system use the **New Technology LAN Manager** (**NTLM**) algorithm, which converts the user's password into an NTLM hash, which is stored in the **Security Account Manager** (**SAM**) database on Windows-based operating systems.

> **Important note**
> The SAM file is stored in the `C:\Windows\System32\config` location within Microsoft Windows operating systems.

Systems that are connected to a network, such as servers and networking devices, are susceptible to online password attacks. IT professionals commonly configure servers and networking devices with remote access management using various networking protocols such as **Remote Desktop Protocol (RDP)** and **Secure Shell (SSH)** to name a few. While remote access protocols are enabled on servers and networking devices, a hacker who's on the network can easily perform a port and service scan to determine which systems have remote access services running. This allows the hacker to perform an online password attack on the target with the enabled remote access service, by launching common user credentials over the network to open a service port on the target.

It's always recommended to use strong and complex passwords, but this is not always practiced by many professionals within various industries, even in the IT industry. Such malpractices often lead to a hacker gaining unauthorized access to a critical system due to missing or default passwords. A good practice is to implement a lockout policy that measures the number of failed login attempts for the username and locks the account as a warning of suspicious activities. For instance, three failed login attempts within a specific period can trigger the policy to lock the account, thus reducing the likelihood of the hacker being able to compromise the user account.

What if a file or folder is password protected? Hackers can perform offline password attacks, which focus on retrieving the password for a password-protected file such as a document that's on a stored drive, such as a USB flash drive or local storage drive. In an offline password attack, the hacker will need to retrieve the digest or hash value of the password that was used to encrypt or lock the file.

Various tools are created by hackers, security researchers, and cybersecurity professionals to perform online and offline password-based attacks. Some of these tools are designed to perform brute-force attacks, such as attempting every possible combination of a password against the target, while other tools use a dictionary, which is a wordlist containing many possible words, where one of them is likely to be the real password. These wordlist/dictionary files can easily be generated and found on the internet.

> **Important note**
> The `SecLists` repository is well-known within the cybersecurity community as it contains wordlists that contain popular and common usernames and passwords that are used during security assessments: `https://github.com/danielmiessler/SecLists`.

Hence, IT professionals must configure their systems with password policies to enforce the following:

- Password complexity
- Password expiration
- Password recovery
- Password history
- Password reuse

- Password length
- Disablement
- Lockout

Within large organizations, using the **Active Directory Domain Services** (**AD DS**) role within Microsoft Windows Server allows IT professionals to create password policies in the form of a **Group Policy Object** (**GPO**) that's applied to groups, users, and computer accounts. This allows IT professionals to easily manage password policies within the organization.

Having completed this section, you have learned about common network-based attacks and threats that can compromise systems within an organization. Next, you will explore various types of wireless-based attacks that are commonly performed by threat actors.

Understanding wireless attacks

Wireless networking has advanced over the years and become a major convenience for many users within organizations and at home. Wireless networking allows users to connect a mobile device with a wireless network interface card to an access point, which provides access to resources and services on a wired network. Users no longer need to sit in a stationary position while using their computers; they can connect their laptops and smartphones to access points and use the internet and share resources with others on their network.

In a wired network, a hacker will need physical access to the network cables and network devices to install a network implant. However, the radio frequency that's emitted from an access point covers a small geographic area, such as around a building or house. This allows hackers to sit within the vicinity of a wireless network that belongs to an organization and attempt various wireless attacks, such as the following:

- Rogue access points and evil twins
- De-authentication attacks

Over the next few subsections, you will explore the preceding types of wireless attacks.

Rogue access points and evil twins

Hackers can use their laptops, microcomputers such as a Raspberry Pi, or even microcontrollers such as an ESP8266 to perform wireless attacks on IEEE 802.11 networks. Typically, hackers can create a fake access point using their laptop or Raspberry Pi device to create a wireless network to trick victims into connecting to it. Typically, the **Service Set Identifier** (**SSID**) or wireless network name is set to lure users into connecting to the rogue access point. When a victim connects their device to the rogue access point, the hacker can intercept and redirect traffic to malicious websites.

Another common technique is where a hacker can sit outside an organization, perform a wireless network discovery scan to determine the organization's SSIDs, then set up an evil twin access point within the same SSID as the one used by the organization. This technique simply disguises the fake access point as a trusted access point because it's broadcasting the same SSID or network name as the organization.

Cybersecurity professionals use various tools and strategies to locate rogue wireless devices, such as unauthorized wireless clients and access points within the vicinity. The following screenshot shows the output of a popular wireless security assessment tool known as **Aircrack-ng** that's discovering all wireless networks within the vicinity that are operating on the 2.4 GHz frequency:

```
CH 14 ][ Elapsed: 1 min ][ 2021-09-12 13:10

 BSSID              PWR  Beacons    #Data, #/s  CH   MB   ENC CIPHER  AUTH ESSID

 9C:3D:CF:          -25     149        2     0    4  540   WPA2 CCMP   PSK  ! ▷_◁ !
 68:7F:74:01:28:E1  -36      76        1     0    6  130   WPA2 CCMP   PSK  Corp_Wi-Fi
 38:4C:4F:          -72      52       46     0    1  195   WPA2 CCMP   PSK  Digicel_WiFi_T28R
 B4:39:39:          -83      26       73     0   11   65   WPA2 CCMP   PSK  Hyundai E504
 2C:9D:1E:          -88       9        3     0    7  195   WPA2 CCMP   PSK  Digicel_WiFi_fh4w
 80:02:9C:          -92       1        0     0   11  130   WPA2 CCMP   PSK  WLAN11_113CAD
 04:C3:E6:           -1       0        2     0    9   -1   WPA               <length:  0>
 38:4C:4F:          -88       2        1     0    1  195   WPA2 CCMP   PSK  Doh Study It
 A8:2B:CD:          -88       5        0     0   11  130   WPA2 CCMP   PSK  Digicel_WiFi_94J3

 BSSID              STATION           PWR   Rate    Lost    Frames  Notes  Probes

 (not associated)   98:09:CF:         -38    0 - 1      0        5
 68:7F:74:01:28:E1  D8:50:E6:2F:F9:2B  -27    0 - 6      0        5
 68:7F:74:01:28:E1  18:31:BF:1A:92:D1  -40    0 - 1      0       25
 38:4C:4F:          2C:C5:46:         -84   24e- 1e  1772      103
 38:4C:4F:          B0:C0:90:         -86   24e- 1      0        9
 38:4C:4F:          B8:C3:85:         -89   24e- 1      0       36
 38:4C:4F:          88:29:9C:         -89    0 - 1      0        2
 38:4C:4F:          E4:C8:01:         -90   12e- 1      0        6
```

Figure 15.17 – Discovering wireless network

As shown in the preceding screenshot, the upper portion shows the **Basic Service Set Identifier (BSSID)** of an access point; the BSSID is the MAC address of the device. Additionally, the power level (**PWR**) indicates the approximate distance between the access point and your device. The **Beacons** column indicates the number of beacons captured from the access point. You can see the channel (**CH**), encryption (**ENC**), cipher, authentication method (**AUTH**), and the name of the wireless network as the **Extended Service Set Identifier (ESSID)**. The lower region of the screenshot shows which stations (clients) are connected to a specific access point via the BSSID value.

> **Tip**
> To learn more about Aircrack-ng, please visit https://www.aircrack-ng.org/.

Aircrack-ng is one of many popular tools within the industry that helps cybersecurity professionals during their wireless security assessments. However, network professionals can use this tool to determine whether a rogue wireless access point is within the vicinity or not.

Deauthentication attacks

As mentioned previously, if a hacker wants to trick the users of an organization into connecting to a wireless network that's owned and managed by the hacker, implementing an evil twin allows the hacker to configure the same SSID as the organization. However, the employees' wireless devices that are currently associated with the legitimate access point will not automatically disassociate and join the evil twin wireless network created by the hacker. Therefore, the hacker will need to use a technique to *knock off* (disassociate) currently associated wireless clients from the legitimate access point.

A hacker can use a deauthentication attack to disassociate (disconnect) wireless clients from the target access point that's owned by the organization, causing them to associate with the evil twin access point that's within the vicinity. By default, when wireless clients are disassociated from an access point, they will attempt to re-establish an association with the same access point that they were previously connected to. However, since a disassociation attack focuses on targeting a specific access point based on its BSSID, all previously associated clients will automatically connect to any nearby access points that are broadcasting the same SSID, hence connecting to the evil twin that's owned and managed by the hacker.

Hackers can launch a deauthentication attack that targets a wireless network indefinitely or sends a few disassociation wireless frames for a few seconds or minutes. Some enterprise wireless access points can detect rogue access points, evil twins, and deauthentication attacks that are occurring within the vicinity. Additionally, cybersecurity professionals can use various tools such as Aircrack-ng and **TCPdump** to detect wireless deauthentication attacks on their network and the source of the attack.

Having completed this section, you have learned about rogue access points, evil twins, and deauthentication attacks on wireless networks. Next, you will explore social engineering attacks.

Delving into human and environmental attacks

As more people and organizations are using the internet, hackers are always looking for new and sophisticated techniques to trick their potential victims into revealing their user credentials for their online user accounts on popular websites, such as those for e-commerce, payment transactions, and banking. Additionally, hackers are noticing that organizations are investing a lot into fortifying their network infrastructure with countermeasures against common cyberattacks and newly emerging threats. Due to this, companies are implementing a multi-layered approach using security solutions, technologies, people, and strategies to create a **Defense in Depth** approach.

Social engineering

Seasoned hackers will not attempt to compromise an organization's internal network while launching the attack from the internet, external to the organization's network infrastructure. Instead, they will attempt to compromise the network from the inside. Hackers commonly use a technique that does not always require the use of a computer but one that is designed to hack the human brain. Since the human mind does not contain traditional antivirus programs or cyber-threat detection solutions like a computer system does, each person has a consciousness, which allows them to make their own decisions and choices each day. The technique of **social engineering** allows a hacker to psychologically trick a person into revealing confidential information such as user credentials or performing an action such as downloading a malware-infected file onto their computer.

For instance, a hacker can make a call to the target organization's customer service department while pretending to be an IT professional within the company. They tell the user they're from IT, that a virus is currently on the company's network, and that they are working quickly to contain it before it infects other systems. They also tell the user to quickly download and install an *update* from a custom URL, before their system gets infected with the virus and all their data is lost permanently. If the user does not pause and think through the situation thoroughly, the user may just install malware created by the hacker to provide backdoor access to the compromised system and network. This is a type of social engineering attack known as **vishing**; it's performed over a telephone system where the attacker calls the potential victim while pretending to be someone trustworthy.

A social engineering attack is only successful if the victim reveals sensitive information or performs the intended action that's expected by the hacker. However, the following are common key elements that improve the success of a social engineering attack:

- **Authority**: Pretending to be someone with higher authority can convince the potential victim into revealing sensitive information or performing the desired action

- **Intimidation**: Inflicting fear in a potential victim with the expectation that the person will comply

- **Consensus**: This element focuses on tricking the potential victim into thinking everyone is doing the same action and that it's quite normal for them to do the same, which is incorrect

- **Scarcity**: Implying scarcity involves telling the potential victim there's limited time to perform an action and if that time runs out, there will be huge consequences

- **Urgency**: Applying urgency to a situation denotes the importance or priority of the situation

- **Familiarity**: Creating a familiar situation with the potential victim such as discussing a past mutual experience can help build trust

- **Trust**: Once the hacker establishes trust with the victim, it's easy to take advantage of it

Next, you will discover various types of social engineering attacks.

Types of social engineering attacks

In **phishing**, the attacker sends fake email messages while pretending to be from a trusted organization and is requesting the user to click a link to a malware-infected web server or to a fake website to capture their user credentials. Additionally, malware-infected attachments are sent within phishing emails by an attacker with a message instructing the potential victim to open the attachment.

The following screenshot shows a phishing email that seems to be originating from a popular e-commerce website:

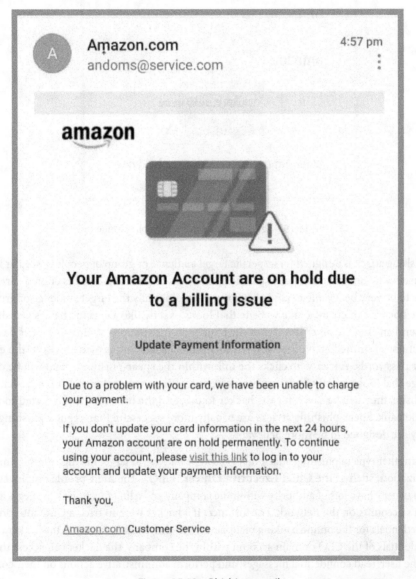

Figure 15.18 – Phishing email

As shown in the preceding screenshot, most of the email message looks trustworthy as the company's logo, fonts, and colors are used. However, the sender's details show that the message didn't originate from Amazon's domain name – the sender's name contains an unusual character that looks very similar to an "**m**," as shown here:

Figure 15.19 – Sender's name in the phishing email

A **spear-phishing** attack is designed for a specific target audience or group of people of similar interest, such as all users who are customers of a specific bank. A spear-phishing email is crafted carefully so that it seems to be very believable to anyone who reads it, especially the target audience or group. For instance, the hacker can create a fake website that looks exactly like a specific bank's website, then create and send an email to all customers of the bank with instructions stating that their passwords need to be changed immediately; they will tell them to click the link provided within the email to change their passwords. A user who clicks the link within the spear-phishing email will be directed to a web page that looks exactly like their bank's website. When they enter their user credentials on the fake website, they will be saved for the hacker to use, and the user will be redirected to the real website of the bank. Spear-phishing attacks are usually more successful than regular phishing emails because they are designed to be more believable.

Whaling is another type of phishing attack that is used by hackers to target the high-profile employees of an organization, such as the **Chief Executive Officer** (**CEO**). The high-profile employees of an organization usually have lots of authority within the company and a lot of technical privileges assigned to their user's accounts on the network. For instance, if a hacker were to trick a CEO into providing their user credentials for the online banking platform, the hacker can sell money. If the hacker can gain the user credentials of the CEO domain account within the company, the hacker can access the email mailbox of the user, read confidential messages, and perform administrative actions on their computer.

The following are additional types of social engineering attacks:

- **Vishing**: This type of social engineering attack is performed over a telephone system where the attacker calls the potential victim while pretending to be someone from a trusted organization.

- **Smishing**: This type of social engineering attack is performed by sending the potential victim a phishing message via **Short Message Service (SMS)**.

- **Tailgating**: This is where an unauthorized person attempts to gain access to a secure area within a company when an employee does not close a door properly, thus allowing the unauthorized person to tail the employee through the secure area. With tailgating, no one knows that the malicious actor "slipped" into the secure area through a door that was slowly closing.

- **Piggybacking**: With piggybacking, someone from the secured area holds the doors open for the malicious actor to *help* them. Often, the malicious actor will have their hands/arms full of boxes or carrying something.

- **Shoulder surfing**: This technique is commonly used by people who are looking over a user's shoulder while they are entering confidential or sensitive data into their computer. Shoulder surfing involves the attacker intending to gain the user credentials of the potential victim.

- **Dumpster diving**: Disposing of documents or devices that contain sensitive and confidential information can lead to impersonation. Some hackers will check a person's trash for any documents or devices for data and attempt to use that data for identity theft or to gain unauthorized access to their online accounts.

Having completed this section, you have learned about the fundamentals of social engineering attacks and various types of attacks. Now, let's summarize this chapter.

Summary

In this chapter, you have explored common types of network-based attacks such as DDoS, botnets, on-path, and even DNS-based attacks. Additionally, you learned how hackers use various techniques to trick users on a wireless network into connecting to a rogue access point that's owned and managed by the hacker. Lastly, you discovered how hackers can use social engineering to trick a person into revealing sensitive information or performing an action.

I hope this chapter has been informative for you and is helpful in your journey toward learning networking and becoming a network professional. In the next chapter, *Chapter 16, Implementing Network Security*, you will learn how to implement various network security solutions to mitigate various types of cyberattacks and threats.

Questions

The following is a short list of review questions to help reinforce your learning and help you identify areas that may require some improvement:

1. Which of the following types of attacks focuses on compromising the availability of a server?

   A. On-path

   B. Phishing

   C. DDoS

   D. All of the above

2. Which type of network-based attack is needed to intercept communication between two or more devices?

   A. VLAN hopping

   B. On-path

   C. DNS

   D. DHCP

3. Which of the following attack is needed for a MiTM attack to be successful?

   A. Phishing

   B. Rogue DHCP server

   C. VLAN hopping

   D. ARP poisoning

4. Which of the following attacks best describes a hacker modifying the DNS cache on their victim's system by sending fake DNS response messages?

   A. DNS poisoning

   B. DNS hijacking

   C. DNS flooding

   D. Domain hijacking

5. Which of the following allows a hacker to gain unauthorized access to another VLAN on the network?

   A. VLAN access port

   B. VLAN hijacking

   C. VLAN hopping

   D. All of the above

6. Which of the following messages are blocked on untrusted ports when DHCP Snooping is enabled on a network? (Choose two)

    A. DHCP Offer

    B. DHCP Request

    C. DHCP Acknowledgement

    D. DHCP Discover

7. Which type of attack can a hacker perform to force wireless clients to disconnect from an access point?

    A. Rogue access point

    B. Brute-force

    C. Disassociation

    D. Deauthentication

8. Which of the following attacks is performed using a telephone to trick a user into installing a malware-infected file?

    A. Social engineering

    B. Vishing

    C. Smishing

    D. Spear-phishing

9. Which of the following attacks allows a hacker to take control of a trusted domain name on the internet?

    A. DNS poisoning

    B. DNS hijacking

    C. DNS flooding

    D. Domain hijacking

10. Which technique does a hacker use to change their identity on a Layer 2 network?

    A. Hostname spoofing

    B. MAC spoofing

    C. IP spoofing

    D. All of the above

Further reading

To learn more about the topics that were covered in this chapter, check out the following links:

- *Network Attacks and Network Security Threats*: `https://www.cynet.com/network-attacks/network-attacks-and-network-security-threats/`

- *Wireless attacks and mitigation*: `https://resources.infosecinstitute.com/topic/wireless-attacks-and-mitigation/`

- *Social engineering*: `https://www.techtarget.com/searchsecurity/definition/social-engineering`

16
Implementing Network Security

Cybersecurity professionals are continuously working to stay at least one step ahead of hackers and protect their organizations from new and emerging cyberattacks and threats. Different types of hackers compromise organizations and user accounts with different motives, such as for fun or just to prove a point to others within the community, while more organized groups of hackers typically work together for financial gain. The age of ransomware shook the world as no one was ready for such a type of threat that affected many organizations and continues to be a major one. The idea of encrypting data and asking for a ransom was a good approach to easily gain money and cryptocurrencies from victims.

While many cybersecurity professionals warn victims to not pay the ransom as there's no guarantee of retrieving their data, many organizations have given in and paid the ransom with the hope that good faith will prevail and their most valuable asset – data – will be available once more. While no single system is perfectly secured against cyberattacks and threats, network security professionals use best practices and technologies on their network to reduce the risk of cyberattacks and protect their assets from hackers. Without network security solutions, organizations are simply left open to potential attacks from hackers around the world.

In this chapter, you will learn about common techniques used by network security professionals to improve the security posture of their network infrastructure and reduce the risk of a cyberattack. You will learn about network hardening techniques and their benefits, wireless security solutions and how they are used to mitigate wireless attacks, how to securely access your network using popular remote access methods, and various physical security practices within organizations.

In this chapter, we will cover the following topics:

- Network hardening techniques
- Wireless security techniques
- Remote connectivity methods
- Importance of physical security

Let's dive in!

Network hardening techniques

Cyberattacks occur all the time; each day, there are many reports of unknown cyberattacks that have been discovered by various security organizations and security researchers around the world. However, many organizations do not realize their systems and networks have been compromised by a threat actor until months after the attack has occurred. The longer an organization takes to discover its systems and networks have been breached, the more time the hacker has to dig deeper into the network and install multiple backdoors while going undetected. Hence, implementing network hardening techniques reduces the risk of being compromised while improving the security of the network.

Implementing network security best practices helps network professionals ensure their network infrastructure, such as its network devices and security appliances, are properly secured against hackers, cyberattacks, and threats. While networking devices are designed to forward frames and packets to their destinations, network devices such as switches and routers have an operating system. If a hacker gains access to an organization's network and discovers an outdated version of an operating system on a router or switch, the hacker can use an exploit to compromise the vulnerable operating system and take control of the device. This allows the hacker to redirect traffic or mirror users' traffic.

Additionally, if the hacker can find a vulnerability within a security appliance such as an organization's firewall, the hacker can attempt to exploit it and gain control of the device. If the firewall is compromised, the hacker can insert, modify, and delete rules on the firewall to permit malicious or suspicious traffic to enter and leave the organization's network undetected.

The following are best practices for improving the security posture of your network infrastructure:

- **Secure Simple Network Management Protocol (SNMP)**: SNMP is a common network protocol used by network professionals to manage their network devices and security appliances over a network. SNMP allows an **SNMP Manager** to gather information from the **SNMP Agent** that's running on the network and security devices within a company. Additionally, SNMP helps network professionals monitor the performance and health status of their network and apply configuration changes to devices. SNMPv1 and SNMPv2 have bad security features such as no data encryption or authentication mechanisms, so these versions are not recommended to be used. However, SNMPv3 supports data encryption and user authentication between the SNMP Manager and SNMP Agent.

- **Router Advertisement (RA) Guard**: Within an IPv6 network, RA messages are used to create a stateless configuration. The IPv6 clients on the network send **Router Solicitation (RS)** messages to search for any IPv6-enabled routers on the network. When an IPv6-enabled router receives an RS message, it responds with RA messages back to the client. The RA Guard security feature is used to prevent a hacker from sending unsolicited or spoofed RA messages to clients on a network. The RA Guard security feature inspects and validates the authenticity of the RA messages from the sender.

- **Port security**: Port security is used to mitigate a **Content Addressable Memory** (**CAM**) Table Overflow attack from occurring on a network. In a CAM Table Overflow attack, the hacker injects thousands of frames with spoofed **Media Access Control** (**MAC**) addresses into a switch's port. The CAM table on a Cisco switch is used to store learned MAC addresses; if the CAM table is full and continues to receive new source MAC addresses, the switch will flood any incoming frames out of all other ports. Therefore, the switches become a hub, allowing a hacker to capture any frames sent into the switch from other devices on the network. Additionally, port security is used to prevent unauthorized devices from connecting to the network and accessing resources. It inspects the source MAC address for any incoming frames into the switch's port and prevents frames with unauthorized source MAC addresses.

- **Enable DHCP snooping**: DHCP snooping is used to prevent both DHCP spoofing and rogue DHCP servers on a network. DHCP spoofing occurs when a rogue DHCP server is connected to a network and provides false IP configurations to clients on the network. DHCP spoofing is dangerous within any organization because clients can lease incorrect IP addresses to **Domain Name System** (**DNS**) servers and the default gateway that's owned and managed by a hacker on the network. When DHCP snooping is enabled on a switch, it builds a DHCP snooping binding database, which records the clients' MAC addresses, IP addresses, DHCP lease times, binding types, **Virtual Local Area Network** (**VLAN**) numbers, and interface information on each untrusted switch port. DHCP snooping prevents any DHCP Offer and DHCP Acknowledgment messages from entering untrusted ports on a switch.

- **Enable Dynamic ARP Inspection (DAI)**: DAI prevents **Man-in-the-Middle** (**MiTM**) and on-path attacks on a network. Additionally, DAI mitigates **Address Resolution Protocol** (**ARP**) poisoning and spoofing from occurring within an organization's network. It leverages the entries within the DHCP snooping binding table and inspects the source MAC addresses that are learned on an untrusted port and match a client's IP address. Once DAI is enabled on a switch, all ports are untrusted by default.

- **Enable Control Plane Policing (CoPP)**: The control plane on a networking device is responsible for controlling how the entire network device operates and functions. The control plane is like the brain of the device – it manages both Layer 2 and Layer 3 forwarding mechanisms, routing and switching protocols, IPv4 and IPv6 routing tables, **Spanning-Tree Protocol** (**STP**), and more within the device. CoPP is used to protect the control plane within the network device by filtering any unsolicited inbound messages from threat actors that are seeking to gain unauthorized access to the device.

- **Implement private VLANs**: A private VLAN creates an isolated port/interface on a network switch. Therefore, any device that's connected to a switch port that is assigned to a private VLAN will be isolated from other VLANs on the switch and network.

- **Disable unneeded switch ports**: Sometimes, network professionals do not disable unused or unneeded ports on their network switches. This leaves the network physically open, allowing anyone to connect an unauthorized device to the network. Disabling unused or unneeded switch ports simply allows the network professionals to administratively shut down the interface via the switch's operating system, thus preventing unauthorized access to the network via those unused or unneeded switch ports.

- **Disable unneeded network services**: On a network, you will commonly find servers and network devices that have been configured to provide common network services and resources to clients. However, IT professionals sometimes forget to disable any network services that are no longer needed by clients on the network. For instance, if a network switch or router has Telnet enabled, a threat actor who's on the network can attempt an on-path attack to intercept any login credentials between the IT professionals' devices and the Telnet-enabled devices since Telnet sends messages in plaintext.

- **Change default passwords**: Devices are usually shipped to customers with a default password that's configured by the vendor of the product. Many times, IT professionals do not always change the default username and password on these devices, which often leads to their network being compromised by a hacker. Hackers seek the easiest method to compromise their targets. Imagine if you were a hacker and you were able to log into someone else's router using the default credentials of the device; this means that anyone can do the same.

- **Password complexity/length**: Setting a unique password on each user account or system reduces the likelihood of account takeover by a hacker. However, not everyone likes setting complex passwords on each user account. Configuring weak passwords increases the likelihood of a hacker being able to successfully use a dictionary or brute-force password attack and retrieve the password. There are many wordlist files on the internet that contain common and popular passwords used by people. A hacker can simply use a common wordlist and retrieve your passwords. Hence, IT professionals need to configure and enforce password complexity criteria for all users within their organization.

- **Change the default VLAN**: Managed network switches are shipped from their vendors with all physical ports assigned to a default VLAN. The default VLAN is simply the primary VLAN that is loaded onto a managed switch after the switch is powered on. Many new out-of-the-box switches have all their ports assigned to VLAN 1 by default, so if you connect end devices to any of the ports on a new switch, communication is allowed between all ports. Using the default VLAN is not recommended because a seasoned hacker who understands networking will know how easy it is to compromise all devices on the same VLAN. It's recommended to implement multiple VLANs within an organization, such as assigning a unique VLAN to each organizational department. Overall, do not use the default VLAN.

- **Patch and firmware management**: Patch and firmware management are a set of procedures and processes that involve acquiring, testing, distributing, and applying system and firmware updates to devices within a network. For instance, IT professionals should download firmware and patches from the vendor's website and not third-party websites on the internet. IT professionals should install the patches on company systems that are connected to a test environment, allowing the IT professionals to use these systems regularly for 2 weeks or more to identify any issues with the newly patched systems. If no issues are found during the testing phase, they can roll out the patches systematically to one organizational department at a time and monitor whether users are reporting any issues of system instability or application crashes.

- **Implement an Access Control List (ACL)**: Routers allow network professionals to implement ACLs to filter traffic between networks. ACLs can filter traffic based on the five tuples: source IP address, destination IP address, source MAC address, destination MAC address, and protocol. Essentially, routers can function as a **packet filtering firewall** within an organization. While packet filtering firewalls are unable to filter application-layer traffic compared to next-generation firewalls, they can still provide a basic layer of security between IP networks.

- **Role-based access**: Role-based access is a type of access control model that is designed to only permit a user with the privileges needed to perform their job duties, nothing more. This type of access control model can be assigned to users via **Group Policy Objects** (**GPOs**) within a Windows-based environment with Microsoft Windows Server. For instance, a GPO can be created by the systems administrator or security professional who defines the user privileges for all employees who work within the customer service department of an organization. Implementing **role-based access control** (**RBAC**) ensures a person with a specific job role has all the necessary privileges to perform their job efficiently while ensuring the user doesn't abuse any additional privileges while being logged into any system on the network.

- **Firewall rules**: By default, all firewalls have an **implicit deny** rule that simply denies any traffic from any source to any destination. This rule is typically found as the last rule within the access control list on the firewall. Simply put, the implicit deny rule will automatically block any traffic that's not explicitly allowed through the firewall by the security professional. The implicit deny rule is needed to ensure all unwanted traffic is blocked, thus allowing the security professional to create rules to permit specific traffic types only while blocking everything else. **Explicit deny** rules are created by a security professional to deny (block) specific traffic between a source and a destination. The primary difference between the implicit deny and explicit deny is that the implicit deny rule is automatically created by the firewall, while the explicit deny rules are created by the security professional.

Additionally, firewall rules are used to filter traffic between networks that are directly connected to the firewall appliance. These firewall rules are created by security professionals using various criteria such as source IP address, destination IP address, source port number, destination port number, network protocol type, transport layer protocol type, application layer type, and so on. It's recommended that these rules are organized so that more specific firewall rules are placed at the top of the list while less specific and general firewalls are placed beneath. An example of a specific firewall rule is a security professional who wants to restrict HTTP traffic from a PC on the internal network to a destination web server on the internet. Here, a general firewall rule would restrict all traffic from one network to another.

- **Security Information and Event Management (SIEM)**: A SIEM is a security system that collects all the logs of devices on a network, performs data de-duplication, and helps security professionals quickly identify potential threats on their network. Simply put, security professionals configure their network devices, security appliances, and servers to send their log messages to the SIEM. The SIEM will both correlate and analyze all the logs collected in real time and trigger alerts for any potential security event on the network. Typically, within medium to large organizations, security professionals implement a SIEM system centrally in their network to assist with monitoring security events in real time.

Having completed this section, you have learned about some common techniques and best practices that are used to improve the security posture and harden a network infrastructure within an organization. Next, you will discover best practices for securing a wireless network.

Wireless security techniques

Wireless networking allows users to connect their wireless, mobile devices to an access point to access the resources on a wired network and vice versa. There are many advantages to implementing a wireless network infrastructure within homes and organizations, with the most obvious benefit being that wireless networking reduces the number of physical cables needed to allow clients to access the network. It's as simple as installing one or more access points so that they're physically connected to a network switch and configuring the wireless settings with each access point to broadcast a **Service Set Identifier** (**SSID**) and network details.

While wireless networking supports mobility, allowing users to roam around the vicinity of a wireless network, many threats and wireless-based attacks are commonly used by hackers to compromise the security of an access point, which compromises the wireless network and its users. For instance, since an access point uses radio frequencies emitted from antennas to transmit **Wireless Local Area Network** (**WLAN**) frames, a threat actor does not need physical access to the access point – they simply need to be within range of the wireless signal generated from the access point to launch an attack against it. Furthermore, if a threat actor were to gain unauthorized access to the wireless network, non-tech-savvy people would not think about frequently checking their network for any unauthorized users and devices.

Many organizations and home users are not always aware that their networks and systems have been compromised by a hacker until it's too late. At this point, the hacker can gain control over critical systems and **Internet of Things** (**IoT**) devices and create multiple backdoors into the network. For instance, imagine that a hacker has compromised a home wireless network and can identify and compromise a home security monitoring system that's connected to the same network. The hacker can either choose to monitor the victims' activities or disable their security monitoring solution. Hence, it's important to secure wireless networks using best practices to reduce the risk of a potential cyberattack and various threats.

SSID considerations

Typically, when setting up a wireless network for a home, office, or organization, it's important to consider the SSID or the network name. Many organizations commonly configure their SSIDs using the name of their company, thus providing the convenience for employees to easily discover and connect to their wireless network. However, this convenience also helps a hacker who's within the vicinity to easily find the company and its wireless network. Hence, setting the SSID as the name of your organization makes your wireless network a target.

Furthermore, many businesses commonly use the default SSID that's configured on the access point by the vendor. For instance, vendors commonly pre-configure their access points with an SSID that contains the name of the vendor and device model. A hacker can use this information to research any known security vulnerabilities of a specific device and attempt to exploit its security weaknesses.

The following screenshot shows the common user interface of a Cisco Linksys E1000 access point:

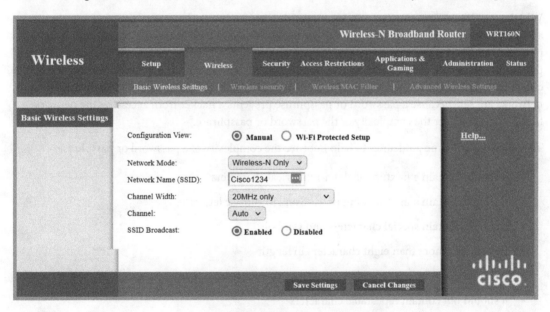

Figure 16.1 – Access point wireless settings

As shown in the preceding screenshot, when logged into an access point, selecting **Wireless | Basic Wireless Settings** will allow you to configure the network mode, SSID, and channel on the device. The access point is using the default SSID that's pre-configured by the vendor before it's shipped. It's recommended to change the default SSID and set a network name that does not identify your specific network or organization. This technique does not prevent but deters a threat actor.

> **Important note**
> Do not use **Wi-Fi Protected Setup** (**WPS**) as there are many unresolved security vulnerabilities.

Additionally, the **SSID Broadcast** feature allows you to configure the access point to advertise the SSID to all wireless clients within the vicinity. By default, the **SSID Broadcast** feature is enabled, which makes it easier to discover the wireless network. However, disabling this feature will allow the access point to still advertise its presence without including the SSID within the WLAN frames, which means wireless clients will not detect the SSID within their list of nearby available wireless networks. From a cybersecurity perspective, a seasoned hacker can discover a hidden wireless network within a few minutes or less. Therefore, disabling the **SSID Broadcast** feature will not prevent a hacker from discovering the hidden wireless network and launching wireless-based attacks.

Password considerations

Whether you're implementing a wireless network within a home or an organization, you should always set strong, complex passwords to reduce the likelihood of a hacker being able to retrieve those passwords and gain access to your network. I've seen many organizations configure weak and guessable passwords during my career and while it might be surprising to aspiring network professionals, it's quite a common and bad practice within many industries. While some companies think their wireless networks are safe because a password or passphrase prevents a hacker from accessing the network, they need to consider the complexity of the password or passphrase.

The following are some guidelines to help improve the complexity of a password or passphrase:

- It should contain a mixture of alpha-numerical characters
- It should contain a mixture of uppercase and lowercase letters
- It should contain special characters and symbols
- It should be more than eight characters in length
- It should not contain easily identifiable data such as names, dates, or places
- It should not contain repeatable characters

If you're having difficulties creating unique complex passwords, consider using an online password generator. The following are a few examples:

- LastPass Password Generator: `https://www.lastpass.com/features/password-generator`
- Bitwarden Password Generator: `https://bitwarden.com/password-generator/`
- 1Password Password Generator: `https://1password.com/password-generator/`

The following screenshot shows an example of a password that meets the criteria that were chosen within the password generator:

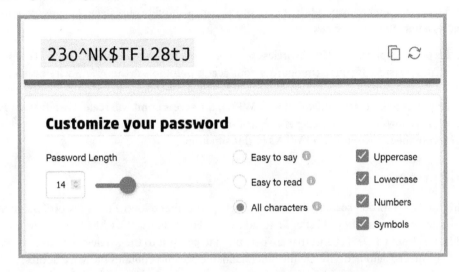

Figure 16.2 – Complex password

The **Pre-Shared Key (PSK)** field within the wireless security settings on an access point allows network professionals to configure a password or passphrase as the PSK value. This PSK is used with the data encryption algorithm to encrypt the data as it is sent over the wireless network.

The following screenshot shows the wireless security window of a Cisco Linksys E1000:

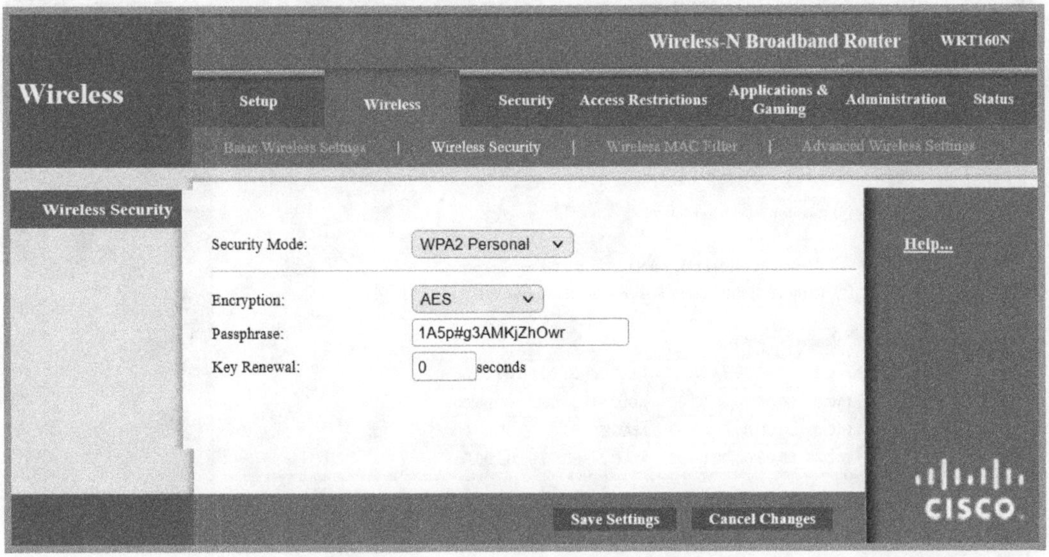

Figure 16.3 – Wireless security window

As shown in the preceding screenshot, the **WPA2 Personal** wireless security standard was selected, and a complex password was configured as the PSK value. Keep in mind that the wireless security feature is disabled by default on access points; network professionals shouldn't use default configurations as it can lead to a potential cyberattack.

Older access points support the WPA2 wireless security standard, while newer access points support WPA3, the latest version. If you're configuring your access point to use the WPA3 wireless security standard, ensure your wireless clients also support WPA3. If you're connecting wireless clients that use WPA2 to an access point that's configured with WPA3, the access point will scale down from WPA3 to WPA2, which allows the wireless clients to establish a connection. Hence, the wireless network will not benefit from the improvements of WPA3 in this situation.

MAC filtering

MAC filtering is a common security feature of access points that allows a network professional to configure either a whitelist or blacklist of MAC addresses. For instance, the whitelist contains a set of MAC addresses from wireless clients that are permitted to connect to the wireless network; all other devices will be denied automatically. On the other hand, the blacklist contains the MAC addresses that are not allowed to access the wireless network. Creating the whitelist (*permit*) or blacklist (*prevent*) helps network professionals add an extra layer of security to their wireless network.

If a hacker can retrieve the password or passphrase of the wireless network, the hacker will not be able to connect to the wireless network if their device's MAC address is restricted when MAC filtering is active.

The following screenshot shows the user interface of the MAC filtering feature on a Cisco Linksys E1000:

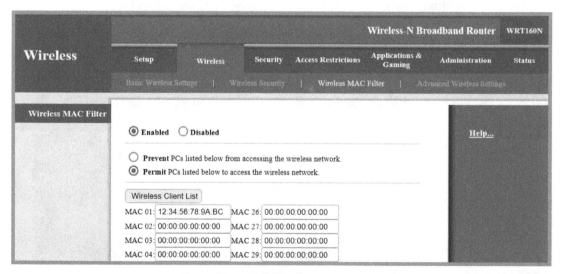

Figure 16.4 – MAC filtering user interface

As shown in the preceding screenshot, the MAC filtering feature is enabled, and it's configured to permit the set of MAC addresses within the list. Therefore, network professionals need to ensure the MAC addresses of authorized devices are included within the list of permitted addresses.

While MAC filtering is an additional layer of security on wireless networks, a seasoned hacker can determine the MAC address of any wireless clients that are associated with an access point. While MAC filtering can be bypassed, it is still considered to be a layer of security on a wireless network.

Antennas and power levels

Without antennas on an access point, it simply won't be able to transmit radio frequency signals to nearby wireless clients. The type, placement, and power levels on these wireless antennas affect the coverage of the wireless signals that are generated from the access point. For instance, some access points contain internal antennas while others support external detachable antennas. The main difference between antenna implementation is quite obvious – that is, the internal antennas can't be removed or changed by the user, while the external antennas usually can be removed. Additionally, access points with external antennas are known to provide better coverage compared to those with internal antennas.

The following figure shows the detachable antennas of an access point:

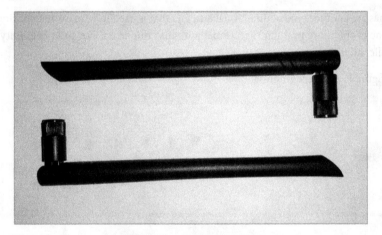

Figure 16.5 – Detachable antennas

As shown in the preceding figure, these are *omnidirectional* antennas, which are designed to transmit radio frequencies in all directions at the same time. The omnidirectional antennas are common on access points as they provide excellent coverage for office spaces within buildings and homes.

Sometimes, network professionals implement a wireless network to bridge two buildings over a large distance, ranging from a few meters to kilometers in distance. Using *parabolic* antennas, network professionals can implement one antenna on the rooftop of each building while ensuring there's a line of sight between them to create a point-to-point connection.

The following diagram shows a visual representation of using parabolic antennas between buildings:

Figure 16.6 – Parabolic antennas

As shown in the preceding diagram, parabolic antennas have a dish-like shape, which allows the antennas to radiate the radio frequencies in a specific direction compared to omnidirectional antennas. Network professionals can achieve distances over a few kilometers using parabolic antennas, provided there are good weather conditions and a line of sight between the source and destinations. If one parabolic antenna is misaligned, the throughput, latency, and connection quality will be greatly affected. Fortunately, vendors who sell commercial parabolic antennas usually provide an application that allows network professionals to test the signal quality between parabolic antennas and measure the throughput between sites.

The *yagi* antennas are another type of directional antenna that is used in wireless networking. This type of antenna is one of the more popular directional antennas due to its size and portability compared to large parabolic antennas.

The following figure is of a yagi antenna:

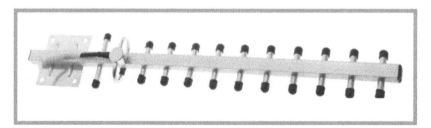

Figure 16.7 – Yagi antenna

The access point provides sufficient power to each antenna. Some access points allow network professionals to reduce the power levels on the antennas to reduce the coverage of the wireless signal within the vicinity. As an aspiring network professional, you've probably been thinking, why reduce the coverage area? Isn't the goal to ensure there is sufficient coverage to allow all authorized users to access the network? Simply put, network professionals need to ensure their wireless networks provide sufficient coverage to all their authorized users within the vicinity, such as their office spaces within a building. However, these wireless signals can penetrate the wall of the building and spread to public spaces such as the neighboring buildings and the people who are walking along the street.

A hacker can be sitting at a coffee shop across the street and detect your organization's wireless network because the signal is strong enough to travel outside the compound. Reducing the power levels on the antennas via the user interface of the access point will reduce the range/coverage of the wireless signal, thus reducing the likelihood of a hacker being able to detect the wireless network from a long distance. However, it's important to understand that reducing the power levels will reduce the coverage area, and authorized users may be affected.

Geofencing and captive portals

Geofencing is a feature within some mobile operating systems, laptops, and applications that leverages the **Global Positioning System (GPS)** and even **Radio Frequency Identification (RFID)** on mobile devices to define a geographical boundary within the real world. IT professionals can configure a company-owned mobile device with geofencing to trigger a set of rules when the device either enters or leaves the building (geographic boundary). For instance, many geofencing applications use Google Maps/Earth to define the boundaries using a satellite view of the area, while other applications allow you to define the longitude and latitude positions on a web-based map.

Organizations can take advantage of geofencing on company-owned devices. For example, if a device is within an authorized geofence virtual barrier, various features and applications will be readily available for the user of the device. If the user carries the device outside the virtual barrier, an automated restriction will be applied to various features and applications on the mobile device.

Captive portals are commonly used within hotels and coffee shops to provide a web page that lists the terms and conditions for using the wireless network. Captive portals are commonly used for marketing purposes and provide login pages for users. For instance, when connecting to the free Wi-Fi at a local shop, you'll be presented with a captive portal before you are granted access to the internet. On the captive portal, you will see the terms and conditions, along with some essential marketing advertisements. Once you've accepted the agreement, you'll be able to access the network. Captive portals are also used within hotels, providing a web portal to allow authorized guests to authenticate themselves before accessing the internet.

Client isolation

Implementing client isolation allows network professionals to logically place specific wireless clients into an isolated network, preventing any communication between the isolated client and other devices that are associated with the access point. Imagine if an organization allowed guest devices and company-owned IoT devices to be connected to the same wireless network, allocate IP addresses from the same subnet, and directly communicate with each other. If a guest connects a malware-infected mobile device to the company's wireless network, the malware can attempt to exploit the security vulnerabilities found on the IoT devices on the same wireless network.

One recommendation would be to improve the security posture of the IoT devices that are on the network. However, IoT devices do not run the same type of operating systems as traditional computers and servers – they run specialized firmware that is strictly created by the vendor of the device. Additionally, IoT devices depend on their vendor to provide regular firmware updates to resolve any bugs and security issues that may arise. However, not all vendors focus on developing updates for the firmware of their devices after the device is manufactured or even after a couple of years. For instance, Android OS is one of the most popular mobile operating systems within the mobile industry. The company, Android, has set its mark on providing operating system updates for 2 to 3 years after the launch and security updates up to 5 years after launch.

It's recommended to set up wireless client isolation, such as creating a guest wireless network for all guest devices to join the network. The guest wireless network only provides access to the internet and restricts access to any internal networks. Many organizations that provide complimentary Wi-Fi access to their customers often create a guest wireless network to allow their visitors and customers to access the internet while restricting their access to the corporate network and resources. Additionally, network professionals can create another wireless network that's isolated for all company-owned IoT devices. Therefore, all IoT devices are on one network, the guest devices are connected to another, and employees are connected to a third wireless network.

Wireless authentication protocols

The **Extensible Authentication Protocol** (**EAP**) is a framework that's commonly used on IEEE 802.11 wireless networks; it defines how systems are authenticated onto the network. There are different variations of EAP that are commonly used on wireless networks that use **Wi-Fi Protected Access** (**WPA**) and **Wi-Fi Protected Access 2** (**WPA2**).

The following are the different variations of EAP:

- **EAP over LAN**: This type of EAP is used on networks that support IEEE 802.1X for **Network Access Control** (**NAC**), which allows devices on a wired network to authenticate to an **Access Control Server** (**ACS**) running the **Remote Authentication Dial-In User Service** (**RADIUS**) service.

- **Lightweight EAP** (**LEAP**): This is a Cisco-proprietary version of EAP that uses passwords only and not digital certificates during the authentication process. This version of EAP was on Microsoft's version of **Challenge-Handshake Authentication Protocol** (**CHAP**), known as **MS-CHAP**, so it contains the same security concerns.

- **Protected EAP** (**PEAP**): This variation of EAP was designed by various organizations such as Cisco, Microsoft, and RSA Security to provide EAP for authentication. This version encapsulates the EAP message within a **security** (**TLS**) tunnel and uses digital certificates to improve the authentication process on both wired and wireless networks.

- **EAP Flexible Authentication via Secure Tunneling (EAP-FAST)**: This version of EAP was created by Cisco as a replacement for LEAP, which was implemented on wireless networks that used **Wired Equivalent Privacy (WEP)** as the wireless security standard.

- **EAP over TLS (EAP-TLS)**: This version of EAP is transported over TLS tunnels for better security. EAP-TLS uses mutual authentication where both the client and server exchange digital certificates.

- **EAP Tunnel TLS (EAP-TTLS)**: This version of EAP also supports TLS tunneling over the network. In EAP-TTLS, only the server needs a digital certificate.

Next, you will discover various installation considerations that can improve the performance of a wireless network.

Installation considerations

Before implementing a wireless network within an organization, it is important to perform a wireless LAN survey to determine the number of access points needed and the placement of these devices within the building or company. Typically, a network professional will use a laptop computer with a wireless monitoring application such as **InSSIDer** to monitor the wireless signal strength, an access point that's preferred by the company, a floor plan of the building, an electrical extension cord, and writing materials.

The network professional will connect the access point to a power outlet and leave it on the floor, then use the wireless monitoring application while walking further away from the access point to observe the wireless signal strength and mark the areas on the floor plan where the signal is weaker. Then, it connects the access point to an area where the signal is weak or absent to continue performing the site survey. This process is repeated until the network professional has covered the entire floor plan, indicating the placement of all access points and their coverage areas. This allows the network professional to determine the number of access points needed to provide maximum coverage and their placement within the building or compound.

The following figure shows a typical scale from a wireless monitoring application:

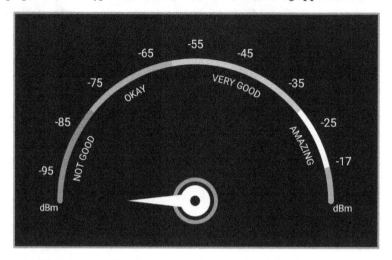

Figure 16.8 – Wireless signal scale

As shown in the preceding figure, this scale helps network professionals easily determine whether their mobile device, such as a laptop or smartphone, is too far away from the access point, or whether the wireless signal is too weak. Therefore, you want to ensure all the wireless clients on the network have *amazing* to *very good* signal. There might be a few clients who will experience *okay* signals on their mobile devices, but you need to remember that as devices move further away from the closest access point, the signal will become weaker.

> **Tip**
> There are many free Wi-Fi analyzer applications that all perform the same core functions: measure signal strength and operating channels and identify nearby wireless networks.

The following screenshot shows a **WiFi Analyzer** application detecting nearby wireless networks and their operating channels:

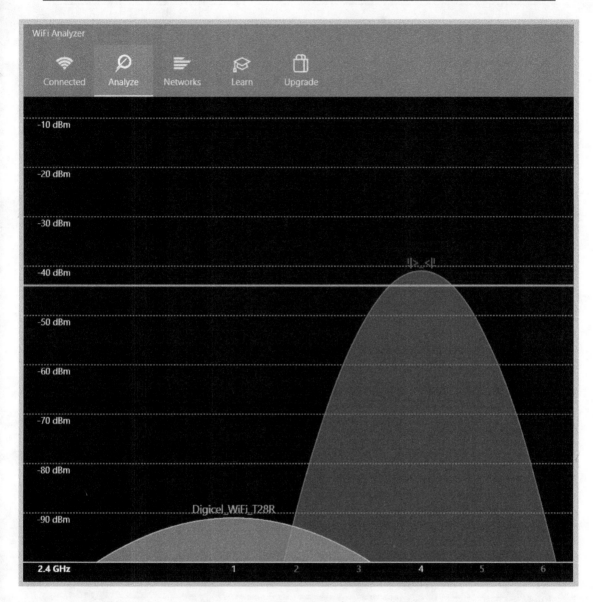

Figure 16.9 – WiFi Analyzer

As shown in the preceding screenshot, the **WiFi Analyzer** application can show the number of wireless networks found within the vicinity, their signal strength based on the location of the device running the wireless monitoring application, and the operating channels of each wireless network. Network professionals should ensure their wireless networks are not using any channels that overlap with other nearby access points.

Remote connectivity methods

A **Virtual Private Network** (**VPN**) provides a secure channel for communication over an unsecure network such as the internet. VPNs allow organizations to interconnect their remote offices securely without the need for a managed solution such as a **Wide Area Network** (**WAN**) from a regional **Internet Service Provider** (**ISP**). Many organizations around the world prefer a WAN because the service provider is responsible for establishing, maintaining, and troubleshooting any issues with the service to the customer. However, managed services from service providers cost money and not all organizations have the financial resources for such services. An alternative, cost-efficient solution is to implement a VPN to interconnect remote branch offices around the world. Many enterprise routers and firewall appliances support VPN technologies and allow network professionals to implement both **site-to-site** and **client-to-site** VPNs without spending a lot of money on managed services.

> **Important note**
>
> The *client-to-site VPN* was previously known as a *remote access VPN*.

VPNs use a set of technologies such as authentication protocols, data encryption algorithms, and integrity-checking algorithms to ensure a secure, encrypted tunnel is established to provide confidentiality, integrity, and authenticity. A site-to-site VPN allows organizations to interconnect their remote offices using a secure and free method over the internet. To set up a site-to-site VPN, the following resources are needed at each remote branch office:

- An internet connection
- A VPN router or firewall
- A static IP address

The following diagram shows a site-to-site VPN interconnecting two office locations:

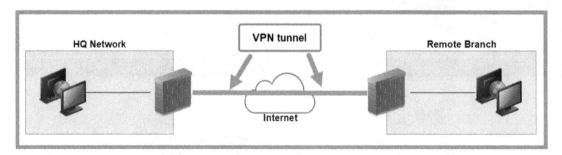

Figure 16.10 – Site-to-site VPN

As shown in the preceding diagram, two branch offices are both interconnected using a site-to-site VPN. Additionally, a firewall is placed on the internet edge at each location and is assigned a static, public IP address on both devices. If the IP address on each device changes, the VPN tunnel will be broken. Furthermore, if a user at the remote branch wants to access a service at the head office, the user's traffic will be sent from their computer to the firewall; then, it's sent through the VPN tunnel directly to the firewall at the head office. While the traffic is passing through the VPN tunnel, it is encrypted to prevent any unauthorized users and devices from seeing the data. Once the firewall at the head office receives the message, it's decrypted and forwarded to the destination server on the network.

> **Important note**
> The device that is providing the VPN service, such as a firewall, is referred to as a **VPN concentrator**.

When using a site-to-site VPN, internal users are not aware that their messages are being encrypted and decrypted as they're being sent between remote offices. This is because the data encryption and decryption process takes place on the branch firewalls and not on their computers. Site-to-site VPNs have many benefits, such as cost savings and security, but the disadvantage is that network professionals are responsible for configuring, maintaining, and resolving any issues with the VPN service between remote branches.

> **Important note**
> There are free, open source firewalls that allow network and security professionals to implement site-to-site and remote access VPNs such as **pfSense** (https://www.pfsense.org/).

Client-to-site VPNs are more common in organizations that support teleworkers and remote working. As its name suggests, a remote access VPN is a type of VPN solution that allows a remote worker to securely connect and access resources on the corporate network. Remote workers can securely connect from the comfort of their homes, hotels, coffee shops, or anywhere with an internet connection. The VPN ensures all data between the teleworker's computer and the corporate network is encrypted to provide confidentiality and data security.

The following diagram shows a client-to-site VPN:

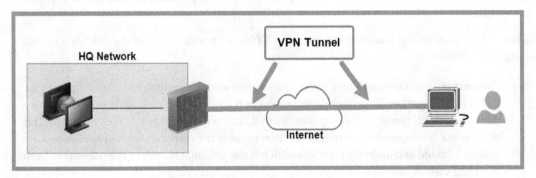

Figure 16.11 – Remote access VPN

When using a client-to-site VPN, a VPN client is installed on the teleworker's computers, and a VPN firewall is configured on the corporate network to access inbound VPN connections and apply policies to the authorized users. When the user wants to access resources on the corporate network, the user launches the VPN client and enters their user credentials, such as a username and password, to authenticate to the VPN firewall on the company's network. This type of VPN establishes a secure tunnel between the user's computer and the firewall over the internet.

The following screenshot shows the simplified user interface of the Cisco AnyConnect Secure Mobility Client on a user's computer:

Figure 16.12 – VPN client user interface

Typically, VPN clients allow a user to select a pre-configured profile that contains the details needed to establish a connection to the firewall over the internet. The user simply needs to enter their credentials and connect.

Network professionals can configure client-to-site VPNs to operate in one of the following modes on the user's device:

- **Full tunnel**: This allows outbound traffic from the teleworker's computer to be sent through the VPN tunnel. Therefore, if the user wants to access a resource on the internet, the traffic is routed through the VPN tunnel to the corporate firewall, then out to the internet, and vice versa. This mode is not recommended for remote workers because the corporate firewall applies policies to both inbound and outbound traffic, which has the potential to restrict the teleworker from accessing various websites.

- **Split tunnel**: If the teleworker has to access a resource on the corporate network, the VPN client ensures the traffic is routed through the VPN tunnel, while all other traffic is routed directly through the internet.

A **clientless VPN** is a type of VPN solution that does not require a VPN client on the teleworker's computer. This type of VPN allows the teleworker to log in via a web portal using a standard web browser to access the company's resources. A clientless VPN provides data encryption using TLS over an HTTPS connection between the client's web browser and the firewall. This type of VPN is suitable for providing users with quick and easy access to resources that can be embedded into a web portal.

Remote access methods

As an aspiring network professional, you will need to remotely connect and access systems over your network. Various *in-band management* methods allow an IT professional to securely access a system over a network, some of which are as follows:

- **Remote desktop connection**: The Microsoft Windows operating system uses the **Remote Desktop Protocol** (**RDP**), which allows IT professionals to establish a remote desktop connection between their computer and the destination system. On a remote desktop connection, the IT professionals will see a graphical user interface of the destination system as if they're right there, allowing them to remotely control the system.

- **Virtual Network Computing (VNC)**: VNC is a common remote access method that uses the **Remote Frame Buffer** (**RFB**) protocol. It is commonly used by IT professionals for its wide support on many operating systems and being mostly open source to users. VNC allows IT professionals to share the desktop experience and control the system remotely over a network.

- **Remote desktop gateway**: Within large organizations, IT professionals commonly implement a remote desktop gateway, which allows a user to secure access to RDP-enabled servers from outside the organization's network. For instance, let's say there's an IT professional who is working from home and securely connects to the remote desktop gateway using an SSL or TLS tunnel. Once connected to the remote desktop gateway, the IT professional will be able to use RDP to connect to any internal RDP-enabled server.

- **Secure Shell (SSH)**: SSH allows IT professionals to securely connect to a remote device using the Terminal. SSH is a secure protocol that provides terminal access to remote systems. This differs from Telnet, which is unsecure and does not encrypt data between the source and destination.

- **Virtual Desktop Infrastructure (VDI)**: After setting up a virtual machine within a data center or on the cloud, the user can connect to a pre-built desktop environment, allowing the user to interact with the desktop environment from any device, such as a mobile device with a web browser. The connection between the mobile device and the VDI on the cloud uses a secure connection such as SSH or TLS with HTTPS.

But what if the internet service is down or portions of the internal network within an organization are unavailable? How will network professionals connect to their network devices and security appliances for troubleshooting? Implementing **out-of-band management** allows network professionals to access devices when a network connection is unavailable. On many networking devices, there are USB, serial, or console interfaces, which allow network professionals to physically access the management interface of the device. Additionally, some network devices allow network professionals to connect an internet modem directly to a management port on the device, allowing remote access to the device.

Having completed this section, you have discovered the importance and concepts of VPN and remote connectivity methods. In the next section, you will explore physical security.

Importance of physical security

As an aspiring network professional, it's important to understand the role physical security plays within organizations and the various techniques that are used to protect assets from malicious activities. Without physical security, anyone can simply walk into restricted areas within a company and access systems, or steal and even tamper with assets. Organizations must implement various detection and prevention controls within their compound to reduce the risk of a physical threat.

> **Important note**
> Detection methods are simply deterrents and do not prevent a physical threat from occurring, while prevention methods allow security professionals to implement a type of preventative control to stop the threat from occurring.

The following are common detection methods:

- **Camera**: Implementing a **Closed Circuit Television** (CCTV) system provides security personnel with visibility into various areas within a compound or remote location. Some camera systems can identify various objects and support motion detection. Often, these camera systems are all connected and record footage over time.

- **Asset tracking tags**: Asset tracking tags allow IT professionals to create a record of every asset owned by the company. Additionally, these tags can be placed on anything such as laptops, network devices, security appliances, and other equipment. The information from asset tags can be integrated with financial records and audits within the company. These tags help IT professionals track when the device was acquired, its warranty, and other relevant information.

- **Tamper detection**: Since IT professionals cannot physically watch all the equipment within the company all the time, implementing tamper detection on devices allows the system to monitor itself for any form of tampering done by the user. For instance, manufacturers implement a physical seal that is broken if the device is opened; this can only be replaced by a service agent or vendor. Additionally, IT professionals can implement hardware tampering sensors within the chassis (case) that identify if the case was opened or removed.

The following are common prevention methods:

- **Employee training**: Training all employees regularly on the dos and don'ts helps improve the physical security within the organization. Implementing proper signage that's visible to everyone helps ensure everyone understands what's allowed and what's not.

- **Access control hardware**: Organizations commonly implement physical security such as gates and locks to prevent unauthorized access to the building or various zones within the compound. These access control hardware systems are usually connected to a network, which allows security professionals to perform real-time monitoring and control over these systems.

- **Badge readers**: Many organizations implement an electronic system that uses a pin or card system, which allows the employee to use the pin or card to access the building. This system is closely managed and controlled, allowing security professionals to monitor who accesses the area and when.

- **Biometrics**: This is a common type of authentication system that allows a user to use themselves to authenticate and verify their identity to the system. Biometrics involves fingerprint, retina, facial, and voice metrics to verify someone's identity. A user needs to be enrolled in the system before it can be effective. For instance, once a user's fingerprint has been scanned, it's converted into a mathematical representation and stored on the system.

- **Access control vestibule**: This was previously known as a **mantrap**, which prevents unauthorized people from tailgating an employee into a secure area within a building. It's usually a very small room that contains two doors: one door allows access into the vestibule and another allows them to exit. However, only one door can be opened at a time; the other door is locked. Therefore, a person has to open one door to enter the vestibule and close it upon entering; then, they will be allowed to open the other door to exit the vestibule.

- **Locking cabinets**: Server racks should be locked at all times when an IT professional is not performing any physical work on the servers. However, the responsibility of locking the ranks is managed by the owner.

- **Smart lockers**: These are safe and automated lockers that allow a retailer to deliver items to customers at a specific location. When the customer arrives, they enter a code or pin to access the smart locker and collect their purchased items. Smart lockers reduce the risk of theft.

The following are some common asset disposal methods:

- **Asset disposal**: Asset disposal focuses on how to securely destroy assets or media that contain sensitive data. Without properly destroying the data, anyone can attempt to retrieve the data and use it for malicious purposes.

- **Factory reset/wipe configuration**: Clearing the device's configurations ensures no one will be able to determine how the device was used within an organization or determine either the VLAN or IP configurations. A factory reset will restore the original default configurations on the device and remove any customized settings.

- **Sanitize devices for disposal**: Before disposing of storage media, it's important to sanitize or wipe the media devices thoroughly to ensure data is not recoverable.

Having completed this section, you have learned about various techniques and methods that can be used to improve physical security within an organization. Now, let's summarize this chapter.

Summary

In this chapter, you learned about popular and common network security solutions and strategies that are used within organizations to prevent and mitigate various types of cyberattacks and threats. Most importantly, they are used to improve the security posture of the network infrastructure. You also learned about network hardening techniques, wireless security solutions, remote access methods and technologies, and how physical security plays an important role within many organizations.

I hope this chapter has been informative for you and is helpful in your journey toward learning networking and becoming a network professional. In the next chapter, *Chapter 17, Network Troubleshooting*, you will focus on performing network troubleshooting to resolve issues that are common on modern networks.

Questions

The following is a short list of review questions to help reinforce your learning and help you identify areas that may require some improvement:

1. Which of the following can be used to prevent an unauthorized device from accessing the resources on a wired network?

    A. Router guard

    B. DHCP snooping

    C. Port security

    D. Root guard

2. Which of the following can be used to prevent MAC spoofing on an internal network?

    A. Dynamic ARP inspection

    B. Router guard

    C. MAC snooping

    D. Root guard

3. Which of the following can be used to ensure only authorized clients are associated with an access point?

    A. Disable the SSID broadcast

    B. Implement AES encryption

    C. Implement MAC filtering

    D. All of the above

4. What can a network professional do to reduce the coverage of a wireless network?

    A. Turn off the access point when it's not in use

    B. Reduce the power levels on the antennas

    C. Decrease the bandwidth on the wireless network

    D. Increase the power levels on the antennas

5. How can an organization ensure applications on their company-owned mobile devices are accessible only when the user is within the office?

    A. Remove the application from the mobile device when it's not in use

    B. Turn on the GPS on the device

    C. Implement WPA3 on the wireless network

    D. Implement geofencing

6. Which of the following allows organizations to interconnect remote offices using a secure method over the internet?

    A. Client-to-site VPN

    B. Remote desktop connection

    C. Clientless VPN

    D. Site-to-site VPN

7. Which of the following is an unsecure remote access method?

    A. Telnet

    B. SSH

    C. HTTPS

    D. RDP

8. Which of the following is a deterrent security control?

    A. Biometrics

    B. Cameras

    C. Locks

    D. All of the above

9. Which of the following prevents tailgating?

    A. Smart locker

    B. CCTV

    C. Access control vestibule

    D. None of the above

10. Which of the following wireless security standards is not recommended on wireless networks?

    A. WPA2

    B. WPA3

    C. WPS

    D. All of the above

Further reading

To learn more about the topics that were covered in this chapter, check out the following links:

- *Small Business Network Security Checklist*: https://www.cisco.com/c/en/us/solutions/small-business/resource-center/security/network-security-checklist.html

- *What Is Wi-Fi Security?*: https://www.cisco.com/c/en/us/products/wireless/what-is-wi-fi-security.html

- *Differences among WEP, WPA, WPA2 and WPA3 wireless security protocols*: https://www.techtarget.com/searchnetworking/feature/Wireless-encryption-basics-Understanding-WEP-WPA-and-WPA2

- *VPN (virtual private network)*: https://www.techtarget.com/searchnetworking/definition/virtual-private-network

17

Network Troubleshooting

As an aspiring network professional, designing and implementing networks is an amazing experience. However, understanding how to identify, troubleshoot, and resolve issues makes a better network professional within the industry. While network implementation and operations are important, network troubleshooting is equally important. Being excellent at network troubleshooting allows a network professional to validate their understanding of the technology to determine the true probable cause of issues by using their knowledge from learning about networking, their wisdom, and skills from experiences to resolve the issues and implement preventative controls. While troubleshooting is a problem-solving skill within the field of networking, it takes some time to develop and improve upon each time a new issue occurs.

In this chapter, you will explore network troubleshooting methodology and approaches used by network professionals within the industry to identify and resolve network-related issues using a systematic and efficient technique. You will also learn how to identify various types of wired and wireless connectivity issues, their probable causes, and how to resolve them. Additionally, you will discover common hardware- and software-based troubleshooting tools to assist you as a network professional, as seen in the following list:

- Network troubleshooting methodology
- Cable connectivity issues
- Wireless connectivity issues
- Common network issues
- Hardware-based troubleshooting tools
- Software-based troubleshooting tools

Let's dive in!

Network troubleshooting methodology

Proper network troubleshooting follows a systematic approach. Rather than guessing solutions to problems based on unclear information and random theories, network professionals who follow a proper troubleshooting methodology perform a specific, organized process that helps them to be more efficient in their problem-solving operations.

The following is a step-by-step network troubleshooting methodology:

1. Identify the problem.
2. Establish a theory of probable cause.
3. Test the theory to determine the cause.
4. Establish a plan of action to resolve the problem and identify potential effects.
5. Implement the solution or escalate as necessary.
6. Verify full system functionality and, if applicable, implement preventive measures.
7. Document findings, actions, outcomes, and lessons learned.

Let's look at each step in detail:

1. **Identify the problem**: The first step in troubleshooting any network issue is to identify the problem that has arisen properly. In many instances, network professionals are presented with symptoms of the problem through reports from other users, automated reports by monitoring software, or their own observations. Often, these symptoms do not provide all of the information on the issue. It is, therefore, essential for the network professional to gather as much data as possible regarding the problem.

2. **Establish a theory of probable cause**: By gathering additional data, network professionals are able to understand the *root cause* of the issue better and determine whether a single issue exists on the network or whether the symptoms relate to multiple problems that need to be segmented and worked on individually. Additional data can be gathered from devices involved in the issue, log files in log management software, and other reports stored locally on the device or remote management software. Data may also be gathered by questioning users involved in the issue, attempting to duplicate the issue (while observing the network more closely), or assessing what changes have been implemented on the network recently.

3. **Test the theory to determine the cause**: Once sufficient data has been gathered in relation to the problem that has manifested itself on the network, network professionals then utilize the data they have gathered to establish a theory of probable cause or, in other words, to make an educated assumption about the cause of the issue. In establishing this theory, it is important not to overlook any of the obvious possible causes of the issue. Many issues that may appear complex at first glance may be caused by simple occurrences on the network. To formulate their explanation of the cause of the issue, network professionals may follow several approaches, including segmenting the problem into multiple smaller problems or working through each layer

of the **Open Systems Interconnection (OSI)** model, either from top to bottom or vice versa. These approaches may even be combined to form a more cohesive explanation of the cause.

Once a proper theory has been established, network professionals must test their formulated theory concerning the cause of the issue. This test will illustrate whether the theory was correct. If the theory is correct, the network professional can continue with the troubleshooting process to determine an appropriate resolution to the issue. If the theory is shown to be incorrect, then return to the previous step to establish an alternative theory to test. At this stage, the network professional may also request help from other staff members or escalate the issue if desired.

4. **Establish a plan of action to resolve the problem and identify potential effects**: Once a theory regarding the cause of the issue is proven to be correct, the network professional must move on to establishing a plan of action to resolve the issue. At this stage, sufficient data has likely been gathered to formulate a proper solution to the problem. However, the network professional may still need to consult with other staff members to establish a plan for the proper resolution of the issue. In many cases, the resolution process can affect business processes and, as such, the network professional must work alongside team members to identify potential repercussions of the resolution plan and to both test the plan and schedule an appropriate time to implement it so that it impacts business processes as little as possible.

5. **Implement the solution or escalate as necessary**: After establishing and verifying the plan of action, the network professional can finally implement the formulated solution. Depending on the anticipated impact on other processes, this plan of action may have to be implemented during off-periods in an approved maintenance window. It may also be necessary to request the aid of other personnel in the organization or to escalate the solution to other staff members for implementation. For instance, if the plan involves a significant number of devices under the jurisdiction of another staff member, it may be appropriate to escalate the plan to that member.

6. **Verify full system functionality and, if applicable, implement preventive measures**: After implementing the plan of action, it is necessary to perform testing on all affected systems to verify full system functionality. This step ensures that no other business processes are unduly affected by the solution. Depending on the circumstance, it may also be necessary to implement preventative measures to prevent the issue from recurring. For instance, if the issue that occurred involved power outages due to loosened power cables, it would be appropriate to secure the cables to both the outlet and the **Power Supply Unit (PSU)** to ensure that the cable does not come undone again.

7. **Document findings, actions, outcomes, and lessons learned**: Lastly, it is important to keep a record of the entire process. Although the issue and its resolution may seem impossible to forget at the time of the incident, network professionals often forget the issue entirely within the space of a few months. Through proper documenting of the issue, from the initial report to the final testing of the implemented solution, network professionals can save themselves a lot of stress by being able to simply reference their documentation when similar issues arise in the future.

Having completed this section, you have learned a common network troubleshooting methodology that's used by many network professionals within the industry. Next, you will deep dive into exploring common issues on a wired network.

Cable connectivity issues

In this section, we will address some of the most common connectivity and performance issues that transpire on wired networks. As most of these issues exist at layer 1 and layer 2 of the OSI model, higher-layer protocols will frequently exhibit issues when these problems exist since these higher-layer protocols depend on the services offered by the lower layers. It is therefore recommended that network professionals become familiar with the symptoms of these issues and perform a bottom-to-top troubleshooting methodology when they suspect that these problems are present.

Link lights/status indicators

Most equipment, such as switches, routers, and firewalls, includes lights on each physical interface where cables can be plugged into the equipment, which helps network professionals to diagnose physical layer issues on those links. Lighting schemes differ between different equipment vendors, but a lack of lights on an interface generally corresponds to no signal being received across the link for that interface. Network professionals can therefore use the presence or absence of link lights on the interfaces to determine whether links are functioning properly or whether troubleshooting is required.

Damaged cables and connectors

The first step in troubleshooting a physical layer issue should always be to search for bends or breaks in the cabling or connectors (including in the pins of the connectors). These issues can be diagnosed through physical inspection or by utilizing a multimeter or cable tester to check continuity across cables and pins (to search for open circuits or shorts between circuits). These issues are usually remedied by simply replacing the damaged component in the link or by replacing the entire cable if deemed necessary.

Incorrect TX/RX alignment

Rather than being linked to damaged cables or connectors, some issues can be traced to misaligned pins or connectors on equipment, resulting in the **TX** (transmitting) and **RX** (receiving) sides of both ends not corresponding correctly. On copper cables, this may be due to wires being crimped improperly, while on fiber cables, this may be due to the incorrect placement of each duplex connector. For copper cables, therefore, the remedy is usually to re-crimp the cables with the proper pin-out or utilize ports with a **Medium-Dependent Interface (MDIX)** if required, while fiber cables simply require a reversal of the connectors at one end of the link.

The following diagram illustrates this issue of incorrect TX/RX alignment:

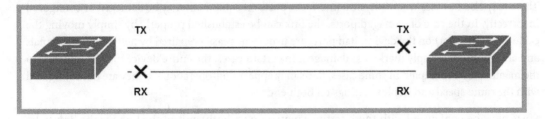

Figure 17.1 – TX/RX transmission issue

As shown in the preceding diagram, both switches are unable to send or receive messages to the other due to incorrect TX and RX alignments.

Attenuation

Attenuation refers to the reduction in amplitude of a signal as it propagates through a system due to the losses present in the system. Attenuation may be caused by a number of factors, including resistance in copper cables, absorption in fiber cables, and reflection in fiber connectors. Attenuation is the physical phenomenon that limits the maximum length of a link since equipment requires a particular minimum threshold of signal power to communicate across the link. In diagnosing attenuation issues, it is important to observe whether link lights are present on equipment, note the maximum link length for the cables/transceivers used in the link, and utilize tools such as light meters to measure the received signal strength at both ends of the cable.

Crosstalk and Electro-Magnetic Interference (EMI)

Crosstalk refers to the phenomenon whereby electrical signals transmitted in one circuit induce an undesirable electrical signal in another. In the field of networking, crosstalk manifests itself most frequently in twisted-pair copper cabling. A number of techniques have already been employed to reduce crosstalk in these cables, including twisting the cables and wrapping the cables in shielding, but crosstalk may still occur due to cables being untwisted at the ends. In many newer category cables, such as Cat 7, it is necessary to maintain the twists straight up to the connector end.

While crosstalk deals with interference generated from within the cable, EMI deals with interference sourced from outside the cable, which may be generated by a number of components, including microwave ovens and generators. Crosstalk and EMI problems may manifest themselves as cables unable to support the speeds they should or as a high number of errors across the cables. These problems may be remedied by techniques such as ensuring that twists remain right up to the connector, using cables with more shielding, or moving the copper cables away from significant sources of interference.

Bad ports/transceivers

There may also be cases where physical interfaces/ports on equipment may be damaged or configured incorrectly. In the case of damaged ports, the link can be established properly by simply moving the cable to another port on the device. Bad ports are usually not easily repaired by network professionals and are commonly simply marked as damaged. In certain cases, the entire device may be returned to the manufacturer for repair. In some cases, ports may appear non-operational if they are not configured with the same speed and duplex settings on both ends.

Ports must be configured with these settings matching on both ends of the link for the link to be established. Additionally, links may not be established due to the transceivers used at both ends. These transceivers may be incorrect for the type of link being established. For instance, a transceiver designed for **Multi-Mode Fiber** (**MMF**) may be inserted into a port while the link uses a **Single-Mode Fiber** (**SMF**) cable, the transceiver may be manufactured for a different device (many devices require transceivers manufactured from the same vendor), or the transceiver may simply be damaged. These situations can be remedied by sourcing the correct type of transceiver from the correct vendor, ensuring that the same type of transceiver is used on both ends of the link, and switching the transceiver to a known working module.

VLAN mismatch

While troubleshooting connectivity issues on switches that support and employ VLAN tagging, it is important to check how the ports on both ends of a link are configured. VLANs segment broadcast domains and are (usually) also implemented with different networks assigned to each VLAN. Therefore, it is important to check that the port undergoing troubleshooting is assigned to the correct VLAN ID. It is also important to ensure that the VLAN being tested has been created in all relevant switches in the network, as switches do not usually pass VLANs that have not been created on them.

Sub-optimal performance

Even if connectivity has been established across a link, there may be cases where performance across the link is sub-optimal. For instance, network professionals may notice high amounts of latency, such as a delay between transmitting and receiving packets across a link or jitter – the variation in latency across a link. This may be caused by factors such as the length of the cable since the signals used to transmit packets across a link takes some time to travel or interference across the link.

Additionally, network professionals may notice that links are not performing at their rated speeds due to the aforementioned factors or due to incorrect cable types being used. For example, a Cat 6 cable may not be able to deliver 10 Gbps across the full 100 m, as a Cat 6a cable might be able to. Due to these links operating at lower speeds, bottlenecks may be created in the network.

If a transmission is being performed across several links, the transmission would only be able to run at the speed of the slowest link in the chain. Many of these issues can be remedied by replacing copper cables with fiber cables. Since light pulses travel faster than electrical signals, latency in fiber cables is usually lower than in copper cables. Fiber cables also do not suffer from EMI or crosstalk. Additionally, fiber cables also have maximum link lengths that are much higher than copper cables, allowing speeds to be maintained across longer runs of cables.

The following diagram illustrates a common bottleneck scenario:

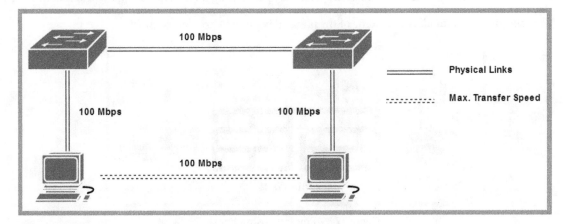

Figure 17.2 – Sub-optimal issue

In this section, we have covered many of the issues commonly seen on wired networks in the hope that you can now troubleshoot these issues much more quickly. In the following section, you will discover prevalent issues often found on wireless networks.

Wireless connectivity issues

Wireless networks are becoming more and more ubiquitous around the world as they free us from many of the technical difficulties of wired networks. However, they also introduce a number of complications that must be considered. In this section, we will explore some of the most common issues that technicians face in wireless networks.

Physical layer issues

Wireless signals face even more obstructions than signals in wired media, as these wireless signals propagate in unguided media. **Radio frequency** (**RF**) signals between Access Points and client devices often have to propagate through various objects and materials, including concrete walls, glass, and other electronic items. While propagating through these materials, these signals may undergo phenomena, such as reflection, where the signals bounce off certain surfaces such as metallic objects; refraction, where the signals bend due to traveling through two dissimilar media; and absorption, where the signals lose a lot of their power while propagating through different materials.

As a result of this, latency and jitter across wireless networks are often significantly higher than in wired networks since RF signals may take a longer time to travel across wireless media, and each RF signal can take a variety of different paths, each with its own corresponding delay. Network professionals must, therefore, properly assess the environment in which their wireless networks will be used and try to minimize the number of obstructions present by positioning their Access Points appropriately.

The following diagram illustrates some of the physical issues on a wireless network:

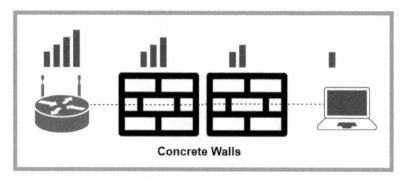

Figure 17.3 – Physical obstructions

As shown in the preceding diagram, the walls are absorbing the radio frequency that is emitted from the Access Point. As a result, the laptop computer is experiencing poor reception of the wireless signal. Hence, the user will experience poor network performance.

Antenna issues

To mitigate some of these physical layer issues, network professionals should properly plan their antenna choice and placement in the network. Omnidirectional antennas are the most popular antennas supplied with Access Points, but they may not be the most appropriate for all situations. Omnidirectional antennas radiate power approximately uniformly in all directions and are, therefore, well-suited to environments where wireless coverage needs to extend to fill an entire room and where the Access Points can be placed in the center of the room.

However, there may be other environments that require the use of directional antennas, which radiate power in one direction only. In these environments, antenna placement becomes even more critical, as technicians must ensure that the signal is radiated in the proper direction.

Signal power issues

Many wireless network issues are caused by clients simply not receiving sufficient **Effective Isotropic Radiated Power** (**EIRP**), better referred to as *power settings* or *signal power* for proper operation. Wireless signals are attenuated by a number of factors, including the reflection, refraction, and absorption phenomena, as discussed previously. Additionally, wireless signals lose power as they propagate through physical media (air in most environments). Therefore, even in the absence of any objects to cause additional losses, signal power is reduced as the distance to the transmitter is increased, resulting in a maximum distance at which a client device can communicate with an Access Point. To increase this maximum distance, network professionals may increase the power levels on their Access Points. However, this does not necessarily increase the range of the network unless the client power levels are also increased.

Interference

In addition to signal power levels, network professionals must also consider the levels of interference in their wireless networks. Wireless networks operate using particular frequency bands. For instance, the IEEE 802.11n protocol commonly operates on 20 MHz channels, meaning that even though 11–14 channels are available for use, depending on the region in which the devices are operating, these channels cannot all be used as channel overlaps will occur.

For this reason, network professionals must plan their wireless networks properly, ensuring that adjacent networks utilize channels with proper spacing to avoid overlaps and interference, thereby ensuring that clients meet or exceed their minimum threshold **Signal-to-Noise Ratio** (**SNR**), the ratio of the wireless signal power to the power of external noise and interference signals required for optimal performance.

The following diagram illustrates the non-overlapping channels used in many IEEE 802.11n networks:

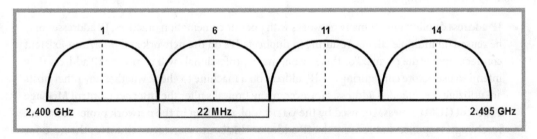

Figure 17.4 – Non-overlapping channels

As shown in the preceding diagram, channels 1, 6, and 11 are non-overlapping channels on IEEE 802.11 wireless networks, which use the 2.4 GHz frequency. Channel 14 is only permitted for usage in Japan.

Client configuration issues

In many instances, network professionals may discover that their wireless networks are configured correctly, but a single client is not configured properly for the network they are trying to access. Some common client issues include the client device not being able to support the correct frequency; for example, the client device may only support 2.4 GHz networks, while the nearest Access Point to it only supports 5 GHz. Another common issue is the client device is connected to the wrong **Service Set Identifier** (**SSID**); hence it's trying to access the incorrect network, or the client device is configured with incorrect passphrases or wireless security standards, resulting in it not being able to authenticate and join the wireless network. These issues must be treated on a case-by-case basis, requiring the network professional to compare the configuration on problematic clients with the desired configuration and then reconfigure the devices as required.

In this section, we've covered many common issues experienced while administering wireless networks. In addition to these wireless-specific issues, network professionals frequently experience several network service issues that impact clients on their networks. In the following section, we will describe some of these common issues.

Common network issues

Many issues network professionals encounter while troubleshooting networks are limited to particular client devices. In these cases, network professionals notice that all of the other clients on the network are operating correctly while the client in question exhibits issues. Here, network professionals should examine the network configuration on the client machine itself, paying particular attention to the possibility of the following:

- **IP address duplication**: In many networks with poor documentation practices, IP addresses may be reused on multiple clients, resulting in duplicate IPs on the network and poor/non-existent connectivity for the clients. For this reason, many professionals will ping the IP address they intend to use before configuring the IP address on a machine to check whether any other hosts are utilizing the intended address. However, many firewalls filter the **Internet Control Message Protocol** (**ICMP**) messages used by the ping tool, resulting in the network professional not receiving a response and reusing the IP address. This issue, therefore, reinforces the need for proper documentation.

- **MAC address duplication**: Although **Media Access Control** (**MAC**) addresses are not usually explicitly configured on host machines in the same way that IP addresses are, specialized software exists that allows hosts to utilize MAC addresses other than those embedded in their **Network Interface Card** (**NIC**). Therefore, rogue agents on the network may spoof MAC addresses of machines on the network for nefarious purposes, preventing communication to the original host machine. Network professionals should be aware of this possibility and actively search the network for rogue agents that might be spoofing their valid MACs and implementing preventative measures such as layer 2 security controls.

- **Incorrect gateway and subnet mask**: IP addresses only form one part of a client's layer 3 configuration. The subnet mask and gateway form another critical part of the configuration, telling the host the size of the network that it is a part of, and letting it know which device it should communicate with to transport packets out of its own network. Therefore, network professionals must verify these configuration parameters and ensure that they match the network that the client is part of.

- **Incorrect DNS/NTP servers**: Client machines are usually configured to communicate with several servers that provide particular services that the client needs. Two of the most important services are name resolution services provided by **Domain Name System (DNS)** servers and time synchronization services provided by **Network Time Protocol (NTP)** servers. Network professionals must verify that both these servers are configured correctly on the client machines. DNS services can be verified by using the `nslookup` or `dig` tools. For time synchronization services, network professionals should verify the correct time zone is set on the client and that the NTP server is responding.

In addition to these client configuration issues, some networks may suffer from **Dynamic Host Configuration Protocol (DHCP)**-related issues. These issues may include the following:

- **Exhausted DHCP scope**: Network professionals may notice new clients connecting to the network are not being assigned addresses from the DHCP pool. In some of these cases, it may be that the pool is simply exhausted on the DHCP server, and there are no more addresses to lease to new clients. In these cases, the network professional may consider expanding the pool, adding additional pools, or reducing the lease time to ensure that addresses are available for use more quickly.

- **Expired IP address**: In certain situations, host machines may not be able to communicate with DHCP servers to renew their IP address leases. In these cases, the host's address may expire, and the host will be forced to request a new address. To prevent these situations, reservations may be created on the DHCP server.

- **Rogue DHCP server**: In some instances, network professionals may notice DHCP messages from servers other than those they configured. In these cases, it may be necessary to locate these rogue DHCP servers and disconnect the machines manually or explicitly configure particular ports on their networks to allow DHCP servers and deny server messages from all other ports.

In some networks, misconfigured security policies may prevent proper network operation. Some of the most common security problems include the following:

- **Untrusted digital certificates**: Web browsers may complain about untrusted digital certificates for several reasons. In some cases, the certificate may be signed by a trusted **Certificate Authority (CA)** but may be rejected by the browser due to a number of issues, such as missing intermediary certificates or misconfigured or expired certificates. In other cases, the server may be using a self-signed certificate that has not been imported into the client's certificate store. Most web browsers provide the network professional with some information about the problematic certificate, which helps in the troubleshooting process.

- **Incorrect network or host firewall settings**: In some networks, firewalls at particular points may block valid traffic from reaching their intended destination. The firewalls (either host-based or network-based) may be configured with **Access Control Lists (ACLs)** that drop traffic to valid destination addresses or ports and require the network professional to trace the traffic through the entire path in the network and determine which node along the path drops the traffic. The network professional should always be aware of implicit denying rules that may exist in ACLs that silently discard traffic on the network.

Lastly, some issues may be simply due to hardware or software failures. Many system processes and hardware devices often become stuck due to problematic software functions or components, requiring the network professional to restart the particular software process or hardware device. In some instances, these devices may need to be upgraded or replaced if the network professional notices that they are becoming stuck and impacting services too frequently.

Having completed this section, you have discovered common network issues that can create a problem on the network. In the next section, you will learn how to use hardware-based tools to resolve physical issues within your network.

Hardware-based troubleshooting tools

Let's first investigate some of the common hardware devices used to troubleshoot and repair both copper-based and fiber-based networks:

- **Crimper**: A crimper is a tool used to attach copper cables to connectors. In modern networks, this is most often used to attach a twisted-pair copper cable to RJ45 connectors, but crimpers also exist for other types of copper cables. The main purpose of a crimper is to press electrical contacts down into the individual copper cables, thereby establishing electrical connectivity between the cables and the connectors. Additionally, they press the plastic hammer down onto the outer sheath of the cable, thereby fixing the connector to the cable. Crimpers usually contain parts to peel the outer sheath and trim the length of the individual copper wires.

The following photo shows a crimping tool:

Figure 17.5 – Network crimper/crimping tool

- **Cable tester**: After copper cables are crimped on both ends, cable testers are usually used to ensure that proper electrical connectivity is established and that electrical signals can traverse the cable properly. Most cable testers simply send a test signal from one end of the tester and verify that the signal is received on all pairs at the other end of the cable. More advanced (and more expensive) cable testers, however, can also measure and display the physical properties of the cable under test.

The following photo shows a cable tester tool:

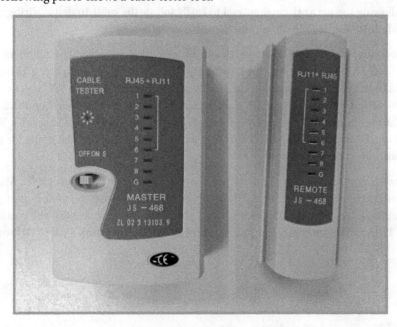

Figure 17.6 – Cable tester

- **Punchdown tool**: Rather than crimping the ends of the copper cable, the ends may be attached to 66 or 110 blocks. Punchdown tools are used to push individual cables from twisted-pair cables into their slots on the blocks and to cut off excess wiring at the end of the slots.

The following photo shows an example of a punchdown tool:

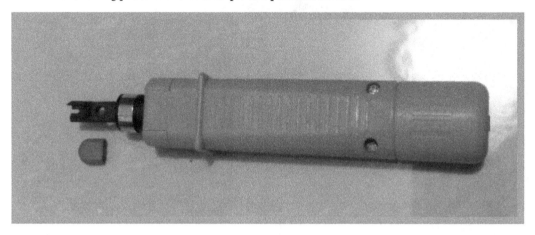

Figure 17.7 – Punchdown tool

- **Tone and probe tool**: A tone and probe tool is a device used to help network professionals to trace copper cables. The tone generator is attached to the start of the cable, and the probe (which generates a loud sound once it is held close to the cable under test) is run along the cable, allowing the network professional to easily follow the cable in dense wiring closets or racks, where it may be difficult to trace the cable visually.

- **Loopback adapter**: A physical loopback adapter is a device attached to equipment to feed a transmitted (TX) signal back into the receiving (RX) interface of the equipment. These adapters may be created for copper interfaces/cables by connecting the TX and RX cables or for fiber cables by connecting the TX and RX connectors or cables in duplex fiber. Loopback adapters are useful for diagnosing physical layer issues. For instance, a loopback adapter may be used at the end of a **Wide Area Network** (**WAN**) circuit to demonstrate that the cables for the WAN circuit are operating correctly.

- **Multimeter**: A multimeter may be used to test several parameters on copper cables. Multimeters can be used to test end-to-end continuity in cables, to check whether the cable is damaged, or to match cable ends as part of cable tracing work. They can also be used to test voltages in circuits such as **Power over Ethernet** (**PoE**) circuits and **Power Distribution Unit** (**PDU**) outlets.

The following photo shows a multimeter tool:

Figure 17.8 – Multimeter

Several other tools are commonly used in diagnosing optical networking issues. One such tool is an **Optical Time Domain Reflectometer** (**OTDR**). OTDRs inject a series of light pulses into fiber cables and record the scattered or reflected pulses they receive in return. Based on these received pulses, they can characterize fiber cables. OTDRs are commonly used to document fiber cables and to estimate points at which fiber cables are damaged, allowing fiber repair teams to greatly increase their efficiency in repairing damaged cables. OTDRs usually require operators to select the wavelength of the test pulse and display attenuation characteristics of the fiber according to the selected wavelength.

Another popular tool used for troubleshooting optical networks is a **light meter** or **optical power meter**. These tools also require operators to select their desired wavelength, allowing them to measure the optical power received on a fiber. These tools are essential in optical networks since equipment in these networks has particular minimum optical signal strengths, below which they cannot establish links. Light meters allow network professionals to measure optical signal strengths and determine whether the signal meets the minimum threshold for the equipment. Optical signal strength is usually referenced in **decibel-milliwatts** (**dBm**).

Lastly, network professionals often require the use of **spectrum analyzers**, which are used to examine radio frequency signals in the frequency domain, displaying the amplitude (strength) of signals for their frequency. These analyzers are commonly used to test electrical signals but may also be used to test other types of signals through appropriate transducers. Spectrum analyzers may be used to investigate interference or signal strength in a wireless network, the bandwidth of a particular signal across a wire, or the effectiveness of RF shielding in a particular cable.

In addition to these hardware tools, network professionals also commonly use a wide range of software tools in their troubleshooting methodology. In the next section, you will examine some of these software tools.

Software-based tools and commands

In this section, we will discuss some of the most common software tools and commands that technicians use to gather data within their networks.

Packet sniffer

A **packet sniffer** is a program used to capture packets traversing a network. **TCPdump** is a command-line packet sniffer, while other packet sniffers may have a graphical user interface, such as **Wireshark**. A packet sniffer is commonly combined with a protocol analyzer so that network professionals can capture and analyze traffic using a single piece of software. Under normal network configurations, packet sniffers can only capture unicast traffic directed at the host machine, multicast, and broadcast traffic on the network.

The following screenshot shows TCPdump capturing live packets on a network:

```
kali@kali:~$ sudo tcpdump -i eth0
[sudo] password for kali:
tcpdump: verbose output suppressed, use -v[v]... for full protocol decode
listening on eth0, link-type EN10MB (Ethernet), snapshot length 262144 bytes
21:45:08.929088 ARP, Request who-has 172.16.17.18 (9c:3d:cf:    (oui Unknown)) tell 172.16.17.13, length 46
21:45:08.930201 ARP, Reply 172.16.17.18 is-at 9c:3d:cf:    (oui Unknown), length 46
21:45:08.973816 IP 172.16.17.15.51396 > 172.16.17.18.domain: 26188+ PTR? 18.17.16.172.in-addr.arpa. (43)
21:45:08.976978 IP 172.16.17.18.domain > 172.16.17.15.51396: 26188 NXDomain* 0/0/0 (43)
21:45:08.977257 IP 172.16.17.15.38794 > 172.16.17.18.domain: 33110+ PTR? 13.17.16.172.in-addr.arpa. (43)
21:45:08.979758 IP 172.16.17.18.domain > 172.16.17.15.38794: 33110 NXDomain* 0/0/0 (43)
21:45:09.074155 IP 172.16.17.15.50398 > 172.16.17.18.domain: 8107+ PTR? 15.17.16.172.in-addr.arpa. (43)
21:45:09.077671 IP 172.16.17.18.domain > 172.16.17.15.50398: 8107 NXDomain* 0/0/0 (43)
21:45:09.996006 IP 172.16.17.13.9993 > root-mia-01.zerotier.com.9993: UDP, length 28
```

Figure 17.9 – A TCPdump packet capture

Therefore, network professionals usually configure monitoring ports on switches or utilize hubs to repeat traffic from other sources to their monitoring hosts. Packet sniffers and protocol analyzers can be used to perform in-depth investigations into networks, allowing network professionals to view the protocols and payloads involved in conversations between host machines. When capturing packets using a packet sniffer application such as TCPdump or Wireshark, it's recommended to set the network interface card in promiscuous mode.

The following screenshot shows that the Wi-Fi 4 adapter is set to capture network traffic using promiscuous mode on Wireshark:

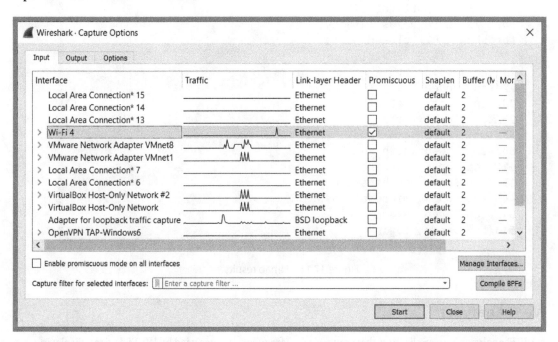

Figure 17.10 – Promiscuous mode

Promiscuous mode allows the network adapter to pass/process all network packets it receives, allowing a packet sniffer application to process each packet and display the information found within the packets.

Port scanner

A **port scanner** is a program used to identify open Transport layer service ports such as **Transmission Control Protocol** (TCP) and **User Datagram Protocol** (UDP) service ports on a machine. Port scanners are useful for assessing which services are running on a host machine since many ports are associated with specific services and application layer protocols. By utilizing port scanners, network professionals can assess the attack surface on their host machines and ensure that only necessary ports are left open.

A **Network Mapper** (**Nmap**) tool is used for scanning hosts or networks and identifying available hosts, running services, open ports, operating systems, and a variety of other information about the target system or network. This tool is commonly used for security audits and network documentation, aiding users in discovering additional information about their networks.

The following screenshot shows the output of Nmap, a common port scanner:

```
kali@kali:~$ nmap 172.30.1.26
Starting Nmap 7.91 ( https://nmap.org ) at 2021-06-23 08:50 EDT
Nmap scan report for 172.30.1.26
Host is up (0.0010s latency).
Not shown: 977 closed ports
PORT      STATE SERVICE
21/tcp    open  ftp
22/tcp    open  ssh
23/tcp    open  telnet
25/tcp    open  smtp
53/tcp    open  domain
80/tcp    open  http
111/tcp   open  rpcbind
139/tcp   open  netbios-ssn
445/tcp   open  microsoft-ds
512/tcp   open  exec
513/tcp   open  login
```

Figure 17.11 – Nmap results

Wi-Fi analyzer

A **Wi-Fi analyzer** is an application that scans wireless frequency ranges used by Wi-Fi devices, displaying information such as SSIDs, channels, Wi-Fi modes, and SNR from different Access Points within the range of the host machine. These analyzers are an important part of wireless network planning, arming network professionals with the knowledge required for tasks such as avoiding interference and scanning for rogue APs in the vicinity.

The following snippet shows the output of a Wi-Fi analyzer application on a laptop computer:

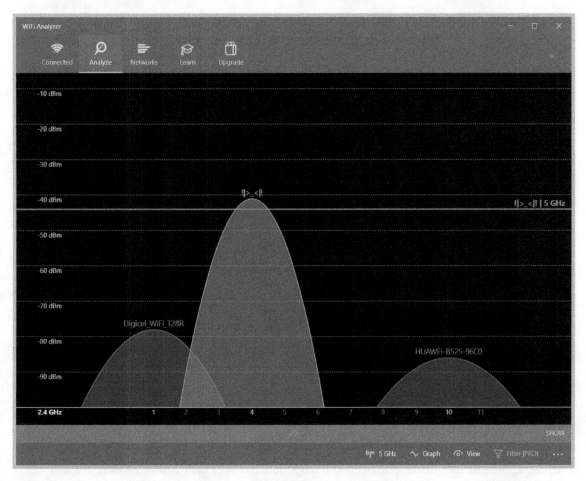

Figure 17.12 – A Wi-Fi analyzer application

As shown in the preceding screenshot, the application helps network professionals determine the channel being used by your current wireless network and those around you. Additionally, you can determine the **Received Signal Strength Indication** (**RSSI**), better referred to as the *signal strength* being received on your device.

Bandwidth speed tester

A **bandwidth speed tester** is an application used for testing the achievable throughput (speed) on a link. Speed tests are essential to ensure that links are performing as expected, and are an important part of ensuring that a **Service-Level Agreement** (**SLA**) is being met by the service provider. In running these speed tests, it is important to note the server used to perform the test, as many factors can affect the results, including the latency to the speed test server and the utilization of the link and server used for testing.

The following are common online speed test websites:

- Speedtest by Ookla – `https://www.speedtest.net/`

- Fast – `https://fast.com/`

> **Tip**
> The **iPerf** application allows network professionals to set up an iPerf server and client over a network and test the throughput between two systems to determine the bandwidth on an internal network or between branch offices. To learn about iPerf, please visit `https://iperf.fr/`.

Command-line tools

In addition to these applications, network professionals commonly utilize a number of command-line programs. These tools are called by entering their names in a command line or terminal window, along with any necessary options for the tool.

Address Resolution Protocol

Address Resolution Protocol (**ARP**) allows a host to resolve an IP address to a MAC address over a network. The ARP tool allows for viewing and modification of ARP table entries, allowing the user to understand and manipulate IP address to MAC address mapping on their host machine.

The following snippet shows the usage of the ARP tool on a Windows-based system:

```
C:\Users\glens>arp /h

Displays and modifies the IP-to-Physical address translation tables used by
address resolution protocol (ARP).

ARP -s inet_addr eth_addr [if_addr]
ARP -d inet_addr [if_addr]
ARP -a [inet_addr] [-N if_addr] [-v]

  -a            Displays current ARP entries by interrogating the current
                protocol data.  If inet_addr is specified, the IP and Physical
                addresses for only the specified computer are displayed.  If
                more than one network interface uses ARP, entries for each ARP
                table are displayed.
  -g            Same as -a.
  -v            Displays current ARP entries in verbose mode.  All invalid
                entries and entries on the loop-back interface will be shown.
  inet_addr     Specifies an internet address.
  -N if_addr    Displays the ARP entries for the network interface specified
                by if_addr.
  -d            Deletes the host specified by inet_addr. inet_addr may be
                wildcarded with * to delete all hosts.
  -s            Adds the host and associates the Internet address inet_addr
                with the Physical address eth_addr.  The Physical address is
                given as 6 hexadecimal bytes separated by hyphens. The entry
                is permanent.
  eth_addr      Specifies a physical address.
  if_addr       If present, this specifies the Internet address of the
                interface whose address translation table should be modified.
                If not present, the first applicable interface will be used.
Example:
  > arp -s 157.55.85.212   00-aa-00-62-c6-09  .... Adds a static entry.
  > arp -a                                    .... Displays the arp table.
```

Figure 17.13 – ARP tool

As shown in the preceding screenshot, various `arp` commands allow a network professional to view, edit, or delete entries from the ARP cache on the host computer.

Ping

The **Ping** tool sends **ICMP Echo Request** packets to remote hosts and processes the corresponding **ICMP Echo Reply** packets, allowing for measurement of metrics such as **Round Trip Time (RTT)**, a measure of latency, jitter, and packet loss on a link.

The following screenshot shows an example of the output generated by the ping tool:

```
C:\Users\glens>ping 8.8.8.8

Pinging 8.8.8.8 with 32 bytes of data:
Reply from 8.8.8.8: bytes=32 time=72ms TTL=116
Reply from 8.8.8.8: bytes=32 time=68ms TTL=116
Reply from 8.8.8.8: bytes=32 time=68ms TTL=116
Reply from 8.8.8.8: bytes=32 time=68ms TTL=116

Ping statistics for 8.8.8.8:
    Packets: Sent = 4, Received = 4, Lost = 0 (0% loss),
Approximate round trip times in milli-seconds:
    Minimum = 68ms, Maximum = 72ms, Average = 69ms
```

Figure 17.14 – Testing end-to-end connectivity

The following are common response messages from the ping tool and their meanings:

- **Request timeout**: The destination host has ICMP disabled, or the ICMP messages are unable to return to the sender

- **Destination host/network unreachable**: The sender or default gateway is unable to reach the destination host, possibly due to a missing route

- **Expired in transit**: The **Time to Live (TTL)** has expired (reached 0) before arriving at the destination host

By knowing the different responses and their meaning from the ping tool, a network professional will have a better idea of potential issues on the network.

Traceroute

The **traceroute** tool utilizes the TTL field of ICMP packets to map the path that a data packet takes to a particular destination, showing the IP address of every layer 3 node that the packet passes or hops through on its way to the destination, along with several measurements of RTTs for each hop. The command tracert is used on Windows-based systems, while the traceroute command is used on Linux-based systems.

The following screenshot shows the output from traceroute:

```
C:\Users\glens>tracert 8.8.8.8

Tracing route to dns.google [8.8.8.8]
over a maximum of 30 hops:

  1    68 ms    67 ms    68 ms   209.107.204.164
  2    67 ms    68 ms    69 ms   151.139.64.10
  3    69 ms    68 ms    67 ms   151.139.64.6
  4    68 ms    68 ms    69 ms   151.139.64.7
  5    73 ms    67 ms    69 ms   72.14.209.104
  6    71 ms    69 ms    68 ms   108.170.253.1
  7    69 ms    69 ms    69 ms   142.250.60.159
  8    69 ms    67 ms    67 ms   dns.google [8.8.8.8]

Trace complete.
```

Figure 17.15 – A traceroute output

As shown in the preceding screenshot, the traceroute tool checks the path the packet is using from the source to the destination, verifying the IP addresses and hostname of next-hop devices and measuring the latency between each hop along the way.

Pathping

The **Pathping** tool (available on Windows hosts) combines the functionality of the ping and traceroute tools, first determining the path between a source and its destination and then measuring RTT and packet loss to each of the nodes along the path.

NSlookup

The **NSlookup** tool allows users to perform DNS resolutions, querying specific DNS entries to display their associated records. These tools can be used for tasks such as verifying that a host is able to resolve DNS entries correctly or for querying specific DNS servers for records.

The following screenshot shows an example of the output generated by the NSlookup tool:

```
C:\Users\glens>nslookup
Default Server:   UnKnown
Address:   2606:4700:4700::1112

> www.google.com
Server:   UnKnown
Address:   2606:4700:4700::1112

Non-authoritative answer:
Name:      www.google.com
Addresses:   2607:f8b0:4006:81d::2004
             142.251.40.164
```

Figure 17.16 – Using NSlookup to resolve a hostname

> **Important note**
> The **Nslookup** tool works on Windows and Linux-based systems; however, **dig** is supported on Linux-based systems to perform DNS troubleshooting.

Ipconfig, ifconfig, and IP

The `ipconfig` tool is used on Windows-based systems, while `ifconfig` is used on Linux-based devices and displays information about the interfaces on a host machine, displaying parameters such as the IP addresses and subnet masks configured on each interface. It is used as a way to verify the configuration on host interfaces.

The following are various `ipconfig` commands:

- `ipconfig /all`: Display full configuration information
- `ipconfig /release`: Release the IPv4 address for the specified adapter
- `ipconfig /release6`: Release the IPv6 address for the specified adapter
- `ipconfig /renew`: Renew the IPv4 address for the specified adapter
- `ipconfig /renew6`: Renew the IPv6 address for the specified adapter
- `ipconfig /flushdns`: Purge the DNS Resolver cache
- `ipconfig /registerdns`: Refresh all DHCP leases and re-register DNS names
- `ipconfig /displaydns`: Display the contents of the DNS Resolver cache

The `ifconfig` command is used on Linux-based operating systems to verify the current IP configurations on the system and the `ip address` command is used on Linux-based systems to view the IP addresses on the interfaces.

The following are additional useful Linux-based commands:

- The `ip route show` command displays the default gateway on a Linux-based system
- The `route add default gw <gateway address>` command allows you to manually insert a default route on a Linux-based system
- The `ip route add default via <destination-network/mask> dev <interface-ID>` command allows you to manually insert a static route in the routing table of the Linux-based system
- Use the `dhclient -r` command to release a DHCP address on a Linux-based system

iptables and route

The `iptables` and `ip6tables` tool is a Linux utility used to manipulate IP packets according to a set of defined rules. This utility allows users to manipulate firewall rules to accept or drop packets according to particular addresses or ports on the packets, or to manipulate packets to implement features such as **Network Address Translation (NAT)**.

The `route` tool is used to configure the routing table in both Windows and Linux hosts, allowing for manual manipulation of routes to specific networks from host machines. It allows users to statically define paths for traffic to specific networks and is especially important on hosts with multiple NICs.

Netstat

The `netstat` tool lists open TCP and UDP connections on a device, showing open ports, the addresses that those ports are bound to, and the states of the connections. This tool is useful in checking which services are bound to which sockets, allowing users to diagnose issues with services or perform security audits on devices.

The following are various Netstat commands that are used on the Windows-based operating system:

- `netstat -a`: This command allows you to display all connections and listening ports on the location system.
- `netstat -e`: Allows you to display Ethernet statistics on the local system.
- `netstat -f`: Allows you to view **Fully Qualified Domain Names (FQDNs)** for their foreign IP address.
- `netstat -n`: Shows the IP addresses and port numbers in numerical format.
- `netstat -o`: Shows the owning **Process ID (PID)** associated with each connection.

- `netstat -p proto`: Displays the connections for the protocol specified by protocol type, such as IP, IPv6, ICMP, ICMPv6, TCP, TCPv6, UDP, or UDPv6.

- `netstat -q`: Shows all the connections, listening ports, and bound non-listening TCP service ports. The bound non-listening service ports may or may not be associated with an active connection on the system.

- `netstat -r`: Shows the routing table of the local system.

- `netstat -s`: Shows per-protocol statistics.

- `netstat -t`: Shows the current connection offload state.

- `netstat -x`: Shows any NetworkDirect connections, listeners, and shared endpoints.

- `netstat -y`: Shows the TCP connection template for all connections.

> **Important Note**
>
> Netstat in Linux has a different syntax. For instance, `netstat -tulpn` will display TCP, UDP in listening mode, the PID, and the numerical address.

Having completed this section, you have discovered various software-based and command-line tools that network professionals commonly use to verify connectivity and assist with troubleshooting network-related issues within their organization.

Summary

During the course of this chapter, you have learned how to use a network troubleshooting methodology to identify issues to resolve and implement preventative measures. Network professionals need to develop a critical-thinking mindset that can solve problems by quickly analyzing current issues, noticing trends in network performance, and predicting potential issues. Being an out-of-the-box thinker has many advantages, especially when you're working in the field of information technology. In addition, it helps develop your troubleshooting and problem-solving skills a lot more quickly.

Furthermore, you have discovered how various issues on wired and wireless networks can affect the availability of network services and resources to clients within an organization. Additionally, you have learned how hardware- and software-based tools can be used to identify and resolve various networking issues and assist network professionals with their day-to-day duties.

Lastly, I know the journey of preparing for the *CompTIA Network+ N10-008* certification isn't easy, and there are many challenges along the path to success. I would personally like to thank you very much for your support in purchasing a copy of my book. Congratulations on making it to the end while acquiring all these amazing new skills in learning about network fundamentals, network implementation, network operations, network security, and troubleshooting. I hope everything you have learned throughout this book has been informative and helpful in your journey toward becoming an awesome network professional and prepares you for the official certification and beyond.

Questions

The following is a short list of review questions to help reinforce your learning and help you identify areas that require some improvement:

1. A client has reported an issue with their machine connecting to the WLAN. A network professional has just finished establishing a theory of probable cause for the issue. What is the technician's next step?

    A. Identify the issue

    B. Document the issue

    C. Test the theory to determine the cause

    D. Verify full system functionality

2. A network professional has noticed that the end of one of their Cat 5 cables is damaged. What tool will they require to repair the end of the cable?

    A. A crimper

    B. A light meter

    C. An OTDR

    D. A packet sniffer

3. A network professional has rebooted a server and wants to verify that the server rebooted successfully and is online again. Which of the following tools would best fulfill this task?

    A. Route

    B. Ipconfig

    C. Ping

    D. Wi-Fi scanner

4. A network professional has received reports that their web server is no longer serving traffic correctly. They have logged into the server and captured a minute's worth of requests to the server. What tool will now enable them to analyze these requests?

    A. Traceroute

    B. Wi-Fi analyzer

    C. Protocol analyzer

    D. Packet sniffer

5. A network professional has received a request from a client to run 200 m of Cat 6 cable between two systems. Which of the following phenomena must the network professional discuss with the client to explain why signals cannot travel for 200 m across Cat 6 cable without suffering significant degradation?

    A. Attenuation

    B. Incorrect pin-out

    C. Reflection

    D. Bottlenecks

6. A client is having issues connecting to their Wi-Fi network. Upon further investigation, the network professional has discovered the user is attempting to connect to the wrong network. Which of the following best describes this occurrence?

    A. Incorrect passphrase

    B. Incorrect security type

    C. Incorrect SSID

    D. Low power levels

7. A security administrator is analyzing a trace of some traffic on their network. They notice that several hosts on this particular wireless network have received IP addresses from a server that is not recognized. What is the most likely presence on this network?

    A. A malicious NTP server

    B. A rogue DHCP server

    C. A firewall

    D. An unresponsive service

8. A network administrator has configured a small WLAN with a DHCP server for a few HR personnel in an office. Several months later, the HR team triples in size. The personnel is now complaining that several of their devices cannot access the network. Which of the following is most likely the cause of the issue?

    A. A rogue DHCP server

    B. An incorrect ACL

    C. An exhausted DHCP scope

    D. Incorrect time

Further reading

To learn more on the subject, check out the following links:

- *A Guide to Network Troubleshooting*: https://www.comptia.org/content/guides/a-guide-to-network-troubleshooting

- *How to crimp network cables*: https://www.wikihow.com/Crimp-Rj45

- *MXToolBox*: https://mxtoolbox.com/

18
Practice Exam

The following practice questions are designed to help reinforce your learning and better equip you in achieving the CompTIA Network+ N10-008 certification.

Questions

1. You're a network professional who has recently started working for a new company and needs to improve the Wi-Fi performance within the building for lots of users. Upon inspecting the specifications of the wireless clients, you notice they are using both 2.4 GHz and 5 GHz. Which of the following meets the need to support all clients?

   A. IEEE 802.11n

   B. IEEE 802.11ac

   C. IEEE 802.11b

   D. IEEE 802.11ax

2. You're a network professional within a company and suspect a rogue device is spoofing their MAC address on the network. Which of the following is most suitable for detecting this type of attack?

   A. Port security

   B. **Domain Name System (DNS)**

   C. **Reverse Address Resolution Protocol (RARP)**

   D. **Internet Message Access Protocol (ICMP)**

3.   The users on your wireless network have been reporting issues about lots of unusual response times while accessing resources. You do some basic troubleshooting, such as pinging the default gateway from your company, and notice there's lots of jitter. You suspect that there may be wireless interference from nearby wireless devices and networks. Which of the following will help you determine the root cause and assist in troubleshooting?

   A. Spectrum analyzer

   B. Network mapper

   C. Bandwidth analyzer

   D. All of the above

4.   The users on your wireless network are complaining about intermittent connectivity when they are trying to access a resource on the internet. Whenever the user disconnects from the access point and reconnects using the web-based captive portal, connectivity is restored. Which of the following will help you determine the probable cause of the issue?

   A. Verify the wireless security standard is configured properly

   B. Check the vicinity for a rogue access point device

   C. Check whether there's a session timeout that's configured on the captive portal settings on the wireless network

   D. Verify the user is entering the correct password when accessing the wireless network

5.   You're a network administrator for a large company and while you're heading to the network closet, you notice an unknown individual is following you to the secure area. Which of the following is the unknown person trying to do?

   A. Shoulder surfing

   B. Impersonation

   C. Social engineering

   D. Tailgating

6.   Users who are connected to a specific segment on a network started reporting latency issues. Upon checking the networking devices on the affected area of the network, you noticed there are increasing amounts of CRC errors while users are communicating. Which of the following OSI layers should you start your troubleshooting process on?

   A. Layer 7

   B. Layer 1

   C. Layer 3

   D. Layer 2

7. Recently, your organization has added 150 users who all use virtual machines daily. The users began to report issues such as very slow desktop response times. Upon investigating the network utilization, you found no evidence of packet collisions, congestion, or latency issues. Which of the following are the most likely probable causes of the issue? (Choose two)

   A. CPU

   B. Jitter

   C. Device temperature

   D. Disk space

   E. Memory

   F. Network bandwidth

8. Within your organization, new devices are experiencing issues connecting to the network. Upon investigating the issue, you notice the DHCP pool is exhausted but you do not want to create a new DHCP pool for the network. Which of the following solutions can you use to resolve the issue?

   A. Implement another DHCP server

   B. Reduce the time set on the lease

   C. Add a new router

   D. Add more VLANs

9. A network professional wants to collect the IPv6 and MAC addresses of all devices within the internal network of the company. Which of the following protocol would assist in this process?

   A. **Address Resolution Protocol (ARP)**

   B. **Spanning-Tree Protocol (STP)**

   C. **Neighbor Discovery Protocol (NDP)**

   D. All of the above

10. You want to create an alias for existing DNS records on your DNS server within your company. Which of the following DNS record types will be most suitable for this task?

    A. CNAME

    B. MX

    C. A

    D. PTR

11. Your organization has a WAN solution that interconnects the two offices together. The head office location has the company's intranet web server, which allows all users to access company resources and important documents. All users are able to access the internet but unable to access the intranet web server using their standard web browser. Which of the following best describes the probable cause of this issue?

A. Check the time server settings

B. Check the network switch configurations

C. Check the default router/gateway configurations

D. Check whether the correct DNS server addresses are provided within the DHCP scope

12. You're a network administrator within an organization and are trying to determine the physical address of a client device that's connected to the network. Which of the following should you check on the switch the device is connected to?

A. Log files

B. VLAN configuration

C. MAC table

D. Routing table

13. Which of the following can a network administrator implement on a critical server to ensure the server remains connected to the network if there's a failure on a switch?

A. Load balancer

B. Multiple PDUs

C. RAID

D. NIC teaming

14. Your organization is looking into improving the performance, such as speed, to distribute content efficiently on the internet and wants to ensure there's excellent latency when there's a lot of load on the server. Which of the following is most suitable for your organization?

A. NIC teaming

B. Cloud computing

C. Load balancing

D. All of the above

15. Within an organization, a user is reporting they are unable to access network resources after some changes were made within the department. Which of the following should you do first in your troubleshooting?

A. Perform end-to-end connectivity testing using ping

B. Ask the user what changes were made

C. Check the IP configurations on the device

D. Check the physical network cables

16. You're a network administrator within an organization. Each time you re-build/crimp the end of a Cat 6 networking cable to create a crossover cable between two switches, it takes additional time to do so. Which of the following technologies can be used to reduce the need for a new cabling certification each time you rebuild the end of the cables?

    A. MDIX

    B. LLDP

    C. LACP

    D. PAgP

17. You are assigned a task to create an inventory of all devices that are connected to the company's internal network. Which of the following software-based applications will be most suitable to assist you in this task?

    A. Port scanner

    B. SSH

    C. IP scanner

    D. Terminal emulator

18. You are implementing a wireless network within your company to support high density while using a frequency that is known for low interference. Which of the following IEEE 802.11 operating frequencies would be most suitable?

    A. 2.5 GHz

    B. 2.4 GHz

    C. 5.5 GHz

    D. 5 GHz

19. You are implementing a new network switch within an office space with a lot of users. You want to ensure the switch is configured to prevent unauthorized access to the physical network. Which of the following will be most suitable for this task?

    A. Dynamic ARP inspection

    B. Port security

    C. DHCP snooping

    D. SSH

20. Which of the following allows cybersecurity professionals to efficiently track and document known security vulnerabilities within the industry?

    A. Publishing your findings on your personal website

    B. Sharing information via email to other vendors

    C. **Common Vulnerabilities and Exposures (CVE)**

    D. All of the above

21. As a network administrator, you want to mitigate the risk of a hacker compromising the email accounts of the employees within your company. The hacker will attempt to retrieve the email addresses and passwords of the users. Which of the following is most suitable to mitigate this type of attack? (Choose two)

    A. Setting up a captive portal

    B. Implementing a geofencing policy

    C. Implementing two-factor authentication

    D. Implementing an implicit deny rule on the firewall

    E. Implementing a complex password policy

22. After configuring LACP on the network switch, you've connected to network cables from the switch to your server to increase the bandwidth between the server and switch. However, the network bandwidth has not increased. Which of the following needs to be configured on the server to complete the overall configuration?

    A. NIC teaming

    B. Load balancing

    C. Clustering

    D. Dual-homing

23. A network professional is configuring the IP addresses for a server on the network and is provided with 192.168.0.0/20. Which of the following subnet masks should be configured on the server?

    A. 255.255.240.0

    B. 255.255.224.0

    C. 255.255.248.0

    D. 255.255.0.0

24. Which of the following is the maximum supported MTU on a wired network within an organization?

    A. 1852

    B. 1600

C. 1492

D. 1500

25. Which of the following tools will provide a network administrator with the protocol, source IP address, source service port, destination IP address, destination service port, and state of a connection?

A. `ifconfig`

B. `traceroute`

C. `netstat`

D. `nslookup`

26. You're currently troubleshooting a network issue. After you've determined the likely cause of the issue, what should you do next?

A. Implement the solution

B. Verify systems functionality

C. Test the theory to determine the cause

D. Establish a plan of action

27. You are tasked with implementing a security solution on the network to notify you of which unauthorized devices are attempting to access the network. Which of the following is most suitable?

A. Proxy

B. **Intrusion Detection System (IDS)**

C. Firewall

D. Access point

28. A telecommunication technician has just finished installing a new cable modem at a customer's office. Which of the following cable types is most suitable for connecting the cable modem to the ISP's network?

A. Single-mode fiber

B. Multi-mode fiber

C. Cat 7

D. Coaxial

29. Which of the following helps network professionals determine a physical issue on a network cable that's connected to a network switch?

A. Runts

B. CRC

C. Giants

D. All of the above

30. Ethernet LANs within organizations use which of the following physical network topologies to interconnect client devices?

A. Star

B. Bus

C. Ring

D. Mesh

31. Your IT manager is interested in setting up a disaster recovery site and wants to ensure there is low downtime to critical operations and business processes. By setting up resources at two different data centers and ensuring all data and applications are always up to date, the company can easily fail over quickly to one of the available data centers. Which of the following best describes this type of recovery site?

A. Cold site

B. Hot site

C. Warm site

D. All of the above

32. Which of the following documents would reduce the risk of unnecessary modifications to the network without prior approval while maintaining version control within the company?

A. Incident response plan

B. Acceptable usage policy

C. Business continuity plan

D. Change management policy

33. Most traffic within a data center is east-west, rather than north-south. Which of the following action would create lots of east-west traffic?

A. Duplicating one virtual server to another physical server

B. Performing a backup to a cloud service provider

C. Performing an update to a server that's within the data center

D. All of the above

34. When debugging is enabled on a networking device such as a switch, it seems to not be responding to requests. Which of the following should you check first on the device?

A. Authentication logs

B. System logs

C. CRC error

D. CPU utilization

35. Within a building, you need to implement multiple access points on each floor to support multiple clients. All access points will be configured with the same SSID. Which of the following best describes this type of wireless deployment?

    A. Mesh

    B. Independent service set

    C. Ad hoc

    D. Extended service set

36. A network professional is trying to ping 192.168.2.101 from a host machine with the address 192.168.1.100 but is receiving multiple destination unreachable messages. Which of the following is missing from the sender's configuration?

    A. IP address

    B. Subnet mask

    C. Default gateway

    D. Loopback address

37. Your organization is using a new ISP for internet connectivity. The network administrator is provided with a new IP address scheme that's different from the previous ISP. The new ISP provides 196.27.6.0/26 to the network administrator; however, internet connectivity is lost. Upon checking the organization's default gateway, it is using the following configurations on the interface that's facing the ISP:

    - IP address = 196.27.6.68

    - Subnet mask = 255.255.255.224

    - Gateway = 196.27.6.65

    Which of the following best describes the issue?

    A. Incorrect IP address

    B. Incorrect subnet mask

    C. Incorrect gateway address

    D. All of the above

38. Which of the following statements is true about most **Infrastructure as a Service (IaaS)** solutions?

    A. Likely to replace an on-premises server with a cloud solution

    B. Likely to replace application hosting on-premises with a cloud solution

C. Likely to replace the need for IT staff

D. Likely to prevent cyber-attacks and threats

39. As a network professional, you may need to prioritize internet traffic based on the application and users on the internal network. Which of the following can assist you in this task?

A. Load balancer

B. Administrative distance

C. OSPF

D. Bandwidth management

40. You need to discover the name servers for a remote host on the internet. Which of the following commands or tools will be able to assist you?

A. `ifconfig`

B. `dig`

C. `tracert`

D. `arp -a`

41. Which of the following is commonly used within organizations to review previous upgrades performed on systems?

A. Change management

B. Standard operating procedures

C. Ask the IT professional who performed the previous upgrades

D. Ask the IT manager about the previous upgrades

42. A new switch is added to the network monitoring platform used within an organization. The network administrator wants to know which metrics can be collected from the devices on the monitoring system. Which of the following can be collected and utilized?

A. Syslog

B. Traps

C. **Management Information Base (MIB)**

D. Sets

43. The network professional within an organization is implementing a dynamic routing protocol such as OSPF within the network. Which of the following replaces the hubs on the network?

A. Firewall

B. Reverse proxy

C. WLAN controller

D. Layer 3 switches

44. Your organization provides a guest wireless network but you notice there are users from the building next door who are connecting to the guest network and downloading inappropriate content. Which of the following can you do to mitigate this problem?

    A. Implement port security on the switch

    B. Change the wireless channel to channel 11

    C. Reduce the power levels on the access points

    D. Set up dynamic ARP inspection

45. Which of the following is most suitable for securely interconnecting two different data centers together to replicate data?

    A. VPN

    B. VNC

    C. RDP

    D. SSH

46. A hacker on the network is attempting to inject popular words and phrases into a password prompt to gain access to a networking device. Which of the following best describes this type of attack?

    A. Brute-force attack

    B. Dictionary attack

    C. Offline password attack

    D. None of the above

47. Which of the following technologies allows a network professional to implement fault tolerance for their default gateway?

    A. CDP

    B. LLDP

    C. LACP

    D. FHRP

48. The DHCP server within your company is configured to provide IP addresses from the block 172.18.41.0/27 to clients on a guest wireless network. However, there are many users who have reported that they are unable to connect to the network. Which of the following can be done to mitigate this issue?

    A. Implement a new VLAN

    B. Add another DHCP server

C. Reduce the lease duration

D. All of the above

49. Which of the following will indicate the duplex settings are mismatched on both ends of a link between two devices?

A. No link light on the interface

B. Giants

C. Runts

D. CRC errors

50. Which of the following is commonly used by network professionals to manage a large wireless network with multiple access points at different branches of an organization?

A. LACP

B. Network monitoring application

C. Lightweight access point

D. Wireless controller

51. You need to implement a device that can operate as a VPN concentrator and perform threat and content filtering for your company. Which of the following is most suitable?

A. Next-generation firewall

B. VPN router

C. Layer 3 switch

D. Forward proxy

52. Which of the following is required for a network professional to configure load balancing between two servers to ensure network connectivity when a failover occurs?

A. NAT

B. Virtual IP

C. Subnet mask

D. All of the above

53. The users within your organization report the wireless network connection drops often, disconnecting their devices from the network, and reconnects after a while. Which of the following is the probable cause of this issue?

A. **Effective Isotropic Radiated Power (EIRP)** is too high

B. EIRP is too low

C. The SSID is incorrect

D. None of the above

54. Which layer of the OSI model allows a network professional to inspect the details of an IP header?

A. Layer 4

B. Layer 7

C. Layer 2

D. Layer 3

55. After implementing redundant links between two switches on a network, which of the following is needed to prevent network instability?

A. RDP

B. STP

C. LACP

D. CDP

56. Which of the following allows an ISP to exchange routing information with another ISP?

A. BGP

B. RIP

C. EIGRP

D. OSPF

57. Which of the following can a network professional use to determine the exact point that is broken on a fiber cable?

A. Tone and prober

B. Cable tester

C. OTDR

D. None of the above

58. Which of the following authentication protocols allows network professionals to centrally managed credentials, policies, and logging on different networking devices within an organization?

A. Firewall

B. SSO

C. Two-factor authentication

D. RADIUS

59. You need to install new applications on multiple Windows-based systems at remote offices. Which of the following will best assist you in performing this task?

    A. VNC

    B. SSH

    C. RDP

    D. Telnet

60. During video conferencing meetings within an organization, users have reported poor quality of the video and audio feeds. Which of the following can be used to improve the performance of the video meetings?

    A. Ether channels

    B. LLDP

    C. Static routing

    D. QoS

61. A network architect has designed a plan for connecting hosts in a new office, but he has realized that he needs to provide more physical ports for these hosts. Which of the following Layer 2 devices would be most appropriate to provide these ports?

    A. A router

    B. A switch

    C. A hub

    D. A WAP

62. An engineer is examining frames from a particular host machine that is exhibiting issues on the network and notices that headers from higher-level protocols are present in the frame. This is due to the process of:

    A. De-encapsulation

    B. Connectionless transport

    C. Encryption

    D. Encapsulation

63. A security administrator has received notice that management wishes to block access to a particular application on port 80, but not interfere with other traffic communicating through that same port. What device will be most suitable to implement this rule?

    A. A router

    B. A switch

C. A firewall

D. All of the above

64. A network administrator is analyzing TCP traffic in an effort to better understand connection-oriented transmissions. What types of PDUs should be analyzed?

   A. Frames

   B. Datagrams

   C. Segments

   D. Packets

65. The fiber team has just received a report that a truck has pulled down overhead cables in a particular area and that services will be interrupted until splicing works can be completed. What layer of the OSI model can this best be classified as affecting?

   A. Physical

   B. Application

   C. Transport

   D. Network

66. An engineer has purchased a wireless repeater that works by simply retransmitting the bits that it receives over its coverage area. What layer does this device most likely operate at?

   A. Network

   B. Data link

   C. Application

   D. Physical

67. How many bits are there in an **Internet Protocol** (**IP**) version 4 address?

   A. 48

   B. 128

   C. 64

   D. 32

68. How many usable IP addresses are there in a Class C address?

   A. 256

   B. 200

   C. 254

   D. 255

69. What is the default subnet mask of 172.18.1.1?

    A. 255.0.0.0

    B. 255.255.0.0

    C. 255.255.255.0

    D. 255.224.0.0

70. How many usable IPv4 addresses are there in a /29 network?

    A. 6

    B. 8

    C. 10

    D. 12

71. Which of the following is a public IPv4 address?

    A. 172.16.56.89

    B. 192.168.47.96

    C. 10.11.12.48

    D. 172.15.58.5

72. Which of the following is a private IPv4 address?

    A. 172.33.5.98

    B. 172.19.5.63

    C. 12.52.69.41

    D. 192.167.59.21

73. How many bits are there in an IP version 6 address?

    A. 32

    B. 48

    C. 128

    D. 127

74. Which of the following is the binary equivalent of 235?

    A. 11101011

    B. 10101010

    C. 11100101

    D. 00101011

75. What is `10101010` in decimal?

    A. 179

    B. 200

    C. 185

    D. 170

76. If a device is communicating with one another device over a network, what type of transmission is taking place?

    A. Anycast

    B. Multicast

    C. Broadcast

    D. Unicast

77. A manager has asked their team of network technicians to source a box of twisted-pair cables, which are to be used in an indoor, low-noise environment to provide speeds of 1 Gbps. What type of cable would best fit the manager's requirements?

    A. UTP Cat 3

    B. STP Cat 5e

    C. STP Cat 6a

    D. UTP Cat 5e

78. A network technician has determined that they need to run 80 m of twisted-pair copper cabling near some high-voltage transmission lines. They require this link to operate at 10 Gbps. Which of the following cable types would most likely fit their needs?

    A. UTP Cat 6

    B. STP Cat 6a

    C. STP Cat 6

    D. STP Cat 5e

79. A manager is planning to connect two remote sites of their business using a WAN connection. The connection needs to span a distance of 8 km. What type of cable would be most suitable for this connection?

    A. STP Cat 6a

    B. SMF

    C. MMF

    D. UTP Cat 5e

80. A network technician is on the phone with a vendor and needs to request transceivers for their router. They require 40 Gbps of capacity on each of the ports of the router. Assuming that the router supports it, which of the following transceivers should be requested?

    A. SFP

    B. SFP+

    C. QSFP

    D. GBIC

81. A network technician has recently taken control of an aging network and has received several complaints about slow speeds at times when many users are utilizing the network. Upon further inspection, they notice that user devices are connected to the network through hubs. What devices should they invest in first to best alleviate this issue?

    A. Routers

    B. WAPs

    C. Switches

    D. Modems

82. A network administrator is trying to set up a link to a remote office 5 km away. Unfortunately, their switches at both offices only support copper cables. What device will allow them to establish a wired connection to the remote office?

    A. WAP

    B. Media converter

    C. Hub

    D. NGFW

83. A network engineer is planning to better segment their enterprise network, creating several subnetworks for each floor and prioritizing traffic for certain mission-critical functions. Which device would best aid the engineer in this task?

    A. Modem

    B. Router

    C. L2 switch

    D. Proxy server

84. A network technician has gotten tired of continually adding and removing user accounts from every device on their network every time a new staff member joins or leaves the team. What appliance would best solve this issue?

    A. Firewall

    B. Switch

C. Proxy server

D. RADIUS server

85. A security administrator has been tasked with purchasing a firewall, a VPN concentrator, and an IPS solution. Instead of purchasing individual appliances for each requirement, what should the administrator consider?

A. A router

B. A hub

C. A **Unified Threat Management (UTM)** appliance

D. A WAP

86. Which wireless security standard uses TKIP?

A. WEP

B. WPA

C. WPA2

D. WPA3

87. An attacker is trying to exhaust a web server by sending a continuous stream of fake requests. What is the attacker trying to do?

A. Scan the network

B. Install a virus

C. DoS

D. Create a backdoor

88. An attacker has called an organization's help desk, pretending to be someone else to gather confidential information from the receiver. What is the attacker attempting to do?

A. Tailgating

B. Piggybacking

C. Social engineering

D. Insider threat

89. A type of virus that is triggered after a predefined set of actions has occurred is known as what?

A. Ransomware

B. Logic bomb

C. Spyware

D. Insider threat

90. A malware that encrypts and holds a victim's data hostage is known as what?

    A. Ransomware

    B. Logic bomb

    C. Spyware

    D. Insider threat

91. Which DNS record is responsible for specifying an email server?

    A. SOA

    B. NS

    C. CNAME

    D. MX

92. Which command is used to view the ARP cache on a Windows system?

    A. `arp -n`

    B. `arp -a`

    C. `netstat -a`

    D. `netstat -n`

93. Using a VPN will assist in mitigating which of the following threats?

    A. Cross-site scripting

    B. Cross-site request forgery

    C. Eavesdropping

    D. SMTP enumeration

94. How can a network security professional prevent an unauthorized network device from gaining access to a network segment?

    A. Implement a firewall

    B. Implement port security

    C. Implement an IPS

    D. Implement a web security appliance

95. On which layer of the OSI model does ARP spoofing occur?

    A. Data link

    B. Internet

    C. Network access

    D. Network

96. If an attacker is able to retrieve the master file containing all the records of an internal network or a DNS server, which type of attack is taking place?

    A. DNS zone transfer

    B. DNS poisoning

    C. DNS hijacking

    D. DNS lookup

97. You would like to keep track of components within your organization. Which of the following would you use?

    A. CCTV

    B. Asset tags

    C. Tamper detection

    D. Badges

98. You would like to implement a technique that will indicate whether an employee has attempted to remove any tagging on the components. Which of the following would you use?

    A. CCTV

    B. Asset tags

    C. Tamper detection

    D. Badges

99. The IT department has implemented a lot of network appliances throughout the organization. The IT manager thinks that creating a unique account separately on each appliance is a bit tedious. Which of the following can they use to make the process easier?

    A. AAA

    B. RADIUS

    C. Two-factor authentication

    D. Security token

100. Which of the following is recommended to mitigate a rogue DHCP server on a network?

    A. DHCP inspecting

    B. Dynamic ARP inspection

    C. DHCP snooping

    D. DHCP binding

Answers

1. D
2. C
3. A
4. C
5. D
6. B
7. A, E
8. B
9. C
10. A
11. D
12. C
13. D
14. C
15. B
16. A
17. C
18. D
19. B
20. C
21. C, E
22. A
23. A
24. D
25. C
26. C
27. B
28. D
29. B
30. A

31. B
32. D
33. A
34. D
35. D
36. C
37. B
38. A
39. D
40. B
41. A
42. C
43. D
44. C
45. A
46. B
47. D
48. C
49. D
50. D
51. A
52. B
53. B
54. D
55. B
56. A
57. C
58. D
59. C
60. D
61. B
62. D

63. C

64. C

65. A

66. D

67. D

68. C

69. B

70. A

71. D

72. B

73. C

74. A

75. D

76. D

77. D

78. B

79. B

80. C

81. C

82. B

83. B

84. D

85. C

86. B

87. C

88. C

89. B

90. A

91. D

92. B

93. C

94. B

95. A
96. A
97. B
98. C
99. B
100. C

Assessments

In the following pages, we will review all the practice questions from each of the chapters in this book and provide the correct answers.

Chapter 1 – Exploring the OSI Model and TCP/IP

1. C
2. C
3. D
4. B
5. A
6. D
7. C
8. A
9. B
10. C

Chapter 2 – Network Topologies and Connections

1. B
2. A
3. C
4. D
5. C
6. B
7. B
8. D
9. C
10. C

Chapter 3 – Ethernet Technology and Virtualization

1. C
2. D
3. A
4. B
5. A
6. C
7. C
8. B
9. A
10. C

Chapter 4 – Understanding IPv4 and IPv6 Addressing

1. A
2. C
3. D
4. A
5. C
6. C
7. D
8. A
9. B
10. D

Chapter 5 – Applied IPv4 Subnetting

1. C
2. D
3. B
4. C
5. A
6. D

7. C
8. B
9. A
10. C

Chapter 6 – Exploring Network Protocols and Services

1. B
2. D
3. C
4. A
5. D
6. A
7. B
8. D
9. C
10. C

Chapter 7 – Data Center Architecture and Cloud Computing

1. B
2. D
3. A
4. C
5. B
6. D
7. A
8. B
9. B
10. A

Chapter 8 – Network Devices

1. B
2. D
3. A
4. D
5. C
6. B
7. A
8. D
9. C
10. B

Chapter 9 – Routing and Switching Concepts

1. C
2. B
3. D
4. B
5. A
6. C
7. A
8. D
9. B
10. C

Chapter 10 – Exploring Wireless Standards and Technologies

1. B
2. C
3. D
4. C
5. A

6. C
7. C
8. B
9. A
10. C

Chapter 11 – Assuring Network Availability

1. D
2. B
3. D
4. A
5. B
6. C
7. A
8. B
9. C
10. C

Chapter 12 – Organizational Documents and Policies

1. D
2. A
3. C
4. D
5. B
6. B
7. D
8. A
9. B
10. B

Chapter 13 – High Availability and Disaster Recovery

1. C
2. B
3. D
4. B
5. A
6. D

Chapter 14 – Network Security Concepts

1. C
2. D
3. A
4. B
5. D
6. C
7. D
8. A
9. D
10. B

Chapter 15 – Exploring Cyber Attacks and Threats

1. C
2. B
3. D
4. A
5. C
6. A, C
7. D
8. B
9. D
10. B

Chapter 16 – Implementing Network Security

1. C
2. A
3. C
4. B
5. D
6. D
7. A
8. B
9. C
10. C

Chapter 17 – Network Troubleshooting

1. C
2. A
3. C
4. C
5. A
6. C
7. B
8. C

Index

D

  antennas and power levels 557, 558
  captive portals 559
  client isolation 559, 560
  geofencing 559
  installation considerations 561-563
  MAC filtering 556
  password considerations 554, 556
  SSID considerations 553
  wireless authentication protocols 560, 561
Wireshark 233, 399
  download link 36
Wireshark OUI lookup tool
  reference link 25
Wireshark, sample capture
  reference link 37
wiring diagram 464
**Worldwide Interoperability for
    Microwave Access (WiMAX) 423**
worm 494

X

XCP-ng
  URL 118

Y

yagi antennas
  using 558

Z

zero-day vulnerabilities 492
Zero Touch Provisioning 295
zero trust 504

Packt.com

Subscribe to our online digital library for full access to over 7,000 books and videos, as well as industry leading tools to help you plan your personal development and advance your career. For more information, please visit our website.

Why subscribe?

- Spend less time learning and more time coding with practical eBooks and Videos from over 4,000 industry professionals

- Improve your learning with Skill Plans built especially for you

- Get a free eBook or video every month

- Fully searchable for easy access to vital information

- Copy and paste, print, and bookmark content

Did you know that Packt offers eBook versions of every book published, with PDF and ePub files available? You can upgrade to the eBook version at packt.com and as a print book customer, you are entitled to a discount on the eBook copy. Get in touch with us at customercare@packtpub. com for more details.

At www.packt.com, you can also read a collection of free technical articles, sign up for a range of free newsletters, and receive exclusive discounts and offers on Packt books and eBooks.

Other Books You May Enjoy

If you enjoyed this book, you may be interested in these other books by Packt:

Network Automation with Go

Nicolas Leiva, Michael Kashin

ISBN: 9781800560925

- Learn Go programming language basics via network-related examples

- Find out what features make Go a powerful alternative for network automation

- Explore network automation goals, benefits, and common use cases

- Discover how to interact with network devices using a variety of technologies

- Integrate Go programs into an automation framework

- Take advantage of the OpenConfig ecosystem with Go

- Build distributed and scalable systems for network observability

Python Network Programming Techniques

Marcel Neidinger

ISBN: 9781838646639

- Programmatically connect to network devices using SSH (secure shell) to execute commands
- Create complex configuration templates using Python
- Manage multi-vendor or multi-device environments using network controller APIs or unified interfaces
- Use model-driven programmability to retrieve and change device configurations
- Discover how to automate post modification network infrastructure tests
- Automate your network security using Python and Firepower APIs

Packt is searching for authors like you

If you're interested in becoming an author for Packt, please visit authors.packtpub.com and apply today. We have worked with thousands of developers and tech professionals, just like you, to help them share their insight with the global tech community. You can make a general application, apply for a specific hot topic that we are recruiting an author for, or submit your own idea.

Share your thoughts

Now you've finished *CompTIA Network+ N10-008 Certification Guide*, we'd love to hear your thoughts! Scan the QR code below to go straight to the Amazon review page for this book and share your feedback or leave a review on the site that you purchased it from.

https://packt.link/r/180323606X

Your review is important to us and the tech community and will help us make sure we're delivering excellent quality content.

Download a free PDF copy of this book

Thanks for purchasing this book!

Do you like to read on the go but are unable to carry your print books everywhere?

Is your eBook purchase not compatible with the device of your choice?

Don't worry, now with every Packt book you get a DRM-free PDF version of that book at no cost.

Read anywhere, any place, on any device. Search, copy, and paste code from your favorite technical books directly into your application.

The perks don't stop there, you can get exclusive access to discounts, newsletters, and great free content in your inbox daily

Follow these simple steps to get the benefits:

1. Scan the QR code or visit the link below

https://packt.link/free-ebook/978-1-80323-606-3

2. Submit your proof of purchase
3. That's it! We'll send your free PDF and other benefits to your email directly

Printed in the USA
CPSIA information can be obtained
at www.ICGtesting.com
LVHW081915141123
763925LV00006B/408